AA
Sai✔ KT-388-278

OXFORD EC LAW LIBRARY

General Editor: F. G. Jacobs
Advocate General, The Court of Justice
of the European Communities

EC EMPLOYMENT LAW

OXFORD EC LAW LIBRARY

The aim of this series is to publish important and original studies of the various branches of European Community Law. Each work will provide a clear, concise, and critical exposition of the law in its social, economic, and political context, at a level which will interest the advanced student, the practitioner, the academic, and government and Community officials.

Other Titles in the Library

The European Union and its Court of Justice
Anthony Arnull

EC Sex Equality Law
second edition
Evelyn Ellis

The General Principles of EC Law
Takis Tridimas

European Community Law of State Aid
Andrew Evans

EC Company Law
Vanessa Edwards

EC Competition Law
third edition
D. G. Goyder

External Relations of the European Communities
I. MacLeod, I. D. Hendry and Stephen Hyett

Directives in European Community Law
Sacha Prechal

EC Tax Law
Paul Farmer and Richard Lyal

The European Internal Market and International Trade
Piet Eeckhout

The Law of Money and Financial Services in the European Community
second edition
J. A. Usher

Legal Aspects of Agriculture in the European Community
J. A. Usher

Trade and Environmental Law in the European Community
Andreas R. Ziegler

EC Employment Law

Second Edition

CATHERINE BARNARD

University Lecturer in Law and Fellow of Trinity College, Cambridge

OXFORD
UNIVERSITY PRESS

OXFORD

UNIVERSITY PRESS

Great Clarendon Street, Oxford OX2 6DP

Oxford University Press is a department of the University of Oxford.
It furthers the University's objective of excellence in research, scholarship,
and education by publishing worldwide in

Oxford New York

Athens Auckland Bangkok Bogotá Buenos Aires Calcutta
Cape Town Chennai Dar es Salaam Delhi Florence Hong Kong Istanbul
Karachi Kuala Lumpur Madrid Melbourne Mexico City Mumbai
Nairobi Paris São Paulo Shanghai Singapore Taipei Tokyo Toronto Warsaw
with associated companies in Berlin Ibadan

Oxford is a registered trade mark of Oxford University Press
in the UK and in certain other countries

Published in the United States
by Oxford University Press Inc., New York

© Catherine Barnard 2000

The moral rights of the author have been asserted
Database right Oxford University Press (maker)

First published 2000

All rights reserved. No part of this publication may be reproduced,
stored in a retrieval system, or transmitted, in any form or by any means,
without the prior permission in writing of Oxford University Press,
or as expressly permitted by law, or under terms agreed with the appropriate
reprographics rights organizations. Enquiries concerning reproduction
outside the scope of the above should be sent to the Rights Department,
Oxford University Press, at the address above

You must not circulate this book in any other binding or cover
and you must impose this same condition on any acquirer

British Library Cataloguing in Publication Data

Data available

Library of Congress Cataloging in Publication Data

Data available

ISBN 0–19–876564–9
ISBN 0–19–876565–7 (pbk.)

1 3 5 7 9 10 8 6 4 2

Typeset in Photina
by RefineCatch Limited, Bungay, Suffolk
Printed in Great Britain by
Biddles Ltd., Guildford and King's Lynn

General Editor's Foreword

This book on EC employment law is, on many counts, a welcome addition to the Oxford EC Law Library.

Employment law has had from the outset of the European Community a fundamental place in its very conception and in the founding Treaties; it has maintained that position throughout the Community's evolution, with both Community legislation and the case-law of the Court of Justice making substantial contributions to the protection of employees in the Member States; and with the Treaty of Amsterdam it has taken on a new impetus.

In the founding Treaties, the free movement of workers throughout the Community, without any discrimination on grounds of nationality, was a cardinal principle, which also informed far-reaching legislation on both employment rights and social security.

Equal pay for men and women, and equal treatment of men and women in employment, were also among the first and most significant contributions of Community law to the national laws of the Member States.

Both these fundamental principles have powerfully reinforced the rights of workers, sometimes in ways which might not have been expected—for example in their impact on retirement ages, on pensions, and on affirmative action. The author's discussion of these fundamental but complex concepts of equality and discrimination, and their various ramifications, succeeds in being both illuminating and highly practical.

In addition, a body of employment legislation of a more general character has given the Community a specific social policy, sometimes controversial in its scope. These areas of legislation are examined under the general heads of Health, Safety, and Working Conditions; Employment Rights on the Restructuring of Enterprises; and Collective Labour Law. Many major items of legislation are considered, such as the working time directive, the acquired rights directive, the collective redundancy directive, the insolvency directive, and many others. Throughout, the author combines legal analysis with an examination of the policy implications.

As she shows, the subject is likely to maintain its momentum. Various new directions in employment law and in social policy are heralded by the Treaty of Amsterdam, and the agreement of the United Kingdom to sign the Social Chapter seems likely to have important implications not only for the effects of new employment measures in the UK but also for the future development of the subject.

This book will not merely give its readers a knowledge of the reach, and much of the detail, of EC employment law; it will give them a new understanding of its basic concepts and underlying policy aims and the capacity for an informed and critical assessment of a subject of great social and economic importance.

Francis G. Jacobs

Author's Preface

This book aims to provide a comprehensive examination of the law and policy in the employment field of the EU. It considers both the law-making process in respect of EC social policy and the rules which result. It also analyses the now extensive case law of the European Court of Justice which has, at different times, been creative, imaginative, and conservative. The book does not examine the individual employment laws of the Member States, nor does it consider the means by which European Community rules have been implemented by the Member States. These topics require their own consideration. It does, however, consider how aspects of Community law are informed by and derived from national employment laws.

Chapter 1 considers the Union's stumbling progress towards developing 'social policy', or more particularly 'employment law' at Community level. It considers the rationale for such a policy and the pressures which operate to constrain its development. It also examines the new Employment Title, introduced by the Amsterdam Treaty, which has indicated a sharp change of emphasis in the Community's focus. Chapter 2 examines how these pressures shape the law-making process in respect of social policy. The remaining chapters consider the substance of Community employment law. Chapters 3 and 4 consider the individual rights initially provided by the Treaty of Rome—the rules relating to the free movement of persons, especially as they affect individual workers and the self-employed, and the right to equality, primarily on the grounds of sex but also, after Amsterdam, in respect of other grounds, notably race. Chapter 5 examines the ramifications that the free movement and sex equality provisions have in respect of social security. Chapter 6 considers further aspects of individual employment rights, notably health and safety and, closely allied to this, working conditions. Chapter 7 examines the individual and collective rights conferred by the Directives of the late 1970s, concerning businesses in times of transformation—covering the transfers of undertakings, collective redundancies, and insolvency. Finally, Chapter 8 discusses the collective dimension of Community employment rules, focusing primarily on rights to information and consultation.

The first and revised editions of this book were published by John Wiley. OUP kindly agreed to publish the second edition and I am extremely grateful for their patience during its gestation. I owe particular thanks to Michaela Coulthard and Matthew Cotton at OUP, to Kate Elliott for her assiduous copy-editing and to Jonathon Price for his proof-reading skills. The renumbering of the Treaties has not made the task of writing the second edition easy. The social field was particularly badly affected because in effect two sets of renumbering occurred, once at Amsterdam itself when the Social Policy Agreement (SPA) was incorporated into the Treaty of Rome and again when the whole Treaty was renumbered. Thus, the health and safety legal basis Article 118a became Article 118 at Amsterdam and then Article 137 subsequently. Confusingly, Article 3 SPA became Article 118a at Amsterdam and then Article 138. The destination tables reflect the changes at Amsterdam and not the reality of the provisions. Where possible, I have listed the Article numbers as they were pre-Amsterdam and then as they are now. When talking historically I have used the old numbers followed by the new. When talking of today I have used the new numbers followed by the old.

Many people have been extremely generous with their time and patience in the completion of this project. Thanks are due especially to Professor Jon Clark, Dr Simon Deakin, Dr Nicholas Emiliou, Lorraine Fletcher, Professor Rosa Greaves, Clive Lewis, Professor Roy Lewis, Simon Steel, and Christine Warry for their advice and expertise in fine-tuning sections of the text; to a number of research assistants, notably Patrick Goodall, for their hard work; to various Commission officials, principally in DG V and the legal service, who spared the time to talk to me; to colleagues first at the University of Southampton and subsequently at the University of Cambridge for moral and practical support; to Laura Peters Cordy who managed the Herculean task of pulling the whole text together; and to my family for all their love and support. Finally, I owe my greatest debt of gratitude to John Cary for the good sense, good humour, and good cooking which have kept the book on course.

Catherine Barnard
27 March 2000

Contents

List of Tables

List of Figures

Table of Cases from the European Court of Justice

*References printed in **bold** refer to the page number where a substantial discussion of the Case commences.*

Table of Cases from the Court of First Instance

Table of Cases from the European Court and Commission of Human Rights

Table of Cases from the EFTA Court

Table of Cases—National

Table of European Commission Decisions

Table of ILO Freedom of Association Committee Decisions

Table of Acts, Agreements, and Conventions

References printed in **bold** *refer to the page number where a substantial discussion of the Act, Agreement, or Convention commences.*

Table of Decisions

References printed in **bold** refer to the page number where a substantial discussion of the Decision commences.

Table of EC Directives

References printed in **bold** refer to the page number where a substantial discussion
of the Directive commences.

Table of Proposed Directives

Table of National Legislation

Portugal

Spain

United Kingdom

Table of European Community Regulations

References printed in **bold** *refer to the page number where a substantial discussion of the Regulation commences.*

Table of Proposed European Community Regulations

Table of European Community Treaties

*References printed in **bold** refer to the page number where a substantial discussion of the Treaty commences.*

1

The Evolution of EC 'Social' Policy

While there is an identifiable body of EC law which can loosely be described as 'labour' or 'social' policy, its coverage is far from comprehensive and certainly does not represent a replication of national social policy on the EC stage. Further, the development of social policy is by no means linear: phases of great activity have been matched by lengthy phases of inertia. This chapter charts the evolution of EC social policy[1] and considers the forces and principles driving this development. The resulting policy is a product of its social, political, and economic context and its shape has been heavily influenced by the individual national legal systems.

A. THE DEVELOPMENT OF EC SOCIAL POLICY

1. The Treaty of Rome

Although the Treaty of Rome did contain a Title on Social Policy, its provisions were largely exhortatory and conferred little by way of direct rights on citizens.[2] This is illustrated by Article 117 [new and heavily amended Article 136], which provided the 'Member States agree upon the need to promote improved working conditions and an improved standard of living for workers, so as to make possible their harmonisation while the improvement is being maintained'. Similarly, Article 118 EEC [new Article 140] failed to provide legally enforceable rights. It entrusted the Commission with the task of promoting 'close cooperation between the Member States and facilitate the coordination of their action in all social policy fields', particularly in matters

---

[1] For more detail, see Nielsen and Szyszczak, *The Social Dimension of the European Community* (2nd edn, Handelshøjskolens Forlag, Copenhagen, 1997); Collins, *The European Communities, The Social Policy of the First Phase* (Martin Robertson, London, 1975); Shanks, *The European Social Policy Today and Tomorrow* (Pergamon, Oxford, 1977); La Terza, *Diritto Communitario and Lavoro* (Pirola Editore, Milan, 1992), ch. 4; Teague, *The European Community, the Social Dimension, Labour Market Policies for 1992* (Kogan Page, London, 1989), esp. ch. 4; Blanpain and Engels, *European Labour Law* (Kluwer, Deventer, 1993); Lyon-Caen and Lyon-Caen, *Droit Social International et Européen* (8th edn, Dalloz, Paris, 1993); Bercusson, *European Labour Law* (Butterworths, London, 1996); Rodière, *Droit Social de l'Union Euopéenne* (Dalloz, Paris, 1999); Baylos, Grau, Caruso, D'Antona, and Sciarra, *Dizionario di Diritto del Lavoro Communitario* (Monduzzi, Rome, 1996).

[2] Hallstein, *Europe in the Making* (1972), 119, cited in Watson, 'The Community Social Charter' (1991) 28 *CMLRev*. 37, 39.

relating to employment, labour law and working conditions, basic and advanced vocational training, social security, prevention of occupational accidents and diseases, occupational hygiene, the right of association, and collective bargaining between employers and workers. The limited scope of this Article was highlighted by *Germany, UK and Others v. Commission*[3] where the Court ruled that Article 118 gave the Commission only procedural powers to set up consultations within the subjects covered. It could not be used to impose on Member States results to be achieved, nor could it prevent Member States from taking measures at national level.

The other social provisions were similarly limited in scope. Article 121 EEC [new Article 144] permitted the Council to assign to the Commission tasks in connection with the 'implementation of common measures', in particular as regards social security for migrant workers; Article 122 [new Article 145] required the Commission to include a separate chapter on 'social developments' within the Community in its annual report to the European Parliament,[4] and Article 128 [new and amended Article 150] required the Council to 'lay down general principles' for implementing a common vocational training policy. The only provision which might have contained some substance was Article 119 [new and amended Article 141] on equal pay for men and women for equal work; and even that obligation was addressed to the Member States and not to individual employers.

This raises the question why a Title on 'Social Policy' should contain such limited ambitions. The answer may lie in part with the original objectives of the European *Economic* Community. When the Community was first established its objectives were to create a common market,[5] consisting of free movement of products (goods and services) and production factors (labour and capital). The view was that economic integration—the removal of artificial obstacles to the free movement of labour, goods, and capital—would in time ensure the optimum allocation of resources throughout the Community, the optimum rate of economic growth, and thus an optimum social system.[6] This in turn would lead, according to the Preamble, to the 'constant improvement of the living and working conditions of their peoples'. This represented a victory for the classic neo-liberal market tradition: there was no need for a European-level social dimension because high social standards were 'rewards' for efficiency, not rigidities imposed on the market.[7]

Thus, the founders of the EC were highly influenced by the idea that regula-

---

[3] Joined Cases 281, 283, 285, 287/85 *Germany, UK and Others v. Commission* [1987] ECR 3203.

[4] The Parliament may also request the Commission to draw up reports on any particular problems relating to social conditions.

[5] Arts. 2 and 3.

[6] Shanks, 'Introductory Article: The Social Policy of the European Community' (1977) 14 *CMLRev*. 14.

[7] See further Hervey, *European Social Law and Policy* (Longman, Harlow, 1998), 7.

tory competition between states would produce allocatively efficient results. The success of this model is, however, dependent on there being perfect mobility on the part of the consumers of laws and full autonomy on the part of the law-makers. Thus in the eyes of the EU's founders, in the absence of market failure, the role of the EC was simply to provide the conditions of perfect mobility (the market-creating function of the law) but not to interfere with the state's ability to regulate. This can be seen in the Spaak report,[8] drawn up by the foreign ministers prior to the signing of the Treaty of Rome. It considered that free movement of labour was crucial to social prosperity. By allowing workers to move to find available work, they would go from areas where labour was cheap and plentiful to areas where there was demand. As a result, it was thought that wage rates would tend to rise. Consequently, free circulation of labour would facilitate an equalization in the terms and conditions of competition.[9] To achieve this goal, Articles 48–66 [new Articles 39–55] were introduced into the Treaty to remove obstacles to the free movement of workers, and complemented by Article 123 [new Article 146] establishing the European Social Fund, designed to make the employment of workers easier and to increase their geographic and occupational mobility.[10] Article 51 [new Article 42] provided a basis for EC regulation in the social security field, based on a policy of co-ordination and not harmonization.[11]

In other areas the Spaak report envisaged only limited action to ensure the functioning of the Common Market. It rejected the idea of trying to harmonize the fundamental conditions of the national economy—its natural resources, its level of productivity, the significance of public burdens— considering that any harmonization might be the result, as opposed to a condition precedent, of the operation of the Common Market and the economic forces which it released. In the social field this anticipated Article 117 EEC which, as we have seen, failed to provide any legal basis for Community social legislation, but simply stated that Member States believed that an improvement in working conditions 'will ensue not only from the functioning of the Common Market . . . but also from the approximation of provisions laid down by law, regulation or administrative action'.

Spaak relied heavily on the earlier Ohlin report of ILO experts.[12] This report had argued for the transnational harmonization of social policy in some areas, such as equal pay, but, invoking the economic theory of comparative

---

[8] Rapport des Chefs de Délégations, Comité Intergouvernemental, 21 Apr. 1956, 19–20, 60–1.

[9] Ibid., 78.

[10] There was also a social dimension to the Common Agricultural Policy (Art. 39 [new Art. 33]) in the form of grants from the European Agricultural Guidance and Guarantee Fund (EAGGF).

[11] See Hervey, above n. 7, 15.

[12] International Labour Office, 'Social Aspects of European Economic Cooperation' (1956) 74 *International Labour Review* 99.

advantage, rejected a general role for harmonization of social policy. It argued that differences in nominal wage costs between countries did not, in themselves, pose an obstacle to economic integration because what mattered was unit labour costs, taking into account the relationship between nominal costs and productivity. Because higher costs tended to accompany higher productivity, differences between countries were less than they seemed. Ohlin also suggested that the system of national exchange rates, which could be expected to reflect general prices and productivity levels within states, would cancel out the apparent advantage of low-wage states,[13] so avoiding a race to the bottom—the phenomenon of standards of social protection either being depressed in states with higher standards or at least prevented from rising, by increased competition from states with substantially lower social standards.[14] Consequently, Ohlin argued that the market itself would ensure that conditions of competition were not distorted. The strength of this argument and its influence on the debate about the function of EC social policy are considered below.

Although opposed to general intervention in the social sphere, Spaak did say that action must correct or eliminate the effect of specific distortions which advantage or disadvantage certain branches of activity (market perfecting). By way of example, the authors of the Spaak report cited a list of areas including working conditions of labour, such as the relationship between the salaries of men and women, working time, overtime and paid holidays, and different policies relating to credit. This suggested that the Community should act in these fields only. However, Kahn-Freund has suggested that the Spaak committee's views were not as clearly reflected as might have been the case,[15] perhaps because the relevant provisions were drafted only at the end of a crucial conversation between the French and German Prime Ministers.[16] At the time of the Treaty negotiations there were important differences in the scope and content of social legislation in force in the states concerned.[17] France, in particular, had a number of rules which favoured workers, including legislation on equal pay for men and women, and rules permitting French workers longer paid holidays than in other states.[18] French workers were also entitled to overtime pay after fewer hours of work at basic rates than elsewhere. This raised concerns that the additional costs

---

[13] The significance of this point will be considered later in the context of Economic and Monetary Union.

[14] See further below, nn. 140–173.

[15] Kahn-Freund, 'Labour Law and Social Security', in *American Enterprise in the European Common Market: A Legal Profile*, eds. Stein and Nicholson (University of Michigan Law School, Ann Arbor, Mich., 1960), 300. See Barnard, 'The Economic Objectives of Article 119', in *Sex Equality Law in the European Union*, eds. Hervey and O'Keeffe (Wiley, Chichester, 1996).

[16] Ibid., citing Katzenstein, 'Der Arbeitnehmer in der europäischen Wirtschaftsgemeinschaft', (1957) 31 *Betriebs-Berater* 1081.

[17] This draws on Ellis, *EC Sex Equality Law* (Clarendon, Oxford, 1998), 60.

[18] Ibid.

borne by French industry would make French goods uncompetitive in the Common Market. Consequently, the French argued that an elimination of gross distortions of competition was not enough, and that it would be necessary to assimilate the entire labour and social legislation of the Member States, so as to achieve a parity of wages and social costs. The Germans, however, were strongly committed to keeping a minimum level of government interference in the area of wages and prices. The resulting compromise was reflected in the Treaty's social policy provisions. Articles 117 and 118 EEC on the need to improve working conditions and co-operation between states, even if textually broad, were legally shallow, reflecting the German preference for *laissez-faire*.[19] Article 119 [new Article 141] on equal pay and Article 120 [new Article 143] on paid holiday schemes and the third protocol on 'Certain Provisions Relating to France' on working hours and overtime,[20] by contrast, are specific provisions designed to protect French industry.[21]

This debate should not, however, disguise the fact that generally Member States believed that labour law was a domestic issue and, at a time of unprecedented activity at national level with workers gaining new legal rights and welfare benefits, there was little pressure for harmonization at Community level. Member States considered social policy lay at the very heart of national sovereignty,[22] and viewed it as an important vehicle to preserve 'the integrity and political stability of their respective political regimes'.[23] As a result, they were keen to keep social policy outside the supranational competence of the Commission. That being said, the Commission noted in its *First General Report on the Activities of the Community* in 1958[24] that 'it bears particular responsibilities in this field [of social policy] and intends to neglect no sphere in which it may prove possible to "promote close cooperation"'. With surprising prescience, it observed that 'It is convinced that in the future the Community will be judged by a large part of public opinion on the basis of its

[19] Forman, 'The Equal Pay Principle under Community Law' (1982) 1 *LIEI* 17.

[20] This provided that the Commission was to authorize France to take protective measures where the establishment of the common market did not result, by the end of the first stage, in the basic number of hours beyond which overtime was paid for and the average rate of additional payment for overtime in the industry did not correspond to the average obtaining in France in 1956. It does not seem that France has called upon this safeguard clause: Budiner, *Le Droit de la femme à l'égalité de salaire et la Convention No. 100 de l'organisation internationale du travail* (Librairie Générale de Droit et de Jurisprudence, Paris, 1975).

[21] According to the French Advocate General Dutheillet de Lamothe in Case 80/70 *Defrenne v. SABENA (No. 1)* [1971] ECR 445, 'It appears to be France which took the initiative, but the article [119] necessitated quite long negotiations'. However, the content of Art. 119 was strongly influenced by ILO Convention No. 100 on equal pay. See Hoskyns, *Integrating Gender* (Verso, London, 1996).

[22] Ross, 'Assessing the Delors' Era and Social Policy', in *European Social Policy: Between Fragmentation and Integration*, eds. Leibfried and Pierson (Brookings Institution, Washington D.C., 1995), 360.

[23] Streeck, 'Neo-voluntarism: A New Social Policy Regime' (1995) 1 *ELJ* 31.

[24] 17 Sept. 1958. The Social Affairs Council did not even meet between 1964 and 1966: see Hervey, above n. 7, 16.

direct and indirect successes in the social field'.[25] It also noted that the reference in the Preamble to the Treaty to 'both economic and *social* progress' and to 'constantly improving the living and working conditions of their peoples' made it clear that 'the objectives of a social character are placed on the same footing as those of an economic character',[26] albeit that 'the legal framework of the Community's action in the social field is less rigid'.[27]

2. A Change of Direction

The non-intervention by the Community in the social field did not last. On the eve of the accession of three new Member States in 1973, the heads of government meeting in Paris issued a communiqué, stating that the Member States:

emphasised that vigorous action in the social sphere is to them just as important as achieving Economic and Monetary Union. They consider it absolutely necessary to secure an increasing share by both sides of industry in the Community's economic and social decisions.[28]

This change of approach can be explained in part by reference to the social unrest in Western Europe in 1968,[29] and in part by an economic recession in Europe. The feeling was that the Community required a human face to persuade its citizens that the social consequences of growth were being effectively tackled and that the Community was more than a device enabling business to exploit the common market.[30] Failure to address this might have jeopardized the whole process of economic integration. This was the first sign that the growth-based, neo-liberal ideology of the European Economic Community was not actually delivering on its promises and that a social dimension was necessary to address the problems faced by the 'losers'—both individuals and companies—suffering from the consequences of European economic integration. Thus, this phase of development of social policy owes more to the recognition that social policy measures were necessary to maintain and support the established social order than to any market-creating ideology of the law.

In response, the Commission drew up an Action Programme[31] containing three objectives: the attainment of full and better employment in the Community, the improvement of living and working conditions, and increased involvement of management and labour in the economic and social decisions of the Community and of workers in the life of the undertaking. This precipi-

---

[25] Para. 103.
[26] Para. 102.
[27] Para. 103.
[28] EC Bull. 10/1972, paras. 6 and 19.
[29] Wise and Gibb, *Single Market to Social Europe* (Longman, Harlow, 1993), 144.
[30] Shanks, above n. 1, 378.
[31] [1974] OJ C13/1.

tated a phase of remarkable legislative activity. Directives were adopted in the field of sex discrimination,[32] and the whole field of sex equality assumed a new importance as a result of judgments by the Court in the *Defrenne* cases,[33] in particular its ruling that Article 119 [new Article 141] was directly effective. An action programme and a number of Directives were adopted in the field of health and safety and, in the face of rising unemployment, measures were taken to ease the impact of mass redundancies,[34] the transfer of undertakings,[35] and insolvent employers.[36] At the same time, the European Regional Development Fund[37] was introduced in order to address the problems of socio-economic convergence in the Community.

This legislation, although quite extensive, was confined to certain areas of employment law, as strictly understood, and not to the broader social sphere as originally envisaged by the 1972 communiqué. Further, this legislation had to be adopted under the general Treaty bases, Articles 100 and 235 [new Articles 94 and 308], both requiring the unanimous agreement of all the Member States. This ensured Member State control over the supranational regulation of employment rights.

Enthusiasm for developing a European social policy began to wane by the start of the 1980s. The new Conservative government in the UK, led by Margaret Thatcher, insisted on strict limits to the growth of Community social policy. Signalling the end of the corporatist era, the British government was fundamentally opposed to the notion that workers' participation had an essential role in the management of change.[38] It strongly advocated deregulation of the labour markets in order to ensure maximum flexibility of the workforce, in line with the American model, and argued for the need to adapt to new technology and the necessity of reducing the burden of regulation on business in order to enable business to compete in a global market.[39] This view represented an extreme form of the neo-liberal market tradition. Put simply, the Thatcherite view was that society is comprised of individuals, each of whom could compete within the market place: no further state intervention, especially in the social field was necessary or desirable.[40] This philosophy

---

[32] Directive 75/117 on equal pay [1975] OJ L45/19, Directive 76/207 on equal treatment [1976] OJ L39/40 and Directive 79/7 on equal treatment in social security [1979] OJ L6/24.

[33] Case 80/70 *Defrenne (No. 1)* [1971] ECR 445, Case 43/75 *Defrenne (No. 2)* v. *SABENA* [1976] ECR 455 and Case 149/77 *Defrenne (No. 3)* v. *SABENA* [1978] ECR 1365. See further Ch. 4.

[34] Directive 75/129/EEC [1975] OJ L48/29, as amended.

[35] Directive 77/187/EEC [1977] OJ L61/27, as amended.

[36] Directive 80/987/EEC [1980] OJ L283/23.

[37] Regulation 724/75 [1975] OJ L73/8. See now Regulation 2052/88 [1988] OJ L185/9, amended by Regulation 2081/93 [1993] OJ L193/5 and replaced by Regulation 1783/1999 [1999] OJ L213/1. See generally Scott, *Development Dilemmas in the European Community: Rethinking Regional Development Policy* (Open University Press, Buckingham, 1995).

[38] See e.g. the demise of the Fifth Directive on Company Structure and the draft Vredling Directive, discussed in Ch. 8.

[39] See e.g. *Employment: the Challenge to the Nation*, Cmnd 9474.

[40] Hervey, above n. 7, 7.

ran into direct conflict with the regulatory stance adopted by the Commission. While the Commission recognized the need for a flexible and adaptable work-force, it did not equate flexibility with deregulation and it refused to renege on its commitment to safeguarding the rights of employees.[41] However, since at that stage, all social policy measures required unanimity in Council the UK was able to veto any proposals to which it objected.[42] Such stagnation was not confined to the social field. Disillusion with the tenets of Community policy and wranglings over budgetary contributions brought the Community legis-lative process shuddering almost to a halt. The arrival of Jacques Delors as President of the Commission, and his proposal for a Single Market to be completed by 1992,[43] represented, at least in the medium term, an end to this inertia.

3. The Single Market and the Community Social Charter 1989

The Single European Act 1986 and the Single Market programme were again premised on the idea that liberalization of trade would lead to economies of scale and economic growth from which the greatest number of Community citizens would benefit. This view was endorsed by Cecchini in his report on the costs of non-Europe, where he recognized that the most important aspect of the 1992 process was the medium term impact of market integration on employment, raising the prospect of 'very substantial job creation'.[44] This was really the only recognition of the social consequences of the Single Market.

Although the idea of adding a social dimension to the internal market programme was discussed, particularly by the European Parliament, the Single European Act (SEA) eventually made few concessions to those who argued for greater social competence. The Community did, however, commit itself to strengthening economic and social cohesion in the Community (Art-icle 130a [new Article 158]), with the aim of reducing disparities between the levels of development of the various regions and the backwardness of the least favoured regions, including rural areas, and to developing the 'dialogue between management and labour at European level', institutionalizing the so-called social dialogue (Article 118b [new and amended Article 139]). Other-wise, Article 8a [new Article 14], setting the deadline of 31 December 1992

---

[41] See further Hepple, 'The Crisis in EEC Labour Law' (1987) 16 *ILJ* 77, 81.

[42] Measures on equality and health and safety were, however, adopted in this period. This can be explained in part by the fact that UK legislation already guaranteed fairly substantial protection in these fields.

[43] See generally Schmitt von Sydow, 'Basic Strategies of the Commission's White Paper', in *1992: One European Market*, eds. Bieber, Dehousse, Pinder and Weiler (Nomos Verlagsgesellschaft, Baden-Baden, 1988) 79.

[44] Cecchini, *The European Challenge: 1992, the Benefits of a Single Market* (Gower, Aldershot, 1988), p. xix.

for the completion of the internal market programme, talked only of the free movement of persons as a fundamental objective of the internal market.

For practical purposes perhaps the most significant innovation for social policy introduced by the SEA was the extension of qualified majority voting to the field of health and safety[45] by Article 118a [new and amended Article 137], although matters 'relating to the rights and interests of employed persons' (Article 100a(2) [new Article 95(2)]) still required unanimous agreement in Council. Article 118a(1) required Member States to 'pay particular attention to encouraging improvements, especially in the working environment, as regards the health and safety of workers'. Article 118a(2) then gave the Council the power to adopt minimum standards directives which allowed Member States to maintain or introduce 'more stringent measures for the protection of working conditions compatible with this Treaty' (Article 118a(3)).[46]

Directives adopted under Article 118a therefore continued to allow some space for regulatory competition. The provisions of Article 118a represented an important shift in thinking. First, they demonstrated that the Community would not harmonize all labour standards but merely set a floor of basic rights. Secondly, the language of 'protection' indicated a change in emphasis away from social standards being viewed as a consequence of the internal market but as having a role to play in worker protection. The true significance of Article 118a became apparent only as the British hostility to the EU's social policy became firmly entrenched: all social measures no longer needed to be adopted with a unanimous vote. This facilitated the adoption of certain important measures, such as the Working Time Directive,[47] the Pregnant Workers' Directive,[48] and the Young Workers' Directive[49] under the Social Charter Action Programme.[50]

The lack of a true social dimension accompanying the SEA once again prompted concern in some quarters that the ambitious single market programme would not succeed unless it had the support of the Community citizens. This concern was combined with the realization that the Single Market programme would also produce negative consequences for employees: as the European market opened up uncompetitive firms would go out of business and large companies might relocate to areas of the Community where social costs were lower. In both cases unemployment would result. For these reasons Jacques Delors set out his plans for 'L'Espace Social Européen',[51] arguing that

[45] This became the Art. 189c [new Art. 252] procedure after the Treaty on European Union and the Art. 251 procedure after Amsterdam.

[46] This is considered further in Ch. 2.

[47] Council Directive 93/104/EC [1993] OJ L307/18.

[48] Council Directive 92/85/EEC [1992] OJ L348/1.

[49] Council Directive 94/33/EC [1993] OJ L216/12.

[50] See below, text attached to n. 65.

[51] This is not a new concept: the French government had been talking in these terms since 1981. See further, Vandamme, 'De la Politique Social a l'Espace Social Européen' [1983] *Revue du Marché Commun* 562. Mitterand had issued a memorandum to Council on the creation of a European Social Area.

The creation of a vast economic area, based on the market and business cooperation, is inconceivable—I would say unattainable—without some harmonisation of social legislation. Our ultimate aim must be the creation of a European social area.[52]

This coincided with growing pressure for the establishment of a people's Europe designed to give the 'individual citizen a clearer perception of the dimension and the existence of the Community'[53]—in other words a recognition that 'Europe exists for its citizens, and not the other way round'.[54] This demonstrated a growing recognition that social and economic conditions are not in fact divisible, that economic efficiency must be balanced by welfare objectives to 'humanize' the market, for reasons of fairness and distributive justice.[55] This is sometimes described as the market-correcting[56] or the social justice approach to social policy. As Hervey points out, this model is based on notions of solidarity, a position which views social welfare as a collective activity rather than the responsibility of individuals, and social citizenship, the normative claim that egalitarian provision of welfare needs is superior to individual neo-liberal provision.

The social dimension of the internal market took more concrete form with the signing of a political declaration, the Community Charter of Fundamental Social Rights, by all the Member States except Britain during the Strasbourg summit in 1989. Although the European Parliament was most anxious that the Charter be incorporated into Community law by means of a binding instrument,[57] when finally adopted the preamble described it merely as a 'solemn proclamation of fundamental social rights'. It therefore has no legal effect,[58] a view confirmed by Advocate General Jacobs in *Albany*.[59] Thus, while the Charter represented an important political signal of a commitment to the social dimension, many were disappointed with its content.[60] Vogel-Polsky described it variously as a 'bitter failure' and putting 'non-decision into a concrete form';[61] Metall described it as 'a non-binding wish list' full of

---

[52] EC Bull. 2/1986, 12.

[53] The Adonnino Report, *A People's Europe: Reports from the ad hoc Committee*, Bull. Supp. 7/1985, 14. See also Commission, *Towards a People's Europe*, European File 3/86.

[54] President of the Council, 14 July 1993, cited in Commission, *A Citizen's Europe* (Brussels, 1993), 9.

[55] Hervey, above n. 7, 10.

[56] See further, below, text attached to nn. 134–135.

[57] See [1991] OJ C96/61 and [1989] OJ C120/5.

[58] Cf. Riley, 'The European Social Charter and Community Law' (1989) 14 *ELRev*. 80 and the reply by Gould, 'The European Social Charter and Community Law. A Comment' (1989) 14 *ELRev*. 80.

[59] Case C–67/96 *Albany International BV v. Stichting Bedrijfspensioenfonds Textielindustrie*, judgment of 21 Sept. 1999, para. 137.

[60] See esp. Bercusson, 'The European Community's Charter of Fundamental Social Rights of Workers' (1990) 53 *MLR* 624; Watson, 'The Community Social Charter' (1991) 28 *CMLRev*. 37; Silvia, 'The Social Charter of the European Community: A Defeat for European Labor' (1990–91) 44 *Industrial and Labour Relations Review* 626.

[61] 'What Future is there for a Social Europe Following the Strasbourg Summit?' (1990) 19 *ILJ* 65.

'rubber formulations' and loopholes that was 'not worth the paper on which it was printed'.[62] Silvia attributes this failure in part to British intransigence within the Council, combined with a willingness on the part of the other EC governments to take advantage of the UK's position, and in part to the failure by the European Trade Union movement either to raise convincingly the spectre of social unrest if it was dissatisfied, or persuasively to promise electoral benefits to ministers if they adopted more radical social policy proposals.[63]

In one sense the Charter was not a radical document: its Preamble still contained an endorsement of the old philosophies, that the completion of the internal market was the 'most effective means of creating employment and ensuring maximum well being in the Community', earlier references to combating *un*employment having been removed. On the other hand, it contains twenty-six rights which Member States have the responsibility to guarantee and it does recognize that the 'same importance' be attached to the social aspects as to the economic aspects which must be 'developed in a balanced manner'. The ambitions of the final version of the Charter were also more limited than the Commission had intended. Earlier drafts of the Charter talked of improvements in the social field for *citizens*. The final version specified that the Charter detailed rights for *workers*.[64] This suggests that the concept of a European social area had been abandoned for the present; and that the social aspect of the internal market had been substituted in its place.

The rights contained in the Social Charter 1989 were to be implemented through the Social Charter Action Programme[65] and any measures adopted were to be based on the EC Treaty and therefore binding on the UK. The Action Programme put forward by the Commission, when its power and prestige may have been at its highest point, proposed that forty-seven different instruments be submitted by 1 January 1993. However, these forty-seven proposals included only seventeen directives,[66] of which ten dealt with narrow health and safety matters, such as safety of the workplace,[67] safety of work equipment,[68] safety of VDUs,[69] and manual handling of loads.[70] This contrasted unfavourably with the proposals for almost 300 directives

---

[62] German Metal Workers' Union, quoted in Silvia, above, n. 60.

[63] Ibid., 640. See also Jacobs, 'Social Europe in Delay' (1990) 6 *IJCLLIR* 26, 35.

[64] See Bercusson, above n. 60, 626.

[65] COM(89)568 final Brussels, 29 Nov. 1989.

[66] Social Europe 1/90, Commission of the European Communities (Brussels, 1990) contains the full text of the Social Charter, the Action Programme, background material and comments. Reports on the progress of the implementation of the Action Programme can be found in COM(91)511 final, summarized in ISEC/B1/92, and Szyszczak, 'First Report on the Application of the Community Charter of the Fundamental Social Rights of Workers' (1992) 21 *ILJ* 149, ISEC/B25/93 COM(93) 668 final.

[67] Council Directive 89/654/EEC [1989] OJ L393/1. See further Ch. 6.

[68] Council Directive 89/655/EEC [1989] OJ L393/13.

[69] Council Directive 90/270/EEC [1991] OJ L156/14.

[70] Council Directive 90/269/EEC [1990] OJ L156/9.

submitted as part of the White Paper for Completing the Internal Market.[71] Nevertheless, the Action Programme led to the enactment of important pieces of social legislation aimed at protecting individual workers, including directives on proof of the employment contract,[72] posted workers,[73] and, taking advantage of the new legal basis, Article 118a, the Commission also managed to secure the adoption of directives on pregnant workers,[74] working time,[75] and young workers.[76]

The Social Charter itself was not, however, confined to a commitment to individual employment rights. The Charter contained a strong endorsement of collective rights: freedom of association,[77] the right to negotiate and conclude collective agreements,[78] possibly resulting in 'contractual relations', and the right to resort to collective action in the event of a conflict of interests, including the right to strike.[79] These rights have not, however, been reflected in any legislation, although the role of collective bargaining was given a considerable boost by the Treaty on European Union.

4. The Treaty on European Union

By the early 1990s, the Community had to come to terms with three main trends in economic and industrial relations, common across virtually all Member States.[80] The first concerned the structural transformation of the economy, involving the internationalization of corporate structures and the sectoral redistribution of the labour force away from agriculture and traditional industries to services, particularly private services. The second trend concerned the economic crises leading to major recessions in the early 1980s and again in the early 1990s. These were accompanied by relatively high levels of unemployment and, with some exceptions, relatively low levels of inflation. The third trend was the change in the political climate in the 1980s, reflected in a general move to the right in national government policy-making together with a shift in the economic balance of power away from employees and trade unions and towards employers and managers. Employment relations were characterized by greater flexibility in recruitment, deployment, and

---

[71] COM(85)310 final.
[72] Council Directive 91/533/EEC [1991] OJ L288/32.
[73] Council Directive 96/71/EC [1997] OJ L18/1.
[74] Council Directive 92/85/EEC [1992] OJ L348/1.
[75] Council Directive 93/104/EC [1993] OJ L307/18.
[76] Council Directive 94/33/EC [1993] OJ L216/12.
[77] Art. 11.
[78] Art. 12.
[79] Art. 13.
[80] See Barnard, Clark, and Lewis, *The Exercise of Individual Employment Rights in the Member States* (Department of Employment, London, 1995).

rewards, and the de-centralization of decision-making, mainly through collective bargaining but also increasingly through the exercise of managerial prerogative.

The enactment of the Treaty on European Union with its significant amendments to the Treaty of Rome[81] represented the Community's response to these changes. The desire to combat unemployment and encourage non-inflationary growth were now placed at the forefront of the Community's agenda. Article 2 EC said that the Community's tasks would be to promote throughout the Community 'sustainable and non-inflationary growth respecting . . . a high level of employment and of social protection, the raising of the standard of living and quality of life, and economic and social cohesion and solidarity among Member States'. In order to achieve these objectives the Community was given some additional activities, listed in Article 3, which included 'a policy in the social sphere comprising a European Social Fund', 'the strengthening of economic and social cohesion', and 'a contribution to education and training of quality'.[82] The Edinburgh European Council helped to provide the financial support to achieve these objectives. Agreement was reached to increase the Community's own resources from 1.2 per cent of GDP in 1993 to 1.27 per cent by 1999[83] in order to precipitate a 'big bang effect'[84] to achieve growth.

These new tasks and activities were reflected in the relabelling of the social policy section as 'Social policy, education, vocational training and youth'. Articles 123–128 on the European Social Fund were combined (Articles 123–125 [new Articles 146–148]) and Articles 126 and 127 [new Articles 149 and 150] formed a new chapter covering education, vocational training, and youth, where the Community was given new, but closely circumscribed competence. The question of competence was brought into sharp focus by the inclusion of Article 3b [new Article 5] into the Treaty. This provides:

The Community shall act within the limits of the powers conferred upon it by this Treaty and of the objectives assigned to it therein.

In areas which do not fall within its exclusive competence, the Community shall take action, in accordance with the principle of subsidiarity, only if and insofar as the objectives of the proposed action cannot be sufficiently achieved by the Member States and can therefore, by reason of the scale or effects of the proposed action, be better achieved by the Community.

Any action by the Community shall not go beyond what is necessary to achieve the objectives of this Treaty.

---

[81] See, generally, Lo Faro, 'EC Social Policy and 1993: The Dark Side of European Integration' (1992) 14 *Comparative Labour Law Journal* 1, esp. 27ff.

[82] Art. 3 (i), (j) and (p), respectively. See further below, the text attached to nn. 298–354.

[83] This proposal represents a weaker version of the Delors II package (COM(92)2000) which proposed an increase in the EC total resources to 1.37 per cent of GNP, discussed in Shackleton, 'Keynote Article: the Delors II Budget Package' (1993) 31 *JCMS* 11.

[84] Kenner, 'Economic and Social Cohesion: The Rocky Road Ahead' [1994/1] *LIEI* 1.

Thus, for the first time the Treaty recognized the doctrine of attribution of powers, the principle of subsidiarity with the presumption that Member States should act unless the action could be better achieved by the Community, and proportionality.[85]

The other key development at Maastricht in the context of a social dimension was the inclusion of the concept of 'Citizenship of the Union'.[86] According to Article 8 [new Article 17], every person holding the nationality of one of the Member States became a citizen of the Union. The rights conferred on citizens by Article 8(a)–(e) [new Articles 18–22] were, however, limited:

- the right to move and reside freely within the territory of the Member States, subject to the limitations and conditions laid down by the Treaty;[87]
- the right to vote and stand as a candidate at municipal and European Parliament elections;[88]
- the right to diplomatic and consular protection in the territory of third countries where the citizen's own Member State is represented;[89]
- the right to petition the European Parliament and to apply to the ombudsman.[90]

These provisions were highly criticized for their limited scope and vision.[91] Weiler argued that for citizenship not to be 'trivialized' to the point of 'embarrassment'[92] it must draw on rights 'scattered'[93] across the Treaty, including the social provisions.[94]

One of the most contentious aspects of the draft Treaty related to the significant changes proposed to Articles 117–122 EEC in order to expand the EC's social competence. This was met by stubborn resistance on the part of the UK and, in order to secure the UK's agreement to the Treaty on European Union as a whole, it was agreed to remove these changes from the main body of the Treaty and place them in a separate Protocol and Agreement (the Social Policy Agreement (SPA)) and the Social Policy Protocol (SPP)) which would not apply to the UK. The UK therefore secured an opt out from the

---

[85] These principles are considered further in Ch. 2.

[86] Art. 8 [new Art. 17].

[87] Art. 8a [new Art. 18]. See further Ch. 3.

[88] Art. 8b [new Art. 19].

[89] Art. 8c [new Art. 20].

[90] Art. 8d [new Art. 21].

[91] Shaw, 'The Many Pasts and Futures of Citizenship in the European Union' (1997) 22 *ELRev.* 554.

[92] Weiler, 'European Citizenship and Human Rights', in *Reforming the Treaty on European Union*, eds. Winter, Curtin, Kellermann, and de Witte (Kluwer, Deventer, 1996), esp. 65, cited in Shaw, above n. 91.

[93] Shaw, above, n. 91.

[94] See e.g. Shaw, above, n. 91; Reich, 'A European Constitution for Citizens: Reflections on the Rethinking of Union and Community Law' (1997) 3 *ELJ* 131, 146–151.

so-called Social Chapter as well as from the provisions on EMU. This was the first clear example of what became known as two-speed Europe or variable geometry[95] and paved the way for Denmark to opt out of other sections of the Treaty to ensure a positive vote in the second Danish referendum.

At the time there was much debate about the legal status of this opt-out. The prevailing view[96] was that the Protocol was an agreement by the twelve Member States that only eleven were to be bound by the new social provisions.[97] According to Article 239 EC [new Article 311], protocols annexed to the Treaty form an integral part of the Treaty. The Protocol on social policy was therefore part of the Treaty and thus part of Community law. Similarly, since the Protocol provided that the agreement on social policy was annexed to the Protocol, which in turn was annexed to the Treaty, the Agreement also formed part of Community law. This view was not without its critics[98] who argued variously that the Social Chapter constituted an intergovernmental agreement or that the Agreement on social policy was not part of the Protocol on social policy but was an independent arrangement made between the eleven.[99] The debate was effectively settled in favour of the Social Chapter being part of Community law when the Court was prepared to rule in the *UEAPME* case[100] on the legality of the Parental Leave Directive 96/34/EC adopted under the Social Chapter.[101]

As far as substance is concerned, the SPA was significant for two reasons. First, it broadened the scope of Community competence in the social field.[102] It extended the range of measures which could be decided by qualified

[95] See, generally, Towers, 'Two Speed Ahead: Social Europe and the UK after Maastricht' (1992) 23 *IRJ* 83; Shaw, 'Twin-track Social Europe—The Inside Track', in *Legal Issues of the Maastricht Treaty*, eds. O'Keeffe and Twomey (Wiley, Chichester, 1994), 295. Such 'flexibility', as it is now called, was constitutionalized at Amsterdam; Ehlermann, 'Differentiation Flexibility, Closer Cooperation: the New "Provisions of the Amsterdam Treaty"' (1998) 4 *ELJ* 246, 247; Shaw, 'The Treaty of Amsterdam: Challenges of Flexibility and Legitimacy' (1998) 4 *ELJ* 63, 66; Weatherill, '"If I'd Wanted You to Understand I would have Explained it Better": What is the Purpose of the Provisions on Closer Cooperation Introduced by the Treaty of Amsterdam?', in *Legal Issues of the Amsterdam Treaty*, eds. O'Keeffe and Twomey (Hart, Oxford, 1999).

[96] Watson, 'Social Policy after Maastricht' (1993) 31 *CMLRev.* 481, 488, *Maastricht and Social Policy—Part Two*, 239, EIRR 19, Whiteford, 'Social Policy after Maastricht' (1993) 18 *ELRev.* 202.

[97] The Social Protocol opens with the statement that 'THE HIGH CONTRACTING PARTIES [the twelve], NOTING that eleven Member States . . . wish to continue along the path laid down in the 1989 Social Charter; that they have adopted among themselves an agreement to this end'.

[98] Weiss, 'The Significance of Maastricht for European Social Policy' (1992) 8 *IJCLLIR* 3; Barnard, 'A Social Policy for Europe: Politicians 1 Lawyers 0' (1992) 8 *IJCLLIR* 15; Vogel-Polsky, *Evaluation of the Social Provisions of the Treaty on European Union*, Report prepared for the Committee on Social Affairs, Employment and the Working Environment of the European Parliament, DOC EN/CM/202155, cited in Watson, above, n. 96, 481, 491. See also the submissions made in *R v. Secretary of State for Foreign and Commonwealth Affairs, ex parte Lord Rees Mogg* [1993] 3 CMLR 101.

[99] Cf. Watson, above n. 96, 491–4 and Whiteford, above, n. 96, 203–4.

[100] Case T–135/96 *UEAPME v. Council* [1998] ECR II–2335, considered further in Ch. 2.

[101] [1996] OJ L145/4. See further Ch. 4 for details of the Directive.

[102] See further Ch. 2.

majority vote as part of the co-operation procedure[103] to include working conditions, information and consultation of workers, equality between men and women with regard to labour market opportunities and treatment at work, and the integration of those excluded from the labour market (Article 2(1) and (2) SPA [new Article 137(1) and (2)]). In addition, the Council of Ministers could adopt, by unanimity, measures in the area of social security and social protection of workers, protection of workers when their employment contract is terminated, representation and collective defence of the interests of workers and employers, including co-determination and conditions of employment for legally resident third country nationals (Article 2(3) [new Article 137(3)]). However, Article 2(6) [new Article 137(6)] expressly excluded from the EC's competence under this Article 'pay, the right of association, the right to strike or the right to impose lock-outs'.

The second reason for the SPA's significance lay with the greater role it envisaged for the Social Partners (representatives of management and labour) under Articles 3 and 4 SPA: not only would they be consulted both on the possible direction of Community action and on the content of the envisaged proposal,[104] but they could, if they chose, also negotiate collective agreements[105] which could be given *erga omnes* effect by a Council 'decision'.[106] The details of this method of legislating are considered in Chapter 2. For the present it is sufficient to note three points. First, these new provisions were the direct result of the 'Val Duchesse' social dialogue between the intersectoral (cross-industry) Social Partners (UNICE and CEEP on the employers' side and ETUC on the workers') which started in 1985. On 31 October 1991 they reached an agreement which formed the basis of Articles 3 and 4 SPA [new Articles 138 and 139]. Thus, for the first time in the social field *private* agents are making public policy.[107] Secondly, this bipartite social dialogue highlights the multi-faceted nature of the principle of subsidiarity. Although the Social Partners are negotiating (a form of 'horizontal' subsidiarity), they are doing so at European level at a time when decentralized collective bargaining is the trend in many States.[108] Thirdly, some see the Social Partners as key

---

[103] As amended to take account of the UK's absence (44 votes out of a possible 66 needed). This is now the Art. 251 [ex Art. 189b] procedure.

[104] Art. 3(2) and (3) [new Art. 138(1) and (2)].

[105] Art. 4(1) [new Art. 139(1)]. See generally Bercusson, 'Maastricht—a Fundamental Change in European Labour Law' (1992) 23 *IRJ* 177 and 'The Dynamic of European Labour Law after Maastricht' (1994) 23 *ILJ* 1.

[106] Art. 4(2) [new Art. 139(2)]. The term 'decision' is not used in the sense of Art. 249 [ex Art. 189] but has been interpreted to mean any legally binding act, in particular, directives.

[107] See further Ch. 8. Obradovic, 'Accountability of Interest Groups in the Union Law-Making Process', in *Lawmaking in the European Union*, eds. Craig and Harlow (Kluwer, Deventer, 1998), 355.

[108] e.g. in the UK most leading firms have abandoned industry-wide agreements and moved towards single employer bargaining: Edwards *et al.*, 'Great Britain: From Partial Collectivism to Neoliberalism to Where?', in *Changing Industrial Relations in Europe*, eds. Ferner and Hyman (Blackwell, Oxford, 1998).

players in the creation of a 'civil society' at European level, which is so essential to giving the newly created 'citizens' confidence in and commitment to the EU. In the words of the Economic and Social Committee:

Civil society is a collective term for all types of social action, by individuals or groups, that do not emanate from the state and are not run by it. . . . The participatory model of civil society also provides an opportunity to strengthen confidence in the democratic system so that a more favourable climate for reform and innovation can develop.[109]

5. From Maastricht to Amsterdam

With the Social Charter Action Programme nearing its natural conclusion and with the new Social Chapter at its disposal, the Commission began to examine the future direction of Community social policy in the light of the trends in economic and industrial relations outlined in section 4 above, focusing especially on the serious levels of unemployment. Its response was to issue a White Paper on Growth, Competitiveness, and Employment,[110] a Green Paper on European Social Policy,[111] leading to a White Paper on Social Policy putting forward specific proposals.[112] The striking feature about these documents is the emphasis placed on social goals, such as the promotion of high levels of employment and the elimination of social exclusion, and the move away from harmonization of social rights to a greater reliance on convergence, which has been extensively used in the context of social security, technocratic support, and soft law.[113] Particularly in the field of employment, harmonization is gradually being replaced by 'management by objectives' or the open method of co-ordination based on policy guidelines, setting benchmarks, concrete targets and a monitoring system to evaluate progress via peer group review.[113A]

In the White Paper the Commission recognized that the SPA provided a new basis for Union action which it intended to use 'to ensure a dynamic social dimension of the Union'.[114] However, recognizing that the UK would not be

[109] Opinion of the Economic and Social Committee on 'The Role and Contribution of Civil Society Organisations in the Building of Europe' [1999] OJ L329/30.

[110] Bull. Supp. 6/93.

[111] COM(93)551, 17 Nov. 1993 and ECOSOC's response 94/C148/10. See Kuper, 'The Green and White Papers of the European Union: The Apparent Goal of Reduced Social Benefits' (1994) 4 *Journal of European Social Policy* 129, and Kenner, 'European Social Policy—New Directions' (1994) 10 *IJCLLIR* 56.

[112] COM(94)333, 27 July 1994.

[113] Cullen and Campbell, 'The Future of Social Policy-Making in the EU', in Craig and Harlow (eds.), *Lawmaking in the European Union* (Kluwer, London, 1998) 263. See below nn. 277–278 and Ch. 2.

[113A] Commission Communication on the Social Policy Agenda COM (2000)379 final, 7.

[114] COM(94)333, 13.

bound by any measure adopted on such a basis, the Commission noted the 'strong desire of all Member States to proceed as twelve wherever possible' and hoped that 'Union social policy action will in future once again be founded on a single legal framework'.[115] This was achieved with the election of the new Labour government in May 1997. One of the first steps taken by the new government was to agree to sign up to—or opt back into—the Social Chapter.[116] As a result, at the IGC in Amsterdam an amended chapter on social provisions, incorporating and revising both Articles 117–121 of the EC Treaty and the SPA, was included in the EC Treaty in a new section in the Amsterdam Treaty entitled 'The Union and the Citizen'.

Three significant changes, were, however, made to the text of the new Title on Social Policy. The first concerns the revised Article 117 [new Article 136], which refers to 'The Community and the Member States, having in mind fundamental social rights such as those set out in the European Charter signed at Turin on 18 October 1961 and in the 1989 Community Charter of Fundamental Social Rights'. While the (eleven) Member States had, in the SPA agreed at Maastricht, referred to their wish to 'implement the 1989 Social Charter on the basis of the *acquis communautaire* . . .', the reference to the 1961 Social Charter adopted by the Council of Europe is new, although the Court had referred to it as a source of fundamental rights in various cases.[117] The importance of Article 117 [new Article 136] had already been emphasized by the Court in *Sloman*.[118] It said that the objectives of Article 117 [new Article 136], although in the nature of a programme, constituted an important aid for the interpretation of other provisions of the Treaty and of secondary legislation on the social field. Yet there is a mismatch between the EC's Title on Social Policy and the two Charters. Both the Community and Council of Europe Charters refer to extensive collective rights, including the right of association, the right to strike, and the right to impose lock-outs. These continue to be excluded from the EC's Title on Social Policy (Article 137(6) [ex Article 2(6)]).

The second change can be found in Article 137 [old Article 118], which replaces the co-operation procedure with the co-decision procedure found in Article 251 [ex Article 189b], introduced by the Treaty on European Union. Further, the use of the Article 251 [ex Article 189b] procedure has been extended to enable the Council to 'adopt measures designed to encourage co-operation between Member States through initiatives aimed at improving

---

[115] Ibid. See also COM(93)600, the Commission's Communication concerning the application of the SPA.

[116] See Barnard, 'The United Kingdom, the "Social Chapter" and the Amsterdam Treaty' (1997) 26 *ILJ* 275.

[117] Case 149/77 *Defrenne (No. 3)* [1978] ECR 1365, para. 28; Case 126/86 *Zaera v. Instituto Nacional de la Securidad Social* [1987] ECR 3697, para. 14.

[118] Joined Cases C–72 and C–73/91 *Sloman Neptun v. Bodo Ziesemer* [1993] ECR I–887, para. 26.

knowledge, developing exchanges of information and best practices, promoting innovative approaches and evaluating experiences in order to combat social exclusion'.

The third change concerns the importance of equality between men and women. The significance of this principle has been reinforced with its inclusion in Article 2 EC as one of the tasks of the Community and as one of the activities of the Community in Article 3. This now provides that 'In all the activities referred to in this Article, the Community shall aim to eliminate inequalities, and to promote equality, between men and women'. Perhaps more importantly, Article 119 [new Article 141] on equal pay has been amended significantly. In particular, Article 141(3) [ex Article 119(3)] finally provides an express legal basis for the Council to adopt measures, again in accordance with the Article 189b [new Article 251] co-decision procedure, 'to ensure the application of the principle of equal opportunities and equal treatment of men and women in matters of employment and occupation, including the principle of equal pay for equal work or work of equal value'. There is, however, some overlap between Article 119(3) [new Article 141(3)] and Article 118(1) [new Article 137(1)] which allows for Community action in the field of 'equality between men and women with regard to labour market opportunities and treatment at work'.[119] The other striking change to Article 119 can be found in the paragraph 4, which recognizes the principle of positive action, first introduced by Article 6(3) SPA.[120] The significance of this will be considered in Chapter 4.

Although the UK agreed to sign the new Social Chapter in the Amsterdam Treaty, the Treaty remained silent on the question of how the UK would incorporate the pre-ratification legislation as a matter of Community law. In the event the Community (re)adopted the existing Directives (European Works Councils (EWCs),[121] Parental Leave,[122] Part-time Work,[123] and Burden of Proof[124]) under the existing legal bases provided for by the EC Treaty and set the UK new deadlines to comply.

Thus, during the five years of the UK opt-out from the Social Chapter only four pieces of legislation were adopted,[125] and two of these, the Parental Leave Directive and the Part-time Work Directive, were adopted through the

[119] Given that the legislative procedures are the same under each Art., the overlap is not perhaps of great significance.

[120] See Betten and Shrubsall, 'The Concept of Positive Sex Discrimination in Community Law—Before and After the Treaty of Amsterdam' (1998) 14 *IJCLLIR* 65.

[121] Council Directive 94/95/EC [1994] OJ L254/64, as amended by Council Directive 97/74/EC [1998] OJ L10/22; consolidated legislation [1998] OJ L10/20.

[122] Council Directive 96/34/EC [1996] OJ L145/4, as amended by Council Directive 97/75 [1998] OJ L10/24.

[123] Council Directive 97/81/EC [1998] OJ L14/9, as amended by Council Directive 98/23/EC [1998] OJ L131/10; consolidated legislation [1998] OJ L131/13.

[124] Council Directive 97/80/EC [1997] OJ L14/16, as amended by Council Directive 98/52/EC [1998] OJ L205/66.

[125] McGlynn, 'An Exercise in Futility: The Practical Effects of the Social Policy Opt-out' (1998) 49 *NILQ* 60.

auspices of the Social Partners. It seems that despite the avowed intention of
the eleven in the SPP 'to continue along the path laid down in the 1989 Social
Charter' they did so with little enthusiasm in the absence of the UK. Further,
even in the absence of the UK, British companies were still affected by legislation adopted under the Social Chapter. This can be seen most clearly in respect
of the EWC Directive.[126] British multi-nationals with plants on the Continent
were obliged to set up EWCs and many extended them to their UK employees
(for example, United Biscuits, BP, ICI, Courtaulds, GKN, and NatWest), even
though the UK government had not participated in negotiating the legislation.
Foreign-owned companies such as Panasonic and TNT also set up consultative
bodies in response to the Directive and included their British operations.

   The other significant developments at Amsterdam for social policy were
first the inclusion of a new legal basis (Article 6a [new Article 13]) prohibiting discrimination on a number of grounds; and secondly, the introduction
of a new Title on Employment heralded by the inclusion in Article 2 of a new
task of 'a high level of employment and of social protection'. This highlighted
a shift in emphasis in the EU from measures protecting those in employment
to addressing the high levels of *un*employment in Europe. Part of this strategy
is to modernize the organization of work, as demonstrated by the Commission's Green Paper, *Partnership for a New Organisation of Work*.[127] As will be
seen, the Social Partners have a central role to play in this process. The
implementation of the Employment Title will be considered below.

B. THE NATURE AND PURPOSE OF EC SOCIAL POLICY

1. Introduction

The discussion in the previous section indicates that the development of the
so-called social dimension has been spasmodic: the resulting rules represent a
patchwork of European social regulation rather than a fully fledged social
policy with welfare institutions and cradle-to-grave protection.[128] It makes no
provision for what is generally agreed to be the central core of social policy:
social insurance, public assistance, health and welfare services, and housing
policy.[129] There is no evidence of the creation of a European welfare state and

---

[126] Wedderburn, 'Consultation and Collective Bargaining in Europe: Success or Ideology?'
(1997) 26 *ILJ* 1.

[127] COM(97)127.

[128] This section draws heavily on Barnard, 'EC "Social" Policy', in *The Evolution of EU Law*, eds.
Craig and de Búrca (OUP, Oxford, 1999).

[129] Majone, 'The European Community: Between Social Policy and Regulation' (1993) 31
JCMS 153, 158. However, the EC Treaty does contain a chapter on education, vocational training, and youth and titles on culture, public health, and consumer protection. The cases on health
testing of staff at the institutions also demonstrate some awareness of the wider dimension of
social policy. See e.g. Case C–404/92 P *Commission* v. *X* [1994] ECR I–4737.

the EU certainly does not have the budget for it. However, the existing body of EC regulation is often referred to as 'European social policy', not least by the EC Treaty itself.[130] In reality, this terminology masks what has been to date employment-related social policy—and an eclectic body of employment law at that. As Freedland points out, it is concerned with equal pay and equal treatment between men and women, rather than with discrimination in employment generally; with collective dismissals and acquired rights on transfer of undertakings, rather than with the termination of employment more generally; with particulars of the terms of the contract rather than the terms themselves; with consultation of workers' representatives on certain issues rather than with collective representation and workers' organizations as a whole; and with working time and health and safety rather than with the quality of working conditions more generally.[131] It is with the area of social policy concerned with employment law, both individual and collective, that this book is concerned, and not with social law and policy as more broadly understood.[132] It will examine the body of Community law which supplements, complements, and sometimes constrains existing national social policy.[133]

Traditionally, social policy is viewed as serving a social justice/social cohesion or a market-correcting[134] function. Marshall defines social policy as the use of 'political power to supersede, supplement or modify operations of the economic system in order to achieve results which the economic system would not achieve on its own, . . . guided by values other than those determined by market forces'.[135] Elements of this can be detected in the development of EC social legislation. On the other hand, as Streeck has observed:

Economic governance through fragmented sovereignty and international relations is more suited to market-making by way of negative integration and efficiency enhancing regulation than to institution building and redistributive intervention, or market distortion.[136]

Thus Streeck argues that the Treaty of Rome charged the Community with

---

[130] Title XI [old Title VIII] is headed 'Social Policy, Education, Vocational Training and Youth'. Ch. 1, which contains Arts. 136–145 [ex Arts. 117–122], is entitled 'Social Provisions'. See also the Commission's 'White Paper on Social Policy', COM(94)333.

[131] Freedland, 'Employment Policy' in Davis, Lyon-Caen, Sciarra, and Simitis (eds.), *European Community Labour Law: Principles and Perspectives* (Clarendon, Oxford, 1996), 278–79. However with the greater competence given to the Community at Maastricht and then Amsterdam (see above, nn. 102–103), this is beginning to change.

[132] For more on these broader issues, see Hervey, above n. 7.

[133] Pierson and Leibfried, 'The Making of Social Policy', in *European Social Policy: Between Fragmentation and Integration*, eds. Leibfried and Pierson (Brookings Institution, Washington D.C., 1995). Streeck, 'Neo-voluntarism: A New Social Policy Regime' (1995) 1 *ELJ* 31, 32.

[134] Streeck, 'From Market Making to State Building? Reflections on the Political Economy of European Social Policy', in Leibfried and Pierson (eds.), above nn. 133, 399.

[135] Marshall, *Social Policy* (Hutchinson, London, 1975), 15.

[136] Streeck, above n. 133, 34. See also above n. 133, Leibfried and Pierson's references to a 'multi-level system of governance'.

developing *a new kind of social policy*, one concerned with *market making rather than market correcting*, aimed at creating an integrated European labour market and enabling it to function efficiently, rather than with correcting its outcomes in line with political standards of social justice.[137]

In other words, the existing body of EC employment-related social policy represents regulation in support of a free or common market to ensure, in the words of Article 96 [ex Article 101], the conditions of competition are not distorted. This analysis does not, however, take into account the EC's policies in the field of vocational training to help the unemployed find work, or to improve the skills of those in work. Such policies could be described as 'market-enforcing' and, as we shall see, have an important role to play in buttressing Community social policy. The market-making thesis has had a considerable influence on the shape of Community social policy and the relevance and influence of this thesis will now be considered.

2. EC Social Policy as Market-making

It seems that the market-making thesis comprises three limbs: first, the creation of a 'European-wide labour market',[138] by removing obstacles to the mobility of (market-creating) workers;[139] secondly, removing distortions to competition by, seeking to harmonize costs on firms and, thirdly, market-perfecting. This involves, on the one hand, setting rules which the market would provide if it were operating efficiently. On the other hand, market perfecting involves setting EC standards designed to stop Member States from using the freedom to control their own social policy for 'malign' rather than 'benign' purposes—to deregulate national labour standards in order to gain a competitive advantage leading to a race to the bottom by states and social dumping by business. It is often difficult to disentangle these strands in the debates about the creation of EC social policy.

The clearest example of aspects of the market-making thesis can be found with the inclusion of Article 119 [new Article 141] on equal pay in the Treaty. As we have seen, it is clear that the debate between the French and German governments prior to the signing of the Treaty of Rome[140] revolved principally around economic interests—concerns about loss of competitiveness on the part of France—and not the social interests of the workers in the EC (although its drafting was inspired by ILO Convention No. 100).[141] The

---

[137] Streeck, above n. 134, 399.
[138] Streeck, above n. 134, 397.
[139] Considered further above, n. 8.
[140] See above, text attached to nn. 16–21.
[141] Hoskyns, *Integrating Gender: Women, Law and Politics in the European Union* (Verso, London, 1996), ch. 3.

French were particularly concerned about discriminatory pay rates resulting from collective agreements in Italy. At that time France had one of the smallest differentials between the salaries of male and female employees (7 per cent compared to 20 to 40 per cent in the Netherlands and in Italy).[142] This risked placing those parts of French industry employing a very large female workforce, such as textiles and electrical construction, in a weaker competitive position than identical or similar industries in other Member States employing a largely female workforce at much lower salaries.[143]

Consequently, Article 119 [new Article 141] was included in the Treaty to impose parity of costs on the Member States and to prevent such destructive competition. This point was noted, albeit somewhat obliquely, by the French Advocate General Dutheillet de Lamothe in *Defrenne (No. 1)*,[144] the first case to consider the application of Article 119 [new Article 141]. Advancing the market-making thesis, he said that although Article 119 [new Article 141] had a social objective it also had an economic objective

for in creating an obstacle to any attempt at 'social dumping' by means of the use of female labour less well paid than male labour, it helped to achieve one of the fundamental objectives of the common market, the establishment of a system ensuring that 'competition is not distorted'.

He continued that 'This explains why Article 119 of the Treaty is of a different character from the articles which precede it in the Chapter of the Treaty devoted to social provisions'.

It therefore seems that the social provisions of the Treaty 'respond above all to the fear that unless employment costs are harmonised, economic integration will lead to competition to the detriment of countries whose social legislation is more advanced'.[145] This suggests a role for exhaustive EC social

---

[142] Budiner, *Le Droit de la femme a l'égalité de salaire et la Convention No. 100 de l'organisation internationale du travail* (Librairie Générale de Droit et de Jurisprudence, Paris, 1975), citing Sullerot, *L'emploi des femmes et ses problèmes dans les Etats Membres de la Communauté Européene* (CEC, Brussels 1972), 177. See generally Barnard, above n. 15.

[143] Budiner, above n. 142, citing Jean-Jacques Ribas, 'L'égalité des salaires feminins et masculins dans la Communauté économique européene' (Nov. 1966), *Droit Social*, para. 1, and Clair, 'L'article 119 du Traité de Rome. Le Principe de l'égalisation des salaires masculins et feminins dans la CEE' (Mar. 1968), *Droit Social*, 150. In addition, France had ratified ILO Convention No. 100 by Law No. 52–1309 of 10 Dec. 1952 (Journal Officiel, 11 Dec.1952). By 1957 the Convention had also been ratified by Belgium, France, Germany, and Italy, but not by Luxembourg and the Netherlands. (Luxembourg ratified the Convention in 1967 and the Netherlands in 1971. All fifteen states of the European Union have now ratified the Convention.)

[144] Case 80/70 [1971] ECR 445. In Case 69/80 *Worringham and Humphreys* v. *Lloyd's Bank* [1981] ECR 767 Advocate General Warner again referred back to Advocate General Dutheillet de Lamothe's statement in *Defrenne (No. 1)* that the first purpose of Art. 119 was to 'avoid a situation in which undertakings established in Member States with advanced legislation on the equal treatment of men and women suffer a competitive disadvantage as compared with undertakings established in Member States that have not eliminated discrimination against female workers as regards pay'.

[145] Author's translation of Valticos, *Droit international du travail*, para. 180, cited in Budiner, above n. 142, 3.

legislation. This sits uncomfortably with the new emphasis on subsidiarity and, in particular, directives setting minimum standards (considered further in Chapter 2) whose objective is not to eliminate the differences between the laws of the Member States but to prevent distortions of competition where standards in any Member State are—or might become—unacceptably low. This suggests that EC social legislation has an underlying market-correcting function. The Court, pursuing in Streeck's words its own 'distinctive integrationist agenda',[146] has recognized the social dimension of the 'social' provisions. In its landmark judgment in *Defrenne (No. 2)*,[147] the Court said:

Article 119 pursues a double aim. *First*, . . . the aim of Article 119 is to avoid a situation in which undertakings established in states which have actually implemented the principle of equal pay suffer a competitive disadvantage in intra-Community competition as compared with undertakings established in states which have not yet eliminated discrimination against women workers as regards pay.

Having recognized the economic purpose of Article 119, the Court then continued:

Second, this provision forms part of the social objectives of the Community, which is not merely an economic union, but is at the same time intended, by common action to ensure social progress and seek the constant improvement of living and working conditions of their peoples. . . . This double aim, which is at once economic and social, shows that the principle of equal pay forms part of the foundations of the Community.

The Court again recognized the dual purpose of the Community's social provisions in *Commission v. UK*.[148] It said that in the Directives on Collective Redundancies and Acquired Rights[149] 'the Community legislature intended both to ensure comparable protection for workers' rights in the different Member States and to harmonise the costs which such protective rules entail for Community undertakings'.[150] Further, the legislation of the 1970s cannot be explained solely in terms of harmonization of costs. Measures such as those on sex equality, transfers of undertakings, collective redundancies, and insolvency suggested a project of market-correcting as well as market-making for Community social policy.[151]

It therefore seems that the Community has seen social policy in terms of a dichotomy combining a market-led conception of employment regulation,

---

[146] Streeck, above n. 133, 39.

[147] Case 43/75 [1976] ECR 455. This was emphasized in Case C–50/96 *Deutsche Telekom v. Schröder*, judgment of 10 Feb. 2000, paras. 53–55. This case also emphasized that EC law set minimum standards (*in casu* non-retroactivity) which Member States were free to improve on (para. 59).

[148] Case C–382/92 *Commission v. UK* [1994] ECR I–2435 and Case C–383/92 [1994] ECR I–2479.

[149] Directives 75/129/EEC [1975] OJ L48/29 and 77/187/EEC [1977] OJ L61/27, respectively.

[150] See further Deakin, 'Labour Law and Market Regulation' in Davies *et al.* (eds.), above n. 131.

[151] Streeck, above n. 134, 399.

augmented by some market-enforcing measures, with some recognition of the market-correcting or social function of such regulation. This prompts Freedland to suggest that the evolution of EC employment law has always depended on the possibility of legitimating it in economic policy terms as well as social policy terms. He argues that this is a possibility which is made all the more attainable by the fact that the proponents of economic policy have felt the need to lay claim to a social legitimation.[152] This can be detected in recent Commission documents. In its White Paper on Social Policy[153] the Commission talks of:

the establishment of a framework of basic minimum standards, which the Commission started some years ago, provides a bulwark against using low social standards as an instrument of unfair economic competition and protection against reducing social standards to gain competitiveness, and is also an expression of the political will to maintain the momentum of social progress.[154]

The Commission's desire to justify its social policy proposals in economic terms has, however, created difficulties.[155] In the Explanatory Memorandum accompanying its proposals for a draft directive on atypical work the Commission said that 'relative cost differences resulting from different kinds of rules on different types of employment relationships, . . . may provide comparative advantages which constitute veritable distortions of competition'.[156] However, the Commission's arguments were weakened by its attempts to suggest that while harmonization of indirect wage costs resulting from social security taxation and employment regulation should take place, harmonization of direct costs (rules governing wages and salaries) was unnecessary because 'differences in productivity levels attenuate these differences in unit labour costs to a considerable degree'. Such a distinction has little merit from either an economic or a legal standpoint and it had the effect of rejecting the very argument put forward in 1957 for the adoption of Article 119 [new Article 141].[157]

The deregulatory agenda adopted by the British Conservative government reawakened concerns about negative competitiveness leading to social dumping. These concerns were brought into sharp focus by the highly-publicized Hoover affair. Hoover decided to close its factory in Longvic, near Dijon, with the loss of 600 out of 700 jobs, and to transfer its activities to the Cambuslang plant, near Glasgow in Scotland, resulting in the recruitment of 400 workers on twenty-four-month fixed-term contracts.[158] This followed the

---

[152] Freedland, above n. 131, 287.
[153] COM(94)333, 27 July 1994.
[154] Ibid., Introduction, para. 19.
[155] Deakin, above n. 150, 77–8.
[156] COM(90)228. See further Ch. 6.
[157] Deakin and Wilkinson, 'Rights vs Efficiency? The Economic Case for Transnational Labour Standards' (1994) 23 *ILJ* 289, 302–3.
[158] See EIRR 230, 16.

conclusion of a collective agreement between management and the British Amalgamated Engineering and Electrical Union (AEEU) providing for improved flexibility of labour, new working patterns, a no-strike deal, and a pay freeze. At the same time Rockwell Graphic systems announced that 110 jobs were to be lost out of 272 at its Nantes plant with production being relocated to Preston in England. Martine Aubry, the French Minister for labour, and the French Prime Minister both said that Hoover's decision constituted 'social dumping'.[159]

Social dumping is the vogue term used to describe a variety of practices by both Member States and employers. In essence it concerns behaviour designed to give a competitive advantage to companies due to low labour standards[160] rather than productivity. Companies that move in response to a deliberate lowering of standards by the State are said to be engaged in social dumping. This in turn might precipitate a race-to-the-bottom, with Member States competing to deregulate to attract capital or at least to retain existing capital.

Social dumping inevitably leads to calls for transnational social legislation to prevent this race-to-the-bottom. The Commission relied on this rhetoric to justify the enactment of Community social legislation:

Legislating for higher labour standards and employee rights has been an important part of the Union's achievements in the social field. The key objectives have been both to ensure that the creation of the single market did not result in a downward pressure on labour standards or create a distortion of competition, and to ensure that working people also shared in the new prosperity. The main areas of focus have been equal treatment of men and women, free movement of workers, health and safety, and—to a limited extent—labour law.[161]

Further, in the Commission's Green Paper on European Social Policy it said that:

a commitment to high social standards and to the promotion of social progress forms an integral part of the [TEU]. A 'negative' competitiveness between Member States would lead to social dumping, to the undermining of the consensus making process ... and to danger for the acceptability of the Union.[162]

However, some argue that such legislation would be inefficient[163] and would have the effect of killing the poorer States with kindness,[164] depriving them of their comparative advantage—their cheaper workforce—and their

---

[159] EIRR 230, 16. John Major, the then British Prime Minister, is reported as saying in response 'France can complain all it likes. If investors and business choose to come to Britain rather than pay the costs of socialism in France, let them call it "social dumping". I call it dumping socialism': *Financial Times*, 6 Mar. 1993.

[160] See also Hepple, 'New Approaches to International Labour Regulation' (1997) 26 *ILJ* 353, 355.

[161] COM(94)333, Ch. III, para. 1.

[162] COM(93)551, 46.

[163] See e.g. Fischel, 'The "Race to the Bottom" Revisited—Reflections on Recent Developments in Delaware's Corporation Law' (1982) 31 *Northwestern University Law Review* 913.

[164] *The Economist*, 23 June 1990, 17.

vehicle for improvement.[165] Yet, crucially the EC has (little or) no competence over pay[166] and, as we have seen, due to the Member States' desire to protect their own sovereignty, it has only limited competence in respect of other types of working conditions, so its hands are severely tied. This largely prevents it from protecting Member States with higher standards from the decisions of the others. However, under pressure from the Germans, the EC has enacted the Directive on Posted Workers[167] in order to preserve the local system of wage-setting and collectively negotiated, levy-based 'social funds' in the German construction industry.[168] Here we have an example of how EC social legislation, in its market-making function, serves as a safety net to prevent the dismantling of national employment protection measures as well as serving a (limited) market-correcting function.[169]

However, despite the rhetoric there is in fact little evidence of the states being engaged in an active policy of deregulation of labour standards for the purpose of gaining a competitive edge,[170] a point noted by the OECD which said 'there is no compelling evidence that "social dumping" has occurred so far in OECD countries'.[171] Schonfield added 'The dangers of "social dumping" have been exaggerated with only isolated examples of competitive undercutting of pay and conditions by firms exploiting labour cost differences between countries'.[172] On the other hand, he noted that there was evidence from Germany that companies are increasingly using the possibility of relocation as a bargaining counter to achieve changes in working practices at home.[173]

It would therefore seem that the development of the Community's 'social' policy is constrained—perhaps fatally—by the need to operate both within an economic and social framework. As we shall see, this leads, on the one hand, to some inconsistent decisions by the Court concerning the interface between Community law on market integration and national law and, on the other, to a patchwork of Community social legislation aimed at both harmonization and minimum standards. Of course, national social policy faces similar

---

[165] Kiernan and Beim, 'On the Economic Realities of the European Social Charter and the Social Dimension of EC 1992' (1992) 2 *Duke Journal of Comparative and International Labour Law* 149.

[166] See above, text attached to n. 103.

[167] Directive 96/71/EC [1997] OJ L181/1. See Davies, 'Posted Workers: Single Market or Protection of National Labour Law Systems' (1997) 34 *CMLRev.* 571.

[168] See Streeck, above n. 133, 42, and Simitis, 'Dismantling or Strengthening Labour Law: the Case of the European Court of Justice' (1996) 2 *ELJ* 156, 163.

[169] See further above, text attached to nn. 138–146.

[170] Barnard, 'Social Dumping and Race to the Bottom: Some Lessons for the European Union from Delaware?' (2000) 25 *ELRev.* 57.

[171] OECD, 'Labour Standards and Economic Integration', in *Employment Outlook 1994* (OECD, Paris, 1994), 138.

[172] Reported by Taylor, 'Wage Bargaining Diversification under EU Single Market', *Financial Times*, 7 Apr. 1997.

[173] See e.g. the concessions made by German workers at Bosch and Daimler Benz because of threats of locating to new plants abroad (see 'Can Europe compete', *Financial Times*, 28 Feb. 1994).

dilemmas but the dichotomy is brought into sharper focus in the Community context due to its original economic objectives[173A] and to the absence of the underpinnings of a welfare state or fundamental civil and social rights.

3. EC Social Policy and the European Court of Justice

Any historical review of the development of EC social policy would not be complete without reference to the important role played by the European Court of Justice. We have already seen how the Court reinvigorated Article 141 [ex Article 119] on equal pay in the *Defrenne* cases by saying that it was directly effective.[174] This highlights what Davies identifies as the Court's pre-occupation, especially strong in the early years, of ensuring that those parts of Community law which were intended to govern relations between and among legal persons in day-to-day life did in fact give rise to legal rights and obligations within the judicial system of the Member States.[175] The social policy cases, with their direct impact on individuals, therefore presented the Court with the opportunity to develop important principles of enforcement, such as the direct effect of directives.[176]

At the same time the Court showed itself willing to bolster the substantive protection provided by the social legislation. For example, it ruled that the Equal Treatment Directive 76/207 prohibited discrimination against trans-sexuals[177] and women on the grounds of their pregnancy,[178] but allowed 'soft quotas';[179] it recognized that Directive 77/187 on transfers of undertakings could apply to contracting-out,[180] even in the public sector;[181] and, perhaps most controversially, it ruled in *Barber*[182] that Article 119 [new Article 141] required equality in respect of occupational pension age, despite the deroga-tion to Directive 86/378/EEC for equal treatment in respect of occupational pensions.

[173A] See Streit and Mussler, 'The Economic Constitution of the European Community: From "Rome" to "Maastricht" ' (1995) 1 *ELJ* 5.

[174] See above, n. 33.

[175] Davies, 'The European Court of Justice, National Courts, and the Member States', in Davies *et al.* (eds.), above n. 131.

[176] Case 152/84 *Marshall v. Southampton Area Health Authority (No. 1)* [1986] ECR 723; Case C–188/89 *Foster v. British Gas* [1990] ECR I–3313.

[177] Case C–13/94 *P v. S* [1996] ECR I–2143, but not homosexuals (see Case C–249/96 *Grant v. S. W. Trains* [1998] ECR I–621).

[178] Case C–177/88 *Dekker v. Stichting Vormungscentrum voor Jong Volwassenen* [1990] ECR I–3941, Case C–32/93 *Webb v. EMO Air Cargo* [1994] ECR I–3567.

[179] Cf. Case C–450/93 *Kalanke v. Freie Hansestadt Bremen* [1995] ECR I–3051 with Case C–409/95 *Marschall v. Land Nordrhein-Westfalen* [1997] ECR I–6363.

[180] Case C–209/91 *Rask and Christensen v. ISS Kantineservice* [1992] ECR I–5755. Cf. Case C–13/95 *Süzen v. Zehnacker Gebäudereinigung GmbH Krankenhausservice* [1997] ECR I-1259.

[181] Case C–29/91 *Dr Sophie Redmond v. Bartol* [1992] ECR I–3189.

[182] Case C–262/88 *Barber v. Guardian Royal Exchange* [1990] ECR I–1889.

In more recent years, the Court has developed a second, linked area of interest—ensuring that the procedural and remedial laws of the Member States governing the enforcement of causes of action derived from Community law are effective. Once again the Court has used the social cases as the principal vehicle to develop this concept. For example, in *Johnston*[183] the Court said that the requirement of judicial control stipulated by Article 6 of the Equal Treatment Directive 76/207 reflected a general principle of law. Further, in *Von Colson*[184] the Court said that the Equal Treatment Directive required that the sanction chosen by the Member State must be such as to guarantee real and effective judicial protection.[185] In *Marshall (No. 2)*[186] the Court accepted that a limit on the total amount of compensation a tribunal could award a complainant and the absence of any power to award interest amounted to a breach of Article 6 of Directive 76/207 which required adequate reparation for the loss and damage sustained.

This desire to make Community law effective in the national systems culminated in the Court's decision on state liability in *Francovich (No. 1)*, a case concerning the Italian government's failure to implement Directive 80/987/EEC on employees' rights on their employer's insolvency.[187] The Court ruled that in order to ensure the full effectiveness of Community law, and as part of the state's duty under Article 5 to take all appropriate measures to fulfil its Community law obligations, the State was liable for 'loss and damage caused to individuals as a result of breaches of Community Law'.[188]

The Court's decisions have not gone without criticism. Some ask whether, given the limited law-making powers in the social field, it is legitimate for the Court to expand both its own power and that of the Community into this area. On the other hand others argue that the Court, by giving a voice to individual litigants and pressure groups, may well have increased the participative element of democracy in the Union as a whole.[189] If the latter view is favoured, then the Court's own legitimacy is undermined by, at times, poorly reasoned judgments and a lack of consistency. For example, in those areas where the Court has shown itself most determined to enforce rights and, often, to increase the level of national protection, there are signs that it is

[183] Case 222/84 *Johnston v. RUC* [1986] ECR 1651.

[184] Case 14/83 *Von Colson and Kamann v. Land Nordrhein-Westfalen* [1984] ECR 1509.

[185] Para. 23.

[186] Case C–271/91 [1993] ECR I–4367. The UK removed these limitations by passing SI 2798/1993 Sex Discrimination and Equal Pay (Remedial) Regulations 1993. It also extended this protection to race relations—Race Relations (Remedies) Act 1994. See also Case C–180/95 *Draehmpaehl v. Urania Immobilienservice ohG* [1997] ECR I–2195; cf. Case C–66/95 *R v. Secretary of State for Social Security, ex parte Sutton* [1997] ECR I–2163; cf. Case C–246/96 *Magorrian v. Eastern Health and Social Services Board* [1997] ECR I–7153.

[187] Joined Cases C–6 and 9/90 *Francovich v. Italian Republic (No. 1)* [1991] ECR I–5357. See also Ch. 7.

[188] Para. 35.

[189] See Fredman, 'Social Law in the European Union: The Impact of the Lawmaking Process', in *Lawmaking in the European Union*, eds. Craig and Harlow (Kluwer, Deventer, 1998), 402.

beginning to back-track. In *Süzen*[190] the Court threatened to undermine the whole complex edifice of worker protection on contracting out in respect of transfers of undertakings, and in *ex parte Sutton*[191] the Court significantly undermined the effectiveness of its earlier ruling in *Marshall (No. 2)* in the context of Directive 79/7.

But perhaps most critical for the purpose of the discussion in this chapter is the challenge the Court's decisions have posed to the integrity of the national system of labour and social protection in the interests of market-creating at EU level.[192] For example, in *Macrotron*[193] the Court held that the German Federal Employment Office was not entitled to maintain its statutory monopoly over 'employment placement services'. The Court said it was abusing its dominant position contrary to Articles 86 and 90(1) [new Articles 82 and 86] because the statutory service could not meet demand and tolerated private head-hunters, even though their activities were illegal. Similarly, in *Porto di Genova*[194] the Court said that Article 90(1) EC [new Article 86] precluded national rules which conferred on an undertaking established in that State (but not individual dockers)[195] the exclusive right to organize dock work and required it to have recourse to a dock work company formed exclusively of national workers. Although the facts of *Porto di Genova* were exceptional (the company was abusing its monopoly to demand payment for unrequested services, to offer selective reductions in prices and by refusing to have recourse to modern technology), the most striking feature of the Court's judgment, as Deakin points out,[196] was the almost complete disregard shown for social arguments which could have been made in favour of the dock labour monopoly. In particular, no reference was made to the need to combat casualization of labour.

On the other hand, in some cases the Court has striven to uphold national social regulation. For example, when interpreting Article 30 [new Article 28] on the free movement of goods, the Court has found that national measures

---

[190] Case C–13/95 [1997] ECR I–1259.

[191] Case C–66/95 [1997] ECR I–2163.

[192] Above n. 8. See generally Wedderburn, 'Workers' Rights: Fact or Fake' (1991) 13 *Dublin University Law Journal* 1; Davies, 'Market Integration and Social Policy in the Court of Justice' (1995) 24 *ILJ* 49; and Lyon-Caen, 'Droit Social et droit de la concurrence. Observations sur une rencontre', in *Orientations Sociales du Droit Contemperain: Ecrits en l'honneur de Pr. Jean Savatier* (PUF, Paris, 1992).

[193] Case C–41/90 *Höfner and Elser v. Macrotron* [1991] ECR I–1979; see also Case C–55/96 *Non-Contentious Proceedings brought by Job Centre Coop arl* [1997] ECR I–7140. See, generally, Ricci, 'Il controverso rapporto fra principi comunitari della concorrenza e normative nazionali del lavoro il caso Job Centre II' (1998) 2 *Diritto delle relazioni industriali* 145.

[194] Case C–179/90 *Merci Convenzionali Porto di Genova v. Siderurgica Gabrielli* [1991] ECR I–5889. See also Case C–163/96 *Criminal Proceedings against Silvano Raso* [1998] ECR I–533; Decision of the Commission 97/744/EC *Re Italian Ports Employment Policy: The Community v. Italy* [1998] 4 CMLR 73.

[195] Case C-22/98 *Criminal Proceedings against Bew, Verweire, Smeg and Adia Interim*, judgment of 16 Sep. 1999.

[196] Deakin, above n. 150, 75.

designed to ensure worker protection—such as legislation prohibiting employment of workers on Sunday[197] or prohibiting night work in bakeries[198]—while potentially a restriction on trade either did not breach Community law or could at least be justified by mandatory or public interest requirements. Similarly, in *Rush Portuguesa*[199] the Court ruled that host states were entitled to apply their labour laws to the employees of subcontractors from another Member State while the employees were working on the host state's territory without infringing Article 59 [new Article 49].[200] The Court has also been prepared to take social factors into account in areas which do not impact on the four freedoms. For example, in *Beentjes*[201] the Court said that the exclusion of a company tendering for a contract on the ground that it was not in a position to employ the long-term unemployed was compatible with Council Directive 71/305/EEC on the award of public works contracts,[202] if it has no direct or indirect discriminatory effect on tenderers from other Member States of the Community.[203] Similarly, when interpreting Article 92 [new Article 87] prohibiting Member States from granting aid which distorts or threatens to distort competition, the Court has found that the exemption of small business from the national system of protection of employees against unfair dismissal did not constitute a state aid.[204] Following this decision, the Court has also ruled that a law exempting the Italian post office from the requirement that employees be appointed on indefinite contracts only did not constitute a state aid.[205]

[197] Case C–312/8 *Union départementale des syndicats CGT de l'Aisne* v. *Conforama* [1991] ECR I–977 and Case C–332/89 *Criminal Proceedings against Marchandise* [1991] ECR I–1027. Cf. Case C–398/95 *SETTG* v. *Ypourgos Ergasias* [1997] ECR I–3091 where the Court said that a restriction to the free movement of services could not be justified on the grounds of 'maintaining industrial peace as a means of bringing a collective dispute to an end and thereby preventing any adverse effects on an economic sector and consequently on the economy of the state'.

[198] Case 155/80 *Oebel* [1981] ECR 1993. See, generally, Poiares Maduro, *We, the Court, The European Court of Justice and the European Economic Constitution* (Hart, Oxford, 1998).

[199] Case C–113/89 *Rush Portuguesa Ltda* v. *Office Nationale d'Immigration* [1990] ECR 1417.

[200] See also Case C–43/93 *Vander Elst* v. *OMI* [1994] ECR I–3803 and Case C–272/94 *Criminal Proceedings against Guiot* [1994] ECR I–1905. See now Council Directive 96/71/EC on the posting of workers [1997] OJ L18/1, discussed by Davies, 'Posted Workers: Single Market or Protection of National Labour Law Systems?' (1997) 34 *CMLRev.* 571, and considered further in Ch. 3.

[201] Case 31/87 *Beentjes* v. *Minister van Landbouw en Visserij* [1988] ECR 4635. See Bovis, 'A Social Policy Agenda in European Public Procurement Law and Policy' (1998) 14 *IJCLLIR* 137.

[202] [1971] OJ Spec. Ed (II)/682.

[203] The Court said that an additional specific condition of this kind must be mentioned in the contract notice (para. 36).

[204] Case C–189/91 *Kirshammer Hack* v. *Sidal* [1993] ECR I–6185. See also Joined Cases C–72/91 and C–73/91 *Sloman* [1993] ECR I–887, where the Court held that only benefits granted directly or indirectly out of state resources were to be regarded as an aid. Consequently, a German rule allowing employment contracts for seamen not to be subject to German law did not constitute a state aid. Cf. Commission Decision 2000/128/EC [2000] OJ L42/1 concerning aid granted by Italy to promote employment and Commission Decision 2000/394/EC [2000] OJ L150/50 on aid to firms in Venice and Chioggia by way of relief from social security contributions.

[205] Joined Cases C–52, C–53 and C–54/97 *Viscido* v. *Ente Poste Italiane* [1998] ECR I–2629.

The potentially damaging scope of the state aid rules to the integrity of national social legislation was highlighted by the Court's decision in *Commission* v. *France*.[206] The Commission decided that the financial participation of the French Fonds National de l'Emploi (FNE), a state body, in paying for measures included in the social plan drawn up by a company faced with large-scale redundancies, constituted a state aid contrary to Article 92(1) [new Article 87(1)] and therefore had to be notified to the Commission. The Commission did, however, conclude that, in the event, the aid was not illegitimate, since it fell under an exception provided by Article 92(3)(c) (which allows aid where it is made 'to facilitate the development of certain economic activities or of certain economic areas, where such aid does not adversely affect trading conditions to an extent contrary to the common interest'). The French government challenged the Commission's initial finding that the payment by FNE came under Article 92 at all, because, if correct, it meant that France would have to notify all similar payments in future to the Commission. The Commission would then have the power to nullify the payments if they did not, in its view (subject to review by the Court), fall under the relevant derogation.

The pre-existing case law drew a distinction between measures of general application, which were not aid, and subsidies payable to particular undertakings, which were. According to Advocate General Jacobs:

measures taken within the framework of employment policy are usually not state aid. However, where public funds are used to reduce the salary costs of undertakings, either directly (for example by recruitment premiums) or indirectly (for example by reductions in fiscal or social charges), the distinction between state aid and general measure becomes less clear. The existence of discretion serves to identify those financial measures promoting employment which are liable to distort competition and affect trade between Member States.

The Court followed this lead and concluded that since the French legislation gave the administration some discretion in the amounts of subsidy which it could grant to a particular employer, there was a state aid.

The Court has, however, recognized in certain cases that an application of the competition provisions Articles 85, 86, and 90 [new Articles 81, 82, and 86] might undermine not only national labour laws but also the entire edifice of national social security systems. This has led it to develop—albeit imperfectly and rather hesitantly—the principle of national solidarity.[207] According to this principle, where the activity is based on national solidarity, it is not an economic activity and therefore the body concerned cannot be

---

[206] Case C–241/94 *French Republic* v. *Commission* [1996] ECR I–4551. See also Case C–256/97 *Proceedings relating to DMT* [1999] All ER(EC) 601. See Barnard and Deakin, 'European Community Social Policy: Progression or Regression?' (1999) 30 *IRJ* 55.

[207] Hervey, 'Social Solidarity: A Buttress against Internal Market Law?', in *Social Law and Policy in an Evolving European Union*, ed. Shaw (Hart, Oxford, 1999).

classed as an undertaking to which Articles 81 and 82 [ex Articles 85 and 86] apply. This principle, when applied, indicates a certain supremacy for social protection over the Single Market.

The principle of solidarity was first recognized in the case of *Poucet and Pistre*.[208] In that case the Court held that certain French bodies administering the sickness and maternity insurance scheme for self-employed persons engaged in non-agricultural occupations and the basic pension scheme for skilled trades were not to be classified as undertakings for the purpose of competition law. The schemes provided a basic pension[209] and affiliation was compulsory. The pension scheme operated on a redistributive basis with active members' contributions being directly used to finance the pensions of retired members; and the schemes had a social objective in that they were intended to provide cover for the beneficiaries against the risks of sickness or old age regardless of their financial status and state of health at the time of affiliation. The principle of solidarity was embodied in the *redistributive* nature of the pension scheme. It was also reflected by the grant of pension rights where no contributions had been made and of pension rights that were not proportional to the contributions paid. Finally, there was solidarity between the various social security schemes, with those in surplus contributing to the financing of those with structural difficulties. The Court said:

It follows that the social security schemes, as described, are based on a system of compulsory contribution, which is indispensable for the application of the principle of solidarity and the financial equilibrium of those schemes.

. . . [O]rganisations involved in the management of the public social security system fulfil an exclusively social function. That activity is based on the principle of national solidarity and is entirely non-profit-making. The benefits paid are statutory benefits bearing no relation to the amount of the contribution.

Accordingly, that activity is not an economic activity . . .

However, in *FFSA* (also known as *Coreva*)[210] the Court 'clarified' its case law. The case concerned a French supplementary retirement scheme for self-employed farmers.[211] The Court noted that in *FFSA* membership of the scheme was optional, that the scheme operated in accordance with the principle of capitalization, rather than on a redistributive basis as in *Poucet*, and that the benefits to which it conferred entitlement depended solely on the amount of contributions paid by the recipients and the financial results

---

[208] Joined Cases C–159 and C–160/91 *Poucet and Pistre v. AGF and Cancava* [1993] ECR I–637.

[209] These are helpfully summarized by Advocate General Jacobs in his Opinion in Case C–67/96 *Albany*, judgment of 21 Sep. 1999, para. 317.

[210] Case C–244/94 *Fédération Française des Sociétés d'Assurances* [1995] ECR I–4013 discussed by Laigre, 'L'intrusion du droit communautaire de la concurrence dans le champ de la protection sociale' [1996] *Droit Social* 82.

[211] Case C–67/96 *Albany*, judgment of 21 Sep. 1999, para. 325.

of the investments made by the managing organization. It concluded that the managing body therefore carries on an economic activity in competition with life assurance companies and so the Community competition rules, in particular Article 85 [new Article 81], applied. Neither the social objective pursued (it was created by the Government in order to protect a population whose income was lower and whose average age was higher than those of other socio-economic categories and whose basic old-age insurance was not sufficient), nor the fact that it was non-profit-making, nor the requirements of solidarity (for example, contributions were not linked to the risks incurred and there was no prior questionnaire or medical examination and no selection took place), nor the other rules concerning, in particular, the restrictions to which the managing organization was subject in making investments, altered the fact that the managing organization was carrying on an economic activity. On the question of solidarity the Court said:

First, . . . the principle of solidarity is extremely limited in scope, which follows from the optional nature of the scheme. In those circumstances, it cannot deprive the activity carried on by the body managing the scheme of its economic nature.

Secondly, whilst the pursuit of a social purpose, the requirements of solidarity and the other rules . . .—in particular, the rights and obligations of the managing body and the persons insured, the rules of that body and the restrictions to which it is subject in making its investments—may make the service provided by the Coreva scheme less competitive than the comparable service provided by life insurance companies, such limitations do not prevent the activity carried on by the [managing body] from being regarded as an economic activity.

Finally, the mere fact that the [managing organisation] is a non-profit-making body does not deprive the activity which it carries on of its economic character since . . . that activity may give rise to conduct which the competition rules are intended to penalise.

In the light of *FFSA* it is not surprising that the Court found in *Albany*[212] that a pension fund charged with the management of a supplementary pension scheme set up by a collective agreement concluded between organizations representing employers and workers in a given sector, to which affiliation has been made compulsory by the public authorities for all workers in that sector, was an undertaking within the meaning of Article 85 *et seq.* [new article 81 *et seq.*] of the Treaty. It noted that the scheme operated in accordance with the principle of capitalization where, unlike in *Poucet*, the amount of the benefits provided by the Fund depended on the financial results of the investments made by it, in respect of which it was subject, like an insurance company, to supervision by the Insurance Board. The Court said that neither the fact that the Fund was non-profit-making, nor that it pursued a

---

[212] Case C–67/96, judgment of 21 Sep. 1999, para. 87.

social objective, nor that it demonstrated elements of solidarity[213] affected this conclusion. On the other hand, the solidarity elements did justify the exclusive right of the fund to manage the supplementary scheme under Article 90(2) [new Article 85(2)] and so there was no breach of Articles 86 and 90(1) [new Articles 82 and 86(1)] respectively.

Although the Court's initial enthusiasm for the principle of solidarity seems to have rather cooled after *FFSA*, the principle was successfully invoked in *Sodemare*.[214] The Court ruled that Articles 52 and 58 [new Articles 43 and 48] on freedom of establishment did not preclude a Member State from allowing only non-profit-making private operators to participate in the running of its social welfare system by concluding contracts which entitled them to be reimbursed by the public authorities for the costs of providing social welfare services of a health-care nature. Having noted that Community law did not detract from the powers of the Member States to organize their social security systems,[215] the Court added:

> It is clear from the documents before the Court that that system of social welfare, whose implementation is in principle entrusted to the public authorities, is based on the principle of solidarity, as reflected by the fact that it is designed as a matter of priority to assist those who are in a state of need owing to insufficient family income, total or partial lack of independence or the risk of being marginalized, and only then, within the limits imposed by the capacity of the establishments and resources available, to assist other persons who are, however, required to bear the costs thereof, to an extent commensurate with their financial means, in accordance with scales determined by reference to family income.[216]

The Court accepted the Italian government's reasoning that since non-profit-making private operators, by their very nature, are not influenced by their need to derive profit from the provision of services, they can pursue social aims as a matter of priority.

Thus, in *Sodemare* the Court used the principle of solidarity to reinforce its view that Community law is not just about unrestricted access for all

---

[213] The solidarity was reflected by the obligation to accept all workers without a prior medical examination, the continuing accrual of pension rights despite exemption from contributions in the event of incapacity for work, the discharge by the fund of arrears of contributions due from an employer in the event of the latter's insolvency and by the indexing of the amount of the pensions in order to maintain their value. The principle of solidarity was also apparent from the absence of any equivalence, for individuals, between the contribution paid, which is an average contribution not linked to risks, and pension rights, which are determined by reference to an average salary. Such solidarity makes compulsory affiliation to the supplementary pension scheme essential. Otherwise, if 'good' risks left the scheme, the ensuing downward spiral would jeopardize its financial equilibrium (para. 75). This would increase the cost of pensions for workers, particularly those in small and medium-sized undertakings with older employees engaged in dangerous activities, to which the Fund could no longer offer pensions at an acceptable cost (para. 108).

[214] Case C–70/95 *Sodemare v. Regione Lombardia* [1997] ECR I–3395.

[215] Para. 27.

[216] Para. 29.

economic operators to the market in other Member States.[217] However, subsequently in *Decker*[218] and *Kohll*[219] the Court ruled that a Luxembourg law
which required prior authorization to purchase spectacles from an optician
established outside Luxembourg, or to receive dental treatment outside
Luxembourg, where authorization was not required for equivalent goods or
services within Luxembourg, contravened Articles 30 and 59 [new Articles
28 and 49] respectively and could not be justified.

It therefore seems that where domestic labour market and more general
social regulation collides with European Single Market (de)regulation the
Court has shown itself to be least sure-footed. The outcomes of the cases
are unpredictable, the standards applied are unclear and national labour
protection is undermined as a result. On the other hand, the Court has
equipped itself with the necessary tools to fend off such attacks, whether
through the principle of solidarity or public interest justifications, if it cares
to use them. The inclusion of a more pronounced social dimension to the
Community by the Amsterdam Treaty might help rebalance the competing
interests. There are signs that the Court has begun to recognize this. In
Albany[220] it said:

[I]t is important to bear in mind that, under Article 3(g) and (i) of the EC Treaty (now,
after amendment, Article 3(1)(g) and (j) EC), the activities of the Community are to
include *not only* a 'system ensuring that competition in the internal market is not
distorted' *but also* 'a policy in the social sphere'. Article 2 of the EC Treaty [now, after
amendment, Article 2 EC] provides that a particular task of the Community is 'to
promote throughout the Community a harmonious and balanced development of
economic activities' and 'a high level of employment and of social protection'
(emphasis added).

4. Fundamental Rights

The problem facing the Court is that the Treaty of Rome dictates the economic imperative of the creation of a single market. Unlike national constitutions, the original Treaty contained virtually no reference to civil, political,
and social rights: the only fundamental rights were the economic freedoms of
movement. This put the Community on a potential collision course with the
Member States. However, in a jurisprudence which has been well docu-

---

[217] In the context of free movement of goods, cf. Case C–267/91 *Criminal proceedings against
Keck and Mithouard* [1993] ECR I–6097.

[218] Case C–120/95 *Decker v. Caisse de maladie des employés privés* [1998] ECR I–1831.

[219] Case C–158/96 *Kohll v. Union des caisses de maladie* [1998] ECR I–1931. See the report
commissioned by the European Commission, *Implications of Recent Jurisprudence on the Coordination of health care systems*, http://europa.eu.int/comm/employment_social/soc-prot/disable/
synt–en.pdf.

[220] Case C–67/96, judgment of 21 Sep. 1999, para. 54.

mented,[221] the Court dealt with potential threats to its supremacy by affirming that Community law respects fundamental human rights.[222] Subsequently, the Court has recognized economic, commercial, and property rights, rights of the defence, traditional civil and political liberties, rights created by Community Treaties and legislation, social rights and administrative law principles, as fundamental rights which are general principles of law.[223] In particular it has given prominence to the principle of equality.[224] It has required both the Community institutions and the Member States, when acting in the Community law field, to respect these fundamental rights.[225] This jurisprudence was confirmed at Maastricht by Article F(2) TEU [new Article 6(2)] which requires that 'The Union shall respect fundamental rights, as guaranteed by the European Convention for the protection of Human Rights and Fundamental Freedoms signed in Rome on 4 November 1950 and as they result from the constitutional traditions common to the Member States, as general principles of Community law'.[226] After the Treaty of Amsterdam, the Court now has jurisdiction to ensure that Article 6(2) is observed by the institutions of the Union.[227]

The growing importance of fundamental rights can be seen in two recent pieces of Community legislation. The first resulted from the Court's decision in *Commission* v. *France*,[228] concerning the failure by the French police to stop French farmers interfering with free movement of goods. The Court ruled that Article 30 [new Article 28] applies where a Member State abstains from 'adopting the measures required in order to deal with obstacles to the free movement of goods which are not caused by the State'.[229] The legality or

---

[221] See generally Hartley, *The Foundations of European Community Law* (4th edn, Clarendon, Oxford, 1998), 132–42; Craig and de Búrca, *EU Law, Text, Cases and Materials* (OUP, Oxford, 1998), ch. 7; Mancini, 'A Constitution for Europe' (1989) 26 *CMLRev.* 595; Coppel and O'Neill, 'The European Court of Justice: Taking Rights Seriously?' (1992) 12 *Legal Studies* 227, 228–31.

[222] See e.g. Mancini and Keeling, 'Democracy and the European Court of Justice' (1994) 57 *MLR* 175, 187.

[223] This classification is derived from de Búrca, 'The Language of Rights and European Integration', in *New Legal Dynamics of European Union*, eds. Shaw and More (Clarendon, Oxford, 1995), 30–4.

[224] See esp. Case C–13/94 *P* v. *S and Cornwall County Council* [1996] ECR I–2143. See Barnard, '*P* v. *S* : Kite Flying or a New Constitutional Approach', in *The Principle of Equal Treatment in EC Law*, eds. Dashwood and O'Leary (Sweet and Maxwell, London, 1997), and the discussion in Ch. 4.

[225] See e.g. Case C–260/89 *ERT* v. *DEP* [1991] ECR I–2925, para. 41; Case C–353/89 *Commission* v. *Netherlands* [1991] ECR I–4069, para. 30; Case C–23/93 *TV10* v. *Commissariat voor de Media* [1994] ECR I–4795, para. 24; *Opinion 2/94 (Accession to the ECHR)* [1994] ECR I–1759, para. 33.

[226] See also new Art. 7 TEU which provides that in the case of a serious and persistent breach of the principles mentioned in Art. 6(1), the Council may decide to suspend a Member State from its Treaty rights.

[227] Art. 46(d) TEU. The Court's jurisdiction is in principle restricted to Community law. With the exception of Arts. 35 and 40 of the EU Treaty, the Court's jurisdiction does not cover actions regarding the second and third pillars.

[228] Case C–265/95 [1997] ECR I–6959.

[229] As Muylle points out, the ruling of the Court in *Commission* v. *France* could also be applied to obstacles to the free movement of goods caused by structural difficulties, e.g. failing infrastructure or traffic jams: Muylle, 'Angry Farmers and Passive Policemen: Private Conduct and Free Movement of Goods' (1998) 23 *ELRev.* 467, 471.

otherwise of the obstruction must be a relevant consideration in assessing the appropriateness of the measures taken in response. This issue was acknowledged in Council Regulation 2679/98[230] which set up an intervention mechanism to safeguard free trade in the Single Market and was adopted unanimously by the Member States following the Court's decision in the French farmers' case. Article 2 provides:

This Regulation may not be interpreted as affecting in any way the exercise of fundamental rights, as recognised in Member States, including the right or freedom to strike.[231]

The second piece of legislation is Directive 95/46/EC on data protection,[232] whose most striking feature is the emphasis it places on fundamental rights. In the first preambular paragraph, for example, it refers to the objectives of the Community to include 'preserving and strengthening peace and liberty and promoting democracy on the basis of the fundamental rights recognised in the constitution and laws of the Member States and in the European Convention for the Protection of Human Rights and Fundamental Freedoms'.[233] The second preambular paragraph provides that 'whereas the data processing systems are designed to serve man; whereas they must, whatever the nationality or residence of natural persons, respect their fundamental rights and freedoms, notably the right to privacy'.[234] Article 6 lays down the principles relating to data quality.[235] Article 8(1) prohibits the collection of personal data revealing 'racial or ethnic origin, political opinions, religious or philosophical beliefs, trade-union membership, and processing of data concerning health or sex life'. This provision does not apply where, for example, 'processing is necessary for the purposes of carrying out the obligations and specific rights of the controller [employer] in the field of employment law in so far as it is authorised by national law providing for adequate safeguards'.[236] Article

---

[230] [1998] OJ L337/8.

[231] Regulation 2679/98 was accompanied by a Resolution of the Council and representatives of the Member States of 7 Dec. 1998 on the free movement of goods [1998] OJ L337/10.

[232] Directive 95/46/EC of the European Parliament and Council on the protection of individuals with regard to the processing of personal data and on the free movement of such data [1995] OJ L281/31. See generally Simitis, 'Reconsidering the Premises of Labour Law: Prolegomena to an EU Regulation on the Protection of Employees' Personal Data' (1999) 5 ELJ 45. See also 'European Communities: The Data Protection Directive' EIRR 297 Oct. 1998, 14.

[233] See also preambular paras. 10 and 37. This Directive gives 'substance to and amplifies the rights contained in Council of Europe Convention 1981 on the Protection of Individuals with regard to Automatic Processing of Personal Data'.

[234] See also Art. 1(1).

[235] This requires Member States to provide that personal data must be, inter alia, processed fairly and lawfully; collected for specified, explicit, and legitimate purposes; adequate, relevant, and not excessive; accurate and kept in a form which permits identification of data subjects for no longer than is necessary.

[236] Art. 8(2)(b). The prohibition also does not apply where the processing is carried out in the course of legitimate activities by a foundation, association, or any other non-profit-seeking body with a political, philosophical, religious, or trade union aim (Art. 8(2)(d)).

9 requires Member States to provide for exemptions from the rules on processing personal data carried out solely for journalistic purposes or for the purpose of artistic or literary expression, only if they are necessary to reconcile the right to privacy with the rules governing freedom of expression. Articles 10 and 11 lay down details of the information to be given to the individual and Article 12 provides details about the individual's right of access to data. Articles 14 and 15 make provision for the individual's right to object to the processing of data relating to them.

In the light of both legislative and judicial developments many have argued for a Bill of Rights to be included in the Treaty, to put fundamental civil, political, and social rights on the same footing as the four economic freedoms, and to reflect the changing nature of Europe from an Economic Community to Union.[237] For example, the Comité des Sages, set up to examine the future of the Community Social Charter 1989,[238] argued that if the Union wished to become 'an original political entity, it must have a clear statement of the citizenship it is offering its members. Inclusion of civic and social rights in the Treaties would help to nurture that citizenship and prevent Europe from being perceived as a bureaucracy assembled by technocratic elites far removed from daily concerns'.[239] It suggested that the EU should include in the Treaty a minimum core of rights and at a later stage set in motion a consultation process which would update and complete the list. The Amsterdam Treaty took one small step in this direction. As we have seen, Article 136 [old Article 117] requires the Community and the Member States to have 'in mind fundamental social rights' as defined in the European Social Charter 1961 and the 1989 Community Charter of Fundamental Social Rights.[240] It is not clear whether these rights can now be considered as 'general principles inspiring Community policy'.[241]

More recently, the Simitis Committee was set up to examine the possible

---

[237] See, *inter alia*, Blanpain, Hepple, Sciarra and Weiss, *Fundamental Social Rights: Proposals for the European Union* (Peeters, Leuven, 1996), 1; Bercusson, Deakin, Koistinen, Kravitou, Mückenberger, Supiot and Veneziani, 'A Manifesto for a Social Europe' (1997) 3 *ELJ* 189; Lo Faro, 'The Social Manifesto: Demystifying the Spectre Haunting Europe' (1997) 3 *ELJ* 300; The Supiot Report, *Transformation of Labour and Future of Labour Law in Europe*, June 1998; *A Human Rights Agenda for the European Union for the Year 2000*, ed. Alston (OUP, Oxford, 1999).

[238] *For a Europe of Civic and Social Rights*, Report by the Comité des Sages chaired by Maria de Lourdes Pintasilgo, Brussels, Oct. 1995–Feb. 1996, Commission, DGV.

[239] The responses of the European Parliament, ECOSOC and the ETUC to the Commission's Green Paper on Social Policy also called for 'the establishment of the fundamental social rights of citizens as a constitutional element of the European Union' COM(94)333, 69. The *Molitor Report* (COM(95)288 final/2, 39) on legislative and administrative simplification also called for the adoption of a Bill of Rights. See also Kenner, 'Citizenship and Fundamental Rights: Reshaping the Social Model', in *Trends in European Social Policy: Essays in Memory of Malcolm Mead*, ed. Kenner (Dartmouth, Aldershot, 1995), esp. 78–84.

[240] See above, text attached to nn. 57–79.

[241] Larsson, 'A Comment on the "Manifesto for Social Europe"' (1997) 3 *ELJ* 304, 306.

inclusion of a Bill of Rights in the Nice IGC.[242] The committee reported that a 'comprehensive approach to the guarantee of fundamental rights is urgently required It argued that 'Fundamental rights must be visible' and justifiable. According to the Committee, the current lack of visibility of fundamental rights 'not only violates the principle of transparency, it also discredits the effort to create a "Europe of citizens" '. The Committee added that 'Clearly ascertainable fundamental rights stimulate the readiness to accept the European Union and to identify with its growing intensification and expanding remits'.[243] The Committee therefore concluded that the ECHR,[244] which has become a 'common European Bill of Rights', should be incorporated in its entirety into Community law,[245] with the addition of certain complementary clauses:

- the right to equality of opportunity and treatment without any distinction such as race, colour, ethnic, national, or social origin, culture or language, religion, conscience, belief, political opinion, sex or gender, marital status, family responsibilities, sexual orientation, age, or disability;[246]
- freedom of choice of occupation;
- the right to determine the use of personal data;
- the right to family reunion;
- the right to bargain collectively and to resort to collective action in the event of a conflict of interests; and
- the right to information, consultation and participation, in respect of decisions affecting the interests of workers.

Giving fundamental rights to Union citizens might help reconcile the growing tension between the desire for decentralization—subsidiarity—and the need for the Community to have an identifiable and meaningful face.

The importance of a rights-based approach has been brought into sharp focus by the accession of the former Eastern bloc countries to the Union, with the prospect of varying forms of 'flexible' integration.[247] Blanpain *et al.* have argued that these models could work only if there is a clear definition of specific social objectives and a statement of fundamental social rights.[248]

---

[242] *Affirming Fundamental Rights in the European Union: Time to Act*, Report of the Expert Group on Fundamental Rights, Brussels, Feb. 1999. The EU heads of government meeting at Tampere in Oct. 1999 set up a committee to begin drafting an EU Charter of fundamental rights.

[243] See e.g. Cappelletti, *The Judicial Process in Comparative Perspective* (Clarendon, Oxford, 1989), 395.

[244] Namely, Arts. 2–13 of the ECHR together with the relevant rights in the Protocols.

[245] A Treaty amendment would be required for this. Art. 308 [ex Art. 235] does not provide an adequate legal basis: *Opinion 2/94 (Accession to the ECHR)* [1994] ECR I–1759.

[246] See now Art.13 [ex Art. 6a] included by the Amsterdam Treaty which provides a legal basis for the Community to enact non-discrimination legislation in most of these areas. See further Ch. 4.

[247] Blanpain, Hepple, Sciarra and Weiss, *Fundamental Social Rights: Proposals for the European Union* (Peeters, Leuven, 1996), 1. See also Lodge, 'Preface: The Challenge of the Future', in *The European Community and the Challenge of the Future*, ed. Lodge (2nd edn, Pinter, London, 1993).

[248] Blanpain *et al.*, above n. 247.

However Hepple sounds a note of caution.[249] He argues that much rights talk is rhetorical and acquires meaning only in specific social and political contexts. He argues that it is necessary to distinguish those principles from which rights flow which are fundamental to democratic societies from particular economic and social policies which are conditioned by the level of socio-economic development of a particular country. Rights tend to be individualistic and individualize what may well be, in the social field, a collective problem. Rights also put considerable power in the hands of the courts, particularly the Court of Justice, which, as we have seen, has shown itself at times to be unaware of the broader social issues. Nevertheless, the European Council meeting in Cologne in June 1999 decided to draw up a charter of fundamental rights of the EU. It said that 'Protection of fundamental rights is a founding principle of the Union and an indispensable prerequisite for her legitimacy. . . . There appears to be a need, at the present stage of the Union's development, to establish a Charter of fundamental rights in order to make their overriding importance and relevance more visible to the Union's citizens'. The Charter is to contain the fundamental rights and freedoms and basic procedural rights guaranteed by the European Convention on Human Rights. It must also take account of the economic and social rights contained in the European Social Charter and the Community Social Charter 1989.[250] The Council is to consider how this charter might be incorporated into the Treaties, as a political declaration or as a legally binding instrument which might apply to the Community institutions and to the Member States when acting in the sphere of Community law. The drafting Convention has proposed a list of economic and social rights as well as civil and political right. The subject civil and social rights under discussion are:[250A]

- freedom to choose an occupation;
- workers' right to information and consultation within the undertaking;
- rights of collective bargaining and action under the conditions laid down by national legislation and practice;
- right to limitation of maximum working hours, to rest periods and to annual leave;
- right to safe and healthy working conditions;
- protection of young people in respect of the age at which they can start work and working conditions;
- right to protection against unjustified or abusive termination of employment;
- right to reconcile their family and professional lives, including the right to maternity leave and parental leave;

[249] 'The Future of Labour Law' (1995) 24 *ILJ* 303.
[250] The detail of those negotiating the Charter are contained in the conclusions to the Tampere summit in Oct. 1999.
[250A] CHARTE 4316/00, 16 May 2000.

- right of third country nationals working lawfully in the territory of the Member States to equal treatment;
- provision shall be made in accordance with each Member State's rules for social security benefits in the event of maternity, illness, dependence, old-age, and unemployment. Provision is also to be made for social assistance and housing benefit to guarantee a decent existence to anyone lacking sufficient resources;
- access to medical care and prophylactic measures in accordance with each Member States's rules;
- provision is to be made for social and vocational integration measures for the disabled.

The draft Charter also contains reference to environmental and consumer protection. It is not supposed to establish any competence or any new task for the Community or the Union or modify any existing tasks or competences. Any limitation on the exercise of rights or freedoms must be necessary for the protection of legitimate interests in a democratic society and proportionate.

While this document may be of considerable importance in the future, many of the substantive areas outlined above (with the notable exception of termination of employment) overlap considerably with provisions in the EC Treaty, the Community Social Charter 1989 and the Council of Europe Social Charter 1961. The substance of these provisions is discussed in detail elsewhere in this book.

C. NEW EMPHASIS: GROWTH AND EMPLOYMENT

1. The Need to Address Unemployment

The Union placed greater emphasis on the need to tackle unemployment after the Maastricht Treaty was signed. For example, the Commission's White Paper on European Social Policy of 1994 identified job creation as a top priority. It said that the pursuit of more good, stable jobs was both a central objective of the Union and a means of addressing more effectively many of the Union's wider social objectives.[251] Subsequently, in the opening para-graphs of its Social Action Programme 1998–2000,[252] the Commission said that 'Employment policy has moved decisively to the top of the European Agenda'. This view was restated by the Vienna European Council: 'Employment is the top priority of the European Union'[253] and again at Cologne: 'Higher employment continues to be Europe's top objective'.[254]

[251] COM(94)333, 17.
[252] COM(98)259, 1.
[253] Bull. 12/98, para. 26.
[254] Cologne European Council Presidency Conclusions, para. 7.

Unemployment levels in the EU are compared unfavourably with those in the US where the rate of unemployment is now lower than it is on average in Europe, and where the rate of job creation has been much higher over the last two decades.[255] In 1996 the unemployment rate stood at around 5 per cent in the US compared to the average unemployment rate of the fifteen EU Member States of virtually 11 per cent.[256] Between 1971 and 1994 civilian employment increased by 55 per cent in the US, but only by 11 per cent in the EU.[257] The EU also has a much higher number of long-term unemployed. In the US only 9.7 per cent of the unemployed had been out of work for 12 months or more in 1995, while in the EU this ratio varied between 17 per cent in Austria and more than 60 per cent in Belgium and Italy, with most countries having shares of long-term unemployment between 30–50 per cent. Women and older male workers,[258] unskilled workers, and young workers with low levels of schooling have been disproportionately affected.[259]

Some commentators prefer to use the employment rate, defined as the proportion of the working age population in employment, as a more effective indicator of the performance of an economy since it measures how the economy is able to provide jobs for all those who are able to work.[260] It focuses attention on employment as well as the employment potential of the non-employed, including both 'economically inactive' people and the unemployed. Even by this standard the EU compares unfavourably with the US. Twenty years ago, the EU's employment rate was 64 per cent, while that of the US was 62 per cent. By 1997, however, the EU rate had dropped to 60.5 per cent, while that of the US had increased to 74 per cent, a spread of almost 14 percentage points.[261] As the Commission's Communication on 'Community Policies in Support of Employment' points out, if the performance of the three best Member States or of the US were taken as a benchmark, an additional 30 million or more people could be employed, raising EU employment from 150 million to 180 million, substantially improving public finances and making pension systems more sustainable.[262]

The need for reducing unemployment is clear.[263] First, the low employment rate in Europe means that there is a high level of unused labour stock. To bring such potential to work would represent a sizeable contribution to

---

[255] Scharpf, *Governing in Europe: Effective and Democratic?* (OUP, Oxford, 1999), 123.

[256] OECD Employment Outlook, Table A and *Employment in Europe* (OPEC, Luxembourg, 1997), 117.

[257] OECD, *Labour Force Statistics 1971–1996* (OECD, Paris, 1997).

[258] COM(99)127, 2.

[259] Scharpf, above n. 255, 124, citing OECD, *Employment Outlook*, July 1996.

[260] The measure of unemployment may be misleading since in the US the figures exclude a number of economically inactive, especially the large prison population.

[261] COM(99)572, Employment Rates Report 1998: Employment Performance in the European Union.

[262] COM(99)127.

[263] See above n. 261.

economic growth for the EU, beyond the long-term growth trend resulting from labour productivity increases. Secondly, an ageing population[264] needs to be supported by higher employment. This would mean more individuals contributing to welfare schemes, thereby helping to fund social security systems faced with an ageing population. Thirdly, employment is important for social cohesiveness. As the Employment Rates Report argues, as many individuals as possible should have an attachment to the world of work, should contribute to, as well as participate in, active society, and should enjoy the benefits of progress and prosperity. High levels of employment are also important to close the gender gap. As the Employment Rates Report points out, women and men should be able to participate in work on equal terms with equal responsibilities in order to develop the full growth potential of the national economies. In 1997 the gap between male and female employment rates was 20 per cent, although it had declined from 26 per cent in 1990. The justifications for a policy of employment and growth were summarized by the Resolution of the Amsterdam European Council on Growth and Employment:[265]

This approach, coupled with stability based policies, provides the basis for an economy founded on principles of inclusion, solidarity, justice and a sustainable environment, and capable of benefiting all its citizens. Economic efficiency and social inclusion are complementary aspects of the more cohesive society that we all seek.

2. The Employment Title and the Luxembourg Process

For a while, in the mid-1990s, there was an active debate about whether to use centralized expenditure to stimulate demand, and thus employment, through investments in infrastructure and public works and thus employment.[266] This received some impetus from the publication of the 1993 White Paper on *Growth, Competitiveness and Employment*,[267] but the Member States refused to countenance a significant increase in the Commission's budget. Instead, a new policy emerged based on the centralized co-ordination of employment policies. This first became apparent in the Essen summit in 1994 which identified five priority fields of action to promote job creation:[268]

- greater investment in vocational training, especially for young people and for life-long learning;

[264] In 1985, life expectancy for men aged 60 was 17.5 years, and the employment rate of men aged 55–64 was 54 per cent. Ten years later, life expectancy for men aged 60 had increased to 19 years, but employment rates for the 55–64 age group had fallen to 47 per cent.

[265] 97/C236/02. See also Resolution of the European Council on the European Employment Pact, paras. 1, 3 and 4, June 1999.

[266] Barnard and Deakin, 'A Year of Living Dangerously? EC Social Policy Rights, Employment Policy and EMU' (1998) 2 *IRJ European Annual Review* 117.

[267] EC Bull. Supp. 6/93.

[268] EC Bull. 12/94.

- an increase in the employment-intensiveness of growth through more flexible organization of work, moderation of wage settlements, and support for job creation in growing sectors such as environmental and social services;
- a reduction in non-wage labour costs;
- a move from a passive to an active labour market policy, eliminating disincentives, providing suitable income support measures and reviewing the effectiveness of instruments of labour-market policy;
- improved measures to help people hit particularly hard by unemployment, especially unqualified school leavers, the long-term unemployed, unemployed women, and older job seekers.

A number of the areas for intervention identified by the Essen Council were clearly deregulatory in character,[269] stressing the reduction of the 'tax wedge' of indirect labour costs and the need for greater flexibility in the utilization of labour. However, other areas assumed a more proactive role for the state in the form of subsidies for training and the reintegration of excluded groups into the labour market.[270] The Essen Council also laid down a monitoring procedure, under which the Member States were required to report back on the steps they had taken. A benchmarking exercise was conducted to promote best practice, focusing on long-term unemployment, youth unemployment, and equal opportunities. The policy was taken further by the Florence Council of 1996 which endorsed a 'Confidence Pact' on employment put forward by the Commission, and by the Dublin Council of 1997 which issued a 'Declaration on Employment'.

Despite the fact that there has been little evaluation of the success of the Essen strategy,[271] the approach adopted at Essen, with its emphasis on co-ordination of policy, is a defining feature of the new Employment Title introduced by the Amsterdam Treaty.[272] According to Article 125 [ex Article 109n], the key provision of the new Title,

Member States and the Community shall, in accordance with the Title, work towards developing a co-ordinated strategy for employment and particularly for promoting a skilled, trained and adaptable workforce and labour markets responsive to economic change with a view to achieving the objectives defined in Article 2 of the Treaty on European Union and in Article 2 of this Treaty.

Both Article 2 TEU and Article 2 EC commit the Union to a 'high level of employment'. Although it appears from Article 125 that action is to be jointly conducted by Member States and the Community, the principal actors are in

---

[269] See Deakin and Reed, 'Between Social Policy and EMU: The New Employment Title of the EC Treaty', in *Social Law and Policy in an Evolving European Union*, ed. Shaw (Hart, Oxford, 2000), forthcoming.

[270] See COM(94)333.

[271] Pochet, 'The New Employment Chapter of the Amsterdam Treaty' (1999) 9 *JESP* 271, 275.

[272] See also Biagi, 'The Implementation of the Amsterdam Treaty with Regard to Employment: Coordination or Convergence?' (1998) 14 *IJCLLIR* 325.

fact the Member States. Article 126 [ex Article 109p] requires the Member States to co-ordinate their policies for the promotion of employment (which is to be regarded as an issue of 'common concern')[273] within the Council, in a way consistent with the broad economic guidelines laid down within the framework of EMU,[274] which are issued annually by the Council as part of the process of ensuring economic stability and convergence. According to Article 127 [ex Article 109p] the Community must encourage co-operation between the States by supporting and, if necessary, complementing their action. The European Council must also draw up guidelines according to Article 128 [ex Article 109q] which the Member States are obliged to take into account in their employment policies. Under Article 129 [ex Article 109r] the Council may adopt incentive measures designed to encourage co-operation between Member States,[275] and to support their action in the field of employment by 'initiatives aimed at developing exchanges of information and best practices, providing comparative analysis and advice as well as promoting innovative approaches and evaluating experiences, in particular by recourse to pilot projects'. The scope of this provision is curtailed by two Declarations included at the request of Germany, which limit the amount of funding available and specify that any such programme must not last longer then five years.

Some commentators are critical of the approach adopted by the Employment Title. Goetschy and Pochet,[276] for example, questioned whether there was a need for a joint approach at all, given that unemployment has been reduced in a number of States using different methods. They also argued that the choice of a 'diplomatic' type process involving Ecofin (the Economic and Finance Council), the Social Affairs Council, and the European Council was risky in terms of the consistency of diagnosis and solutions. They argue that this process favours consensual solutions (such as vocational training) over possibly more suitable but more controversial solutions (such as reducing labour costs or reducing working time).

Despite such criticisms, and given the concern about high levels of unemployment, the European Council decided to put the relevant provisions on monitoring employment policy of the new Title on Employment into effect before the Treaty of Amsterdam came into force. This was agreed at an Extraordinary meeting of the European Council in Luxembourg on 20–21 November 1997 (the so-called Jobs Summit). Under the 'Luxembourg process' the first guidelines outlining policy areas for 1998 were agreed by the Member

[273] Art. 126(2). The Commission considers a high level of employment to be an employment rate of over 70%: COM(97)497.

[274] Ibid., Art. 126(1).

[275] The decision-making mechanism under the Employment Title is considered in more detail in Ch. 2.

[276] Goetschy and Pochet, 'The Treaty of Amsterdam: a New Approach to Social Affairs' (1997) 3 *Transfer* 607.

States and adopted by the Council of Ministers.[277] The Member States were then obliged to incorporate these guidelines into National Action Plans (NAPs).

Developing the fields of action identified at Essen, the guidelines have centred on four main 'pillars'.[278] The first of the pillars is *employability*, which focuses on the prevention of long-term and youth unemployment by means of vocational education and training[279] and active labour market policies including the placement of young workers in work experience schemes and subsidies to employers offering training. Secondly, the *entrepreneurship* pillar attempts to make the process of business start-ups more straightforward, and incorporates steps to revise regulations affecting small businesses. The *adaptability* pillar encourages negotiation over the improvement of productivity through the reorganization of working practices and production processes. The reduction and re-negotiation of working time, the flexible implementation of labour standards, and information and consultation over training issues have also come under this heading. Finally, the *equal opportunities* pillar has been concerned with raising awareness of issues relating to gender equality in terms of equal access to work, family friendly policies, and the needs of people with disabilities.[280] Table 1.1 indicates the relationship between pillars and guidelines.

While the 1999 guidelines largely repeat the substance of those in 1998,[281] they contain a number of important additions:

- greater emphasis on partnership, particularly with the Social Partners;
- recognizing the need to review tax as well as benefits and training;
- promoting a labour market open to all, emphasizing the need for a coherent set of policies for those who experience particular difficulties in acquiring relevant skills and in gaining access to, and remaining in, the labour market. As a result, each Member State will give 'special attention to the needs of the disabled, ethnic minorities and other groups and individuals who may be disadvantaged, and develop appropriate forms of preventive and active policies to promote their integration into the labour market';
- recognizing the employment potential of the services sector;

Finally, gender mainstreaming has achieved a much greater profile across all four pillars. The guidelines note that 'Women still have particular problems in gaining access to the employment market, in career advancement, in earnings and in reconciling professional and family life'.

---

[277] Council Resolution of 15 Dec. 1997 on the 1998 Employment Guidelines [1998] OJ C30/1.

[278] See Barnard and Deakin, above n. 266, 117.

[279] See Resolution of the Council and Representatives of the Governments of the Member States on the employment and social dimension of the information society [2000] OJ C8/1.

[280] See generally the Commission's 'EQUAL' programme.

[281] Council Resolution on the 1999 Employment Guidelines [1999] OJ L69/2.

Table 1.1 Employment Pillars 1998 and Guidelines 1998 and 1999

Pillars	1998 Guidelines	1999 Guidelines
Employability	• Tackling youth and long-term unemployment by offering the unemployed a fresh start with training or work practice within 6–12 months. • Transition from passive to active measures in respect of benefit and training systems. • Encouraging a partnership approach, involving the social partners to work with the Member States in providing training and life-long learning. • Easing the transition from school to work.	• Member States are to intensify their activities. • This also now applies to taxation. Emphasis also on flexible working arrangements as part of a policy on active ageing. • Emphasis also on training for older workers in the field of information technology. • This particularly applies to young people with learning difficulties. • Promoting a labour market open to all.
Entrepreneurship	• Reducing overhead and administrative costs for businesses, especially SMEs, and promoting self-employment. • Exploiting the opportunities for job creation in the social economy and at local level; making the tax system more employment friendly; examining ways of reducing VAT in labour-intensive sectors not exposed to cross-border competition.[1]	• Importance of SMEs in job creation and training. Need to take steps to encourage their start up and need to encourage 'greater entrepreneurial awareness'. • Emphasis on exploiting the potential of the services sector.[2]
Adaptability	• Modernizing work organization, by encouraging the social partners to negotiate agreements, balancing flexibility and security; and for the states to introduce more adaptable types of contracts while providing adequate levels of security. • Support adaptability in enterprises by encouraging in-house training and investment in human resources.	• Greater emphasis on the role of partnership at all appropriate levels (European, national, sectoral, and enterprise levels).

| *Equal opportunities* | • Tackling gender gaps in employment and unemployment.
• Reconciling work and family life through policies on career breaks, parental leave, and part-time work combined with good quality childcare.
• Facilitating reintegration into the labour market.
• Promoting the integration of people with disabilities into working life. | • New guidelines on gender mainstreaming.
• Positive obligations to bring about balanced representation of women and men and positive steps to promote equal pay.
• Obligations in respect of the disabled covered elsewhere. |

Source: Employment Pillars 1998 and Guidelines, 1998 and 1999.

[1] Council Directive 99/85/EC [1999] (OJ L277/34), amending Directive 77/388/EEC as regards the possibility of applying on an experimental basis a reduced VAT rate on labour-intensive services and Council Decision 2000/185/EC [2000] OJ L59/10 authorizing Member States to apply a reduced rate of VAT.

[2] Reference is made in the 2000 Guidelines to the role of Public Employment Services in identifying local employment opportunities and improving the functioning of local labour markets. See also COM(98)641 'Modernising Public Employment Services to Support the European Employment Strategy'.

The Commission has decided that the four-pillar structure of the Employment Guidelines has provided a good basis for an integrated medium-term approach. For the sake of consistency the Commission has not proposed any new guidelines for 2000 but has merely classified certain existing guidelines.[282]

There has long been a tension between deregulation as a means of achieving the flexibility necessary to help fight against unemployment and the need for social rights. These tensions can be seen very clearly in the Luxembourg strategy. The deregulatory aspects of the Employment Strategy can be most clearly seen in the entrepreneurship pillar and in aspects of the employability and adaptability pillars. On the other hand, the stress on social rights can be found in the equal opportunities pillar as well as in social policy more generally. The Treaty of Amsterdam, itself, does not contain a deregulatory agenda. Not only does the Treaty incorporate the SPA into the new Social Title in the EC Treaty but also Article 2 talks of 'a high level of employment *and* social protection' (emphasis added) and 'equality between men and women', as well as 'sustainable and non-inflationary growth, a high degree of competitiveness and convergence of economic performance'. This indicates the Community's attempts to find a 'third way' between the 'Anglo-Saxon' model of deregulation, low unemployment, and fewer welfare benefits, and the European model of job protection, high unemployment and generous welfare provision. This third way, which seemed to have influenced the governments participating in

[282] Proposal for Guidelines for Member States' Employment Policies 2000. Council Decision 2000/228/EC on guidelines for Member State's employment policies for the year 2000 [2000] OJ L72/15.

the Luxembourg summit, was to create a new European employment model which would balance social protection, competitiveness, and welfare provision with sound finance.[283] The aim is to achieve competitiveness through creating highly productive workplaces, rather than combating unemployment through the creation of low-paid, low-productivity 'entry jobs'.[284] Thus, the new emphasis is on flexibility for firms combined with security for workers.

This is the new theme found in the Commission's Green Paper, *Partnership for a New Organisation of Work*,[285] the Commission's Communications, *Modernising and Improving Social Protection in the European Union*[286] and *Modernising the Organisation of Work*,[287] and the 1998 Employment Guidelines under the Adaptability Pillar. Attempts to reconcile flexibility with security lie in an 'improved organisation of work' which, although unable 'of itself to solve the unemployment problem', may nevertheless 'make a valuable contribution, first, to the competitiveness of European firms, and secondly, to the improvement of the quality of working life and the employability of the workforce'.[288] More specifically, 'the flexible firm could offer a sound basis for fundamental organisational renewal built on high skill, high productivity, high quality, good environmental management—and good wages'.[289]

The flexibility envisaged by the Community can take a variety of forms:[290] *numerical* flexibility allowing the firm to modulate the numbers employed; *working time* flexibility which permits the firm to raise or lower hours through overtime or through variations to normal hours; *financial* flexibility which links remuneration directly to output; and *functional* flexibility which refers to the multi-skilling of workers permitting them to move between tasks and adapt their working practices to new technical or organizational requirements. But, these various types of flexibility will only be achieved if the workers feel secure. As the Commission says in its Communication:

Flexibility internal to the enterprise not only promotes corporate productivity but also the quality of working life. . . . Security for workers can also give benefits to the enterprise in the form of a more stable, versatile and motivated workforce.[291]

[283] Pierson, Forster, and Jones, 'The Politics of Europe: (Un)employment Ambivalence' (1997) 1 *Industrial Relations Journal European Annual Review* 5, 15. See also Kenner, 'The EC Employment Title and the "Third Way": Making Soft Law Work' (1999) 15 *IJCLLIR* 33.

[284] Deakin and Reed, above n. 269.

[285] COM(97)127 final.

[286] COM(97)102 final. See also Commission Communication: *A Concerted Action for Modernising Social Protection* COM(99)347, Council Conclusions on the strengthening of cooperation for modernising and improving social protection [2000] OJ C8/7) and Council Decision 2000/436/EC [2000] OJ L172/26 setting up a Social Protection Committee. See also the role envisaged for the social partners, as the Commission lauched the first stage of consultation on 26 June 2000.

[287] COM(98)592.

[288] Ibid., para. 4.

[289] Ibid., para. 24.

[290] See Deakin and Reed, above n. 269.

[291] COM(98)592, 3.

Thus, social policy is seen as an input into the productive process[292] and not a burden on it.[293] As the Commission said in the White Paper on Social Policy, 'the pursuit of high social standards should not be seen as a cost but also as a key element in the competitive formula',[294] and again in the Medium Term Social Action Programme it talks of encouraging 'high labour standards as part of competitive Europe'.[295]

In the Commission's eyes the Social Partners have a key role in reconciling the objectives of both flexibility and security and thus modernizing working life. In particular they need to focus on training, working time, facilitating the diversification of working relations, and new forms of work, as well as ensuring the optimum conditions for the introduction of new technology and promoting equal opportunities.[296] According to the Commission, workers need to be committed to the process of change. Thus, according to the Green Paper, flexibility within organizations will be encouraged by reinforcing mechanisms for employee participation at the level of the plant or enterprise.[297] This means that the successful conclusion of the Commission's proposed directive on information and consultation of employees at national level has assumed a greater importance.[298]

The Luxembourg process and the incentive measures under Article 129 comprise two limbs of the 'European employment strategy'.[299] The third limb is the role played by the structural funds. This will now be considered.

3. The Structural Funds and Economic and Social Cohesion

As we have seen, much of the concern about high levels of unemployment relates to the implications it has for economic and social cohesion, concepts which have now found express recognition in the Treaty and which lay at the

---

[292] See Deakin and Wilkinson, 'Rights vs Efficiency: the Economic Case for Transnational Labour Standards' (1994) 23 *ILJ* 289, 295–6. See the Commission Communication, 'Modernising and Improving Social Protection in the EU' COM(97)102 and the follow-up 'A Concerted Strategy for Modernising Social Protection' COM(99)347.

[293] See e.g. the views of Addison and Siebert, 'The Social Charter: Whatever Next?' (1992) 30 *BJIR* 495.

[294] COM(94)333, introduction, para. 5. This is wholly consistent with the 'essential objective' expressed in the Preamble to the EC Treaty of 'the constant improvement of the living and working conditions of their peoples'.

[295] *Social Europe* 1/95, 9, 18, 19. See also now the UK government's *Fairness at Work* White Paper, Cm 3968, 1998.

[296] COM(98)592, 4.

[297] COM(97)127, para. 44.

[298] In Mar. 1998 the private sector employers' confederation, UNICE, refused to enter into negotiations with ETUC and CEEP (298 EIRR 1). However, the Commission has now proposed its own draft proposals: COM(98)612. See further Ch. 8.

[299] See generally Goetschy, 'The European Employment Strategy: Genesis and Development' (1999) 5 *EJIR* 117.

heart of the creation of a European civil society.[300] Article 2 EC, as amended
by the Maastricht Treaty, identifies 'economic and social cohesion and
solidarity between Member States' as one of the tasks of the Community and
Article 3(k) [ex Article 3(j)] lists 'strengthening of economic and social cohesion' as one of the activities of the Community. A Title [new XVII, ex XIV][301]
on economic and social cohesion was added by the Single European Act
1986. The aim of this Title is to reduce disparities between the levels of
development of the various regions. The Community is to support the
achievement of these objectives through the use of the (reformed) structural
funds—ESF, ERDF, FIFG and EAGGF (guidance section).[302]

At national level such policies are based on the shared identity of the
citizens of the state which underpins solidarity or cohesion[303] (the binding
together of those who are part of the state by mutual duties of support).[304]
This 'cohesion' justifies the redistribution of resources, financed through taxation, which is necessitated by social policy. At Community level, by contrast,
the justification for such policies was initially expressed more in terms of
economic integration: that disadvantages experienced by regions on the
periphery of the EU must be corrected to enable them to have an equal
opportunity[305] to compete in the single internal market.[306] More recently,
the justification for the existence of such funds has been in terms both of
combating high levels of unemployment[307] and the promotion of a 'European' identity through citizenship of the Union. Thus, 'national' justifications
have begun to influence the Community debate, although there is still much
less of a sense of solidarity between the nationals of the fifteen Member States
(and even less within the twenty or more States of an expanded Europe)
than within the national context.[308] This makes a major expansion of the EC
structural funds politically unacceptable.[309]

---

[300] Opinion of the Economic and Social Committee 1999/C329/10 [1999] OJ C329/30, 32.

[301] Arts. 158–162 [ex Art. 130a—e)]. See also point 10 of the Community Social Charter
1989.

[302] The details of the funds are considered below. The Treaty of Amsterdam also introduced a
legal basis [new Art. 138(2)] for the Council acting under the Art. 251 [ex Art. 189b] procedure
to encourage co-operation between Member States to combat social exclusion.

[303] Hervey, *European Social Law and Policy* (Longman, Harlow, 1998), 175.

[304] These ideas emerge in para. 1 of the Preamble to Council Recommendation 92/441/EEC
[1992] OJ L245/46 on common criteria concerning sufficient resources and social assistance in
social protection systems (see further Ch. 5) which says: 'Whereas reinforcing social cohesion
within the Community requires the encouragement of solidarity with regard to the least priv-
iledged and most vulnerable people'. See also the Preamble to Council Recommendation 92/442/
EEC [1992] OJ L245/49.

[305] COM(92)84.

[306] Hervey, above n. 303, 176–7.

[307] See e.g. Council Regulation 1260/1999 [1999] OJ L161/1, discussed below, and the
accompanying Commission Communication (99/C267/02).

[308] Hervey, above n. 303, 193.

[309] See the Commission's 'Agenda 2000' report.

The diverse justifications for the structural funds can be seen in the strategic priorities for 2000–2006.[310] These are:

- regional competitiveness,
- social cohesion and employment, and
- the development of urban and rural areas.

Underpinning these priorities is the 'basic democratic principle' of equality for men and women which is 'no longer an option but an obligation'.

For the purposes of addressing the problems of unemployment, the most important structural fund is the European Social Fund (ESF),[311] set up by the Treaty of Rome in response to the problem of declining industries, especially coal and steel. The original Article 3(i) talked of 'the creation of a European Social Fund in order to improve employment opportunities of workers and to contribute to the raising of their standard of living'. Subsequently Article 3(i) [new Article 3(j)], amended by the Maastricht Treaty, talks of 'a policy in the social sphere comprising a European Social Fund'. Substantive provisions can be found in Articles 146–148 [ex Articles 123–125].[312] Article 146 [ex Article 123] now provides that:

In order to improve employment opportunities for workers in the internal market and to contribute thereby to raising the standard of living, a European Social Fund is hereby established . . ; it shall aim to render the employment of workers easier and to increase their geographical and occupational mobility within the Community, *and to facilitate their adaptation to industrial changes and to changes in production systems, in particular through vocational training and retraining.*[313]

The ESF is one of the four structural funds. The other three funds are the ERDF introduced in 1975,[314] whose aim is to help redress 'the main regional imbalances in the Community through participation in the development and structural adjustment of regions whose development is lagging behind and in the conversion of declining industrial regions';[315] EAGGF (guidance section),[316] whose aim is to help those excluded by restructuring

---

[310] Commission Communication concerning the Structural Funds and their co-ordination with the Cohesion Fund: Guidelines for Programmes in the Period 2000 to 2006 (1999/C267/02) [1999] OJ 267/2, 3.

[311] See generally http://europa.eu.int/comm/dg05/esf. See also Art. 157 [ex Art. 130] on industry where the Community and the Member States' action is to be aimed at *inter alia*, 'speeding up the adjustment of industry to structural changes'.

[312] Going back even further, the Treaty of Paris, which established the European Coal and Steel Community, contained provisions relating to training and support for workers affected by industrial restructuring.

[313] The section in italics was added by the Treaty on European Union.

[314] European Regional Development Fund: Regulation 724/75 [1975] OJ L73/1 with Art. 235 [new Art. 308] as its legal basis.

[315] Art. 160 [ex Art. 130c].

[316] European Agricultural Guidance and Guarantee Fund. Art. 159 [ex Art. 130b] the Guidance section is concerned with redistribution and its budget is insignificant (no more than 5 per cent of the total). See Hervey, above n. 303, 176.

of the agricultural sector; and the new FIFG on fisheries.[317] The Title on Economic and Social Cohesion introduced by the SEA [new XVIII, ex XIV] brought these funds under a single umbrella. The new Title and a commitment to reform the structural funds were introduced as a *quid pro quo* for agreement on the 1992 Single Market programme by governments representing the poorer regions of the EU who feared that the removal of non-tariff barriers would disproportionately affect them because of their inferior infrastructure, higher unemployment, lower skill levels, and lower productivity.

The promised reform of the structural funds took place in 1988. A parent Regulation[318] and a specific Regulation concerning each fund[319] were adopted and revised in 1993[320] after the Maastricht Treaty to ensure more transparency.[321] The Maastricht Treaty also provided for the inclusion of a Cohesion Fund, this time to assist those Member States likely to be disproportionately affected by the advent of EMU (Spain, Greece, Portugal, and Ireland). The Cohesion Fund[322] is designed to provide a financial contribution to projects in the field of the environment and Trans European Networks (TENs).[323]

Four principles underpinned the reforms of the structural funds in 1988 and 1993. First, they concentrated resources on six priority objectives which included combating long-term unemployment and facilitating the integration of young workers and those excluded from the labour market into employment,[324] and facilitating the adaptation of workers to industrial changes and

---

[317] The FIFG (Financial Instrument of Fisheries Guidance) was set up after the Edinburgh European Council in Dec. 1992.

[318] Regulation 2052/88 [1988] OJ L185/9 and Coordination Regulation 4253/88 [1988] OJ L374/1.

[319] ERDF: Council Regulation (EEC) 4254/88 [1988] OJ L374/15; ESF: Council Regulation (EEC) 4255/88 [1988] OJ L374/21; EAGGF: Council Regulation (EEC) [1988] OJ L374/25.

[320] Regulation 2081/93 [1993] OJ L193/5; Coordination Regulation 2082/93 [1993] OJ L193/20. The specific Regulations are 2083/93 [1993] OJ L193/34 (ERDF) now replaced by Regulation 1783/1999 [1999] OJ L213/1, 2084/93 [1993] OJ L193/39 (ESF) now replaced by Regulation 1262/1999 [1999] OJ L161/48 and 2085/93 [1993] OJ L193/44 (EAGGF) now replaced by Regulation 1257/1999 [1999] OJ L160/80.

[321] This was especially important in the light of the increased budget for structural funds: total expenditure was ECU 147.47 billion between 1994 and 1999. This constitutes 33 per cent of the Community budget as compared with 20 per cent for the preceding period.

[322] Council Regulation (EC) No. 1164/94 [1994] OJ L130/1 as amended by Regulations 1264/99 [1999] OJ L161/57 and 1265/99 [1999] OJ L161/62. The European Investment Bank (Arts. 266 and 267 [ex Arts. 198d and 198e]) also has an important role to play in the redistribution of Community resources. According to Art. 267 [ex Art. 198e] the Bank, operating on a non-profit-making basis, shall grant loans and make guarantees which contribute to the 'balanced and steady development of the Common Market in the interest of the Community'.

[323] Art. 161 [ex Art. 130d]. The Maastricht Treaty also introduced a Committee of the Regions designed to advise on the formation of regional policy in the EC (Art. 263 [ex Art. 198a]).

[324] Objective 3.

to changes in production systems.[325] The ESF was used to achieve these objectives. Secondly, financing was based on programmes and not individual projects. Thirdly, the regulations required additionality[326] in spending over and above national spending, and, fourthly, the reforms placed much greater emphasis on partnership by involving EU institutions, national governments, regional authorities, and the Social Partners more closely, in particular in respect of the ESF.[327]

In 1999 a new set of Regulations were adopted covering the period 2000–2006.[328] Based on the principles underpinning the 1988 and 1993 reforms, they placed greater emphasis on transparency and the 'fundamental principle' of effectiveness.[329] The Regulations also reduced the number of objectives of the structural funds to three: Objective 1 (least developed regions), Objective 2 (regions with serious structural problems and the former Objectives 2 and 5b) and Objective 3 (Human Resources, 'supporting the adaptation and modernisation of policies and systems of education, training and employment').[330] With a budget of EUR 24.05 billion (12.3 per cent of the total),[331] the ESF[332] is to be used to achieve Objective 3. Article 1 of the new ESF Regulation provides:

the Fund shall support measures to prevent and combat unemployment and to develop human resources and social integration into the labour market in order to promote a high level of employment, equality between men and women, sustainable development, and economic and social cohesion. In particular, the Fund shall contribute to the actions undertaken in pursuance of the European Employment Strategy and the Annual Guidelines on Employment.

Article 2 then sets out five areas of intervention for the ESF which are consistent with the four pillars of the Employment Guidelines:

- to develop active policies to combat unemployment, to prevent the unemployed moving into long-term unemployment, to help the long-term

---

[325] Objective 4. In addition, specific reference was made to promoting equal opportunities in the labour market between men and women and providing pathways to employment for people at risk of social exclusion. Definitions were made more flexible, extending eligibility to people at risk of long-term unemployment or exclusion from the world of work, as well as those already in either of these situations.

[326] 'Additionality' means that every sum provided by the Community must be matched by the same amount by the Member State.

[327] See Scott, *Development Dilemmas in the European Community: Rethinking Regional Development Policy* (OUP, Oxford, 1995), 26.

[328] Regulation 1260/1999 [1999] OJ L161/1 replacing Regulation 2052/88 [1988] OJ L185/9 and Coordination Regulation 4253/88 [1988] OJ L374/1. See also Commission Communication concerning the Structural Funds 1999/C267/02 [1999] OJ C267/2.

[329] Preambular para. 25 of Regulation 1260/1999 [1999] OJ L161/1.

[330] Art. 1 of Regulation 1260/1999 [1999] OJ L161/1.

[331] Art. 7(1) of Regulation 1260/1999 [1999] OJ L161/1.

[332] Regulation 1262/1999 [1999] OJ L161/48 replacing Regulation 4255/88 [1988] OJ L374/21.

unemployed back into the job market, and to provide support for those entering the job market—either young people starting work for the first time or those returning to work;

- to promote social inclusion[333] and equality of opportunity for everyone to access work;
- to develop education and training as part of a policy for lifelong learning to enhance and sustain employability, mobility, and integration into the labour market;
- to promote a skilled, trained and adaptable workforce, foster innovation and adaptability in work organization, support entrepreneurship and employment creation, and boost human potential in research, science and technology;
- to improve the participation of women in the labour market including their career development, their access to new job opportunities and to entrepreneurship, and to reduce vertical and horizontal segregation in the labour market.[334]

Ross has argued that these well-constructed regional development policies, designed to redistribute wealth from richer to poorer regions, have become 'the most significant instruments for preempting any "race to the bottom" in labour standards and labour-market regulation'.[335] He continues that 'the social policy goal is to buy backward EU regions into the "European model of society"'.[336] This helps to explain why 'there has been very little North–South social dumping in the European Union and remarkably few signs that southern EU Member States are eager to exploit their relative economic and social policy backwardness as a competitive tool. By and large, the South seems persuaded that it should cast its lot with the higher-wage, stronger welfare-state northerners'.[337]

4. Vocational Training

As we have seen, one of the key pillars of ESF expenditure is on training to produce a highly skilled and adaptable workforce. This has long been a

---

[333] See generally Commission Communication *Building an Inclusive Europe* COM(2000) forthcoming and Commission Communication *Social Trends, Prospects and Challenges* COM(2000) forthcoming.

[334] See esp. the launch of the EQUAL programme dealing with 'transnational cooperation to promote new means of combating all forms of discrimination and inequalities in connection with the labour market'.

[335] Ross, 'Assessing the Delors Era and Social Policy' in Leibfried and Pierson (eds.), above n. 133; Scott and Mansell, 'European Regional Development: Confusing Quantity with Quality' (1993) 18 *ELRev.* 87.

[336] Ross, above n. 133, 366.

[337] Ross, above n. 133, 368.

favourite (and largely uncontroversial) theme for the Commission. For example, in its White Paper on Growth, Competitiveness, and Employment 1993,[338] the Commission proposed solutions to unemployment based on increasing the competitiveness of the EU, seeking healthy growth leading to stable jobs, and enhancing flexibility in the labour market with the emphasis on new kinds of jobs. It therefore called for a significant increase in investment in human capital and greater and more effective efforts in vocational training. This implied increasing skill levels, especially in the new technologies, and promoting life-long learning.[339] In its subsequent action plan the European Council identified seven areas for particular attention by the Member States, including improving education and training systems, especially continuing training; and specific measures concerning young people without adequate training. The ESF was to be used to help implement a guarantee to provide access to recognized education or training for all young people under 18.

The achievement of these objectives was facilitated by the inclusion at Maastricht of a new Chapter on Education, Vocational Training, and Youth which confirmed the Community's growing competence in this field.[340] A new DG was established, DG XXII, to take responsibility for this area. The Community's education and vocational training strategy[341] has, however, developed only gradually as a result of an insecure legal basis provided by the foundation Treaties. The original Article 128 EEC [new and amended Article 150] empowered the Council of Ministers only to 'lay down general principles for implementing a common vocational training policy capable of contributing to the harmonious development both of the national economies and the common market'. These principles were elaborated by Council Decision 63/266.[342] The Commission then used these principles and Article 128 as a legal base for Community action[343] which was challenged unsuccessfully by the UK. In *United Kingdom v. Council*[344] the Court said that the wording of Article 128, combined with the need to secure its effectiveness, permitted the Community to enact legal measures providing for Community action in the field of

---

[338] Bull. Supp. 6/93, endorsed at the Brussels European Council of Dec. 1993.

[339] See also the Commission's White Paper on Education and Training COM(95)590 and the Green Paper on Innovation COM(95)688 final.

[340] Arts. 126–127 [new Arts. 149–150] of the EC Treaty. See Shaw, ' "From the Margins to the Centre": Education and Training Law and Policy', in *The Evolution of EU Law*, eds. Craig and de Búrca (OUP, Oxford, 1999).

[341] See generally, Commission, *Education and Training in the European Community: Guidelines for the Medium Term* COM(91)397.

[342] [1963] OJ Spec. Ed. 64/25.

[343] See generally Flynn, 'Vocational Training in Community Law and Practice' (1988) 8 *Yearbook of European Law* 59; Lonbay, 'Education and Law: The Community Context' (1989) 14 *ELRev.* 363; Lenaerts, 'Education in European Community Law after Maastricht' (1994) 31 *CMLRev.* 7.

[344] Case 56/88 [1989] ECR 1615.

vocational training. Vocational training, it subsequently ruled,[345] within the meaning of Article 128 covered both initial training and continuing or advanced training, even if the training had budgetary implications. However, if the proposed Community measure went beyond the sphere of vocational training, Article 235 [new Article 308] had to be added as an additional legal base.[346]

The Treaty on European Union introduced new Community competence for education (Article 149 EC [ex Article 126]) and significantly amended and renumbered Article 128 EEC in respect of vocational training (Article 150 [ex Article 127]). The Community's new competence for education is heavily circumscribed by the principle of subsidiarity and respect for cultural and linguistic diversity.[347] Article 150 [ex Article 127] provides that the 'Community shall implement a vocational training policy which shall support and supplement the action of the Member States, while fully respecting the action of the Member States for the content and organization of vocational training'.[348] Once again the principle of subsidiarity is emphasized, with the Community playing only a supportive role. However, the Community does have the 'carrot' of funding, possibly leading to some convergence in training policy, but harmonization is expressly excluded.

Vocational training was given normative effect by Council Decision 94/819/EC,[349] known as the Leonardo decision, establishing an action programme for the implementation of an EC vocational training policy.[350] This hard law measure is supplemented by two important soft law documents, the *vade mecum* providing guidelines on how the different strands of the programme fit together, and the *Promoters' Guide.*

[345] Joined Cases C–51, C–90 and C–94/89 *United Kingdom v. Council* [1991] ECR I–2757.

[346] Case 242/87 *EC Commission v. Council (Erasmus)* [1989] ECR I–1425. In order to help the Commission implement its common vocational training policy, the European Centre for Vocational Training (CEDEFOP) (Council Regulation (EEC) No. 337/75 of 10 Feb. 1975 [1975] OJ L39/1, as amended) has been established to compile and disseminate documentation relating to recent developments, research, and vocational training structural problems and to encourage the approximation of standards of vocational training, with a view to mutual recognition of certificates and other documents. The European Training Foundation has also been established to contribute to the development of vocational training in Central and Eastern Europe (Regulation (EEC) No. 1360/90 [1990] OJ L131/90, as amended).

[347] Art. 149(1).

[348] See Barnard, 'The Maastricht Agreement and Education: One Step Forward and Two Steps Back?' (1992) 4 *Education and the Law* 123; Johnson, 'From Vocational Training to Education: the Development of a No-frontiers Education Policy for Europe' (1999) 11 *Education and the Law* 199.

[349] [1994] OJ L340/8. See also Decision 1031/2000/EC ([2000] OJ L117/1) of the Parliament and Council establishing the 'Youth' Community Action Programme.

[350] Socrates, the main action programme on education matters (Council Decision 819/95 [1995] OJ L87/10 on the first phase, Decision 253/2000/EC [2000] OJ L28/1 on the second phase, adopted under both Arts. 126 and 127 [new Arts. 149 and 150]) covers higher education ('Erasmus'), school education ('Comenius'), and 'horizontal activities' (i.e. activities at all levels of education), promotion of language skills ('Lingua'), adult education ('Grundtvig'), and open and distance learning and language exchange ('Minerva'). See further Hervey, above n. 303, 114–15, and http://europa.eu.int/comm/dg22/progr.html.

The developments in the field of training and employment more generally highlight the shift in emphasis from the enactment of employment *law* (the body of rules directly concerned with the employment relationship) to the creation of employment *policy* (measures directly concerned with the creation and maintenance of employment, including measures concerned with training).[351] As Freedland observes, vocational training policy seems to lie within a relatively highly consensual area of convergence between economic policy and social policy (particularly if dressed up as education policy):[352] it has always been potentially difficult to deny the generally ameliorative nature of vocational training policy. Therefore vocational training has seemed a good area for Community development and the strengthening of the power base of the Community institutions, and of the Commission in particular. On the other hand, while it may seem overridingly important to ensure that vocational training is provided for all groups in society, especially to the young, this may result in an under-awareness of, or under-concern with, the potential of vocational training arrangements to erode labour standards.[353] He argues that there is a danger that an educational policy in favour of ever greater flexibility and adaptability in vocational training might be conducive to an over-ready endorsement of all forms and types of flexibility as a matter of employment policy. The Community has recently shown some awareness of this problem. Its 1999 Employment Guidelines make reference to the need for women 'to benefit positively from flexible forms of work organisation'.[354]

5. EMU

Economic and monetary union (EMU) is also intended to form an important pillar in the fight again unemployment. The Vienna European Council proclaimed the birth of the euro to be 'a milestone in the process of European integration. The single currency will strengthen Europe's capacity to foster employment growth and stability'.[355] It argued that the creation of the single currency reinforced the need for economic policy co-ordination which has led to the development of instruments to co-ordinate macro-economic policies in order to maintain sustainable growth and productivity, which in turn

---

[351] See Freedland, 'Employment Policy', in *European Community Labour Law: Principles and Perspectives. Liber Amicorum Lord Wedderburn of Charlton*, eds. Davies, Lyon-Caen, Sciarra and Simitis (Clarendon, Oxford, 1996), 97. This he describes as government by *dominium* as opposed to government by *imperium* through harmonization measures. See also Daintith, 'The Techniques of Government' in Jowell and Oliver (eds.), *The Changing Constitution* (3rd edn, Clarendon, Oxford, 1994), 213–14.

[352] Freedland, 'Vocational Training in EC Law and Policy—Education, Employment or Welfare' (1996) 25 *ILJ* 110, 118–19.

[353] Freedland, above n. 131, 307.

[354] Council Resolution on the 1999 Employment Guidelines.

[355] Para. 7. See also Cologne European Council, para. 5.

translates to the maintenance of higher levels of employment, instruments to improve the effectiveness of national employment policies and instruments to accelerate reform in product, service, and capital markets.[356]

The procedures for the implementation of EMU derive initially from the convergence criteria laid down in the Maastricht Treaty.[357] These require the Member States participating in the third stage of EMU (full monetary union leading to the single currency) to maintain retail price inflation within certain limits, restrict national debt to 60 per cent of gross domestic product (GDP), and confine budget deficits to no more than 3 per cent of GDP. The provisions governing excessive levels of national debt and excessive budget deficits (now contained in Article 104 of the EC Treaty [ex Article 104c]) set up a monitoring and reporting process which, in the last resort, can result in sanctions being applied to a Member State; these include requiring the Member State to make a non-interest bearing deposit 'of an appropriate size' with the Community until the budget deficit in question has been cleared, and, in the last resort, the levying of a fine on the Member State.

In addition, Article 99 of the EC Treaty [ex Article 103] provides for the Community to issue 'broad economic guidelines' for the conduct of economic policy by the Member States. Article 99 is supplemented by the Stability and Growth Pact, agreed by the Member States at the Amsterdam European Council, which is contained in two Regulations[358] and a Council Resolution.[359] Regulation 1466/97 on the strengthening of the surveillance of the budgetary procedures and the surveillance and co-ordination of economic policies puts in place an 'early warning system' designed to alert the Council to the possibility that a Member State participating in the third stage of EMU may be running up an excessive deficit. The Council Resolution on the Stability and Growth Pact,[360] although not 'hard law', is also significant for employment policy, in that it 'underlines the importance of safeguarding sound government finances as a means to strengthening the conditions for price stability and for strong sustainable growth conducive to employment creation'. Alongside this measure, the Council issued a further Resolution on growth and employment.[361] This states:

it should be a priority aim to develop a skilled, trained and adaptable workforce and to make labour markets responsive to economic change. Structural reforms need to be comprehensive in scope, as opposed to limited or occasional measures, so as to address

---

[356] Para. 9.

[357] The following is largely taken from Barnard and Deakin, above n. 266, and Deakin and Reed, above n. 269. I am grateful for Simon Deakin's permission to use this.

[358] Council Regulation 1466/97 [1997] OJ L209/1 and Council Regulation 1467/97 [1997] OJ L209/7.

[359] Resolution 97/C236/01 [1997] OJ C236/1.

[360] Ibid.

[361] Resolution 97/C236/02 [1997] OJ C236/3.

in a coherent manner the complex issue of incentives in creating and taking up a job.[362]

It also calls for more 'employment-friendly' tax and social protection systems aimed at 'improving the functioning of the labour market'.[363]

The implications of EMU for both employment and social policy are further detailed in Council Recommendation 97/479,[364] which prescribes the broad economic guidelines envisaged by Article 103 [new Article 99]. The Recommendation sets as the main objectives 'growth, employment and convergence', noting that the Community 'must progressively achieve a high employment rate'. It then identifies five areas for policy co-ordination: the 'growth and stability-oriented macroeconomic policy mix', price and exchange rate stability, sound public finances, better functioning product and services markets, and 'fostering labour market reforms and investment in knowledge'. As part of macroeconomic policy, it is proposed that 'real wage developments should be below the increase in productivity in order to strengthen the profitability of employment-creating investment'. This clearly has immediate and tangible implications for workers. Under labour market reforms, the Recommendation identifies five areas to which priority should be given. These are 'higher employment growth' through wage levels that take into account appropriate regional differences and variations in workers' qualifications; reductions in non-wage labour costs and income taxation; reform of the taxation and social protection systems; new patterns of work organization including more flexible working time arrangements 'tailored to the specific needs of firms and workers'; and adaptation of the training and education system to the need to invest in human capital, including measures aimed at 'improving the employability of the unemployed'.[365]

The Council Resolution on Stability and Growth calls for the co-ordination of economic policies with the procedure laid down in the Employment Title.[366] This was emphasized by the European Council meeting in Vienna where the heads of government agreed that employment policy has to be 'embedded in a comprehensive approach encompassing macro-economic policies directed towards stability and employment-creating growth, economic reform promoting competitiveness, and the Employment Guidelines'.[367] This has meant that the 1999 Broad Guidelines on Economic Policy drawn up in conformity with Article 103(2) EC [new Article 99] demonstrate a 'greater synergy'[368] with the 1999 Employment Guidelines. As a result, the 1999 Guidelines on Economic Policy recognize that:

[362] Ibid., para. 1.
[363] Ibid., para. 4.
[364] [1997] OJ L209/13.
[365] See [1997] OJ L209/18.
[366] Ibid., para. 6.
[367] COM(99)127, 3.
[368] COM(99)127, 3.

Europe's employment challenge is the key priority for economic policy. The successful launch of the euro and a well-functioning EMU set a favourable framework. However, creating the conditions for high and sustainable growth and employment, which is primarily a matter for Member States, will require a comprehensive and coherent strategy that consists of three mutually-reinforcing key components.[369]

These are:

- sound macroeconomic policies that are conducive to growth, employment, and price stability, involving full respect of the Stability and Growth pact and continued appropriate wage developments;
- policies that improve the overall functioning of labour markets and in particular improve employability, entrepreneurship, adaptability, and equal opportunities via a steadfast, prompt, and transparent implementation of the employment guidelines tailored to Member States' conditions; and
- economic reforms that enhance the efficiency and flexibility of goods, services, and capital markets and favour an environmentally sustainable growth path, involving a close monitoring of the single market, a vigorous competition policy, regulatory reforms and more efficient taxation systems.[370]

The Guidelines continue that these 'three components are reflected in the three pillars of the European Employment Pact'.

The so-called 'European Employment Pact' was prepared by the German Presidency and presented to the Cologne Council in June 1999.[371] The first limb comprises the effective implementation of the employment strategy (in essence the Luxembourg process). The second limb, developed at the Cardiff summit in December 1998, involves comprehensive structural reform and modernization to improve the innovative capacity and efficiency of the labour market and the markets in goods, services, and capital.[372] The third limb is described as the 'Cologne Process' and involves the improved interaction between fiscal, wage, and monetary policies. In particular it notes that the primary objective of monetary policy is to maintain price stability. Underpinning this monetary policy must be a wage policy (where wages keep to a sustainable path, with wage developments that are consistent with price stability and job creation) and a fiscal policy which must respect the objectives of the Stability and Growth Pact. At the Lisbon summit in March 2000[373] the Union set itself a new strategic goal 'to become the most competitive and

---

[369] Council Recommendation 99/570/EC [1999] OJ L217/34, 38. See also the earlier Commission Recommendation COM(99)143 final.

[370] Ibid. These themes were further developed in the Commission's Communication on 'Community Policies in Support of Employment' COM(99)127.

[371] Cologne European Council Presidency Conclusions, 3 and 4 June 1999, para. 7.

[372] See esp. the Action Plan on 'Promoting Entrepreneurship and Competitiveness' COM(98)550.

[373] Presidency Conclusions, 24 Mar. 2000, paras. 5–7.

dynamic knowledge-based economy in the world capable of sustainable economic growth with more and better jobs and greater social cohesion'. It said:

Achieving this goal requires an *overall strategy* aimed at:

— preparing the transition to a knowledge-based economy and society by better policies for the information society and R & D, as well as by stepping up the process of structural reform for competitiveness and innovation and by completing the internal market;
— modernising the European social model, investing in people and combating social exclusion;
— sustaining the healthy economic outlook and favourable growth prospects by applying an appropriate macro-economic policy mix.

This Lisbon summit also fixed quantified targets for attaining these objectives, including raising the male employment rate from 61 per cent to 70 per cent by 2010 and to increase the female employment rate from 51 per cent to 60 per cent. Given that the Luxembourg process has already enabled Europe to 'substantially reduce unemployment', the most striking feature of this summit is the emphasis on regaining 'the conditions for *full employment*', and not just a high level of employment, and 'on strengthening regional cohesion in the European Union'. This is still to be achieved through co-ordination 'at all levels, coupled with a stronger guiding and coordinating role for the European Council to ensure more coherent strategic direction and effective monitoring of progress'. This has now been endorsed by the Commission's social policy agenda.[374A]

This complex web of pacts, strategies, and processes, while politically significant, does little to address the fundamental contradiction that governments cannot, on the one hand, reduce the public deficits and keep the overall level of taxes stable, and, on the other, invest in factors of long-term growth (education, research, infrastructure) and maintain the level of expenditure on social security.[374] They also do not address the potential conflict which these contradictions might create within the Commission between DG II (Economic and Financial Affairs) or DG V (Employment and Social Affairs) nor do they allay fears about race-to-the-bottom by the Member States and an erosion of social standards. The argument runs as follows. Given the constraints imposed by the convergence criteria and EMU, Member States have lost or will lose their ability independently to regulate interest rates and exchange rates in their quest for improving their international competitiveness. The one area where they would retain their independence is in respect of the regulation— or rather deregulation—of labour standards, wages, and social security. As a

---

[374A] COM(2000)379.
[374] Pochet, 'The New Employment Chapter of the Amsterdam Treaty' (1999) 9 *JESP* 271, 273. Cf. Traversa, 'The Consequences of European Monetary Union on Collective Bargaining and the National Social Security Systems' (2000) 16 *IJCLLIR* 47 which argues that there is no scientific evidence that EMU has had a particularly negative effect on the level of social protection.

result, there is concern that one of the consequences of EMU might be that so long as Member States retain competence in the field of social policy, they will take advantage of this freedom to lower national labour and social security standards (social devaluation), unless transnational standards are put in place to discourage them from doing this.[375] It will also be recalled that the Ohlin report generally denied the need for transnational labour standards in the 1950s so long as the system of national exchange rates reflected general prices and productivity within States. This would cancel out the apparent advantage of low-wage States. Once there is a uniform exchange rate, the position described by Ohlin may well be different.

6. The Role of the Social Partners

As we have already seen, in the eyes of the Commission the Social Partners have a vital function to play at the micro-level, ensuring the modernization of the firm and in the application of the structural funds.[376] They also have a role at the macro-level where the social dialogue is seen as playing an important part in the formulation of wage determination policies which are compatible with employment growth. This tripartite concertation with the Social Partners occurs largely in the reformed Standing Committee on Employment[377] which the newly created Employment Committee,[378] set up under Article 130 [ex Article 109s] of the Employment Title, is obliged to consult. The role for the Social Partners was highlighted at the Cologne summit in June 1999 where the European Council noted that:

For a consistent policy mix to be implemented successfully, it is helpful to have a fruitful macroeconomic dialogue between Social Partners, fiscal and employment policymakers and monetary policymakers within existing institutions. In the course of this dialogue, the starting position and future prospects could be discussed on the basis of statistical data and analyses, and ideas could be exchanged as to how, while retaining their respective responsibilities and preserving their independence, those involved consider that a policy mix can be achieved that is conducive to growth and employment under conditions of price stability.[379]

---

[375] OECD, above n. 171, 164. See also Peters, 'Economic and Monetary Union and Labour Markets: What to Expect?' (1995) 134 *International Labour Review* 315. For concerns about the impact of EMU on social protection more generally, see Guild, 'How can Social Protection Survive EMU? A United Kingdom Perspective' (1999) 24 *ELRev.* 22.

[376] See above n. 327.

[377] Council Decision 1999/207/EC [1999] OJ L72/33, repealing Decision 70/532/EEC.

[378] Art. 5 of Council Decision 2000/98/EC [2000] OJ L29/21.

[379] Cologne European Council Presidency Conclusions, 3 and 4 June 1999. See also Recommendation 97/249, para. 2(iii) which calls on the Commission to promote social dialogue at Community level 'notably on macroeconomic policy issues'; the Commission Communication of 20 May 1998 on *Adapting and Promoting the Social Dialogue at Community Level* also notes that: 'the incorporation of a new Employment Title in the Amsterdam Treaty and the application of these arrangements has changed the nature of the tripartite dialogue', COM(98)322, at 10.

The economic guidelines also envisage a neo-corporatist role for the Social Partners in tripartite, national-level dialogue over the employment consequences of EMU. The 1999 guidelines provide that 'For wage developments to contribute to an employment-friendly mix, the Social Partners should continue to pursue a responsible course and conclude wage agreements in Member States in line with the general principles set out in previous Broad Economic Policy Guidelines', namely:[380]

- nominal wage increases must be consistent with price stability;
- real wage increases in relation to labour productivity growth should take into account the need to strengthen and maintain the profitability of investment;
- wage agreements should take into account differentials in productivity levels according to qualifications, regions and sectors.

As Deakin and Reed point out, the suggestion in the Council Resolution on growth and employment that the Social Partners should 'fully face their responsibilities within their respective sphere of activity',[381] coupled with the direction in the broad economic guidelines that real wage levels should be pegged below increases in productivity so as to provide incentives for investment, indicates a role in suppressing wage growth which sits unhappily with the traditional role of trade unions. Nevertheless, the importance of social dialogue as a mechanism for promoting the appropriate conditions for growth should not be underestimated; it is reflected in experiences at Member State level. Some Member States, such as Italy, Spain, and France, have a long tradition of tripartite bargaining between government and the Social Partners over labour costs, flexibilization, and wage growth.[382] On the other hand, as Towers and Terry observe,[383] UNICE's refusal to bargain in good faith, particularly in respect of information and consultation and sexual harassment, may hinder efforts to implement the EU's employment strategy which requires a high degree of co-operation and agreement between the Social Partners.

7. Conclusions

In its White Paper on Social Policy[384] the Commission talks of the creation of a 'European Social Model' based around certain shared values:

---

[380] Council Recommendation 99/570/EC [1999] OJ L217/34.

[381] Resolution 97/C236/02, para. 13. See also Biaggi, 'The Economic and Monetary Union and Industrial Relations' (2000) 16 *IJCLLIR* 39.

[382] See Treu, 'European Collective Bargaining Levels and the Competences of the Social Partners', in Davies (ed.), above n. 131, 179.

[383] Towers and Terry, 'Editorial Unemployment and the Social Dialogue' (1999) 30 *IRJ* 272, 276.

[384] COM(94)333, para. 3.

These include democracy and individual rights, free collective bargaining, the market economy, equality of opportunity for all and social welfare and solidarity. These values ... are held together by the conviction that economic and social progress must go hand in hand. Competitiveness and solidarity have both been taken into account in building a successful Europe for the future.

This piecemeal European Social Model provides the bridge between the economic aspect of the Treaty (job creation) and the social dimension of the Treaty (politics of social inclusion, solidarity, and citizenship) and represents a step towards the creation of a European 'civil society'.[385] The justification for establishing a European social policy has changed over time and the techniques for achieving these objectives have also varied. It is to this subject that Chapter 2 turns.

[385] See Opinion of the Economic and Social Committee, above n. 109, 32.

2

Law-making in the Field of Social Policy

Different approaches by the Member States towards social legislation at national level have forced the European Union to consider its own method of legislating at EU level. This chapter examines this problem and the means employed to ensure the principle of subsidiarity is respected and flexibility achieved. The chapter considers both the traditional route to legislation and the innovative method introduced by the Treaty on European Union of legislating by collective agreement, primarily by the cross-industry (interprofessional or intersectoral) social partners but also by the sectoral social partners. This form of autonomous, bipartite dialogue is complemented by the tripartite dialogue encouraged by the Employment and Broad Economic Policy Guidelines.[1] The functioning of the new Employment Title introduced by the Amsterdam Treaty is considered in the final part of this chapter.

A. THE LEGISLATIVE PROCESS

1. Competence

Unlike national constitutions, the European Community enjoys no general competence to enact legislation: it has only specific competences or enumerated powers given to it by the Member States in the Treaties. As Article 5(1) [ex Article 3b(1)] makes clear, 'The Community shall act within the limits of the powers conferred on it by this Treaty and of the objectives assigned to it therein'.[2] These powers may be specific, as in the case of Article 137 [ex Article 118a] concerning health and safety, or more general, as in the case of Articles 94, 95, and 308 [ex Articles 100, 100a, and 235] concerning measures for the attainment of the common market and internal market.[3] Where the Community has exclusive competence, Member States cannot act

---

[1] Commission, *Industrial Relations in Europe—2000*, COM(2000)113, 7.

[2] See Dashwood, 'The Limits of European Community Powers' (1996) 21 *ELRev.* 113.

[3] Art. 100 [new Art. 94] (measures which directly affect the establishment or functioning of the Common Market) was used to adopt the three Directives in the late 1970s on restructuring of enterprises (Directive 75/129 on collective redundancies [1975] OJ L48/29, Directive 77/187 on transfers [1977] OJ L61/126, and Directive 80/987/EEC [1980] OJ L283/23 on insolvency). Directive 75/117 on equal pay was also adopted on the basis of Art. 100 [new Art. 94]. Directives 76/207 and 79/7 on equal treatment were adopted on the basis of Art. 235 [new Art. 308]

in the field irrespective of whether the Community itself has acted.[4] The corollary of this is that where the Member States have not conferred power to act on the Community the Member States retain legal competence. Between these two extremes lie areas where the Community and the Member States are concurrently competent. This means that until the Community acts in these fields the Member States may act, providing they do so within the limits set by the Treaty relating to, for example, free movement of goods and persons under Articles 28, 39, 43, and 49 [ex Articles 30, 48, 52, and 59], non-discrimination on the grounds of nationality under Article 12 [ex Article 6], and the obligation of co-operation with the Community under Article 10 [ex Article 5]. In other words, concurrence still implies the supremacy of Community norms. If, by reason of the scale and effects of the measure,[5] the Community decides it should act, it converts a field of concurrent competence into a field of exclusive competence for the Community.[6] This effect is described in American constitutional law as the doctrine of 'preemption'.[7]

While the attribution of competence to the Community has great significance, both internally and externally,[8] the Treaty does not identify those areas which fall within the exclusive competence of either the Community or the Member States, or those areas which fall within the concurrent competence of the Member States and the Community. In the field of social policy the Community has no competence, at least under Article 137,[9] in respect of pay, the right to strike, or the right to impose lock-outs (Article 137(6) [ex Article 2(6) SPA]). However, the Community probably shares competence with the Member States in respect of Article 100a(2) [new Article 95] concerning 'the rights and interests of employed persons', introduced by the Single European

---

(action by the Community to attain one of the objectives of the Community where the Treaty has not provided the necessary powers). Directives 86/378 and 86/613 on equality in occupational social security and of the self-employed respectively are both based on Arts. 100 and 235 [new Arts. 94 and 308]. Both legal bases require unanimous voting in Council.

[4] See e.g. in the context of Art. 133 [ex Art. 113] *Opinion 1/75* [1975] ECR 1355 and Case 41/76 *Donckerwolke v. Procureur de la République* [1976] ECR 1921.

[5] The principle of subsidiarity contained in Art. 5(2) [ex Art. 3b(2)], is considered below, text attached to nn. 39–47.

[6] If the Community acts again in this field the principle of subsidiarity now does not apply.

[7] See, e.g., Weatherill, 'Beyond Preemption? Shared Competence and Constitutional Change in the European Community', in *Legal Issues of the Maastricht Treaty*, eds. O'Keeffe and Twomey (Chancery, Chichester, 1994); Cross, 'Preemption of Member State Law in the European Economic Community: A Framework for Analysis' (1992) 29 *CMLRev.* 447; Soares, 'Preemption, Conflicts of Powers and Subsidiarity' (1998) 23 *ELRev.* 109.

[8] Where the Community has internal competence it also has authority to enter into international commitments necessary to attain this objective, even in the absence of express provision to that effect: Joined Cases 3, 4 and 6/76 *Kramer and Others* [1976] ECR 1279 and *Opinion 2/91* [1993] ECR I-1061, considered below at n. 11.

[9] See Brinkman, 'Lawmaking under the Social Chapter of Maastricht', in *Lawmaking in the EU*, eds. Craig and Harlow (Kluwer, Deventer, 1998), 244, although the Presidency Note 'IGC 2000: Extension of Qualified Majority Voting—Social Provisions', CONFER 4708/00 says that 'all of . . . [these areas] are excluded from the scope of the Treaty under Article 137(6) TEC'.

Act to which the unanimous voting provisions found in Article 100 [new Article 94] apply, and the areas listed in Article 118a [new Article and significantly amended Article 137]. Article 118a was included in the Treaty by the SEA. Prior to the Social Policy Agreement being incorporated into the EC Treaty it was the only express legal basis included in the social chapter of the Treaty of Rome. Article 118a(1) provided that 'Member States shall pay particular attention to encouraging improvements, especially in the working environment, as regards health and safety of workers'. Article 118a(2) then provided that the Council, acting by a qualified majority vote,[10] was to adopt directives laying down '*minimum requirements* for gradual implementation' (emphasis added) to help achieve the objective laid down in Article 118a(1). According to Article 118a(3), Member States were free to maintain or introduce 'more stringent measures for the protection of working conditions'.

The nature of the Community's competence in respect of social policy, and in particular Article 118a, was considered by the Court in *Opinion 2/91*[11] concerning ILO Convention No. 170 relating to safety in the use of chemicals at work. During the negotiations leading up to the agreement of this Convention, the Commission argued that the subject-matter of the Convention fell within the exclusive competence of the Community. This was disputed by some Member States and the matter was considered by the Court under Article 228(6) [new Article 300(6)]. The Court began by noting that the area covered by the Convention fell within the Title on Social Policy. Referring to Article 118a, it said that the Community 'enjoys an internal legislative competence in the area of social policy'.[12] It continued that since the subject matter of Convention No. 170 coincided with that of several directives adopted under Article 118a,[13] the Convention fell within the Community's area of competence. The Court then distinguished between two situations. On the one hand, it said that in the areas where the Community had laid down only minimum requirements and those standards were inferior to those set by the ILO the Member States had competence under Article 118a(3) to adopt more stringent measures.[14] On the other hand, the Court said that in those areas where the Community had harmonized rules, for example, relating to classification, packaging, and labelling of dangerous substances and preparations,[15] the Community alone had competence.

[10] At Maastricht this was amended to the co-operation procedure contained in Art. 189c [new Art. 252].

[11] [1993] ECR I–1061. See Emiliou, 'Towards a Clearer Demarcation Line? The Division of External Relations Power between the Community and the Member States' (1994) 19 *ELRev*. 76.

[12] Para. 40. On the importance of developing international co-operation see COM(2000)379.

[13] See further Ch. 6.

[14] Para. 18. The Court dismissed the argument made by the Commission that it could be difficult to determine whether one specific measure was more favourable to a worker than another. The Court said that such difficulties could not constitute a basis for exclusive competence.

[15] Council Directive 67/548/EEC [1967] (OJ Spec. Ed. 234), as amended and Directive 88/379/EEC [1988] OJ L187/14.

The ILO Convention also contained provisions about implementation, making express reference to consultation with the social partners. The Court said that in so far as it had been established that the substantive provisions of the Convention came within the Community's sphere of competence, the Community was also competent to undertake commitments for putting those provisions into effect. It recognized that 'as Community law stands at present, social policy and in particular co-operation between the two sides of industry are matters which fall predominantly within the competence of the Member States'[16] but, pointing to Article 118b [new Article 139], which provides that the Commission shall endeavour to develop a dialogue between management and labour at European level,[17] it said these matters had not been 'withdrawn entirely from the competence of the Community'. It added that where the subject-matter of an agreement fell in part within the competence of the Community and in part within the competence of the Member States, there had to be a close association between the two, particularly because unlike the Member States the Community had only observer status at the ILO and so could not itself conclude an ILO Convention.[18]

The legal basis of a measure not only confers on the Community the power to act but it also sets out the legislative procedure by which the measure must be adopted, be it simple consultation with the European Parliament and unanimous voting, the co-operation procedure under Article 252 [ex Article 189c] (abolished by the Amsterdam Treaty, with the exception of the Title on EMU)[19] or the co-decision procedure under Article 251 [ex Article 189b]. When the original Article 118a [new Article 137] was introduced the choice of legal basis became a political football: the Commission made extensive use of the provision since it provided for qualified majority voting which permitted Community social policy measures to be adopted even if the British Conservative government voted against them. The Commission's strategy was eventually challenged by the UK in the *Working Time* case.[20] The Working Time Directive 93/104/EC[21] was adopted under Article 118a, with the UK government abstaining. The UK then challenged the choice of legal basis arguing, *inter alia*, that since the organization of working time envisaged by the Directive was intended to achieve both job creation and social policy objectives, recourse should have been had to Article 100 EC [new Article 94]

---

[16] Para. 30.

[17] Para. 31. Cf. Case C–67/96 *Albany International BV v. Stichting Bedrijfspensioenfonds Textielindustrie*, judgment of 21 Sept. 1999, considered further in Ch. 8.

[18] Paras. 36–37.

[19] Dashwood, 'European Community Legislative Procedures after Amsterdam' (1999) 1 *CYELS* 25, 33.

[20] Case C–84/94 *UK v. Council (Working Time)* [1996] ECR I–5755. See, generally, *The ECJ's Working Time Judgment: The Social Market Vindicated*, CELS Occasional Paper No. 2, 1997; Waddington, 'Towards a Healthier and More Secure European Social Policy' (1997) 4 *Maastricht Journal of European and Comparative Law* 83.

[21] [1993] OJ L307/18. See Ch. 6 for further details of the Directive.

or to Article 235 [new Article 308], both requiring unanimity in Council. It also argued that on a proper interpretation, Article 118a [new Article 137] should be read in conjunction with Article 100a(2) [new Article 95] concerning the rights and interests of employed persons and required a unanimous vote. The Court rejected these arguments. It said that since Article 118a appeared in the section dealing with social provisions it related only to measures concerning the health and safety of workers. The Court reasoned that it therefore constituted a more specific rule than Articles 100 and 100a, an interpretation confirmed by the fact that the provisions of Article 100a was to apply 'save where otherwise provided in this Treaty'.[22]

The UK then argued that the link between health and safety (as narrowly understood under English law) and working time was too tenuous. The Advocate General pointed out that under Danish law the term 'working environment' (*arbejdsmiljø*) contained in Article 118a(1) was a very broad one, not limited to classic measures relating to safety and health at work in the strict sense, but included 'measures concerning working hours, psychological factors, the way work is performed, training in hygiene and safety, and the protection of young workers and worker representation with regard to security against dismissal or any other attempt to undermine their working conditions'. The Court, without referring to the Danish origins of Article 118a, also favoured a broad approach to health and safety. It pointed to the World Health Organization's (WHO) definition of health as 'a state of complete psychic, mental and social well being . . . [which] does not merely consist of an absence of disease or infirmity'. As a result it was able to conclude that 'where *the principal aim* of the measure in question is the protection of the health and safety of workers, Article 118a must be used, albeit such a measure may have ancillary effects on the establishment and functioning of the internal market'.[23]

The Court then examined whether the Directive was correctly based on

[22] An approach favouring a specific basis in preference to a general legal basis is consistent with the Court's earlier jurisprudence, esp. the *Tariff Preference* case (Case 45/86 *Commission v. Council* [1987] ECR I-1493) concerning Arts. 113 [new Art. 133] and 235 [new Art. 308] and, more recently Case C-271/94 *Parliament v. Council* [1996] ECR I-1705 (Art. 129c(1) v. Art. 100a [new Art. 155 v. new Art. 95]). At the same time, possibly unintentionally, the Court in *Working Time* has also followed its ruling in the controversial *Titanium Dioxide* decision (Case C-300/89 *Commission v. Council* [1991] ECR I-2867). In that case, the Court favoured the use of Art. 100a [new Art. 95] over the specific basis of Art. 130s [new Art. 175] on the ground that it incorporated the more democratic co-operation procedure. The Court observed that parliamentary participation 'reflects a fundamental democratic principle that the peoples should take part in the exercise of power through the intermediary of a representative assembly'. The Advocate General made a similar point in *Working Time*. He said 'only a broad interpretation of Art. 118a was capable of ensuring effective supervision by the Parliament in social policy matters, a field in which its role is predominant'. The Court made no reference to this. It is perhaps fortuitous that Art. 118a combined the advantage of being both specific and democratic.

[23] This approach confirms that adopted by the Court in e.g. the *Waste Directive* case (Case C-155/91 *Commission v. Council* [1993] ECR I-939) and Case C-271/94 *Parliament v. Council* [1996] ECR I-1705).

Article 118a. Noting that the Directive was a social policy measure and not a general measure relating to job creation and reducing unemployment, it said that health and safety was the essential objective of the Directive, albeit that it might affect employment as well, and therefore the Directive was properly adopted on the basis of Article 118a. The Court did, however, annul Article 5(2) of the Directive which provided that the minimum weekly rest period 'shall in principle include Sunday'. The Court said that the 'Council has failed to explain why Sunday as a weekly rest day, is more closely connected with health and safety of workers than any other day of the week'. As a result, the provision, 'which is severable from the other provisions of the Directive', had to be annulled.

The outcome of the case is unsurprising and served to reinforce Article 118a as an autonomous legal basis for social policy measures. However, the judgment can be criticized on the grounds that the Court was content with relying on 'self-justifying proclamations' in the Preamble as the basis of making the link between working time and health and safety,[24] without giving a thorough examination either to the scientific evidence produced or considering the impact of the numerous exceptions and derogations to the Directive on the overall health and safety objective.[25]

The SPA substantially amended Article 118a in respect of the then eleven Member States and extended the areas to which qualified majority voting (in the co-operation procedure) applied. It also introduced express new legal bases to which unanimous voting applied. These were incorporated into the EC Treaty at Amsterdam and revised. Thus, according to Article 137(1) and (2), the Community now has competence to adopt, by the Article 251 [ex Article 189b] co-decision procedure, after consulting the Economic and Social Committee and the Committee of the Regions, minimum standards directives, supporting and complementing the activities of the Member States, concerning:

- improvements in particular of the working environment to protect workers' health and safety;
- working conditions;
- the information and consultation of workers;
- the integration of persons excluded from the labour market without prejudice to Article 150 [ex Article 127];
- equality between men and women with regard to labour market opportunities and treatment at work.

Article 137(2) also gives the Council the power to 'adopt measures designed to encourage cooperation between Member States through initiatives aimed

[24] Kenner, 'A Distinctive Legal Base for Social Policy? The Court of Justice Answers a "Delicate Question"' (1997) 22 *ELRev.* 579, 584.
[25] Ellis (1997) 34 *CMLRev.* 1049, 1057. See further Ch. 6.

at improving knowledge, developing exchanges of information and best practices, promoting innovative approaches and evaluating experiences in order to combat social exclusion'.

According to Article 137(3), the Council also has the power to adopt minimum standards directives by unanimous vote, after consulting the European Parliament, the Economic and Social Committee and the Committee of the Regions, concerning:

- social security and social protection of workers;[26]
- protection of workers where their employment contract is terminated;[27]
- representation[28] and collective defence of the interests of workers and employers,[29] including co-determination, subject to paragraph 6 (which provides that the 'provisions of this Article shall not apply to pay, the right of association, the right to strike and the right to impose lock-outs');
- conditions of employment for third country nationals legally residing in Community territory;[30]

[26] According to CONFER 4708/00, 'This indent explicitly empowers the EC to adopt basic minimum social security provisions, whereas Article 42 TEC merely permits it to coordinate social security in order to achieve the free movement of workers. This is a highly sensitive area, primarily because the Member States' political responsibility and budgetary liability are at stake. In addition, the legal concepts, philosophy and funding methods underlying national legislation on social security and the protection of workers still differ widely from Member State to Member State. It proposes that the introduction of qualified majority voting could make it easier to explore coordinated approaches to problems that are widely shared by Member States, whether this be how to fund pensions or to control health expenditure, or the problem of employment. It then says that the IGC might consider the possibility of identifying certain specific social security measures that could be adopted by qualified majority voting on grounds of their relevance to the Union's overall aims; the fundamental principles and basic rules applying to social security would continue to be governed by the unanimity rule.'

[27] CONFER 4708/00 says that this provision may cover redundancy protection measures which relate to the method of terminating the employment contract (agreement?, notification?, unilateral dismissal?, termination by the courts?), to compensation schemes for workers made redundant, and to the conditions for granting unemployment benefit. The potential advantages of facilitating the definition of a common approach on these questions may make this a field in which a switch to qualified majority voting might be considered.

[28] CONFER 4708/00 says that this refers to the information, consultation, and participation of workers in works councils, occupational health and safety committees, civil servants' associations, and trade union representations. It says that a switch to qualified majority voting might be envisaged in this area provided that the measures in question represented an extension of the information and consultation of workers referred to in the fourth indent of Art. 137(1), aspects which are themselves governed by qualified majority voting under Art. 137(2).

[29] CONFER 4708/00 says this refers to the negotiation of collective agreements and covers the parties authorized to conclude such agreements, the form and content of such agreements, the Community level status of such agreements, and their binding nature. The question of a shift to qualified majority voting for measures of this type might arise, perhaps excluding the most sensitive areas, namely arrangements for settling labour disputes (mediation, conciliation, arbitration), which are directly linked to the right to strike.

[30] CONFER 4708/00 says that this provision is directly related to three questions: the crossing of internal borders by third-country nationals, Member States' residence requirements for third country nationals legally residing in another Member State, and freedom of movement for workers. It says that these considerations might lead the Conference to consider the possibility of a

- financial contributions for promotion of employment and job creation without prejudice to the provisions relating to the social fund.[31]

In all cases, the directives must avoid imposing administrative, financial, and legal constraints which would hold back the creation and development of small and medium sized enterprises.[32] This does not, however, mean, according to the first declaration appended to the SPA, that when laying down minimum requirements for the protection of health and safety there is an intention to discriminate 'in a manner unjustified by the circumstances' against employees in small and medium enterprises. The importance of this provision (or at least its predecessor in Article 118a(2), paragraph 2) was recognized by the Court in *Kirshammer-Hack*[33] where, in the context of national legislation exempting small businesses from the protection against unfair dismissal, the Court ruled that such legislation formed part of a group of measures 'intended to alleviate the constraints on small businesses, which play an essential role in economic development and job creation within the Community'. The Court also indicated that 'these undertakings can be the object of special measures'.

Finally, as with (ex) Article 118a(2) and (3), when the Council adopts a measure setting minimum requirements under Article 137(2) or (3) Member States remain free to maintain or introduce more stringent protective measures compatible with the Treaty.[34] In the *Working Time* case[35] the Court said that the phrase 'minimum requirements' in Article 118a(2) [new Article 137(2)] 'does not limit Community action to the lowest common denominator, or even the lowest level of protection established by the Member States'.[36] It meant that Member States were free to adopt more stringent measures than those resulting from Community law,[37] high as those might

---

shift to qualified majority voting; as the conditions of employment for third country nationals legally residing in Community territory relate to the freedom of movement of third country nationals as workers, it would, in order to have parallel procedures, be a fairly logical step to apply to them the same voting rule (i.e. qualified majority) as applies to the freedom of movement of workers who are Member States' nationals.

[31] CONFER 4708/00 says that this provision deals with the provision of funding to promote employment and job-creation overlapping, topping up, or additional to European Social Fund support under Art. 146 EC. Given that the implementing decisions relating to the European Social Fund are adopted by a qualified majority under the co-decision procedure with the European Parliament (Art. 148 EC), the same voting rule could apply to the substance of the fifth indent of Art. 137(3) EC. It should also be noted that the measures eligible for adoption under this provision constitute the legal basis for establishing a heading in the Community budget, a heading which is adopted by a qualified majority.

[32] Art. 137(2) [ex Art. 2(2) SPA]; Art. 118a(2), para. 2.

[33] Case C–189/91 *Kirshammer-Hack v. Sidal* [1993] ECR I–6185.

[34] Art. 137(5) [ex Art. 2(5)].

[35] Case C–84/94 *UK v. Council* [1996] ECR I–5755.

[36] Para. 56.

[37] See also *Opinion 2/91* [1993] ECR I–1061, para. 16, and Case C–2/97 *Società Italiana Petroli SpA v. Borsana* [1998] ECR I–8597.

be.[38] The Advocate General also strongly rejected the contention that 'the Community cannot take action except on the basis of the lowest common denominator, or at the lowest possible level'. He said that this was diametrically opposed to the very conception of Community law where Community action has never been towards levelling down, in particular because Article 2 EC refers to 'harmonious development', to a 'high degree of convergence', and 'to a high level of employment and of social protection'. He said that minimum requirements were not synonymous with low level requirements but meant the compulsory minimum beyond which the Member States were free to adopt legislation according greater protection to the safety and health of workers.

2. Subsidiarity and Proportionality

If the Community does have (non-exclusive) competence to legislate, it must then consider the application of the principle of subsidiarity. As we have already seen in Chapter 1, the principle of subsidiarity—that decisions should be taken as close as possible to those affected—pervades the nature and form of all action by the Community. In the legislative context the principle of subsidiarity is specifically defined by Article 5(2) [ex Article 3b(2)]. It requires that Community action should be taken 'only if and insofar as the objectives of the proposed action cannot be sufficiently achieved by the Member States and can therefore, by reason of the scale and effects of the proposed action, be better achieved by the Community'.[39] This is a decentralized or bottom-up approach to subsidiarity where the power to act belongs first and foremost to the Member States. Article 5(3) [ex Article 3b(3)] then adds that 'any action taken by the Community shall not go beyond what is necessary to achieve the objectives of this Treaty' (the principle of proportionality). This means that in areas such as social policy which do not fall within the Community's exclusive competence the Community can take action only if the tests of effectiveness and scale are satisfied and any measure taken is proportionate.

---

[38] As Szyszczak notes in 'The New Parameters of European Labour Law', in *Legal Issues of the Amsterdam Treaty*, eds. O'Keeffe and Twomey (Hart, Oxford, 1999), such high principles do not always rule the day in practice. e.g. the UK was responsible for watering down the content of the Pregnant Workers' Directive 92/85/EEC [1992] OJ L348/1 to such an extent that the Italian government abstained, claiming that the level of protection was too low for it to accept.

[39] See, generally, Toth, 'A Legal Analysis of Subsidiarity', in *Legal Issues of the Maastricht Treaty*, eds. O'Keeffe and Twomey (Chancery, London, 1994). See also the essays by Steiner and Emiliou in the same vol. For detailed analysis of the application of this principle see Proceedings of the Jacques Delors Colloquium, *Subsidiarity and the Challenge of Change* (EIPA, Maastricht, 1991); Emiliou, 'Subsidiarity: An Effective Barrier Against "the Enterprises of Ambition"' (1992) 17 *ELRev.* 383; Toth, 'The Principle of Subsidiarity in the Maastricht Treaty' (1992) 29 *CMLRev.* 1079.

The Commission has phrased this rather differently.[40] It says that three questions must be answered:

- What is the Community dimension of the problem?
- What is the most effective solution given the means available to the Community and the Member States?
- What is the real added value of common action compared with isolated action by the Member States?[41]

It continues that 'the intensity of the action should leave the Member States all possible room for manoeuvre in its implementation. Subsidiarity requires Community legislation to be limited to what is essential'.

At Amsterdam the Member States took the opportunity to add a Protocol on the application of the principles of subsidiarity and proportionality 'with a view to defining more precisely the criteria for applying them and to ensure their strict observance and consistent implementation by all institutions'.[42] According to Article 5 of the Protocol, for Community action to be justified, both aspects of the subsidiarity principle must be met: 'the objectives of the proposed action cannot be sufficiently achieved by Member States' action in the framework of their national constitutional system and can therefore be better achieved by action on the part of the Community'. The Protocol then provides guidelines to be used in examining whether these conditions are fulfilled:

- the issue under consideration has transnational aspects which cannot be satisfactorily regulated by action by Member States;
- actions by Member States alone or lack of Community action would conflict with the requirements of the Treaty (such as the need to correct distortions of competition or avoid disguised restrictions on trade or strengthen economic and social cohesion) or would otherwise significantly damage Member States' interests;
- action at Community level would produce clear benefits by reason of its scale or effects compared with action at the level of the Member States.

[40] *Commission Report to the European Council on the adaptation of Community legislation to the subsidiarity principle* COM(93)545 final, 1. See also SEC(92) 1990, 27 Oct. 1992.

[41] See also the Commission White Paper COM(94)333, 11. The Preamble to the Community Social Charter makes clear that the implementation of social rights must respect the principle of subsidiarity, i.e. 'responsibility for the initiatives to be taken . . . lies with the Member States or their constituent parts and, *within the limits of its powers*, with the European Community' (emphasis added).

[42] This Protocol takes account of the Interinstitutional Agreement of 25 Oct. 1993 between the European Parliament, the Council, and the Commission on procedures for implementing the principle of subsidiarity and confirms the conclusions of the Birmingham European Council on 16 Oct. 1992. The overall approach to the application of the subsidiarity principle agreed by the European Council meeting in Edinburgh on 11–12 Dec. 1992 will continue to guide the action of the Union's institutions as well as the development of the application of the principle of subsidiarity.

The application of the principle of subsidiarity to employment issues raises particularly difficult questions. First, what is the most effective level? Is it EC level, national level, or perhaps regional or district, sectoral, enterprise, or plant level? Secondly, who should make the decisions—the EC institutions, national or regional authorities, the Social Partners (management and labour), or the individual manager? Thirdly, what type of measures should be taken—normative measures such as directly applicable regulations, directives which confer some discretion on Member States as to their manner of implementation, soft law measures such as recommendations and opinions, or collective agreements? This will be considered below.

The subsidiarity question also raises a fourth issue: what is the appropriate extent of the Community action? Different views exist about precisely when the Community should act in the social field.[43] The first advocates a positive and active role for the Community, regarding the Community as having a duty of care for the social well-being of its citizens as much as the furtherance of their collective economic interests within the framework of a single integrated market. This would justify wide-ranging action by the Community. The second school views the Community as being primarily concerned with economic matters and therefore as being competent to act in the social field only to the extent necessary to prevent distortions of competition arising out of divergences in production costs between Member States due to differences in national social standards, levels of health and safety protection, and other similar matters. The third school claims that the Community should not act since there is no firm evidence on the incidence of differing social standards upon production costs. This last view is not supported by the legislation adopted to date and elements of both the first and second schools have influenced the form, shape, and content of Community action.

The question of subsidiarity was broached, albeit rather hesitantly, by the UK in the *Working Time* case.[44] The UK alleged that Directive 93/104 infringed the principles of subsidiarity and proportionality. The Advocate General dismissed the UK's arguments. Distinguishing between subsidiarity and proportionality, he said:

The two principles operate in turn, at two different levels of Community action. The first (subsidiarity) determines whether Community action is to be set in motion, whereas the second (proportionality) defines its scope. Hence the question of competence is dissociated from that of exercise. In other words, the principle of subsidiarity comes into play before the Community takes action, whilst the principle of proportionality comes into play after such action has been taken.

He then said that in so far as harmonization is an objective of the Directive, it was difficult to criticize the measures adopted by the Council. He said it would

---

[43] Watson, 'The Community Social Charter' (1991) 28 *CMLRev.* 37, 40.
[44] Case C–84/94 *UK v. Council* [1996] ECR I–5755.

be illusory to expect the Member States alone to achieve the harmonization envisaged since it necessarily involved supra-national action.

The Court also rejected the argument of non-compliance with the principle of subsidiarity. It said:

Once the Council has found that it is necessary to improve the existing level of protection as regards the health and safety of workers and to harmonise the conditions in this area while maintaining the improvements made, achievement of that objective through the imposition of minimum requirements necessarily presupposes Community wide action.[45]

Thus, the Court indicates a more centralized, top-down approach to subsidiarity: that in the case of harmonization measures the Community should act.

The Court then examined the application of the principle of proportionality, looking to see whether the means which the Community institution employed were suitable for the purpose of achieving the desired objective and whether they went beyond what was necessary to achieve it. Rejecting the plea,[46] the Court said:

As to the judicial review of these conditions, however, the Council must be allowed a wide discretion in an area which, as here, involves the legislature in making social policy choices and requires it to carry out complex assessments. Judicial review of the exercise of that discretion must therefore be limited to examining whether it has been vitiated by a manifest error or misuse of powers, or whether the institution concerned has manifestly exceeded the limits of its discretion.[47]

It therefore seems that the Court has clipped the wings of Article 5(2) and (3) [ex Article 3b(2) and (3)] and restricted judicial review to the rare case of manifest abuse.

B. THE FORM OF LEGISLATION: DIVERSITY AND FLEXIBILITY

As we have already seen, the principle of subsidiarity applies not only to the level at which legislation is enacted but also to the form which it takes. This is particularly significant in the labour context where the national systems are characterized by their diversity.

1. Regulating Industrial Relations in the Member States

Three main systems of legal regulation of industrial relations can be found in

---

[45] Para. 47.
[46] Para. 57, citing Case C–426/93 *Germany v. Council* [1995] ECR I–3723, para. 42.
[47] Para. 58.

the EU:[48] the Romano-Germanic system, the Anglo-Irish system, and the Nordic system. The hallmark of the Romano-Germanic system, found in countries such as Belgium, France, Germany, Greece, Italy, Luxembourg, and the Netherlands, is that the state plays a central and active role in industrial relations. In addition, in States such as Belgium, France, and Germany, collective agreements can be extended to all workers and employers. Trade union density also tends to be lower in these countries than elsewhere, and falling— in France, for example, trade union membership declined from around 20 per cent in the mid-1970s to below 10 per cent today (see Table 2.1). Typically, the constitutions of these Member States guarantee a core of fundamental rights and freedoms, including the right to engage in collective bargaining and the right to form and join a trade union. The system is also characterized by comprehensive legislation governing various areas of working conditions such as the length of the working day, rest periods, and employee representation. Since the Community was numerically dominated by Member States from the highly regulated Romano-Germanic tradition, in the past this has provided the model for EC legislation on employment rights.

By contrast, the main feature of the Anglo-Irish system has been the limited role played by the State in industrial relations (sometimes known as voluntarism or collective *laissez-faire*). For example, collective agreements apply solely to the parties involved; they are not legally binding,[49] nor can they be extended to the entire workforce by administrative act.[50] Neither the individual nor the collective relationship is subject to extensive legal regulation compared to the Romano-Germanic system, despite a trend

Table 2.1 Union Density Rates

90+	Sweden
80+	Denmark
70+	Finland
40–50	Italy, Austria
30+	UK
20+	Netherlands, Germany, Greece, Portugal
10+	Spain
0–10	France

Source: EIRO Annual Review 1997.

[48] The following discussion draws heavily on Commission, *Comparative Study on Rules Governing Working Conditions in the Member States—a Synopsis* SEC(89) 1137, 30 June 1989, 10 and Due, Madsen and Jensen, 'The Social Dimension: Convergence or Diversification of IR in the Single European Market' (1991) 22 *IRJ* 85, 90–1. See also Fitzpatrick, 'Community Social Law After Maastricht' (1992) 21 *ILJ* 199, 209–13.

[49] S. 179 Trade Union and Labour Relations (Consolidation) Act 1992.

[50] Although Sched. II of the Employment Protection Act 1975, now repealed, did offer a form of *erga omnes* effect.

towards legislative intervention over the last three decades. Consequently, the Anglo-Irish system is characterized by the lack of comprehensive coverage of either collective agreements or legislation and it is the contract of employment which forms the cornerstone of the employment relationship.

In the Nordic system the state also assumes a relatively limited role in industrial relations. The cornerstone of this system is a series of labour market collective agreements, including a permanent basic agreement which is seldom challenged or amended. The State participates only when asked to do so by the parties, and there is very limited general legislative regulation. However, as a result of the high unionization of workers (at 90 per cent Sweden has the highest union density in the EU) which is so characteristic of the Nordic system, the vast majority of workers are covered by collective agreements.

2. The EU's Legislative Response

Many commentators make much of the diversity[51] of industrial relations systems in the Member States and the dangers of simply identifying what is successful in one State and bolting it onto the structures in other States where different political and industrial relations cultures exist.[52] On the other hand, others have advised caution in suggesting that characteristics of employee relations policies are predetermined to be culturally specific.[53] Nevertheless, these different national approaches to the regulation of labour standards has forced the Community to consider its own approach to legislating. Consequently, it has focused on flexibility before the term itself became vogue.[54] First, there has been flexibility in the forms of legislative instrument. Regulations, seen by many as the epitome of uniformity, have never been used to set EC employment standards. The principal regulatory vehicle in the social field has been directives which, by their very nature, allow for a degree of flexibility in the way in which EC norms manifest themselves in the Member States. This flexibility is increased in three ways: first, by the use of framework directives which lay down certain core standards but the detail of their operation is left

---

[51] See e.g. Hyman, 'Industrial Relations in Europe: Theory and Practice' (1995) 1 *EJIR* 17, 35, but cf. Marginson and Sisson, 'European Collective Bargaining: A Virtual Prospect?' (1998) 36 *JCMS* 505, 509, and Hansen, Madsen and Jensen, 'The Complex Reality of Convergence and Diversification in European Industrial Relations Systems' (1997) 3 *EJIR* 357.

[52] For his seminal analysis, see Kahn-Freund, 'On the Uses and Misuses of Comparative Law' (1974) 37 *MLR* 1. For a practical example of the problems experienced with comparative work, see the Supiot Report, *Transformation of Labour and Future of Labour Law in Europe*, June 1998.

[53] Bridgeford and Stirling, 'Britain in a Social Europe: Industrial Relations and 1992' (1991) 22 *IRJ* 263, 263.

[54] This section draws on Barnard, 'Flexibility and Social Policy', in De Búrca and Scott, *Flexible Governance in the EU* (Hart, Oxford, 2000).

to be determined by the Member States and/or the social partners;[55] secondly, through the use of directives aimed at partial harmonization;[56] and thirdly, through the use of directives setting minimum standards which Member States are free to improve upon.[57]

This practice of adopting minimum standards directives was endorsed by the Council Resolution on Certain Aspects for a European Union Social Policy.[58] It points out:

Minimum standards constitute an appropriate instrument for achieving economic and social convergence gradually while respecting the economic capabilities of the individual Member States. They also meet the expectations of workers in the European Union and calm fears about social dismantling and social dumping in the Union.[59]

The Resolution continues that the Council is convinced that a 'comprehensive legislative programme' is not necessary but rather it requires 'agreement on specific fields of action in order to build up the core of minimum social standards gradually in a pragmatic and flexible manner'.[60] The Resolution then provides a framework for Community social legislation. Community legislative acts must:[61]

- take account of the situation in all Member States when each individual measure is adopted and neither overstretch any one Member State nor force it to dismantle social rights;
- avoid going into undue detail but concentrate on basic, binding principles and leave the development and transposition to the Member States individually and, where this is in accordance with national traditions, to the two sides of industry;[62]

---

[55] See e.g. the Framework Directive on Health and Safety 89/391 [1989] OJ L183/9, considered further in Ch. 6 and the Council Directive on the Framework Agreement on Parental Leave 96/34/EC [1996] OJ L145/4, as amended by Council Directive 97/75/EC [1998] OJ L10/24, considered further in Ch. 4.

[56] Directive 77/187/EEC on transfers of undertakings [1977] OJ L61/27, as amended by Council Directive 98/50/EC [1998] OJ L210/88 and Council Directive 98/59/EC on collective redundancies [1998] OJ L225/16 (formerly Council Directive 75/129/EEC [1975] OJ L48/29), as amended by Council Directive 92/56/EEC [1992] OJ L245/3 provide a good example of this. While these directives provide a core of rights, such as the right for the transferor's employees to enjoy the same terms and conditions when transferred to the transferee, the detail of those rights and key definitions, e.g. the meaning of terms 'dismissal' and 'worker representatives', are left to be determined by national law. See further Ch. 7.

[57] See Art. 118a(2) EC [new Art. 137(2)] discussed above, n. 10.

[58] Council Resolution of 6 Dec. 1994 on certain aspects for a European Union Social Policy: a contribution to economic and social convergence in the Union [1994] OJ C368/6.

[59] Para. 10.

[60] Para. 11.

[61] Para. 17.

[62] See also the Commission's Green Paper, *Partnership for a New Organization of Work* (COM(97) 127) which talks of 'the likely development of labour law and industrial relations from rigid and compulsory systems of statutory regulations to more open and flexible legal frameworks' (para. 44). This raises 'fundamental questions concerning the balance of regulatory powers between

- be flexible enough and confine themselves to provisions which can be incorporated into the various national systems;
- include clauses which allow the two sides of industry room for manoeuvre on collective agreements;
- contain review clauses so that they can be corrected in the light of practical experience.

Stressing the diversity of the national systems, the Resolution says that 'unification of national systems in general by means of rigorous approximation of laws [is] an unsuitable direction to follow as it would also reduce the chances of the disadvantaged regions in the competition for location'.[63] The Resolution advocates instead 'gradual convergence of systems—with due regard for economic strength of the Member State—by means of alignment of national goals'.[64]

This approach has now been confirmed by the Protocol on the application of the principles of subsidiarity and proportionality. Articles 6 envisages that:

The form of Community action shall be as simple as possible, consistent with satisfactory achievement of the objective of the measure and the need for effective enforcement. The Community shall legislate only to the extent necessary. Other things being equal, directives should be preferred to regulations and framework directives to detailed measures. Directives as provided for in Article 189 [new Article 149] of the Treaty, while binding upon each Member State to which they are addressed as to the result to be achieved, shall leave to the national authorities the choice of form and methods.

Article 7 adds that, as far as the nature and the extent of Community action is concerned, Community measures should leave as much scope for national decision as possible, consistent with securing the aim of the measure and observing the requirements of the Treaty. It continues that while respecting Community law, care should be taken to respect well-established national arrangements and the organization and working of Member States' legal systems. Where appropriate, and subject to the need for proper enforcement, Community measures should provide Member States with alternative ways to achieve the objectives of the measures.

Another consequence of this desire for flexibility in the form of legislative instruments has been the increasing use of soft law measures. Most of the EC legislation adopted under the 1974 and 1989 Action Programmes was legally binding, hard law.[65] By contrast, the Medium Term Action Programme

---

public authorities (legislation) and the social partners (collective bargaining) and between the social partners and individual employees (individual employment contracts) which may well mean greater scope for derogations from legislative standards through not just collective agreements but also individual contracts of employment' (para. 43).

[63] Para. 18.
[64] Para. 19.
[65] See generally Beveridge and Nott, 'A Hard Look at Soft Law', in *Lawmaking in the European Union*, eds. Craig and Harlow (Kluwer, Deventer, 1998).

1995–7[66] and its successor, 1998–2000[67] were characterized by their heavy reliance on soft law measures[68] which are persuasive rather than coercive in character.[69] This shift had already been flagged by the conclusions of the Edinburgh Council on the implementation of Article 3b [new Article 5] on the principle of subsidiarity.[70] These said that 'Non-binding measures such as recommendations should be preferred where appropriate. Consideration should also be given where appropriate to the use of voluntary codes of conduct'.[71] The Commission endorsed this view, suggesting that recourse to the most binding instruments should only be as a last resort.[72]

Soft law measures have also formed the principal legislative vehicle under the new Employment Title.[73] Presidency conclusions, Commission Communications, annual reports, and even the Employment Guidelines[74] all come into the category of soft law: they are no more than methods of Community guidance or rules which create an expectation that the conduct of Member States will be in conformity with them, but without any accompanying legal obligation.[75] This is 'management by objectives' which as Kenner notes, has certain advantages. The flexibility of soft laws allows the Community institutions to stimulate European integration by building on and around existing Treaty objectives without directly creating legal obligations. They are a kind of informal law-making by exhortation.[76]

Flexibility is not confined to the form of the legislative instruments. Increasingly flexibility manifests itself within the directive—a form of 'internal

[66] COM(95)134 final.

[67] COM(98)259.

[68] See e.g. the Council Resolution on the promotion of equal opportunities through action by the Structural Funds (94/C231/01 [1994] OJ C231/1); Council Recommendation on the balanced participation of men and women in the decision-making process (96/C694/EC [1996] OJ C319/11) and Resolution of the Council and of the Representatives of the governments of the Member States 94/C368/02 on equal participation by women in an employment intensive economic growth strategy in the EU [1994] OJ C368/2.

[69] See also Snyder, 'Soft Law and Institutional Practice in the European Community', EUI Working Paper, Law No. 93/5; Klabbers, 'Informal Instruments before the European Court of Justice' (1994) 31 *CMLRev.* 997; and Kenner, 'EC Labour Law: The Softly, Softly Approach' (1995) 11 *IJCLLIR* 307.

[70] EC Bull. 12/1992, 25–26, Council Conclusions II, Guidelines, 3rd para., point 3.

[71] See generally Sciarra, 'Social Values and the Multiple Sources of European Social Law' (1995) 1 *ELJ* 60, esp. 78–9 and Whiteford, 'W(h)ither Social Policy', in *New Legal Dynamics of European Union*, eds. Shaw and More (Clarendon, Oxford, 1995).

[72] SEC(92)1990 final. Cram, *Policy Making in the EU: Conceptual Lenses and the Integration Process* (Routledge, London, 1997) describes the Commission as a 'purposeful opportunist' in that it uses soft law measures among others to 'soften-up' the Member States, paving the way for the Commission's preferred course of action should a 'policy window' open up.

[73] Considered further below, text attached to nn. 216–252.

[74] See e.g. Council Resolution of 15 Dec. 1997 on the 1998 Employment Guidelines [1998] OJ C30/1. Cf. Council Decision 2000/228/EC on guidelines for Member States' Employment Policies for the Year 2000 [2000] OJ L72/15.

[75] Kenner, 'The EU Employment Title and the "Third Way": Making Soft Law Work?' (1999) 15 *IJCLLIR* 33, 57–8.

[76] Ibid.

flexibility'. Two examples illustrate this. First, Article 13 of the European Works Councils Directive 94/95/EC[77] provides that where an agreement which covered the entire workforce was already in existence by 22 September 1996,[78] the date by which the Directive should have been implemented, the substantive obligations contained in the Directive did not apply. 386 such agreements were signed by the September 1996 deadline,[79] including 58 signed by British companies at a time when the UK had secured an opt-out from the Social Chapter.[80]

The second example of internal flexibility can be found in the provisions allowing Member States more time to implement certain more controversial directives. For example, according to Article 17(1)(b) of the Young Workers Directive 94/33/EC the UK could 'refrain from implementing' certain provisions on working time and night work for a period of four years.[81] The Working Time Directive 93/104/EC[82] also provided for the possibility of an individual opt-out from Article 6 on the maximum forty-eight-hour working week (subject to review before 2003)[83] and delayed implementation of the four weeks' paid annual leave contained in Article 7.[84] This was also introduced largely for the benefit of the UK where the legacy of collective *laissez-faire* meant that the state has traditionally abstained from regulating key aspects of the employment relationship, notably pay and working time, leaving these to be negotiated collectively. These two Directives therefore represented a cultural clash between the Romano-Germanic countries with their history of centralized regulation of issues such as working time, and the abstentionist Anglo-Saxon tradition. The Working Time Directive does, however, envisage a substantial role for the social partners. The Directive provided that not only could the 'social partners' implement the Directive,[85] but 'collective agreements or agreements between the two sides of industry' could be used in setting certain standards, such as the duration and terms on which a rest break can be taken,[86] and derogating from those standards.[87] Thus, the Working Time

---

[77] [1994] OJ L254/64, as amended by Council Directive 97/74/EEC [1998] OJ L10/22. A similar procedure is envisaged in Art. 3 of the proposed Directive on Informing and Consulting Workers, COM(98)612. See further Ch. 8.

[78] 15 Dec. 1999 for the UK: Art. 3(1) of Directive 97/74/EC [1998] OJ L10/22.

[79] See Marginson, Gilman, Jacobi, and Krieger, *Negotiating European Works Councils: an Analysis of Agreements under Article 13*, European Foundation of Living and Working Conditions, EF9839. A particularly high incidence of such agreements can be found in Norway, see Knudsen and Bruun, 'European Works Councils in the Nordic countries: An Opportunity and a Challenge for Trade Unionism' (1998) 4 *EJIR* 131.

[80] See further Ch. 1.

[81] [1994] OJ L216/12.

[82] [1993] OJ L307/18.

[83] Art. 18(1)(b)(i).

[84] Art. 18(1)(b)(ii).

[85] The details of this procedure more generally are considered further below, nn. 132–134.

[86] Art. 4.

[87] Art. 17. This is most unusual: collective agreements usually improve upon statutory protection.

Directive provides a further example of internal flexibility by introducing a new set of actors. It creates a space in which the social partners can negotiate for better standards and—contrary to the Continental legal tradition[88]— for worse. This is an example of 'controlled' or 'negotiated' flexibility'.[89]

The possibility for negotiated European level collective agreements concluded by the European Social Partners introduced by the Maastricht Social Chapter provides a further example of this phenomenon.[90] Once negotiated, these agreements can be extended to cover all workers by means of a 'decision'.[91] These agreements take controlled flexibility one stage further: it is the interprofessional (or sectoral) European-level social partners who are negotiating a framework collective agreement which in turn provides space for the national (interprofessional or sectoral) or subnational (enterprise or plant) level social partners to act. This process also demonstrates a form of subsidiarity—not just in the vertical sense envisaged by Article 5 [ex Article 3b(2)] (Member State or Community level) but in the horizontal or multi-layered sense that different tasks can be assigned to different actors.[92] As the Council Resolution on certain aspects for a European Union Social Policy explains, the Social Partners are 'as a rule closer to social reality and to social problems'.[93] This raises the fundamental question, who are the social partners? Are they truly representative? This will be considered in the next section. For the present it is sufficient to note that the Community now has a twin-track approach to legislation: on the one hand legislative, following the usual channels, and on the other, collective.[94] The legislative process will now be considered.

C. THE LEGISLATIVE PROCESS

Whether Community social legislation is to be adopted via the legislative or the negotiated route the Commission retains the power of initiative for

[88] Wedderburn, 'Collective Bargaining at European Level: the Inderogability Problem' (1992) 21 *ILJ* 245.

[89] This is also described as 'centrally-co-ordinated' regulation (Ferner and Hyman, *Changing Industrial Relations in Europe* (Blackwell, Oxford, 1998), p. xvi) or 'reflexive labour law' (Rogowski and Wilthagen, in *Reflexive Labour Law*, eds. Rogowski and Wilthagen (Kluwer, Deventer, 1994), 7). See also Art. 4a(2) of the amendments to the Transfer of Undertakings Directive 98/50/EC [1998] OJ L201/88, noted by Davies (1998) 27 *ILJ* 365, 369.

[90] See further the text attached to nn. 118–131, below.

[91] This has been interpreted to mean any legally binding instrument, including a directive. See further below, nn. 145–146.

[92] Sciarra, 'Collective Agreements in the Hierarchy of European Community Sources', in *European Community Labour Law: Principles and Perspectives*, eds. Davies *et al.* (OUP, Oxford, 1996), 203.

[93] [1994] OJ C368/6, II.3. See also e.g. Recital 9 of the Parental Leave Directive 96/34/EEC [1996] OJ L145/4.

[94] Bercusson, 'The Dynamic of European Labour Law after Maastricht' (1994) 23 *ILJ* 1; Shaw, 'Twin-track Social Europe—the Inside Track' in O'Keeffe and Twomey (eds.) *Legal Issues of the Maastricht Treaty* (Wiley Chancery, Chichester, 1994).

submitting proposals (see Figure 2.1). Before doing so it must consult the
social partners on the possible direction of Community action.[95]

1. Consultation of Management and Labour

Article 138(1) [ex Article 3(1) SPA] provides that the Commission has the
task of promoting the consultation of management and labour at Community
level. It must also take any relevant measures to facilitate their dialogue by
ensuring balanced support for the parties.[96] This provision was intended to
replace the weaker obligation 'to endeavour to develop the dialogue' contained
in the original Article 118b. The Commission considers that it can be more
active under Article 138(1) than under Article 118b by providing three types
of support: the organization of meetings, support for joint studies or working
groups, and technical assistance necessary to underpin the dialogue.[97]

The Treaty offers no guidance on which organizations should be consulted.
As a result, the Commission set out in a Communication of 1993[98] a number
of criteria to identify those representatives of management and labour whose
representativity,[99] entitled them to be consulted. The criteria applied are,
first, that the associations must be cross-industry or relate to specific
sectors or categories and be organized at European level; secondly, that they
must consist of organizations which are themselves 'an integral and recognised part of Member State social partner structures', have the capacity to
negotiate agreements and be representative of all Member States 'as far as
possible'; and thirdly, that they must have adequate structures to ensure
their effective participation in the consultation process.[100] Despite much

---

[95] Art. 138(2) [ex Art. 3(2) SPA]. For further details of this process, see Brinkman,
'Lawmaking under the Social Chapter of Maastricht' in Craig and Harlow (eds.), above n. 65.

[96] See further Ch. 8. Another form of consultation takes place in cross-industry advisory
committees (social security for migrant workers and freedom of movement for workers (the Commission intends to merge these committees), European social fund, vocational training, safety,
hygiene and health protection at work, and Equal Opportunities for men and women). According
to COM(98)322, the Commission intends to develop and broaden its practice of consultations.

[97] COM(93)600, para. 12.

[98] COM(93)600, para. 24. This list only applies to the consultation stage provided for by Art.
3(2) and (3) SPA [new Art. 138(2) and (3)]: see Case T–135/96 *Union Européenne de l'Artisanat et
des Petites et Moyennes Entreprises' (UEAPME)* v. *Council and Commission* [1998] ECR II–2335,
para. 77.

[99] See Case T–135/96 *UEAPME* [1998] ECR II–2335, para. 72.

[100] This list is a slimmed down version of the criteria proposed by ETUC, CEEP, and UNICE
(*Social Europe* 95/2, 164). The European Parliament proposed that two further criteria be added:
that eligible organizations are composed of groups representing employers or workers with membership that is voluntary at both national and European level; and that they have a mandate from
their members to represent them in the context of the Community social dialogue and can
demonstrate their representativeness: Report A3–0269/94, PE 207.928—fin, cited in
COM(96)448, para. 62. ECOSOC proposed that the criteria should also include the capacity to
negotiate for and bind national structures: Opinion 94/C–397/17, paras. 2.1.12 and 2.1.15
[1994] OJ C397/43.

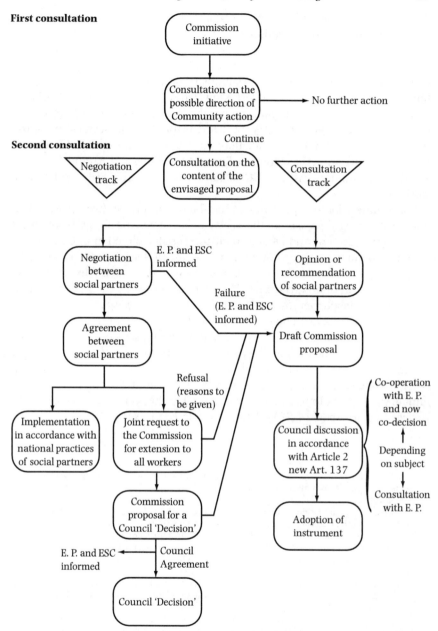

First consultation

Commission initiative

Consultation on the possible direction of Community action → No further action

Continue

Second consultation

Consultation on the content of the envisaged proposal

Negotiation track

Consultation track

Negotiation between social partners

E. P. and ESC informed

Opinion or recommendation of social partners

Failure (E. P. and ESC informed)

Agreement between social partners

Draft Commission proposal

Implementation in accordance with national practices of social partners

Refusal (reasons to be given)

Joint request to the Commission for extension to all workers

Council discussion in accordance with Article 2 new Art. 137

Co-operation with E. P. and now co-decision

↕

Depending on subject

↕

Consultation with E. P.

Commission proposal for a Council 'Decision'

Adoption of instrument

E. P. and ESC informed ← Council Agreement

Council 'Decision'

Figure 2.1 Operational Chart showing the Implementation of the Agreement on Social Policy

Source: COM (93)600, 43, as updated.

disagreement,[101] these criteria were confirmed by the Commission in 1998.[102] The Social Partners' organizations which currently comply with these criteria fall into five categories:[103] general cross-industry organizations (the trade union body ETUC, the employers' organization UNICE, and the public sector employers' association CEEP); cross-industry organizations representing certain categories of workers or undertakings (UEAPME,[104] EUROPMI,[105] CEC,[106] and Eurocadres); specific organizations (the association of European Chambers of Commerce and Industry, EUROCHAMBRES); and sectoral organizations with no cross-industry affiliations such as the Community of European Railways (CER) and Association of European Airlines (AEA) and European Industry Committees with ETUC affiliation such as the EFA (agricultural workers).

Consultation for the purposes of legislation occurs at two stages. First, *before submitting proposals* in the social policy field, the Commission must consult management and labour about the possible direction of Community action.[107] If, after such consultation, due to last no longer than six weeks,[108] the Commission considers that Community action is advisable, the second stage of consultation is triggered. The Commission must then consult management and labour *on the content of the envisaged proposal.*[109] Management and labour then have a choice. One possibility is for them to forward to the Commission an opinion or a recommendation within six weeks.[110] Any measure proposed will then follow the usual legislative route outlined in section 2 below. The other possibility, provided by Article 138(4) [ex Article 3(4) SPA], is for management and labour to inform the Commission of their wish to initiate the process to negotiate Community level agreements provided for in Article 139 [ex Article 4 SPA]. This is considered in section 3.

---

[101] See e.g. the responses to the Commission's Communication concerning the Development of the Social Dialogue at Community Level: COM(96)448.

[102] COM(98)322.

[103] Annex II of Commission's Communication COM(93)600. An updated list of those organizations satisfying the criteria is found in Annex I of COM(98)322.

[104] Union Européenne de l'Artisanat et des Petites et Moyennes Entreprises.

[105] European Association of Craft, Small and Medium-sized Enterprises.

[106] Confédération Européene des Cadres (higher white collar employees and managerial employees).

[107] Art. 138(2) [ex Art. 3(2) SPA]. It also proposes to continue to consult all European or national organizations which might be affected by the Community's social policy. This confirms previous practice (COM(93)600, para. 22).

[108] COM(93)600, 19. Despite some criticisms that the six-week time limit was too short, the Commission has decided to maintain it so as not to put the effectiveness of the process at risk, but may apply it flexibly depending on the nature and complexity of the subject matter (COM(98)322, 9).

[109] Art. 138(3) [ex Art. 3(3) SPA].

[110] Ibid. It seems that there is no obligation on the Commission to take into account the recommendation or opinion issued by management and labour.

2. The Legislative Route

If management and labour do not inform the Commission of their wish to negotiate collectively the measure follows the legislative route. If the measure concerns one of the items listed in Article 137(1) [ex Article 2(1) SPA],[111] for example, improvements in the working environment and working conditions, then the Council will adopt a minimum requirements directive, following the Article 251 [ex Article 189b] procedure, after consulting the Economic and Social Committee, and the Committee of the Regions. If the measure concerns one of the matters listed in Article 137(3) [ex Article 2(3)], for example social security and social protection of workers, then the Council must act unanimously after consulting the European Parliament, the Economic and Social Committee, and the Committee of the Regions. In either case, as we have seen,[112] Member States remain free to maintain or introduce more stringent protective measures compatible with the Treaty[113] and directives must avoid imposing administrative, financial, and legal constraints which would hold back the creation and developments of SMEs.[114]

Once the directives are adopted, Article 137(4) [ex Article 2(4)] provides for the possibility of Member States entrusting the Social Partners, at their joint request, with the implementation. This approach has already been introduced in the more recent directives.[115] This is a further example of 'internal' flexibility. It allows the general language of the directive to be adapted to local conditions, especially at company or plant level. Member States do, however, retain the ultimate responsibility for ensuring that, by the date on which the directive must be transposed, 'management and labour have introduced the necessary measures by agreement'.[116] According to Article 138(4) [ex Article 2(4), paragraph 2, SPA] Member States must take 'any necessary measure enabling it at any time to be in a position to guarantee the results imposed by that Directive'. This may include, as in Belgium, the passing of a Royal Decree which gives *erga omnes* effect to a collective agreement.[117]

[111] See the text between nn. 25–26, above.

[112] See the text attached to nn. 24–25, above.

[113] Art. 137(5) [ex Art. 2(5) SPA].

[114] Art. 137(2) [ex Art. 2(2) SPA].

[115] See e.g. Directive 91/533/EC on conditions applicable to the contract of employment [1991] OJ L288/32, Directive 92/56 on collective redundancies [1992] OJ L255/63 and the Working Time Directive 93/104/EC [1993] OJ L307/18. This corresponds to the implementation requirements of the ILO (Convention Nos. 100, 101, 106, 111, 171, 172) and the Council of Europe (Art. 35(1) of the European Social Charter).

[116] Art. 138(4) [ex Art 2(4)].

[117] In a case decided before the SPA was introduced, the Court considered that Belgium had adequately implemented the Directive on collective dismissals when a collective agreement had been extended *erga omnes* by legislative instruments: see Case 215/83 *Commission* v. *Belgium* [1985] ECR 1039, discussed in Adinolfi, 'The Implementation of Social Policy Directives through Collective Agreements?' (1988) 25 *CMLRev*. 291. Art. 138(4) was introduced to meet the Court's earlier criticisms of implementation of directives by collective agreements: see e.g. Case 1/81 *Commission* v. *Italy* [1982] ECR 2133, considered further in Ch. 7.

3. The Collective Route to Legislation

The collective route constitutes the second limb of this twin-track approach to Community social legislation. The social partners at Community level negotiate agreements which are then extended to all workers by Council 'decision'. Streeck describes this as 'neo-voluntarism', putting the will of those affected by a rule, and the 'voluntary' agreements negotiated between them, above the will or potential will of the legislature.[118] The collective route is triggered when, at the second stage of the consultation process,[119] the social partners inform the Commission that they would like to negotiate Community level agreements.

3.1 Negotiation

If the social partners inform the Commission of their wish to negotiate they have nine months, or longer with the agreement of the Commission,[120] to enter into 'a dialogue at Community level [which] may lead to *contractual relations*, including agreements' (emphasis added).[121] There is no indication of what constitutes an agreement, nor of what is a suitable subject matter for the agreement.[122] The Commission's Communication simply says that the question whether an agreement between social partners constitutes a sufficient basis for the Commission to suspend its legislative action will have to be examined on a case-by-case basis.[123]

The Commission is also not clear about who should negotiate. In its first Communication the Commission said that 'the social partners concerned will be those that agree to negotiate with each other'.[124] Such agreement is

---

[118] Streeck, 'Competitive Solidarity: Rethinking the "European Social Model" ' MPIfG Working Paper 99/8 and Streeck, 'Neo-voluntarism: A New European Social Policy Regime' (1995) 1 *ELJ* 31. See also Jensen, 'Neo-functionalist Theories and the Development of European Social and Labour Market Policy' (2000) 38 *JCMS* 71, 90. See Bernard, 'Privatisation of European Social Law: Reflections around the *UEAPME* Case', in *Social Law and Policy in an Evolving European Union*, ed. Shaw (Hart, Oxford, forthcoming) who argues that this may promote 'privatization' of European social law. For a general discussion see Lo Faro, *Regulating Social Europe: Reality and Myth of Collective Bargaining in the EC Legal Order* (Hart, Oxford, 2000).

[119] COM(93)600, para. 29, although ECOSOC has suggested that it might occur after the first stage of consultation.

[120] Art. 138(4) [ex Art. 3(4) SPA].

[121] 'Contractual relations' is a translation of the French term *relations contractuelles* which means relations based on agreement. It has been suggested that the addition of the phrase 'including agreements' serves only to emphasize that legally-binding contracts are only one potential outcome. Hepple, *European Social Dialogue—Alibi or Opportunity* (IER, London, 1993), 23. See also Art. 118b [new Art. 140] where the social dialogue could 'lead to relations based on agreement'.

[122] The Commission has, however, made clear that certain matters are not appropriate for negotiations such as the Burden of Proof in Sex Discrimination cases (COM(93)600, para. 67).

[123] COM(93)600, para. 30.

[124] Ibid., para. 31.

entirely in the hands of the different organizations. Subsequently, the Commission said that the social partners can develop 'their own dialogue and negotiating structures'.[125] It continued:

it is up to the social partners who sit at the negotiating table and it is up to them to come to the necessary compromises. The respect of the right of any social partner to choose its negotiating counterpart is a key element of the autonomy of the social partners.[126]

The Commission has said that where Article 3(2) [new Article 138(2)] is applied it must assess the validity of an agreement in the light of its content which requires an assessment of whether those affected by an agreement have been represented. It therefore says that the question of representativeness must be examined on a case-by-case basis, as the conditions will vary depending on the subject matter under negotiation. The Commission therefore examines whether those involved in the negotiation have a genuine interest in the matter and can demonstrate significant representation in the domain concerned.[127] To date, in the interests of efficient bargaining, negotiation over agreements which apply generally to all employment relationships[128] has been conducted only by the established general cross-industry organizations (ETUC, UNICE, CEEP[129]) 'based on principles of autonomy and mutual recognition of the negotiation parties'.[130] Although the Commission has said that these three organizations fulfil its own criteria of representativeness,[131] as we shall see, the question of representativity has become a running sore which has threatened to undermine the legitimacy of the collective route to social legislation.

3.2 Implementation

Once an EC-wide collective agreement is reached, Article 139(2) [ex Article 4(2) SPA] provides two methods for its implementation. First, an agreement can be implemented 'in accordance with the procedures and practices specific to management and labour and the Member States'. The second declaration appended to the SPA explains that this means 'developing, by collective bargaining according to the rules of each Member State, the content of the agreements'. However, the declaration continues that this does not imply any

[125] COM(98)322, 12.

[126] Ibid.

[127] COM(96)448, para. 71.

[128] Two sectoral agreements have also been negotiated by European sectoral organizations. These are considered further below nn. 219–220.

[129] These three cross-sector organizations have long enjoyed a favoured position through the social dialogue steering group and have therefore developed a 'substantial body of experience' COM(93)600, para. 25, confirmed in COM(96)448 and COM(98)322.

[130] COM(98)322, 13. See Case T–135/96 *UEAPME* [1998] ECR II–2335, para. 79, 'it is the representatives of management and labour concerned, and not the Commission which have charge of the negotiation stage properly so-called'.

[131] COM(96)26 final, 14.

obligation on the Member States 'to apply the agreements directly or to work out rules for their transposition, nor any obligation to amend national legislation in force to facilitate their implementation'. In other words, in the case of an EC-level agreement, there is no obligation to bargain on these matters at national level or to ensure that they apply to all workers. As Hepple has argued, these provisions attach the social dialogue to the existing structures of collective bargaining and labour law in the Member States. These structures were never intended to take on a new hierarchy of EC-level obligations and, in many cases, are under compelling pressures to decentralize and become more flexible.[132] No agreement has yet been implemented via this route nor is likely to be because of the difficulty in implementation at national level.[133] A very high coverage rate would be necessary, as in Belgium, Sweden, and Finland (see Table 2.1) or a declaration giving *erga omnes* effect (as in Belgium, France, and Germany) which, according to the declaration appended to the SPA, Member States are not obliged to make.[134]

The alternative method for implementation envisaged by Article 137(2) is for management and labour jointly to request the Commission to propose that the Council adopt a 'decision' to implement the agreement in respect of matters covered by Article 137.[135] This would give *erga omnes* effect, extending the collective agreement to all workers. The Council then follows the procedure set out in Article 137 (qualified majority vote for those areas listed in Article 137(1)–(2), unanimity for those areas listed in Article 137(3)), to adopt the measure.[136] The Social Partners had requested that in order to respect the autonomy of the social partners the Commission's proposal should follow the Social Partners agreement 'as concluded' by them[137] but this requirement was deleted from the final version of the SPA. While this appears to give the Commission the discretion to amend the agreement in its proposal to the Council, the Commission has never done so. In practice the agreement has been annexed to the proposal to the Council and the Commission considers that the Council has no opportunity to amend the agreement.[138] This seems to have been acknowledged by the Council: according to its legal service, while the Commission and Council could introduce rules for implementation

[132] Hepple, above n. 121, 31.

[133] Brinkman, above n. 95, 256.

[134] Keller and Sörries, 'The New Social Dialogue–Old Wine in New Bottles?' (1999) 9 *JESP* 110, 119.

[135] The Social Partners are not obliged to do this. They could confine themselves to negotiating a single agreement producing effects *inter partes*: see Case T–135/96 *UEAPME* [1998] ECR II–2335, para. 45.

[136] In Case C–67/96 *Albany*, judgment of 21 Sept. 1999, the Court pointed to this provision and noted that the decision of the public authorities to make affiliation to a pension fund compulsory could not be regarded as requiring or favouring the adoption of agreements, decisions or concerted practices contrary to Art. 85 [new Art. 81] (paras. 67–68).

[137] The Oct. 1991 agreement had provided 'on a proposal from the Commission, with regard to the agreements *as they have been concluded*' (emphasis added): *Social Europe* 2/95, 149.

[138] COM(93)600, para. 38.

or amend those agreed by management and labour, neither could amend the essence of the agreement.[139]

In making its proposals for a 'decision' by the Council,[140] the Commission resumes control of the procedure.[141] In its capacity as guardian of the Treaties, the Commission considers the mandate of the social partners[142] and the 'legality' of each clause in the collective agreement in relation to Community law, and the provisions regarding SMES set out in Article 137(2).[143] The Council, when taking its 'decision' must verify whether the Commission has fulfilled these obligations, otherwise it runs the risk of ratifying a procedural irregularity capable of vitiating the measure ultimately adopted by it.[144]

The use of the term 'decision' as the legal form by which the agreement is implemented is misleading. In Article 249 [ex Article 189 EC] a Decision is defined as being 'binding in its entirety upon those to whom it is addressed'. Decisions are individual in nature and are addressed to undertakings, individuals, or Member States; they are not usually normative in the sense of creating generally applicable Community law. Therefore, the Commission has said that in this context the term 'decision' refers to one of the binding legislative instruments listed in Article 249 [ex Article 189](Regulations, Directives, and Decisions) and that the Commission should choose the most appropriate measure.[145] In the case of the Parental Leave Collective Agreement the Commission said that the content of the agreement and its framework nature suggested that a Directive was the most appropriate legal form, based on Article 2(1) SPA [new Article 137(1)] (equal opportunities for men and women on the labour market). It therefore seems that 'decision' in the context of Article 139(2) has a more general meaning. This is reflected in the German and Danish texts which use 'decide' as a verb rather than in the technical sense of a 'decision'.[146]

The European Parliament has no formal role in this collectively negotiated legislation. Its attitude towards the corporatist pattern of interest representation is ambiguous. On the one hand, it sees the collective approach to legislating as a step towards greater involvement of citizens in policy formation.[147] It

---

[139] Opinion of 31 Mar. 1994, Council Doc. 6116/94, cited in Brinkman, above n. 95.

[140] On the significance of this see below the discussion of Case T–135/96 *UEAPME* [1998] ECR II–2335, para. 86.

[141] Case T–135/96 *UEAPME* [1998] ECR II–2335, para. 84.

[142] Confirmed by Case T–135/96 *UEAPME* [1998] ECR II–2335, para. 85.

[143] COM(93)600, para. 39. This assumption of power was contested by ECOSOC (Opinion 94/C397/17 [1994] OJ C397/40, cited in Bercusson, 'Democratic Legitimacy and European Labour Law' (1999) 28 *ILJ* 153, 162) on the grounds that the Commission has no discretion whether a collective agreement should be put to the Council.

[144] Case T–135/96 *UEAPME* [1998] ECR II–2335, para. 87.

[145] COM(96)26 final, 7. See generally Bercusson and Van Dijk, 'The Implementation of the Protocol and Agreement on Social Policy of the Treaty on European Union' (1995) 11 *IJCLLIR* 3.

[146] Hepple, above, n. 121, 31 (*Beschluß v. Entscheidung*).

[147] Obradovic, 'Accountability of Interest Groups in the Union Lawmaking Process', in Craig and Harlow (eds.), above n. 65, 363–4.

also recognizes that the lack of parliamentary involvement is common in those Member States where collective agreements are given *erga omnes* effect, usually by an *administrative* act.[148] Nevertheless, this absence of Parliamentary involvement has prompted concerns by some MEPS about the possible 'democratic deficit' of a process where the Social Partners dictate social legislation from behind closed doors[149] even though the Commission does intend that the Parliament will have the opportunity to see any proposed decision and deliver an opinion where necessary, despite the wording of the Treaty.[150]

3.3 Application of the Collective Route to Legislation

The first attempt to use this collective route was unsuccessful. It had been intended to break the deadlock over the proposals for a European Works Council.[151] On 8 February 1994, in accordance with Article 3(3) SPA [new Article 138(3)], the Commission initiated the second phase of the consultation process. By the deadline for the second phase of consultation, 30 March 1994, the Social Partners sent their views on the consultation document. However, the Social Partners failed to reach agreement on setting in motion the procedure provided for in Article 4 SPA [new Article 139].[152] Because the Commission considered that a Community initiative on the information and consultation of workers was still warranted, it adopted a further proposal,[153] this time on the legislative footing of Article 2(2) SPA [new Article 137]. The measure was adopted on 22 September 1994.

The collective approach was, however, successful in the (less controversial) case of parental leave. This agreement was reached against a background of further institutional failure. The Commission's proposal for a Council Directive on parental leave and leave for family reasons[154] had been discussed in the Council of Ministers on various occasions between 1985 and 1994 but the unanimity required by Article 100 [new Article 94], the Directive's proposed legal basis, was not obtained. Consequently, the Commission decided to initiate the procedure under Article 3 SPA [new Article 138]. Seventeen employers' and workers' organizations informed the Commission of their views at the

---

[148] See the agreement between management and labour of 31 Oct. 1991, *Social Europe* 2/95, 148, cited in Szyszczak, above n. 38. See above n. 134.

[149] See A3–0091/94 *Resolution on the New Social Dimension of the Treaty on European Union* [1994] OJ C77/30. See also Case T–135/96 *UEAPME* [1998] ECR II–2335, para. 89, considered below, and Betten, 'The Democratic Deficit of Participatory Democracy in Community Social Policy' (1998) 23 *ELRev.* 20. Parliament asked the Commission and the Council to conclude an institutional agreement in order to ensure the consultation and opinion of Parliament before the Council refuses to implement an agreement.

[150] COM(93)600, para. 40.

[151] See e.g. COM(90)581 final [1991] OJ C39/10. For further details see Ch. 8.

[152] For details of the Social Partners' 'talks about talks', see Gold and Hall, 'Statutory European Works Councils: The Final Countdown?' (1994) 25 *IRJ* 177, 179–82.

[153] COM(94)134 final.

[154] COM(83)686 final.

end of the first consultation period but it was the three established partners, UNICE, CEEP, and the ETUC, which, on 5 July 1995, announced their intention of starting negotiations with the assistance of an active conciliator appointed by the parties. A framework agreement laying down minimum requirements designed to facilitate the reconciliation of parental and professional responsibilities for working parents[155] was concluded by the Social Partners on 14 December 1995.

The matter was then placed in the hands of the Commission which proposed that the measure be adopted by a directive. The Explanatory Memorandum accompanying the 'Proposal for a Council Directive on the framework agreement on parental leave concluded by UNICE, CEEP and the ETUC',[156] carefully details the Commission's application of its own Communication on the SPA.[157] First, the Commission considered the representative status of the contracting parties and their mandate.[158] It said that since UNICE, CEEP, and ETUC had committed themselves to an 'autonomous and voluntary process' (the Val Duchesse dialogue) since 1985 they satisfied the criteria defined in the Commission's Communication[159] and they were representative.[160] Secondly, the Commission considered the 'legality' of the clauses of the agreement. It found that none of the clauses contravened Community law, even though the collective agreement contained a clause imposing obligations on the Member States to implement the Commission decision.[161]

The Commission's proposal for a Directive on parental leave contained two articles. The first provided that the parental leave agreement annexed to the Directive was made binding. The original proposal also contained two additional clauses concerning the principle of non-discrimination and sanctions but they were dropped from the final version. The collective agreement itself was placed in a separate annex. The Commission kept the Parliament informed about the various phases of consultation with the Social Partners and also forwarded the proposal to the Parliament and the Economic and Social Committee so that they could deliver their opinion to the Commission and Council. The measure was adopted on 3 June 1996.

A similar model has been followed in the case of part-time work and fixed-term work.[162] It was also followed in the sectoral agreement on the organization of working time by seafarers which was negotiated under the collective

---

[155] Cl. 1(1).

[156] COM(96)26 final.

[157] COM(93)600.

[158] COM(96)26 final.

[159] COM(93)600, para. 24, considered above nn. 103–106.

[160] The Commission forwarded the framework agreement to all of the organizations which it had previously consulted or informed.

[161] The Commission said that it followed from the second declaration annexed to the SPA that collective agreements were likely to create obligations from the Member States.

[162] Council Directive 97/81/EC [1998] OJ L14/9 as amended by Council Directive 98/23/EC [1998] OJ L131/10 and Council Directive 99/70/EC [1999] OJ L175/43, respectively.

route by the European Community Shipowners' Association (ECSA) and the Federation of Transport Workers' Unions (FST)[163] and extended by Directive 99/63/EC[164] to all seafarers on board every commercial seagoing ship registered in the territory of a Member State.

The successful outcome of the negotiations on parental leave was hailed by some as the birth of Euro-corporatism.[165] However, UEAPME, CEC, and EUROCOMMERCE criticized the monopoly created by the established social partners. This led UEAPME, representing small and medium sized employers, to bring judicial review proceedings seeking annulment of the agreement and/ or Directive 96/34 on parental leave,[166] with respect to its application to small and medium sized undertakings. The grounds of review advanced by UEAPME were breach of the principle of equality, breach of Articles 2(2), 3(3), and 4 SPA [new Articles 137(2), 138(3), and 139], the principles of subsidiarity and proportionality, and the principle of *patere legem quam ipse fecisti*. As a 'non-privileged applicant'[167] in the terms of Article 173 [new Article 230] EC, UEAPME first had to overcome the hurdle of admissibility, by showing it had *locus standi* to bring the claim. Article 230 EC provides that 'Any natural or legal person may . . . institute proceedings against a decision addressed to that person or against a decision which, although in the form of a regulation or a decision addressed to another person, is of direct and individual concern to the former'. Thus, a literal interpretation of Article 173 EC would have suggested that UEAPME did not have *locus standi* since the measure was a Directive and not a Decision or a Decision in the form of a Regulation.[168]

Taking into account its character and legal effects, rather than its form,[169] the Court of First Instance (CFI) agreed that Directive 96/34 was not a

---

[163] A European Industry Committee with ETUC affiliation: COM(98)322, Annex 1.

[164] [1999] OJ L167/33. A similar process is under way in respect of a sectoral agreement on the Organization of Working Time of Mobile Staff in civil aviation, see further Ch. 6.

[165] Falkner, 'The Maastricht Protocol on Social Policy: Theory and Practice' (1996) 6 *JESP* 1, and *EU Social Policy in the 1990s: Towards a Corporatist Policy Community* (Routledge, London, 1998).

[166] Case T–135/96 *UEAPME* [1998] ECR II–2335. In Case T–55/98 *Union européenne de l'artisanat et des petites et moyennes entreprises (UEAPME)* v. *Council*, UEAPME started (but then withdrew) a challenge to the Directive part-time work. This section draws on Barnard and Hervey, 'European Union Employment and Social Policy Survey 1998' (1998) 18 *YEL* 618. For an early example of an unsuccessful claim of this sort, see Case 66/76 *CFDT* v. *Council* [1977] ECR 305. CFDT, the second largest trade union confederation, complained that it had not been included among the representative organizations designated to draw up lists of candidates for a consultative committee. The Court dismissed the application because the ECSC Treaty did not empower claimants like CFDT to file such an application.

[167] The 'privileged applicants' are the Member States, the Council, and the Commission; and the European Parliament and European Central Bank, for the purpose of protecting their prerogatives. 'Non-privileged applicants' are all other applicants.

[168] It will, however, be recalled that in Art. 4(2) SPA [new Art. 139(2)] the English version of the Treaty makes reference to the implementation of a collective agreement by a Council 'decision'.

[169] See Case C–298/89 *Gibraltar* v. *EU Council* [1993] ECR I–3605.

'decision' but was a general legislative measure.[170] However, the Court went on to find that, notwithstanding the legislative character of Directive 96/34, it might nevertheless be of direct and individual concern to UEAPME.[171] The Court noted that such individual concern would be present where a measure affected an applicant in a special way 'by reason of certain attributes peculiar to them or by reason of circumstances which differentiate them from all other persons'.[172] UEAPME claimed that this was the case, by reference to the consultation procedures set out in the SPA, as implemented by the Commission. It argued that, as it had been represented in the 'informal' consultation (as we have seen, it was explicitly listed in the Commission's Communication), its exclusion from the formal negotiation stage was unlawful. The CFI did not agree. It said that the consultation stage was separate from the negotiation stage, and there was no general right of those consulted to take part in the negotiations under Articles 3(4) and 4 SPA [new Articles 138(4) and 139] or an individual right to participate in negotiation of the framework agreement.[173]

However, the CFI found that this in itself did not render the action inadmissible. The question was whether 'any right of the applicant has been infringed as the result of any failure on the part of either the Council or the Commission to fulfil their obligations under the SPA procedure'.[174] The CFI said that the Commission and Council were obliged, in carrying out their roles under Articles 3(4) and 4 SPA [new Articles 138(4) and 139], to act in conformity with the principles governing their action in the field of social policy.[175] In particular, the Commission was obliged by Article 3(1) SPA [new Article 138(1)] to promote consultation of management and labour and facilitate dialogue by ensuring balanced support for the parties. This obligation was interpreted by the CFI as imposing a duty on the Commission, when resuming control of the SPA procedure at the joint request of the Social Partners under Article 4(2) [new Article 139(2)], to examine the representativity of the signatories to agreements proposed for implementation at the Community level under Articles 3(4) and 4 SPA [new Articles 138(4) and 139] and the Council had to verify whether the Commission had fulfilled this task. The CFI noted that this was particularly important in the case of this procedure from which, as we have seen, the European Parliament is excluded. It said that participation of the European Parliament in the Community legislative process reflects at Community level 'the fundamental democratic principle that the people

---

[170] Case T–135/96 *UEAPME*, paras. 63–67.

[171] Applying (para. 69) Case C–358/89 *Extramet Industrie v. Council* [1991] ECR I–2501; Case C–309/89 *Codorniu v. Council* [1994] ECR I–1853.

[172] Ibid., para. 69; Case 25/62 *Plaumann v. Commission* [1963] ECR 95; Case C–309/89 *Codorniu* [1994] ECR I–1853.

[173] Para. 82.

[174] Para. 83.

[175] Para. 85.

must share in the exercise of power through a representative assembly'.[176] The Court pointed out that in respect of measures adopted by the Council under the legislative route provided by Article 2 SPA [new Article 137] the democratic legitimacy derives from the European Parliament's participation.[177] By contrast, in respect of measures adopted under the collective route (Articles 3(4) and 4 SPA [new Articles 138(4) and 139]) the European Parliament has no formal involvement. In this case, the 'principle of democracy on which the Union is founded requires . . . that the participation of the people be otherwise ensured, in this instance through the parties representative of management and labour who concluded the agreement which is endowed by the Council . . . with a legislative foundation at Community level'.[178]

Therefore, the Court of First Instance emphasized that the Commission and Council were under a duty to verify that the signatories to the agreement were truly representative. This obliges them to ascertain whether 'having regard to the content of the agreement in question, the signatories, taken together are sufficiently representative'. Thus, the autonomy of the social dialogue is subject to the scrutiny of the Commission, the Council, and ultimately the Court. The Court continued that where that degree of representativity is lacking the Commission and Council must refuse to implement the agreement at Community level.[179] In such a case, the representatives of management and labour which were initially consulted by the Commission under Article 3(2) and (3) SPA [new Article 138(2) and (3)] but which were not parties to the agreement, and 'whose particular representation—again in relation to the content of the agreement—is necessary in order to raise the collective representativity[180] of the signatories to the required level, have the right to prevent the Commission and the Council from implementing the agreement at Community level by means of legislative instrument'.[181] Thus, even after a European collective agreement has been concluded it can be challenged by those organizations excluded from it on the ground of the absence of sufficient collective representativity.

The CFI went on to find that, in this case, the Commission and Council did indeed take sufficient account of the representativity of the parties to the framework agreement on parental leave. Since the Parental Leave Agreement applied to all employment relationships, the signatories, in order to satisfy the

[176] Citing, *inter alia*, Cases C–300/89 *Commission* v. *Council* [1991] ECR I–2867, para. 20; Case 138/79 *Roquette Frères* v. *Council* [1980] ECR 333, para. 33.

[177] Para. 88.

[178] Para. 89.

[179] Para. 90.

[180] Bercusson, above n. 143, argues that this is an inadequate translation of the original French '*une representativité cumulée suffisante*'. He favours the translation found earlier in para. 90, 'the signatories, *taken together*, are sufficiently representative'. This interpretation might include collective organizations which in themselves are not sufficiently representative but when taken together attain that status.

[181] Para. 90.

requirement of sufficient collective representativity, had to be qualified to represent all categories of undertakings and workers at Community level. Since the signatories (ETUC, UNICE, and CEEP) were *general* cross-industry organizations with a general mandate,[182] as distinct from cross-industry organizations representing *certain* categories of workers and undertakings with a specific mandate (the sub-group in which UEAPME was placed), they were sufficiently representative.[183] The CFI also considered that the particular constituency which UEAPME claimed to represent—small and medium sized undertakings—was adequately represented by UNICE, one of the parties to the agreement. The fact that UEAPME represented more small and medium sized undertakings than UNICE and that CEEP represented only the interests of undertakings governed by public law was not sufficient to require UEAPME's participation. UEAPME had failed to show that it was sufficiently different, in terms of its representativity, from all other organizations consulted by the Commission which were not part of the formal negotiation procedure.[184] Thus UEAPME was not affected by Directive 96/34 by reason of certain attributes which were peculiar to it or by reason of a factual situation which differentiated it from all other persons. Therefore, UEAPME was not individually concerned and the CFI found the action inadmissible.[185]

The judgment in the UEAPME case raises general issues concerning the nature of governance and democratic processes in the EU.[186] As we have seen, it has been argued that the social dialogue, and the collective route to legislation in particular, help to legitimize the EU in the eyes of its citizens because it enhances democracy, not by conferring ever wider powers on the European Parliament—quite the converse—but because, as the Court notes,[187] it provides an alternative type of representative democracy.[188] This is based, not on representatives elected by their constituencies on a territorial basis, but on representatives of management and labour selected on a functional basis. The CFI's decision has therefore effectively condoned the 'established' Social Partners of UNICE, CEEP, and the ETUC, thereby ensuring continuity of the social dialogue process begun under the Delors Presidency at the Val Duchesse talks

---

[182] This is a delicate question. In the ETUC decisions to approve agreements may be taken by majority vote; in the case of UNICE negotiations are undertaken only where there is unanimous agreement. The lack of any clear mandate for the parties to the dialogue to represent or to bind their constituent members has caused problems at the level of establishing contractual relations, e.g. the ETUC has been essentially a political lobby group and some major union confederations have not been affiliated to it. See further nn. 192–195.

[183] Paras. 95 and 96.

[184] Para. 111.

[185] The appeal of Case C–316/98 *UEAPME* [1998] ECR II–2335 to the Court was removed from the Court's register on 2 Feb. 1999.

[186] See Armstrong, 'Governance and the Single Market', in *The Evolution of EU Law*, eds. Craig and de Búrca (OUP, Oxford, 1999); Armstrong, *The Problems and Paradoxes of EU Regulatory Reform* (Kogan Page, London, forthcoming).

[187] Case T–135/96 *UEAPME* [1998] ECR II–2335, para. 89.

[188] See the excellent work of Bernard, above n. 118.

of 1985. The CFI did not, however, take the opportunity to undertake a wider consideration of the representativity of the established Social Partners, especially in respect of those who are not members of a trade union at all. Instead, it confined itself to imposing a minimal review requirement on the Commission and Council.

But are the social partners truly representative?[189] Bercusson argues that they are representative of the *interests* of their members, rather than the actual number of those members,[190] from whom they have a mandate to negotiate.[191] As far as the cross-industry (intersectoral) social partners are concerned, the ETUC changed its statutes in 1995 to mandate the ETUC to negotiate by qualified majority decisions[192] with a view to strengthening and intensifying the bargaining capacity of the European-level association. In UNICE a similar change occurred. If required, UNICE can receive a mandate to negotiate but, unlike the ETUC, a consensus of all members is still required in the Council of Presidents for all decisions referring to the social chapter. As Keller and Sörries point out, this internal rule can constrain UNICE's ability to enter into negotiations and to ratify more far-reaching agreements because it takes only one vetoing member to undermine any agreement. This also has the effect of neutralizing the shift to qualified majority voting elsewhere. As far as representativity is concerned, UNICE is the most representative of all categories of private undertakings, although this is questioned by UEAPME.[193] However, in contrast with ETUC, UNICE has no sectoral organization but only national umbrella associations as members. According to UNICE, these sectoral interests are already represented within its national member federations which have sectoral members themselves, albeit that UNICE has started to develop an informal network of sectoral business associations on a voluntary basis to keep its members informed. CEEP covers only public enterprises. This leaves other public employers, notably the civil service,

---

[189] See the Social Partners' Study of 1993, Doc. No. V/6141/93/E. The main findings of the study can be found in COM(93)600, Annex 3. The Commission is currently conducting studies on the representativeness of the European social partner organizations: http://europa.eu.int/comm/dg05/soc-dial/social/index_en.htm.

[190] Bercusson, 'Democratic Legitimacy and European Labour Law' (1999) 28 *ILJ* 153, 159. See also Wedderburn, 'Collective Bargaining or Legal Enactment: the 1999 Act and Union Recognition' (2000) 29 *ILJ* 1, 6; Franssen and Jacobs, 'The Question of Representativity in the European Social Dialogue' (1998) 35 *CMLRev*. 1295, 1309, argue that 'it is essential to judge the representativeness of the totality of the signatory parties, not the representativity of one single organization'.

[191] This reflects the Parliament's proposed criteria for reprensentativity listed in COM(96)448, para. 62, discussed above, n. 100. The following draws heavily on Keller and Sörries, 'The New Social Dialogue: Old Wine in New Bottles?' (1999) 9 *JESP* 110.

[192] Art. 13 of the Constitution. On the problems that might arise if one large national trade union confederation voted against the agreement, see Bercusson, above n. 143, 161.

[193] UNICE and UEAPME have concluded a co-operation agreement (12 Nov. 1998 cited in Bercusson, above, n. 143, 160) outlining 'the modalities of cooperation . . . in social dialogue and negotiation meetings'.

without representation.[194] The ETUC, by contrast, does represent the over-whelming majority of trade unions but some national trade union organiza-tions are not affiliated to the ETUC. Other European organizations, such as CESI and CEC, also wish to be involved.[195]

Thus, while the picture is complicated the established interprofessional social partners do seem to be more representative than the other organizations. But the representativity of the established Social Partners is likely to become more problematic as law-making in the social field expands under the new social policy title. For instance, it is difficult to see how UNICE, CEEP, and the ETUC could represent the various concerns of those who might be affected by action to promote 'the integration of persons excluded from the labour market' (Article 137(1)), a social policy matter covering issues far wider than those of classic labour law agreements which are traditionally the subject of social dialogue. Even in the more traditional labour law areas, as trade union mem-bership continues to decline across the Member States (see Table 2.1), the extent to which trade unions actually represent 'the people', especially women, is questionable. There is a risk, as Betten suggests, that the social dialogue actually leads to a predominance of an interest group in creating rules.[196]

Given the problems with the legitimacy of the social dialogue being derived from the model of representative democracy, some commentators argue that its legitimacy should be seen in terms of the participatory model of democracy instead. At the heart of this model lies the idea that decisions are taken as close to the citizens as possible on subject matters of interest and relevance to the citizens. This is the basis of the social dialogue. As Fredman puts it, the social dialogue is uniquely suited to the development of social policy because it is based on an intimate knowledge by the bargainers of the factual basis of issues discussed, and leads to a synthesis which is all the more effective because it carries with it the commitment of the two sides of industry.[197] Yet, this model is also problematic: 'there is the fundamental inequality of bargaining power between the two sides of the process and the user of bargaining could well entrench such inequalities leading to an unjustifiable concentration of power in the hands of management representatives legitimised under the cloak of Social Dialogue'.[198] This prompts Obradovic to argue that[199] corporatism should supplement but not supplant representative democracy, facilitating consultation and co-ordination between social interests and public bodies.

[194] Franssen and Jacobs, above, n. 143, 1299. See Szyszczak, above n. 148.
[195] COM(93)600, Annex III.
[196] Betten, 'The Democratic Deficit of Participatory Democracy in Community Social Policy' (1998) 23 *ELRev.* 20.
[197] Fredman, 'Social Law in the European Union: the Impact of the Lawmaking Process' in Craig and Harlow (eds.), above n. 65, 386, 410.
[198] Ibid.
[199] Above n. 147, citing Hirst, *Representative Democracy and its Limits* (Polity Press, Cambridge, 1990), 12.

Bercusson adopts an entirely different stance. He argues forcefully that despite the CFI opting for 'the EU constitutional law paradigm of democratic legitimacy' in its analysis of the social dialogue in *UEAPME*, the social dialogue should not be seen as a legislative process at all. With its roots in private law and industrial relations, he advocates that 'European labour law cannot afford to abandon national labour law systems'.[200] However, this approach also presents difficulties. As Fredman notes, the nature of the sanctions available to the parties, especially the unions, in respect of European level collective bargaining is far weaker than at domestic level due to the absence of any economic pressure such as industrial action.[201] The only pressure to reach an agreement, especially on the employer's side, is the prospect that without an agreement the legislative initiative will return to the Community legislator which will lead, at least for employers, to inferior results (less flexibility and fewer derogations).[202] This has been described as 'bargaining in the shadow of the law'.[203] For these very reasons, the union representatives prefer the use of the law, with collective bargaining being used to top up the minimum standards provided by the law[204] since this may well produce superior results for their members. This runs counter to the very essence of the collective route to legislation.

3.4 Sectoral Dialogue

It seems that the issues raised by *UEAPME* will have to be resolved by the EU's legislative, rather than judicial, institutions. Szyszczak[205] notes that the Commission has begun to address some of the problems of representativity by means of developing a sectoral strategy. In its Communication on Adapting and Promoting the Social Dialogue at Community Level,[206] the Commission announced that it would set up a new framework for the sectoral social dialogue. It therefore adopted a Decision[207] on the establishment of new

---

[200] Bercusson, 'Democratic Legitimacy and European Labour Law' (1999) 28 *ILJ* 153, 165.

[201] Fredman, above, n. 197, 408.

[202] Ibid., 409, Keller and Sörries, above n. 134, 115, and Cullen and Campbell, 'The Future of Social Policy Making in the European Union', in *Lawmaking in the European Union* (Kluwer, Deventer, 1998), 272, citing Ross, *Jacques Delors and European Integration* (Polity Press, Cambridge, 1995), 150–1.

[203] Bercusson, 'Maastricht: a Fundamental Change in European Labour Law' (1992) 23 *IRJ* 177, 185.

[204] Fredman, above n. 197, 409. They fear that the Social Dialogue will enable employers to 'avoid the unwelcome attentions of the European Commission and European Parliament and to engage in what will in effect be a social monologue with trade unions weakened by recession and structural changes in the economy'.

[205] Szyszczak, above, n. 148, and Bercusson, above n. 143, 165.

[206] COM(98)332.

[207] It therefore adopted a decision, Commission Decision 98/500/EC [1998] OJ L225/27 on the establishment of Sectoral Dialogue Committees promoting the Dialogue between the Social Partners at European level. On the future of the sectoral dialogue see Keller and Sörries, 'The Sectoral Social Dialogue and European Social Policy: More Fantasy, Fewer Facts' (1998) 4 *EJIR* 331, and 'Sectoral Social Dialogues: New Opportunities or Impasses?' (1999) 30 *IRJ* 330.

sectoral dialogue committees[208] which are to constitute the main forum for sectoral social dialogue (consultation, joint action, and negotiations). The committees are to be set up in all sectors which 'submit a joint request and are sufficiently well organized with a meaningful European presence in line with the established criteria of representativeness'.[209] The committees are to be consulted on developments at Community level having social implications and must develop and promote the social dialogue at sectoral level.[210] A maximum of forty people, representing the two sides of industry equally, can take part in the meetings of the Committees.[211] Each committee, together with the Commission, is to establish its own rules of procedure.[212] The committee must meet at least once a year,[213] the so-called 'high-level plenary meeting'.[214] It is to be chaired by a representative of the employers' or employees' delegations or, at their joint request, by a representative of the Commission.[215] Where the Commission informs the Committee that a matter discussed is confidential, members of the committee are bound not to disclose any information acquired at the meetings of the secretariat.[216] The Commission and the social partners are to review the functioning of the sectoral committee regularly.[217]

At present the social dialogue is being developed in twenty-four sectors at European level.[218] While much of this dialogue has involved identifying relevant problem areas for the social dialogue and trying out common vocabulary, agreements on the reduction of working time in agriculture and on the organization of working time (maritime transport,[219] railways,[220] and airline pilots and cabin crew[220A]) have been negotiated. In its Communication on Adapting and Promoting the Social Dialogue[221] the Commission noted that there was nothing in the SPA (as it then was) 'that limits possible sectoral negotiations thereunder, either as a complement to cross-industry

---

[208] Replacing existing Joint Committees on Maritime Transport, Civil Aviation, Inland Navigation, Road Transport, Railways, Telecomms, Agriculture, Sea Fishing, and Post.

[209] COM(98)332, 8 and Art. 1 of the Commission Decision 98/500/EC, above n. 207.

[210] Art. 2.

[211] Art. 3.

[212] Art. 5(1).

[213] Art. 5(3).

[214] There is to be reimbursement for a maximum of 15 representatives on each side.

[215] Art. 5(2).

[216] Art. 6.

[217] Art. 5(4).

[218] Commission, *Industrial Relations in Europe—2000*, COM(2000)113, 6.

[219] Council Directive concerning the Agreement on the Organization of Working Time of Seafarers concluded by ECSA and FST [1999] OJ L167/33, corrected [1999] OJ L244/64.

[220] On 18 Sept. 1996 the Social Partners meeting in the Joint Committee on Rail Transport reached agreements on including all railway workers, whether mobile or non-mobile, under Directive 93/104.

[220A] Agreement of 22 Mar. discussed at http:/europa.eu.int/comm/dg05/empl&esf/news/pilots.eu.htm.

[221] COM(98)322, 14.

agreements or establishing independent agreements limited to their sector concerned'. A potential problem may arise if the sectoral organizations were to negotiate collective agreements in an area already covered by the intersectoral partners and then pass it on to the Commission for a Council Decision.

D. DECISION-MAKING UNDER THE EMPLOYMENT TITLE

So far this chapter has focused on the legislative processes established under the Treaties of Rome and Maastricht. The Treaty of Amsterdam introduced a new decision-making procedure to implement the Employment Title. As we saw in Chapter 1, the defining feature of the new Employment Title is the emphasis on co-ordination of policy started at Essen. According to Article 125 [ex Article 109n], the key provision of the new Title, 'Member States and the Community shall, in accordance with the Title, work towards developing a coordinated strategy for employment and particularly for promoting a skilled, trained and adaptable workforce and labour markets'. Article 126 [ex Article 109p] makes clear that the principal actors are the Member States. They are required to co-ordinate their policies for the promotion of employment (which is to be regarded as an issue of 'common concern'[222]) within the Council, in a way consistent with the broad economic guidelines laid down within the framework of EMU. However, in an important recognition of the diversity of social policy, the States must have regard to 'national practices related to the responsibilities of management and labour'.[223] The subsidiary role of the Community is reinforced by Article 127 [ex Article 109p]. This calls on the Community to contribute to a high level of employment by encouraging co-operation and supporting the action of the Member States, and by *complementing* their action only 'if necessary' and after respecting 'the competence of the Member States'. This provision is reminiscent of the circumscribed competence of the Community in the fields of education and vocational training (Articles 149 and 150 [ex Articles 126 and 127]),[224] culture (Article 151 [ex Article 128]), and public health (Article 152 [ex Article 129]) where the Community is ostensibly given competence but has very limited options as to how to exercise it. Together these provisions provide a good example of what Kenner describes as 'Third Way' thinking: the

---

[222] Art. 126(2). Sciarra ('The Employment Title in the Amsterdam Treaty: A Multilanguage Legal Discourse' in O'Keeffe and Twomey (eds.) above n. 194) notes the parallel tracks of co-ordination and co-operation in the Employment Title.

[223] Art. 126(2). The Cologne summit expressly recognized the 'autonomy of the social partners in collective bargaining'.

[224] See further Ch. 1.

principal themes are those of shared responsibility between and within the Community and the Member States, and a decentralizing conception of subsidiarity in which the 'the Community enables and the Member States deliver'.[225]

Article 128 [ex Article 109q] contains more detailed provisions governing the process of monitoring and reporting on Member States' activities (see Figure 2.2). Each year the Council and Commission are to make a joint report which is to be considered at a European Council meeting of heads of state,

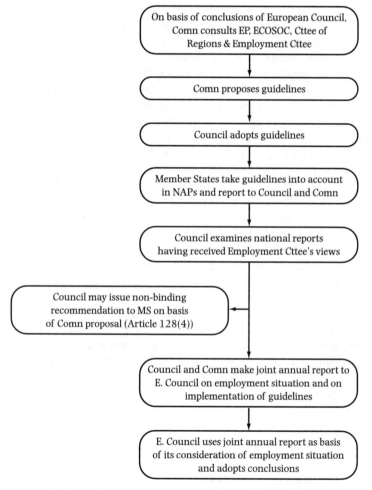

Figure 2.2 The Application of the Monitoring Procedure under the Employment Title

---

[225] Kenner, 'The EC Employment Title and the "Third Way": Making Soft Law Work' (1999) 15 *IJCLLIR* 33, 48.

which will then adopt a set of conclusions. On the basis of these conclusions the Council, acting by qualified majority on a proposal from the Commission, after consulting the European Parliament, the Economic and Social Committee, the Committee of the Regions, and the Employment Committee, must draw up employment guidelines which the Member States 'shall take into account'.[226] These guidelines must also be consistent with the broad economic guidelines issued in relation to EMU.[227]

The newly-created Employment Committee[228] with which the Council must consult, consists of two nominees from each Member State and two from the Commission,[229] selected from among 'senior officials or experts possessing outstanding competence in the field of employment and labour market policy in the Member States'.[230] It has an 'advisory status' to promote co-ordination between Member States on employment and labour market policies. Its tasks are to monitor employment policies both within the Member States and the Commission, and to formulate opinions at the request of the Commission or the Council or on its own initiative. It must also contribute to the preparation of the employment guidelines. In fulfilling its mandate, the Employment Committee must also consult the Social Partners[231] who are represented on the tripartite Standing Committee on Employment.[232] Only European-level social partners are now represented on the Standing Committee: UNICE, CEEP, UEAPME, COPA,[233] and EUROCOMMERCE on the employer's side and ETUC, EUROCADRES, and CEC on the employee side.

Once the employment guidelines for a given year are adopted, Article 128(3) requires each Member State to make an annual report to the Council and the Commission on 'the principal measures taken to implement its employment policy in the light of the guidelines for employment'—the so-called National Action Plans (NAPs). On the basis of these reports, the Council, having received the views of the Employment Committee, must examine the employment policies of the Member States in the light of the guidelines on employment. If, after this examination, the Council considers it appropriate it may, acting by qualified majority on a recommendation from the Commission, 'make recommendations to Member States'.[234] In the light of this examin-

---

[226] Ibid., Art. 128(2).

[227] Art. 99 [ex Art. 103]. See e.g. Council Recommendation 99/570/EC (OJ [1999] L217/34).

[228] Council Decision 2000/98/EC establishing the Employment Committee [2000] OJ L29/21. This replaces the Employment and Labour Market Committee established by Decision 97/16/EC [1997] OJ L6/32.

[229] Art. 130 [ex Art. 109s].

[230] Art. 2 of Decision 2000/98, above n. 228.

[231] Ibid.

[232] Council Decision 1999/207/EC [1999] OJ L72/33) on reform of the Standing Committee on Employment and repealing Decision 70/352/EEC [1970] OJ L273/25. The Preamble to Decision 2000/98/EC says that the Employment Committee should 'collaborate closely with the social partners, in particular with those represented in the Standing Committee on Employment'.

[233] Committee of Agricultural Organizations in the EC.

[234] Art. 128(4).

ation the Council and Commission must then submit a joint report to the European Council for that year on how far the guidelines have been implemented.[235] This recommendation procedure is the main innovation in the new Title: if the employment guidelines are not being observed by a Member State, a recommendation can be issued which is, in effect, a warning for failure to comply with the guidelines.[236] A similar procedure can be found for monitoring the compliance with EMU. However, under EMU, a Member State which fails to observe warnings issued by the Council in relation to excessive levels of national debt and excessive budget deficits may be subject to a fine;[237] under the Employment Title the recommendation is without sanction.

Not only can the Council issue recommendations, it can also act to 'adopt incentive measures designed to encourage cooperation between Member States and to support their action in the field of employment through initiatives aimed at developing exchanges of information and best practices, providing comparative analysis and advice as well as promoting innovative approaches and evaluating experiences, in particular by recourse to pilot projects' (Article 129 [ex Article 109r]). However, these limited measures 'shall not include harmonisation of the laws and regulations of the Member States'. Two Declarations issued at the time of the adoption of the Amsterdam Treaty further limit the usefulness of Article 129.[238] The first sets limits to the validity, duration, and financing of measures under this Article and the second says that incentive measures may not be supported from the structural funds expenditure but from other areas of the Community budget where resources are insignificant compared to those available to the Social Fund. These restrictions were included at the insistence of the German and British governments during the negotiations for the inter-governmental conference, and illustrate again how the Member States resisted any significant expansion in the powers of the central Community organs to act as initiators of expenditure aimed at boosting job creation. Deakin and Reed[239] therefore conclude that the institutional framework put in place by the Employment Title is facilitative rather than prescriptive. Member States continue to have immediate control over their own employment policies which may well be highly diverse in terms of their approach and effects. Harmonizing laws are ruled out and, in respect of the looser power to co-ordinate and vet employment policies, the central organs must observe the principle of subsidiarity.

As we saw in Chapter 1, the first set of employment guidelines for 1998

---

[235] Art. 128(5).

[236] Deakin and Reed, 'Between Social Policy and EMU: The New Employment Title of the EC Treaty' in Shaw (ed.), *Social Law and Policy in an Evolving European Union* (Hart, Oxford, forthcoming).

[237] Art. 104(1) [ex Art. 104c].

[238] Deakin and Reed, above n. 236.

[239] See ibid.

were adopted at the Luxembourg summit in November 1997.[240] The Member States were obliged to incorporate these guidelines into National Action Plans (NAPs) in the early part of 1998[241] and a preliminary assessment was made by the Commission and discussed at the Cardiff Council in June 1998.[242] The Member States subsequently submitted their assessment of their NAPs,[243] and together these formed the basis of the 1998 *Joint Employment Report*[244] by the Commission and Council.[245] As Deakin and Reed observe,[246] for the most part, the 1998 Joint Employment Report consists of a report back from Member States on their practices which, unsurprisingly, demonstrate the high degree of diversity in the way employment policy is addressed. This is reflected in the wide variety of measures which are singled out as examples of good practice. These include subsidy schemes for the integration of the unemployed (Danish youth unemployment policies, the UK's New Deal for young people, and the Irish back-to-work allowance), various schemes of state subsidies for self-employment in Portugal, Germany, Finland, and France, the 1997 Spanish agreement of the Social Partners on employment stability (aimed in part at enhancing competitiveness by reducing the share of temporary employment) and an Austrian package of vocational training and support measures for raising the employment rate of women. Although the value of the exercise was regarded as one of 'peer review' and exchange of 'best practice', in reality the lack of evidence has made it difficult to assess whether these policies should be adopted as reference models for other Member States'.[247] This suggests that the process of monitoring and vetting employment policy initiatives within Member States is a very long way short of achieving any kind of centralized convergence.

The 1998 Joint Report formed the basis for the 1999 Guidelines[248] which Member States had to incorporate into revised NAPs for 1999. Based on these NAPs, the Commission produced a Draft Joint Employment Report 1999,[249] the first after the Treaty of Amsterdam came into force, which formed the basis of the Joint Employment Report that the Commission and Council jointly submitted to the Helsinki summit in December 1999. This concluded that the employment performance of the EU as a whole was improving, but varied across individual Member States, with the EU achieving a growth rate

---

[240] Council Resolution 128/198 of 15 Dec. 1997 on the 1998 Employment Guidelines [1998] OJ C30/1.
[241] http://europa.eu.int/comm/dg05/empl&esf/naps/naps-en.htm.
[242] Anticipating Art. 128(2).
[243] Anticipating Art. 128(3).
[244] See http://europa.eu.int/comm/dg05/empl&esf/empl99/joint_en.htm.
[245] Anticipating Art. 128(5).
[246] See above, n. 236.
[247] *Joint Employment Report*, 1998, 30.
[248] Council Resolution on the 1999 Employment Guidelines.
[249] *Joint Employment Report*, 9 Sept. 1999.

of 2.9 per cent and the creation of 1.8 million jobs. However, little has been done to improve the low employment in the EU, which at 61 per cent is still lagging behind Japan and the US.

The analysis and conclusions in this 1999 Report provided the basis for the new, but little changed, Employment Guidelines for 2000[250] as well as for the Commission's Recommendation to the Council to issue recommendations to Member States under Article 128(4) for the first time on the implementation of their employment policies.[251] These have been drawn up on the basis of a comparative analysis of each country's performance against EU Employment Guidelines, and identify nine priority areas for further action. These are: tackling youth unemployment; preventing adult long-term unemployment; reforming the tax and benefit systems, with a particular focus on older workers and women to reduce disincentives for employment; promoting lifelong learning; creating job opportunities in the services sector; reducing the fiscal pressure on labour; modernizing work organization through the establishment of partnerships at all appropriate levels; tackling gender issues in the labour market; and improving indicators and statistics. Noting that the power to issue recommendations should be used sparingly, the Council followed the Commission's recommendations and issued its own Recommendation on the implementation of Member States' employment policies.[252] The Annex contains a brief summary of the employment situation in each Member State followed by specific recommendations. There is much emphasis on addressing the disincentives in the tax and benefit system which may discourage labour market participation (Belgium, Denmark, Germany), reducing the fiscal pressure on labour (France, Italy, Finland, Sweden), encouraging entrepreneurship (Germany, Greece, Spain, France, Portugal), mainstreaming equal opportunities and taking other measures which facilitate the reconciliation of work and family life (Spain, Ireland, Italy, Luxembourg, Austria, Finland, Sweden, UK) and encouraging a partnership approach to work organization (Greece, Portugal, UK).

* * *

So far this book has examined the development of a Community 'social' policy, the competing interests and goals which underlie this policy and the ways in which those tensions are reflected, addressed, and, at times reconciled, in the law-making process. These themes will be returned to in the context of the four substantive areas of law which form the corpus of Community social law:[253]

---

[250] Council Decision 2000/228/EC [2000] OJ L72/15 on guidelines for Member States' employment policies for the year 2000.
[251] See http://europa.eu.int/comm/dg05/empl&esf/napev-en.htm.
[252] Council Recommendation 2000/164/EC [2000] OJ L52/32.
[253] COM(2000)113, 8.

free movement of workers (primarily Chapter 3),[254] equal opportunities for men and women (Chapter 4 and part of Chapter 5), protection of health and safety in the workplace (Chapter 6), and labour law (Chapters 7 and 8).

---

[254] Social security is considered in Ch. 5.

3

Free Movement of Persons

A. INTRODUCTION

More than 18 million people living in the European Union have moved from their country of origin. About one-third of these migrants come from other Member States, while the remaining two-thirds come from non-Member States.[1] The majority of these migrant workers were recruited during the 'golden' years of the 1950s and 1960s by European firms faced with acute labour shortages. However, while the right of free movement is guaranteed as a fundamental freedom to Community nationals who enjoy protection against discrimination on the grounds of nationality,[2] the position of migrants from non-Member States (referred to as 'third country nationals') is considerably more precarious.

While Article 3(c) of the Treaty of Rome aspired to 'the abolition, as between Member States of obstacles to the free movement of . . . persons',[3] it did *not* provide a general right of free movement for all people: to qualify the individual has to be a national of a Member State engaged in an *economic* activity, as a worker (Articles 38–42 [ex Articles 48–51]), as a self-employed person (Articles 43–48 [ex Articles 52–58]), or as the provider of services (Articles 49–55 [ex Articles 59–66]). Generally, workers go to another Member State to work as employees under the control of an employer; establishment concerns those who leave the Member State in which they have been established in order to establish themselves in another Member State in a self-employed capacity. Establishment connotes some degree of permanence; the provision of services, by contrast, indicates only temporary presence in the host Member State, or indeed no physical presence at all, where the service is provided via electronic means such as telephone, Internet, or fax. In respect of all three fundamental rights Member States can derogate on the grounds of

---

[1] The Veil Report to the Commission on the free movement of persons. The number of EU nationals resident in another Member State is 5.5 million out of a total of 370 million. There are also 12.5 million from non-Member States nationals. For a more detailed discussion, see O'Leary, 'The Free Movement of Persons and Services', in Craig and de Búrca, *The Evolution of EU Law* (OUP, Oxford, 1999).

[2] See e.g. Case 53/81 *Levin* v. *Staatssecretaris van Justitie* [1982] ECR 1035 (Art. 48 [new Art. 39]); Case 2/74 *Reyners* v. *Belgian State* [1974] ECR 631 (Art. 52 [new Art. 43]) and Case 33/74 *Van Binsbergen* v. *Bestuur van de Bedrijfsvereniging voor de Metaalnijveheid* [1974] ECR 1299 (Art. 59 [new Art. 49]).

[3] See further Case 118/75 *Watson and Belmann* [1978] ECR 1185, paras. 16 and 17.

public policy, public security, and public health.[4] There is also a special derogation for employment in the public service.[5]

In *Gebhard*[6] the Court said that the rules on persons, services, and establishment were mutually exclusive, with the provisions of the chapter on services being subordinate to those on establishment.[7] However, common principles apply to all three.[8] As the Court pointed out in *Asscher*,[9] a comparison of Articles 39 and 43 [ex Articles 48 and 52] showed that they are based on the same principles both as regards the entry into and residence in the territory of the Member States by persons covered by Community law, and as regards the application of the prohibition of all discrimination against them on the grounds of nationality. The Court then added that 'the same applies to the pursuit of an economic activity in the territory of the Member States by persons covered by Community law'. By implication the same principles must also apply to service providers. The common feature is that Community law, especially the principle of non-discrimination, applies only when there is movement by the individual from one Member State to another.

1. The Development of the Rights to Free Movement

As we have seen, in the Treaty of Rome the free movement of persons provisions were viewed primarily in economic terms and concerned the rights of entry and residence of economically active citizens of Member States. Since the idea was to mobilize human resources as a production factor[10] the rights to enter and reside in another Member State of the Community were therefore linked to exercising an occupational activity. The problem with this was that 'economic actors' were reluctant to move without their families. As a result, a series of important secondary measures were adopted in the late 1960s and early 1970s to facilitate the free movement of workers and their families; and these were backed up by some important judgments by the Court.[11]

These legislative and judicial steps to realize free movement of persons have been supplemented by two further conventions—the Schengen Convention and the Dublin Convention—both designed to achieve an area without

---

[4] Arts. 39(3), 46, and 55 [ex Arts. 48(3), 56, and 66].

[5] Arts. 39(4), 45, and 55 [ex Arts. 48(4), 55, and 66].

[6] Case C–55/94 *Gebhard v. Consiglio dell'Ordine degli Avvocati e Procuratori de Milano* [1995] ECR I–4165.

[7] The wording of para. 1 of Art. 49 [ex Art. 59] assumed that the provider and the recipient of the service were 'established' in two different Member States; para. 1 of Art. 60 [new Art. 59] specifies that the provisions relating to services apply only if those relating to establishment do not apply.

[8] Case 48/75 *Procureur du Roi v. Royer* [1976] ECR 497.

[9] Case C–107/94 *Asscher v. Staatssecretaris van Financiën* [1996] ECR I–3089, para. 29.

[10] See the Spaak report discussed in Ch. 1.

[11] See section C below.

internal frontiers. The Dublin Convention, signed and ratified by all of the then twelve Member States, provides that an application for asylum lodged in any of the Member States must be examined by one designated Member State. The Schengen Agreements of 1985 and 1990, originally signed by the Benelux Countries, France, and Germany,[12] are designed to remove border formalities at common frontiers, approximate visa formalities, and provide for the co-operation of law enforcement agencies particularly in relation to drugs and firearms.[13] The agreements cover all nationals of the Member States of the EU, regardless of whether they are members of the Schengen area. All are subject to the same (increased) checks on crossing one of Schengen's *external* frontiers, but once within the Schengen area the principle of free movement applies and traditional formalities at the *internal* frontiers have been abolished. The abolition of border controls, however, does not mean an end to the policing powers of the competent authorities. Individuals must also continue to hold, carry, and present identity documents.

At EC level free movement was given a renewed boost by the inclusion of what became Article 7a [new Article 14] into the Treaty of Rome by the Single European Act 1986. This obliged the Community to adopt measures with the aim of progressively establishing the internal market by 31 December 1992. The internal market was defined as 'an area without internal frontiers in which the free movement of goods, persons, services and capital is ensured'. The idea behind this provision, and the measures to be adopted subsequently as part of the 1992 programme, was to enable a person of any nationality (including a national of a non-Member State) to cross the *internal* borders of the EC without being subjected to checks or formalities. This objective has not been realized in its entirety.[14] The Schengen Convention, often presented as the 'testing ground' for the free movement of persons because it was originally meant to come into force before the 1992 deadline, was intended to facilitate the application of Article 7a [new Article 14].[15]

Although the Treaty of Rome envisaged rights only for economically active people, the effect of secondary legislation and judgments by the Court[16] has been that the right of free movement and related rights to benefits in the host State have increasingly been expanded to cover Union citizens more generally. This expansion was also the result of the Council adopting three directives in 1990 conferring more general rights of entry and residence on students,

---

[12] Italy, Portugal, Spain, and Greece acceded to the Convention in 1990, Austria in 1995, Denmark, Sweden, and Finland in 1996.

[13] See generally Schutte, 'Schengen: its Meaning for the Free Movement of Persons in Europe' (1991) 28 *CMLRev.* 549.

[14] However, see the June 1997 Action Plan for the Single Market, Communication of the Commission to the European Council, CSE(97)1 final and the Single Market Scoreboard http://europa.eu.int/comm/dg15/en/update/score.

[15] O'Keeffe, 'The Schengen Convention. A Suitable Model for European Integration?' (1991) 11 *YEL* 185.

[16] See section C below.

retired people, and any other citizens with the means to support themselves.[17] The Treaty on European Union 1992 reflected this changing attitude towards the free movement provisions, giving the 'citizen' a much higher profile. This was reflected in three ways. First, the common provisions of the TEU provided that the Union had among its objectives 'strengthening economic and social cohesion' and strengthening 'the protection of the rights and interests of the nationals of its Member States through the introduction of a citizenship of the Union'.[18] The Union also committed itself to respect the 'national identities of the Member States, whose systems of government are founded on principles of democracy',[19] and to respect fundamental human rights.[20]

Secondly, these objectives took concrete form with the inclusion of a new Part Two in the EC Treaty entitled 'Citizenship of the Union'. This is a direct descendant from the plans to develop a 'People's Europe' in the 1980s. Article 8 [new Article 17] provides that 'Every person holding the nationality of a Member State shall be a citizen of the Union'. The determination of nationality, however, remains a matter of domestic law.[21] The citizens' rights are laid down in Article 8a–e [new Articles 18–22]. These are:

- the right to move and reside freely within the territory of the Member States, subject to the limitations and conditions laid down by the Treaty and by the measures adopted to give it effect (Article 8a(1) [new Article 18(1)]);[22]
- the right to vote in local[23] and European elections[24] (Article 8b [new Article 19]);

---

[17] Three directives were passed based on Art. 235 [new Art. 308]: Council Directive 90/364/EEC [1990] OJ L180/26 on the Rights of Residence for persons of sufficient means (the 'playboy Directive'); Council Directive 90/365/EEC on the rights of residence for employees and self-employed who have ceased their occupational activity [1990] OJ L180/28 and Council Directive 90/366/EEC [1990] OJ L180/30 on the rights of residence for students. The incorrect legal basis had been selected for this last Directive (Case C–295/90 *European Parliament v. Council* [1992] ECR I–4193, see Art. 235 [new Art. 308] instead of Art. 7(2) [new Art. 12(2)]. A new directive has been enacted, Directive 93/96/EC [1993] OJ L317/59.

[18] Art. B [new Art. 2 TEU].

[19] Art. F(1) TEU [new Art. 6(1) TEU].

[20] Art. F(2) TEU [new Art. 6(2) TEU].

[21] Declaration on Nationality of a Member State appended to the TEU. See also Closa, 'Citizenship of the Union and Nationality of the Member States' (1995) 29 *CMLRev.* 487.

[22] The Council may, however 'adopt provisions with a view to facilitating the exercise of the rights referred to in paragraph 1'.

[23] Directive 94/80/EC [1994] OJ L368/38, as amended by Directive 96/30/EC [1996] OJ L122/14 laying down detailed arrangements for the exercise of the right to vote and to stand as a candidate in municipal elections by citizens of the Union residing in a Member State of which they are not nationals.

[24] Directive 93/109/EC [1993] OJ L329/34 on the right to vote and stand as a candidate in elections to the European Parliament for citizens of the Union residing in a Member State of which they are not nationals. This Directive provides that entitlement to vote and to stand as a candidate in the Member State of residence is conferred on persons seeking to do so who are

- the right to diplomatic and consular protection from the authorities of any Member State in third countries[25] (Article 8c [new Article 20]);
- the right to petition the European Parliament in accordance with Article 138d and the right to apply to the ombudsman in accordance with Article 138e (Article 8d [new Article 21]).

The Commission must report every three years on the application of these provisions.[26]

The inclusion of the notion of citizenship was intended to encourage nationals to develop a sense of loyalty to the EU as well as to the Member States, to give them a sense that they were also benefiting from the Single Market project, and to provide a degree of legitimacy for the activities of the EU.[27] According to the literature, citizenship concerns the reciprocity of rights and duties towards the community. It entails membership of the community and membership involves degrees of participation. Marshall has argued that full membership is brought about through rights: civil rights (basic freedoms from state interference), political rights (electoral rights), and social rights (health care, social security and pension).[28] Judged by this standard, the EU has only a nascent form of citizenship. However, the inclusion of Article 8a–e [new Articles 18–22] is politically significant for it signals that the EU sees itself as having some of the attributes of a state. Therefore, it reflects the changing nature of the EU: it marks a shift away from a common market and towards political union.

The third step taken at Maastricht, and essentially the flip side of the coin of free movement, is security. The third (intergovernmental) pillar (Title VI TEU) on co-operation in respect of Justice and Home Affairs was introduced by the TEU to reconcile freedom of movement with protection against crime, drugs, and illegal immigration.[29] The Member States regarded matters concerning

---

citizens of the Union but are not nationals of the Member State where they reside; who satisfy the conditions applicable to nationals of that State in respect of the right to vote and to stand as a candidate, and who are not deprived of those rights in their home Member State.

[25] Decision 95/553/EC of the Representatives of the Governments of the Member States meeting within the Council of 19 Dec. 1995 regarding protection for citizens of the EU by diplomatic and consular representations [1995] OJ L314/73.

[26] See e.g. the second Commission Report on citizenship COM(97)230 final.

[27] Shaw, *Citizenship of the Union: Towards Post-National Membership*, specialized course delivered at the Academy of European Law, Florence, July 1995; Shaw, 'The Many Pasts and Futures of Citizenship in the European Union' (1997) 22 *ELRev.* 554; Reich, 'A European Constitution for Citizens: Reflections on the Rethinking of Union and Community Law' (1997) 3 *ELJ* 131. See also O'Keeffe, 'Union Citizenship', in *Legal Issues of the Maastricht Treaty*, eds. O'Keeffe and Twomey (Chancery, Chichester, 1994); Wiener and della Sala, 'Constitution-Making and Citizenship Practice—Bridging the Democracy Gap in the EU?' (1997) 35 *JCMS* 595; d'Oliveira, 'European Citizenship: Its Meaning and Potential', in *Europe after Maastricht: An Ever Closer Union*, ed. Dehousse (Law Books in Europe, Munich, 1994); Preuß, 'Problems of a Concept of European Citizenship' (1995) 1 *ELJ* 267.

[28] Marshall, *Citizenship and Social Class* (CUP, Cambridge, 1950), 28–9.

[29] See O'Keeffe, 'Recasting the Third Pillar' (1995) 32 *CMLRev.* 893. See also 'The Emergence of a European Immigration Policy' (1995) 20 *ELRev.* 20.

the crossing of external borders, immigration,[30] asylum, drug addiction, fraud, judicial co-operation in civil and criminal matters, customs and police co-operation to be of common interest (points (1) to (3) of Article K.1). However, the determination of which third country nationals should be in possession of a visa was to be decided by the Council under Article 100c of the EC Treaty (now repealed).[31] The inevitable overlaps between the Community pillar (the EC Treaty) and the third pillar (Title VI of the Treaty on European Union) created considerable difficulties, not least because the Court had no jurisdiction to hear cases arising under the third pillar. To address this problem, the Heads of State agreed at Amsterdam to transfer key areas relating to the free movement of persons (namely asylum, immigration, and the rules governing the crossing of external borders) from the third pillar to the first (Community) pillar and created a new Title IV [ex Title IIIa] entitled 'Visas, asylum, immigration and other policies related to free movement of persons'.[32] This is the so-called 'communitarization' of the third pillar.[33] Police co-operation and judicial co-operation in criminal matters, however, remain in the third pillar, now entitled 'Provisions on Police and Judicial Cooperation in Criminal Matters'. Article 29 TEU [ex Article K.1] provides that 'the Union's objective shall be to provide citizens with a high level of safety within an area of freedom, security and justice by developing common action among the Member States in the fields of police and judicial co-operation in criminal matters and by combating racism and xenophobia'. The reference to racism and xenophobia reflects growing concern about the rise in racism across the EU.[34] The Commission has issued a Communication on the subject,[35] a European Monitoring Centre on Racism and Xenophobia has been set up,[36] and the Council has adopted a Joint Action under Article K.3 TEU.[37]

The new Title IV EC has as its objective the progressive establishment of 'an

---

[30] A Recommendation on harmonizing means of combating illegal immigration and illegal employment has been adopted (96/C5/01), as has a Resolution on the status of third-country nationals residing on a long-term basis in the territory of the Member States (96/C80/02).

[31] Council Regulation (EC) 1683/95 of 29 May 1995 laying down a uniform format for visas [1995] OJ L164/1. Council Regulation 2317/95 [1995] OJ L234/1 in respect of visa requirements for third country nationals. The Court annulled this Regulation in Case C–392/95 *Parliament v. Council* [1997] ECR I–3213, while provisionally maintaining its effects. The new Regulation 574/99 [1999] OJ L72/2 was adopted on 12 Mar. 1999. See Hailbronner, 'Visa Regulations and Third Country Nationals in EC Law' (1994) 31 *CMLRev.* 969.

[32] See generally Langrish, 'The Treaty of Amsterdam: Selected Highlights' (1998) 23 *ELRev.* 3.

[33] Monar, 'Justice and Home Affairs in the Treaty of Amsterdam: Reform at the Price of Fragmentation' (1998) 23 *ELRev.* 320.

[34] See also new Art. 13 [old Art. 6a] which provides a legal basis for the Community to adopt measures combating discrimination on the grounds, *inter alia*, of racial or ethnic origin, considered further in Ch. 4.

[35] COM(95)653. See further Gearty, 'Racism, Religious Intolerance and Xenophobia', in *The EU and Human Rights*, ed. Alston (OUP, Oxford, 1999).

[36] Council Regulation (EC) 1035/97 [1997] OJ L151/1; COM(97)489 final.

[37] Joint Action 96/443/JHA [1996] OJ L185/5.

area of freedom, security and justice'.[38] After an initial five-year period when specific institutional provisions apply (for example, the Member States will share the right of initiative with the European Commission[39]), Community decision-making procedures will apply. Under Article 61(a) the Council must adopt 'measures aimed at ensuring the free movement of persons in accordance with Article 14 [ex Article 7a], in conjunction with directly related flanking measures with respect to external border controls, asylum and immigration'. Further, under Article 62 the Council has five years to adopt first, 'measures with a view to ensuring, in compliance with Article 14, the absence of any controls on persons, be they citizens of the Union or nationals of third countries, when crossing internal borders';[40] secondly, 'measures on the crossing of external borders of the Member States which shall establish (a) standards and procedures to be followed by Member States in carrying out checks on persons at such borders; (b) rules on visas for intended stays of no more than three months'; and thirdly, measures setting out the conditions under which nationals of third countries shall have the freedom to travel within the territory of the Member States during a period of no more than three months. On the basis of two protocols added by the Treaty of Amsterdam,[41] the UK and Ireland do not apply some aspects of Article 14 [ex Article 7a EC] regarding the elimination of controls at internal borders, nor are they bound by measures adopted under Title IV but they can opt in to any particular measure. Denmark is also in a special position.[42]

The Court now has jurisdiction to hear cases under Title IV,[43] albeit under modified conditions: the case must be pending before a court or tribunal of a Member State against whose decisions there is no judicial remedy.[44] This modified jurisdiction was introduced to reduce the risk of the Court being overloaded with individual immigration and asylum cases from lower national courts and to ensure that only issues of principle reached the Court.[45] The Court was also given limited jurisdiction under the third pillar (Title VI) TEU to give preliminary rulings. This is an optional jurisdiction: Member States can accept the jurisdiction of the Court to hear references

---

[38] Art. 61. See also Art. B TEU [new Art. 2]. See generally O'Keeffe, 'Can the Leopard Change its Spots? Visas, Immigration and Asylum following Amsterdam', in *Legal Issues of the Amsterdam Treaty*, eds. O'Keeffe and Twomey (Hart, Oxford, 1999).

[39] Art. 67(1).

[40] Art. 62(1). See, for example, COM(2000)27 final on a Proposal for a Council Regulation listing the third countries whose nationals must be in possession of a visa [2000] OJ C 177 E/66.

[41] Protocol B.3 and B.4.

[42] Protocol B.5.

[43] Albors-Llorens, 'Changes in the Jurisdiction of the Court of Justice under the Treaty of Amsterdam' (1998) 35 *CMLRev.* 1273.

[44] Art. 68(1) [ex Art. 73p]. The Court does not have jurisdiction to rule on any measure or decision taken pursuant to Art. 62(1) (measures to ensure the absence of any controls on persons when crossing internal borders) relating to the maintenance of law and order and safeguarding internal security.

[45] Langrish, above, n. 32, 8.

from its courts by making a declaration, and when doing so it may restrict the power to make references to its courts of last resort.[46] The Court also has jurisdiction similar to Art. 230 [ex Art. 173] to review the legality of framework decisions and decisions, but only Member States and the Commission can initiate these actions.[47] In addition, the Court has jurisdiction to resolve disputes between Member States or between Member States and the Commission on the interpretation and application of third pillar measures.

The Treaty of Amsterdam also incorporated the Schengen Convention into the single institutional framework of the Union.[48] This is an example of 'closer co-operation' or flexibility whereby the thirteen Member States (excluding the UK and Ireland) will continue their co-operation under the framework of the EC. The UK, which is opposed to Schengen, and Ireland which harmonizes its position with the UK, are the only Member States not to have signed up to Schengen, and they are excluded, although the protocol provides for the full or partial involvement of both States at some later date,[48A] but only with the unanimous agreement of the other States. Special arrangements are also made for Denmark.

In addition to these developments, the EU has entered into a number of international agreements granting some rights to nationals of non-Member States. The most substantive agreement, the European Economic Area (EEA), extends the EU's own *acquis* to Norway, Iceland, and Liechtenstein.[49] Apart from the EEA, the most extensive EU agreements on migrant workers and social security are Decisions 1/80 and 3/80 concluded by the EEC–Turkey Association Council.[50] This chapter, however, focuses particularly on the rights of Community nationals who wish to work elsewhere in the Community, although reference will be made to the rights of nationals from non-Member States where directly related to the Community national's rights.

2. Direct Effect of Articles 39, 43, and 49 [ex Articles 48, 52, and 59]

It is clear that Articles 39, 43, and 49 [ex Articles 48, 52, and 59] are directly effective and have been since the expiry of the transitional period. In the case

---

[46] Art. 35(1)–(3) [ex Art. K.7]. Even if a Member State has not made a declaration it is entitled to submit statements or written observations (Art. 35(4)).

[47] Art. 35(6).

[48] Protocol B.2. Hedemann-Robinson, 'The Area of Freedom, Security and Justice with Regard to the UK, Ireland and Denmark: The "Opt-in Opt-outs" under the Treaty of Amsterdam', in O'Keeffe and Twomey (eds.), above, n. 38.

[48A] See Council Decision 2000/365/EC OJ [2000] L131/43 concerning the request of the UK to take part in some of the provisions of the Schengen acquis.

[49] [1994] OJ L1/1; [1995] OJ L86/58.

[50] See, further, Peers, 'Towards Equality: Actual and Potential Rights of Third Country Nationals in the European Union' (1996) 33 *CMLRev.* 7.

of Article 39 [ex Article 48] this was first acknowledged by the Court in the *French Merchant Seamen's case*[51] and confirmed in *Van Duyn*.[52] In the latter case the Court ruled that despite the derogations from the principle of free movement contained in Article 48(3) [new Article 39(3)], the provisions of Article 48(1) and (2) [new Article 39(1) and (2)], imposed a sufficiently precise obligation to confer direct effect. The Court also confirmed in *Reyners*[53] that Article 52 [new Article 43] was directly effective and in *Van Binsbergen*[54] that Article 59 [new Article 49] was directly effective.

Directly effective Treaty provisions can have both vertical and horizontal direct effect and so can be relied on by an individual against both the state and a private body. For many years it was not clear whether the Treaty provisions on free movement had both vertical and horizontal direct effect. *Walrave and Koch*[55] suggested the answer was affirmative. The Court said that 'the rule on non-discrimination applies in judging *all legal relationships* in so far as these relationships, by reason either of the place they are entered into or the place where they take effect, can be located within the territory of the Community' (emphasis added). The Court also said that 'prohibition of discrimination does not only apply to the action of public authorities but extends likewise to rules of any other nature aimed at collectively regulating gainful employment and services'. However, subsequent cases have concerned action taken by public authorities[56] or professional regulatory bodies, such as the Bar Council,[57] the Italian football association,[58] or the International Cycling Union[59] and this suggested an extended form of vertical direct effect only.

In *Bosman* the Court left the question open, since the defendants were sporting associations which determined the terms on which professional sportsmen could engage in gainful employment[60] to which, after *Walrave and Koch*, Article 48 [new Article 39] applied. The Court did not, however, expressly rule out the possibility of Article 48 applying to individuals: at paragraph 86 it referred to the possibility of 'individuals' relying on the Article 48(3) [new Article 39(3)] derogations (public policy, public security, and public health). By implication, if individuals can rely on the derogations, they

[51] Case 167/73 *Commission v. France* [1974] ECR 359.
[52] Case 41/74 *Van Duyn v. Home Office* [1975] ECR 1337.
[53] Case 2/74 [1974] ECR 631.
[54] Case 33/74 [1974] ECR 1299.
[55] Case 36/74 *Walrave and Koch v. Association Union Cycliste Internationale* [1974] ECR 1405.
[56] e.g. the Home Office in Case 41/74 *Van Duyn* [1975] ECR 1337 and local authorities in Case 197/84 *Steinhauser v. Ville de Biarritz* [1985] ECR 1819.
[57] Case 71/76 *Thieffry v. Conseil de l'ordre des avocats de la cour de Paris* [1977] ECR 765.
[58] Case 13/76 *Dona v. Mantero* [1976] ECR 1333.
[59] Case 36/74 *Walrave and Koch* [1974] ECR 1405.
[60] Union Royale Belge des Sociétés de Football Association (URBSFA), FIFA, and UEFA. See also Case C–176/96 *Lehtonen v. FRBSB*, judgment of 13 Apr. 2000, which concerned the Belgian Basketball Federation and the International Basketball Federation and Joined Cases C–51/96 and C–191/97 *Deliège v. Ligue francophone de Judo et Disciplines Associées Asbl*, judgment of 11 Apr. 2000, which concerned the Belgian Judo Association.

must be bound by the right and hence the free movement of person provisions have horizontal direct effect. This view seems to have been confirmed in *Clean Car*.[61] The Court noted that the derogations could be relied on by individuals 'to justify such limitations under agreements or other measures adopted by persons governed by private law'. The Court continued that if an employer could rely on a derogation under Article 48(3), 'he must also be able to rely on the same principles under, in particular, Article 48(1) and (2)'.[62] This case therefore suggests that Article 39 has horizontal direct effect. It also makes clear that Article 39 can be invoked not only by the worker affected but also his or her employer. This issue has been finally resolved in *Angonese*[62A] where the Court, drawing on the case law under Article 141 [ex Article 119], said that since Article 48 is designed to ensure there is no discrimination on the labour market it applies to private persons as well as public authorities.

B. NON-DISCRIMINATION ON THE GROUNDS OF NATIONALITY

1. Introduction

At the heart of the free movement of persons lies the principle of non-discrimination on the grounds of nationality expressed in Article 12 EC [ex Articles 7 EEC and 6 EC].[63] It provides:

Within the scope of application of this Treaty, and without prejudice to any special provisions contained therein, any discrimination on grounds of nationality shall be prohibited.[64]

Thus, unless there are any express derogations to the contrary, the principle of non-discrimination on grounds of nationality applies. Articles 39, 43, and

---

[61] Case C–350/96 *Clean Car Autoservice GmbH* v. *Landeshauptmann von Wien* [1998] ECR I–2521.

[62] Para. 24. *Clean Car* is also authority for the fact that the free movement of workers provisions could be relied on not only by a worker but also by an employer in order to employ, in the Member State in which he is established, workers who are nationals of another Member State.

[62A] Case C–281/98 *Angonese* v. *Cassa di Risparmio di Bolzano*, judgment of 6 June 2000, paras. 35–36.

[63] See further Sundberg-Weitman, 'Addressees of the Ban on Discrimination Enshrined in Article 7 of the EEC Treaty' (1973) 10 *CMLRev.* 71 and *Discrimination on the Grounds of Nationality. Free Movement of Workers and Freedom of Establishment under the EEC Treaty* (North-Holland Publishing Co., Amsterdam, 1977).

[64] In Case C–193/94 *Criminal Proceedings against Skanavi* [1996] ECR I–929 the Court said that Art. 6 EC [new Art. 12] applied independently only to situations governed by Community law in respect of which the Treaty lays down no specific prohibition on discrimination. Consequently, where one of the specific Treaty provisions applies, Art. 6 need not be considered. See also Case C–131/96 *Romero* v. *Landesversicherunganstalt Rheinprovinz* [1997] ECR I–3659, para. 10; Case C–176/96 *Lehtonen*, judgment of 13 Apr. 2000, paras. 37–38.

49 [ex Articles 48, 52, and 59] give specific expression to this principle.[65] For example, Article 39(2) [ex Article 48(2)] reads:

Such freedom of movement shall entail the abolition of any discrimination based on nationality between the workers of the Member States as regards employment, remuneration and other conditions of work and employment.[66]

The significance of Article 12 was emphasized by the Court in *Data-Delecta*.[67] It said that the principle of non-discrimination means that 'there must be perfect equality of treatment in Member States of persons in a situation governed by Community law and nationals of the Member States in question'.[68] Therefore, migrants will enjoy better social conditions in some Member States, where nationals benefit from higher social standards, than in others. This point was confirmed in *Perfili*[69] where the Court added that, in prohibiting discrimination on the grounds of nationality, Articles 6, 52, and 59 [new Articles 12, 43, and 49] were not concerned with disparities in treatment arising from differences between the laws in the Member States, so long as they affected all persons subject to them in accordance with objective criteria and without regard to nationality.

Community law outlaws both direct and indirect discrimination.[70] Direct discrimination, which means different and usually less favourable treatment on the grounds of nationality, breaches Articles 39, 43, and 49 [ex Articles 48, 52, and 59]. Such conduct may, however, be lawful if it is caught by one of the derogations expressly provided by the Treaty, namely public health, public security, public policy, and, to a limited extent, employment in the public service. Indirect discrimination, by contrast, involves the elimination of requirements which, while apparently nationality-neutral on their face, have a greater impact or impose a greater burden on nationals of other Member States or have the effect of hindering the free movement of persons.[71] Thus,

[65] Case 1/78 *Kenny* v. *Insurance Officer* [1978] ECR 1489, para. 9.

[66] A similar approach is taken by the secondary legislation, esp. Art. 7(1) of Regulation 1612/68 [1968] OJ Spec. Ed. L257/2.

[67] Case C–43/95 *Data-Delecta* v. *MSL Dynamics* [1996] ECR I–4661. A similar issue was raised in Case C–122/96 *Saldanha and MTS Securities Corporation* v. *Hiross Holding AG* [1998] ECR I–5325.

[68] Therefore, a Swedish law requiring a foreign national to lodge security for costs when no such security could be demanded from Swedish nationals contravened Art. 6 EC [new Art. 12]. See also Case C–274/96 *Criminal Proceedings against Bickel and Franz* [1998] ECR I–7637 where the Court said that Art. 6 required that 'persons in a situation governed by Community law be placed entirely on an equal footing with nationals of the Member State'. On the facts of the case this meant that a German and an Austrian national were entitled to have their criminal case in the Italian region of Bolzano conducted in German, as residents of the region were entitled to do.

[69] Case C–177/94 *Criminal Proceedings against Gianfranco Perfili, civil party: Lloyd's of London* [1996] ECR I–161.

[70] See further Bleckmann, 'Considerations sur l'interpretation de l'article 7 du Traité CEE' (1976) 12 *Revue Trimestrielle de Droit Européen* 469, 477. See also Hilson, 'Discrimination in Community Free Movement' (1999) 24 *ELRev.* 445.

[71] See e.g. Case C–175/88 *Biehl* v. *Administration des Contributions* [1990] ECR I–1779; Case C–111/91 *Commission* v. *Luxembourg* [1993] ECR I–817.

indirect discrimination focuses on the *effect* of a measure. This is recognized by Article 3(1) of Regulation 1612/68[72] which says that provisions laid down by national law will not apply where, 'though applicable irrespective of nationality, their exclusive or principal aim *or effect* is to keep nationals of other Member States away from employment offered' (emphasis added). Indirectly discriminatory measures also breach Articles 39, 43, and 49 unless they can be objectively justified.

2. Direct Discrimination

The Court has been forced to examine the issue of direct discrimination in the context of participation in national sports teams. In *Dona*[73] the Court considered the compatibility with Community law of national rules under which only football players who were affiliated to the Italian Football Federation could take part in matches as professional or semi-professional players, affiliation being open only to players who were Italian. The Court ruled, first, that sport was subject to Community law only in so far as it constituted an economic activity. This included the activities of professional football players who were employed or providing a service.[74] It then said that Community law did not prevent the adoption of rules or of a practice:

excluding foreign players from participation in certain matches for reasons which are not of an economic nature, which relates to the particular nature and context of such matches and are thus of sporting interest only, such as, for example, matches between national teams from different countries.[75]

In reaching this compromise the Court did add that 'This restriction on the scope of the provisions in question must however remain limited to its proper objective'.

Therefore, while the Italian rules imposing a blanket ban on players who were not Italian from playing professional or semi-professional football were incompatible with Community law, it was lawful to exclude foreign players from playing in certain matches (such as national games) for reasons which were not of an economic nature. As a result of this ruling the Commission entered into a 'gentleman's agreement' with UEFA (Union of European Football Associations) under which national associations had to allow each first division team to field at least three foreign players and two 'acclimatized'

---

[72] [1968] OJ Spec. Ed. L257/2.

[73] Case 13/76 [1976] ECR 1333. See also Case 36/74 *Walrave and Koch* [1974] ECR 1405.

[74] Case C–415/93 *Union Royale Belge des Sociétés de Football Association* v. *Bosman* [1995] ECR I–4921.

[75] See also Case C–176/96 *Lehtonen* v. *FRBSB*, judgment of 13 Apr. 2000, paras. 32–34 and Joined Cases C–51/76 and C–191/97 *Deliège*, judgment of 11 Apr. 2000, paras. 41–44. See also Declaration No. 29 on sport annexed to the Treaty of Amsterdam.

foreigners in domestic league matches from the 1992 season—the so-called '3+2 rule'.[76] This rule was challenged in the now infamous case of *Bosman*.[77] The Court, referring to the principle of non-discrimination contained in Article 48(2) [new Article 39(2)] and Article 4 of Regulation 1612/68, said that the principle applied to clauses contained in the regulations of sporting associations which restricted the rights of nationals of other Member States to take part, as professional players, in football matches. The Court said that it was irrelevant that the clauses did not concern the employment of such players, on which there was no restriction, but the extent to which their clubs could field them in official matches. The Court said that in so far as participation in official matches was the essential purpose of a professional player's life, a rule which restricted that participation obviously also restricted the chances of employment of the player concerned. The Court also said that since the nationality clauses did not concern matches between teams representing their countries but applied to all official matches between clubs, and thus to the essence of the activity of professional players, the nationality clauses could not be justified. If this were otherwise Article 48 [new Article 39] would be 'deprived of its practical effect and the fundamental right of free access to employment which the Treaty confers individually on each worker in the Community rendered nugatory'.

3. Indirect Discrimination

The principle of equal treatment not only forbids overt or direct discrimination on the grounds of nationality but also prohibits all covert forms of discrimination which, by the application of other criteria of differentiation, lead in fact to the same result.[78] In *O'Flynn*[79] the Court explained what was meant by covert or indirect discrimination. It said:[80]

[C]onditions imposed by national law must be regarded as indirectly discriminatory where, although applicable irrespective of nationality, they affect essentially migrant workers[81] or the great majority of those affected are migrant workers,[82] where they are indistinctly applicable but can be more easily satisfied by national workers than by

---

[76] *Financial Times*, 27 Jan. 1990 and 19 Apr. 1991.

[77] Case C–415/93 [1995] ECR I–4921.

[78] Case 152/73 *Sotgiu v. Deutsche Bundespost* [1974] ECR 153.

[79] Case C–237/94 *O'Flynn v. Adjudication Officer* [1996] ECR I–2617. See also Case C–281/98 *Angonese*, judgment of 6 June 2000, paras. 41–42.

[80] Paras. 18–19.

[81] Citing Case 41/84 *Pinna v. Caisse d'allocations familiales de la Savoie* [1986] ECR 1, para. 24; Case 33/88 *Allué and Coonan v. Universitá degli studia di Venezia* [1989] ECR 1591, para. 12; Case C–27/91 *URSSAF v. Hostellerie Le Manoir* [1991] ECR I–5531, para. 11.

[82] Case C–279/89 *Commission v. United Kingdom* [1992] ECR I–5785, para. 42, and Case C–272/92 *Maria Chiara Spotti v. Freistaat Bayern* [1993] ECR I–5185, para. 18.

migrant workers[83] or where there is a risk that they may operate to the particular detriment of migrant workers.[84]

It is otherwise only if those provisions are justified by objective considerations independent of the nationality of the workers concerned, and if they are proportionate to the legitimate aim pursued by national law.

Therefore, the Court said, unless objectively justified and proportionate to its aim, the provision of national law must be regarded as indirectly discriminatory and contrary to Community law if it is intrinsically liable to affect migrant workers more than national workers and if there is a risk that it will place migrant workers at a particular disadvantage. The Court added that it is not necessary to find that the measure in question does in practice affect a substantially higher proportion of migrant workers. It is sufficient that it is liable to have such an effect.[85]

The Court's case law has revealed a variety of examples of indirectly discriminatory conduct. Some involve service requirements in the host Member State. For example, in *Ugliola*[86] German law provided that a period spent performing military service in Germany had to be taken into account by an employer when calculating periods of service but not periods of service undertaken abroad. This was indirectly discriminatory since it had a greater impact on non-German nationals working in Germany who were more likely to have done their military service in their own country. The Court said that a non-German national's military service performed in his own Member State should also be taken into account.[87] Similarly in *Schöning-Kougebetopoulou*[88] the Court found that the conditions laid down in a collective agreement (the BAT) for promotion on grounds of seniority which took no account of a person's service abroad 'manifestly work to the detriment of migrant workers who have spent part of their careers in the public service of another Member State. For that reason they are such as to contravene the principle of non-discrimination laid down by Article 48 [new Article 39] of the Treaty and Article 7(1) and (4) of Regulation No. 1612/68'. It added that the finding was not called into question by the fact that some employees of the German public service might encounter the same situation as migrant workers or by the fact that the public service was

[83] Citing Case C–111/91 *Commission* v. *Luxembourg* [1993] ECR I–817, para. 10, and Case C–349/87 *Paraschi* v. *Landesversicherungsanstalt Württemberg* [1991] ECR I–4501, para. 23.

[84] Citing Case C–175/88 *Biehl* [1990] ECR I–1779, para. 14, and Case C–294/90 *Bachmann* v. *Belgium* [1992] ECR I–249, para. 9.

[85] Cf. the position in respect of sex equality and Case C–167/97 *R* v. *Secretary of State for Employment, ex parte Seymour-Smith and Perez* [1999] ECR I–623 considered in Ch. 4.

[86] Case 15/69 *Württembergische Milchverwertung Südmilch AG* v. *Ugliola* [1969] ECR 363.

[87] See also Case C–27/91 *Le Manoir* [1991] ECR I–5531 and Case C–419/92 *Scholz* v. *Opera Universitaria de Cagliari* [1994] ECR I–505.

[88] Case C–15/96 *Kalliope Schöning-Kougebetopoulou* v. *Freie und Hansestadt Hamburg* [1998] ECR I–47. See also Case C–187/96 *Commission* v. *Greece* [1998] ECR I–1095.

governed by different organizational and operational rules in the different Member States.

Other cases have concerned residence requirements which have also been found to be indirectly discriminatory.[89] This point was recognized by the Court in *Clean Car*.[90] The case concerned an Austrian rule that in order to exercise a trade in Vienna the manager had to be resident in Austria. Clean Car brought proceedings contending that its manager, although resident in Berlin, was entitled as an employee in its service and therefore a worker to enjoy the right of free movement established by Article 48 [new Article 39]. The Court noted that although the Austrian rule applied without regard to the nationality of the person to be appointed as manager, national rules under which a distinction is drawn on the basis of residence were liable to operate mainly to the detriment of nationals of other Member States, as non-residents were in the majority of cases foreigners. It therefore constituted indirect discrimination based on nationality, contrary to Article 48(2) [new Article 39(2)] of the Treaty.

Foreign language assistants have also found themselves the subject of indirect discrimination. In *Allué and Coonan*,[91] for example, Italian law limited the duration of contracts of employment of foreign language assistants, without imposing the same limitation on other workers. Since only 25 per cent of foreign language assistants were Italian nationals the fixed-term contracts imposed by the legislation on those working as foreign language assistants essentially concerned workers who were nationals of other Member States. The Court said this rule was indirectly discriminatory. It confirmed that the 'principle of equal treatment of which Article 48(2) [new Article 39(2)] is one embodiment prohibits not only overt discrimination on the ground of nationality but all covert forms of discrimination which, by applying other distinguishing criteria, in fact achieve the same result'.[92] The Court was faced with a similar problem in *Spotti*,[93] this time in respect of a German law which required contracts with foreign language assistants to be for a limited duration. The Court ruled that the German law was indirectly discriminatory contrary to Article 48(2) unless it was justified 'for objective reasons' unrelated to nationality.[94]

---

[89] Case 205/84 *Commission v. Germany* (Insurance Services) [1986] ECR 3755; see also Case C–111/91 *Commission v. Luxembourg* [1993] ECR I–817 where a residence requirement was considered indirectly discriminatory contrary to Art. 7(2) of Regulation 1612/68 on the free movement of workers and Case C–57/96 *Meints v. Minister van Landbouw* [1997] ECR I–6689.

[90] Case C–350/96 [1998] ECR I–2521.

[91] Case 33/88 [1989] ECR 1591.

[92] See also Case 41/84 *Pinna* [1986] ECR 1.

[93] Case C–272/92 [1993] ECR I–5185.

[94] Case C–107/94 *Asscher* [1996] ECR I–3089; Case C–279/93 *Finanzamt Köln v. Schumacker* [1995] ECR I–225; Case C–80/94 *Wielockx v. Inspecteur der Directe Belastingen* [1995] ECR I–2493.

4. Non-discriminatory Measures: Measures which Hinder Free Movement

While many of the earlier cases concerned measures which either directly or indirectly discriminated against non-nationals, more recent cases have concerned measures which, while not discriminatory in the true sense of the term because they do not discriminate either in law or in fact, nevertheless impede access to the market in other Member States in some way. This can be seen in *Bosman*.[95] Not only did Bosman object to the 3+2 rule but he also complained that the rules laid down by sporting associations under which a professional footballer who was a national of one Member State could not, on the expiry of his contract with a club, be employed by another club unless the latter club had paid to the former a transfer, training, or development fee, breached Article 48 [new Article 39]. The rules were not discriminatory, because they also applied to transfers between clubs belonging to different national associations within the same Member States and were similar to those governing transfers between clubs belonging to the same national association. Nevertheless, the Court said that 'the transfer rules constitute *an obstacle to the freedom of movement of workers* prohibited in principle by Article 48 of the Treaty [new Article 39]'[96] (emphasis added). The Court had already adopted this approach in the context of services. In *Säger*,[97] for example, the Court talked of 'the abolition of any restriction, even if it applies without distinction to national providers of services and to those of other Member States when it is liable to prohibit or otherwise impede the activities of a provider of services established in another Member State'.[98] This approach can also be found in the context of the case law on establishment. In *Gebhard*[99] the Court said that national measures breached Article 52 [new Article 43] which were '*liable to hinder or make less attractive* the exercise of fundamental freedoms guaranteed by the Treaty' (emphasis added).

If, however, the national rule is non-discriminatory and there is no direct

---

[95] Case C–415/93 [1995] ECR I–4921. See generally Weatherill (1996) 33 *CMLRev*. 991.

[96] Para. 104. Similarly in Case C–176/96 *Lehntonen*, judgment of 13 April 2000, para. 49 the Court said that rules laid down by a national sporting association which prohibited a basketball club from fielding players from other Member States in matches in the national championship, where the players have been transferred after a specified date, were liable to restrict the freedom of movement of players who wished to pursue their activity in another Member State contrary to Art. 48 [ex Art.39]. On the other hand, in Joined Cases C–51/96 and C–191/97 *Deliège*, judgment of 11 April 2000, the Court said that a rule requiring professional or semi-professional athletes to have been authorized or selected by their federation in order to be able to participate in a high-level international sports competition (which does not involve national teams competing against each other) did not in itself contravene Art. 59 [new Art. 49], as long as it derived from a need inherent in the organization of such a competition.

[97] Case C–76/90 *Säger* v. *Dennemayer* [1991] ECR I–4221.

[98] See also Case C–275/92 *H.M. Customs and Excise* v. *Schindler* [1994] ECR I–1039; Case C–384/93 *Alpine Investments* v. *Minister van Financiën* [1995] ECR I–1141.

[99] Case C–55/94 [1995] ECR I–4165.

hindrance of access of workers to the labour market then there is no breach of Article 39 [ex Article 48]. This was the situation in *Graf*.[100] In that case Graf, a German national, had worked for his Austrian employer for four years when he terminated his contract in order to take up employment in Germany. Under Austrian law, a worker who had worked for the same employer for more than three years was entitled to compensation when his employment came to an end, unless the job terminated on the worker's own initiative. Relying on *Bosman*, Graf argued that this rule contravened Article 48 [new Article 39] because it constituted an obstacle to the free movement of workers. The Court disagreed. It said that the Austrian law was genuinely non-discriminatory and that

it was not such as to preclude or deter a worker from ending his contract of employment in order to take a job with another employer, because the entitlement to compensation on termination of employment is not dependent on the worker's choosing whether or not to stay with his current employer but on a future and hypothetical event, namely the subsequent termination of his contract without such termination being at his own initiative or attributable to him.

Such an event is too uncertain and indirect a possibility for legislation to be capable of being regarded as liable to hinder free movement for workers.[101]

5. Defences and Justifications

As we have seen, directly discriminatory measures breach the Treaty provision but defences can be found in one of the express derogations (public policy, public security, public health, and employment in the public service).[102] By contrast, in the case of indirectly discriminatory and non-discriminatory measures which directly hinder free movement, there is also breach of Articles 39, 43, and 49 [ex Articles 48, 52, and 59] unless they can be objectively justified, in which case there is no breach, or saved by one of the express derogations.

As we have seen in *O'Flynn*, the language of objective justification was used in the context of free movement of workers. In respect of establishment and services, the Court tends to talk about justifications in the 'public' or 'general' interest or 'imperative requirements'.[103] In *Gebhard* (concerning Article 52 [new Article 43]) the Court elaborated on these requirements. It said that national measures liable to hinder or make less attractive the exercise of

---

[100] Case C–190/98 *Graf v. Filzmozer Maschienebau GmbH* [2000] All ER (EC) 170.

[101] Paras. 24–25.

[102] This is the orthodox position: see Case C–288/89 *Stichting Collectieve Antennvoorziening Gouda v. Comissariaat voor de Media* [1991] ECR I–4007. Cf. Case C–120/95 *Decker v. Caisse de Maladie des Employés Privés* [1998] ECR I–1831 and Case C–158/98 *Kohll v. Union des Caisses de Maladie des Employés Privés* [1998] ECR I–1935.

[103] Cases 205/84 *Commission v. Germany* (Insurance Services) [1986] ECR 3755.

fundamental freedoms guaranteed by the Treaty must fulfil four conditions in order not to breach Article 52: they must be applied in a non-discriminatory manner; they must be justified by imperative requirements in the general interest; they must be suitable for securing the attainment of the objective which they pursue; and they must not go beyond what is necessary to attain it.[104] The different terminology might suggest different justifications are allowed in respect of each Treaty provision but this has yet to be clearly articulated by the Court.[105]

For present purposes, the scope of the justifications will be considered in the context of the cases on workers. In *Bosman*[105A] the justifications raised were that in view of the considerable social importance of sporting activities and in particular football in the Community, the aims of maintaining a balance between the clubs by preserving a certain degree of equality and uncertainty as to results and of encouraging the recruitment and training of young players had to be accepted as legitimate. However, the Court also supported Bosman's contention that the application of the transfer rules was not an adequate means of maintaining financial and competitive balance in the world of football. Those rules neither precluded the richest clubs from securing the services of the best players nor prevented the availability of financial resources from being a decisive factor in competitive sport, thus considerably altering the balance between clubs.

The Court also accepted that the prospect of receiving transfer, development, or training fees was likely to encourage football clubs to seek new talent and train young players. However, it said that since it was impossible to predict the sporting future of young players with any certainty and because only a limited number of such players went on to play professionally, those fees were by nature contingent and uncertain and were, in any event, unrelated to the actual cost borne by clubs of training both future professional players and those who would never play professionally. The prospect of receiving such fees could not therefore be either a decisive factor in encouraging recruitment and training of young players or an adequate means of financing such activities, particularly in the case of smaller clubs. As the Advocate General pointed out,

---

[104] Para. 37, citing Case C–19/92 *Kraus* v. *Land Baden-Württemberg* [1993] ECR I–1663, para. 32. See also, in the context of services, Case 205/84 *Commission* v. *Germany* (Insurance Services) [1986] ECR 3755 where the Court made clear that measures liable to hinder trade could be justified on public interest grounds other than nationality, provided the measures taken were proportionate.

[105] See generally Daniele, 'Non-discriminatory Restrictions to the Free Movement of Persons' (1997) 22 *ELRev.* 191.

[105A] Case C–415/93 [1995] ECR I–4921. In Case C–176/96 *Lehntonen*, judgment of 13 April 2000, the Court recognized that transfer periods could be justified on the grounds of ensuring the regularity of sporting competitions. Late transfers could substantially change the sporting strength of one or other team in the course of the championship. This would call into question the comparability of results between the teams taking part in that championship, and consequently the proper functioning of the championship as a whole.

the same aims could be achieved at least as efficiently by other means which did not impede freedom of movement of workers. He suggested two possibilities. First, it would be possible to determine by collective agreement specified limits for the salaries to be paid to the players by the clubs. Secondly, it would be conceivable to distribute the clubs' receipts among the clubs. Specifically, that meant that part of the income obtained by a club from the sale of tickets for its home matches should be distributed to the other clubs. Similarly, the income received for awarding the rights to transmit matches on television could be divided up between all the clubs. The Court therefore concluded that Article 48 [new Article 39] precluded the application of rules laid down by sporting associations under which a professional footballer who was a national of one Member State could not, on the expiry of his contract with a club, be employed by a club of another Member State unless the latter club had paid to the former a transfer fee.

Thus, in *Bosman* the Court adopted a fairly rigorous approach to justification. This was also the case in *Schöning*[106] and *Clean Car*.[107] In *Schöning* the Court considered whether discrimination (based on length of service) could be justified on the ground that the purpose of the collective agreement (BAT) was to reward loyalty to the employer and to motivate the employee by the prospect of improvement in his financial situation. The German Government explained that the BAT covered not only the majority of German public institutions but also other undertakings performing public interest tasks. For this very reason, the Court ruled that to take into account periods of employment completed with one of those institutions in determining seniority for the purposes of promotion could not, given the multiplicity of employers, be justified by the desire to reward employee loyalty. The system afforded employees covered by the BAT considerable mobility within a group of legally separate employers and therefore the discrimination could not be justified.

In *Clean Car* the Court also considered whether discrimination on the grounds of residence could be justified. The Austrian government that the residence requirement was intended to ensure that the manager could be served with notice of fines which might be imposed upon him, that they could be enforced against him and that the manager had to be in a position to act effectively in the business. The Court rejected such justifications, ruling that the residence requirement was either inappropriate for ensuring that the aim pursued was achieved or went beyond what was necessary for that purpose. The Court reasoned that, in the first place, the fact that the manager resided in the Member State in which the undertaking was established and exercised its trade did not itself necessarily ensure that he would be in a position to act effectively as manager in the business. A manager residing in the State but at a considerable distance from the place at which the undertaking exercised its

---

[106] Case C–15/96 [1998] ECR I–47.
[107] Case C–350/96 [1998] ECR I–2521.

trade would normally find it more difficult to act effectively in the business than a person whose place of residence, even if in another Member State, was at no great distance from that at which the undertaking exercised its trade. Secondly, the Court said that other less restrictive measures were available, such as serving notice of fines at the registered office of the undertaking employing the manager and ensuring that they would be paid by requiring a guarantee to be provided beforehand. *Clean Car* and *Schöning* make it clear that the Court is not willing to find justifications easily for indirectly discriminatory measures.

6. Nationality and Reverse Discrimination

The Treaty provisions on free movement of persons apply to workers, the self-employed, and the suppliers of services who are nationals of a Member State. The determination of nationality is a question of *national* rather than Community law.[108] Articles 39, 43, and 49 [ex Articles 48, 52, and 59] can be invoked only by those individuals who move from one Member State to another. This is made explicit in Article 43 [ex Article 52] which refers clearly to 'the freedom of establishment of nationals of a Member State in the territory of another Member State'. This means that the free movement provisions cannot be applied to 'activities which have no factor linking them with any of the situations governed by Community law and which are confined in all aspects within a single Member State'.[109] This means that, in principle, nationals cannot invoke the free movement provisions against their own Member States. This was confirmed in *Knoors*[110] where the Court said 'the provisions of the Treaty relating to establishment and the provisions of services cannot be applied to situations which are purely internal to a Member State'. Therefore, in *Morson and Jhanjhan*,[111] two women of Surinamese origin wishing to join their children who were Dutch nationals living in the

---

[108] This is confirmed by the Declaration on Nationality of a Member State appended to the end of the TEU which provides that 'the question whether an individual possesses the nationality of a Member State shall be settled solely by reference to the national law of the Member States concerned'. See generally Greenwood, 'Nationality and the Limits of Free Movement of Persons in Community Law' (1987) 7 YEL 185, esp. 187–93. In the case of a person with dual nationality, the Court ruled in Case C–369/90 *Micheletti* v. *Dalagacíon del Gobierno en Cantabria* [1992] ECR I–4239 that if a person was able to produce one of the documents referred to in Council Directive 73/148/EEC [1973] OJ L172/14 to prove they were nationals of one Member State, other Member States were not entitled to dispute that status on the ground that the persons concerned were also nationals of a non-Member State, the nationality of which took precedence under the host state's law.

[109] See e.g. Case C–18/95 *Terhoeve* v. *Inspecteur van de Belastingdienst Particulieren* [1999] ECR I–345, para. 26; Joined Cases C–64/96 and C–65/96 *Uecker and Jacquet* v. *Land Nordrhein-Westfalen* [1997] ECR I–3171, para. 16.

[110] Case 115/78 *Knoors* v. *Staatssecretaris van Economishe Zaken* [1979] ECR 399.

[111] Joined Cases 35 and 36/82 *Morson and Jhanjhan* v. *Netherlands State* [1982] ECR 3723.

Netherlands, could not rely on Community law rights to enable them to stay in the Netherlands. The Court found that since the children had never exercised their right of free movement within the Community, the situation was wholly internal to the Member State and consequently Community law did not apply.[112] The same rule applies in the field of freedom of establishment and the provision of services.[113] This may well mean that migrant workers, who can take advantage of their Community law rights, enjoy more favourable treatment than nationals, who cannot—a situation referred to as reverse discrimination.[114]

However, Community nationals who, irrespective of their place of residence and nationality, have exercised their rights of free movement fall within the scope of Community law.[115] A purely hypothetical prospect of employment in another Member State will not suffice to establish a sufficient link with Community law.[116] However, as the Court found in *Surinder Singh*,[117] actual employment may provide the necessary Community law element to allow Community nationals to invoke the free movement provisions against their own Member States. Mr Surinder Singh, an Indian national, married a British citizen, Rashpal Purewal, in England in 1982. From 1983 to 1985, Mr and Mrs Singh lived and worked in Germany. Mrs Singh was employed on a part-time basis and was therefore a worker who was entitled under Community law to be joined by her spouse, irrespective of his nationality.[118] The couple returned to the UK in 1985 to run a business which they had bought. The question was raised whether Mr Surinder Singh was entitled to enter and remain in his wife's state of origin, relying this time on Article 52 [new Article 43], read in conjunction with Article 1(c) of Directive 73/148, which allows a Community national to be joined by her spouse.

The Court found that nationals who have gone to work in another Member State in order to exercise their Community law rights under Articles 48 and 52 [new Articles 39 and 43] were entitled to benefit from the Community

---

[112] See also e.g. Case 180/83 *Moser v. Land Baden-Württemberg* [1984] ECR 2539; Case 175/78 *R v. Saunders* [1979] ECR 1129; Case 44/84 *Hurd v. Jones* [1986] ECR 29; Case 298/84 *Iorio v. Azienda Autonoma delle Ferrovia dell Stato* [1986] ECR 247; Case C–332/90 *Steen v. Deutsche Bundespost* [1992] ECR I–342; Case C–60/91 *Criminal Proceedings against Batista Morais* [1992] ECR I–2085.

[113] Cases C–330–331/90 *Ministerio Fiscal v. Lopez Brea* [1992] ECR I–323. See also Case 136/78 *Ministère public v. Auer (No. 1)* [1979] ECR 437; Joined Cases C–54/88, C–91/88 and C–14/89 *Criminal Proceedings against Nino* [1990] ECR I–3537.

[114] 'Reverse discrimination arises when a national of a Member State is disadvantaged because he or she may not rely on a protective provision of Community law when a national of another Member State in otherwise identical circumstances may rely on that same provision' (Pickup, 'Reverse Discrimination and Freedom of Movement for Workers' (1986) 23 *CMLRev.* 135, 137).

[115] Case C–419/92 *Scholz* [1994] ECR I–505, para. 9.

[116] Case 180/83 *Moser* [1984] ECR 2539.

[117] Case C–370/90 *R v. IAT and Surinder Singh, ex parte Secretary of State for the Home Department* [1992] ECR I–4265. See also Case C–18/95 *Terhoeve* [1999] ECR I–345.

[118] Art. 10 of Regulation 1612/68, considered further below nn. 247–249.

secondary legislation. The Court explained that a national of a Member State might be deterred from exercising her Community law rights of free movement if, on returning to the Member State of origin, the conditions of her entry or residence were not at least equivalent to those which she would enjoy on entering the territory of another State, which would include the right to be accompanied by her spouse.

It seems that in this case there was a sufficient Community law element to enable the Singhs to rely on their Community law rights. Consequently, *Surinder Singh* serves only to confirm the earlier case of *Knoors*,[119] where the Court found that a Dutch plumber who had qualified and worked in Belgium was entitled to rely on his Community law rights to return to establish himself in the Netherlands using his Belgian qualifications. The Court said that his position was 'assimilated to that of another person enjoying their rights and liberties guaranteed by the Treaty'. However, in order to prevent the abuse of Community law, the Court said in *Surinder Singh* that the provisions of the Treaty could not be used as a means of evading the application of national legislation[120] and as a means of prohibiting Member States from taking the necessary measures to prevent such abuse.[121]

The Court's judgment in *Surinder Singh* was predicated on the fact that Mrs Singh was engaged in an economic activity: establishing a business. Her husband's rights of residence were dependent on her continuing to work. However, the position remains unclear if she voluntarily ceased to work. If her position was governed exclusively by Community law, it would seem, as the UK government suggested, that she could be deported on the grounds of public policy, public security, or public health, which would act as a deterrent to her exercising her right of free movement and contravene the general principle of international law that a State may not expel one of its own nationals nor may it deny them entry to its territory.[122] Perhaps the most sensible way of rationalizing these questions would be to say that while Mrs Singh, on returning to the Member State of origin, would enjoy the benefits of being a national, she would also enjoy any more favourable provisions of Community law. Therefore, she could bring her husband with her under

---

[119] Case 115/78 [1979] ECR 399. See also Case C–107/94 *Asscher* [1996] ECR I–3089.

[120] See also Joined Cases C–369/96 and C–376/96 *Arblade* v. *Le Loup and Sofrage SARL*, judgment of 23 Nov. 1999, para. 32, where the Court noted that the activities of the service provider were not wholly or principally directed towards the host State with a view to avoiding the rules which would apply to them if they were established within its territory. Cf. Case C–212/97 *Centros* v. *Erhvervs- og Selskabsstyrelsen* [1999] ECR I–1459, para. 27, where the Court said that the fact that a national of a Member State who wishes to set up a company chooses to form it in a Member State whose rules of company law seem to him the least restrictive and to set up branches in other Member States cannot, in itself, constitute an abuse of the right of establishment.

[121] The Singhs were absent from the UK for two years. The Court appeared to feel that this was long enough to be considered legitimate. On the other hand, in an earlier case decided by an English court, *R* v. *Secretary of State for the Home Department, ex parte Muhammad Ayub* [1983] 4 CMLR 140, three weeks in another Community country was deemed insufficient.

[122] See e.g. Art. 3 of the Fourth Protocol to the European Convention on Human Rights.

Community law rules, even if the national law rules would prevent his admission, but she could not be deported from her own Member State. This approach would minimize the distortion of rules relating to nationality, which have always lain within the competence of the Member States, while remaining consistent with the Community law principle of abolishing obstacles to free movement of workers and improving living and working conditions.

C. FREE MOVEMENT OF WORKERS

Article 39(1) [ex Article 48(1)] lays down the principle that workers should enjoy the right of free movement, which includes the abolition of any discrimination based on nationality, as regards employment, remuneration, and other conditions of work and employment.[123] The right of free movement includes the right to accept offers of employment actually made, to move freely within the territory of the Member States for this purpose, to stay in the Member State for the purpose of the employment, and to remain in the Member State after having been employed.[124] These rights, however, do not apply to employment in the public service[125] and are subject to limitations justified on the grounds of public policy, public security or public health.[126]

1. Who is a 'Worker'?

The term 'worker' is not defined in the Treaty. Nevertheless the Court has insisted that it be given a broad Community meaning to ensure uniformity of interpretation across all Member States.[127] In *Lawrie-Blum*[128] the Court said that the term 'worker' had to be defined in accordance with objective criteria which distinguish the employment relationship by reference to the rights and duties of the persons concerned. The essential feature of an employment relationship is that 'for a certain period of time a person performs services for and under the direction of another person in return for which he receives remuneration'. In *Levin*[129] the Court added the criterion that the work must be 'genuine and effective' and not purely marginal and ancillary. The key issue is whether a relationship of subordination exists which is for the

---

[123] Art. 39(2) [ex Art. 48(2)].
[124] Art. 39(3) [ex Art. 48(3)].
[125] Art. 39(4) [ex Art. 48(4)].
[126] Art. 39(3) [ex Art. 48(3)].
[127] See Case 75/63 *Unger v. Bestuur* [1964] ECR 1977; Case 53/81 *Levin* [1982] ECR 1035, paras. 11–12; Case 139/85 *Kempf v. Staatssecretaris van Justitie* [1986] ECR 1741, para. 15; Case 66/85 *Lawrie-Blum v. Land Baden-Württemberg* [1986] ECR 2121, para. 16.
[128] Case 66/85 [1986] ECR 2121, paras. 16–17.
[129] Case 53/81 [1982] ECR 1035.

national court to decide.[130] Both the sphere of employment[131] and the nature
of the legal relationship between employer and employee, whether involving
public law status or a private law contract,[132] are immaterial. Therefore, in
Lawrie-Blum the Court found that a trainee teacher had to be regarded as a
worker for the purpose of Article 48(1) [new Article 39(1)].

A guarantee of work is not actually necessary before the case falls within
Article 39. In *Raulin*[133] the employment contract described Raulin as an
'*oproepkracht*' (on-call worker), where no work was actually guaranteed and
often 'the person involved works only a very few days per week or hours per
day'; nor was the '*oproepkracht*' obliged to take up the work offered. The Court
said that to be regarded as a worker, 'a person must perform effective and
genuine activities to the exclusion of activities on such a small scale as to be
purely marginal and ancillary'.[134] The Court said an '*oproepkracht*' could be a
worker but it was a matter for the national court to decide, taking into
account the irregular nature and limited duration of the services actually
performed.

The work must constitute an economic activity within the meaning of
Article 2 EC. Generally, the pursuit of an activity as an employed person or
the provision of services for remuneration satisfies this requirement.[135] Thus,
as we have seen, sportsmen and women, including footballers, can be workers.[136] But this may not always be the case. For example, participation in a
community-based religion or another form of philosophy may not fall within
the field of application of Community law. This point was raised in the case of
Steymann.[137] Steymann worked as a plumber for a Bhagwan community as
part of its commercial activities. In return, the community looked after his
material needs and paid him pocket money. The Court considered that since
this might constitute an indirect *quid pro quo* for genuine and effective work
Steymann could be considered a worker. In *Bettray*,[138] by contrast, the Court
found that paid activity provided by the state as part of a drug rehabilitation
programme did not represent 'real and genuine economic activity'. This case
is, however, exceptional: generally a person would be considered a worker
when engaged in most other lawful activities.

[130] Case C–337/97 *Meeusen v. Hoofddirectie van de Informatie Beheer Groep*, judgment of 8 June
1999. According to Case C–107/94 *Asscher* [1996] ECR I–3089 the director of a company of
which he is the sole shareholder is not a worker, but in *Meeusen* the Court said that result cannot
be automatically transposed to his spouse.
[131] Case 36/74 *Walrave and Koch* [1974] ECR 1405.
[132] Case 152/73 *Sotgiu* [1974] ECR 153.
[133] Case C–357/89 *Raulin v. Minister van Onderwijs en Wetenschappen* [1992] ECR I–1027.
[134] Para. 10.
[135] See e.g. Case 13/76 *Dona* [1976] ECR 1333. See also Case C–3/90 *Bernini v. Minister van
Onderwijs en Wetenschappen* [1992] ECR I–1071.
[136] Case C–415/93 *Bosman* [1995] ECR I–4921; Case C–176/96 *Lehntonen*, judgment of 13
Apr. 2000 (basketball players).
[137] Case 196/87 *Steymann v. Staatssecretaris van Justitie* [1988] ECR 6159.
[138] Case 344/87 *Bettray v. Staatssecretaris van Justitie* [1989] ECR 1621.

The Court has also been faced by a number of cases concerning part-time workers. The first case, *Levin*,[139] concerned a British woman working in the Netherlands as a chambermaid. She earned less than the minimum required for subsistence, as defined by Dutch law. Nevertheless, the Court decided that the rules relating to free movement of workers also applied to part-time workers, even though part-timers earned less than the minimum wage of a particular Member State, provided that they were seriously engaged in a 'genuine and effective' economic activity. In addition, such activity should not be on such a small scale as to be purely marginal and ancillary.[140] Once identified as a worker, Levin could benefit from her Community rights, which in this case included entitlement to a residence permit. Her motives for entering the country were also irrelevant, because, as the Court recognized, part-time employment constitutes for a large number of people an effective means of improving their living conditions. The Court reasoned that if the enjoyment of rights conferred by the principle of free movement of workers were reserved solely to those in full-time employment and earning at least the minimum wage, the effectiveness of Community law would be impaired.

The Court had a further opportunity to refine its definition of 'effective and genuine' work in *Kempf*.[141] Kempf worked as a part-time music teacher, giving twelve music lessons a week. Although his income was supplemented by social security benefits paid out of public funds, the Dutch court had found that his work was not on such a small scale as to be purely marginal and ancillary. The Court then made clear that once a finding of effective and genuine employment had been established it was irrelevant whether the worker subsisted on the income, or whether the income was used to supplement other family income, as in *Levin*,[142] or was supplemented by money from public funds.

Although the provisions of Article 39 [ex Article 48] explicitly apply to those who have already found work in another Member State[143] the Court has extended the definition of worker to include those seeking work but not those who have lost their jobs. This was confirmed by *Martínez Sala*[144] where the Court said that 'Once the employment relationship has ended, the person concerned *as a rule* loses his status of worker, although that status may produce certain effects after the relationship has ended[145] and a person who is genuinely seeking work must be classified as a worker' (emphasis added).[146]

---

[139] Case 53/81 [1982] ECR 1035.

[140] In Case C–357/89 *Raulin* [1992] ECR I–1027 the Court said that the national court, when assessing the effective and genuine nature of the activity, can take account of the duration of the activities.

[141] Case 139/85 [1986] ECR 1741.

[142] Case 53/81 [1982] ECR 1035.

[143] Art. 39(3) [ex Art. 48(3)] also envisages that the worker has already found a job before leaving for the host State.

[144] Case C–85/96 *Martínez Sala* v. *Freistaat Bayern* [1998] ECR I–2691.

[145] See Case 39/86 *Lair* v. *Universität Hannover* [1988] ECR 3161 discussed below, n. 226.

[146] Para. 32.

The period allowed for the worker to remain in the host Member State looking for work depends on the rules of that State but workers must be allowed at least three months,[147] unless they are dependent on social security, in which case they may be asked to leave.[148] In the UK the period for which it is possible to remain looking for work is six months.[149] In the case of *ex parte Antonissen*[150] the Court found that this was compatible with Community law. If after the expiry of the six-month period the worker can show that he or she has genuine chances of being engaged, they cannot be required to leave the host State. In *Commission* v. *Belgium*[151] the Court said that a Belgian law which required a work seeker to leave the country automatically on the expiry of three months breached Article 48 [new Article 39].

2. The Rights Consequent on Being a Worker

Once it is established that a person is a worker, he or she has access to a variety of rights under three principal secondary measures: Directive 68/360[152] on the rights of entry and residence, Regulation 1612/68 on free movement of workers, and Regulation 1251/70 on the right to remain. These will be considered in turn.

2.1 Rights of Entry and Residence: Directive 68/360

The Court has held that the provisions of the Treaty relating to free movement of persons are intended to facilitate the pursuit by Community citizens of occupational activities of all kinds throughout the Community, and preclude measures which might place Community citizens at a disadvantage when they wish to pursue an economic activity in the territory of another Member State.[153] They have the right, derived directly from the Treaty, to leave their country of origin to enter the territory of another Member State and reside there in order to pursue an economic activity.[154] Provisions which preclude or deter nationals of a Member State from leaving their country of origin in order to exercise their right to freedom of movement constitute an obstacle to that freedom even if they apply to all workers.[155] Consequently, in

---

[147] In certain circumstances work seekers are entitled to social security benefits for three months under Art. 69, Regulation 1408/71. See further Ch. 5.

[148] Declaration of Council accompanying Directive 68/360 [1968] OJ Spec. Ed. L257/13, and Regulation 1612/68 [1968] OJ Spec. Ed. L257/2.

[149] Statement of Changes to the Immigration Rules (HC 169).

[150] Case C–292/89 *R* v. *IAT, ex parte Antonissen* [1991] ECR I–745.

[151] C–344/95 *Commission* v. *Belgium* [1997] ECR I–1035.

[152] [1968] (II) OJ Spec. Ed. L257/13.

[153] Case 143/87 *Stanton* v. *INASTI* [1988] ECR 3877, para. 13.

[154] Art. 39(3)(b) and (c). See also Case C–363/89 *Roux* v. *Belgium* [1991] ECR I–273, para. 9.

[155] Case C–10/90 *Masgio* v. *Bundesknappschaft* [1991] ECR I–1119, paras. 18–19.

Bosman[156] the Court said that the rights guaranteed by Article 48 [new Article 39] would be rendered meaningless if the Member State of origin could prohibit nationals wishing to engage in gainful employment from leaving in order to establish themselves in another Member State. As a result, the Court concluded that the rules on transfer fees constituted an obstacle to freedom of movement for workers, since they directly affected players' access to the employment market in other Member States and contravened Article 48 [new Article 39] unless they pursued a legitimate aim compatible with the Treaty.

Directive 68/360 merely facilitates the exercise of the worker's right of free movement.[157] This Directive applies in particular to the worker's departure from one Member State and the entry into and residence in the host Member State. The Directive also applies to a worker's family,[158] as defined by Article 10 of Regulation 1612/68.[159] Directive 68–360 provides the following rights:

(a) Right to Depart

The right to move freely includes the right to depart from a Member State, not necessarily the state of origin, where the worker and his or her family currently live.[160] Nationals, and members of their families, may leave the Member State on the production of a valid identity card or passport, specifying the person's nationality, which the Member State is obliged to issue or renew.[161] The passport[162] must be valid for all Member States and for any States through which the holder must pass when travelling between Member States.[163] Having produced a passport or identity card, the Member State may not demand from the worker an exit visa or similar document.[164] Article 10 recognizes derogations on grounds of public policy and public health.

(b) Right to Enter

Member States must allow workers and their families to enter the territory of the host State on the production of an identity card or passport.[165] No entry visa or other entry formality can be demanded from workers[166] and their families except from a member of the worker's family who is not an EC

---

[156] Case C–415/93 [1995] ECR I–4921, para. 94; Case C–18/95 *Terhoeve* [1999] ECR I–345, para. 37; and Case C–190/98 *Graf* [2000] All ER (EC) 170, para. 22.

[157] See further Case 249/86 *Commission v. Germany* [1989] ECR 1263.

[158] Art. 1.

[159] [1968] OJ Spec. Ed. L257/2. See further text attached to nn. 247–249, below.

[160] Art. 2.

[161] Art. 2(1).

[162] If the passport is the only document with which the person may lawfully leave the country, it must be valid for at least five years.

[163] Art. 2(3).

[164] Art. 2(4).

[165] Art. 3(1).

[166] Case 157/79 *R v. Pieck* [1980] ECR 2171. The term 'entry visa' or equivalent requirement covers any formality for the purpose of granting leave to enter the territory of a Member State which is coupled with a passport or identity card check at the frontier.

national.[167] The compatibility of such border formalities with the notion of a 'Europe without internal frontiers' has been raised in two enforcement proceedings brought by the Commission. In the first, *Commission v. Belgium*,[168] the Belgian authorities asked, on a non-systematic basis, non-Belgian Community nationals residing in Belgium to produce their residence or establishment permit. The Court said that such controls could constitute a barrier to free movement if they were carried out in a systematic, arbitrary, or unnecessarily restrictive manner. However, on the facts, this was not the case. In the second case, *Commission v. Netherlands*,[169] the Court ruled that national legislation providing that citizens of Member States could be required to answer questions put by border officials regarding the purpose and duration of their journey and the financial means at their disposal, was incompatible with Directive 68/360.

(c) Residence

Member States must grant the right of residence to workers and their families on production of the listed documents.[170] As proof of the right of residence a permit must be issued to workers and their families.[171] Therefore, in *Giagounidis*[172] the Court ruled that the host Member State had to grant the right of residence to a worker who produced a valid identity card, even if the card did not authorize its holder to leave the territory of the State in which it was issued. Community law also allows a Member State to carry out checks on compliance with the obligation to be able to produce a residence permit at all times, provided that it imposes the same obligation on its own nationals as regards their identity cards.[173] In the event of failure to comply with that obligation, the national authorities are entitled to impose penalties comparable to those attaching to minor offences committed by their own nationals, such as those laid down in respect of failure to carry an identity card, provided that they do not impose a penalty so disproportionate that it becomes an obstacle to the free movement of workers.[174] Member States are also not allowed to treat nationals of other Member States residing in the host State disproportionately differently, as regards the degree of fault and the scale of fines, from nationals when they commit a comparable infringement of the obligation to carry a valid identity document.[175]

---

[167] Art. 3(2). In Case 157/79 *Pieck* [1980] ECR 2171 the Court extended the prohibition on host Member States demanding any entry visa to cover any formality for granting leave to enter a territory.

[168] Case 321/87 *Commission v. Belgium* [1989] ECR 997.

[169] Case C–68/89 [1991] ECR I–2637.

[170] Art. 4(1). The right of entry and residence of a student cannot be made conditional on the granting of a residence permit: Case C–357/89 *Raulin* [1992] ECR I–1027.

[171] Art. 4(2) and Case 48/75 *Royer* [1976] ECR 497.

[172] Case C–376/89 *Giagounidis v. Stadt Reutlingen* [1991] ECR I–1069.

[173] Case 321/87 *Commission v. Belgium* [1989] ECR 997, para. 12.

[174] Case 265/88 *Criminal proceedings against Messner* [1989] ECR 4209, para. 14.

[175] Case C–24/97 *Commission v. Germany* [1998] ECR I–2133, para. 15.

The residence permit must be valid throughout the territory of the Member State which issued it, it must be valid for five years, and automatically renewable.[176] Breaks in residence not exceeding six consecutive months and absence on military service will not affect the validity of residence permits.[177] However, completion of the formalities for obtaining a residence permit will not hinder the immediate start of employment under a contract concluded by the applicants:[178] the worker's right to reside is not dependent upon the possession of a residence permit since, according to *Watson and Belmann*,[179] the right of residence is a fundamental right derived from the Treaty. In that case the Court found that an Italian law providing that migrants would be deported if they failed to register with the Italian authorities within three days of entering Italy was disproportionate.[180]

This residence permit issue re-emerged in the recent and important decision in *Martínez Sala*.[181] Sala, a Spanish national, had been living in Germany since 1956. She had held various residence permits which had expired and a series of documents saying that she had applied for an extension of her permit. It was during this period that she gave birth and applied for a child allowance. Her application was rejected by the German authorities on the grounds that she did not have German nationality, a residence entitlement, or a residence permit. The Court said that for the purposes of recognition of the right of residence, a residence permit can have only declaratory and probative force.[182] On the facts of this case, possession of a residence permit was constitutive of the right to the benefit. The Court therefore said that it was discriminatory for a Member State to require a national of another Member State, who wished to receive a benefit such as a child allowance, to produce a document which was constitutive of the right to the benefit and which was issued by its own authorities, when its own nationals were not required to produce any document of that kind.

A valid residence permit cannot be withdrawn from a worker solely on the ground that he or she is no longer in employment either due to temporary incapacity as a result of illness or accident or because of *involuntary* unemployment, confirmed by the competent employment office.[183] As far as temporary workers are concerned, workers entering a Member State for a period of between three months and a year must be given a temporary

---

[176] Art. 6.

[177] Art. 6(2).

[178] Art. 5.

[179] Case 118/75 [1976] ECR 1185.

[180] See also Case 265/88 *Messner* [1989] ECR 4209.

[181] Case C–85/96 [1998] ECR I–2691.

[182] See, to this effect, Case 48/75 *Royer* [1976] ECR 497, para. 50.

[183] Art. 7(1). When the residence permit is renewed for the first time the period of residence may be restricted, but not to less than 12 months, where the worker has been involuntarily unemployed in the Member State for more than 12 consecutive months.

residence permit, valid for the period of employment.[184] A temporary residence permit must also be issued to a seasonal worker employed for a period of more than three months.[185] However, in the case of workers staying for less than three months, entry documents will suffice without the need for a residence permit.[186] In the case of frontier workers,[187] the State where the workers are employed may issue them with a special permit valid for five years, and automatically renewable.[188]

The necessary residence documents must be issued and renewed free of charge, or on payment of an amount not exceeding the dues and taxes charged for the issue of identity cards to nationals.[189] Member States must also take the necessary steps to simplify the formalities and procedure for obtaining the relevant documents.[190] Therefore the Court found in *Commission* v. *Belgium*[191] that the Belgian requirement for issuing registration certificates which involved several stages, where a charge was levied at each stage and where the total sum was higher than that paid by nationals, breached Article 9(1).

2.2 Regulation 1612/68 on the Free Movement of Workers

Regulation 1612/68[192] is designed to facilitate the free movement of both workers and their families. The Council, when enacting this Regulation, 'took into account, first, the importance for the worker, from a human point of view of having his entire family with him and, secondly, the importance, from all points of view, of the integration of the worker and his family into the host Member state without any difference in treatment in relation to nationals of that State'.[193]

(a) Employment Conditions

Article 1 of Regulation 1612/68 reiterates the substance of Article 39 [ex Article 48]: any national of a Member State 'has the right to take up an

---

[184] Art. 6(3).

[185] Ibid., para. 2.

[186] Art. 8(1)(a).

[187] Frontier workers are those who have their residence in the territory of a Member State to which he returns, as a rule, each day or at least once a week but are employed in another Member State.

[188] Art. 8(1)(b).

[189] Art. 9(1).

[190] Art. 9(3).

[191] Case C–344/95 *Commission* v. *Belgium* [1997] ECR I–1035.

[192] [1968] OJ Spec. Ed. L257/2, amended by Regulation (EEC) 312/76 [1976] OJ L3/2 and Council Regulation (EEC) 2434/92 [1992] OJ L25/1. Previously measures existed which protected the national labour market: Regulation 15/1961 allowed a migrant worker to take a job in another Member State where, after three weeks, no national was available to take the job. This was changed by Regulation 38/1964 and Directive 64/240.

[193] Case 249/86 *Commission* v. *Germany* [1989] ECR 1263, para. 11.

activity as an employed person, and to pursue such activity, within the territory of another Member State', enjoying the same priority as a national. The
worker may conclude and perform contracts of employment in accordance
with the laws of the host State.[194] Any provisions which discriminate (either
directly or indirectly[195]) against foreign nationals or which are designed to
hinder foreign nationals from obtaining work are not permissible.[196]

The most important exception to this provision concerns 'conditions relating to linguistic knowledge required by reason of the nature of the post to be
filled'.[197] This provision was successfully relied upon by the Irish government
in *Groener*.[198] Groener, a Dutch woman, previously employed under a temporary contract of employment at a design college, was refused a permanent post
on the ground that she did not speak Gaelic. The Court upheld the requirement of the language qualification, even though it was not necessary to use
Gaelic in the job, because it was a clear policy of national law to maintain and
promote the use of the Irish language as a means of expressing national
culture and identity.[199] The Court continued that the Community did not
prohibit the adoption of a policy for the protection and promotion of a language which is both the national language and first official language.[200] It
concluded that since the role of teachers in the education process was an
important one in the implementation of such a policy, and that so long as
the language requirement was not disproportionate, it could fall within the
exception of Article 3(1).

Article 4(1) provides that national provisions which restrict, by number or
percentage, the employment of foreign nationals in any undertaking do not
apply to nationals of the other Member States. Therefore a French requirement that there be a ratio of three French seamen to one non-French seaman
on a merchant ship contravened Article 4(1).[201] If there is a requirement that
an undertaking is subject to a minimum percentage of national workers being
employed, nationals of the other Member States are counted as national
workers.[202] Article 6 provides that although the engagement and recruitment

---

[194] Art. 2.

[195] See text attached to nn. 73–94, above.

[196] Art. 3(1). Art. 3(2) lists particular examples, including prescribing a special recruitment
procedure for foreign nationals, restricting the advertising of vacancies in the press, and imposing additional requirements on applicants from other Member States of subjecting eligibility for
employment to conditions of registration with employment offices.

[197] Art. 3(1).

[198] Case 379/87 *Groener* v. *Minister for Education* [1989] ECR 3967; cf. Case C–281/98
Angonese, judgment of 6 June 2000, para. 43.

[199] e.g. Irish courses were compulsory for children receiving primary education and optional
for those receiving secondary education.

[200] See also Case C–274/96 *Bickel and Franz* [1998] ECR I–7637 where the Court observed that
in a Community based on the free movement of persons 'the protection of linguistic rights and
privileges of individuals is of particular importance'.

[201] Case 167/73 *Commission* v. *France (French Merchant Seamen)* [1974] ECR 359.

[202] Art. 4(2). This must be read in the light of Directive 63/607 [1963–64] OJ Spec. Ed. 52.

of a worker must not depend on medical, vocational, or other criteria which are discriminatory on the ground of nationality, the foreign worker may have to undergo a vocational test, if the employer expressly requests this when making his offer of employment.

(b) Employment and Equality of Treatment

Title II of the Regulation provides specific examples of the application of the principle of non-discrimination on the ground of nationality. Article 7(1) says that a migrant worker must not be treated 'differently from national workers in respect of any conditions of employment and work, in particular as regards remuneration, dismissal, and should he become unemployed, reinstatement or reemployment'.[203] Therefore in *Sotgiu*[204] it was held unlawful to treat an Italian postal worker working for Deutsche Bundespost less favourably than a German worker in the payment of an allowance for living away from home.

Article 7(2)[205] provides that a worker[206] will enjoy the same social and tax advantages as national workers. As far as taxation is concerned, recent cases have revealed the extent to which the application of national rules on taxation might have an indirectly discriminatory effect on foreign workers.[207] For example, *Schumacker*[208] concerned a Belgian national who lived in Belgium with his family but worked in Germany. His wages were subject to German income tax on a limited taxation basis due to the fact that he was a non-resident. This meant that he was denied certain benefits which were available to resident taxpayers. The Court recognized that national rules which drew a distinction based on residence, where non-residents were treated less favourably than residents, were liable to operate mainly to the detriment of nationals of other Member States since non-residents were, in the main, foreigners.

The Court then refined its definition of discrimination. It said that 'discrimination can arise only through the application of different rules to comparable situations or the application of the same rule to different situations'. In respect of direct taxes it said that the situations of residents and non-residents in a given state were not generally comparable since there were

---

[203] Art. 7(1) applies only to payments made by virtue of statutory or contracted obligations incumbent on the employer as a condition of employment: see Case C–315/94 *Peter de Vos v. Stadt Bielefeld* [1996] ECR I–1417.

[204] Case 152/73 [1974] ECR 153. See also Case 15/96 *Ugliola* [1969] ECR 363.

[205] For a detailed examination of this provision see O'Keeffe, 'Equal Rights for Migrants: The Concept of Social Advantages in Article 7(2), Regulation 1612/68' (1985) 5 YEL 92.

[206] Art. 7(2) applies to workers only, and not to work seekers: see Case 316/85 *CPAS de Courcelles v. Lebon* [1987] ECR 2811, although see now Case C–85/96 *Martínez Sala* [1998] ECR I–2691 and O'Leary, 'Putting Flesh on the Bones of European Union Citizenship' (1999) 24 ELRev. 68.

[207] It has always been clear that direct taxation falls within the competence of the Member States. However, as the Court pointed out in Case C–246/89 *Commission v. UK* [1991] ECR I–4585, the powers retained by the Member States in respect of taxation must be exercised consistently with Community law.

[208] Case C–279/93 [1995] ECR I–225.

objective differences between them from the point of view of the source of the income and the possibility of taking account of their ability to pay tax or their personal and family circumstances. Since this constituted different treatment of non-comparable situations this in itself did not constitute discrimination. However, on the facts of the case, a non-resident taxpayer who received all or almost all of his income in the State where he worked was objectively in the same situation as a resident in that State who did the same work there. Both were taxed in that State alone and their taxable income was the same, yet discrimination arose, because the non-resident taxpayer did not have his personal and family circumstances taken into account—either in his State of residence, because he received no income there, or in his State of employment, because he was not resident there. Consequently, his overall tax burden would be greater and he would be at a disadvantage compared to the resident taxpayer.

Article 7(2) also applies to 'social advantages'. The Court in *Even*[209] defined social advantages as benefits

which, whether or not linked to a contract of employment, are generally granted to national workers primarily because of their objective status as workers or *by virtue of the mere fact of their residence on the national territory* and the extension of which to workers who are nationals of other Member States therefore seems suitable to facilitate their mobility within the Community [emphasis added].

The concept of social advantage embraces benefits granted as of right,[210] benefits granted on a discretionary basis,[211] benefits granted after employment has terminated,[212] and even benefits not directly linked to employment such as language rights[213] and rights to bring in unmarried companions.[214] Article 7(2) also applies to beneficiaries who are not resident in the territory of the providing Member State.[215] This is particularly important in the case of frontier workers.[216]

The decision in *Even* paved the way for Article 7(2) to be applied not just to workers *qua* workers but also their families *qua* lawful residents (see the emphasis above). The Court justified this on the grounds that, first, Article

[209] Case 207/78 *Ministère public* v. *Even* [1979] ECR 2019.
[210] See e.g. Case C–111/91 *Commission* v. *Luxembourg* (child-birth loan) [1993] ECR I–817; Case C–85/96 *Martínez Sala* [1998] ECR I–2691, para. 28 (childraising allowance granted automatically to persons fulfilling certain objective criteria).
[211] Case 65/81 *Reina* v. *Landeskreditbank Baden-Württemberg* [1982] ECR 33 (free childbirth loan).
[212] See e.g. Case C–57/96 *Meints* [1997] ECR I–6689, para. 36 (simple payment to agricultural workers whose contract of employment is terminated). There is no *de minimis* rule for social advantages: Case C–237/94 *O'Flynn* [1996] ECR I–2617.
[213] Case 137/84 *Mutsch* [1985] ECR 2681.
[214] Case 59/85 *Netherlands* v. *Reed* [1986] ECR 1283.
[215] Case C–57/96 *Meints* [1997] ECR I–6689, para. 50; Case C–337/97 *Meeusen*, judgment of 8 June 1999, para. 21.
[216] Case C–337/97 *Meeusen*, judgment of 8 June 1999.

7(2) was essential to encourage free movement not just of workers but also of their families, without whom the worker would be discouraged from moving;[217] and secondly, it encouraged the integration of migrant workers into the working environment of the host country.[218] The broad scope of Article 7(2) 'social advantages' was made clear in the cases of *Christini*[219] and *Castelli*.[220] In *Christini* the French railways had a scheme which offered a fare reduction for large families. Christini, an Italian national resident in France and the widow of an Italian who had worked in France, was refused the reduction on the ground of her nationality. SNCF argued that Article 7(2) applied only to advantages connected with the contract of employment but the Court disagreed. It said that in view of the equality of treatment that Article 7(2) was designed to achieve, the substantive area of application had to be delineated so as to include all social and tax advantages, whether or not attached to the contract of employment, including reductions in fares for large families. It added that Article 7(2) applied to those lawfully entitled to remain in the host Member State, irrespective of whether the 'trigger' for the rights, the worker, was alive.

The Court adopted a similarly broad approach in *Castelli*. Castelli, an Italian national, lived in Belgium with her son. She had never worked in Belgium. She was refused a Belgian income guaranteed to old people on the grounds that she was not Belgian and that no reciprocal agreement existed between Belgium and Italy. Nevertheless, the Court found that the concept of social advantage in Article 7(2) should include the unconditional grant of income guaranteed to old people payable to a dependent relative in the ascending line, reasoning that the concept of equal treatment in Article 7(1) of Regulation 1612/68 was also intended to prevent discrimination against a worker's dependent relatives.

The significance of Article 7(2) has become particularly apparent in the context of maintenance grants for attending vocational training courses. Article 7(3) provides that a worker shall 'have access to training in vocational schools and retraining centres' under the same conditions as national workers. In *Gravier*[221] the Court defined vocational training broadly to include any

[217] See e.g. Case 94/84 *ONEM v. Deak* [1985] ECR 1873 where a Hungarian national, the son of an Italian working in Belgium, applied for unemployment benefit. Since unemployment benefit was found to constitute a social advantage within the meaning of Art. 7(2), the son was entitled to receive it, irrespective of the fact that he was not a Community national.

[218] See also Joined Cases 389 and 390/87 *Echternach and Moritz v. Minister van Onderwijs en Wetenschappen* [1989] ECR 723; Case C–308/93 *Bestuur van de Sociale Verzekeringsbank v. Cabanis-Issarte* [1996] ECR I–2097.

[219] Case 32/75 *Christini v. SNCF* [1975] ECR 1085. See also Case C–278/94 *Commission v. Belgium* [1996] ECR I–4307 (tideover benefits); Case C–185/96 *Commission v. Greece* [1998] ECR I–6601.

[220] Case 261/83 *Castelli v. ONPTS* [1984] ECR 3199.

[221] Case 293/83 *Gravier v. Ville de Liège* [1985] ECR 593 where the Court also confirmed that the principle of non-discrimination contained in Art. 7 EEC/Art. 6 EC [new Art. 12] applied to fees but not to maintenance grants.

form of education which prepares for a qualification or which provides the necessary training or skills for a particular profession, trade, or employment. Subsequently, in *Blaizot*,[222] the Court confirmed that vocational training could be received at universities, except in the case of courses intended for students 'wishing to improve their general knowledge rather than prepare themselves for a particular occupation'. A grant for attending such a training course is considered a 'social advantage' within the meaning of Article 7(2).[223] The potential benefit of the broad scope of Article 7(2) was shown in *Matteucci*.[224] Matteucci was the daughter of an Italian worker working in Belgium. She was educated in Belgium and it was assumed that she was now a worker in her own right, teaching rhythmics. She applied for a scholarship, available on a bilateral basis (Belgium–Germany) to study singing in Berlin but her application was rejected on the ground that she was not Belgian. The Court said that this was contrary to Article 7(2): a bilateral agreement reserving scholarships for nationals of the two Member States which were the parties to the agreement could not prevent the application of the principle of equality under Community law.

Matteucci's case was a strong one: she had lived and worked in Belgium all her life. But the case law on Article 7(2) is open to exploitation by those who work in another Member State for a short period of time and then claim entitlement to social advantages in the form of a grant for further study in the host Member State. The Court had to deal with this problem in two important cases. The first case, *Brown*,[225] concerned a student with dual French and British nationality who had lived in France for many years but had a place at Cambridge University to read engineering. He was sponsored by Ferranti in the UK and worked for the company for eight months before starting his course. He then claimed that he was a worker and was entitled to a grant from the British government under Article 7(2). The Court, however, refused to recognize that he was a worker because he had become a worker exclusively as a result of his admission to university.

The second case, *Lair*,[226] concerned a French woman who had moved to Germany where she worked on a series of part-time contracts. She then decided to study for a degree at the University of Hannover and sought a maintenance grant for that purpose. The Court held that a grant awarded for maintenance and vocational training with a view to pursuing university

---

[222] Case 24/86 *Blaizot v. Université de Liège and Others* [1988] ECR 379. See also Traversa, 'L'interdiction de discrimination en raison de la nationalité en matière d'accès à l'enseignement' (1989) 25 *Revue Trimestrielle de Droit Européen* 45.

[223] Case C–3/90 *Bernini* [1992] ECR I–1071 where the Court ruled that descendants of workers could rely on Art. 7(2) to obtain study finance under the same conditions as children of national workers. This also applies to non-resident children of a migrant worker: see Case C–337/97 *Meeusen*, judgment of 8 June 1999, para. 25.

[224] Case 235/87 *Matteucci v. Communauté française de Belgique* [1988] ECR 5589.

[225] Case 197/86 *Brown v. Secretary of State for Scotland* [1986] ECR 3205.

[226] Case 39/86 [1988] ECR 3161. See also Case C–357/89 *Raulin* [1992] ECR I–1027, para. 21.

studies leading to a professional qualification could constitute a social advantage within the meaning of Article 7(2). It then recognized that people who have previously pursued an effective and genuine activity in the host Member State but who were no longer employed could, nevertheless, be considered workers. A maintenance grant will be paid under Article 7(2) provided there is a link between the previous occupational activity[227] and the studies in question.[228] However, no link is required in the case of a migrant worker who has become involuntarily unemployed and is obliged by conditions on the job market to undertake occupational retraining in another field of activity.

The Court has imposed further limitations on the burgeoning scope of Article 7(2). The case of *Lebon*[229] concerned a French woman living in Belgium with her father who received a Belgian retirement pension. She wished to be granted the Belgian minimum means of subsistence (minimex) as a social advantage based on the fact that she was the descendant of a worker.[230] The Court, however, ruled that descendants did not retain the right to equal treatment with regard to a social benefit when they reached the age of 21, were no longer dependent on the worker and did not have the status of worker. Although it is not clear whether these three conditions should be read disjunctively or conjunctively, perhaps in the light of the subsequent discussions on the question of dependency in the judgment, the list is disjunctive.[231] Therefore, if Lebon could show that she was still dependent on her father she might have been entitled to the minimex.

The Court also found that Article 7(2) did not apply on the facts in *Even*.[232] The case concerned Belgian regulations providing that a retirement pension, normally granted at 65, could start to run at the request of an individual up to five years preceding the normal pension age, albeit with a reduction of 5 per cent per year of early payment. This reduction was not made in the case of Belgian nationals who served in the allied forces during the Second World War and who received an invalidity pension granted by an allied country for incapacity for work attributable to an act of war. Even, a French national living in Belgium, was in just such a position, receiving an invalidity pension from the French government and wishing to receive the full Belgian state pension. The Court concluded that the relevant Belgian legislation could not be considered an advantage granted to a national worker. It explained that the Belgian legislation benefited those who had given wartime service to their

---

[227] The host State cannot make the right to the same social advantages conditional upon a minimum period of prior occupational activity, see Case 39/86 *Lair* [1988] ECR 3161, para. 44.

[228] If no link exists between the study and the previous occupational activities the person does not retain the status as a migrant worker, see Case C–357/89 *Raulin* [1992] ECR I–1027.

[229] Case 316/85 [1987] ECR 2811 and Case C–3/90 *Bernini* [1992] ECR I–1071.

[230] She had received the minimex in her own right but it was discontinued as there was no evidence that she was looking for work.

[231] A view supported by Case C–3/90 *Bernini* [1992] ECR I–1071, para. 25.

[232] Case 207/78 [1979] ECR 2019.

own country and 'its essential objective is to give those nationals an advantage by reason of the hardships suffered for that country'. A similar issue was raised in *de Vos*.[233] De Vos, a Belgian national, was employed as a doctor by the German municipality of Bielefeld which paid contributions to a supplementary old-age and survivor's insurance scheme on his behalf. These contributions were not paid while he did his military service in Belgium. Had he been a German national German law required employers to pay the contributions while the employee did military service in the German army. The Court said that such an advantage, which was essentially linked to the performance of military service, could not be considered to be granted to national workers because of their objective status as workers or by virtue of the mere fact of their residence on the national territory, as defined by the *Even*[234] formula, and thus did not have the essential characteristics of social advantages as referred to in Article 7(2).

Finally, in *O'Flynn*[235] the Court limited the scope of 'social advantage' in a different way. O'Flynn, an Irish national resident in the UK, applied for a funeral payment to pay for the burial of his son in Ireland. His application was refused on the ground that the burial had not taken place in the UK, as required by British law. O'Flynn argued that the territorial condition was indirectly discriminatory against migrant workers. The Court agreed. It said that a national provision which made a grant of a payment to cover funeral expenses incurred by a migrant worker conditional on the burial or cremation taking place in the Member State concerned infringed Article 7(2) of Regulation 1612/68. However, the Court said that the Member States could limit the allowance to a lump sum or reasonable amount fixed by reference to the normal cost of a burial in the UK. Thus, as Peers explains,[236] taking these cases as a whole, the *Even* formula is somewhat misleading: in the Court's practice government measures will be classified as 'social advantages' if they are available to workers as workers, to residents as residents *or* to specified classes of persons as specified classes of persons, unless the class of person in question is defined by a criterion inherently and inseparably related to the nationality of the Member State, such as military-related benefits.

The area which has not been satisfactorily clarified is the relationship between Article 7(2) of Regulation 1612/68 and the social security Regulation 1408/71. It does seem, however, that a benefit which is excluded from Regulation 1408/71 on the ground that it is social assistance, may still constitute a social advantage under Regulation 1612/68[237] or it may fall within

---

[233] Case C–315/94 [1996] ECR I–1417.

[234] Case 207/78 [1979] ECR 2019.

[235] Case C–237/94 [1996] ECR I–2617.

[236] Peers, '"Social Advantages" and Discrimination in Employment: Case Law Confirmed and Clarified' (1997) 22 *ELRev.* 157, 164.

[237] Case 249/83 *Hoeckx v. Openbaar Centrum voor Maatschappenlijk Welzijn Kalmthout* [1975] ECR 973.

the scope of both Regulations.[238] This can be seen in *Martínez Sala*.[239] The Court, considered that a childraising allowance granted as of right to those fulfilling certain objective criteria was a family benefit within the meaning of Article 4(1)(h) of Regulation 1308/71 *and* a social advantage within the meaning of Article 7(2) of Regulation 1612/68. The Court said that since Regulation 1612/68 was of general application Article 7(2) may be 'applied to social advantages which at the same time fall specifically within the scope of Regulation 1408/71'.[240]

Article 7(4) provides that any clause of a collective or individual agreement or of any other collective regulation concerning eligibility for employment, employment, remuneration, and other conditions of work or dismissal shall be null and void in so far as it lays down or authorizes discriminatory conditions in respect of workers who are nationals of the other Member States. This provision was considered in *Schöning*. The Court ruled that a discriminatory clause in a collective agreement was 'null and void under Article 7(4) of Regulation No. 1612/68'.[241] The Court then looked at the consequences which ensued from Article 7(4), pending the adoption by the parties to the collective agreement of the amendments necessary to eliminate the discrimination. It agreed with Mrs Schöning-Kougebetopoulou and the Commission that it was appropriate to apply the Court's case law on the principle of equal pay for men and women. In this area the Court has ruled that where a provision is discriminatory on the grounds of sex, the members of the disadvantaged group (women) are to be treated in the same way and to have applied to them the same rules as the other workers (men). The Court has said that, failing correct implementation of Article 119 [new Article 141] on equal pay in national law, those rules remain the only valid point of reference.[242] Therefore, in the context of free movement of workers, the national court must apply the same rules to the members of the group disadvantaged by that discrimination as those applicable to the other workers, without requiring or waiting for the discriminatory clause to be abolished by collective negotiation or by some other procedure.

Article 8(1) provides that migrant workers must also enjoy equality of treatment with nationals in respect of trade union membership and the exercise of rights related to trade union membership, 'including the right to vote and to be eligible for the administration or management posts of a trade

---

[238] Case 63/76 *Inzirillo* [1976] ECR 2057. See further Ch. 5.
[239] Case C–85/96 [1998] ECR I–2691.
[240] Para. 27.
[241] Para. 30.
[242] See the judgments in Case C–154/92 *Van Cant v. Rijksdienst voor Pensionen* [1993] ECR I–3811, para. 20; Case C–184/89 *Nimz v. Freie und Hansestadt Hamburg* [1991] ECR I–297, para. 18; Case C–33/89 *Kowalska v. Freie und Hansestadt Hamburg* [1990] ECR I–2591, para. 20; and Case 286/85 *McDermott and Cotter v. Minister for Social Welfare and Attorney General* [1987] ECR 1453, para. 19, considered further in Ch. 4.

union'.[243] Migrant workers are also eligible to participate in workers' representative bodies in the undertaking, such as works councils. The Court has extended the scope of Article 8(1) to cover rights analogous to trade union rights. In *Association de Soutien*[244] the Court ruled that Article 8(1) prohibited national legislation which denied migrant workers the right to vote in elections for members of a professional institute, to which they were required to be affiliated, and to which they had to pay contributions. This was particularly important where the institute was responsible for defending the interests of affiliated workers and exercised a consultative role in legislation. Workers may, however, be excluded from taking part in the management of bodies governed by public law and from holding office governed by public law.[245]

Finally, Article 9 provides that workers must enjoy all the rights and benefits accorded to national workers in matters of housing, including ownership, and the right to put their names on housing lists in the region where they are employed. Therefore in *Commission* v. *Greece*[246] a restriction on a foreigner's right to own property in Greece was found to infringe the free movement rules.

(c) Workers' Families

The Preamble to Regulation 1612/68 states that free movement is a fundamental right 'of workers and their families' and it requires that obstacles to the mobility of workers should be eliminated, in particular as regards 'the worker's right to be joined by his family' and 'the conditions for the integration of that family into the host country'. Article 10(1) allows a worker's spouse, descendants who are under the age of 21 or who are dependants, and their dependent relatives in the ascending line—irrespective of nationality—to install themselves with a worker who is a national of one Member State and who is employed in the territory of another Member State. In addition, Article 10(2) requires Member States to 'facilitate the admission' of any member of the family who does not fall within the provisions of Article 10(1) if they are dependent on the worker or living under the roof of the worker in the country where the worker lived previously. The rights of all these people are entirely dependent on the rights of the worker unless and until they acquire their own independent status as workers.

The term 'spouse' has been narrowly and conventionally construed by the

---

[243] See further Evans, 'Development of European Community Law regarding the Trade Union Rights and Related Rights of Migrant Workers' (1979) 28 *ICLQ* 354; Case C–118/92 *Commission* v. *Luxembourg* [1994] ECR I–1891.

[244] Case C–213/90 *Association de Soutien aux Travailleurs Immigrés* v. *Chambre des Employés Privés* [1991] ECR I–3507.

[245] Art. 8. It seems that this provision was introduced at the request of the French because of the politically important bodies to which French trade unions may send representatives. See Evans, above n. 243, 361ff.

[246] Case 305/87 *Commission* v. *Greece* [1989] ECR 1461.

Court. In *Reed*[247] an English woman wished to join her cohabitee in the Netherlands. The Court ruled that she could not rely on Article 10 of the Regulation 1612/68 because she was not a spouse. However, on the facts of the case the applicant was successful because under Dutch law foreigners in a stable relationship with a Dutch national were entitled to reside in the Netherlands. It would therefore amount to discrimination on the grounds of nationality in breach of Article 7 [new Article 12] and Article 48 [new Article 39] of the Treaty, and Article 7(2) of Regulations 1612/68, if Reed could not remain.

In *Diatta*[248] the situation of a woman who was separated from her worker husband was considered. A Senegalese woman married a French national who lived and worked in Belgium. Eventually she separated from her husband and lived in separate accommodation, intending to divorce. As a result she was refused a renewal of her residence permit on the ground that she was no longer a member of the family of an EC national and that she did not live with her husband. The Court, however, ruled that Article 10 did not necessarily require members of a migrant's family to live permanently with him. If cohabitation of spouses was a mandatory condition for a residence permit, the worker could at any moment cause the expulsion of his spouse from the Member State by throwing her out of the house. As the Court recognized: 'It was not for the Court to decide whether a reconciliation was still possible'. Therefore it seems that separated couples must be allowed to remain in the host country. This decision is compatible with the Court's approach in *Commission v. Germany*[249] that Regulation 1612/68 must be interpreted in the light of the requirement of the respect for family life set out in Article 8 of the European Convention on Human Rights.

A divorced spouse may well not be in such a favourable position. Although this point has not been directly discussed, the Court did say in *Diatta*[250] that a 'marital relationship cannot be regarded as dissolved so long as it has not been terminated by the competent authority'. This suggests that on the completion of all the formal stages of divorce proceedings the spouse's dependent right of residence in the Member State would cease.

The definition of dependency for the purposes of Article 10(1) has been less

---

[247] Case 59/85 [1986] ECR 1283. Cf Case C–356/98 *Kaba* v *Secretary of State for the Home Department*, judgment of 11 April 2000, where the Court ruled that legislation of a Member State which requires spouses of migrant workers who are nationals of other Member States to have resided in the territory of that Member State for four years before they become entitled to apply for indefinite leave to remain, but which required residence of only 12 months for the spouses of persons who were settled in that territory, did not constitute discrimination contrary to Article 7(2) of Regulation 1612/68. See generally the Veil Report which advocates *inter alia* more flexible rules for bringing families together (http://europa.eu.int/comm/dg15/en/people/hlp/somm.htm).

[248] Case 267/83 *Diatta* v. *Land Berlin* [1985] ECR 567.

[249] Case 249/86 *Commission* v. *Germany* [1989] ECR 1263, para. 10.

[250] Case 267/83 [1985] ECR 567.

controversial. In *Lebon*[251] the Court made clear that dependency is a question of fact. A dependant is 'a member of the family who is supported by the worker'. Once it has been found that a person is a dependant there is no need to determine the reasons for recourse to the worker's support or to raise the question whether the persons concerned are able to support themselves by taking up paid employment. The Court has justified such a broad interpretation by reference to the fact that Article 39 [ex Article 48], as a fundamental freedom must be construed broadly, and also by reference to the German language version (*Unterhalt gewahren*) and the Greek language version (*efoson synthreitai*) which are 'particularly clear in that respect'.

Article 10(3) provides that workers must have available for their families 'housing considered as normal for national workers in the region where he is employed'. This provision must not give rise to discrimination between national workers and workers from other Member States nor does it impose a requirement that workers and their families must share the same household.[252] The purpose of Article 10(3) is both to implement public policy and to protect public security by preventing immigrants from living in precarious conditions.[253] In *Commission v. Germany*[254] German legislation went one stage further. It made the renewal of a residence permit for members of the families of Community migrant workers conditional on their living in appropriate housing, not only at the time when they arrived in the country, but for the entire duration of their residence. The Court, however, said that the requirement in Article 10(3) applied solely as a condition under which each member of the worker's family was permitted to come to live with the worker. Once the family had been brought together, the position of the migrant worker was not different from a national. The German legislation was therefore found to be in breach of Article 10(3).

Article 11 permits a worker's spouse, dependent children, or children under 21 to take up any activity as an employed or self-employed person throughout the territory of the host State, even if they are not nationals of any Member State. This was illustrated by the case of *Gül*.[255] Gül, a Cypriot doctor trained in Germany, was married to a British citizen who worked in Germany as a hairdresser. As the spouse of a Community national within the meaning of Article 10(1), Gül should have been entitled to work under Article 11. He was, however, refused a permanent practising certificate because he was not a Community national. The Court ruled that the clear wording of Article 11 entitled a spouse of whatever nationality to take up employment as an employed person, whatever the activity.

---

[251] Case 316/85 [1987] ECR 2811.
[252] Case 267/83 *Diatta* [1985] ECR 567.
[253] Ibid., para. 10.
[254] Case 249/86 *Commission v. Germany* [1989] ECR 1263.
[255] Case 131/85 *Gül v. Regierungspräsident Düsseldorf* [1986] ECR 1573.

Article 12 requires the 'children of a national of a Member State' who is or has been employed in the territory of another Member State, to be admitted to that State's general educational, apprenticeship or vocational training courses[256] under the same conditions as the nationals of that State, if the children are residing in that territory. Indeed, Member States are obliged to encourage these children to attend such courses and, if necessary, make special efforts to ensure that the children can take advantage of educational and training facilities on an equal footing with nationals.[257] The reference to 'same conditions' is broadly construed. In the early case of *Casagrande*[258] the Court ruled that 'conditions' did not refer solely to conditions relating to admission but extended to 'general measures intended to facilitate educational attendance'. This would include a grant for maintenance and training. Therefore, it was unlawful for the German authorities to refuse a monthly maintenance grant to the daughter of an Italian working in Germany on the ground of her nationality.[259] The Court emphasized the importance of studying, and therefore studying assistance, to make it possible for the children to 'achieve integration in the society of the host country'.

These considerations also apply to those children who arrive in the host State before school age.[260] They also apply irrespective of the place where the children pursue their studies. In *Di Leo*[261] the daughter of an Italian migrant worker, who had been employed in Germany for twenty-five years, wished to study medicine in Italy, having received her primary and secondary education in Germany. She was refused an educational grant because she was pursuing a course in her country of origin. This was found to contravene Article 12. Finally, in *Gaal*[262] the question raised was whether, given the limitation imposed in Article 10, the right to equal treatment set out in Article 12 might still be invoked by a child of a migrant worker who was 21 years of age or older and who was no longer a dependant of that worker. The Court refused to make a link between Article 10 and Article 12 of the Regulation. Referring to its earlier decision in *Echternach*,[263] the Court said that the principle of equal

---

[256] These are to be read disjunctively: Joined Cases 389 and 390/87 *Echternach and Moritz* [1989] ECR 723.

[257] Case 9/74 *Casagrande v. Landeshauptstadt München* [1974] ECR 2323. Council Directive 77/486/EEC [1977] OJ L199/139 on the education of children of migrant workers requires, first, that free tuition is available, including the teaching of the official language of the host State (Art. 2); secondly, it also provides that the host Member State must promote the teaching of the children's mother tongue and culture (Art. 3).

[258] Case 9/74 [1974] ECR 773.

[259] See also Joined Cases 389 and 390/87 *Echternach and Moritz* [1989] ECR 723 and Case C–308/89 *Di Leo v. Land Berlin* [1990] ECR I–4185.

[260] Joined Cases 389 and 390/87 *Echternach and Moritz* [1989] ECR 723.

[261] Case C–308/89 [1990] ECR I–4185.

[262] Case C–7/94 *Landesamt fur Ausbildungsforderung Nordrhein-Westfalen v. Gaal* [1995] ECR I–1031.

[263] Joined Cases 389 and 390/87 [1989] ECR 723.

treatment found in Article 12 extended to all forms of education, whether vocational or general, including university courses. It then said that the same principle required that the child of a migrant worker should be able to continue his studies in order to complete his education successfully. The Court then concluded that Article 12 also encompassed financial assistance for those students who were already at an advanced stage in their education, even if they were already 21 or over and were no longer dependent on their parents.

(d) The EURES (European Employment Service) Network

The most significant recent amendment to Regulation 1612/68 has been the introduction of the Eures System, replacing the outdated Sedoc,[264] in order 'to ensure the greatest possible transparency of the Community labour market'.[265] Article 15 now requires the specialist service in each Member State to send to its counterparts in the other States, and to the European Coordination Office,[266] details of vacancies which could be filled by nationals of other Member States, details of vacancies addressed to non-Member States, details of applications for employment by those who have formally expressed a wish to work in another State, and information, by region and by branch of activity, on applicants who have declared themselves actually willing to accept employment in another country.

2.3 Regulation 1251/70: The Right to Remain in the Host Member State

Regulation 1251/70[267] gives effect to Article 39(3)(d) [ex Article 48(3)(d)] which provides for the right to remain in the territory of a Member State after having been employed in that State. It applies to workers and their families who want to remain permanently in the territory of the host State (State A). Article 2 provides that workers will have the right to remain in three situations:

- retirement, provided they have been employed for the last twelve months[268] and resided in the host Member State continuously for more than three years;[269]
- incapacity, provided they have resided for more than two years in the host

---

[264] Sedoc stands for European system for the international clearing of vacancies and applications for employment.

[265] Preamble to Council Regulation (EEC) No. 2434/92 [1992] OJ L245/1.

[266] DG V has been designated as the European Coordination Office, Commission Decision 93/569/EEC [1993] OJ L274/32.

[267] [1970] OJ Spec. Ed. L142/24, 402.

[268] Periods of involuntary unemployment, recorded at the unemployment office and absences due to illnesses or accidents are considered as periods of employment (Art. 4(2)).

[269] Residence is not affected by temporary periods of absence not exceeding three months a year, nor by longer absences to comply with obligations of military service (Art. 4(1)).

Member State and have ceased to work due to some permanent incapacity. However, if the incapacity is due to an accident at work or an occupational disease entitling the worker to a pension for which an institution of the state is entirely or partially responsible, no condition is imposed as to length of residence;

- frontier workers, provided after three years of continuous employment and residence in State A they work as employees in State B, while retaining residence in State A to which they return each day or at least once a week. The periods of employment completed in State B are treated as having been completed in State A.

The conditions as to length of residence and employment do not apply if the worker's spouse is a national of the host Member State, State A, or has lost the nationality of the host State through marriage.[270]

The worker's family is entitled to remain in the host Member State in the situations prescribed by Article 3:

- if the worker is entitled to remain;[271]
- if the worker dies during his working life, before having acquired the right to remain, but:

    (i)   the worker resided there continuously for two years; or
    (ii) the death resulted from an accident at work or occupational disease; or
    (iii) the surviving spouse is a national of the host State or has lost that nationality through marriage to the worker.

Those who are entitled to remain must exercise that right within two years of the right coming into existence.[272] No formality is required on the part of the person exercising the right to remain[273] but he or she must be issued with a residence permit free of charge valid throughout the territory for at least five years.[274] Finally, the right to equality of treatment, established by Regulation 1612/68 also applies to people coming within this provision.[275]

---

[270] Art. 2(2).
[271] See Art. 2 above.
[272] Art. 5(1).
[273] Art. 5(2).
[274] Art. 6(1). Periods of non-residence not exceeding six consecutive months will not affect the validity of the residence permit.
[275] Art. 5(2).

D. RIGHT OF ESTABLISHMENT AND THE PROVISION OF SERVICES

1. Introduction

The distinction between the right of establishment (Article 43 [ex Article 52]) and the closely related right of freedom to provide services (Article 49 [ex Article 59]) relates to the question of permanence in the host Member State:[276] while a person who stays in the host State permanently is likely to be covered by the rules relating to establishment, a person there on a temporary[277] basis is likely only to be providing services. As the Court said in *Gebhard*,[278] the temporary nature of the activities has to be determined 'in the light, not only of the duration of the provision of the service but also of its regularity, periodicity or continuity'. The Court said the fact that the provision of services is temporary does not mean that the provider of services may not equip himself with some form of infrastructure in the host Member State (including an office, chambers, or consulting rooms) in so far as such infrastructure is necessary for the purposes of performing the services in question. On the facts of the case, Gebhard, a German national authorized to practise as a *Rechtsanwalt* in Germany, opened chambers in Milan where he described himself as *avvocato*.[279] This prompted complaints from a number of Italian practitioners and disciplinary proceedings from the Milan Bar Council. The Court said that given that Gebhard was pursuing his professional activities on a stable and continuous basis in another Member State from an established professional base his case had to be considered under the chapter on establishment rather than the chapter relating to services.

2. Article 43 [ex Article 52]: Right of Establishment

Article 43[280] [ex Article 52] concerns 'the actual pursuit of an economic activity through a fixed establishment in another Member State for an indefinite period'[281] and embraces two basic rights: the right to take up and pursue activities on a self-employed basis, often as a professional person, and the right to set up and manage undertakings, in particular companies and

---

[276] Case 2/74 *Reyners* [1974] ECR 631; Case 11/77 *Patrick v. Belgian State* [1977] ECR 1119.

[277] Art. 50(2) [ex Art. 60(2)].

[278] Case C–55/94 [1995] ECR I–4165.

[279] See now the Lawyers' Directive 98/5/EC [1998] OJ L77/36.

[280] See also General Programme for the abolition of Restrictions of Freedom of Establishment (OJ Spec. Ed. IX/7).

[281] Case C–221/89 R v. *Secretary of State for Transport, ex parte Factortame* [1991] ECR I–3905, para. 20.

firms.[282] As the Court explained in *Gebhard*,[283] the right of establishment is granted both to legal persons within the meaning of Article 58 [new Article 48] and to natural persons who are nationals of a Member State of the Community. Subject to the exceptions and the conditions laid down in the Treaty, Article 52 [new Article 43] allows all types of self-employed activity to be taken up and pursued on the territory of any other Member State, undertakings to be formed and operated, and agencies, branches, or subsidiaries to be set up. Consequently, a person may be established in more than one Member State through the setting up of branches, agencies, and subsidiaries in the case of companies or through the establishment of a second professional base in the case of members of the professions.[284] The Court concluded that:

the concept of establishment within the meaning of the Treaty is therefore a very broad one, allowing a Community national to participate, on a stable and continuous basis, in the economic life of a Member State other than his state of origin and to profit therefrom, so contributing to social and economic penetration within the Community in the sphere of activities as self-employed persons.[285]

These rights in Article 43, which are directly effective,[286] may only be exercised under the conditions laid down by the law for the nationals of the country where the establishment is effected. Consequently, no discrimination on the ground of nationality—either directly or indirectly—is permitted by any law, regulation or administrative practice nor in any other non-discriminatory treatment which hinders access to the market.[287] These obligations must be respected not only by the Member States but also by professional bodies such as the Bar Council[288] and local authorities.[289] Indirectly discriminatory or non-discriminatory national restrictions which hinder access to the market may, however, be justified.[290] In *Gebhard*[291] the Court said that

---

[282] This second element will not be considered further in this book.

[283] Case C–55/94 [1995] ECR I–4165.

[284] See e.g. Case 107/83 *Ordre des avocats au barreau des Paris* v. *Klopp* [1984] ECR 2971 where a German national and a member of the Düsseldorf bar applied to take an oath as *avocat* at the French bar. He also applied to complete the necessary period of training while remaining a member of the Düsseldorf bar and retaining his residence and chambers there. His application was rejected on the ground that an *avocat* may establish chambers in one place only, which must be in the region of Paris, to ensure the availability of *avocats* both to the courts and to their clients. The Court said that the requirement of having only one set of chambers would mean that lawyers established in one Member State could exercise their rights under Art. 52 [new Art. 43] only by abandoning their first place of establishment. This was inconsistent with Art. 52 [new Art. 43].

[285] Para. 25. See generally Lonbay (1996) 33 *CMLRev.* 1073.

[286] Case 2/74 *Reyners* [1974] ECR 631.

[287] Case 48/75 *Royer* [1976] ECR 497. See more recently Case 38/87 *Commission* v. *Greece* [1989] ECR 4415.

[288] Case 71/76 *Thieffry* [1977] ECR 765.

[289] Case 197/84 *Steinhauser* [1985] ECR 1819. See also Case C–168/91 *Konstantinidis* v. *Stadt Altensteig-Standesamt* [1993] ECR I–1191 (documents relating to civil status).

[290] See text attached to nn. 103–107, above.

[291] Case C–55/94 [1995] ECR I–4165.

the national rule must be non-discriminatory, justified by imperative require-ments in the general interest, suitable, and proportionate.[292] These imperative requirements might relate to the organization of a profession, qualifications, professional ethics, supervision and liability, and rules stipulating that the person must hold certain qualifications or be a member of a professional body.[293]

The obligation not to discriminate is far reaching. Not only does it apply to conditions of access to the profession but it also applies to any other benefit or opportunity which facilitates the pursuit of the profession. This can be seen in *Steinhauser*[294] and *Konstantinidis*.[295] In *Steinhauser* the city of Biarritz refused to allow Steinhauser, a German artist, to participate in a tendering procedure for the allocation of rented lock-ups, used for the exhibition and sale of craft products, on the grounds that he was not French. The local authority argued that Article 52 [new Article 43] applied only to conditions intended to regu-late the right to take up a specific activity and not to any other rules. The Court, however, insisted on a broad ambit for Article 52: it included the right not only to take up activities as a self-employed person but also to pursue those activities in the broadest sense. It referred to the General Programme for the Abolition of Restrictions on the Freedom of Establishment,[296] which expressly excludes the imposition of conditions on the power to exercise rights normally attached to the activity of a self-employed person, including submit-ting of tenders. The Court was therefore able to conclude that the renting of premises for business purposes furthered an occupation and fell within the scope of Article 52 [new Article 43].

In *Konstantinidis* the applicant, a Greek national, worked in Germany as a self-employed masseur and assistant hydrotherapist. His name was entered into the marriage register as Konstadinidis but he argued that the correct transliteration of his name was Konstantinidis. He argued that the distortion of his name exposed him to the risk of potential clients confusing him with other masseurs and thereby interfered with his business, contrary to Article 52 [new Article 43]. The Court ruled that while there was nothing in the

---

[292] On the importance of the principle of proportionality, see also Case C–193/94 *Skanavi* [1996] ECR I–929 where the Court ruled that while it was lawful for the Member State to impose an obligation on migrants to exchange their driving licences, Member States may not impose a penalty so disproportionate to the gravity of the infringement in the event of failure to exchange the licence that this becomes an obstacle to the free movement of persons, particularly if the penalty consisted of imprisonment. Therefore, treating a person who has failed to have exchanged his driving licence as if he were driving without a licence, thereby causing criminal penalties, would also be disproportionate, especially since a criminal conviction might have con-sequences for the exercise of a trade or profession by an employed or self-employed person, particularly with regard to access to certain activities or offices, which would constitute a further, lasting restriction on free movement.

[293] See also Case 7/76 *Thieffry* [1977] ECR 765 and text attached to nn. 105–107 above.

[294] Case 197/84 [1985] ECR 1819.

[295] Case C–168/91 [1993] ECR I–1191.

[296] OJ Spec. Ed. 2nd Series IX/7 Restrictions, A.

Treaty to prevent transliteration of a Greek name into Latin characters, the rules concerning the method of transliteration were incompatible with Article 52 in so far as their application to Greek nationals interfered with the unfettered exercise of the right of establishment.

Thus, the Court has taken a fairly robust approach to the principle of non-discrimination combined with a purposive reading of free movement. This can also be seen in the context of taxation. In *Wielockx*[297] a self-employed Belgian national residing in Belgium who received his whole income from a partnership in a physiotherapy practice in the Netherlands was not allowed under Dutch law to set up a pension reserve qualifying for deductions under the same tax conditions as a resident taxpayer. Once again, the Court concluded that he suffered from discrimination contrary to Article 52 [new Article 43].[298]

3. Qualifications

Article 43 [ex Article 52] is subject to the limitation that the rights may be exercised under the conditions laid down by the law of the country where the establishment is effected for its own nationals. This raises particular problems in respect of qualifications and membership of professions governed by strict rules of conduct. These requirements may represent a significant disincentive for free movement. Although Articles 44 and 47 [ex Articles 54 and 57] allow the Council to adopt Directives for the mutual recognition of diplomas, certificates and other evidence of formal qualifications, for many years the requirement of unanimity[299] slowed the process and it was left to the Court to address the problem.

3.1 No Community Legislation Adopted

If Community law has not laid down provisions to secure the objective of freedom of establishment, the Member States and legally recognized professional bodies[300] retain the jurisdiction to adopt the necessary measures[301] provided they comply with the obligations of co-operation laid down by Article 10 [ex Article 5][302] and the principle of non-discrimination.[303] However, the Court has been willing to circumscribe this freedom by giving a broad interpretation to Article 43 [ex Article 52]. In *Patrick*,[304] for example, a British

---

[297] Case C–80/94 [1995] ECR I–2493.

[298] See generally Vanistendael, 'The Consequences of *Schumacker* and *Wielockx*: Two Steps forward in the Tax Procession of *Echternach*' (1996) 33 *CMLRev*. 255.

[299] Now the Art. 251 [ex Art. 189b] procedure applies.

[300] Case 7/76 *Thieffry* [1977] ECR 765.

[301] Case 292/86 *Gullung v. Conseils de l'ordre des avocats du barreau de Colmar* [1988] ECR 111.

[302] Case 222/86 *UNECTEF v. Heylens* [1987] ECR 4097.

[303] Case C–61/89 *Criminal Proceedings against Bouchoucha* [1990] ECR I–3569.

[304] Case 11/77 [1977] ECR 1199.

architect applied for authorization to practise in France. His application was rejected on the ground that there was neither a diplomatic convention between the UK and France concerning the mutual recognition of certificates, nor an EC directive on recognition of architectural qualifications.[305] The Court held, however, that the failure to enact harmonization Directives 'has become superfluous with regard to implementing the rule on nationality' since this was sanctioned by the Treaty itself with direct effect. The Court concluded that the fact that those directives had not been issued did not entitle the Member State to deny an applicant the right of freedom of establishment. This followed the earlier case of *Reyners*[306] where a Dutch national, the holder of the legal diploma giving the right to take up the profession of *avocat* in Belgium, was excluded from the profession in Belgium by reason of his nationality. The Court found that he could rely on Article 52 [new Article 43] directly to secure the protection of his Community law rights.

Similarly, in *Thieffry*[307] a Belgian advocate held a Belgian diploma of Doctor of Laws which had been recognized by a French university as equivalent to the French licenciate's degree in law. He subsequently obtained a French advocate's certificate, having passed a French examination, but was refused admission to the Paris bar on the ground that he lacked a French degree. The Court said Article 52 [new Article 43] was directed towards 'reconciling freedom of establishment with the application of national professional rules justified by the general good, in particular relating to the organization, qualifications, professional ethics, supervision and liability, provided that such application is effected without discrimination'.[308] However, on the facts the Court held that the Paris bar's requirement constituted an unjustified restriction on the freedom of establishment, particularly because Thieffry held a diploma recognized as an equivalent qualification by the competent authority in France and had passed the French bar exams. Had there been no recognition of his degree he could have been lawfully denied admission to the French bar.[309] However, in *Kraus*[310] the Court ruled that, in order to prevent abuse, it was compatible with Articles 48 and 52 [new Articles 39 and 43] for Germany to prevent one of its own nationals, who had been awarded a

---

[305] However, see now Council Directive 85/384/EEC [1985] OJ L223/85 on the mutual recognition of formal qualifications in architecture. See also Case C–310/90 *Nationale Raad van de Orde der Architecten v. Egle* [1992] ECR I–177.

[306] Case 2/74 [1974] ECR 631.

[307] Case 7/76 [1977] ECR 765. On the general question of mutual recognition of legal qualifications see Skarlatos, 'European Lawyer's Right to Transnational Legal Practice in the Community' [1991/1] *LIEI* 49.

[308] Case 7/76 *Thieffry* [1977] ECR 765.

[309] However, in Case C–319/92 *Haim v. Kassenzahnärtzliche Vereinigung Nordrhein* [1994] ECR I–425, the Court ruled that recognition by a Member State of qualifications awarded by non-Member States, even if they have been recognized as equivalent in one or more Member States, does not bind the other Member States.

[310] Case C–19/92 [1993] ECR I–1663. The case arose before the period for transposition of Directive 92/51 [1992] OJ L209/25 had expired. See n. 335 below.

postgraduate qualification by another Member State (an LLM from the University of Edinburgh), from using the title without obtaining prior administrative authorization by the German authorities. This was subject to the condition that the authorization procedure was intended only to verify that the academic title was duly awarded, the procedure was easily accessible, the administrative charge was not excessive, any refusal was subject to judicial review, and that the penalties prescribed for non-observance were not disproportionate.[311]

These cases were, however, merely precursors to the Court's important decision in *Vlassopoulou*.[312] Vlassopoulou, a Greek lawyer, worked in Germany advising on Greek and EC law. Her application to join the local German bar was rejected on the ground that she had not pursued her university studies in Germany, nor had she sat the two State exams or completed the preparatory stage, although she did hold a German doctorate. The Court ruled that Member States could not ignore an applicant's existing qualifications, which had to be compared with those required by national rules to see if the applicant had the appropriate skills to join the equivalent profession. If the comparison revealed that the applicant only partially fulfilled the necessary qualifications then the host Member State could require the applicant to demonstrate she had the 'missing' knowledge and qualifications. Member State authorities then had to take into account the applicant's knowledge and professional experience acquired. This judgment effectively pre-empted Council Directive 89/48/EEC on mutual recognition of higher education diplomas and the complementary Directive 92/51/EEC.[313]

3.2 Community Legislation Adopted

Despite the Court's best endeavours, the legal requirements in the various Member States relating to the possession of qualifications for admission to certain professions constituted a restriction on the effective exercise of the freedom of establishment. This has been eased by the adoption of harmonization legislation.[314] At first the Council adopted a vertical approach,

---

[311] Para. 42.

[312] Case C–340/89 *Vlassopoulou* v. *Ministerium für Justiz* [1991] ECR I–2357, noted Lonbay, 'Picking over the Bones: The Rights of Establishment Reviewed' (1991) 16 *ELRev*. 507. See also Hopkins, 'Recognition of Teaching Qualifications; Community Law in the English Context' (1996) 21 *ELRev*. 435. This approach was approved in respect of a Community national with a Turkish dental qualification who had practised in a Member State but lacked the qualifications required by Council Directive 78/686/EEC, see Case C–319/92 *Haim (No. 1)* [1994] ECR I–425. On damages see Case C–424/97 *Haim (No. 2)* v. *KVN*, judgment of 4 July 2000. See also Case C–164/94 *Georgios Aranitis* v. *Land Berlin* [1996] ECR I–135 concerning a diploma in geology and Case C–55/94 *Gebhard* [1995] ECR I–4165, para. 38.

[313] Lonbay, above, n. 312, 516.

[314] See generally Laslett, 'The Mutual Recognition of Diplomas, Certificates and other Evidence of Formal Qualifications in the European Community' [1990/1] *LIEI* I.

attempting to harmonize professions sector by sector. This process was interminably slow: for example, the Directive on architects[315] took many years to agree and the Directive on Lawyers' Services[316] applied only to services and not to establishment. Consequently, a new approach was adopted as part of the single market programme: horizontal harmonization based on the principle of mutual recognition established by the Court in *Cassis de Dijon*[317] and applied subsequently in *Vlassopoulou*.[318] Directive 89/48[319] on the mutual recognition of diplomas provided the first example of this approach.

The Directive applies to all areas of activity for which a higher education diploma is required and applies to any national of a Member State wishing to pursue a regulated profession in a host Member State in a self-employed capacity or as an employed person.[320] The Directive does not apply to professions which are the subject of a separate Directive establishing arrangements for mutual recognition of diplomas.[321] A regulated profession is one which involves the pursuit of a regulated professional activity or range of activities which constitute this profession in a Member State.[322] Regulated professional activities are defined as being engaged in a professional activity in so far as taking up or pursuit of such activity is subject directly or indirectly to the

---

[315] Council Directive 85/384/EEC [1985] OJ L223/85 and Case C–447/93 *Dreessen* v. *Conseil national de l'ordre des architectes* [1994] ECR I–4087. See also Council Recommendation 85/386/EEC concerning the holders of a diploma in architecture awarded in a third country [1985] OJ L223/28.

[316] Council Directive 77/249/EEC [1977] OJ L78/17. See Case 427/85 *Commission* v. *Germany* [1988] ECR 1123; Case C–294/89 *Commission* v. *France* [1991] ECR I–3591 and Case 427/85 *Commission* v. *Germany Re Lawyer's Services* [1988] ECR 1123. See also now EP and Council Directive 98/5/EC [1998] OJ L77/36 to facilitate practice of the profession of lawyer on a permanent basis in a Member State other than that in which the qualification was obtained. See also Directives on doctors (75/363/EEC [1975] OJ L167/14), nurses responsible for general care (77/452/EEC [1977] OJ L176/1), dentists (78/686 EEC [1978] OJ 233/1), vets (78/1026/EEC [1978] OJ L362/1), all supplemented by Council Directive 81/1057/EEC [1985] OJ L385/25. See also Directives on midwives (80/154/EEC [1980] OJ L33/1), pharmacists (86/433/EEC [1985] OJ L253/37), general practitioners (86/457/EEC [1986] OJ L267/26) and carriers of goods by waterway (87/540/EC [1987] OJ L322/20). Council Directives 75/362/EEC, 75/363/EEC and 86/457/EEC have now been consolidated in Council Directive 93/16/EEC [1993] OJ L165/1. See Case C–93/97 *ASBL* v. *Flemish Government* [1998] ECR I–4837 and Case C–131/97 *Carbonari* v. *Università de Studi di Bologna* [1999] ECR I–1103.

[317] Case 120/78 *Rewe-Zentral* v. *Bundesmonopolverwaltung für Branntwein* [1979] ECR 649.

[318] Case C–340/89 [1991] ECR I–2357.

[319] [1989] OJ L19/16. Council Resolution 2000/C 141/02 on Mutual Recognition ([2000] OJ C141/5). See Pertek, 'La Reconnaissance mutuelle des diplomes d'enseignement superieur' (1989) 25 *Revue Trimestrielle de Droit Européen* 623. See also Guide for Users of the general system for the recognition of qualifications, XV/E/8417/94–EN, and Code of Conduct approved by the Group of Co-ordinators for the general system of recognition of Diplomas.

[320] Art. 2(1).

[321] Art. 2(2).

[322] Art. 1(c).

possession of a diploma.[323] This includes the pursuit of an activity under a professional title or a professional activity relating to health.[324] A diploma is defined to mean a certificate or other formal qualification which:[325]

- has been awarded by a competent authority[326] in a Member State;
- shows that the holder has successfully completed a post-secondary course of at least three years' duration, or equivalent part-time, at a university or establishment of higher education, and, where appropriate, has successfully completed the professional training required in addition to the post-secondary course;[327] and
- shows that the holder has the professional qualifications required to take up or pursue a regulated profession in that Member State.

Article 3 lays down the basic principle of automatic recognition by the host State (see Figure 3.1). It provides that where, in a host State, the taking up and the pursuit of a regulated profession are subject to the possession of a diploma, the competent authority may not, on the grounds of inadequate qualifications, refuse to authorize a national of another Member State to take up or pursue that profession on the same conditions as apply to its own nationals, provided either that the applicant holds a diploma (as defined above) or has pursued that profession for at least two years during the previous ten years in a State that does not regulate that profession and possesses evidence of one or more formal qualifications.[328] In addition, Community nationals who fulfil the conditions for taking up a regulated profession in their territory can use the professional title of the host Member State corresponding to that profession.[329]

Article 4 contains the exception to the basic principle: recognition by the

---

[323] Art. 1(d). It also applies to a professional activity pursued by members of an association or organization whose purpose is the promotion and maintenance of high professional standards and which is recognized in a special form by a Member State, and awards a diploma to its Members, ensures that its members respect the rules of professional conduct which it prescribes and confers on them the right to use a title or designatory letters, or to benefit from a status corresponding to a diploma. The annex contains a list of such organizations.

[324] Art. 1(d), para. 2.

[325] Art. 1(a).

[326] Competent authorities are designated by Member States in accordance with Art. 9(1).

[327] This education and training must have been received mainly in the Community, or the holder must have three years' professional experience certified by the Member State which recognized a third country diploma, certificate, or other evidence of formal qualifications. However, Council Recommendation 89/49/EEC, concerning nationals of Member States who hold a diploma conferred by a third state ([1989] OJ L19/24), recommends that governments should allow nationals of Member States who hold diplomas, certificates, or other evidence of formal qualifications awarded in third states—whose position is comparable to those in Art. 3—to take up and pursue regulated professions within the Community by recognizing these diplomas. See also Case C–319/92 *Haim* [1994] ECR I– 425.

[328] These qualifications must have been awarded by a competent authority in a Member State, have shown that the holder has completed a post-secondary course of at least three years' duration and have prepared the holder for the pursuit of his profession.

[329] Art. 7(1).

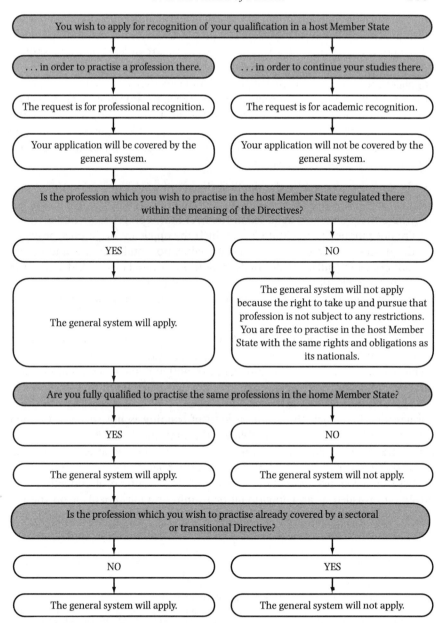

Figure 3.1 General System for the Recognition of Professional Qualifications

Source: Summary of the conditions which must be satisfied in order to be covered by the general system, Commission, *Guide for Users of the General System for the Recognition of Professional Qualifications.*

host State after compensation in the form of an adaptation period, an aptitude test, or prior professional experience. It provides that, notwithstanding Article 3, where the applicant's education and training are at least one year shorter than those required by the host State the Member State may also require the applicant to produce evidence of professional experience. This may not exceed the shortfall in supervised practice, nor be twice the duration of the shortfall in education and training required by the host State.[330] In any event the professional experience may not exceed four years.[331] The Member State may also require the applicant to take an aptitude test or complete an adaptation period not exceeding three years when:[332]

- the matters covered by the applicant's training and education differ substantially from those covered by the diploma required by the host State; or
- where the profession regulated in the host State comprises activities which are not pursued in the State from which the applicant originates, provided the difference corresponds to specific education and training and covers matters which differ substantially from those covered by the evidence of the formal qualifications adduced by the applicant; or
- the activities regulated by the host State are not regulated by the State of origin.

Usually it is for the individual to choose between the aptitude test or adaptation period[333] but in the case of the legal profession, or other professions which depend on the precise knowledge of national law when giving advice, the host Member State decides which of the two alternatives should apply.[334]

The Community has extended the system of mutual recognition to those professions for which the required level of training is not so high. Council Directive 92/51/EEC[335] closely follows the pattern of Directive 89/48/EEC. Directive 92/51 makes a distinction between level one and level two training. It recognizes 'certificates' which show that the holder, after having followed a course of secondary education, has completed a course of education and training provided at an educational or training establishment or on the job (level one).[336] It also recognizes 'diplomas' which show that the holder has

---

[330] Art. 4(1)(a).
[331] Ibid., para. 4.
[332] Art. 4(1)(b).
[333] Ibid., para. 2.
[334] Ibid. Art. 4(1)(a) and (b) cannot be applied cumulatively.
[335] [1992] OJ L209/25 as amended by Commission Directives 94/38/EEC [1994] OJ L217/8, 95/43/EC [1995] OJ L184/21, 97/38 [1997] OJ L38/31, 2000/5/EC [2000] OJ L54/42. Council Resolution of 18 June 1992 ([1992] OJ C187/1) accompanying Directive 92/51 EEC invites the Member States to allow nationals of the European Community who have been awarded diplomas, certificates, or other qualifications by third countries to take up and pursue professions in the Community by recognizing these diplomas and certificates in their territories. See also COM(97) 638 final.
[336] Art. 1(1)(b).

completed either a post-secondary course of at least one year's duration and the necessary professional training or one of the education or training courses listed in an annex to the Directive (level two).[337] Level three training, which includes degrees granted after three years' study in an institution of higher education and the necessary professional qualifications thereafter, also known as a 'diploma' course, is covered by Directive 89/48. As far as Directive 92/51 is concerned, these certificates and diplomas are to be recognized by the host State[338] but, as with Directive 89/48, compensatory measures may be required from a migrant worker whose education and training differ substantially from those provided in the host State. These compensatory measures include an adaptation period which does not exceed three years, or an aptitude test[339] where the training received differs substantially from that required by the host State.

The Directive also makes provisions for a conflict between the levels of training required by different Member States for the same profession. If State A requires level 2 training and State B level 1 and the worker moves from A to B, the worker is deemed to be over-qualified and will normally need only to possess the diploma.[340] If, however, the worker moves from State B to State A the worker must produce the certificate and undergo either a period of adaptation or an aptitude test.[341]

As we have seen, Directive 89/48/EEC on a general system for the recognition of higher-education diplomas requires lawyers either to sit an aptitude test or to complete an adaptation period before they can establish themselves in another Member State on the basis of recognition of his or her diploma. The new Lawyers Directive 98/5/EC[342] represents a new phase in the recognition of professional qualifications aimed at facilitating establishment in other Member States, because it specifically recognizes that a person's authorization in his or her home Member State must be taken into account, as well as his or her diplomas. The Directive enables lawyers to practise permanently and without restriction, under their original professional title, in another Member State on the same basis as the host country's own lawyers. Lawyers who are fully qualified in one Member State will simply have to register with the bar or other competent authority in the host Member State on the basis of their registration in the home Member State, without the need for either a test or an adaptation period. The Directive will also make it easier to acquire the professional title of the host Member State, after effectively and regularly pursuing an activity involving the law of the Member State in question, including Community law, for a period of three years.

---

[337] Art. 1(1)(a).
[338] Arts. 3 and 5 respectively.
[339] This has been the solution adopted in the case of ski instructors in France (14 July 1999).
[340] Art. 5.
[341] Art. 9.
[342] [1998] OJ L77/36.

4. Secondary Legislation Facilitating Freedom of Establishment and the Freedom to Provide Services

The secondary legislation concerning establishment and services parallels the provisions on workers. Directive 73/148/EEC[343] on rights of entry and residence is loosely equivalent to Directive 68/360; Directive 75/34/EEC[344] on the right to remain permanently in a Member State after having been self-employed there is equivalent to the general principle of non-discrimination in Article 43 [ex Article 52] and Regulation 1251/70. There is no equivalent to Regulation 1612/68 on the rights of workers to equal treatment, although Article 12 [ex Article 6] can be used to fill this gap to ensure that the self-employed and their families who are lawfully resident receive equal treatment and other social advantages.[345]

Article 1 of Directive 73/148/EEC provides that Member States must abolish restrictions on the movement and residence of nationals wishing to establish themselves in another Member State as self-employed persons, those wishing to provide services in another Member State, and nationals wishing to go to another Member State to receive services. In addition, the same obligations are imposed on Member States in respect of members of a worker's family as defined in Article 10(1) and (2) of Regulation 1612/68. Articles 2 and 3 govern the rights concerning departure from one Member State and the entry into another Member State and Articles 4(1), 5, and 7 provide details of the grant of residence permits for those wishing to establish themselves in the host Member State. The right of residence for persons providing and receiving services will be commensurate to the period during which the services are provided.[346] If the period exceeds three months, the host Member State will issue a right of abode as proof of the rights of residence. Where the period is less than three months, an identity card or passport will suffice, although the Member Sate may require the person concerned to report his or her presence on the territory.

The right for the self-employed and their families to remain in the host State contained in Directive 75/34/EEC is governed by the same conditions as to residence and periods of employment as prescribed by Regulation 1251/70 for workers, subject to minor adjustments in recognition of the different nature of the types of employment. Consequently, if the Member State does not grant certain categories of self-employed workers the right to an old-age pension, the retirement age of the self-employed is considered to be 65.

---

[343] [1973] OJ L172/14.
[344] [1975] OJ L14/10.
[345] See e.g. Case C–337/97 *Meeusen*, judgment of 8 June 1999, para. 28.
[346] Art. 4(2).

5. Articles 49 and 50 [ex Articles 59 and 60]: Freedom to Provide and Receive Services

5.1 Interpretation of the Provisions

Articles 49 and 50 [ex Articles 59 and 60] on the freedom to provide services,[347] another fundamental freedom of the Treaty, are also directly effective.[348] The provisions are based on the premise that the provider of a service must be established in a Member State of the Community (although not necessarily as a national of that State) other than the one where the services are to be provided. Although the Treaty talks of the freedom to provide services, the Court has also extended the scope of Article 49 to permit a person to travel to *receive* services. This was first established by the Court in *Luisi and Carbone*[349] where it said that the freedom to receive services was the corollary of the freedom to provide services.[350] Services, as defined by Article 50 [ex Article 60], are normally provided for remuneration,[351] and include activities of an industrial or commercial character, the exercise of a profession and the activities of craftsmen. The Court has also found that medical services,[352] including abortion,[353] employment services, where an employment agency supplies staff to other companies,[354] services provided to a tourist and to

---

[347] See also General Programme for the Abolition of Restrictions of Freedom to provide services: OJ Spec. Ed. IX/3.

[348] Case 33/74 *Van Binsbergen* [1974] ECR 1229.

[349] Joined Cases 286/82 and 26/83 *Luisi and Carbone* v. *Ministero del Tesoro* [1984] ECR 377. This had already been recognized in Art. 1 of Directive 73/148 [1973] OJ L172/14 and by the Advocate General in Case 118/75 *Watson and Belmann* [1976] ECR 1185. Article 49 also applies to the situation where neither party travels. See p. 110.

[350] See also Case 186/87 *Cowan* v. *Le Trésor public* [1989] ECR 195 where the Court confirmed that the prohibition on discrimination is applicable to recipients of services within the meaning of the Treaty including, on the facts of this case, the freedom of a tourist to be protected from harm occurring in the host State and the right to obtain compensation provided for under national law when the risk, in this case being mugged on the Paris metro, materialized. See also Case C–348/96 *Criminal Proceedings against Calfa* [1999] ECR I–11, para. 16.

[351] Case 352/85 *Bond van Adverteerders* v. *Netherlands* [1988] ECR 2085. Joined Cases C–51/96 and C–191/97 *Deliège*, judgment of 11 Apr. 2000, para. 56 (a high-ranking athlete's participation in an international competition is capable of constituting the provision of services even if some of those services are not paid for by those for whom they are performed). This fact was used by the Court in Case C–159/90 *SPUC* v. *Grogan* [1991] ECR I–4685 to avoid having to decide whether Art. 40.3.3 of the Irish constitution preventing abortion was contrary to Art. 59 [new Art. 49]. See further *AG* v. *X* [1992] 2 CMLR 277 on a decision of the Irish Supreme Court concerning the freedom of travel to receive an abortion, and Protocol 17 to the Treaty on European Union which provides that 'Nothing in the Treaty on European Union, or in the Treaties establishing the European Communities, or in the Treaties or Acts modifying or supplementing those Treaties shall affect the application in Ireland of Article 40.3.3 of the Constitution of Ireland'. See also Phelan, 'The Right to Life of the Unborn v Promotion of Trade in Service and the Normative Shaping of the European Union' (1992) 55 *MLR* 670.

[352] Joined Cases 286/82 and 26/83 *Luisi and Carbone* [1984] ECR 377.

[353] Case C–159/90 *Grogan* [1991] ECR I–4685.

[354] Case 279/80 *Criminal Proceedings against Webb* [1981] ECR 3305.

people travelling for the purposes of education or business,[355] all constitute services within the meaning of the Treaty.

The object of Article 49 [ex Article 59] is to remove obstacles to the freedom to provide services. As the Court said in *Gouda*,[356] Article 59 [new Article 49] of the Treaty entails:

in the first place, the abolition of any discrimination against a person providing services *on the grounds of his nationality or the fact that he is established in a Member State other than the one in which the service is provided* . . . [emphasis added].

Thus, the categories of unlawful discrimination have been extended in the context of services to cover not only nationality but also discrimination on the grounds of residence. It is unlawful to insist on residence in the territory where the service is to be provided since, according to the Court in *Van Binsbergen*,[357] this may have the consequence of 'depriving Article 59 [new Article 49] of all useful effect, in view of the fact that the precise object of the Article is to abolish restrictions on the freedom to provide services imposed on persons who are not established in the state where the service is to be provided'. Therefore, a Dutch law requiring a legal adviser to be resident in the Netherlands in order to appear before a Dutch tribunal was not compatible with Article 59 [new Article 49].

Gouda also made clear that indirectly discriminatory measures, such as licensing requirements, imposed upon providers of services represented an obstacle to the freedom to provide services contrary to Article 59 by prohibiting or otherwise impeding 'the activities of a provider of services established in another Member State where he lawfully provides similar services'.[358] The obstacle to the freedom to supply the services lies in the fact that the service provider may have to obtain a licence both in the state of establishment and in the place where the service is provided. In *Commission* v. *Germany* (insurance services)[359] the Court said that this was incompatible with Article 59 [new Article 49] unless five conditions were satisfied: first, the licensing requirement must be justified by imperative reasons relating to the public interest; secondly, the licensing requirement must apply to all persons and undertakings operating in the state; thirdly, that there was no Community legislation governing activities in this field; fourthly, that the public interest was not already protected by the rules of the state of establishment; and fifthly, that the same result could not be obtained by less restrictive rules.[360]

---

[355] Case 186/87 *Cowan* [1989] ECR 195.
[356] Case C–288/89 [1991] ECR I–4007.
[357] Case 33/74 [1974] ECR 1229.
[358] See Case C–76/90 *Säger* [1991] ECR I–4221 para. 12.
[359] Case 205/84 *Commission* v. *Germany* (Insurance Services) [1986] ECR 3755.
[360] To this the Court has added in Case C–288/89 *Gouda* [1991] ECR I–422 that the national provisions must be such as to guarantee the achievement of the intended aim as well as being proportionate to that objective.

This case marked a significant shift in the jurisprudence of the Court towards the idea that in principle the *home state* controls the activities of the provider of services.[361] Any additional control by the host State must be justified.[362]

The Court has recognized certain categories of public interest requirements.[363] This list, which is not exhaustive, includes professional rules to protect the recipients of services,[364] protection of workers,[365] consumer protection,[366] conservation of national historic and artistic heritage and the widest possible dissemination of knowledge. The last two headings are derived from *Commission* v. *Italy*[367] and the other so-called *Tourist Guide* cases.[368] Italian law insisted that tourist guides held a licence which was issued after the person had passed an exam leading to a specific qualification. The Court said that tourist guides fell within the rules on freedom to provide services in two ways: first, because tour companies could employ guides and so the tour company was providing services and, secondly, the tour company could also engage self-employed tour guides established in other Member States and so the service was being provided by the guide to the tour company. Since the services were for a limited duration and were provided for remuneration they fell within the definition in Article 60 [new Article 50]. The Italian government justified the existence of its tour guide licensing rules with reference to consumer protection and the desire to conserve its national historic and artistic heritage. The Court, while recognizing these categories of public interest, said that the Italian legislation was not proportionate. It suggested that the licensing requirement forced tour companies to use local, established guides who might not be familiar with the language, interests, and specific expectations of the tour companies. The Court argued that the competitive pressures on tour groups enabled them to be selective in their choice of tour guides, and this would provide a control on the quality of services provided by the guide.

The Court has, however, recognized some limits on the scope of these justifications. In *Ypourgos Ergasias*[369] the Court said that a national restriction

---

[361] See the fourth requirement listed in Case 205/84 *Commission* v. *Germany* [1986] ECR 3755.

[362] See Case C–76/90 *Säger* [1991] ECR I–4221, Case C–288/89 *Gouda* [1991] ECR I–4007 and the *Tourist Guide* cases: Case C–154/89 *Commission* v. *France* [1991] ECR I–659; Case C–180/89 *Commission* v. *Italy* [1991] ECR I–709; Case C–198/89 *Commission* v. *Greece* [1991] ECR I–727; Case C–375/92 *Commission* v. *Spain* [1994] ECR I–923.

[363] Case 205/84 *Commission* v. *Germany* (Insurance Services) [1986] ECR 3755. See also nn. 105–107 above.

[364] Cases 110 and 111/78 *Ministère public* v. *Van Wesemael* [1979] ECR 35; Case 96/85 *Commission* v. *France* [1986] ECR 1475.

[365] Case 279/80 *Webb* [1981] ECR 3305; Joined Cases 62/81 and 63/81 *Seco SA and Another* v. *EVI* and *Desquenne and Giral* [1982] ECR 223.

[366] Case 205/84 *Commission* v. *Germany* (Insurance Services) [1986] ECR 3755.

[367] Case C–180/89 [1991] ECR I–709.

[368] See above, n. 362.

[369] Case C–398/95 *SETTG* v. *Ypourgos Ergasias* [1997] ECR I–3091.

could not be justified on the grounds of 'maintaining industrial peace as a means of bringing a collective dispute to an end and thereby preventing any adverse effects on an economic sector and consequently on the economy of the state'.

5.2 Posted Workers

(a) The Case Law

As a result of the Treaty rules on the provision of services and the EC Directives on public procurement[370] transnational subcontracting has burgeoned. Consequently, companies established in one State, having been awarded a contract in another Member State (the host State), have relocated their employees to the host Member State to supply the particular service. For the host State this has raised the spectre of 'social dumping'[371]—that service providers take advantage of cheaper labour standards in their own States to win a contract in the host State.[372] The potential problems facing the host country in this situation were highlighted by the case of *Rush Portuguesa*.[373]

Rush Portuguesa, a Portuguese company, entered into a subcontract with a French company to carry out work in connection with building a railway line in France. In order to fulfil the contract Rush Portuguesa used its own workforce. This contravened French rules about the employment of non-Community nationals under which only the French Office d'Immigration could recruit foreign workers.[374] The Court ruled that Articles 59 and 60 [new Articles 49 and 50]:

preclude a Member State from prohibiting a person providing services established in another Member State from moving freely on its territory *with all his staff* and preclude that Member State from making the movement of staff in question subject to restrictions such as a condition as to engagement *in situ* or an obligation to obtain a work permit[375] [emphasis added].

The Court said the imposition of such conditions discriminated against guest service providers in relation to their competitors established in the host

---

[370] See e.g. Council Directives 92/50/EEC on the coordination of procedures on the award of public services [1992] OJ L209/1 amended to implement WTO Agreement on government purchasing ([1994] OJ L336/1) by Directive 97/52/EC ([1997] OJ L328/1), Directive 93/36/EEC on public supply contracts [1993] OJ L199/1; 93/37/EEC on public works contracts [1993] OJ L199/54; and 93/38 on utilities [1993] OJ L199/84.

[371] See further Ch. 1 and Rodière, *Droit Social de l'Union Européene* (LGDJ, Paris, 1998), 148.

[372] This point was also noted by the Commission which talked of the risk that 'in addition to disadvantages for workers this will give rise to distortions of competition between undertakings' (Social Charter Action Programme section 4). See further the text attached to n. 419, below.

[373] Case C–113/89 *Rush Portuguesa v. Office national d'immigration* [1990] ECR I–1417.

[374] This case arose shortly after Portugal's accession to the Community, when the rules on freedom to provide services were in force but not those relating to the free movement of workers.

[375] Para. 12.

country who were able to use their own staff without restrictions. The Court went one stage further in *Vander Elst*.[376] It confirmed that Articles 59 and 60 [new Articles 49 and 50] also precluded Member States from obliging guest service providers which lawfully and habitually employed nationals of non-Member States to obtain and pay for work permits for those workers with the imposition of an administrative fine as the penalty for infringement, on condition that the workers did not seek access to the labour market in the host State and return to their country of origin or residence after completion of their work.

In *Guiot*[377] the Court adopted a rather different approach. It said that a national law which required an employer providing a service in the host Member State to pay employer's contributions to the social security fund of the host Member State, in addition to the contributions paid to the social security fund in the State in which the employer was established, placed an additional financial burden on the employer which was liable to restrict the freedom to provide services. However, it then went on to consider whether the national legislation could be justified by the public interest relating to the 'social protection of workers in the construction industry'.[378] The Court said that 'this is not the case where the workers in question enjoy the same protection, or essentially similar protection, by virtue of employer's contributions already paid by the employer in the Member State of establishment'.[379] This was a matter for the national court to decide.[380]

Generally, the conditions of employment of the temporary staff are governed by the rules applicable in the country where the company is established. These conditions may be inferior to those in the host Member State. This was of particular concern to the Germans who were anxious to preserve the local system of wage setting and collectively negotiated, levy-based 'social funds' in the German construction industry[381] from the threats

---

[376] Case C–43/93 *Vander Elst v. Office des Migrations Internationales* [1994] ECR I–3803.

[377] Case C–272/94 *Criminal proceedings against Guiot* [1996] ECR I–1905. The Court also adopted this approach in Joined Cases C–369 and C–376/96 *Arblade*, judgment of 23 Nov. 1999.

[378] See the discussion above, n. 365.

[379] Para. 17. See also Joined Cases C–369 and C–376/96 *Arblade*, judgment of 23 Nov. 1999, para. 80, concerning '*timbres-intempéries*' and '*timbres-fidélité*'. The Court also said that the host State could not require the service provider to draw up social or labour documents such as labour rules, a special staff register, and an individual account for each worker in the form prescribed by the rules of the host State, where the social protection of workers is already safeguarded by the home State. The host State also could not require the service provider to keep social documents, such as a staff register, for five years after the service provider has ceased to employ the workers in the host State at the address of an agent in the host State.

[380] On the facts the Court observed that the Belgian and Luxembourg contributions at issue in practice covered the same risks and had a similar, if not identical purpose (para. 19).

[381] See Streeck, 'Neo-voluntarism: A New Social Policy Regime' (1995) 1 *ELJ* 31, 42, and Simitis, 'Dismantling or Strengthening Labour Law: The Case of the European Court of Justice' (1996) 2 *ELJ* 156, 163.

posed by cheap migrant labour.[382] Therefore, in *Rush Portuguesa* the Court ruled that:[383]

Community law does not preclude Member States from extending their legislation, or collective labour agreements entered into by both sides of industry, to any person who is employed, even temporarily, within their territory, no matter in which country the employer is established; nor does Community law prohibit Member States from enforcing those rules by appropriate means.[384]

The Court emphasized this in *Arblade*.[385] It said that Community law allowed the host Member State to require the service provider to pay the minimum wage fixed by collective agreement, provided that the provisions of the collective agreement were sufficiently precise and accessible and they did not render it impossible or excessively difficult in practice for the employer to determine the obligations with which he was to comply. It also said that the host Member State could insist that the service provider keep social and labour documents available on site or in an accessible and clearly identified place in the host State, where such a measure was necessary to enable it effectively to monitor compliance with the host State's legislation which is justified by the need to safeguard the social protection of workers. The decision in *Rush Portuguesa* gave the green light to the enactment, under pressure from the Germans, of the Directive on Posted Workers.[386]

(b) The Posted Workers Directive 96/71/EC

Personal and Material Scope of the Directive

Directive 96/71 on the posting of workers in the framework of the provision

---

[382] In Germany the Arbeitnehmer-Entsendungsgesetz was approved by Parliament on 26 Feb. 1996 (see May 1996 EIRR 268, 15). The legislation stipulates that all employers based outside the country and sending one or more employees to work in Germany must abide by provisions laid out in the relevant collective agreement, relating to minimum pay and certain conditions of employment, such as minimum holiday pay. These employers must also make payments into the relevant social security funds unless they are already paying into social security funds in their own country or have already done so. Employers with headquarters outside Germany but which are sending employees to work in the country must register in writing with the relevant local authorities in Germany before work commences. Employers must supply the name of the employee concerned, the commencement and expected duration of the employment, and the location of the site where the work is to be carried out. These provisions are valid from the first day of employment in Germany. Employers which contravene this legislation are liable to fines of up to 100,000 DM (£43,800). The Ministry of Labour and customs offices are to be responsible for ensuring that employers comply with this law. As EIRR points out, this legislation puts Germany on a par with other EU countries, most notably France, which has national legislation on minimum pay and conditions for posted workers. In answer to written question E–2507/97 by Frédéric Striby MEP, the Commission said that the German law was in accordance with Community law, provided that the inspections carried out to ensure the compliance with the minimum wage were not discriminatory or disproportionate.

[383] Para. 18.

[384] Citing Joined Cases 62/81 and 63/81 *Seco SA and Another* [1982] ECR 223.

[385] Joined Cases C–369 and C–376/96, judgment of 23 Nov. 1999.

[386] Directive 96/71/EC [1996] OJ L18/1. See Davies, 'Posted Workers: Single Market or Protection of National Labour Law Systems' (1997) 34 *CMLRev.* 571.

of services,[387] based on Articles 57(2) and 66 [new Articles 47(2) and 55], is intended to promote the transnational provision of services which requires a 'climate of fair competition and measures guaranteeing respect for the rights of workers'.[388] It aims to coordinate the legislation in the Member States and to lay down a hard core of mandatory EC rules which must be respected by undertakings assigning their employees to work in another Member State. The Directive applies to undertakings established in a Member State[389] which, in the framework of the transnational provision of services, post workers to the territory of another Member State (the host State).[390] The posting of workers can take one of three forms:[391]

(a) undertakings posting workers to the territory of a Member State on their account and under their direction, under a contract concluded between the undertaking making the posting and the party for whom the services are intended, operating in that Member State, provided there is an employment relationship between the undertaking making the posting and the worker during the period of posting;

(b) undertakings posting workers to an establishment or to an undertaking owned by the group in the territory of a Member State, provided there is an employment relationship between the undertaking making the posting and the worker during the period of posting (this second category, referred to as intra-firm or intra-group mobility,[392] has been included to prevent an undertaking from opening a subsidiary in another Member State purely to place some of its workers there to carry out temporary assignments, and thereby to avoid the scope of the Directive);

(c) undertakings which are temporary employment or placement agencies (temp agencies) hiring out workers to a user undertaking established or operating in the territory of another Member State, provided there is an employment relationship between the temp agency and the worker during the period of posting.[393]

In all three cases the key feature is the employment relationship existing between the service-providing undertaking which is established in a Member State and the posted worker.

---

[387] [1996] OJ L18/1. See also COM(93)225 final–SYN 346.

[388] Preambular para. 5.

[389] Art. 1(1). Art. 1(4) provides that undertakings established in non-Member States must not be given more favourable treatment than undertakings established in a Member State.

[390] Art. 1(1).

[391] Art. 1(3).

[392] Arts. 1 and 2.

[393] Art. 3(9) provides that Member States may provide that workers employed by temp agencies must guarantee to temps the terms and conditions which apply to temporary workers in the Member State where the work is carried out.

A posted worker means a worker, as defined by the law of the host State, who for a limited period, carries out his work in the territory of a Member State other than the State in which he normally works.[394] According to Article 3, whatever the law applicable to the employment relationship, the undertakings identified above must guarantee posted workers the host State's terms and conditions of employment in respect of:

- maximum work periods and minimum rest periods;
- minimum paid holidays;
- minimum rates of pay,[395] as defined by the host State's law and/or practice, including overtime. This does not apply to supplementary occupational retirement pension schemes;
- the conditions of hiring out of workers, in particular the supply of workers by temp agencies;
- health, safety, and hygiene at work;
- protective measures with regard to the terms and conditions of employment of pregnant women or women who have recently given birth, of children, and young people;
- equality of treatment between men and women and other provisions on non-discrimination.

These terms and conditions can be laid down by law, regulation, or administrative provision.[396] In the case of building work, including all work relating to the construction, repair, upkeep, alteration, or demolition of buildings,[397] the terms and conditions can be laid down by law, regulation, or administrative provision and/or by collective agreements or arbitration awards which have been declared 'universally applicable',[398] that is, they must be observed by all undertakings in the geographical area and in the profession or industry concerned. In countries such as the UK where no such system exists, Member States may, if they so decide, base themselves on collective agreements or arbitration awards which are generally applicable to all similar undertakings in the geographical area and in the profession or industry concerned, and/or collective agreements which have been concluded by the most representative

---

[394] Art. 2(1) and (2). For the position on social security see Art. 14 of Regulation 1408/71 [1971] OJ L149/2 as amended, discussed in Ch. 5. See also Case C–202/97 *Fitzwilliam Executive Search Ltd* v. *Bestuur van het Landelijk Instituut Sociale Verzekeringen* [2000] All ER (EC) 144.

[395] Allowances specific to the posting shall be considered to be part of the minimum wage, unless they are paid in reimbursement of expenditure actually incurred on account of the posting, such as expenditure on travel, board, and lodging (Art. 3(7), para. 2).

[396] Art. 3(1).

[397] Esp. excavation, earth-moving, actual building work, assembly and dismantling of prefabricated elements, fitting out or installation, alterations, renovation, repairs, dismantling, demolition, maintenance, upkeep, painting and cleaning work, improvements (Annex).

[398] Art. 3(1), explained in Art. 3(8).

employers' and labour organizations at national level,[399] and which are applied throughout the national territory, provided that their application ensures equality of treatment in the matters listed in the bullet points above between undertakings in a similar position.[400] These provisions will not prevent the application of terms and conditions of employment which are more favourable to workers.[401] Article 3(10) allows Member States, on a basis of equality of treatment, to apply to national undertakings and to undertakings of other Member States terms and conditions of employment on matters other than those referred to in the bullet points above in the case of public policy provisions, and terms and conditions of employment laid down in collective agreements or arbitration awards concerning activities other than those relating to building.[402]

In order to implement this Directive, Member States must, in accordance with national legislation or practice, designate one or more liaison offices or one or more competent national bodies.[403] They must also make provision for co-operation between the public authorities which, in accordance with national legislation, are responsible for monitoring the terms and conditions of employment. This co-operation must, in particular, consist of replying (free of charge) to reasoned requests about information on transnational supply of workers, including manifest abuses or possible cases of unlawful transnational activities.[404] The Commission and the public authorities must co-operate, especially in respect of any difficulties which may arise in the application of Article 3(10).

Remedies and the Brussels and Rome Conventions

Article 5 of Directive 96/71 requires the Member States to 'take appropriate measures in the event of failure to comply with this Directive'. They must ensure that 'adequate procedures are available to workers and/or their representatives for the enforcement of the obligations under this Directive'.[405]

---

[399] According to the Commission, this means that Member States can include agreements or awards which are complied with by the great majority of 'national-level undertakings'. The key factor is the extent to which the national level undertakings are real potential competitors to the service provider.

[400] Equality of treatment shall be deemed to exist where national undertakings in a similar position are subject, in the place in question or in the sector concerned, to the same obligations as posting undertakings as regards the matters listed in the bullet points on p. 172 above and are required to fulfil such obligations with the same effects.

[401] Art. 3(7).

[402] Art. 4(2) requires the Commission and the competent public authorities to co-operate in order to examine any difficulties which may arise in the application of Art. 3(1).

[403] Art. 4(1). Member States must notify the other Member States and the Commission of the liaison offices and/or competent bodies.

[404] It can also be inferred from Case 113/89 *Rush Portuguesa* [1990] ECR I–1417 that the provisions on the freedom to provide services must not be abused to achieve some other purpose (para. 17).

[405] Art. 5.

Article 6 provides that in order to enforce the right to the terms and conditions guaranteed by Article 3, judicial proceedings may be instituted in the Member State in whose territory the worker is or was posted, without prejudice, where applicable, to the right, under existing international conventions on jurisdiction, to institute proceedings in another Member State.[406] This coincides with the principle laid down in Article 5 of the Brussels Convention.[407] In derogation from the general principle[408] that persons domiciled in a contracting State shall, whatever their nationality, be sued in the courts of that State, Article 5 of the Brussels Convention provides:

A person domiciled in a contracting state may, in another contracting state be sued— (1) in matters relating to a contract in the courts for the place of performance of the obligation in question; [in matters relating to individual contracts of employment, this place is that where the employee habitually carries out his work or if the employee does not habitually carry out his work in any one country, the employer may also be sued in the courts for the place where the business which engaged the employee was or is now situated].[409]

In *Mulox*[410] the Court had to consider the application of the principles laid down in Article 5(1) before its amendment by the San Sebastian Convention. Geels, a Dutch national domiciled in France, sued his employer, Mulox, a limited company established under English law in London, in the French courts for terminating his contract of employment. Geels had set up his office in France but marketed Mulox products in Germany, Belgium, the Nether-

---

[406] Art. 6. See Art. 6 of the Rome Convention considered at p. 176 below. Art. 20 of the Rome Convention recognizes the principle of the precedence of Community law. Consequently, the Convention does not affect the application of provisions which, in relation to a particular matter, lay down choice-of-law rules relating to contractual obligations and which are or will be contained in the acts of institutions of the European Communities or in national laws harmonized in implementation of such acts.

[407] Convention of 27 Sept. 1968 on Jurisdiction and the Enforcement of Judgments in Civil and Commercial Matters, as amended by the Convention of 9 October 1978 on the Accession of Denmark, Ireland and the UK [1979] OJ L304/1. This was amended by Art. 4 of the San Sebastian Convention of 26 May 1989 which provided for the accession of Spain and Portugal to the Brussels Convention [1989] OJ L285/1. The discussion which follows draws heavily on the very clear exposition of the law provided by Advocate General Jacobs in his Opinion in Case C–125/92 *Mulox IBC Ltd v. Geels* [1993] ECR I–4075.

[408] The exceptions are justified by the fact that 'there must be a close connection between the dispute and the court with jurisdiction to resolve it' (Jenard Report [1979] OJ C59/1/22). Exceptions must be narrowly construed: Case 189/87 *Kalfelis v. Schröder* [1988] ECR 5565, para. 8.

[409] Added by the San Sebastian Convention. The amendments made to Art. 5(1) of the Brussels Convention by the San Sebastian Convention were modelled on the Lugano Convention (16 Sept. 1988 [1988] OJ L319/9), extending the principles of the Brussels Convention to the countries of the European Free Trade Association). Under the San Sebastian Convention, the jurisdiction based on the place of the business which engaged the employee is available only to the employee. Under the Lugano Convention it is available to both parties. Unlike the Lugano Convention, the San Sebastian Convention provides that the employer may be sued at a particular place without pretending that that is the place of performance of any obligation under the contract.

[410] Case C–125/92 [1993] ECR I–4075.

lands, and Scandinavia. Referring to earlier case law,[411] the Court pointed out that employment contracts differ from other contracts by virtue of the 'lasting bond which brings the worker to some extent within the organizational framework of the business' and consequently the link between the place where the activities are pursued which determines the application of mandatory rules and collective agreements. The Court therefore recognized that, given the peculiarities of contracts of employment, it was the courts of the place where the work was carried out which were best suited to resolving disputes in which one or more obligations under the contract of employment gave rise. The Court also added that the provisions of the Convention should be interpreted so as to take account of the need to ensure adequate protection for the socially weaker contracting party, namely the employee. Such adequate protection was better assured if the cases relating to contracts of employment fell within the jurisdiction of the courts in the place where the employee discharged his obligations to the employer to carry out the work agreed. The Court said that it was in this place that the employee could, at less cost, apply to the tribunals or defend himself before them. Consequently, the place of performance of the relevant obligation was the place where the employee carried out the activities agreed with the employer. This approach has how been confirmed in *Rutten*[411A] in the context of the Brussels Convention in its amended form. The Court also made clear that in order to determine the place 'where the employee habitually carries out his work' when the work is carried out in more than one place, the test is the place where the employee has 'established the effective centre of his working activities and where, or from which, he in fact performs the essential part of his duties vis-à-vis his employer'.

While the Brussels Convention lays down rules concerning the forum of the dispute, the Rome Convention of 19 June 1980[412] on rules concerning the law applicable to contractual obligations, which came into force on 1 April 1991, lays down choice-of-law rules for application in contractual disputes. The basic rule, laid down in Article 3, is that a contract is governed by the law chosen by the parties. However, Article 6(2) provides that:

a contract of employment shall, in the absence of choice in accordance with Article 3, be governed:

(a) by the law of the country in which the employee habitually carries out his work in performance of the contract, even if he is temporarily employed in another country; or

---

[411] Case 133/81 *Ivenel v. Schwab* [1982] ECR 1891; Case 266/85 *Shenavai v. Kreischer* [1987] ECR 239; and Case 32/88 *Six Constructions v. Humbert* [1989] ECR 341.

[411A] Case C–383/95 *Rutten v. Cross Medical Ltd* [1997] ECR I–57, para. 23.

[412] [1988] OJ L266/1. See also the Report by Giuliano and Lagarde [1980] OJ C282/1. See also AG Jacobs' Opinion in the Case C–383/95 *Rutten* [1997] ECR I–57, para. 17.

(b) if the employee does not habitually carry out his work in any one country, by the law of the country in which the place of business through which he was engaged is situated;

unless it appears from the circumstances as a whole that the contract is more closely connected with another country in which case the contract shall be governed by the law of that country.[412A]

According to Article 6(1), the choice of law made by the parties is not to have the result of depriving the employee of the protection afforded to him by the mandatory rules of the law which would be applicable under Article 6(2) in the absence of choice. The Rome Convention applies in each contracting State to contracts made after the date on which the Convention entered into force with respect to that State.[413] The Court of Justice does not yet have jurisdiction to interpret the Rome Convention. However, in *Schwab*[414] the Court did refer to the Rome Convention and indicated that it was desirable to interpret Article 5(1) of the Brussels Convention in such a way as to confer jurisdiction on the courts of the country whose substantive law governed the contract of employment.

Exceptions to and Derogations from the Directive

The provisions of the Directive do not apply to seagoing personnel in the merchant navy.[415] In addition to this total exclusion, Article 3 lists four potential derogations. First, Article 3(1) provides that Member States may choose not to apply the rules relating to minimum rates of pay and paid holidays to skilled or specialist workers employed by an undertaking involved in a contract for supplying goods, where the workers are engaged in the initial assembly or installation of goods which is an integral part of the contract, and the period of posting does not exceed eight days.[416] Secondly, Article 3(3) provides that Member States may, after consulting employers and labour, in accordance with the traditions and practices of each Member State, decide not to apply the provision relating to pay in the case of all posted workers, with the exception of those employed by a temp agency, where the posting does not exceed one month. Thirdly, Article 3(4) provides that Member States

---

[412A] Cf. Art. 6(2)(b) Rome Convention and Art. 5(1), final phrase Brussels Convention. Art. 6 will presumably be interpreted in the same way as Art. 5(1). Brussels Convention (see ss.3(1) and (2) contracts (Applicable Law) Act 1990 in the UK; Case C–125/92 *Mulox* [1993] ECR I–4075; Case C–383/95 *Rutten* [1997] ECR I–57.

[413] Art. 17.

[414] Case 133/81 [1982] ECR 1891; cf. the two Protocols [1989] OJ L48 which could confer jurisdiction on the ECJ.

[415] Art. 1(2).

[416] Art. 3(6) provides that the length of the posting shall be calculated on the basis of a reference period of one year from the beginning of the posting. In calculating the one-year period, account shall be taken of any previous periods for which the post has been filled by a posted worker. This provision does not apply to the building activities described above: see Art. 3(2).

may, in accordance with national laws or practices, provide that exemptions may be made from the provisions relating to pay in the case of all posted workers with the exception of those employed by a temp agency, and from a decision of a Member State within the meaning of Article 3(3), by means of a collective agreement,[417] where the posting does not exceed one month.[418] Fourthly, Article 3(5) provides that Member States may provide for exemptions to be granted from the provisions relating to pay and holidays in the case of all posted workers, with the exception of those employed by a temp agency, on the grounds that the amount of work to be done is not significant.[419]

It is not clear how much use will be made of these derogations since, following the social dumping thesis, it is usually not in the host State's interests to exempt service providers from the domestic rules. This is the position taken by the UK which has not taken advantage of any derogations.

Conclusions

The Directive does not try to harmonize the rules of the Member States relating to working conditions but only identifies those employment conditions which the guest undertaking must respect. However, the disparity between the rules of the different Member States in these core areas will be reduced as the Community passes further legislation in the social field. Significantly, those working conditions which this Directive identifies as important largely correspond to the areas in which Community legislation has already been passed or proposed.

Will the Directive fulfil its objectives? If the Directive is intended to facilitate the provision of services, it could be argued that the imposition of additional burdens on service providers hinders rather than facilitates the provision of services, albeit that the Court approved this interference in *Rush Portuguesa*.[419A] If, on the other hand, the Directive is intended to harmonize costs and stop social dumping the setting of only minimum standards suggests this is unlikely. For example, it is sufficient that the guest provider of services pays only the *minimum* wage rates. Most companies established in the host State will pay workers at rates above the minimum level. Therefore, the guest service provider still retains a competitive advantage, albeit one whose significance has been reduced. If, however, the objective is worker protection then the Directive may well have succeeded. In the UK the government has decided to extend all rights required by the Directive to posted workers.

---

[417] As defined in Art. 3(8).

[418] Art. 3(4).

[419] Art. 3(5). Member States must lay down the criteria to determine whether the work is considered non-significant.

[419A] German references have been made on this point: Cases C–49/98, 50–54/98 *Finalarte Sociedade de Construcao Civil v. Urlaubs – und Lohnausgleichskasse der Bauwirtschaft.*

The European Commission has now proposed two further directives on the cross-border provision of services.[420] The first covers the right of businesses established in the EU to provide services in another Member State using non-Community staff who are lawfully established in the EU. The second proposal covers self-employed workers from non-Community countries who are lawfully established in the EU. The two proposals primarily provide for the introduction of an 'EC service provision card' which would be issued by the Member State where the Community business or self-employed person is established. The card would be valid for a limited period (a maximum of twelve months) and would not be automatically renewable. This would ensure compliance with the rules governing the free movement of services (the principal place of work must continue to be the place where the business is established). The initiative does not cover the family members of nationals of the non-member countries concerned. Based on principles laid down by the Court in *Vander Elst*, the EC service provision card would cover only temporary postings. The card would ensure that businesses no longer have to complete so many procedures (to meet conditions with regard to visas, residence permits, and work permits) in every Member State where their staff provide services. The second proposal specifically targets non-Community nationals established as self-employed workers in a Member State, with the aim of extending to them the freedom to provide services. This possibility is expressly provided for in the Treaty (Article 59(2)) and is necessary to coincide with the proposal on the secondment of employed persons.

E. DEROGATIONS FROM THE PRINCIPLE OF FREE MOVEMENT OF PERSONS

1. Public Policy, Public Security, Public Health

Article 39(3) [ex Article 48(3)] authorizes derogations from the fundamental principle of free movement of workers on three grounds: public policy, public security, and public health. Articles 46 and 55 [ex Articles 56 and 66] contain the same derogations for establishment and services respectively. All derogations to a fundamental freedom of the Community must be interpreted strictly so that their scope cannot be determined unilaterally by each Member State, without being subject to control by the Community institutions,[421] and must be read subject to the general principles of law, including fundamental

---

[420] COM(99)3 final—2.
[421] Case 41/74 *Van Duyn* [1974] ECR 1337, para. 18; Case C–348/96 *Calfa* [1999] ECR I–11, para. 23.

human rights.[422] Member States do, however, retain a certain amount of discretion, within the limits of the Treaty, to determine what constitutes public policy in the light of their national needs.[423]

The bare bones of these derogations are fleshed out by the provisions of Directive 64/221.[424] Although based on Article 46(2) [ex Article 56(2)], the Directive applies to all three categories of free movement of persons as well as to spouses and members of their families.[425] The Directive relates to all measures concerning entry into the territory, issue or renewal of residence permits, and expulsion from the territory[426] but it cannot be used 'to service economic ends'.[427] It applies to legislative measures and individual decisions taken in applying the legislation,[428] as well as to judicial decisions.[429]

1.1 Public Policy and Public Security

The starting point for determining what constitute public policy and public security is Article 3(1) of Directive 64/221 which is directly effective.[430] This provides that measures taken on the grounds of public policy must be 'based exclusively on the *personal* conduct of the individual concerned'.[431] The corollary of this, as the Court pointed out in *Bonsignore*,[432] is that extraneous matters unrelated to the particular individual, such as making an example of him or her as a deterrent to others, may not be taken into account. Bonsignore was convicted of a firearms offence and of causing the death of his brother by negligence. A deportation order was made against him for reasons of a 'general preventive nature', based on the deterrent effect that the deportation of an alien found in illegal possession of a firearm would have in immigrant circles where there had been a resurgence of violence. The Court said that in these circumstances the deportation would contravene Article 3

---

[422] See Case C–260/89 *ERT v. DEP* [1991] ECR I–2925 where the Court said that the application of the derogations in Arts. 56 and 66 [new Arts. 46 and 55] must be appraised in the light of the general principle of freedom of expression in Art. 10 of the European Convention on Human Rights.

[423] Case 41/74 *Van Duyn* [1974] ECR 1337; Joined Cases 115 and 116/81 *Adoui and Cornuaille v. Belgian State* [1982] ECR 1665, para. 8; and Case 36/75 *Rutili v. Ministre de l'intérieur* [1975] ECR 1219.

[424] [1964] OJ Spec. Ed. 850/64. See also Commission Communication to the Council and the European Parliament on the Special Measures concerning the movement and residence of citizens of the Union which are justified on the grounds of public policy, public security or public health 1999: http://europa.eu.int/comm/dg15/en/update/citi/citiz.htm.

[425] Art. 1.

[426] Art. 2.

[427] Art. 2(2).

[428] Case 36/75 *Rutili* [1975] ECR 1219.

[429] Case 30/77 *R v. Bouchereau* [1977] ECR 1999.

[430] Case 41/74 *Van Duyn* [1974] ECR 1337, para. 15.

[431] See also Woolridge, 'Free Movement of EEC Nationals: The Limitation Based on Public Policy and Public Security' (1977) 2 *ELRev.* 190.

[432] Case 6/74 *Bonsignore v. Oberstadtdirektor of the City of Cologne* [1975] ECR 297.

of Directive 64/221. Deportation may be ordered only in the case of breaches of the peace and public security caused by the individual concerned.

The question of what constitutes personal conduct was also considered in *Van Duyn*.[433] Van Duyn was refused entry into the UK to work as a secretary for the Church of Scientology. Although membership of this church was not prohibited by English law, the activities of the church were considered to be 'socially harmful'. The Court was asked to decide whether membership of a particular organization could constitute personal conduct. First, it ruled that a person's past association could not, in general, justify a decision refusing him the right to move freely within the Community. By contrast, a person's present association with an organization could constitute personal conduct, because present association reflected a voluntary participation in the activities of an organization, as well as an identification with its aims and designs.[434] The Court also said that the personal conduct did not need to be unlawful before a Member State could invoke the public policy exception. It was sufficient that the conduct was deemed to be 'socially harmful' and that the State had taken administrative measures to demonstrate its disapproval of the particular activities.

More controversially, the Court also suggested that the host State could refuse a national of another Member State benefit of the rules on the free movement of persons, even though the State did not place a similar restriction on its own nationals.[435] Subsequent case law has implicitly reversed this part of the judgment: it is now clear that Member States must apply the doctrine of non-discrimination as far as possible, subject to the condition that pursuant to international law Member States have no authority to refuse entry or expel their own nationals from the territory of their own State.[436] Therefore, if conduct on the part of the State's own nationals is not subject to serious repressive measures, it cannot be a cause for expulsion of other citizens of the Union. This can be seen in *Adoui and Cornuaille*[437] where two French prostitutes were refused permission to reside in Belgium on public policy grounds, despite the fact that prostitution was not prohibited by Belgian legislation.[438] The Court said that Member States were not entitled to base the exercise of their discretion on 'assessments of certain conduct which would have the effect of applying an arbitrary distinction to the detriment of nationals of other Member States'. This decision confirmed the approach adopted by the

---

[433] Case 41/74 [1974] ECR 1337.

[434] Para. 17.

[435] The Court was heavily influenced by the principle of international law that a State is precluded from refusing its own nationals the right of entry or residence.

[436] See further Case C–171/96 *Pereira Roque v. Governor of Jersey* [1998] ECR I–4607, paras. 49–50; see further Case C–348/96 *Calfa* [1999] ECR I–11, para. 20.

[437] Joined Cases 115 and 116/81 [1982] ECR 1665.

[438] Although certain incidental activities, such as the exploitation of prostitution by third parties and various forms of incitement to debauchery, were unlawful.

Court in the earlier case of *Rutili*.[439] The French Minister confined the activities of Rutili, a noted political agitator, to certain regions of France. The Court held that this could only be justified if the Member State imposed similar restrictions on its own nationals. The Court also made clear that restrictions could not be imposed on the right of individuals to free movement unless their 'presence or conduct constitutes a genuine and sufficiently serious threat to public policy'. In interpreting the limitations to this fundamental freedom the Court referred to Articles 8 to 11 of the European Convention on Human Rights.[440] The Court, in recognizing the application of the principle of proportionality, concluded that no restrictions in 'the interests of national security or public safety [sic] are permitted other than such as are necessary for the protection of those interests "in a democratic society"'.

The concept of personal conduct was further narrowed in *Bouchereau*.[441] The Court said that the public policy exception could only be invoked to justify restrictions on the free movement of workers provided that 'there was a genuine and sufficiently serious threat *affecting one of the fundamental interests of society*' (emphasis added). A simple infringement of the social order by breaching the law (possessing drugs on the facts of the case) would not suffice. In *Adoui*[442] the Court concluded that the personal conduct (being a prostitute) could not be deemed sufficiently serious to justify the application of the derogations, where the host Member State did not adopt with respect to the same conduct on the part of its own nationals 'repressive measures or other genuine and effective measures intended to combat such conduct'.

The Court in *Bouchereau*[443] also had the opportunity to consider the relevance of previous criminal convictions. Bouchereau, a French national working in England, was convicted of unlawful possession of drugs. Six months earlier he had pleaded guilty to a similar offence and had been given a twelve-month conditional discharge. The magistrate now wished to deport him on the ground of public policy. Article 3(2) of Directive 64/221 provides that previous criminal convictions will not themselves constitute reasons for taking measures on the grounds of public policy. The Court decided that the existence of a criminal conviction could only be taken into account in so far as the circumstances which led to that conviction were evidence of personal conduct constituting a *present threat* to the requirements of public policy by showing a propensity to commit the similar acts again. The importance of this requirement was emphasized in *Calfa*.[444] The Court had to consider the

---

[439] Case 36/75 [1975] ECR 1219.

[440] For a discussion of the role played by the European Convention in shaping the case law on Art. 39(3) [ex Art. 48(3)], see Hall, 'The European Convention on Human Rights and Public Policy Exceptions to the Free Movement of Workers under the EEC Treaty' (1991) 16 *ELRev*. 466.

[441] Case 30/77 [1977] ECR 1999.

[442] Joined Cases 115 and 116/81 [1982] ECR 1665.

[443] Case 30/77 [1977] ECR 1999.

[444] Case C–348/96 [1999] ECR I–11.

expulsion of an individual for life from the host State, Greece, on the ground that she was convicted of obtaining and being in possession of drugs for her own use. The Court ruled that an expulsion order could be made against a Community national only if, besides her having committed an offence under national drugs laws, her personal conduct created a genuine and sufficiently serious threat affecting one of the fundamental interests of society. On the facts of the case expulsion for life automatically followed a criminal conviction, without any account being taken of the personal conduct of the offender or of the danger which that person represented for the requirements of public policy. The Court therefore ruled that the conditions for the application of the public policy exception provided for in Directive 64/221, as interpreted by the Court, were not fulfilled and that the public policy exception could not be successfully relied upon to justify such a restriction on the freedom to receive services.

While the category of public policy and public security is usually considered from the point of view of personal conduct, the Annex to Directive 64/221 also lists diseases and disabilities which might threaten public security or public policy. The Annex identifies drug addiction, profound mental disturbance, and manifest conditions of psychotic disturbance with agitation, delirium, hallucinations, or confusion as falling within this category. This list is closely related to the exclusions on the grounds of public health considered below.

Neither the Treaty nor the Directive specifies what measures can be taken against an individual by the State when acting to protect the public interest. The most obvious measure would be deportation[445] but the draconian nature of such a step was recognized by the Court in *Watson and Belmann*.[446] It ruled that deportation for failing to comply with the residence formalities within a reasonable time after arriving in a country was disproportionate, for deportation 'negates the very right conferred and guaranteed by the Treaty'. Similarly, Article 3(3) of Directive 64/221 provides that the expiry of an identity card or passport used by a person to enter the host country will not suffice to justify deportation.[447] The Court has, however, recognized that other measures would be lawful. In *Rutili*[448] the Court said that restricting a person's right of residence to a limited area in the country, provided that similar measures would also be applied to nationals, was compatible with Community law.

---

[445] See Barav, 'Court Recommendation to Deport and the Free Movement of Workers in EEC Law' (1981) 6 *ELRev.* 139.

[446] Case 118/75 [1976] ECR 1185.

[447] In these circumstances, the State which issued the identity card or passport must allow the holder to re-enter its territory, even if the document is no longer valid or the nationality of its holder is in dispute (Art. 3(4)).

[448] Case 36/75 [1975] ECR 1219.

1.2 Public Health

The public health derogation can be invoked only to justify refusal of entry or first issue of a residence permit.[449] The public health grounds are those diseases or disabilities contained in the exhaustive list found in the Annex to the Directive. The recognized diseases are those subject to quarantine listed in International Health Regulation No. 2 of the World Health Organization of 25 May 1951: tuberculosis, syphilis, or other infectious or contagious diseases or contagious parasitic diseases if they are subject to provisions for protection of nationals of the host country. Migrants who are HIV positive or who suffer from AIDS find themselves in a particularly invidious position.[450] The practice of Member States has been to deny admission to such people,[451] although there is no express provision for this in the Directive.[452] However, in its Communication on the derogations, the Commission rejects the use of any measures which could lead to 'social exclusion, discrimination or stigmatisation of persons with HIV/AIDS'.[453] More generally, the Commission observes that the public health grounds are 'somewhat outdated' given the current level of integration in the EU and the development of new means to handle public health problems. It concludes that 'restrictions of free movement can no longer be considered a necessary and effective means of solving public health problems'.

1.3 Procedural Matters

Directive 64/221 lays down minimum procedural requirements to protect migrant workers faced with measures taken against them on public policy, public security, and public health grounds. First, they are entitled to be informed officially[454] of the grounds of public policy, public security, or public health upon which the decisions taken in their cases are based, unless this is contrary to the interests of the security of the State.[455] This statement of reasons must be precise and comprehensive to enable the migrant to take

---

[449] Diseases or disabilities occurring after a first residence permit has been issued will not justify refusal to renew the residence permit or expulsion from the territory: see Art. 4(2).

[450] See Van Overbeek, 'AIDS/HIV infection and the Free Movement of Persons within the Community' (1990) 27 *CMLRev.* 791.

[451] Ibid., 792.

[452] In this context of the Community's treatment of its own staff or job applicants with HIV is instructive. The Court has ruled that the requirement that every person undergo a medical examination does not infringe Art. 8 of the ECHR. However, the Court did examine the conclusions of the Council as the Ministers of Health which said that employees who are HIV positive but who do not show any symptoms of AIDS should be looked on as normal employees fit for work [1989] OJ C28/2. The Court said that the administration must treat these conclusions as rules of practice, otherwise the principle of equal treatment would be infringed, see Case T–10/93 *A v. EC Commission* [1994] ECR II–179, IA–119, II–387.

[453] See above, n. 424, 12.

[454] Art. 7.

[455] Art. 6.

effective steps to prepare a defence.[456] Secondly, except in cases of urgency, the period provided for leaving the country must not be less than fifteen days, for those who have not yet been granted their residence permit, and one month in all other cases.[457] Thirdly, according to Article 8, 'The person concerned shall have the same legal remedies in respect of any decision concerning entry, or refusing the issue or renewal of a residence permit, or ordering expulsion from the territory, as are available to nationals of the state concerned in respect of acts of the administration'. In *ex parte Shingara and Radiom*[458] the Court was asked to consider whether, on a proper construction of Article 8 the words 'the same legal remedies' refer (a) to specific remedies available in respect of decisions concerning *entry* by nationals of the State concerned (*in casu*, an appeal to an immigration adjudicator) or (b) only to remedies available in respect of acts of the administration generally (*in casu*, an application for judicial review).

The Court said that Article 8 did not govern the ways in which remedies were to be made available, for instance by stipulating the courts from which such remedies could be sought, but it did mean that a Member State could not, without being in breach of the obligation imposed by Article 8, organize legal remedies governed by special procedures affording lesser safeguards than those pertaining to remedies available to nationals in respect of acts of the administration. By contrast, where national law provided no specific procedures for the remedies available for persons covered by the Directive, the Article 8 obligation was fulfilled if nationals of other Member States enjoyed the same remedies as those generally available against acts of the administration in that Member State. The Court then said that the remedies available to nationals of other Member States in the circumstances defined by the Directive could not be assessed by reference to the remedies available to nationals concerning the right of entry because the two situations were not comparable: whereas in the case of nationals the right of entry was a consequence of the status of being a national, so that there could be no margin of discretion for the State as regards the exercise of that right, the special circumstances which might justify reliance on the concept of public policy as against nationals of other Member States might vary over time and from one country to another, and it was therefore necessary to allow the competent national authorities a margin of discretion. Consequently, the Article 8 obligation was satisfied if nationals of other Member States enjoyed the same remedies as those available against acts of the administration generally in that Member State.

---

[456] Case 36/75 *Rutili* [1975] ECR 1219, para. 39; Joined Cases 115 and 116/81 *Adoui and Cornuaille* [1982] ECR 1665, para. 13.
[457] Art. 7.
[458] Joined Cases C–65 and C–111/95 *The Queen v. Secretary of State for the Home Department, ex parte Singh Shingara and Abbas Radiom* [1997] ECR I–3343.

The provisions of Article 9 complement those of Article 8. This requires that the administrative authority making the final adjudication cannot, save in cases of urgency, take a decision until the competent authority has given its view. This competent authority must not be the same body as the one empowered to take the decision and the migrant must enjoy 'the same rights of defence and assistance or representation as the domestic law of that country provides for'.[459] Article 9(1) is sufficiently well-defined as to have direct effect.[460] Article 9(1) envisages the intervention of a competent authority in three situations: first, where there is no right of appeal to a court of law; secondly, where such appeal may be only in respect of the legal validity of the decision; and thirdly, where the appeal cannot have suspensory effect. The role of the competent authority is to make an exhaustive examination of all the facts and circumstances, including the expediency of the proposed measure to be taken, before a final decision is made.[461] Member States can decide on the procedure by means of which a person appears before the competent authority; the Member States do not have to allow an individual to make a direct approach.[462] The migrant must be informed of the outcome of the authority's decision but is not entitled to know the identity or professional status of those making up the competent authority.[463]

The Directive does not define the term 'competent authority', requiring only that it be 'independent of the administration', but it gives the Member States a margin of discretion as regards the nature of the authority. Article 9 does not require the authority to be a court or tribunal or composed of members of the judiciary.[464] However, in *ex parte Santillo* the Court recognized that a recommendation for deportation made by a criminal court at the time of conviction could constitute an opinion given by a competent authority, providing that the court had taken account of Article 3(2) of Directive 64/221 that the mere existence of criminal convictions did not automatically constitute grounds for deportation. Nor does Article 9 require that the members of the authority be appointed for a specified period. The essential requirement is for the authority to perform its duties in absolute independence; that it must not be directly or indirectly subject to any control by the administrative body empowered to take the measures provided for in the Directive; and that the authority follow a procedure which enables the person concerned, on the terms laid down by the Directive, effectively to present his defence.[465] Provided that requirement is satisfied, it is not unlawful for the

---

[459] Joined Cases C–297/88 and C–197/89 *Dzodzi* v. *Belgium* [1990] ECR I–3763, para. 62.
[460] Case 131/79 *R* v. *Secretary of State for Home Affairs, ex parte Santillo* [1980] ECR 1585.
[461] Ibid. and Joined Cases 115 and 116/81 *Adoui and Cornuaille* [1982] ECR 1665.
[462] Joined Cases 115 and 116/81 *Adoui and Cornuaille* [1982] ECR 1665.
[463] Ibid.; Case C–175/94 *R* v. *Secretary of State for the Home Department, ex parte Gallagher* [1995] ECR I–4253.
[464] Case C–175/94 *ex parte Gallagher* [1995] ECR I–4253.
[465] Ibid.

remuneration of the members of the authority to be charged to the budget of the department which is also responsible for the administrative authority.[466]

According to the Court in *ex parte Santillo*,[467] Article 9(1) can only operate as a real safeguard if all the factors to be taken into account by the administration are placed before the competent authority, if the opinion of the competent authority is sufficiently proximate in time to the decision ordering the expulsion to ensure that there are no new factors to be taken into consideration, and if both the administration and the person concerned can understand the reasons which led the competent authority to give its opinion, except where it is contrary to the interests of the state to provide such reasons. The defendant in *ex parte Santillo* had been convicted in December 1973 of buggery, rape, and assault. He was sentenced to eight years' imprisonment and the court also recommended deportation. Five years later, in September 1978, the Secretary of State made a deportation order against Santillo to take effect when his prison sentence was completed. With remission for good behaviour Santillo completed his prison sentence in April 1979. The Court said that a lapse of time amounting to several years between the recommendation for deportation and the decision by the administration was liable to deprive the recommendation of its function as an opinion within the meaning of Article 9. The Court added that it was essential that the social danger resulting from the foreigner's presence should be assessed at the very time when the decision ordering expulsion was made, since the factors to be taken into account, particularly concerning conduct, were likely to change in the course of time.[468]

The competent authority plays a more limited role where no residence permit has been issued, or a first permit has been refused. According to Article 9(2) the decision can only be referred to the competent authority at the migrant's request. The migrant can then make a case in his or her own defence, unless this is contrary to national security.[469] In *Pecastaing*[470] the Court said that the migrant could not be deported until the procedure had been completed, except in an emergency.

Article 9(2) was also at issue in *ex parte Shingara and Radiom*.[471] The national court asked whether a national of a Member State who had been refused entry into another Member State for reasons of public order or public security had a right of appeal in respect of measures adopted subsequently which prevented his entering that State, even if the first decision had not been

---

[466] Joined Cases 115 and 116/81 *Adoui and Cornuaille* [1982] ECR 1665, para. 16.

[467] Case 131/79 [1980] ECR 1585.

[468] The national court, however, found that no new facts justified setting aside the deportation order, see [1981] 3 CMLR 212 and [1981] 2 WLR 370. See also O'Keeffe, 'Practical Difficulties in the Application of Article 48 of the EEC Treaty' (1982) 19 *CMLRev*. 35.

[469] Art. 9(2).

[470] Case 98/79 *Pecastaing v. Belgian State* [1980] ECR 691.

[471] Joined Cases C–65 and C–111/95 [1997] ECR I–3343.

the subject of an appeal or an opinion. The Court said that a Community national expelled from a Member State could apply for a fresh residence permit, and, if that application was made after a reasonable time, it had to be examined by the competent administrative authority in that State, which had to take into particular account the arguments put forward to establish that there had been a material change in the circumstances which justified the first decision ordering expulsion. Decisions prohibiting entry into a Member State of a national of another Member State constituted derogations from the fundamental principle of freedom of movement. Consequently, such a decision could not be of unlimited duration.

The general principles of law developed by the Court, derived from the European Convention on Human Rights, underpin the application of the law in this area. As the Court said in *Wachauf*,[472] fundamental rights form part of the Community legal order, and are binding on the Member States when they implement Community rules. Consequently, Member States must, as far as possible, apply those rules. These general principles include the right to a fair hearing[473] and the right to have access to the judicial process.[474] The substance of these general principles was considered by the Court in *Heylens*.[475] The Court said that the existence of a remedy of a judicial nature against any decision of a national authority refusing the benefit of that right was essential in order to secure for the individual effective protection of that right. This requirement reflects a general principle of Community law which underlies the constitutional traditions common to the Member States and has been enshrined in Articles 3 and 6 of the European Convention on Human Rights.[476] The Court added that the national authority is under a duty to inform the migrant of the reasons on which the decision is based. This is particularly important in a case concerning a fundamental right, the free movement of workers, so that the migrant can defend that right under the best possible conditions.

2. Public Service Exception

It has been traditional for Member States to reserve certain jobs, usually in the public service, to their own nationals.[477] This has been recognized by Article

---

[472] Case 5/88 *Wachauf v. Bundesamt für Ernährung und Forstwirtschaft* [1989] ECR 2609.

[473] Case 17/74 *Transocean Marine Paint v. Commission* [1979] ECR 1063.

[474] Case 222/84 *Johnston v. RUC* [1986] ECR 1651.

[475] Case 222/86 [1987] ECR 4097.

[476] See also Case 222/84 *Johnston* [1986] ECR 1651.

[477] For further details see Morris, Fredman, and Hayes, 'Free Movement and the Public Sector' (1990) 19 *ILJ* 20; Groenendijk, 'Nationality and Access to Employment in the Public Service: Law and Practice in the Netherlands' [1989] *Netherlands International Law Review* 107; Lenz, 'The Public Service in Article 48(4) EEC with Special Reference to the Law in England and in the Federal Republic of Germany' [1989/2] *LIEI* 75.

39(4) [ex Article 48(4)] which provides that the principles of free movement of workers and non-discrimination on the ground of nationality do not apply to employment in the public service, and more specifically to access to employment in the public service.[478] Articles 45 and 55 [ex Articles 55 and 66] say that the provisions of the chapter on freedom of establishment do not apply to activities which in that State are connected 'even occasionally with the exercise of official authority'.[479] The justification for the Article 39(4) [ex Article 48(4)] exception is that these particular posts presume a special relationship of allegiance to the state and a 'reciprocity of rights and duties which form the foundation of the bond of nationality'.[480] These provisions represent further exceptions to fundamental freedoms and consequently must also be narrowly construed,[481] limiting their scope to what is 'strictly necessary for safeguarding the interests of the state which that provision allows the Member States to protect'.[482]

The most striking illustration of the application of Article 39(4) [ex Article 48(4)] can be found in the case of *Commission v. Belgium*.[483] The Belgian government restricted posts on Belgian railways, including trainee drivers, shunters, and signallers, and posts within the City of Brussels, including hospital nurses, plumbers, and electricians, to Belgian applicants only. This denied nationals of other Member States access to a large number of positions. The Court explained that the jobs envisaged by Article 48(4) [new Article 39(4)] 'involve direct or indirect participation in the exercise of powers conferred by public law[484] and duties designed to safeguard the interests of the state or of other public authorities'. The Court continued that these jobs are 'characteristic of specific activities of public service insofar as it is invested with the exercise of public power and the responsibility for safeguarding the general interests of the state'. It is not clear whether these requirements should be read cumulatively.[485] A cumulative reading would be consistent with the view that Article 39(4) must be interpreted restrictively; but support can be found in the decision in *Commission v. Italy*[486] that the requirements should be read disjunctively.

The Court, in developing a Community law definition of employment in the public service, adopts a functional rather than an institutional (organic) approach. The institutional approach regards the institution together with its

---

[478] Case 152/73 *Sotgiu* [1974] ECR 153.

[479] The same applies to freedom to supply services, see Art. 56 [ex Art. 66].

[480] Case 149/79 *Commission v. Belgium* [1980] ECR I–3881. See also Handoll, 'Article 48(4) and Non-National Access to Public Employment' (1988) 13 *ELRev.* 223.

[481] Case 152/73 *Sotgiu* [1979] ECR 153, para. 4.

[482] Case 225/85 *Commission v. Italy* [1987] ECR 2725.

[483] Case 149/79 [1980] ECR 3881.

[484] See further Lenz, above, n. 477, 102–3.

[485] Cf. Handoll, above n. 480; Lenz, above n. 477, 99–100; Morris *et al.*, above n. 477, 23.

[486] Case 225/85 [1987] ECR 2725, paras. 9 and 10.

personnel as a whole, regardless of individual functions.[487] The functional approach applies only to workers exercising certain functions within that sector.[488] In *Sotgiu*[489] the Court refused to examine the nature of the legal relationship between the employee and the employing administration, nor the job description (workman, clerk, or official), nor whether the person was employed under public or private law. Instead, the Court has taken into account the nature of the tasks and responsibilities inherent in the post, dealing with each situation on a case by case basis.[490] In a somewhat inconsistent line of case law, the Court has recognized that local authority posts for architects, supervisors, and some nightwatchmen would fall within the Article 39(4) [ex Article 48(4)] exception,[491] as would posts involving management (of public bodies) and those involved in advising the State on scientific and technical questions. However, consistent with the fundamental objective of encouraging free movement of persons, most posts fall outside Article 39(4), such as a teaching post in a state school,[492] a state nurse,[493] a foreign language assistant in a university,[494] a local government employee,[495] a seaman,[496] a job in research which did not involve sensitive research work,[497] and a post in the lower echelons of the civil service.[498] Article 39(4) may, however, represent a barrier to promotion for non-nationals because, as the Court pointed out in *Commission v. Italy*,[499] Community law does not prohibit a Member State from reserving for its own nationals those posts within a career bracket which involve participation in the exercise of powers conferred by public law or safeguarding the general interests of the State.

While it is difficult to draw any clear principle from the case law, it does appear that posts in which the exercise of public law powers is purely marginal and ancillary to the principal functions of the posts fall outside Article 39(4) [ex Article 48(4)]. This seems to be the view taken by the Commission

---

[487] The French have argued in favour of an institutional approach which they say is integral to the French administrative structure. For a discussion of these views see Rapacciuolo, 'The Scope of Article 48(4) of the EEC Treaty', *Social Europe* 1/89.

[488] Lenz, above n. 477, 95; Handoll, above n. 480, 228.

[489] Case 152/73 [1974] ECR 153.

[490] Case 149/79 *Commission v. Belgium* [1980] ECR 3881.

[491] Ibid.

[492] Case 66/85 *Lawrie-Blum* [1986] ECR 2121. Employment as a secondary school teacher also does not fall within Art. 48(4) [new Art. 39(4)]: Case C–4/91 *Bleis* v. *Ministère de l'education nationale* [1991] ECR I–5627.

[493] Case 307/84 *Commission v. France* [1986] ECR 1725 where under French law a nurse had to be French to have a permanent job in a public hospital.

[494] Case 33/88 *Allué and Coonan* [1989] ECR 1591.

[495] Case 149/79 *Commission v. Belgium* [1980] ECR 3881.

[496] Case C–37/93 *Commission v. Belgium* [1993] ECR I–6295.

[497] Case 225/85 *Commission v. Italy* [1987] ECR 2625.

[498] Case 66/85 *Lawrie-Blum* [1986] ECR 2121 and Case C–4/91 *Bleis* [1991] ECR I–5627 (post in a French secondary school).

[499] Case 225/85 *Commission v. Italy* [1987] ECR 2625.

in its Communication and action programme designed to eliminate restrictions in areas of the public sector. It has listed jobs in the public sector to which, in normal circumstances, Article 48(4) [new Article 39(4)] does not apply, including public health care services, employment in state educational institutions, research for non-military purposes in public establishments and public bodies responsible for administering public, commercial services, including, for example, public transport, gas, or electricity distribution, air or maritime navigation, post and telecommunications, and broadcasting. It suggested that Article 48(4) would, however, apply to the police and other forces of order, the armed forces, the judiciary, tax authorities, and the diplomatic service.[500] Following on from this Communication, the Commission started enforcement proceedings against defaulting Member States. Luxembourg, for example, was condemned for restricting to its own nationals posts in the public sectors of research, education, health, inland transport, post, telecommunications, and in the water, gas, and electricity distribution services.[501]

The *Sotgiu*[502] case made clear that Article 48(4) [new Article 39(4)] applies only to conditions of access to employment; it does not authorize discriminatory conditions of employment once access has been granted. Sotgiu, an Italian national, was employed by the German postal service. His employers refused to pay him a separation allowance which was granted to German workers who were employed away from their homes, on the ground that he was employed in the public service which was exempt from the non-discrimination provisions under Article 48(4). The Court rejected this argument. It ruled that Article 48(4) applied only to access to the public service; it could not be used to justify discriminatory measures against workers who have joined the public service, since the fact of being admitted to the service denied the existence of those very interests which justified the derogation.

As we have seen, an equivalent derogation to Article 39(4) [ex Article 48(4)] exists in the context of establishment and services: Article 45 [ex Article 55]. This talks of the 'exercise of official authority' rather than 'employment in the public service' but the objectives of Article 45 are similar to those of Article 39(4) and the jurisprudence on Article 39(4) would apply by analogy.[503] The nature of what constitutes official authority was discussed

---

[500] [1988] OJ C72/2; Watson (1989) 14 *ELRev.* 415. Unfortunately, this list does not coincide precisely with the cases found by the Court to fall within Art. 39(4) [ex Art. 48(4)].

[501] Case C–473/93 *Commission v. Luxembourg* [1996] ECR I–3263. See also Case C–173/94 *Commission v. Belgium* [1996] ECR I–3265 and Case C–290/94 *Commission v. Greece* [1996] ECR I–3285 where Greece was also condemned for limiting posts in radio and television broadcasting and orchestras to Greek nationals only.

[502] Case 152/73 [1979] ECR 153.

[503] See also Case C–42/92 *Thijssen v. Controldienst voor de verzekeringen* [1993] ECR I–4047, where the Court held that the office of an approved Commissioner responsible for the monitoring of insurance undertakings did not constitute the exercise of official authority.

in *Reyners*.[504] A question was raised whether the principle of non-discrimination on the grounds of nationality should not apply to the profession of
avocat, on the ground that *avocats* were connected with the public service of
administration of justice. The Court said that Article 55 [new Article 45] had
to be narrowly construed: it applied only to those activities which had a
'direct and specific connection with official authority'. It would not be possible
to extend the application of Article 55 [new Article 45] to a whole profession
unless such activities were linked with the profession in such a way that
freedom of establishment would result in imposing on the Member State concerned the obligation to allow the exercise, even occasionally, of official
authority. This would not apply to the legal profession where contacts with
the courts, although regular and organic, did not constitute the exercise of
official authority since it was possible to separate the exercise of official
authority from the professional activity taken as a whole.

Questions have been raised about the compatibility of Articles 39(4) and
45 [ex Articles 48(4) and 55] with the objectives of the internal market and
more specifically with the notion of Community citizenship laid down by
Article 17 [ex Article 8(1)]. Articles 39(4) and 45 represent a continued
respect for *national* sovereignty at a time when efforts are being made to
promote *Union* consciousness. Nevertheless, no attempt has been made to
amend these derogations.

F. CITIZENSHIP AND THE FREE MOVEMENT PROVISIONS

It will be recalled that the Treaty on European Union introduced the concept
of citizenship of the Union for all those holding the nationality of one of the
Member States. The first right granted to all citizens is the right to move and
reside freely within the territory of the Member States, subject to the limitations and conditions laid down by this Treaty and by the measures adopted to
give it effect (Article 18(1) [ex Article 8a(1)]).[505] The question is whether
Article 18(1) confers rights beyond those already found in Articles 39, 43,
and 49 [ex Articles 48, 52, and 59] of the Treaty and the secondary legislation. The English courts have been forced to examine these issues in two cases,
ex parte Vitale and Do Amaral[506] and *ex parte Adams*.[507] The *Adams* case
concerned an order made by the Home Secretary under the Prevention of

---

[504] Case 2/74 [1974] ECR 631.
[505] The Council may, however 'adopt provisions with a view to facilitating the exercise of the
rights referred to in paragraph 1' (Art. 18(2) [ex Art. 8a(1)]) in accordance with the Art. 251
procedure, save as otherwise provided in the Treaty.
[506] R v. *Secretary of State, ex parte Vitale and Do Amaral* [1995] All ER (EC) 946.
[507] R v. *Secretary of State, ex parte Adams* [1995] All ER(EC) 177.

Terrorism (Temporary Provisions) Act 1989 excluding Gerry Adams, the leader of Sinn Fein, the political wing of the IRA, from mainland Britain. He challenged the order on the basis that it contravened Article 8a(1) [new Article 18(1)]. The Divisional Court thought that Gerry Adams at least had an arguable case based on Article 8a(1), even though the case appeared to concern a purely internal situation. Steyn LJ also suggested that Article 8a(1) might have direct effect, and that the right to move freely in the Union and the right of free speech were fundamental rights. He did, however, agree to refer the matter to the Court of Justice to determine the ambit of Article 8a(1). With the changed political situation in Northern Ireland, the reference was subsequently withdrawn. However, in *Kremzow*[508] the Court seems to have ruled out the possibility of using Article 8a [new Article 18] to apply to intra-state movement.

While the *Adams* case concerned the right to move freely, *Vitale and Do Amaral* concerned the right to reside. The applicants were citizens of Italy and Portugal. They received income support for approximately six months when the Home Office requested them to leave the country. It explained that they were not lawfully resident in the UK under Community law because they were not in employment or genuinely seeking work with a reasonable prospect of success. The applicants then sought judicial review of the Home Secretary's decisions, contending that as citizens of the Union they had a directly effective and unlimited right to reside freely in the UK under Article 8a [new Article 18]. Judge J argued that the rights of free movement and to reside freely were neither free-standing nor absolute: they were subject to the limitations and conditions laid down in the Treaty. Consequently, he concluded that 'Article 8a [new Article 18] does not provide every citizen of the Union with an open-ended right to reside freely within every Member State', nor is the restriction limited to the three areas identified in Article 48(3) [new Article 39(3)]. He then argued that since Articles 48, 52, and 59 [new Articles 39, 43, and 49] remained unrepealed and unamended, and the relevant body of secondary legislation continued to exist, Article 8a(1) did not significantly extend the rights of free movement and residence already accorded to nationals of Member States under the Treaty or pursuant to the Council Directives. The Court of Appeal upheld Judge J's ruling and rejected Vitale's appeal.[509] Staughton LJ said that if Article 8a(1) had been intended to sweep aside the limitations upheld in *ex parte Antonissen* and to confer a general unfettered right of residence, leaving in place only those limitations expressly referred to in Article 48(3) [new Article 39(3)] which could be justified on the grounds of public policy, public security, and public health, then it would have been necessary to have made that explicit by amendment of Article 48 [new

---

[508] Case C–299/95 *Kremzow v. Republik Österreich* [1997] ECR I–2629. See also Joined Cases C–64 and C–65/96 *Uecker and Jacquet* [1997] ECR I–3171.

[509] *R v. Secretary of State for the Home Department, ex parte Vitale, The Times,* 26 Jan. 1996.

Article 39]. The Court added that it seemed equally clear that Article 8a(1) could not be taken to have replaced the 1990 Directives and that Article 8a(1) had to be read as being subject to the limitation found in these Directives, namely that the visiting national should not become a burden on the social assistance system of the Member State. The Court concluded that 'there was at the moment no unqualified right of residence of the kind claimed by the applicant'.

The Court of Justice has also been somewhat reluctant to put flesh on the bones of the citizenship provisions. Typically it has made passing reference to the citizenship provisions to reinforce its interpretation of other Treaty provisions, in particular the principle of non-discrimination found in Article 12 [ex Article 6]. For example, in *Bickel and Franz*[510] the Court said:

Article 59 [new Article 49] therefore covers all nationals of Member States who, independently of other freedoms guaranteed by the Treaty, visit another Member State where they intend or are likely to receive services. Such persons—and they include both Mr Bickel and Mr Franz—are free to visit and move around within the host State. Furthermore, pursuant to Article 8a [new Article 18] of the Treaty, '[e]very citizen of the Union shall have the right to move and reside freely within the territory of the Member States, subject to the limitations and conditions laid down in this Treaty and by the measures adopted to give it effect'.

The Court continued that, under the principle of non-discrimination, Bickel and Franz were entitled to treatment no less favourable than that accorded to nationals. Similarly, in *Skanavi*[511] the Court was asked to consider Article 8a(1) [new Article 18(1)] in the context of Article 52 [new Article 43]. The Court said that Article 6 EC [new Article 12] concerning the principle of non-discrimination on the grounds of nationality applied independently only to situations governed by Community law in respect of which the Treaty laid down no specific prohibition on discrimination. The same would apply to Article 8a [new Article 18]. Since, on the facts of the case, Article 52 [new Article 43] applied there was no need to consider Article 8a(1) [new Article 18(1)].

In the more important case of *Martínez Sala*[512] the Court adopted a similar approach to citizenship and non-discrimination. It will be recalled that the case concerned the right to child benefit for a Spanish woman resident in Germany, but lacking the necessary residence permit. The Court said that as a national of a Member State lawfully residing in the territory of another Member State, albeit refused a residence permit, she came within the scope *ratione personae* of the provisions of the Treaty on European citizenship.[513] It then said:

[510] Case C–274/96 [1998] ECR I–7637.

[511] Case C–193/94 [1996] ECR I–929.

[512] Case C–85/96 [1998] ECR I–2691. See Friess and Shaw, 'Citizenship of the Union: First Steps in the European Court of Justice' (1998) 4 *European Public Law* 533 and O'Leary, 'Putting Flesh on the Bones of European Union Citizenship' (1999) 24 *ELRev.* 68.

[513] Para. 61.

Article 8(2) [Article 17(2)] of the Treaty attaches to the status of citizen of the Union the rights and duties laid down by the Treaty, including the right, laid down in Article 6 of the Treaty, not to suffer discrimination on grounds of nationality within the scope of application *ratione materiae* of the Treaty.[514]

It follows that a citizen of the European Union, such as the appellant in the main proceedings, lawfully resident in the territory of the host Member State, can rely on Article 6 of the Treaty in all situations which fall within the scope *ratione materiae* of Community law, including the situation where that Member State delays or refuses to grant to that claimant a benefit that is provided to all persons lawfully resident in the territory of that State on the ground that the claimant is not in possession of a document which nationals of that same State are not required to have and the issue of which may be delayed or refused by the authorities of that State.

The decision in *Martínez Sala* suggests a shift away from recognition of rights related to economic-based free movement towards the grant of rights *per se* to Community nationals.[515] Yet for every *Martínez Sala*, *Lawrie-Blum*,[516] and *Cowan*[517] there are decisions such as *Brown*[518] and *Bettray*.[519] The Court is unpredictable. As O'Leary points out,[520] even at its most 'human' the Court has never lost sight of the economic (and hence political) realities, especially the need to ensure that government deficit and debt to GDP do not exceed 3 per cent and 60 per cent respectively to satisfy the requirements of EMU.

[514] Para. 62.
[515] O'Leary, above n. 512, 385.
[516] Case 66/85 [1986] ECR 2121.
[517] Case 186/87 [1989] ECR 195.
[518] Case 197/86 [1988] ECR 3205.
[519] Case 344/87 [1989] ECR 1621.
[520] O'Leary, above n. 512, 386.

4

Equality Law

A. INTRODUCTION

The quest for sex equality has been the central and most highly developed pillar of the EC's social policy. For the Commission, equal opportunities is the 'legal framework reflecting social policy at European level [which] has been a catalyst for change in the Member States'.[1] The importance of equal opportunities to the Community is underlined in the Commission's vision of a 'European social model'. This is based around the 'values of democracy and individual rights, free collective bargaining, the market economy, equality of opportunity for all and social welfare and solidarity'.[2] Equal opportunities also appears as one of the four pillars around which the employment guidelines[3] are structured.

It is not entirely clear why sex equality[4] has maintained such a unique hold on the attentions of administrators and the litigators for so long. It is true that women represent more than a third of the workforce, are more likely to occupy 'atypical' jobs, especially part-time jobs, and are particularly affected by long-term unemployment. Perhaps, as Ellis suggests, the attainment of sex equality serves political and economic goals: on an economic level, it is important to prevent competitive distortions in a now quite highly integrated market; and on a political level, sex equality provides a relatively innocuous, even high-sounding platform, by which the Community can demonstrate its commitment to social progress.[5] However, Community law does not, and possibly cannot, really address the deep rooted causes of inequality—institutionalized discrimination, inflexibility of work patterns, and the absence of adequate child care. Nevertheless, within the more limited confines of the workplace, both the legislature and the judiciary have been active in achieving sexual equality.

While EC discrimination law insists on equality between the sexes in all

---

[1] White Paper on Social Policy COM(94)333, 41.

[2] Ibid.

[3] Council Resolution of 15 Dec. 1997 on the 1998 Employment Guidelines [1998] OJ C30/1. See further Ch. 1.

[4] For a comprehensive discussion of this subject, see Ellis, *EC Sex Equality Law* (Oxford EC Law Library, Oxford, 1998). See also Arnull, *The European Union and its Court of Justice* (Oxford EC Law Library, Oxford, 1999).

[5] Ellis, above n. 4, 61–2.

aspects of work, it has only recently acquired the competence to address discrimination on the grounds of race or ethnic origin, religion, colour, sexual orientation, age and disability.[6] It is, however, the desire to achieve sex equality which has captured the Community's attention since 1957 and forms the principal subject matter of this chapter.

1. The Development of EC Sex Equality

Article 141 [ex Article 119] of the Treaty of Rome establishes the principle that men and women should receive equal pay for equal work and for work of equal value. Article 119 on equal pay for equal work was introduced into the Treaty of Rome largely to serve the economic purpose: of 'correcting or eliminating the effect of "specific distortions which advantage or disadvantage certain branches of activity".[7] France insisted on the inclusion of the provision since it feared that its worker protection legislation, including its laws on equal pay, would put it at a competitive disadvantage in the Common Market due to the additional costs borne by French industry.[8] Thus, the original economic rationale for including sex equality legislation in the Treaty was a negative one: to stop social dumping.[9] More recently Community documents recognize a more positive economic justification for equal opportunities: as an input into growth of the Member States since equal opportunities practices can be used to attract and retain the most efficient staff. The role of the EC is thus to create a floor of rights in which equal opportunities can be realized. As the Commission's White Paper on Social Policy recognized, the 'adaptability and creativity of women is a strength which should be harnessed to the drive for growth and competitiveness in the EU'.[10]

Given the emphasis when the Treaty of Rome was drafted (and even today) on the creation of a European *Economic* Community, it comes as little surprise that there was no reference to the social and moral justification for sex

---

[6] Art. 13 [ex Art. 6a]. See further below, text attached to nn. 510–528.

[7] The Spaak report, 61 (author's translation). Comité Intergouvernemental Crée par la conférence de Messine, Rapport des Chefs de Délégations aux Ministères des Affaires Etrangères of 21 Apr. 1956. The Committee, comprising the heads of delegations, was established at the Messina conference in June 1955 under the chairmanship of M Paul Henri Spaak, then Belgian foreign minister. See generally Barnard, 'EC Sex Equality Law: A Balance Sheet', in *The EU and Human Rights*, ed. Alston (OUP, Oxford, 1999) on which this section draws heavily.

[8] See Kahn-Freund, 'Labour Law and Social Security', in *American Enterprise in the European Common Market: A Legal Profile*, eds. Stein and Nicholson (University of Michigan Press, Ann Arbor, Mich., 1960), 300, discussed in Barnard, 'The Economic Objectives of Article 119', in *Sex Equality Law in the European Union*, eds. Hervey and O'Keeffe (Wiley, Chichester, 1996); More, 'The Principle of Equal Treatment: From Market Unifier to Fundamental Right', in *The Evolution of EU Law*, eds. Craig and de Búrca (OUP, Oxford, 1999). See also the influence of ILO Convention 100: Hoskyns, *Integrating Gender* (Verso, London, 1996), ch. 4.

[9] See further Ch. 1.

[10] COM(94)333, 41.

equality. Yet, within twenty years the Community had adopted directives on equality, and the Court had started to recognize that the principle of equality was a fundamental right which served a social as well as an economic function. This was first identified in the landmark judgment in *Defrenne (No. 2)*[11] where the Court famously observed:

Article 119 [new Article 141] pursues a double aim. *First*, . . . the aim of Article 119 is to avoid a situation in which undertakings established in states which have actually implemented the principle of equal pay suffer a competitive disadvantage in intra-Community competition as compared with undertakings established in states which have not yet eliminated discrimination against women workers as regards pay. *Second*, this provision forms part of the social objectives of the Community, which is not merely an economic union, but is at the same time intended, by common action to ensure social progress and seek the constant improvement of living and working conditions of their peoples . . . This double aim, which is at once economic and social, shows that the principle of equal pay forms part of the foundations of the Community [emphasis added].

In *Defrenne (No. 3)* the Court took the social dimension of equality one stage further and elevated the principle to the status of a fundamental right. It said 'respect for fundamental personal human rights is one of the general principles of Community law . . . there can be no doubt that the elimination of discrimination based on sex forms part of those fundamental rights'.[12]

As we shall see, despite such statements, the yoke of the economic justification for Community sex equality legislation has been far from cast off. This has significantly curtailed the effectiveness of the Community's policy for women. Such criticisms must, however, be tempered by the fact that it has long been recognized[13] that the Community needs sex equality legislation and neo-liberal arguments that such legislation interferes with freedom of contract did not predominate. By contrast, in the US such arguments have attracted considerable attention. For example, Posner has argued that sex discrimination laws, if successful, diminish social welfare; that the laws are ineffective in meeting their goals, and that where the

---

[11] Case 43/75 *Defrenne (No. 2)* v. *SABENA* [1976] ECR 455.

[12] Case 149/77 *Defrenne (No. 3)* v. *SABENA* [1978] ECR 1365, 1378. See also Case 152/84 *Marshall* v. *Southampton and South West Hampshire Area Health Authority (Teaching)(No.1)* [1986] ECR 723, para. 36; Case 151/84 *Roberts* v. *Tate & Lyle Industries Ltd* [1986] ECR 703, para. 35; Case C–132/92 *Birds Eye Walls Ltd* v. *Roberts* [1993] ECR I–5579, para. 17; Case C–408/92 *Smith* v. *Avdel Systems* [1994] ECR I–4435, para. 25; and Case C–167/97 *R* v. *Secretary of State for Employment, ex parte Seymour-Smith and Perez* [1999] ECR I–623, para. 75. See also Docksey, 'The Principle of Equality between Women and Men as a Fundamental Right Under Community Law' (1991) 20 *ILJ* 258 and Tridimas, *The General Principles of EC Law* (OUP, Oxford, 1999). Only the staff of the Community institutions can rely on the general principles of law directly. In this context the Court has applied the principle to non-discrimination on the grounds of religion: see Case 30/75 *Prais* v. *Council* [1976] ECR 1589.

[13] See the discussion about the Spaak report in Ch. 1.

laws have met their goals, the laws have actually harmed their intended beneficiaries.[14]

His views naturally have their critics. Donohue argues that discrimination laws can promote efficiency by more rapidly eliminating discriminators, by inducing potential productivity, and by reducing the inefficiencies associated with statistical discrimination.[15] Hepple is also critical of the 'fashionable economic model of society', where markets are seen as sets of unplanned, spontaneous exchanges rewarding individual efforts and abilities.[16] He argues that this approach leads to the conclusion that the woman seeking part-time work loses the opportunity of being paid at the same rate as a man doing full-time work because of her preference for looking after children. In this model the woman is assumed to be a calculating person able freely to choose her economic relations. Her preferences for caring are valued only in the process of exchange. Her right, as a human being, to equal treatment and respect is not seen as a social value in itself. The economic model does not correspond to the real world in which individuals do not have a free choice, precisely because of differences in wealth, social class, gender, and race.

The EC's approach has tended towards a more middle way between social regulation and neo-liberalism. It sees equal opportunities as acceptable so long as they do not interfere significantly with the operation of the Single Market.[17] Inevitably attitudes have changed over time, with different approaches to equality prevailing at various stages so that progress has, by no means, been linear.[18]

The Social Action Programme following the Paris Communiqué in 1972 aspired to create a 'situation in which equality between men and women obtains in the labour market throughout the Community, through the improvement of economic and psychological conditions, and of the social and educational infrastructure'.[19] Three important Directives were passed as a result:

---

[14] Posner, 'An Economic Analysis of Sex Discrimination Laws' (1989) 56 *U.Chicago L.Rev.* 1311.

[15] Donohue, 'Prohibiting Sex Discrimination in the Workplace: An Economic Perspective' (1989) 56 *U.Chicago L.Rev.* 1337.

[16] Hepple, 'The Principle of Equal Treatment in Article 119 EC and the Possibilities for Reform', in *The Principle of Equal Treatment in E.C. Law*, eds. Dashwood and O'Leary (Sweet & Maxwell, London, 1997), 141.

[17] See e.g. Case C–127/92 *Enderby* v. *Frenchay Health Authority* [1993] ECR I–5535. At para. 26 the Court said 'The state of the employment market, which may lead an employer to increase the pay of a particular job in order to attract candidates, may constitute an objectively justified ground'. See further below, text attached to nn. 115–149, and the temporal limitations on the retrospectivity of judgments: Case C–262/88 *Barber* v. *Guardian Royal Exchange* [1990] ECR I–1889; Case C–109/91 *Ten Oever* v. *Stichting Bedrijfspensioenfonds* [1993] ECR I–4879.

[18] See generally Neilson, 'Equal Opportunities for Women in the European Union: Success or Failure?' (1998) 8 *JESP* 64.

[19] See Council Resolution of 21 Jan. 1974 concerning a Social Action Programme [1974] OJ L14/10.

- Directive 75/117/EEC[20] on equal pay for male and female workers, enshrining the principle of 'equal pay for equal work' laid down in Article 119 [new Article 141], and introducing the concept of 'equal pay for work of equal value', now supplemented by two codes of practice intended to give practical advice on measures to ensure the effective implementation of equal pay.[21]
- Directive 76/207/EEC[22] on equal treatment with regard to access to employment, vocational training, promotion, and working conditions, aimed at eliminating all discrimination, both direct and indirect, in the world of work and providing an opportunity for positive measures.
- Directive 79/7/EEC[23] on the progressive implementation of equal treatment with regard to statutory social security schemes.

There followed three Action Programmes targeted specifically at equal opportunities for men and women.[24]

In the 1980s, at a time of stagnation in Community social policy, two specific Directives were adopted on equality:

- Directive 86/378/EEC[25] on implementation of equal treatment in occupational schemes of social security. The Directive was amended by Directive 96/97/EC[26] in the light of the *Barber*[27] judgment.
- Directive 86/613/EEC[28] on equal treatment for men and women carrying out a self-employed activity, including agriculture.

The 1989 Social Action Programme[29] implementing the Community Social Charter 1989 led to the enactment, on the basis of Article 118a EC [new Article 137], of a Directive on pregnancy:

- Directive 92/85/EC[30] improving the health and safety of workers who are pregnant or have recently given birth.

[20] [1975] OJ L45/19.

[21] COM(94)6; COM(96)336 final.

[22] Council Directive 76/207/EEC [1976] OJ L39/40. The Directive was based on Art. 235 [new Art. 308]. Member States had 30 months to implement the Directive from the date of notification. In addition, they had four years to revise discriminatory laws designed to protect one group whose justification is no longer well founded (Art. 9(1)). An amendment has now been proposed COM(2000)334 final.

[23] [1979] OJ L6/24. This is considered in detail in Ch. 5.

[24] Action Programme 1982–5 [1982] OJ C186/3, EC Bull. 5–1982, point 2.1.48 and EC Bull. 7/8–1982, point 2.1.67; Equal Opportunities for Women Medium-term Community Programme 1986–90; EC Bull. Supp. 3/86 and EC Bull. 6–1986, point 2.1.116; Third Medium-term Action Programme COM(90)449 final; Fourth Medium-term Action Programme (1996–2000); Council Decision 95/593/EC [1995] OJ L335/37.

[25] [1986] OJ L225/40.

[26] [1997] OJ L46/20.

[27] Case 262/88 *Barber* v. *Guardian Royal Exchange* [1990] ECR I–1889.

[28] [1997] OJ L359/56.

[29] COM(89)568.

[30] [1992] OJ L245/23. This was the ninth individual directive within the meaning of Art. 16(1) of Directive 89/391/EEC.

The Social Policy Agreement (SPA) annexed to the Treaty on European Union (the Maastricht Treaty), from which the UK initially secured an opt-out, led to the enactment of two further measures:[31]

- Directive 96/34/EC on reconciling family and working life (parental leave).[32] This was the first Directive adopted under the new procedure provided for by the SPA, allowing the Social Partners to negotiate a framework agreement which was then extended to all workers by a Directive.[33]
- Directive 97/80/EC[34] on the burden of proof in cases of discrimination based on sex. Under the terms of this Directive, the onus is on defendants accused of discrimination at work to prove that the principle of equal treatment has not been violated.

A change of government in the UK in 1997 meant that these two measures were readopted under Article 100 EC [new Article 94] and now apply to the UK.[35]

A variety of soft law measures have also been adopted.[36] The most recent ones relate to the integration of equal opportunities into the Structural Funds,[37] balanced participation by men and women in decision-making,[38] women and science,[39] and equal participation by women in an employment intensive growth strategy in the EU.[40] Although these texts are not legally binding they form part of the 'softening up process' paving the way for the Commission's preferred course of action should a 'policy window' open up.[41]

The Treaty of Amsterdam explicitly introduced equality between men and women as one of the tasks (Article 2) and activities (Article 3) of the Community. In addition, it introduced a new Article, Article 13 [ex Article 6a] allowing the Council, acting unanimously on a proposal from the Commis-

---

[31] In addition, directives were adopted on part-time work (Directive 97/81/EC [1998] OJ L14/9) and fixed-term work (Directive 99/70/EC [1999] OJ L175/43). These will be considered in Ch. 6.

[32] [1996] OJ L145/4, amended by Directive 97/75/EC [1998] OJ L10/24, consolidated [1998] OJ L10/11.

[33] See Ch. 2. See also the Directives on Part-Time Work 97/81/EC [1998] OJ L14/9, as amended by Directive 97/81/EC [1998] OJ L131/10, consolidated in [1998] OJ L131/13 and Fixed-Term Work 99/70/EC [1999] OJ L175/43 considered in Ch. 6.

[34] [1998] OJ L14/6, amended by Directive 98/52/EC [1998] OJ L205/66.

[35] The Social Partners were also consulted with regard to combating sexual harassment at work: COM(96)373 (first round consultation) and SEC(97)373 (second round consultation). UNICE pulled out of their negotiations in September 1997.

[36] See e.g. Council Resolution on the promotion of equal opportunities for women [1986] OJ L203/2.

[37] 94/C231/01 [1994] OJ C231/1. See also Council Regulation (EC) 2836/98 of 22 Dec. 1998 on integrating of gender issues in development cooperation [1998] OJ L354/5.

[38] Council Resolution of 27 Mar. 1995 [1995] OJ L168/3 and Council Recommendation 96/694/EC [1996] OJ L319/11.

[39] Council Resolution of 20 May 1999 [1999] OJ C201/1.

[40] 94/C368/02.

[41] Cram, *Policy Making in the EU: Conceptual Lenses and the Integration Process* (Routledge, London, 1997). On the role of soft law measures see Ch. 2.

sion, to take action to combat any form of discrimination, including that based on sex. Elsewhere, Article 119 [new Article 141] on equal pay was amended significantly. Article 141(1) [ex Article 119(1)] extended the definition of equal pay for equal work with reference to 'or work of equal value'.[42] The new Article 141(3) [ex Article 119(3)] has finally provided an express legal basis for the Council to adopt measures, in accordance with the Article 251 [ex Article 189b] co-decision procedure, 'to ensure the application of the principle of equal opportunities and equal treatment of men and women in matters of employment and occupation, including the principle of equal pay for equal work or work of equal value'.[42A] Finally, the new Article 141(4) allows Member States to adopt or maintain positive-action measures for the under-represented sex in respect of professional careers.

Institutional support for the realization of equality has also been provided: there are special committees concerned with women's issues in the European Parliament, including the Committee on Women's Rights and Equal Opportunities, an Equal Opportunities Unit within DGV of the European Commission,[43] and an Advisory Committee on Equal Opportunities for men and women.[44] In addition, the Equal Opportunities Working Party of Members of the Commission examines and monitors the integration of the gender dimension into all relevant policies and programmes. At its instigation the Commission adopted, on 21 February 1996, a communication on incorporating equal opportunities for women and men into all Community policies and activities.[45]

Further, the Commission has made efforts to promote specific measures aimed at improving the situation of women in practice, particularly with regard to employment, through successive multi-annual action programmes designed and implemented in partnership with the Member States. The fourth medium-term Community action programme (1996–2000)[46] aimed at incorporating equal opportunities into the process of defining and

---

[42] See the proposals made in Dashwood, *Reviewing Maastricht: Issues for the 1996 IGC* (Sweet & Maxwell, London, 1996), esp. 297. Art. 1 of Directive 75/117/EEC already makes provision for this and, as the Court pointed out in Case 96/80 *Jenkins* v. *Kingsgate* [1981] ECR 911, Art. 1 'is principally designed to facilitate the practical application of the principle of equal pay outlined in Article 119 [new Art. 141] of the Treaty [and] in no way alters the content or scope of that principle as defined in the Treaty'.

[42A] COM(2000)334 has been proposed on this basis.

[43] On a more independent basis the Centre for Research on Women (CREW) has been established, as have the European Network of Women (ENOW) and the Women's Lobby. See further Szyszczak, 'L'Espace Social Européen, Reality, Dreams or Nightmare' [1990] *German Yearbook of International Law* 284, 298.

[44] Established by Commission Decision 82/43/EEC [1982] OJ L20/35, as amended by Decision 95/420/EEC [1995] OJ 249/43.

[45] COM(96)67 and the Commission's Progress Report COM(98)122. See also the Commission's Guide to 'Gender Impact Assessment', http://europa.eu.int/comm/dg05/equ-opp/index_en. htm. The Commission has also begun to put its own house in order: Commission Decision 2000/407/EC [2000] OJ L154/34 relating to gender balance within the committees and expert groups established by it.

[46] Council Decision 95/593/EC [1995] OJ L335/37.

implementing the relevant policies at Community, national, and regional levels (mainstreaming); and, on 12 February 1997, the Commission adopted its first annual report on equal opportunities for women and men in the EU (1996).[47] This reviews progress with regard to equality at Member State and Union level and represents an instrument for monitoring equal opportunities policies.[48] Finally, as we have seen, promotion of equal opportunities forms one of the four key pillars of the European Employment Strategy initiated in Luxembourg in November 1997.[49] In the 1999 Employment Guidelines[50] the Commission emphasized the need to pursue integration of equal opportunities for men and women into all aspects of employment policies, notably by guaranteeing active employment market policies for the vocational integration of women proportionate to their rate of unemployment and by promoting women in the context of entrepreneurship. The 2000 Guidelines focus on facilitating reintegration of men and women into the labour market after a period of absence.[51]

2. The Meaning of Equality

It is clear that equality has a central role to play in the EU. But what is meant by the term equality?[52] The principle of equality cannot stand alone: it needs an answer to the question 'equal to what?' Aristotle had an answer. He said that 'Equality in morals means this: things that are alike should be treated alike'. This is often described as the principle of formal equality or the similarly situated test.[53] But who is alike? The very nature of human beings is that they are all unique—and different. It is a moral judgement as to who is alike. This leads Westen to conclude that the concept of equality is tautological. He says equality 'tells us to treat like people alike; but when we ask who "like people" are, we are told they are "people who should be treated alike". Equality is an empty vessel with no substantive moral content of its own. Without moral standards, equality remains meaningless, a formula that has nothing to say about how we should act'.[54]

Since equality provides no internal guidance on the relevance of particular characteristics of individuals or groups, the principle of non-discrimination

---

[47] Luxembourg, OPEC, 1997.

[48] The third and most recent annual report can be found in COM(99)106 final. For the second annual report, see the DGV's home page, above n. 45.

[49] See further Ch. 1.

[50] [1999] OJ C69/2.

[51] Proposal for Guidelines for Member States' Employment Policies 2000.

[52] This section draws on Barnard, 'The Principle of Equality in the Community Context. *P, Grant, Kalanke* and *Marschall*: Four Uneasy Bedfellows?' (1998) 57 *CLJ* 352.

[53] Aristotle, *Ethica Nicomachea* V.3.1131a–1131b (Ross, trans., 1925), cited in Westen, 'The Empty Idea of Equality' (1982) 95 *Harvard Law Review* 537, 543.

[54] Westen, above n. 53, 547.

helps to fill this vacuum. At Community level this can be seen in Article 141 [ex Article 119] which provides for 'Equal pay without discrimination on the grounds of sex'.[55] Article 2(1) of Directive 76/207 says that the 'principle of equal treatment' means 'there shall be no discrimination whatsoever on grounds of sex either directly or indirectly by reference in particular to marital or family status', with the added guide that the Directive is intended to 'promote equal opportunity for men and women'.[56] It is the legislature which has defined the principle of non-discrimination, prohibiting, as Article 2(1) makes clear, both direct and indirect discrimination. Further, it is the legislature, and not the Court, which has taken the policy decision and identified which people should be treated alike. In the Community context it has decided that women should be treated like men (and married people like non-married people),[57] and now the Court had added that trans-sexuals should be treated like a person of the sex they had belonged to previously.[58]

In the context of sex discrimination, the formal equality model articulated so clearly by Aristotle requires women to be treated like men. Yet, as we have seen, the choice of a (male) comparator can be problematic. Are men and women really similarly situated? Can and should women aspire to a male life pattern?[59] Many women are not in a position to compete as equals since their domestic and caring responsibilities preclude this. This means that they often take time out to fulfil these roles and/or seek part-time work which suits their domestic responsibilities, since inadequate and often expensive childcare facilities limit their flexibility. Consequently the limited, formal notion of equality adopted by the law can assist only the minority who are able to conform to the male stereotype but cannot reach or correct underlying structural impediments.[60] As Fredman puts it, this formal equality model reinforces the liberal ideas of 'the primacy of the neutrality of law, the rights of the individual as individual, and the freedom of the market'.[61] Further, she argues, equal treatment of individuals who are not socially equal perpetuates inequalities.[62] This leads some to advocate a more substantive notion of equality, one aimed

---

[55] Art. 1 of Directive 75/117 explains that the principle of equal pay outlined in Art. 119 means 'the elimination of all discrimination on grounds of sex'.

[56] Art. 2(4).

[57] See below, n. 261.

[58] Case C–13/94 *P v. S and Cornwall County Council* [1996] ECR I–2143.

[59] See further Mackinnon, *Feminism Unmodified—Discourses on Life and Law* (Harvard University Press, Cambridge, 1987), 32–45; Mackinnon, 'Reflections on Sex Equality under Law' (1991) 100 *Yale Law Journal* 1281; on the British Sex Discrimination Act 1975 see Lacey, 'Legislation against Sex Discrimination—Questions from a Feminist Perspective' (1987) 14 *Journal of Law and Society* 411.

[60] Fredman, 'European Community Discrimination Law' (1992) 21 *ILJ* 119, 121.

[61] Fredman, *Women and the Law* (Clarendon, Oxford, 1997), 383.

[62] Fredman, 'Reversing Discrimination' (1997) 113 *LQR* 575.

at achieving equality of outcome or results.[63] This demands not merely that persons should be judged on individual merit, but that the real situation of many women which may place them in a weaker position on the market should be addressed.[64] This marks a shift away from the individual to the group, looking at the way in which individuals' opportunities are determined by their social and historical status. This suggests a more positive role for the principle of equality which goes beyond the Aristotelian notion of formal equality and aims instead at equality as a societal goal. This might involve some form of positive action[65] or even positive discrimination[66] to achieve equality in the longer term. However, from the Aristotelian perspective any form of positive discrimination, albeit for benign motives, faces the accusation that it is itself discriminatory, this time against the dominant group (men) and therefore contravenes the principle of equality.

3. The EC Model of Equality: Equal Opportunities

If legislative approaches to sex equality range from formal equality at one end of the spectrum to a substantive approach to equality at the other end, the EC 'equal opportunities model' lies somewhere in between. This is based on the idea that true equality cannot be achieved if individuals begin the race from different starting points.[67] The aim is therefore to equalize the starting points through a combination of formal and substantive equality measures. While focusing on the importance of the individual, it does recognize that sex-based policies may be used as a transitional remedial measure to address structural discrimination. Therefore, Article 2(4) is included in Directive 76/207.[68] This provides that the Directive shall be 'without prejudice to measures which promote *equal opportunity* for men and women, in particular by removing existing inequalities which affect women's opportunities'. However, despite the existence of Article 2(4) and the recognition that Community law outlaws both direct *and* (unintentional) indirect discrimination, the concept of formal rather than substantive equality has wielded considerable influence in the

[63] In Case C–136/95 *Caisse Nationale d'Assurance Vieillesse des Travailleurs Salariés (CNAVTS)* v. *Evelyne Thibault* [1998] ECR I–2011 the Court claimed that the result pursued by the Directive was substantive, not formal, equality (para. 26).

[64] Fenwick and Hervey, 'Sex Equality in the Single Market: New Directions for the European Court of Justice' (1995) 32 *CMLRev.* 443, 445.

[65] Positive action allows for a variety of measures ranging from encouragement to apply for positions where women are under-represented and vocational training, to, more substantively, reorganizing working life and greater provision for childcare.

[66] Positive discrimination goes further and allows for the imposition of quotas or goals for the under-represented sex. See further below nn. 303–337A.

[67] Fredman, above n. 61, 384.

[68] See also Art. 141(4), considered below, n. 337.

Court's interpretation of Community legislation.[69] For example, in *Hofmann*[70] the Court made clear that Directive 76/207 was not 'designed to settle questions concerning the organisation of the family or to alter the division of responsibility between parents'.[71] In *Helmig*[72] the Court ruled that there was no discrimination when part-timers, who were predominantly women, did not receive overtime rates for hours worked over their normal contractual hours but less than the full-time hours, even though the social consequences for part-timers to work one hour's overtime is likely to be more disruptive than for full-timers.[73] These decisions serve to highlight the fact that while the Court will require non-discrimination in the world of work, it is reluctant to look at the effects of its decisions in the domestic sphere. The creation of an artificial distinction between the world of work and the family further prejudices the many women who are not 'well-assimilated' to the male norm and denies them *de facto* equality.[74] This approach perpetuates, in Mackinnon's words, the male experience of the world, since it allows male power and male interests to be concealed within apparently universal and objective standards.[75]

In some cases the Court has, however, shown itself to be sensitive to the arguments in favour of substantive equality. For example, in *Thibault*[76] it said that 'the result pursued by the Directive [76/207] is substantive, not formal, equality'. This can be seen in the Court's ruling in *Marschall*[77] on positive

---

[69] See generally Mancini and O'Leary, 'The New Frontiers of Sex Equality Law in the European Union' (1999) 24 *ELRev.* 331.

[70] Case 184/83 *Hofmann* v. *Barmer Ersatzkasse* [1984] ECR 3047. See Hervey and Shaw, 'Women, Work and Care: Women's Dual Role and Double Burden in EC Sex Equality Law' (1998) 8 *Journal of European Social Policy Law* 43.

[71] See also Case 170/84 *Bilka-Kaufhaus* v. *Weber von Hartz* [1986] ECR 1607 where the Court stopped short of imposing a positive requirement on companies to organize their occupational pension schemes in such a way as to accommodate the needs of their employees, and Case C–297/93 *Grau-Hupka* v. *Stadtgemeinde Bremen* [1994] ECR I–5535 where the Court said that since Community law on equal treatment did not oblige Member States to take into account in calculating the statutory pension years spent bringing up children, the national rules also did not breach Art. 119 [new Art. 141].

[72] Case C–399/92 *Stadt Lengerich* v. *Helmig* [1994] ECR I–5727. On the serious consequences of this decision see the House of Lords' decision in *Barry* v. *Midland Bank* [1999] IRLR 581.

[73] See Rubinstein [1995] *IRLR* 183.

[74] See Cullen, 'The Subsidiary Woman' (1994) 16 *JSWL* 407, 408.

[75] Mackinnon, above n. 59, 244.

[76] Case C–136/94 [1998] ECR I–2011, repeated in Case C–207/98 *Mahlburg* v. *Land Mecklenburg-Vorpommern*, judgment of 3 Feb. 2000, para. 26. See also Case 109/88 *Handels- og Kontorfunktionærernes Forbund i Danmark* v. *Dansk Arbejdsgiverforening, acting on behalf of Danfoss (Danfoss)* [1989] ECR 3199 where the Court ruled that a criterion rewarding employees' mobility—their adaptability to variable hours and places of work—may work to the disadvantage of female employees who, because of household and family duties, are not as able as men to organize their working time with such flexibility. Similarly, the criterion of training may work to the disadvantage of women in so far as they have had less opportunity than men for training or have taken less advantage of that opportunity. In both cases the employer may only justify the remuneration of such adaptability or training by showing it is of importance for the performance of specific tasks entrusted to the employee.

[77] Case C–409/95 *Marschall* v. *Land Nordrhein-Westfalen* [1997] ECR I–6363.

discrimination[78]. The Court, in upholding the State's law which gave preference to a woman in a tie-break situation, subject to a saving clause operating in favour of the man, said that this national rule was compatible with Article 2(4) because:

even where male and female candidates are equally qualified, male candidates tend to be promoted in preference to female candidates particularly because of prejudices and stereotypes concerning the role and capacities of women in working life and the fear, for example, that women will interrupt their careers more frequently, that owing to household and family duties they will be less flexible in their working hours, or that they will be absent from work more frequently because of pregnancy, childbirth and breastfeeding.[79] For these reasons, the mere fact that a male candidate and a female candidate are equally qualified does not mean that they have the same chances.[80]

The Court also showed some sympathy with the position of job-sharers in *Hill*.[81] It said that almost all job-sharers were women, most of whom chose that option 'in order to be able to combine work and family responsibilities which invariably involve caring for children'. The Court then added:

Community policy in this area is to encourage and, if possible, adapt working conditions to family responsibilities. Protection of women within family life and in the course of their professional activities is, in the same way as for men, a principle which is widely regarded as being the natural corollary of the equality between men and women, and which is recognized by Community law.

4. Direct and Indirect Discrimination on the Grounds of Sex

4.1 The Concept of Discrimination

Article 141 and Directive 76/207 require equal pay or equal treatment without either direct or indirect discrimination based on sex. Direct or 'overt' discrimination involves one sex being treated less favourably than the other: in the case of *Macarthys*[82] this meant that the woman received less pay than the man doing the same job. The motive or intention to discriminate is not a

---

[78] See further below, text attached to nn. 303–337.

[79] See also the views of the Federal Labour Court when the *Kalanke* case returned to it (Nr 226), Urteil of 5 Mar. 1996—1 AZR 590/92 (A). It said that it was impossible to distinguish between opportunity and result, especially in the case of engagement and promotion because the selection itself was influenced by circumstances, expectations and prejudices that typically diminish the chances of women.

[80] Paras. 29 and 30.

[81] Case C–243/95 *Kathleen Hill and Ann Stapleton v. Revenue Commissioners* [1998] ECR I–3739, para. 42. Cf. McGlynn and Farrelly, 'Equal Pay and the "Protection of Women within Family Life"' (1999) 24 *ELRev*. 202.

[82] Case 129/79 *Macarthys v. Smith* [1980] ECR 1275.

necessary element of direct discrimination: it is enough that the effect of the measure is discriminatory.[83]

Indirect discrimination arises when the application of a gender-neutral criterion or practice[84] in fact disadvantages a much higher percentage of women that men, unless that difference can be justified by objective factors unrelated to any discrimination on the grounds of sex.[85] The definition developed by the Court has now been adopted by the legislative. The Burden of Proof Directive 97/80[86] provides:

Indirect discrimination exists where an apparently neutral provision, criterion or practice disadvantages a substantially higher proportion of the members of one sex, unless that provision, criterion or practice is appropriate and necessary and can be justified by objective factors unrelated to sex.[87]

The notion of indirect discrimination is designed to target those measures which are discriminatory in *effect*. At first the Court had some difficulty in appreciating the full ambit of indirect discrimination. In *Jenkins*,[88] a case where part-time workers received a lower hourly rate than full-time workers, the Court looked at the employer's intention[89] to see whether discrimination had occurred. Confining indirect discrimination to intentional acts only would have significantly limited its effectiveness. In *Bilka-Kaufhaus*,[90] however, the Court recognized that the prohibition on discrimination also included *unintentional* indirect discrimination, where the employer does not intend to discriminate but the effects of any policy are discriminatory.[91] In particular, indirect discrimination has been a useful tool to address less favourable treatment of part-time workers[92] and job-sharers on the grounds that considerably fewer men than women work part-time[93] or job-share. Unless the differential

---

[83]   Case 69/80 *Worringham v. Lloyd's Bank* [1981] ECR 767.

[84]   Case 170/84 *Bilka-Kaufhaus* [1986] ECR 1607; Case C–127/92 *Enderby* [1993] ECR I–5535.

[85]   Case 171/88 *Rinner-Kühn v. FWW Spezial-Gebäudereinignung* [1989] ECR 2743.

[86]   [1998] OJ L14/6, amended by Directive 98/52/EC [1998] OJ L205/66.

[87]   Art. 2(2). Cf. the definition of indirect discrimination in the proposed 'horizontal' directive on equal treatment 2000/C 177 E/07 which focuses on the individual and not the group. See below n. 553.

[88]   Case 96/80 [1981] ECR 911.

[89]   Para. 14. The employer, who had previously paid men and women at different rates, changed his system so that he paid part-timers, the majority of whom were women, less than full-timers. There was a concern that the employer had replaced a directly discriminatory system by an intentionally indirectly discriminatory system.

[90]   Case 170/84 [1986] ECR 1607; Case 171/88 *Rinner-Kühn* [1989] ECR 2743.

[91]   The culpability of the employer should be reflected in the remedy.

[92]   See now the Part-time Work Directive 97/81/EC [1998] OJ L14/9, considered in Ch. 6.

[93]   See Case 96/80 *Jenkins* [1981] ECR 911; Case 170/84 *Bilka-Kaufhaus* [1986] ECR 1607; Case 171/88 *Rinner-Kühn* [1989] ECR 2743; Case 33/89 *Kowalska v. Freie und Hansestadt Hamburg* [1990] ECR I–2591; Case C–360/90 *Arbeiterwohlfahrt der Stadt Berlin eV v. Bötel* [1992] ECR I–3589; Case C–184/89 *Nimz v. Freie und Hansestadt Hamburg* [1991] ECR I–297; Case C–1/95 *Gerster v. Freiestadt Bremen* [1997] ECR I–5253; and Case C–100/95 *Kording v. Senator für Finanz* [1997] ECR I–5289.

treatment can be objectively justified, the part-time workers are entitled to have the same scheme applied to them as that applied to other workers, on a basis proportional to their working time.[94]

Hill[95] provides a good example of indirect discrimination. The case concerned the situation of workers who converted from job-sharing to full-time work. These workers were at a disadvantage compared with those who had worked on a full-time basis for the same number of years since, when converting to full-time work, a job-sharing worker was placed on the full-time pay scale at a level below that which she previously occupied on the pay scale applicable to job-sharing staff and, consequently, at a level lower than that of a full-time worker employed for the same period of time. The Court pointed out that Community law precludes the application of a national measure which, although formulated in neutral terms, works to the disadvantage of far more women than men, unless that measure is based on objective factors unrelated to any discrimination on grounds of sex.[96] The Court noted that 99.2 per cent of clerical assistants who job-shared were women, as were 98 per cent of all civil servants employed under job-sharing contracts. It therefore concluded that in those circumstances a provision which, without objective justification, adversely affected the legal position of job-sharers had discriminatory effects based on sex.

The concept of indirect discrimination in the context of sex equality is complex and raises many more difficulties than the equivalent term in free movement of persons since, as we have seen in *Hill*, the Court requires detailed evidence of disparate impact rather than merely a potential impact.[97] The most common areas of difficulty concern the questions:

- What is the appropriate pool of comparators?
- What is meant by 'disadvantages a substantially higher proportion of the members of one sex'?
- When should the discrimination be judged—when the measure is adopted, when it is brought into force, or when the employee actually suffers the discrimination?

These questions have elicited divergent views in the national courts[98] and a reference to the Court in *Seymour-Smith*.[99] This case raised the issue whether

[94] Case C–102/88 *Ruzius Wilbrink v. Bestuur van de Bedrijfsvereniging voor Overheidsdiensten* [1989] ECR 4311.

[95] Case C–243/95 [1998] ECR I–3739.

[96] Citing, to that effect, Case C–343/92 *De Weerd, née Roks and Others v. Bestuur van de Bedrijfsvereniging voor de Gezondheid* [1994] ECR I–571, para. 33, and Case C–444/93 *Megner and Scheffel v. Innungskrankenkasse Rheinhessen-Pfalz* [1995] ECR I–4741, para. 24.

[97] Cf. Case C–237/94 *O'Flynn v. Adjudication Officer* [1996] ECR I–2617 considered in Ch. 3.

[98] See e.g. *R v. Secretary of State for Education, ex parte Schaffter* [1987] IRLR 53; *Staffordshire County Council v. Black* [1995] IRLR 234; *London Underground v. Edwards (No. 2)* [1997] IRLR 157 (EAT) and Court of Appeal [1998] IRLR 253.

[99] Case C–167/97 [1999] ECR I–623.

a two-year service requirement[100] prior to bringing a claim for unfair dismissal in the UK was indirectly discriminatory against women contrary to
Article 119 [new Article 141]. On the question of what is the appropriate
pool of comparators, English law asks the question: how many men and
women in the workplace (in the case of an individual employer) or the workforce as a whole (especially where legislation is being challenged) *can* comply
with the requirement? Traditionally, English law has not looked at the opposite, 'failure rates', question: how many men and women can*not* comply? The
answer to this question might produce a very different statistical result.[101] In
Seymour-Smith the Court seemed to accept an amalgam of the 'can' and
'cannot' comply tests. It said that the best approach to comparing statistics
was to consider:

[o]n the one hand, the respective proportions of men in the workforce *able* to satisfy
the requirement of two years' employment under the disputed rule and of those *unable*
to do so, and on the other, to compare those proportions as regards women in the
workforce [emphasis added].[102]

Subsequently it focused on the 'can' comply test.[103]

The Court then went on to consider the tests for disparate impact. There
are, in effect, four options as to the legal test for establishing that a measure
has a disparate impact on women.[104] The first is a rule-of-thumb of the kind
adopted in the US Equal Employment Opportunity Commission Uniform
Guidelines on Employee Selection Procedures.[105] These state that a selection
rate for any race, sex, or ethnic group which is less than four-fifths (80 per
cent) of the group with the highest rate will generally be regarded as evidence
of adverse impact. Smaller differences in selection rates may nevertheless
constitute adverse impact where they are 'significant' in both statistical and
practical terms or where a user's actions have discouraged applicants disproportionately. This rule has the advantage of being relatively easy to apply.

The second option is an impressionistic or 'eyeball' approach which asks, as
the British Sex Discrimination Act 1975 does, whether or not the difference in
impact is 'considerable'. The UK government argued for this approach, attaching to the word 'considerable' the meaning of a 'large disparity'. The advantage of this approach is that it does not rely solely on numbers, which may
be an unreliable guide since they depend upon the size and male/female

---

[100] The two-year service requirement has now been reduced to one year by SI 1999/1436,
Unfair Dismissal and Statement of Reasons for Dismissal (Variation of Qualifying Period) Order
1999.

[101] See Deakin and Morris, *Labour Law* (Butterworths, London, 1998), 582–3.

[102] Para. 59.

[103] See e.g. para. 60.

[104] This is taken from Barnard and Hepple, 'Indirect Discrimination: Interpreting *Seymour-
Smith*' (1999) 58 *CLJ* 399.

[105] *Federal Register*, Vol. 43, No. 166, 25 Aug. 1978.

composition of the employer's workforce or (in the case of a legislative measure) the national labour force.

A third approach, for which the applicants argued, is to ask whether there
is an inherent risk that a measure adopted by a Member State will have a
disparate impact as between men and women.[106] This approach has the
advantage of allowing the tribunal to use its general knowledge and to look
outside the pool for comparison to take account of social facts, such as the fact
that ten times as many women as men are likely to be single parents and
responsible for a child.

The fourth approach, for which the European Commission argued, was to
adopt a 'statistically significant' test, whereby a provision is indirectly discriminatory where it affects a significantly different number of members of
one sex.[107] This test was said to enable the national court to determine
whether a difference in impact is due to a mere chance or whether it reflects a
social fact or structural phenomenon.

The Court did not consider the first of these options (the four-fifths rule),
and failed to give any clear guidelines on whether the second, third, or fourth
option was to be preferred. Instead, the Court suggested that there were two
tests for disparate impact. The first test can be found at paragraph 60 where it
said that the test was whether a 'considerably smaller proportion of women
than men' was able to satisfy the two-year requirement (i.e. the second or
third option).[108] It then went on to adopt a test of statistical significance (the
fourth option).[109] At paragraph 61 it then proposed an alternative test for
disparate impact. It said that there would be evidence of apparent sex discrimination 'if the statistical evidence revealed a lesser but persistent and
relatively constant disparity over a long period between men and women who
satisfy the requirement of two years' employment'. The Court did not have
the evidence to propose an answer to the paragraph 61 test[110] but it did
suggest an answer to the paragraph 60 test. It said that the statistics in this
case (77.4 per cent of men and 68.9 per cent of women could comply when
the two-year rule was introduced in 1985) 'do not appear, on the face of it, to
show that a considerably smaller proportion of women than men is able

---

[106] [1999] IRLR 253, 258. This accords with the important decision of the Court of Appeal in
the English case of *London Underground Ltd v. Edwards* [1998] IRLR 364 upholding a tribunal
finding that a rostering system requiring an early morning start had an adverse impact on
women with family responsibilities, even though only one of 21 women train drivers positively
complained about the arrangements.

[107] Para. 57.

[108] Para. 60.

[109] Para. 62.

[110] When the case returned to the House of Lords the majority considered that the para. 61
test, but not the para. 60 test, had been satisfied. Therefore, there was evidence of indirect
discrimination but the national law was not unlawful because it could be objectively justified
under the more dilute test considered below, nn. 131–149.

to fulfill the requirement imposed by the disputed rule'.[111] The Court seems to be equating statistical significance with a 'considerable' difference, since, where the sample is relatively small, a difference of less than 10 per cent is insufficient to prove indirect sex discrimination.[112]

Seymour-Smith also considered the question of when should the discrimination be judged. The statistics in this case showed that over the period 1985 to 1993 the proportions of men and women who had two years' or more service with their current employer ranged for men, from a minimum of 72.5 per cent to a maximum of 78.4 per cent, and for women from a minimum of 63.8 per cent to a maximum of 74.1 per cent. Throughout the period 1985 to 1991 the ratio of the proportion of men qualified to the proportion of women qualified was about 10:9 reducing to about 20:19 in 1993. Therefore, the impact appears to have diminished over time. This makes it crucial to determine the moment in time at which the disparate impact test is to be applied, not least because the objective justification which existed at one time may not exist at another. The Court failed to give an unequivocal answer to this question, preferring to throw it back to the national court, stating that 'the point in time at which the legality of a rule of the kind at issue in this case is to be assessed by the national court may depend on various circumstances, both factual and legal'.[113] It was suggested that if the authority was alleged to have acted *ultra vires* (as in these judicial review proceedings), then this was in principle the time when the rule was adopted[114] but in cases of application of the rule to an individual, it was the time of application which was relevant.

4.2 Defences and Justifications

According to the orthodoxy, there is no defence to a claim of *direct* discrimination unless an express derogation is provided. While the Equal Treatment Directives 76/207 and 79/7 contain such derogations[115] there are no equivalents in the field of pay. In the case of *indirect* discrimination, by contrast, the discriminatory conduct, as we have seen, may be objectively justified on grounds other than sex.[116] In *Bilka-Kaufhaus*[117] the Court laid down a

---

[111] Para. 64. Similarly, in Case C–226/98 *Jørgensen v. Foreningen af Speciallæger*, judgment of 6 Apr. 2000, para. 34 the Court said that the provision affected 'only 22 specialized medical practitioners, of whom 14 were women, out of a total of 1680, of whom, 302 were women. It seems doubtful that such data could be treated as significant.'

[112] For criticisms of this approach see Barnard and Hepple, above n. 104.

[113] Para. 46.

[114] Para. 47 and implicit in para. 63.

[115] Art. 2(2)–(4) of Directive 76/207; Art. 7(1) of Directive 79/7.

[116] Case 96/80 *Jenkins* [1981] ECR 911, para. 114. See Hervey, 'Justification of Indirect Sex Discrimination in Employment: European Community Law and United Kingdom Law Compared' (1991) 40 *ICLQ* 807 and *Justifications for Sex Discrimination in Employment* (Butterworths, London, 1993), ch. 8.

[117] Case 170/84 [1986] ECR 1607, para. 36.

three-stage test for justifications for the national court to apply in respect of indirectly discriminatory conduct by employers: the measures chosen must 'correspond to a real need on the part of the undertaking, are appropriate with a view to achieving the objectives pursued and are necessary to that end'. In subsequent cases the Court has provided considerable guidance on the meaning of this test. It has said that objective justifications may take account of economic factors relating to the needs and objectives of the under-taking.[118] This may include permitting the employer to pay full-timers more than part-timers in order to encourage full-time work,[119] and paying certain jobs more in order to attract candidates when the market indicates that such workers are in short supply.[120] It does not include paying job-sharers less solely on the ground that avoidance of such discrimination would involve increased costs.[121]

On the other hand generalizations about certain categories of workers—such as the belief that part-time workers are not as integrated in, or as dependent upon, the undertaking employing them as full-time workers—do not constitute objectively justified grounds.[122] This point was reinforced in *Hill* where the Court sent out a strong message that it required concrete evidence before accepting a justification. Therefore, the Irish government's argument that its reward system maintained staff motivation, commitment, and morale was 'no more than a general assertion unsupported by objective criteria'.

The Court is also suspicious of justifications based on mobility and training. In *Danfoss*[123] it recognized that a criterion for awarding a pay increase to reward employees' mobility—their adaptability to variable hours and places of work—may work to the disadvantage of female employees who, because of household and family duties, are not as able as men to organize their working time with such flexibility. Similarly, the criterion of training may work to the disadvantage of women in so far as they have had less opportunity than men for training or have taken less advantage of that opportunity. In both cases the employer may only justify the remuneration of such adaptability or

---

[118] Case 96/80 *Jenkins* [1981] ECR 911.

[119] See e.g. Case C–170/84 *Bilka-Kaufhaus* [1984] ECR 1607 where Bilka-Kaufhaus argued that the employment of full-time workers entailed lower ancillary costs and permitted the use of staff throughout opening hours. In general part-time workers refused to work in the late after-noons and on Saturdays.

[120] Case C–127/92 *Enderby* [1993] ECR I–5535. If the national court can determine precisely what proportion of the increase in pay is attributable to market forces, it must necessarily accept that the pay differential is objectively justified to the extent of that proportion.

[121] Case C–243/95 *Hill* [1998] ECR I–3739, para. 40. In Case C–226/98 *Jørgensen*, judgment of 6 Apr. 2000, para. 42, the Court said that budgetary considerations could not in themselves justify discrimination on grounds of sex. However, measures intended to ensure sound manage-ment of public expenditure on specialized medical care and to guarantee people's access to such care could be justified if they met a legitimate objective of social policy, were appropriate and necessary.

[122] Case 171/88 *Rinner-Kühn* [1989] ECR 2743.

[123] Case 109/88 [1989] ECR I–3199.

training by showing it is of importance for the performance of specific tasks entrusted to the employee.[124]

A common justification raised by employers is seniority. At first, the Court accepted this without criticism. In *Danfoss* the Court said that a criterion which rewarded length of service, while operating to the prejudice of women in so far as women have entered the labour market more recently than men or more frequently take a career break did not require justification. The Court reasoned that since length of service went hand in hand with experience, and since experience generally enabled employees to perform their duties better, the employer was free to reward length of service without having to establish the importance service had in the performance of specific tasks entrusted to the employee. In *Nimz*[125] the Court modified its approach. It said that:

Although experience goes hand in hand with length of service, and experience enables the worker in principle to improve performance of the tasks allotted to him, the object-ivity of such a criterion depends on all the circumstances in a particular case, and in particular on the relationship between the nature of the work performed and the experience gained from the performance of the work upon completion of a certain number of working hours. However it is a matter for the national court [to determine].

Gerster[126] and *Kording*[127] also concerned the application of length of service rules for the purposes of promotion and accreditation. In *Gerster* part-time workers had their service counted at either zero (for part-time work at less than half time), two-thirds (for part-time work at one-half to two-thirds time), or full-time (for part-time work over two-thirds time). As the Advocate General pointed out, such a system totally lacked the internal coherence necessitated by the requirement of objective justification. While not going as far as its Advocate General, the Court pointed out, as it had previously held in *Nimz*, that:

it is impossible to identify objective criteria . . . on the basis of an alleged special link between length of service and acquisition of a certain level of knowledge and experi-ence, since such a claim amounts to no more than a generalisation concerning certain categories of worker.[128]

Rather it said, an individual assessment must be made by the national court, on the basis of all the circumstances of the individual case, and the nature of the work and the experience acquired through time by the particular employee.

The Court has also examined the validity of the justification that the dis-crimination was the result of separate structures of collective bargaining. In

---

[124] Cf. Case C–309/97 *Angestelltenbetriebsrat der Wiener Gebietskrankenkasse v. Wiener Gebiets-krankenkasse*, judgment of 11 May 1999, para. 19.
[125] Case C–184/89 [1991] ECR I–297.
[126] Case C–1/95 [1997] ECR I–5253.
[127] Case C–100/95 [1997] ECR I–5289.
[128] Para. 39.

Enderby[129] the Court ruled that the fact that rates of pay of two jobs of equal value, one carried out almost exclusively by women and the other predominantly by men, were arrived at by collective bargaining was not sufficient objective justification for the difference in pay between the two jobs. The Court reached this conclusion despite the fact that the collective bargaining was carried out by the same parties, and, taken separately, had in itself no discriminatory effect. However, in *Dansk Industri*[130] the Court seems to have relaxed its view. It said that the national court may take into account the fact that the elements of pay are determined by collective bargaining in its assessment of whether the differences between the two groups of workers were due to objective factors unrelated to sex.

So far we have considered objective justification in the context of indirectly discriminatory conduct by employers. In the context of indirectly discriminatory *legislation* the Court initially formulated a similar test to that in *Bilka* for objective justification. In *Rinner-Kühn*,[131] a case concerning indirectly discriminatory employment legislation, the Court ruled that the Member State could justify such legislation provided that it could show that the means chosen met a necessary aim of its social policy and that the legislation was suitable for attaining that aim. In *De Weerd*[132] the Court applied *Rinner-Kühn* in the context of social security. More recently, however, the Court has shown signs of diluting this test, at least in the context of social security cases. *Nolte*[133] and *Megner*[134] concerned German social security law under which individuals working less than fifteen hours per week and whose income did not exceed one-seventh of the monthly reference wage[135] were termed 'minor' or 'marginal' part-time workers. Since these workers were not subject to the statutory old-age insurance scheme covering invalidity and sickness benefit, they did not have to pay contributions. They were also exempt from paying contributions for unemployment benefit. Although the legislation affected considerably more women that men, the German government argued that the exclusion of persons in minor employment corresponded to a structural principle of the German social security scheme, that there was a social demand for minor employment and that if it subjected marginal workers to compulsory insurance there would be an increase in unlawful employment (black employment) and an increase in avoidance techniques (for instance, false self-employment).

---

[129] Case C–127/92 [1993] ECR I–5535.
[130] Case C–400/93 *Specialarbejderforbundet i Danmark v. Dansk Industri* [1995] ECR I–1275.
[131] Case 171/88 [1989] ECR 2743.
[132] Case C–343/92 [1994] ECR I–571.
[133] Case C–317/93 *Nolte v. Landesversicherungsanstalt Hannover* [1996] ECR I–4625.
[134] Case C–444/93 *Megner* [1995] ECR I–4741.
[135] The average monthly salary of persons insured under the statutory old-age insurance scheme during the previous calendar year.

The Court began by citing *De Weerd*[136] and repeated the standard *Rinner-Kühn* test for objective justification. It said that social policy was a matter for the Member States which had a broad margin of discretion and could choose the measures capable of achieving the aim of their social and employment policy. It then said:

It should be noted that the social and employment policy aim relied on by the German government is objectively unrelated to any discrimination on the grounds of sex and that, in exercising its competence, the national legislature was *reasonably entitled* to consider that the legislation in question was necessary in order to achieve that aim [emphasis added].[137]

The Court reached similar conclusions in *Laperre*[138] and *Van Damme*.[139] The test of 'reasonableness' applied here is significantly weaker than the more rigorous test envisaged by *Rinner-Kühn* and the subsequent cases. It is also striking that the Court itself decided in *Megner* that 'the legislation in question was necessary to achieve a social policy aim unrelated to any discrimination on the grounds of sex',[140] even though in *Lewark* the Court said that drawing such conclusions was a task for the national court. The Court reached this conclusion without citing any evidence, or considering whether the social policy aim in question could be achieved by other means.[141] The Court also accepted that, with the exception of mere budgetary considerations,[142] almost any other social policy reason (provided it meets the proportionality test) will justify indirect discrimination in state social security schemes.[143]

In *Seymour-Smith*[144] the Court was asked to choose between the *Rinner-Kühn* and *Nolte/Megner* test in the context of *employment* legislation. The answer was inconclusive. The Court's initial observations favoured the *Rinner-Kühn* test. The Court said 'It must also be ascertained, in the light of all the relevant factors and taking into account the possibility of achieving the social policy aim [encouragement of recruitment[145]] in question by other means, whether such an aim appears to be unrelated to any discrimination

---

[136] Case C–343/92 [1994] ECR I–571.

[137] Para. 30.

[138] Case C–8/94 *Laperre v. Bestuurcommissie beroepszaken in de provincie Zuid-Holland* [1996] ECR I–273.

[139] Case C–280/94 *Posthuma-van Damme v. Bestuur van de Bedrijfsvereniging voor Detailhandel* [1996] ECR I–179.

[140] It decided similarly in Case C–317/93 *Nolte* [1996] ECR I–4625, and Case C–8/94 *Laperre* [1996] ECR I–273.

[141] The Court's approach contrasts with the decision of the House of Lords in the UK in *R v. Secretary of State for Employment, ex parte EOC* [1994] IRLR 176 that the Secretary of State had failed to show that discriminatory service thresholds could be objectively justified.

[142] Case C–343/92 *De Weerd* [1994] ECR I–571.

[143] Case C–280/94 *Posthuma-van Damme* [1996] ECR I–179 and Case C–8/94 *Laperre* [1996] ECR I–273.

[144] Case C–167/97 [1999] ECR I–623.

[145] The Court accepted that this was a legitimate aim of social policy (para. 71).

based on sex and whether the disputed rule, as a means to its achievement, is capable of advancing that aim'.[146] The UK government, introducing the language of reasonableness, maintained that a Member State should merely have to show that it was reasonably entitled to consider that the measure would advance a social policy aim. The Court recalled that in *Nolte/Megner* it had observed that, in choosing the measures capable of achieving the aims of their social and employment policy, the Member States have a broad margin of discretion. It added:

75. However, although social policy is essentially a matter for the Member States under Community law as it stands, the fact remains that the broad margin of discretion available to the Member States in that connection cannot have the effect of frustrating the implementation of a fundamental principle of Community law such as that of equal pay for men and women.

76. Mere generalisations concerning the capacity of a specific measure to encourage recruitment are not enough to show that the aim of the disputed rule is unrelated to any discrimination based on sex nor to provide evidence on the basis of which it could reasonably be considered that the means chosen were suitable for achieving that aim.

The Court then reformulated the test for justification in its answer to the national court in terms of the *Nolte/Megner* test:

77. Accordingly, the answer to the fifth question must be that if a considerably smaller percentage of women than men is capable of fulfilling the requirement of two years' employment imposed by the disputed rule, it is for the Member State, as the author of the allegedly discriminatory rule, to show that the said rule reflects a legitimate aim of its social policy, that that aim is unrelated to any discrimination based on sex, and that it could reasonably consider that the means chosen were suitable for attaining that aim.

So where do we stand? It is still not clear which test is being applied: judges favouring a more rigorous approach to equality got their way in paragraphs 75 and 76; those favouring a more market-oriented concept winning through in paragraph 77. There seem now to be at least three tests for objective justification: the strict *Bilka* test for indirectly discriminatory conduct by employers, recently affirmed in *Hill*,[147] the weaker *Seymour-Smith* test for indirectly discriminatory employment legislation, and the very dilute test for social security legislation in *Nolte/Megner*. This view is supported by the Court's decision in *Krüger*.[148] The case concerned the exclusion of those employed in 'minor' employment, as defined in *Nolte/Megner*, from an end-of-year bonus paid by the employer under a collective agreement. The Court said that the case concerned a situation 'which is different from . . . *Nolte* and *Megner*'.[149] It said:

---

[146] Para. 72.
[147] Case C–243/95 [1998] ECR I–3739 (job sharers returning to full-time work).
[148] Case C–281/97 *Krüger* v. *Kreiskrankenhaus Ebersberg*, judgment of 9 Sept. 1999.
[149] Para. 29.

In this case, it is not a question of either a measure adopted by the national legislature in the context of its discretionary power or a basic principle of the German social security system, but of the exclusion of persons in minor employment from the benefit of a collective agreement which provides for the grant of a special annual bonus, the result of this being that, in respect of pay, those persons are treated differently from those governed by that collective agreement.

This confirms that employers cannot rely on the more lenient test of justification available to the State. The Court itself then went on to find that the exclusion was indirectly discriminatory.

As we have seen, the Court seems to have recognized that *direct* discrimination cannot be objectively justified[150] except by reference to any derogations expressly provided for by the legislation. The absence of any such derogations from Article 141 has, at times, created difficulties. For example, in *Roberts*[151] the employer paid a former male employee a bridging pension between the ages of 60 and 65 but not a former female employee who received the equivalent from the State. The woman therefore received less pay from her employer than a man. Ostensibly she suffered direct discrimination but there were no derogations available for the employer. This prompted the Commission in *Roberts*[152] to suggest that direct discrimination could be objectively justified 'since the very concept of discrimination, whether direct or indirect, involves a difference in treatment which is unjustified'. The Advocate General also said that the Court has not stated that direct discrimination can never be justified by objective factors,[153] making it arbitrary to permit the possibility of justifying a clear inequality of treatment dependent on whether that inequality is direct or indirect. On the other hand, in *Grant*[154] Advocate General Elmer reasserted the orthodox position. He said 'direct discrimination cannot be justified by reference to objective circumstances'.

Although the Court did not expressly rule on this point in *Roberts*, in *Smith*[155] it did contemplate taking objective justification into account in the context of not applying the equality principle to pension benefits payable immediately post the *Barber* judgment.[156] Similarly, in *Webb*[157] the Court ruled in the context of the Equal Treatment Directive that the termination of a

---

[150] Case C–262/88 *Barber* [1990] ECR I–1889, para. 32, and Case C–177/88 *Dekker* v. *Stichting Vormingscentrum voor Junge Volwassen Plus* [1990] ECR I–3941, para. 12.

[151] Case C–132/92 [1993] ECR I–5579. See further Ch. 5.

[152] Ibid.

[153] See e.g. Case C–217/91 *Spain* v. *Commission* [1993] ECR I–3923, para. 37: 'The principle of equal treatment viewed as a general principle of Community law requires that similar situations shall not be treated differently and that different situations shall not be treated in the same manner unless such differentiation is objectively justified'.

[154] Case C–249/96 *Grant* v. *South West Trains* [1998] ECR I–621, para. 38.

[155] Case C–408/92 [1994] ECR I–4435.

[156] Paras. 30 and 31.

[157] Case C–32/93 *Webb* v. *EMO Air Cargo* [1994] ECR I–3567.

contract for an indefinite period on grounds of the woman's pregnancy, which constitutes direct discrimination '*cannot be justified* by the fact that she is prevented, on a purely temporary basis, from performing the work for which she has been engaged' (emphasis added). By implication this does suggest that termination of a fixed-term contract on the grounds of pregnancy might be justified.[158]

Ellis has argued that those advocating that direct discrimination should be capable of being objectively justified misunderstand the structural elements of discrimination. Since discrimination means detrimental treatment which is grounded on sex, it consists of two elements—harm and causation. The concept of justification is used in relation to indirect discrimination, where the root cause of the detrimental treatment is not clear and the defendant is seeking to show that its cause is unrelated to sex. In direct discrimination cases, where it is proved that the detrimental treatment is grounded upon the plaintiff's sex, cause has been established and there is no room to argue about justification. Further, she argues, the introduction of a concept of justification into direct discrimination would have the effect of extending the range of defences open to the employer in an open-ended manner contrary to the intentions of the drafters of the legislation[159] and would seriously undermine discrimination law as it now stands.

Should the distinction between direct and indirect discrimination itself be maintained? Some argue not. For example, in *Roberts*[160] the Advocate General said that direct and indirect discrimination could not always be distinguished with clarity;[161] in *Enderby*[162] the Court did not attempt to make a distinction between direct and indirect discrimination. It merely said that the fact that rates of pay of two jobs of equal value, one carried out almost exclusively by women and the other predominantly by men, were different led to the requirement that the employer show that the difference is based on objectively justified factors unrelated to any discrimination on the grounds of sex. Despite these problems, the distinction between direct and indirect discrimination should be maintained so that the framework of the legislation remains intact.

---

[158] The justification will not include the financial loss which an employer who appointed a pregnant woman would suffer during her maternity leave (Case C–207/98 *Mahlburg*, judgment of 3 Feb. 2000, para. 29).

[159] Ellis, 'The Definition of Discrimination in European Community Sex Equality Law' (1994) 19 *ELRev.* 563.

[160] Case C–132/92 [1993] ECR I–5579.

[161] e.g. while *Roberts* looked like a case of direct discrimination, if emphasis were laid on the fact that the employer calculates the bridging pension in the same way but the result of such calculation is that for five years women receive a lower bridging pension, this constitutes indirect discrimination.

[162] Case C–127/92 [1993] ECR I–5535.

4.3 Discrimination Based on Sex

For the discrimination to be unlawful it must be based on sex. At first, it seemed that the Court would construe the concept of 'sex' broadly. For example, in *Liefting*[163] it recognized that 'gender-plus' (e.g. gender and marriage) discrimination was caught by Article 141. In that case employer contributions to a pension scheme discriminated against female civil servants married to (male) civil servants. Although there was no allegation that women were being discriminated against generally, the Court found that discrimination against this particular category of female civil servant was nevertheless caught by Article 119 [new Article 141].[164]

The broad approach to the term 'sex' was also followed in *P* v. *S*[165] where the Court considered that the term 'sex' included sex change in the context of the Equal Treatment Directive. Therefore, a male to female transsexual dismissed on the grounds of her sex change had a remedy in EC law. *P* v. *S* provides a good example of a case where the Court was influenced by the fundamental nature of the principle of equality. It argued that 'the Directive is simply the expression, in the relevant field, of the principle of equality, which is one of the fundamental principles of Community law'.[166] The Court then reasoned that since the right not to be discriminated against on grounds of sex is one of the fundamental human rights whose observance the Court has a duty to ensure, the scope of the Directive could not be confined simply to discrimination based on the fact that a person was of one sex or the other.[167] It then said that in view of the purpose and the nature of the rights which it sought to safeguard, the scope of the Directive applied to discrimination arising from the gender reassignment of the person concerned, since 'such discrimination is based, essentially if not exclusively, on the sex of the person concerned'.[168] To justify its decision the Court said 'To tolerate such

---

[163] Case 23/83 *Liefting v. Academisch Ziekenhuis bij de Universiteit van Amsterdam* [1984] ECR 3225.

[164] See also Case C–7/93 *Bestuur van het Algemeen Burgerlijk Pensioenfonds v. Beune* [1994] ECR I–4471 (discrimination against married men) and Case C–128/93 *Fisscher v. Voorhuis Hengelo and Stichting Bedrijfspensioenfonds voor de Detailhandel* [1994] ECR I–4583 (discrimination against married women). In *Beune* the Court ruled that married men placed at a disadvantage by discrimination must be treated in the same way and have the same rules applied to them as married women.

[165] Case C–13/94 *P* v. *S* [1996] ECR I–2143; Barnard, 'Some are more Equal than Others: the Decision of the Court of Justice in *Grant* v. *South-West Trains*' (1999) 1 *Cambridge Yearbook of European Legal Studies* 147.

[166] See also the Advocate General's Opinion at para. 22: 'The Directive is nothing if not an expression of a general principle and a fundamental right . . . Respect for fundamental rights is one of the general principles of Community law, the observance of which the Court has a duty to ensure'.

[167] Paras. 18–19. The Court reached this conclusion even though Advocate General Tesauro pointed out that it was indisputable that the *wording* of the principle of equal treatment laid down by the Directive referred to the traditional man/woman dichotomy.

[168] Paras. 20–21. See Wintemute, 'Sexual Orientation Discrimination', in *Individual Rights and the Law in Britain*, eds. McCrudden and Chambers (Clarendon, Oxford, 1995).

discrimination [against transsexuals] would be tantamount, as regards such a person, to a failure to respect the dignity and freedom to which he or she is entitled, and which the Court has a duty to safeguard'.[169] This is a quite remarkable decision. It seems that a strong opinion on the part of the Advocate General was highly influential. He declared:

I am well aware that I am asking the Court to make a 'courageous' decision. I am asking it to do so, however, in the profound conviction that what is at stake is a universal fundamental value, indelibly etched in modern legal traditions and in the constitutions of the more advanced countries: the irrelevance of a person's sex with regard to the rules regulating relations in society. . . . I am quite clear, I repeat, that in Community law there is no precise provision specifically and literally intended to regulate the problem . . . [but] I consider that it would be a great pity to miss this opportunity of leaving a mark of undeniable civil substance, by taking a decision which is bold but fair and legally correct, inasmuch as it is undeniably based on and consonant with the great value of equality.[170]

In *Grant*,[171] however, the Court drew the line at extending the concept of 'sex' to include sexual orientation. It began by rejecting the authority of a decision of the UN Human Rights Committee in *Toonen* v. *Australia*[172] that under Article 28 of the International Covenant of Civil and Political Rights, the term 'sex' was to be taken as including sexual orientation, on the grounds that the Committee was 'not a judicial institution [and] whose findings have no binding force in law',[173] and that its views did not 'in any event appear to reflect the interpretation so far generally accepted of the concept of discrimination based on sex which appears in various international instruments concerning the protection of fundamental rights'.[174] Therefore, the Court determined the scope of Article 119 [new Article 141] only by having regard to its wording and purpose, its place in the scheme of the Treaty, and its legal context,[175] and concluded that Community law did not cover discrimination based on sexual orientation.

The Court's reluctance to extend the definition of 'sex' further is probably based on respect for the separation of powers. It said:

It should be observed, however, that the Treaty of Amsterdam amending the Treaty on European Union, the Treaties establishing the European Communities and certain related acts, signed on 2 October 1997, provides for the insertion in the EC Treaty of an Article 6a [new Article 13] which, once the Treaty of Amsterdam has entered into force, will allow the Council under certain conditions (a unanimous vote on a proposal

---

[169] Para. 22.

[170] Para. 24.

[171] Case C–249/96 [1998] ECR I–621. Cf. the decision of the European Court of Human Rights concerning Art. 8 of the European Convention in *Smith and Grady* v. *United Kingdom* [1999] IRLR 734.

[172] Communication No. 488/1992, views adopted on 31 Mar. 1994, 50th session, point 8.7.

[173] Para. 46.

[174] Para. 47.

[175] Ibid.

from the Commission after consulting the European Parliament) to take appropriate action to eliminate various forms of discrimination, including discrimination based on sexual orientation.[176]

As we have seen unlawful discrimination occurs only if it is on the grounds of sex. If the discrimination occurs for reasons other than sex then this is compatible with Community law. For example, in *Danfoss*[177] the Court said that a criterion for awarding a pay increase based on the quality of work done by the employee is 'undoubtedly wholly neutral from the point of view of sex'.[178] The Court reiterated the point in the complex case of *Dansk Industri*[179] where the Court had to consider a collective agreement in a Danish ceramics factory under which the majority of workers opted to be paid largely on a piecework basis. Their pay consisted of a fixed element, paid as a basic hourly wage, and a variable element, paid by reference to the number of items produced. In April 1990 a comparison was made between the average hourly wage of three sub-groups of workers.[180] The workers' union considered that the difference in pay between the predominantly female blue-pattern painters and the male automatic machine operators breached the requirement under Article 119 [new Article 141] of equal pay for work of equal value.

The Court said that while the principle of equal pay applied to piecework pay systems the mere finding that there was a difference in the average pay of two groups of workers, calculated on the basis of the total individual pay of all the workers belonging to the group, did not suffice to establish that there was pay discrimination, since that difference might be due to differences in the individual output of the workers constituting the two groups, rather than to a difference between the units of measurement applicable to the two groups. Further, the Court said that it was for the national court to decide whether a pay differential relied on by a worker belonging to a group consisting predominantly of women as evidence of sex discrimination against that worker compared with a worker belonging to a group consisting predominantly of men was due to a difference between the units of measurement, which would contravene Article 119 [new Article 141], or to a difference in output, which would not.

---

[176] Para. 48.

[177] Case 109/88 [1989] ECR 3199.

[178] Although it did say that if the application of such a wholly neutral criterion systematically works to the disadvantage of women, then the only explanation is that the employer has misapplied the criterion and so cannot objectively justify its application.

[179] Case C–400/93 [1995] ECR I–1275.

[180] This found that the average hourly pay of the automatic machine operators (an all-male group of 26 turners) was Danish Krone (DKR) 103.93, including a fixed element of DKR 71.69, the pay of the blue-pattern painters (155 women and 1 man) was DKR 91, including a fixed element of DKR 57 and the pay of the ornamental plate painters (an all-female group of 51) was DKR 116.20, including a fixed element of DKR 35.85.

4.4 Identifying the Comparator

Article 141 provides that 'men and women should receive equal pay for equal work'. This suggests that there must always be a comparator of the opposite sex,[181] usually chosen by the applicant.[182] The choice of the comparator can be crucial. In *Grant*, the applicant, a lesbian, was denied benefits (concessionary train fares) for her female partner. She claimed, *inter alia*, direct discrimination on the grounds of sex since her (heterosexual) male colleague had received those benefits for his female partner. The Court, however, chose a homosexual male as the comparator. Grant lost her case since both (homosexual) men and women would have been treated equally, albeit equally badly. Had the Court chosen a heterosexual male comparator, as Grant had argued, there would have been discrimination on the grounds of sex.[183] In *P v. S*, by contrast, the case concerning the dismissal of a male to female transsexual on the grounds of her sex change, the comparator selected was a person of the sex to which P was deemed to have belonged prior to the gender reassignment. Discrimination was found. As the Advocate General recognized, had the Court chosen a female to male transsexual, as the UK government had argued, the result might have been different.

It seems that not only must the comparator be of the opposite sex but must also be a real, identifiable person and not a 'hypothetical worker'.[184] This prevents a woman from arguing that she was the victim of discrimination because if she had been a man she would have received a higher salary. The Court excluded such claims in *Macarthys* on the ground that they would necessitate comparative studies of entire branches of industry which would require further Community legislation. While hypothetical comparators do present considerable problems of proof, the requirement for an actual comparator potentially limits the effectiveness of the equality legislation in sectors predominated by women. Under UK law hypothetical comparators are allowed in the context of the Sex Discrimination Act 1975 but not under the Equal Pay Act 1970.[185]

---

[181] The French version of the Directive makes this explicit: there must be discrimination '*entre les hommes et les femmes*'.

[182] This is the British rule: *Ainsworth v. Glass Tubes & Components Ltd* [1977] IRLR 74.

[183] Cf. *Baehr v. Lewin* 852 P.2d 44 (Hawaii 1993). See further Barnard, 'Some are More Equal than Others: the Case of *Grant v. South-West Trains*' (1999) 1 *Cambridge Yearbook of European Law* 147; Bell, 'Shifting Conceptions of Sexual Discrimination at the Court of Justice: from *P v. S* to *Grant v. SWT*' (1999) 5 *ELJ* 63.

[184] Case 129/79 *Macarthys* [1980] ECR 1275. This argument was based on the distinction the Court had drawn between direct and indirect discrimination. If the comparator were to be a hypothetical male this would be classed as indirect, disguised discrimination which would require comparative studies of entire industries. At that stage Art. 119 [new Art. 141] was directly effective only in respect of direct discrimination. Since the law has now changed this approach may require reassessment. See also Case C–200/91 *Coloroll Pension Trustees Ltd v. Russell* [1994] ECR I–4389.

[185] In a case concerning pregnancy, Case C–177/88 *Dekker* [1990] ECR I–3941, the Court found direct discrimination without looking for a male comparator. See below, nn. 196–198.

The pool from which the comparator can be drawn is further limited by the additional requirement, thought to be derived from *Defrenne (No. 2)*[186], that the comparator must be employed in the same establishment or service as the applicant. This requirement prevents a woman from making comparisons with colleagues in other establishments belonging to the same employer or with comparators working for different employers in the same industry. It also prevents female workers, in a sector dominated by women, relying on Article 141 to make cross-industry comparisons. However, in *Defrenne (No. 2)* the Court actually said that the principle of equal pay applies '*even more* in cases where men and women receive unequal pay for equal work carried out in the same establishment or service, whether public or private'[187] (emphasis added). Consequently the Advocate General in *Commission* v. *Denmark*[188] has expressed doubts about the validity of the single workplace rule which might defeat the purpose of the principle of equal pay.[189]

The Court has also stressed that the woman and her comparator must be in 'identical situations',[190] albeit that they do not have to work contemporaneously.[191] This requirement was used in *Roberts*[192] to deny the woman her claim. It will be recalled in that case that the employer paid a man a bridging pension between the ages of 60 and 65 but paid Mrs Roberts a reduced bridging pension because she received a state pension at the age of 60 which her male comparator did not. The Court ruled that no discrimination occurred since the 'difference as regards the objective premise, which necessarily entails that the amount of the bridging pension is not the same for men and women, cannot be considered discriminatory'. Similarly, in *Abdoulaye*[193] the Court said that it was not contrary to Article 119 [new Article 141] for women but not men to receive a maternity bonus since the two situations were not comparable.

In *Dansk Industri*[194] the Court provided guidance for identifying the comparator group. It said that the two groups must encompass all the workers who can be considered to be in a comparable situation, taking into account

---

[186] Case 43/75 [1976] ECR 455. Cf. *Lawrence* v. *Regent Office Care* [1999] IRLR 148 (EAT).
[187] Para. 22.
[188] In Case 143/83 *Commission* v. *Denmark* [1985] ECR 427.
[189] COM(94)6 final.
[190] Case C–132/92 *Roberts* [1993] ECR I–5579. See also Case C–342/93 *Gillespie and Others* v. *Northern Health and Social Services Board and Others* [1996] ECR I–475; Case C–249/97 *Gruber* v. *Silhouette International Schmied GmbH*, judgment of 14 Sept. 1999; Case C–309/97 *Wiener Gebietskrankenkasse*, judgment of 11 May 1999; and Case C–333/97 *Lewen* v. *Lothar Denda* [2000] All ER (EC) 261, para. 38. Such differences in circumstances (such as the hours worked) may, however, constitute an objective justification: Case C–236/98 *Örebro läns landsting*, judgment of 30 Mar. 2000, para. 61.
[191] Case 129/79 *Macarthys* [1980] ECR 1275.
[192] Case C–132/92 [1993] ECR I–5579. See also Case C–342/93 *Gillespie* [1996] ECR I–475.
[193] Case C–218/98 *Abdoulaye* v. *Régie Nationale des Usines Renault SA*, judgment of 16 Sept. 1999.
[194] Case C–400/93 [1995] ECR I–1275.

factors such as the nature of the work, training requirements, and working conditions. The group must also comprise a relatively large number of workers. The national court must ensure that any differences are not due to purely fortuitous or short-term factors or to differences in the individual output of the workers concerned. Consequently, it said that a comparison is not relevant where it involves groups formed in an arbitrary manner so that one comprises predominantly women and the other comprises predominantly men with a view to carrying out successive comparisons.[195] In other words, it is not possible to carve a group of women and a group of men out of larger groups merely to bring an equal pay claim.

The principal drawback with the requirement of a comparator in the context of sex equality is that, as we have seen, it takes the male as the norm and assumes that a woman is like a man and should be placed in the same position as a man. In some contexts, notably pregnancy, this makes no sense. Comparisons adopted by some courts between a pregnant woman and a sick man are artificial, inaccurate and misleading. This point was recognized in both *Dekker*[196] and *Webb*.[197] In *Dekker* a woman was refused a job on the ground that she was pregnant; another woman was appointed and there were no male candidates. Nevertheless, the Court found that discrimination had occurred. It reasoned that since employment can be refused because of pregnancy only to a woman, such a refusal constituted discrimination on the grounds of sex. In *Webb* the Court confirmed that 'there can be no question of comparing the situation of a [pregnant] woman ... with that of a man similarly incapable for medical or other reason'. These cases suggest that a male comparator is not needed when a woman has clearly been disadvantaged by the use of a sex-specific criterion, such as pregnancy (the asymmetrical approach), whereas a comparison must be carried out where discrimination can only be established on the basis of the different treatment accorded to men (the symmetrical approach).[198]

---

[195] Para. 36.
[196] Case C–177/88 [1990] ECR I–3941.
[197] Case C–32/93 [1994] ECR I–3567, para. 24.
[198] Banks, 'Equal Opportunities for Women and Men', *Social Europe* 3/91, 65.

B. EQUAL PAY: ARTICLE 141 [EX ARTICLE 119] AND THE EQUAL PAY DIRECTIVE 75/117

1. Introduction

Article 141(1) and (2) [ex Article 119] provide:

1. Each Member State shall ensure that the principle of equal pay for male and female workers for equal work *or work of equal value*[199] is applied.
2. For the purpose of this Article, 'pay' means the ordinary basic or minimum wage or salary or any other consideration, whether in cash or in kind, which the worker receives directly or indirectly, in respect of his employment, from his employer.

Equal Pay without discrimination based on sex means:

(a) that pay for the same work at piece rates shall be calculated on the basis of the same unit of measurement;
(b) that pay for work at time rates shall be the same for the same job.[200]

The significance of Article 119 first became apparent in the case of *Defrenne (No. 2)*.[201] Defrenne was an air hostess employed by Sabena Airlines. Although she did identical work to a male cabin steward she was paid less than her male counterpart. She claimed that she was discriminated against contrary to Article 119 [new Article 141]. The Court, recognizing that the principle of equal pay forms part of the 'foundations of the Community', decided, despite strong objections by the Member States, that Article 119 was 'directly applicable' both horizontally and vertically, and 'may thus give rise to individual rights which the courts may protect'.[202] However, realizing the number of potential claims arising from this decision which might seriously affect the solvency of many companies, the Court ruled that in the interests of legal certainty the direct effect of Article 119 could not be relied on to support the claims of people prior to the date of the judgment (8 April 1976), except in the case of workers who had already brought legal proceedings.

2. The Definition of Pay

Article 141(1) [ex Article 119] defines 'pay' broadly. It refers to the 'ordinary basic minimum wage or salary', which includes pay received as piece rates[203]

---

[199] Added by the Treaty of Amsterdam. For other amendments see above, text attached to n. 42.

[200] The wording of Art. 119 is based on Art. 2(1) of ILO Convention 100, 1951 (UNTS, Vol. 165, 303).

[201] Case 43/75 [1976] ECR 455. See also Case C–50/96 *Deutsche Telekom* v. *Schröder*, judgment of 10 Feb. 2000, para. 31.

[202] Para. 24. See also Case C–28/93 *Van den Akker* v. *Stichting Shell Pensioenfonds* [1994] ECR I–4527, para. 21.

[203] See also Case C–400/93 *Dansk Industri* [1995] ECR I–1275, above n. 179.

or time rates, 'and any other consideration, whether in cash or in kind, which the worker receives directly or indirectly in respect of his employment from his employer'. The Court has added further glosses to this definition. It has said that pay can be 'immediate or future' provided that the worker receives it, albeit indirectly,[204] in respect of his employment from his employer.[205] Thus, in *Garland* the Court found that concessionary travel facilities granted voluntarily to ex-employees fell within the scope of Article 119 [new Article 141].[206] The legal nature of the facilities is not important (they can be granted under a contract of employment, a collective agreement,[207] as a result of legislative provisions,[208] with the exception of social security[209] to which Directive 79/7 applies,[210] or made *ex gratia*[211] by the employer[212]) provided that they are granted in respect of employment.[213] The important point is that the pay does not need to be contractual in origin: it can be legislative or voluntary.[214] Therefore, the Court has ruled that sick pay,[215] redundancy payments resulting from voluntary or compulsory redundancy,[216] unfair dis-

---

[204] Since Art. 141 also applies to money received indirectly from an employer, it would cover occupational pensions paid out of a trust fund, administered by trustees who are technically independent of the employer: see Case C–262/88 *Barber* [1990] ECR I–1889; Joined Cases C–270 and C–271/97 *Deutsche Post AG v. Sievers and Schrage*, judgment of 10 Feb. 2000; Joined Cases C–234 and C–235/96 *Deutsche Telekom AG v. Vick and Conze*, judgment of 10 Feb. 2000 and Case C–50/96 *Schröder*, judgment of 10 Feb. 2000.

[205] Case 80/70 *Defrenne (No. 1) v. Belgian State* [1971] ECR 445.

[206] Case 12/81 *Garland v. British Railways Board* [1982] ECR 359.

[207] Case C–281/97 *Krüger*, judgment of 9 Sept. 1999, para. 17.

[208] See Cases 43/75 *Defrenne (No. 2)* [1976] ECR 455, para. 40, and C–262/88 *Barber* [1990] ECR I–1889.

[209] Case 80/70 *Defrenne (No. 1)* [1971] ECR 445. In Case C–7/93 *Beune* [1994] ECR I–4471 the Court sought to clarify the criteria necessary to identify state social security schemes. It ruled that a pension scheme directly governed by statute is a strong indication that the benefits provided by the scheme are social security benefits. It then added that Art. 119 [new Art. 141] does not embrace social security schemes or benefits such as retirement pensions directly governed by statute, which apply to general categories of employees where no element of collective bargaining is involved. Finally, the Court recognized that although these schemes are funded by the contributions of workers, employers, and possibly the public authorities, the funding is determined not so much by the employment relationship between the employer and the worker as by considerations of social policy.

[210] See further Ch. 5.

[211] *Ex gratia* payments are 'advantages which an employer grants to workers although he is not required to do so by contract': Cases C–262/88 *Barber* [1990] ECR I–1889, para. 19, and Case 12/81 *Garland* [1982] ECR 359.

[212] Case C–360/90 *Bötel* [1992] ECR I–3589.

[213] Cf. the position with additional voluntary contributions which are not granted in respect of employment: see Case C–200/91 *Coloroll* [1994] ECR I–4389.

[214] Case C–457/93 *Kuratorium für Dialyse- und Nierentransplantation eV v. Lewark* [1996] ECR I–243.

[215] Case 171/88 *Rinner-Kühn* [1989] ECR 2743.

[216] Case C–262/88 *Barber* [1990] ECR I–1889 concerned *compulsory* redundancy. Case 19/81 *Burton v. British Rail* [1982] ECR 555 concerned voluntary redundancy where the Court suggested that Directive 76/207 did not apply to discriminatory age conditions. The Court seems *sotto voce* to have overruled this decision (see Curtin, 'Scalping the Community Legislator: Occupational Pensions after *Barber*' (1990) 27 *CMLRev.* 475, 482) and it seems likely that Art. 41 would apply to both.

missal compensation,[217] occupational pensions,[218] survivors' benefits,[219] bridging pensions,[220] additional statutory redundancy payments,[221] maternity benefits paid under legislation or collective agreements,[222] special bonus payments made by the employer[223] (including an end-of-year bonus[224] and an 'inconvenient hours' supplement[224A]), concessionary train fares,[225] and a severance grant payable on the termination of an employment relationship[226] all constitute pay within the meaning of Article 141 [ex Article 119]. Similarly, compensation in the form of paid leave or overtime pay for participation in training courses given by an employer to Staff Committee members[227] and rules governing the automatic reclassification to a higher salary grade can constitute pay.[228]

As the definition of pay gets broader it might be thought that the role for Directive 76/207 will diminish, especially since Article 141 has both vertical and horizontal direct effect. However, in *Gillespie*[229] the Court emphasized that there was a clear distinction between equal pay matters governed by Article 119 [new Article 141] and equal treatment in respect of working conditions covered by Directive 76/207, with no room for overlap.

---

[217] Case C–167/97 *Seymour-Smith* [1999] ECR I–623. In Case C–249/97 *Gruber*, judgment of 14 Sept. 1999, the Court said that 'termination payments' constitute pay.

[218] Case 170/84 *Bilka-Kaufhaus* [1986] ECR 1607 (supplementary pensions); Case C–262/88 *Barber* [1990] ECR I–1889 (contracted-out pensions).

[219] Case C–109/91 *Ten Oever* [1993] ECR I–4879; Case C–147/95 *DEI* v. *Efthimios Evrenopoulos* [1997] ECR I–2057.

[220] Case C–132/92 *Roberts* [1993] ECR I–5579.

[221] Case C–173/91 *Commission* v. *Belgium* [1993] ECR I–673.

[222] Case C–342/93 *Gillespie* [1996] ECR I–475. The Court did, however, rule that neither Art. 119 [new Art. 141] nor Art. 1 of Directive 75/117 required that women should continue to receive full pay during maternity leave, nor did those provisions lay down any specific criteria for determining the amount of benefit to be paid to them during that period. See also Case C–218/98 *Abdoulaye*, judgment of 16 Sept. 1999, para. 14.

[223] Case 58/81 *Commission* v. *Luxembourg* [1982] ECR 2175 where a special 'head of household' allowance was deemed to be pay. Individual pay supplements to basic pay (Case 109/88 *Danfoss* [1989] ECR 3199) and increments based on seniority (Case 184/89 *Nimz* [1991] ECR 297) are considered to be pay. So, presumably, would shift premia, overtime, and all forms of merit and performance pay constitute 'pay' within Art. 141 (COM(94)6 final).

[224] Case C–281/97 *Krüger*, judgment of 9 Sept. 1999; Case C–333/97 *Lewen* [2000] All ER (EC) 261 a Christmas bonus paid on a voluntary basis as an incentive for future work or loyalty to the undertaking constituted pay (para. 22).

[224A] Case C–236/98 *Jämställdhetsombudsmannen* v. *Örebro läns landsting*, judgment of 30 Mar. 2000, para. 42.

[225] Case C–249/96 *Grant* [1998] ECR I–621.

[226] Case C–33/89 *Kowalska* [1990] ECR I–2591. Such payments are deemed to be deferred pay.

[227] Case C–360/90, *Bötel* [1992] ECR I–3589.

[228] Case C–184/89 *Nimz* [1991] ECR I–297.

[229] Case C–342/93 [1996] ECR I–475, para. 24. See also Case C–281/97 *Krüger*, judgment of 9 Sept. 1999, para. 14.

3. The Meaning of Equal Pay

3.1 Equal Pay for the Same Work

It is clear that 'equal work' embraces at least the concept of equal pay for the same or similar work even if the work of the applicant and her comparator is not performed contemporaneously.[230] Thus, in *Macarthys*,[231] the plaintiff successfully brought an action based on Article 119 [new Article 141] against her employers claiming that she had been discriminated against on the grounds of her sex. She worked as a warehouse manageress earning £50 a week. Her predecessor, a man, had earned £60 a week. According to the Court, an assessment of whether the work was equal was 'entirely qualitative in character in that it is exclusively concerned with the nature of the services in question'. It did not matter that the man and woman did not work at the same time, since the Court said that the scope of Article 119 'may not be restricted by the introduction of a requirement of contemporaneity'.

On the other hand, the Court ruled in *Wiener Gebietskrankenkasse*[232] that the term 'the same work' does not apply 'where the same activities are performed over a considerable length of time by persons the basis of whose qualification to exercise their profession are different'. Therefore, graduate psychologists, most of whom were women, could not claim equal pay with medical doctors who were paid 50 per cent more, even though both groups worked as psychotherapists and the patients were charged the same irrespective of whether they were treated by a psychologist or a doctor.

3.2 Equal Pay for Work of Equal Value

The principle of equal pay for work of equal value, originally found in Article 1 of Directive 75/117[233] and now in the amended Article 141(1), is intended to redress the undervaluing of jobs undertaken primarily by women where they are found to be as demanding as different jobs more usually undertaken by men. A job classification or job evaluation scheme,[234] while not obliga-

---

[230] Directive 75/117, Art. 1.

[231] Case 129/79 [1980] ECR 1275.

[232] Case C–309/97, judgment of 11 May 1999.

[233] See above, n. 42. Art. 1 provides 'The principle of equal pay for men and women outlined in Article 119 of the Treaty, means for the same work or for work to which equal value is attributed, the elimination of all discrimination on the grounds of sex with respect to all aspects and conditions of employment'.

[234] Job classification is a non-analytical process used to categorize jobs. Job evaluation, used in the UK and Ireland, is a more analytical approach to assessing the relative demands of a job. The analytical approach involves breaking the jobs down into their component elements for the process of comparison, whereas the non-analytical approach considers the relative worth of the job based on a whole job comparison. While analytical schemes are more objective the whole process is still subject to judgments made by evaluators which reflect their own background, experience and attitudes (COM(94)6 final).

tory,[235] offers one method of determining whether a man and woman's work is of equal value. This is recognized by Article 1(2) of Directive 75/117 which provides that:

Where a job classification system is used for determining pay, it must be based on the same criteria for both men and women and so drawn up so as to exclude any discrimination on the grounds of sex.

The contents of a job classification system were discussed in *Rummler*.[236] A German printing firm adopted a grading scheme which classified jobs according to the previous knowledge required, concentration, effort, exertion, and responsibility. Grade II jobs involved slight to medium muscular effort; Grade III jobs medium to high muscular effort; and Grade IV jobs involved on occasion high levels of muscular exertion. Mrs Rummler's job was classified as Grade III. She argued that it should have been classified as Grade IV because it involved lifting packages of 20kg which, *for her*, was heavy physical work. She therefore asked that account be taken of her own (subjective) characteristics.

The Court said that the nature of the work had to be considered objectively. It recognized that a criterion which took account of an objectively measurable level of physical strength needed to do the job was compatible with Article 1(2) provided that the work, by its very nature, did require physical exertion. However, the Court said that when calculating the amount of physical exertion needed, a criterion based solely on the values of one sex, for example, the average strength of a woman, brought with it the threat of discrimination since it might result in work requiring use of greater physical strength being paid in the same way as work requiring less physical strength. The Court did, however, accept that even though a strength criterion might generally favour male employees, the classification system was not discriminatory on this ground alone. Instead, the Court said that the scheme must be considered overall and, in order for it to accord with the principles of the Directive, it had to be designed so that, if the nature of the work permitted, 'it includes as "work to which equal value is attributed" work in which other criteria are taken into account for which female employees may show particular aptitude'. Thus, as the United Kingdom government suggested, a system based on the criterion of muscular effort is only discriminatory if it excludes from consideration the activation of small groups of muscles which typifies manual dexterity where women tend to score highly. The Court concluded that it was the task of national courts to decide in individual cases whether the job classification scheme in its entirety permitted fair account to be taken of all the criteria on the basis of which pay was determined.

[235] Case 61/81 *Commission* v. *UK* [1982] ECR 2601.
[236] Case 237/85 *Rummler* v. *Dato-Druck* [1986] ECR 2101.

A job classification system is not the only method for determining whether work is of equal value. A national court may have to decide the question for itself. In *Commission v. United Kingdom*[237] the Court said that the individual must have the right to initiate an equal value claim in the national court, notwithstanding objections from her employer, since Article 6 of Directive 75/117 required Member States to endow an authority with the requisite jurisdiction to decide whether different jobs are of equal value, even though national courts might have difficulty in applying such an abstract concept.

The Court has not yet decided the question of how equal in value the men's and women's work must be to receive equal pay. Since the Court has insisted that 'equal work be remunerated with equal pay'[238] this suggests that only work of exactly equal value should receive equal pay. The Court has also not expressly considered the question whether Article 141 should secure a woman proportionate pay, that is, an increase in pay when her work is valued at, for example, 60 per cent of the man's, yet she receives only 40 per cent of his pay.[239] However, in *Rummler*[240] the Court said that it follows from the principle that equal work must be remunerated with equal pay that work performed must be remunerated according to its nature. This case, when read in conjunction with Article 136 [new Article 117] and the Directive on Part-time Workers,[241] suggests that part-time workers should receive a proportionate share of full-time earnings.[242] This might indicate that any sex-based wage discrimination should be eliminated under the Directive.

3.3 Equal Pay for Work of Greater Value

Article 141(1) also covers the situation where the woman is doing work of greater value than the man, is being paid less than the man, and wishes to be paid the same as the man. This was the situation in *Murphy*.[243] The Court said that since the principle of equal pay forbids women engaged in work of equal value to men from being paid less than men on the grounds of sex, *a fortiori* it

---

[237] Case 61/81 [1982] ECR 2601. The Member States have adopted different mechanisms for resolving whether, in the light of the nature and demands of the different jobs, the work is of equal value. In Belgium, France, Italy, and Luxembourg, disputes may be resolved by labour inspectorates, while under Irish legislation any dispute on the subject of equal pay can be referred to one of three equality officers (COM(94)6 final).

[238] Case 237/85 *Rummler* [1986] ECR 2101.

[239] See perhaps Case C–127/92 *Enderby* [1993] ECR I–5535. See further Rubinstein, 'The Equal Treatment Directive and UK Law', in *Women, Employment and European Equality Law*, ed. McCrudden (Eclipse, London, 1987).

[240] Case 237/85 [1986] ECR 2101.

[241] Directive 97/81/EC [1997] OJ L14/9, as amended by Council Directive 98/23/EC [1998] OJ L131/10, and consolidated [1998] OJ L131/13.

[242] See also Case C–102/88 *Ruzius Wilbrink* [1989] ECR 4311.

[243] Case 157/86 *Murphy v. Bord Telecomm Eireann* [1988] ECR 673.

prohibits a difference in pay where the woman is engaged in work of higher value. To adopt a contrary interpretation would be 'tantamount to rendering the principle of equal pay ineffective and nugatory' since an employer could circumvent the principle by assigning additional duties to women who could then be paid a lower wage.

4. The Material Scope of the Principle of Equal Pay

The prohibition of discrimination applies not only to acts of employers, both in respect of the contract of employment and unilateral acts,[244] but also to action by public authorities and collective agreements. This will now be considered.

4.1 Discriminatory Legislation

Article 3 of the Equal Pay Directive 75/117/EEC requires Member States to abolish all discrimination arising from laws, regulations, or administrative provisions which are contrary to the principle of equal pay. In reality Member States have not always satisfied this requirement and so the Court has used Article 141 to eliminate any remaining discriminatory legislative provisions. For example, in *Rinner-Kühn*[245] a German law obliged an employer to pay sick pay to employees who worked more than ten hours a week or 45 hours a month. The Court found that such a provision resulted in discrimination against female workers and contravened Article 119 [new Article 141] unless it could be objectively justified.[246]

A series of references has also been made concerning German legislation on compensation paid to a worker for taking part in training courses connected with staff representation. The legislation provided that both full- and part-time workers attending training courses could be compensated up to the limit of their respective normal working hours. In *Bötel*[247] the Court found that this legislation discriminated against part-time workers and thus against women because, while both part-time and full-time employees participated in the same number of hours of training, part-timers received less compensation due to the lower number of hours worked. The Court said that this method of compensation was a disincentive to part-time workers from attending such training courses and acquiring further skills and knowledge.

---

[244] Case C–333/97 *Lewen* [2000] All ER(EC) 261, para. 26.
[245] Case 171/88 [1989] ECR 2743.
[246] See above, text attached to nn. 116–149.
[247] Case C–360/90 [1992] ECR I–3589. See Barnard and Hervey, 'European Union Employment and Social Policy Survey 1996 and 1997' (1997) 17 *YEL* 435, 473.

This decision led to considerable concern in Germany since it interfered with the special status of works and staff councils in the organization of German national employment policy and labour relations. In particular, it interfered with the principle that members of staff councils carry out their duties without loss of earnings but without any financial incentives to take on such a responsibility. As a result, in *Lewark*[248] the Court was asked to reconsider its decision in *Bötel*.[249] Once again the Court recognized that the application of the legislation discriminated against women contrary to Article 119 [new Article 141] unless it could be objectively justified, which was a matter for the national court. The Court, however, did note that such legislation was likely to deter part-time workers from performing staff council functions or from acquiring the knowledge necessary for performing them, which made it more difficult for part-time workers to be represented by qualified staff council members.[250] It confirmed this view in *Freers*.[251] This statement might be seen as a suggestion from the Court that the requisite non-discriminatory justification was not present here,[252] since women are significantly under-represented in collective bargaining structures.[253]

4.2 Discrimination arising from Collective Agreements

Article 4 of the Equal Pay Directive 75/117/EEC obliges Member States, disregarding principles relating to the autonomy of the Social Partners, to take the necessary measures to ensure that provisions appearing in collective agreements, wage scales, wage agreements, or individual contracts of employment, which are contrary to the principle of equal pay, are declared null and void or can be amended.[254] Subsequently, in *Kowalska*[255] the Court confirmed that Article 119 [new Article 141] also applied to terms contained in collective agreements. Thus, the Court found that a provision in a collective agreement excluding part-time workers from the payment of a

---

[248] Case C–457/93 [1996] ECR I–243.

[249] Case C–360/90 [1992] ECR I–3589.

[250] Cf. the decisions of the Court in *Lewark* and *Bötel* with that in Case C–399/92 *Helmig* [1994] ECR I–5727, a case where part-timers did not receive the higher rate of overtime pay until they worked in excess of the normal working hours for full-timers. See above, n. 72.

[251] Case C–278/93 *Freers and Speckmann* v. *Deutsche Bundespost* [1996] ECR I–1165. See Shaw, 'Works Councils in German Enterprises and Article 119 EC' (1997) 22 *ELRev.* 256.

[252] Ibid.

[253] Cockburn, 'Strategies for Gender Democracy: Women and the European Social Dialogue', *Social Europe* Supp. 4/95, and 'Women's Access to European Industrial Relations' (1995) 1 *EJIR* 171.

[254] See generally Lester and Rose, 'Equal Value Claims and Sex Bias in Collective Bargaining' (1991) 20 *ILJ* 163.

[255] Case C–33/89 [1990] ECR I–2591. See also Case 109/88 *Danfoss* [1989] ECR 3199; Case C–281/97 *Krüger*, judgment of 9 Sept. 1999.

severance grant on termination of their employment infringed Article 119 unless it could be objectively justified. Similarly, in *Nimz*[256] a collective agreement provided that the full period of service of employees working for at least three-quarters of normal working time was to be taken into account when reclassifying salary grades, whereas only one-half of the period of service was taken into account in the case of employees whose working hours were between one-half and three-quarters of normal work-ing time. This latter group comprised a considerably smaller percentage of men than women. The Court ruled that Article 119 [new Article 141] precluded such indirectly discriminatory agreements unless the employer could prove that such provisions were objectively justified.[257] The Court also emphasized that the national court was obliged, first, to set aside any dis-criminatory provision in a collective agreement immediately without requesting or waiting for its removal by collective bargaining, and secondly, to apply to the discriminated group the same arrangements applicable to other employees, which were, according to the Court the only valid point of reference.

5. Conclusions

Although the principle of equal pay has been enshrined in the EC Treaty since 1957, women still earn, on average, a quarter less than men.[258] Eurostat has conducted some research into the hourly earnings of women in four coun-tries (Sweden, Spain, France, and the UK). It found that Sweden is the country which comes nearest of the four to equal remuneration for men and women where the average earnings for women are 84 per cent of those for men, compared with 73 per cent in Spain and France and 64 per cent in the UK (see Table 4.1).

Eurostat found that in three of these Member States the female managers are the worst remunerated occupational group in comparison with their male counterparts. In the fourth Member State, the UK, they actually come off even worse, receiving only two-thirds of male earnings. Women in the lower-paid non-manual occupations (clerks, and service workers, shop and market sales workers) come nearest to male earnings in the same occupations. The research also discovered that there was a noticeable trend consistent in all four countries—the older the age-group of women con-sidered, the further they fall short of the average earnings of their male

---

[256] Case C–184/89 [1991] ECR I–297.

[257] Ibid.; see also Cases 143/83 *Commission v. Denmark* [1985] ECR 427 and C–127/92 *Enderby* [1993] ECR I–5535.

[258] The EU average is 76.3 per cent (1999). See further http://europa.eu.int/en/comm/ eurostat/compres/en/5499/6305499a.htn

Table 4.1 Hourly Earnings of Women as Percentage of Men's.[1] Full-time and Part-Time Workers, Excluding Bonuses and Overtime

	E	F	S	UK
OCCUPATION				
Managers	69.7	70.2	80.1	65.8
Professionals	77.4	78.9	87.7	82.9
Technicians and associate professionals	82.7	86.1	84.6	68.9
Clerks	76.4	92.5	95.5	89.8
Service and sales workers	79.1	70.5	96.2	80.7
Craft and related trades workers	70.6	67.0	88.7	61.3
Plant and machine operators	73.5	76.3	92.0	74.5
Elementary occupations	83.9	76.2	87.4	73.6
ECONOMIC ACTIVITY				
Mining and quarrying	66.7	57.9	78.8	75.3
Manufacturing	69.7	72.1	85.2	66.3
Electricity, gas and water supply	82.6	72.1	77.5	76.1
Construction	94.8	93.0	78.2	74.5
Total industry	**73.6**	**74.1**	**84.3**	**67.4**
Wholesale and retail trade; repair of motor vehicles	70.7	61.0	84.3	62.4
Hotels and restaurants	79.4	61.1	79.7	75.7
Transport, storage and communication	85.9	92.4	93.6	82.3
Financial intermediation	75.5	63.1	64.2	51.4
Real estate, renting and business activities	69.4	68.5	76.4	62.8
Total services	**71.1**	**70.6**	**82.1**	**62.6**
AGE				
Less than 20 years	92.9	98.0	90.7	91.0
Between 20 and 24 years	86.6	94.1	94.5	82.6
Between 25 and 29 years	86.5	88.4	88.4	79.7
Between 30 and 44 years	77.8	77.1	86.1	63.1
Between 45 and 54 years	74.4	69.3	79.8	53.6
55 years and more	70.6	64.5	77.4	58.1
EDUCATION				
Less than upper secondary level	73.8	73.8	87.3	70.9
Upper secondary level	74.2	78.7	82.1	70.8
Third level (university or otherwise)	64.9	66.5	80.4	68.4
TOTAL	**72.7**	**72.9**	**84.0**	**64.4**
After discounting main structural effects (occupation, economic activity, education)	**78.2**	**76.6**	**86.8**	**75.4**

Source: *Eurostat, Statistics in Focus, Population and Social Conditions, How Evenly are Earnings Distributed?* 1997/15, 7.

[1] Because of the differences which have already been noted in the patterns of full-time and part-time work of men and women, and in overtime work, a comparison of male and female earnings is best carried out on the basis of hourly rates, excluding bonuses and overtime payments.

contemporaries. Similarly the most highly-qualified women, those with third-level education, receive more pay than women with lower qualifications but actually earn a smaller percentage of male earnings. However, Eurostat found that even when women's earnings are recalculated to remove structural effects (educational qualifications, occupation, and industry) women's earnings come closer to men's, but there still remains an hourly earnings difference between a man and a woman with a comparable educational background in the same occupation and industry, of 13 per cent in Sweden, 22 per cent in Spain, 23 per cent in France, and almost 25 per cent in the UK.

The pay gap is due to a variety of factors. First, women are segregated both in terms of occupation and establishment. Women working in predominantly female occupations attract consistently lower rates of pay than men. This is particularly the case where women work part-time, as the facts of *Enderby* highlight. In that case the majority of the speech therapists were women working part-time while the majority of pharmacists were men working full-time. Speech therapists earned up to 60 per cent less than pharmacists.

The second explanation for the difference in pay is that even where men and women do the same kind of work in the same organizations women tend to attract lower pay because they are concentrated in lower paying specialisms, they occupy lower status jobs, and the method of remuneration impacts differently on men and women (by, for example, rewarding seniority or flexibility). Further, women's skills are often undervalued.

The importance of combating discrimination on the grounds of sex has also been highlighted by research conducted by the Equal Opportunities Commission. This argues that, in the absence of discrimination, women's earnings would rise by 14 per cent and the gender pay gap would fall from 23 per cent to 7 per cent. The biggest increase would be experienced by single women relative to married men, where, in the absence of discrimination (defined as men and women with the same labour market characteristics receiving the same pay), single women's pay would rise by almost 40 per cent.[259]

---

[259] *Gender and the Earnings Gap: Unequal Treatment or Unequal Workers?*, considered in (1997) 73 EOR 4.

C. EQUAL TREATMENT

1. The Material Scope of the Directive

The principle of equal treatment is defined by Article 2(1) to mean that 'there shall be no discrimination whatsoever on grounds of sex either directly or indirectly by reference in particular to marital or family status'. The language of Article 2(1) is far-reaching. It outlaws any discrimination 'whatsoever' on the grounds of sex.[260] It also excludes discrimination on the grounds of marital and family status. This precludes discrimination against those who are married and those, presumably, who have children, irrespective of their marital status.[261] The principle of equal treatment found in Article 2(1)[262] applies to access to employment, including promotion (Article 3), vocational training (Article 4), and working conditions, including dismissal (Article 5). It applies to all types of employment, including employment in the public service.[263] Social security is, however, excluded from the scope of the equal treatment principle. Article 1(2) provides that 'with a view to ensuring the progressive implementation of the principle of equal treatment in matters of social security, the Council . . . will adopt provisions defining its substance, its scope and the arrangements of its application'. The Court has consistently held that Article 1(2), as a derogation from a fundamental principle, must be narrowly construed.[264] Therefore, in *Jackson*[265] the Court said that a benefit could not be excluded from the scope of the Directive simply because it was formally part of the social security system; it might fall within the scope of the Directive if its subject matter was access to employment, including vocational training and working conditions.[266] In *Meyers*[267] the Court considered that family credit, a social security benefit 'designed to encourage workers who are poorly paid to continue working and to meet family expenses',[268] fell within the scope of Directive 76/207. It said that family credit, which was necessarily linked to an employment relationship, was concerned with access to employment under Article 3 of Directive 76/207, since the prospect of receiving family credit might encourage an unemployed worker to accept work.

---

[260] See above, text attached to nn. 163–180.

[261] The phrase 'family status' may also embrace those with other caring responsibilities including looking after elderly relatives. Presumably, 'marital status' could also apply to those who are no longer married, either because of death or divorce, or those who are unmarried.

[262] See above, nn. 55–58.

[263] Case 248/83 *Commission v. Germany* [1985] ECR 1459.

[264] Case 151/84 *Roberts* [1986] ECR 703 and Case 152/84 *Marshall (No. 1)* [1986] ECR 723.

[265] Case C–63–64/91 *Jackson v. Chief Adjudication Officer* [1992] ECR I–4737.

[266] The fact that the Court in Case C–78/91 *Hughes v. Chief Adjudication Officer* [1992] ECR I–4839 found that family credit fell within Regulation 1408/71 and also did not prevent the benefit from falling within the scope of Directive 76/207. See further Ch. 5.

[267] Case C–116/94 *Meyers v. Adjudication Officer* [1995] ECR I–2131.

[268] See the judgment in Case C–78/91 *Hughes* [1992] ECR I–4839.

In *Meyers* the Court also gave a very broad interpretation to Article 5 of the Directive, refusing to confine 'working conditions' to those conditions set out in a contract of employment or applied by the employer in respect of a worker's employment. It said that a benefit such as family credit constituted a working condition within the meaning of Article 5. This is consistent with its earlier case law. In *Burton*[269] the Court said that the phrase 'working conditions, including the conditions governing dismissal' had to be 'widely construed so as to include termination of the employment relationship between a worker and his employer, even as part of a voluntary redundancy scheme'. This idea was developed further in *Marshall (No. 1)*[270] where the Court made it clear that compulsory retirement fell within the scope of Article 5.[271] It was therefore unlawful for any employer to have different retirement ages for men and women.

2. Exceptions

Three express exceptions to the principle of equal treatment are provided for in the Directive: first, where the sex of the worker constitutes a determining factor (Article 2(2)); secondly, where women need to be protected, particularly as regards pregnancy and maternity (Article 2(3)); and thirdly, where the State has implemented 'positive action' programmes (Article 2(4)). These exceptions, being derogations from an individual right laid down in the Directive, must be interpreted strictly,[272] must be regularly reviewed,[273] and are subject to the principle of proportionality.[274] Although the Member States retain a reasonable margin of discretion as to the detailed arrangements for the implementation of these exceptions,[275] the list of exceptions is exhaustive, as the Court made clear in *Johnston*.[276] It said that it was not prepared to subject the principle of equal treatment to, for example, any general reservation as regards measures taken on the grounds of public safety.

---

[269] Case 19/81 [1982] ECR 555.

[270] Case 152/84 [1986] ECR 723.

[271] See also Case C–13/94 *P* v. *S* [1996] ECR I–2143. The conditions determining whether an employee who was unfairly dismissed was entitled to obtain reinstatement or re-engagement are also covered by the Equal Treatment Directive (and not Art. 141), see Case C–167/97 *Seymour-Smith* [1999] ECR I–623; Case C–236/98 *Örebro läns landsting*, judgment of 30 Mar. 2000, para.60, where the Court ruled that the reduction in working time related to working conditions (and not pay under Art. 119 [new Art. 141]).

[272] See e.g. Case C–450/93 *Kalanke* v. *Freie und Hansestadt Bremen* [1995] ECR I–3051.

[273] See also Arts. 3(2)(c), 5(2)(c), 9(1)–(2). See also Case 222/84 *Johnston* v. *Chief Constable of the RUC* [1986] ECR 1651.

[274] Ibid., para. 36.

[275] See e.g. Case 184/83 *Hofmann* [1984] ECR 3047, para. 27.

[276] Case 222/84 [1986] ECR 1651.

2.1 Sex of the Worker Constitutes a Determining Factor

According to Article 2(2), Member States have the option not to apply the
principle of equal treatment to 'those occupational activities and, where
appropriate, the training leading thereto, for which, by reason of their nature
or the context in which they are carried out, the sex of the worker constitutes
the determining factor'. Article 2(2) does not oblige Member States to exclude
certain occupational activities from the scope of the Directive, nor does it
require Member States to exercise the power of derogation in a particular
manner.[277] Certain clearly defined occupations such as singing, acting, dan-
cing, and artistic or fashion modelling fall within this heading.[278] The Court
has also accepted that certain kinds of employment in private households
might fall within Article 2(2)[279] but has ruled that a general exclusion of the
application of the principle of equal treatment to employment in a private
household or in undertakings with no more than five employees went beyond
the objective which could be lawfully pursued under Article 2(2).[280] On the
other hand, the Court has found that it was lawful to limit access by men
to the post of midwife in view of the 'personal sensitivities' which may play
'an important role in relations between midwife and patient'.[281] Similar
reasoning can explain the Court's acceptance that it was lawful to reserve
posts primarily for men in male prisons and for women in female prisons.[282]

More surprisingly, however, the Court accepted in *Johnston*[283] that certain
policing activities in Northern Ireland might be such that the sex of the police
officers constituted a determining factor. In that case the Chief Constable of
the RUC decided not to renew the contract of Mrs Johnston and other women,
and not to give them training in the handling of firearms. The Court accepted
unquestioningly that the justification for this policy was that 'in a situation
characterised by serious internal disturbances the carrying of fire-arms by
policewomen might create additional risks of their being assassinated and
might therefore be contrary to the requirements of public safety'.[284] The
Court did, however, insist that Member States had a duty to assess the activities periodically in order to decide whether, in the light of social developments, the derogation from the general scheme of the Directive should be
maintained.[285] In addition, the Court recognized that it was for the national

---

[277] Case 248/83 *Commission v. Germany* [1985] ECR 1459.
[278] Commission survey on the implementation of Art. 2(2) cited in Case 248/83 *Commission v.*
Germany [1985] ECR 1459.
[279] Case 165/82 *Commission v. UK* [1983] ECR 3431.
[280] Ibid.
[281] Ibid.
[282] Case 318/86 *Commission v. France* [1988] ECR 3559.
[283] Case 222/84 [1986] ECR 1651.
[284] Para. 36.
[285] See also Art. 9(2) and the requirement to notify the Commission of the results of the
assessment and see Case 248/83 *Commission v. Germany* [1985] ECR 1459, para. 37.

court to ensure that the principle of proportionality be maintained. The Court also re-emphasized the limited nature of the derogation in *Commission v. France*.[286] It said that the exceptions provided for in Article 2(2) could relate only to specific activities and that they had to be sufficiently transparent to permit effective supervision by the Commission. Therefore a system of separate recruitment according to sex fell outside Article 2(2).

Despite these caveats, the Court adopted a similarly respectful approach to state policy in *Sirdar*.[287] Mrs Sirdar had been in the British army since 1983 and had served as a chef in a commando regiment since 1990. When she was made redundant she was invited to apply for a job as a chef in the Royal Marines provided that she satisfied a selection board and a commando training course. The invitation was subsequently withdrawn when the authorities realized that she was a woman, due to the policy of excluding women from the regiment. The existence of this policy was justified by the State on the grounds that the presence of women was incompatible with the requirement of 'interoperability'—the need for every Marine, irrespective of his specialization, to be capable of fighting in a commando unit.

Having ruled that Community law in principle applies to the case, since there was no general exception from Community law covering all measures taken for reasons of public security, the Court considered the application of the Article 2(2) derogation to see whether the measures have 'the purpose of guaranteeing public security and whether they are appropriate and necessary to achieve that aim'. The Court said that it was clear from the documents and the findings of the national court that 'the organisation of the Royal Marines differs fundamentally from that of other units in the British armed forces, of which they are the "point of the arrow head"'. They were a small force and were intended to be the first line of attack. The Court noted that it had also been established that, within this corps, chefs were also required to serve as front-line commandos, that all members of the corps were engaged and trained for that purpose, and that there were no exceptions to this rule at the time of recruitment. The Advocate General added that the evidence given by the Royal Marines showed the 'negative effects' which the presence of any female element might have on the operational cohesion of a commando unit, 'resulting from the foreseeable preoccupation of infanteers to protect women, quite apart from the latter's (as yet untested) physical suitability for difficult offensive operations involving hand-to-hand combat for which the marines are trained'. Therefore the Court concluded that 'In such circumstances, the competent authorities were entitled, in the exercise of their discretion as to whether to maintain the exclusion in question in the light of social developments, and without abusing the principle of proportionality, to come to the view that the specific conditions for deployment of the assault units of which

[286] Case 318/86 [1988] ECR 3559.
[287] Case C–273/97 *Sirdar v. Secretary of State for Defence*, judgment of 26 Oct. 1999.

the Royal Marines are composed, and in particular the rule of interoperability to which they are subject, justified their composition remaining exclusively male'.[288] However, in the *dispositif* the Court allowed the national tribunal some room for manoeuvre. It said that 'the exclusion of women from service in special combat units . . . *may* be justified under Article 2(2) . . .' (emphasis added).

In the light of *Johnston* the outcome of this case is unsurprising. It does, however, reveal how easy it is for a Member State (condoned by the Court) to use the derogations as a shield for gender stereotyping and untested assumptions about male soldiers' attitudes to women. However, the limited nature of the exclusion of women in *Sirdar* was emphasized by the Court in *Kreil*.[289] It reiterated the point already made in *Johnston* and *Sirdar* that the principle of proportionality had to be observed in determining the scope of any derogation. Proportionality requires that 'derogations remain within the limits of what is appropriate and necessary in order to achieve the aim in view'.[290] The Court then ruled that the provisions of German law which excluded women from *all* military posts involving the use of arms and which allowed women access only to medical and military music services could not be regarded as a derogating measure justified by the specific nature of the posts in question or by the particular context in which the activities in question were carried out.

2.2 Protection of Women, particularly as regards Pregnancy and Maternity

Article 2(3) permits a derogation from the principle of equal treatment to protect women 'particularly as regards pregnancy and maternity'. In *Johnston*[291] the Court made clear that this provision was intended 'to protect a woman's biological condition and the special relationship which exists between a woman and her child'. The significance of this was made clear by the decision in *Hofmann*.[292] In that case the father took unpaid paternity leave to look after his new-born child while the mother, having completed the initial obligatory period of maternity leave, returned to work. When the father's claim for the state maternity allowance, which was payable to mothers, was refused, he claimed direct discrimination. The Court accepted that Article 2(3) permitted Member States to introduce provisions which were designed to protect both 'a woman's biological condition during pregnancy and thereafter until such time as her physiological and mental functions have returned to

---

[288] Para. 31.
[289] Case C–285/98 *Kreil* v. *Bundesrepublik Deutschland*, judgment of 11 Jan. 2000.
[290] Para. 23.
[291] Case 222/84 [1986] ECR 1651.
[292] Case 184/83 [1984] ECR 3047. For criticisms see e.g. Fenwick and Hervey, above n. 64, and Shaw and Hervey, above n. 70.

normal after childbirth' and 'to protect the special relationship between a woman and her child over the period which follows between pregnancy and childbirth,[293] by preventing that relationship from being disturbed by the multiple burdens which would result from the simultaneous pursuit of employment'.[294] Thus, the Court ruled that Directive 76/207 did not require Member States to grant leave to fathers, even where the parents had decided differently.[295]

While Article 2(3) can be used to justify special protection of women where their condition requires it, the derogation cannot be used to justify a total exclusion of women from a post of indefinite duration because they are pregnant at the beginning[296] or from an occupation, such as the police force, because public opinion demands that women be given greater protection than men, even though the risks are not specific to women.[297] Similarly, as the Court held in *Stoeckel*,[298] women cannot be excluded from nightwork where, with the exception of pregnancy and its aftermath,[299] the risks relating to nightwork are common to men and women.[300] However, in *Levy*[301] the Court recognized that while Article 5 of Directive 76/207 required national

[293] See also Case C–394/96 *Brown* v. *Rentokil* [1998] ECR I–4185.

[294] Both requirements need not be present: in Case 163/82 *Commission* v. *Italy* [1983] ECR 3273 the Court found that an Italian law which gave a woman but not her husband the entitlement to the equivalent of maternity leave when they adopted a child under six years old was justified 'by the legitimate concern to assimilate as far as possible the conditions of entry of the child into the adoptive family to those of the arrival of a new born child in the family during the very delicate initial period'. Although Art. 2(3) was not cited the thinking is very similar to the requirement of safeguarding the 'special relationship' between mother and child.

[295] Cf. the Directive on Parental Leave 96/34 discussed below, nn. 466–486.

[296] Case C–207/98 *Mahlburg*, judgment of 3 Feb. 2000, para. 25.

[297] Case 222/84 *Johnston* [1986] ECR 1651 and Case C–285/98, *Kreil*, judgment of 11 Jan. 2000, para. 30. The Commission discussed the implications of the *Johnston* decision in its Communication on Protective Legislation for Women (COM(87)105 final; Council Conclusions of 26 May 1987 on Protective Legislation for Women in the Member States of the European Community [1987] OJ C178/04). It examined all national protective provisions, esp. in the light of Arts. 3(2)(c) and 5(2)(c) of the Equal Treatment Directive which require Member States to revise all protective legislation which is no longer justified. It found that 'a mosaic of extremely varied and highly specific regulations exist, the reasons for which are not clearly defined' and concluded that protective legislation which does not relate to pregnancy or maternity should be made to apply equally to both sexes or be repealed.

[298] Case C–345/89 [1991] ECR I–4047. See also Case C–13/93 *Office national de l'emploi* v. *Minne* [1994] ECR I–371 where discriminatory derogations from the prohibition of nightwork contravened Art. 5 of Directive 76/207/EEC.

[299] Case C–421/92 *Habermann-Beltermann* v. *Arbeiterwohlfahrt* [1994] ECR I–1657, para. 18; and Art. 7 of Directive 92/85 [1992] OJ L348/1 on pregnant workers.

[300] The French law at issue, Art. L213–1 of the French *Code du travail* preventing women from working at night, was based on ILO Convention No. 89. A new, non-discriminatory Convention has now been passed (No. 171) which the ILO hopes all Member States will ratify. See EIRR 219, Apr. 1992. France was condemned for maintaining Art. L213–1 in force, see Case C–197/96 *Commission* v. *France* [1997] ECR I–1489. The Commission is now proposing a fine of 142,425 euros per day on France for non-implementation of the Court's earlier judgment (23 Apr. 1999). Italy has also been condemned for retaining national rules prohibiting nightwork for women, see Case C–207/96 *Commission* v. *Italy* [1997] ECR I–6869.

[301] Case C–158/91 *Minstère public et Direction du travail* v. *Levy* [1994] ECR I–4287.

legislation prohibiting nightwork by women to be set aside, this rule did not apply in cases where the national provision was introduced by virtue of an agreement concluded with a non-member country before the entry into force of the Treaty of Rome.[302]

2.3 Positive Action

Article 2(4) of the Equal Treatment Directive provides that the Directive shall be 'without prejudice to measures which promote equal opportunity for men and women, in particular by removing existing inequalities which affect women's opportunities'. The importance of positive action was recognized by a Commission report on occupational segregation.[303] This concluded, first, that despite rising female participation in the workforce, occupational segregation remains a central characteristic of all European labour markets; and secondly, that although women have made entry into high level jobs, they have also increased their shares of lower level service and clerical work. The authors argued that positive action programmes, particularly those implemented in a favourable labour market, context have a role to play in reducing this segregation.

Positive action is a management approach intended to identify and remedy situations which lead to or perpetuate inequalities in the workplace. It is intended to put women in the position to be able to compete equally with men but does not interfere with the selection process. Thus, positive action aims to complement legislation on equal treatment and includes any measure contributing to the elimination of inequalities in practice. It focuses on balancing family and professional responsibilities, in particular looking at the development of child-care structures, the arrangement of working hours, and the reintegration of women who have taken career breaks into the workplace.[304] Positive discrimination, by contrast, consists of setting recruitment targets or quotas and discriminating in favour of women at the point of selection in order to meet these targets. Although ostensibly contravening the principle of formal equality,[305] such discrimination can be justified in that it compensates for past discrimination, providing an immediate remedy to a long standing problem.[306] The Community has favoured positive action over positive

[302] Art. 234(1) [new Art. 307]. See also Case C–13/93 *Minne* [1994] ECR I–371.

[303] Rubery and Fagan, *Occupational Segregation of Women and Men in the European Community*, Commission of the European Communities, V/5409/93–EN.

[304] See also Advocate General Tesauro's Opinion in Case C–450/93 *Kalanke* [1995] ECR I–3051 and COM(96)88.

[305] See Fredman, above n. 61, 380–3.

[306] But see Parekh, 'A Case for Positive Discrimination', in *Discrimination: The Limits of the Law*, eds. Hepple and Szyszczak (Mansell, London, 1992). See also chs. 16–21 from the same book. For some lively discussion on the positive discrimination debate, see the essays by Kennedy and Delgado, in *Foundations of Employment Discrimination Law*, ed. Donohue III (OUP, New York, 1997).

discrimination. The Council's Recommendation on the Promotion of Positive Action for Women[307] recommends that Member States adopt a positive action policy 'designed to eliminate existing inequalities affecting women in working life and to promote a better balance between the sexes in employment'. The policy is intended, first, to eliminate the prejudicial effects on women which arise from existing attitudes, behaviour, and structures based on the idea of a traditional division of roles in society for men and women; and, secondly, to encourage the participation of women in sectors where they are currently under-represented and at higher levels of responsibility in order to achieve better use of human resources.[308] Article 4 contains a list of the steps that Member States might take, including encouraging women to participate in vocational and continuous training,[309] encouraging women candidates in making applications, adapting working conditions, and adjusting working time. Article 8 emphasizes that the public sector should promote equal opportunities to serve as an example.[310]

The Commission published an extensive guide to positive action[311] listing the organizational advantages of a positive action programme and the means by which to put it into place. Nevertheless, a report produced for the Commission found that 'despite almost a decade of the active promotion of positive action for women progress is slow. . . . Many organisations do not appear to have a policy for equality of opportunity. Even less appear to have a programme of practical actions.'[312] As a result, the third and fourth action Community programmes contain a continued commitment to positive action,[313] including support for programmes such as NOW (New Opportunities for Women) aimed at promoting opportunities for women in the field of employment and training.[314]

Given the sensitivities surrounding positive action it was inevitable that the Court would eventually become drawn into the debate. In some of its earlier case law the Court took a very narrow view of what was permissible. In *Commission* v. *France*[315] it said that the Article 2(4) exception was specifically

---

[307] Recommendation 84/635/EEC [1984] OJ L331/34.

[308] Art. 1.

[309] See further the Commission Recommendation 87/567/EEC of 24 Nov. 1987 on Vocational Training for Women [1987] OJ C342/5; the Council Resolution of 16 Dec. on the Reintegration and Late Integration of Women into Working Life [1988] OJ C333/01.

[310] The Commission itself introduced a positive action programme on 8 Mar. 1988.

[311] *Positive Action. Equal Opportunities for Women in Employment. A Guide*, Commission of the European Communities (1988) CB–48–87–525–EN–C.

[312] *An Evaluation Study of Positive Action in Favour of Women*, ER Consultants (1990), Commission V/587/91–EN, 39. For the Commission's own assessment, see its report to Council COM(88)370 final.

[313] See e.g. II.2 Third Action Programme and Commission Document Implementation of the Third Action Programme on Equal Opportunities 1991–5, Development of Positive Action Measures, Strategy Document and Work Programme 1992–5.

[314] See further Ch.1.

[315] Case 318/86 [1988] ECR 6315. See also Case 111/86 *Delauche* v. *Commission* [1987] ECR 5345.

and exclusively designed to allow measures which, although discriminatory in appearance, were in fact intended to eliminate or reduce actual instances of inequalities which might exist in the reality of social life. It ruled out, however, 'a generalised preservation of special rights for women in collective agreements'. This led one commentator to suggest that special measures—perhaps even positively discriminatory ones—would be excused by Article 2(4) to the extent that they compensated for specific instances of pre-existing inequality, albeit that Article 2(4) would not justify positive discrimination in favour of women in employment generally.[316]

The decision in *Kalanke*[317] casts doubts on any such broad reading of Article 2(4). The case concerned the Bremen law on positive discrimination which, in the case of a tie-break situation, gave priority to an equally-qualified woman over a man if women were under-represented in the workforce.[318] Relying on this provision, the State of Bremen promoted Ms Glißman to the post of section manager in the parks department in preference to Mr Kalanke. He argued that he had been discriminated against on the grounds of sex contrary to Article 2(1) of the Directive 76/207; Bremen relied on the Article 2(4) derogation.

The Court explained that Article 2(4) did permit national measures relating to access to employment, including promotion, which gave a specific advantage to women, with a view to improving their ability to compete on the labour market and to pursue their career on an equal footing with men.[319] However, it said that measures which, at the decision stage, departed from the principle of individual merit contravened Article 2(4). It continued that national rules which guaranteed women 'absolute and unconditional priority for appointment or promotion' went beyond promoting equal opportunities and overstepped the limits of the exception in Article 2(4) of the Directive.[320] Consequently, the Bremen system 'substitutes for equality of opportunity as envisaged in Article 2(4) the result which is only to be arrived at by providing such equality of opportunity'.[321]

---

[316] Ellis, above n. 4, 246.

[317] Case C–450/93 [1995] ECR I–3051.

[318] Under-representation exists where women 'do not make up at least half the staff in the individual pay, remuneration and salary brackets in the relevant personnel group within a department'.

[319] Para. 19, referring to the Preamble of the Recommendation on Positive Action (84/635/EEC [1984] OJ L331/34), above, n. 307.

[320] Para. 22. See also Case C–407/98 *Abrahamsson* v. *Fogelqvist*, judgment of 6 July 2000, where the Court ruled that a national rule which gave automatic priority to a person of the under-represented sex who had adequate qualifications but qualifications which were inferior to those of the person who would otherwise have been appointed, albeit that the difference in qualifications was not important, breached Art 2(4) of the Directive and Article 141(4) EC. This outcome was not affected by the limited number of posts to which the rule applied nor the level of the appointment.

[321] Para. 23.

Advocate General Tesauro's Opinion was equally narrow. He said: 'Giving equal opportunities can only mean putting people in a position to attain equal results and hence restoring conditions of equality between members of the two sexes as regards starting points'. This means removing existing barriers to achieve such a result. He then reasoned that since the man and woman in *Kalanke* had equivalent qualifications they must have had and continued to have equal opportunities: 'they are therefore on an equal footing at the starting block.' Consequently, by favouring the woman, he said this created a position of equality of results which exceeded the scope of Article 2(4). He continued:

In the final analysis, must each individual's right not to be discriminated against on grounds of sex—which the Court itself has held is a fundamental right the observance of which it ensures—yield to the rights of the disadvantaged group, in this case women, in order to compensate for the discrimination suffered by that group in the past?

Put this way the answer was, inevitably, no. He said that positive discrimination brought about a quantitative increase in female employment but it also most affected the principle of equality as between individuals. He concluded:

I am convinced that women do not merit the attainment of numerical—and hence only formal—equality—moreover at the cost of an incontestable violation of a fundamental value of every civil society: equal rights, equal treatment for all. Formal numerical equality is an objective which may salve some consciences, but it will remain illusory and devoid of all substance unless it goes together with measures which are genuinely destined to achieve equality . . . [W]hat is necessary above all is a substantial change in the economic, social and cultural model which is at the root of the inequalities.[322]

The judgment was much criticized for its excessive reliance on the formal non-discrimination model, its focus on the individual, its failure both to show any sensitivity towards the position of women[323] and to respect the principle of subsidiarity, and the absence of any attempt to weigh up any policy arguments. It also cast doubt on the legality of a variety of different forms of positive action. As a result, the Commission issued a Communication on *Kalanke*.[324] It took the view that the Court only condemned the special feature of the Bremen law which automatically gave women the absolute and unconditional right to appointment or promotion over men. Therefore, it considered that only those quota systems which were completely rigid and did not leave any possibility of taking account of individual circumstances were

---

[322] Para. 28.
[323] See e.g. Schiek, 'Positive Action in Community Law' (1996) 25 *ILJ* 239; Prechal (1996) 33 *CMLRev.* 1245; Fredman, above n. 61, 392; Peters, 'The Many Meanings of Equality and Positive Action in Favour of Women under European Community Law—A Conceptual Analysis' (1996) 2 *ELJ* 177.
[324] COM(96)88.

unlawful. It therefore proposed an amendment to Article 2(4) of Directive 76/207/EEC to the effect that:

This Directive shall be without prejudice to measures to promote equal opportunity for men and women in particular by removing existing inequalities which affect the opportunities of the underrepresented sex in the areas referred to in Article 1(1). Possible measures shall include the giving of preference, as regards access to employment or promotion, to a member of the underrepresented sex, provided that such measures do not preclude the assessment of the particular circumstances of the individual case.

The Commission's approach was reflected in the Court's decision in the subsequent case of *Marschall*.[325] Mr Marschall, a teacher, applied for promotion. The District Authority informed him that it intended to appoint a female candidate on the basis of the state law which provided for priority to an equally qualified woman where women were under-represented. However, unlike *Kalanke*,[326] the state law contained a saving clause (*Öffnungsklausel*): priority was given to the woman 'unless reasons specific to an individual [male] candidate tilt the balance in his favour'. Advocate General Jacobs thought that the saving clause did not alter the discriminatory nature of the rule in general. He agreed with Advocate General Tesauro in *Kalanke* that the measures permitted by Article 2(4) were those designed to remove the obstacles preventing women from pursuing the same results on equal terms. He said Article 2(4) did not permit measures designed 'to confer the results on them [women] directly, or, in any event, to grant them priority in attaining those results simply because they are women'. He said that the reasoning in *Kalanke* suggested that the rule in *Marschall* was also unlawful: if an absolute rule giving preference to women on the grounds of sex was unlawful, then a conditional rule which gave preference to men on the basis of admittedly discriminatory criteria must *a fortiori* be unlawful.[327]

The Court disagreed. While recognizing that a rule which automatically gave priority to women when they were equally qualified to men involved discrimination on grounds of sex, it distinguished *Marschall* from *Kalanke* on the basis of the saving clause. Having noted the 'prejudices and stereotypes concerning the role and capacities of women in working life',[328] it said that:

It follows that a national rule in terms of which, subject to the application of the saving clause, female candidates for promotion who are equally as qualified as the male candidates are to be treated preferentially in sectors where they are under-represented may

---

[325] Case C–409/95 [1997] ECR I–6363.

[326] The Bremen law at issue in *Kalanke* did not contain a saving clause. The Federal Labour Court, however, read exceptions into the Bremen law in accordance with the *Grundgesetz*. While this was mentioned to the Court (see para. 9), the questions referred made no reference to these exceptions. It therefore seems that the Court answered the question in *Kalanke* on the basis of the absence of such a clause.

[327] Para. 36.

[328] Paras. 29 and 30: see text attached to nn. 76–81, above.

fall within the scope of Article 2(4) if such a rule may counteract the prejudicial effects on female candidates of the attitudes and behaviour described above and thus reduce actual instances of inequality which may exist in the real world.[329]

The Court then added a proviso. The state rule did not breach Article 2(4) provided that the national rule contained a saving clause. This means that:

in each individual case the rule provides for male candidates who are equally as qualified as the female candidates a guarantee that the candidatures will be the subject of an objective assessment which will take account of all criteria specific to the individual candidates and will override the priority accorded to female candidates where one or more of those criteria tilts the balance in favour of the male candidate. In this respect it should be remembered that those criteria must not be such as to discriminate against the female candidates.[330]

It then said that it was for the national court to determine whether those conditions were fulfilled.

The case therefore suggests that so-called soft quotas (quotas with a saving clause) fall within Article 2(4) as an exception to the equal treatment principle, provided that the proviso is satisfied.[331] The ruling in *Marschall* therefore confines *Kalanke* to the (unusual) situation of an unqualified ('hard') quota rule. However, the qualification introduced by the Court to the types of saving clause permitted, and the limitations on the criteria which may be applied to tilt the balance (back) in favour of the man, in effect restrict the operation of such saving clauses. The criteria applied must be based on the individuals concerned and 'not such as to discriminate against *female candidates*',[332] that is, they must be non-discriminatory in a general sense. Therefore, the criteria applied to bring the saving clause into operation may not be based on generalizations about men, such as, for instance their need to bring home a 'household wage' (an indirectly discriminatory requirement), or the fact that the man is a sole breadwinner[333] (again an indirectly discriminatory assumption), or reasons of seniority.[334] This was Advocate General Jacobs' concern about the use of such a proviso. He said that such a saving clause would have 'the result that the post will be offered to the male candidate on the basis of criteria which are accepted as discriminatory'.[335]

[329] Para. 31.

[330] Para. 33.

[331] On the different types of quota, see Schiek, 'Sex Equality Law after *Kalanke* and *Marschall*' (1998) 4 *ELJ* 148.

[332] Para. 33, italics added.

[333] It was suggested by the national court that this might be precisely one such criterion applied in the assessment. Mr Kalanke had argued that he should have been promoted on social grounds since he had to maintain three dependants (wife and two children) whereas Ms Glißman had no such obligation.

[334] On the question of seniority, see above, nn. 125–128. For an anlysis of the proviso, see Charpentier, 'The European Court of Justice and the Rhetoric of Affirmative Action' (1998) 4 *ELJ* 167.

[335] Barnard and Hervey, 'Softening the Approach to Quotas: Positive action after *Marschall*' (1998) 20 *JSWL* 333.

There is much to suggest that the Court is adopting a more substantive approach to equality in *Marschall*.[336] The new Article 141(4), introduced by the Amsterdam Treaty, amending Article 6(3) of the SPA, may have provided some guidance for the Court. This provides: 'With a view to ensuring *full equality in practice between men and women* in working life, the principle of equal treatment shall not prevent any Member State from maintaining or adopting measures providing for specific advantage, in order to make it easier for the *underrepresented sex* to pursue a vocational activity or to prevent or compensate for disadvantages in their professional careers' (emphasis added). This is a stronger and more generalized formulation than its forbear in the SPA and appears to go further than Article 2(4) of Directive 76/207 to permit positively discriminatory measures.[337]

This broader approach to positive action is also reflected in *Badeck*.[337A] The question was raised whether, following *Kalanke*, the Hessen law on equal rights for women and men and the removal of discrimination against women in the public administration contravened EC law. The Court ruled that it did not. For example, it said that Article 2(1) and (4) of Directive 76/207/EEC did not preclude national rules:

[which] in so far as its objective is to eliminate under-representation of women, in trained occupations in which women are under-represented and for which the State does not have a monopoly of training, allocates at least half the training places to women, unless despite appropriate measures for drawing the attention of women to the training places available there are not enough applications from women,

where male and female candidates have equal qualifications, guarantees that qualified women who satisfy all the conditions required or laid down are called to interview, in sectors in which they are under-represented,

relating to the composition of employees' representative bodies and administrative and supervisory bodies, recommends that the legislative provisions adopted for its implementation take into account the objective that at least half the members of those bodies must be women.

These aspects of the ruling are unsurprising. Two important issues did, however, arise inthe case. The first concerned the legality of the so-called 'flexible result quota' ('*flexible Ergebnisquote*'). This was explained as a rule which, in sectors of the public service where women are under-represented, gives priority to female candidates where male and female candidates for selection have equal qualifications, where this proves necessary for complying with the bind-

---

[336] Cabral, 'A Step Closer to Substantive Equality' (1998) 23 *ELRev.* 481, 486. See also Case C–407/98 *Abrahamsson* v. *Fogelqvist*, judgment of 6 July 2000, para. 48.

[337] See Ellis, above, n. 4, 259. Cf. Case C–407/98 *Abrahamsson*, judgment of 6 July 2000, para. 55. Com (2000) 334 envisages that Art. 141(4) replaces Art. 2(4). It imposes an obligation on the Commission to report on positive measures adopted by the Member States.

[337A] Case C-158/97 *Badeck* v. *Hessischer Ministerpräsident und Landesanwalt beim Staatsgerichtshof des Landes Hessen*, judgment of 28 Mar. 2000.

ing targets in the women's advancement plan, if no reasons of 'greater legal weight' are put forward. These reasons of 'greater legal weight' concern five rules of law, described as 'social aspects' which make no reference to sex, whereby, preferential treatment is given, first, to former employees in the public service who have left the service because of family commitments; secondly, to individuals who worked on a part-time basis for family reasons and now wish to resume full-time employment; thirdly, to former temporary soldiers; fourthly, to seriously disabled people; and, fifthly, to the long-term unemployed.

As a result, the Court said that the priority rule introduced by the Hessen law was not 'absolute and unconditional' in the *Kalanke* sense. It therefore concluded that Article 2(1) and (4) of the Directive did not preclude such a rule provided that that rule guaranteed that candidatures were the subject of an objective assessment which took account of the specific personal situations of all candidates. Following *Marschall* this outcome is not surprising. Of more interest is the Court's (cursory) discussion of the criteria by which the initial selection of candidates occurred, before the flexible quota was applied. For example, capabilities and experience acquired by carrying out work in the home were to be taken into account in so far as they were of importance for the suitability, performance, and capability of candidates. By contrast, seniority, age, and the date of last promotion were to be taken into account only in so far as they were of importance to the job. The family status or income of the partner was immaterial. Further, part-time work, leave, and delays in completing training as a result of looking after children or other dependants could not have a negative effect on the selection process. As the Court simply noted:

Such criteria, although formulated in terms which are neutral as regards sex and thus capable of benefiting men too, in general favour women. They are manifestly intended to lead to an equality which is substantive rather than formal, by reducing the inequalities which may occur in practice in social life. Their legitimacy is not challenged in the main proceedings.

Thus, the Court seems to allow some (indirect) discrimination against men in the application of the selection criteria. Only if a female candidate and a male candidate could not be distinguished on the basis of their qualifications could the woman be chosen according to the flexible quota.

The second interesting aspect of the case concerned the Hessen rule which prescribed binding targets for women for *temporary* posts in the academic service and for academic assistants where women were equally qualified to the men. These targets required that the minimum percentage of women be at least equal to the percentage of women among graduates, holders of higher degrees, and students in each discipline. The *Land* Attorney noted that this minimum quota system came very close to equality as to results which had been rejected in *Kalanke*. Nevertheless, the Court said that this rule was compatible with Community law. It pointed out that this system did not fix an absolute ceiling but only a ceiling by reference to the number of persons who had received appropriate training. It said that this amounted to using an actual fact as a quantitative criterion for giving preference to women.

3. Directive 86/613 on Equal Treatment of the Self-Employed

Directive 86/613[338] applies the principle of equal treatment both to self-employed workers who are defined as 'all those persons pursuing a gainful activity for their own account, under the conditions laid down by national law, including farmers and members of the liberal professions', and to their spouses, not being employees or partners, who habitually participate in the activities of the self-employed worker and perform the same tasks or ancillary tasks. The principle of equal treatment is applied to miscellaneous aspects of self-employed working life. First, it applies to all the self-employed, 'especially in respect of the establishment, equipment or extension of a business or the launching or extension of any other form of self-employed activity, including financial activities'.[339] Secondly, it applies to spouses who form a company, requiring that the conditions imposed on spouses when forming a company must be no more restrictive than the conditions imposed on unmarried persons.[340]

The remaining provisions are characterized by their generality, more akin to a Recommendation or a Resolution than a Directive, since they outline a programme of action for Member States. Thus, Article 7 says that if the Member State provides for a contributory social security scheme for the self-employed, a spouse who participates in the activities of the self-employed worker should be able to join the contributory scheme *voluntarily*.[341] It also provides that Member States should encourage the recognition of the work performed by spouses in these circumstances. Article 8 requires Member States to examine the conditions under which a female self-employed worker and the wife of a self-employed worker who interrupt their occupation on the grounds of pregnancy or motherhood may have access to services supplying temporary replacements or existing national social services or be entitled to cash benefits under a social security scheme.[342] Finally, Article 9 obliges

---

[338] Council Directive 86/613/EEC, based on Arts. 100 and 235 [new Arts. 94 and 308] on the application of the principle of equal treatment between men and women engaged in an activity, including agriculture, in a self-employed capacity, and on the protection of self-employed women during pregnancy and motherhood [1986] OJ L359/56.

[339] Art. 4.

[340] Art. 5. If Art. 5 necessitates a change in domestic legislation on matrimonial rights and obligations, Member States had until 30 June 1991 to comply with this provision of the Directive.

[341] This provision would be of assistance only to those spouses who are earning a sufficient income to enable them to make such contributions.

[342] Art. 8.

Member States to allow those who consider that they have been discriminated against to pursue their claims by judicial process.

Although this Directive was designed to address the problems of self-employed women, particularly those working in agriculture who had complained of a lack of a clearly defined occupational status, of a precarious position in respect of social security entitlements, and of a lack of protection in respect of pregnancy and maternity,[343] its substance is weak and uninspired.[344] The Council was intending to review the Directive before 1 July 1993 but no action has so far been taken.

D. ENFORCEMENT OF EQUALITY RIGHTS

The enforcement of equality rights has proved to be an area of great importance where the Court has, at times, shown considerable imagination in developing its case law. The Court has also used the equality cases to develop principles, such as the vertical direct effect of directives and effective judicial protection, which are of wider constitutional significance.

1. Direct Effect

1.1 Article 141

As we have already seen, the Court made clear in *Defrenne (No. 2)*[345] that Article 119 [new Article 141] was 'directly applicable' and could thus give rise to individual rights which the courts must protect. This means that the prohibition of discrimination applies 'not only to the actions of public authorities, but also extends to all agreements which are intended to regulate paid labour collectively, as well as contracts between individuals'.[346] Thus, Article 141 has both vertical *and* horizontal direct effect. At first the Court suggested that Article 119 [new Article 141] was not directly effective in the context of 'indirect or disguised discrimination' which requires the elaboration by the Community and national legislative bodies of criteria of assessment,[347] but in *Bilka-Kaufhaus*[348] the Court said that individuals could rely on Article 119 to secure the elimination of indirect discrimination. It now seems that although the Court continues to pay lip service to this potential limit on the direct effect

---

[343] COM(84)57 final/2.
[344] See, further, Ellis, above n. 4, 268–70.
[345] Case 43/75 [1976] ECR 455.
[346] See also Case C–28/93 *Van den Akker* [1994] ECR I–4527, para. 21.
[347] Case 43/75 *Defrenne (No. 2)* [1976] ECR 455, para. 19, and Case 129/79 *Macarthys* [1980] ECR 1275, para. 15.
[348] Case 170/84 [1986] ECR 1607.

of Article 141,[349] the limitation is, in reality, redundant for the Court has found Article 141 to be directly effective in areas of great complexity, including occupational pensions and survivors' benefits.[350]

1.2 Directive 76/207

It is well established that provisions of a directive which are unconditional and sufficiently precise and which have not been implemented correctly or at all can have vertical direct effect.[351] This means that an individual may, after the expiry of the period prescribed for implementation, rely on a such provisions directly against the Member State in default.[352] This prevents Member States from taking advantage of their own failure to comply with Community law to deny rights to individuals.[353] The same argument does not apply to private individuals: as the Court explained in *Marshall (No. 1)*, since the binding nature of a directive exists only in relation to 'each Member State to which it is addressed . . . it follows that a Directive may not of itself impose obligations on an individual and that a provision of a Directive may not be relied upon as such against such a person'.[354] Consequently, clear and unambiguous provisions of an unimplemented or incorrectly implemented directive cannot have horizontal direct effect. On the facts of the case, Helen Marshall was able to rely on the principle of equal treatment laid down in Article 2(1), as applied to conditions governing dismissal referred to in Article 5(1), which were directly effective, to complain against her state employer of a discriminatory dismissal. Similarly, in *Johnston*[355] the Court said that Article 2(1) was directly effective when applied to conditions governing access to jobs, vocational training, and advanced vocational training referred to in Articles 3(1) and 4(1) and could be invoked against the Royal Ulster Constabulary. Early cases suggested that the terms of Article 6 of Directive 76/207 on remedies[356] were not, however, sufficiently unconditional or precise to be directly effective.[357] There was merely an

---

[349] See e.g. Case C–262/88 *Barber* [1990] ECR I–1889, para. 37.

[350] Case C–262/88 *Barber* [1990] ECR I–1889 and Case C–109/91 *Ten Oever* [1993] ECR I–5535, respectively.

[351] Case 152/84 *Marshall (No. 1)* [1986] ECR 723.

[352] Case 148/78 *Pubblico Ministero v. Ratti* [1979] ECR 1629 and Case 8/81 *Becker v. Finanzamt Munster-Innenstadt* [1982] ECR 53. See generally De Witte, 'Direct Effect, Supremacy, and the Nature of the Legal Order', in *The Evolution of EU Law*, eds. Craig and de Búrca (OUP, Oxford, 1999); Prechal, *Directives in European Community Law: a Study of Directives and their Enforcement in National Courts* (Clarendon, Oxford, 1995).

[353] Case 152/84 *Marshall (No. 1)* [1986] ECR 723, para. 47.

[354] Ibid., para. 48.

[355] Case 222/84 [1986] 1651.

[356] See below, nn. 396–402.

[357] Case 14/83 *Von Colson and Kamann v. Land Nordrhein-Westfalen* [1984] ECR 1891, para. 27; Case 79/83 *Harz v. Deutsche Tradax* [1984] ECR 1921, para. 27. However, in Case 222/84 *Johnston* [1986] ECR 1651 Art. 6 seemed to have direct effect in so far as it overrode the national rule that denied the plaintiff access to the Court.

obligation to interpret national law in the light of the wording and purpose of the Directive.[358] In *Marshall (No. 2)*,[358A] however, the Court said that the combined provisions of Articles 5 and 6 of the Directive conferred rights on a victim of a discriminatory dismissal which that person must be able to rely upon before the national courts as against the State and authorities which were an emanation of the State. Therefore, it seems that Article 6, when read in conjunction with Articles 3 and 4, will also be directly effective.

The Court has taken three steps to address the hardship caused by the distinction between horizontal and vertical direct effect. First, it has given a broad definition to the term 'State'. In *Marshall (No. 1)*[359] the Court said a person can rely on a directive against the State regardless of the capacity in which the State is acting, whether employer or, as a public authority, such as Southampton and South West Hampshire Area Health Authority (Teaching). Subsequently, in *Foster*[360] the Court defined 'State' as 'organisations or bodies which were subject to the authority and control of the state or had special powers beyond those which result from the normal rules applicable to relations between individuals'. Therefore, Mrs Foster could rely on Article 5(1) of Directive 76/207 against British Gas, at that time a nationalized company, to claim damages for a discriminatory dismissal.[361] The directly effective provisions of the Equal Treatment Directive have also been relied on against constitutionally independent authorities responsible for maintaining law and order,[362] public authorities providing public health services,[363] and a nationalized industry responsible for providing energy.[364] The case of *Dekker*,[365] however, concerned a private employer who was nevertheless held bound to comply with the provisions of the Directive which had not been fully implemented by the Dutch government.[366]

---

[358] Case 14/83 *Von Colson* [1984] ECR 1891, para. 26.

[358A] Case C–271/91 *Marshall v. Sourthampton and South West Hampshire Area Health Authority (Teaching) (No. 2)* [1993] ECR I–4367.

[359] Case 152/84 [1986] ECR 723, para. 49.

[360] Case C–188/89 *Foster v. British Gas* [1990] ECR I–3313, para. 18.

[361] *Foster v. British Gas* [1991] IRLR 268 (House of Lords).

[362] Case 222/84 *Johnston* [1986] ECR 1651.

[363] Case 152/84 *Marshall (No. 1)* [1986] ECR 723.

[364] Case C–188/89 *Foster* [1990] ECR I–3313.

[365] Case C–177/88 [1990] ECR I–3941.

[366] It has been argued that this case is in reality an application of the *Marleasing/Von Colson* 'interpretation' mechanism: see Banks, 'Equal Pay and Equal Treatment for Men and Women in Community Law', *Social Europe* 3/91, ch. 2. A similar point was raised in Case C–421/92 *Habermann-Beltermann* [1994] ECR I–1657. See also Case C–180/95 *Nils Draehmpaehl v. Urania Immobilienservice ohG* [1997] ECR I–2195, and Ward, 'New Frontiers in Private Enforcement of EC Directives' (1998) 23 *ELRev.* 65.

Secondly, in *Von Colson* and *Marleasing*[367] the Court imposed a broad obliga-tion on all state institutions, especially the national courts, arising from both the Directive and Article 10 EC [ex Article 5], to interpret national law, as far as possible, in conformity with the requirements of Community law, subject to the general principles of law, especially the principles of legal certainty and non-retroactivity.[368] Therefore, in *Von Colson* the national court was obliged to interpret the national rules on compensation in the light of Directive 76/207.

The third step taken by the Court was to introduce the principle of state liability in *Francovich*,[369] saying that Community law requires the Member States to make good damage caused to individuals through failure to trans-pose a directive. Subsequently, in *Brasserie du Pêcheur and Factortame (No. 3)*[370] and *British Telecommunications*[371] (cases concerning breaches of Treaty provi-sions involving wide discretion and an incorrectly implemented directive respectively) the Court made clear that the principle of state liability was inherent in the system of the Treaty. It did not merely apply in a situation where the provisions of Community law were directly effective: direct effect was only a 'minimum guarantee' and could not ensure in every case that individuals enjoyed their Community law rights. The Court then established a threefold test for liability: first, the rule of law infringed must be intended to confer rights on individuals; secondly, the breach must be sufficiently serious; and thirdly, there must be a direct causal link between the breach of the obligation resting on the State and the damage suffered by the injured parties. If the State totally failed to transpose a directive the Court ruled in *Dil-lenkofer*[372] that the breach was *per se* sufficiently serious.

In the context of Directive 76/207, Articles 3, 4, and 5 also impose obliga-tions on the Member States to abolish any laws, regulations, or administrative provisions contrary to the principle of equal treatment and to ensure that any discriminatory provisions contained in collective agreements,[373] individual contracts of employment, internal rules of undertakings, or in rules govern-

---

[367] The is also known as the doctrine of indirect effects: see Cases 14/83 *Von Colson and Kamann v. Land Nordrhein-Westfalen* [1984] ECR 1891 and C–106/89 *Marleasing SA v. La Comercial Interna-cional de Alimentacion* [1990] ECR I–4135; and confirmed recently in Case C–185/97 *Coote v. Granada Hospitality Ltd* [1998] ECR I–5199. In Case C–54/96 *Dorsch Consult* [1997] ECR I–4961 the Court said that this minimum guarantee could not justify a Member State absolving itself from taking, in due time, implementing measures sufficient to meet the purpose of each directive.

[368] Case 14/86 *Pretore di Salò v. X* [1987] ECR 2545; Case C–168/95 *Criminal Proceedings against Arcaro* [1996] ECR I–4705.

[369] Joined Cases C–6 and C–9/90 *Francovich and Bonifaci v. Italian State* [1991] ECR I–5357.

[370] Joined Cases C–46/93 *Brasserie du Pêcheur v. Bundesrepublik Deutschland* and C–48/95 *R v. Secretary of State for Transport, ex parte Factortame (No. 3)* [1996] ECR I–1029.

[371] Case C–392/93 *R v. HM Treasury, ex part British Telecommunications* [1996] ECR I–1631.

[372] Joined Cases C–178, C–179, C–188, C–189, and C–190/94 *Dillenkofer and Others v. Bundesrepublik Deutschland* [1996] ECR I–4845.

[373] The Directive covers all collective agreements, irrespective of whether they have legal effects or not because they have important *de facto* consequences for employment relationships: see Case 165/82 *Commission v. UK* [1982] ECR 3431.

ing the independent occupations or professions are declared null and void or are amended.[374] Therefore, individuals not employed by the State but who have suffered discriminatory conduct have good grounds for bringing an action for damages for loss suffered as a result.[375]

2. Burden of Proof

The Court has ruled that in principle the burden of proving the existence of sex discrimination lies with the complainant.[376] It has, however, recognized that adjustments to national rules on the burden of proof may be necessary to ensure the effective implementation of the principle of equality. This can be seen in *Danfoss*.[377] In that case the employer's pay structure provided the same basic wage to all employees but paid additional individual supplements on the basis of mobility, training, and seniority. This resulted in the average wage paid to men being 6.86 per cent higher than that paid to women. This system so lacked in transparency that female employees could only establish differences between their pay and that received by their male colleagues by reference to average pay. Consequently, the Court concluded that the applicants would be deprived of any effective means of enforcing the principle of equal pay before the national courts if the effect of producing such evidence was not to impose upon employers the burden of proving that their pay practices were not in fact discriminatory. Similarly, in *Enderby* the Court concluded that if the pay of speech therapists was significantly lower than that of pharmacists, and the speech therapists were almost exclusively women while the pharmacists were predominantly men, there was a *prima facie* case of discrimination, at least where the two jobs were of equal value and the statistics describing the situation were valid. As a result it was for the employers to show that there were objective reasons for the difference in pay and for the national court to assess whether it could take those statistics into account and to assess whether they covered enough individuals, whether they illustrated purely fortuitous or short-term phenomena, and whether in general they appeared to be significant.[378]

However, in *Dansk Industri*[379] the Court sounded a note of caution. It said that in a piecework pay scheme a *prima facie* case of discrimination did not

---

[374] Arts. (2)(a), (b), 4(a), (b) and 5(2)(a), (b).

[375] Joined Cases C–6 and C–9/90 *Francovich* [1991] ECR I–5357, above n. 369.

[376] Case C–127/92 *Enderby* [1993] ECR I–5535.

[377] Case 109/88 [1989] ECR I–3199. See further Case 318/86 *Commission v. France* [1988] ECR 3559; Case 248/83 *Commission v. Germany* [1985] ECR 1459; Case C–127/92 *Enderby* [1993] ECR I–5535.

[378] See also Case C–400/93 *Dansk Industri* [1995] ECR I–1275; Case C–236/98 *Örebro läns landsting*, judgment of 30 Mar. 2000, para. 53.

[379] Case C–400/93 [1995] ECR I–1275. See above, n. 179.

arise solely because significant statistics disclose appreciable differences between the average pay of two groups of workers, since those statistics might be due to differences in individual output of the workers in the two groups. However, where the individual pay consisted of both a fixed element and a variable element, and it was not possible to identify the factors which determined the rates or units of measurement used to calculate the variable element in the pay, the employer might have to bear the burden of proving that the differences found were not due to sex discrimination. Again, it was for the national court to decide whether the conditions for shifting the burden of proof were satisfied.

This case law, allowing a partial reversal of the burden of proof, has helped to unblock legislation proposed under Articles 100 [ex Article 94] and 235 [ex Article 308],[380] but stuck in Council. Eventually the Commission initiated the procedure under Article 3 of the SPA [new Article 138],[381] which led to the adoption of Directive 97/80 on the burden of proof.[382] The Directive lays down minimum standards[383] which apply to situations covered by Article 119 [new Article 141], the Directives on Equal Pay and Equal Treatment and, in so far as discrimination based on sex is concerned, the Directives on Pregnant Workers' and Parental Leave.[384] It also applies to any civil or administrative procedure concerning the public or private sector which provides for means of redress under national law pursuant to Article 141 and the Equality Directives.[385] The central provision is Article 4. This provides that Member States shall take such measures as are necessary, in accordance with their national judicial systems, to ensure that:

> when persons who consider themselves wronged because the principle of equal treatment has not been applied to them establish, before a court or other competent authority, facts from which it may be presumed that there has been direct or indirect discrimination, it shall be for the respondent to prove that there has been no breach of the principle of equal treatment.[386]

---

[380] The Commission's original proposal can be found at [1988] OJ C176/5.

[381] The first round of consultations was launched on 5 July 1995. The Social Partners' opinions differed. Some did not consider any action in the area to be justified, since a series of national legal instruments and the Court's case law had already achieved the desired aim. Others thought that action should be taken at European level while respecting the principle of subsidiarity. As regards the proper level and nature of the action to be taken, some organizations preferred a binding Community measure and others a less rigid approach, such as a recommendation.

[382] [1998] OJ L14/16, amended by Council Directive 98/52 [1998] OJ L205/66. See Lanquetin, 'Discriminations à raison du sexe' (1998) 7/8 *Droit Social* 688.

[383] Art. 4(2).

[384] Art. 3(1)(a).

[385] Art. 3(1)(b). It does not apply to out-of-court procedures of a voluntary nature or provided for in national law. The Directive also does not apply to criminal procedures, unless otherwise provided by the Member States (Art. 3(2)).

[386] Art. 4(1). Art. 6 contains a non-regression clause and Art. 7 sets 1 Jan. 2001 as a deadline for implementation.

[387] An equivalent provision appears in Art. 7 of Directive 75/117 on equal pay.

In addition, Article 5 contains the new and important obligation on the Member States to 'ensure that measures taken pursuant to this Directive, together with the provisions already in force, are brought to the attention of all the persons concerned by all the appropriate means'.[387] This Directive is extremely unpopular with employers. Nevertheless, the Commission has incorporated its provisions into a package of proposals for anti-discrimination legislation.[388]

3. Judicial Remedies

3.1 Effectiveness of the Remedy

It is a long established principle of Community law that under the duty of co-operation laid down in Article 10 [ex Article 5] EC the Member States must ensure the legal protection which individuals derive from the direct effect of Community law. In the absence of Community rules governing a matter, it is for the domestic legal system of each Member State to designate the courts having jurisdiction and to lay down detailed procedural rules governing actions for safeguarding rights for individuals (the principle of procedural autonomy). However, such rules must not be less favourable than those governing similar domestic actions (the principle of non-discrimination) nor render virtually impossible or excessively difficult the exercise of rights conferred by Community law (the principle of effective judicial protection).[389]

As far as remedies for breach of Article 141 (ex Article 119) are concerned, the Court has required that the amount of *each* individual benefit paid be non-discriminatory.[390] It has also ruled that access to the benefits must be non-discriminatory.[391]

The question of the adequacy of national remedies has been of central importance to the procedural protection conferred by the Equality Directives. Article 6 of the Equal Pay Directive 75/117/EEC requires Member States to

---

[388] COM(99)565. See nn. 577–583 below.

[389] See e.g. Case 33/76 *Rewe-Zentralfinanz eG* v. *Landwirtschaftskammer für das Saarland* [1976] ECR 1989, para. 5. See generally Craufurd-Smith, 'Remedies for Breaches of EC Law in National Courts: Legal Variation and Selection', in *The Evolution of EU Law*, eds. Craig and de Búrca (OUP, Oxford, 1999).

[390] Case C–262/88 *Barber* [1990] ECR I–1889; Case C–236/98 *Örebro läns landsting*, judgment of 30 Mar. 2000, para. 43 where, relying on the principle in *Barber*, the Court said that midwives' basic monthly salary (excluding an anti-social hours allowance) should be compared with the salary of a clinical technician. The same principle of transparency was applied to Directives 76/207 and 86/613 in Case C–226/98 *Jørgensen*, judgment of 6 Apr. 2000, paras. 27 and 36.

[391] Case 170/84 *Bilka-Kaufhaus* [1986] ECR 1607. See further Ch. 5.

ensure that the principle of equal pay is applied,[392] and that effective means are available to ensure that the principle is observed. In addition, Article 2 of the Directive requires Member States to allow those who consider themselves wronged by the failure to apply the principle of equal pay to pursue their claims by judicial process.[393] The Directive also provides some protection against victimization of those who have sought to enforce their rights. Under Article 5 Member States must protect employees against dismissal as a result of making a complaint or starting legal proceedings to seek equal pay.[394] Article 7 of Directive 76/207 contains the equivalent provision in respect of equal treatment. Article 6 of Directive 76/207 requires Member States to introduce into their national legal systems such measures as are necessary to enable all persons who consider themselves wronged by the failure to apply to them the principle of equal treatment to pursue their claims by judicial process.

The Court has, however, circumscribed the Member States' discretion as to the remedies available for sex discrimination. First, as the Court ruled in *Johnston*,[395] Member States cannot exclude judicial control altogether. In *Johnston* the Secretary of State issued a certificate under section 53(2) of the Sex Discrimination Order declaring that the decisions taken by the Chief Constable of the Royal Ulster Constabulary were made for the purpose of safeguarding national security and protecting public safety and public order. Such a declaration constituted conclusive evidence that the conditions for derogating from the principle of equal treatment had been fulfilled and therefore excluded the exercise of any power of review by the courts. The Court held that such a provision deprived an individual of the possibility of asserting the rights conferred by the Equal Treatment Directive by judicial process and was therefore contrary to Article 6 of the Directive. The Court added that Article 6 'reflects a general principle of law which underlies the constitutional traditions common to the Member States,

---

[392] According to the Court, Member States may leave the implementation of the principle of equal pay to representatives of management and labour but this does not discharge Member States from the obligation of ensuring that all workers are afforded the full protection of the Directive, esp. where the workers are not union members, where the sector is not covered by a collective agreement or where the agreement does not fully guarantee the principle of equal pay: Case 143/83 *Commission v. Denmark* [1985] ECR 427.

[393] The similarity of wording between Art. 2 of Directive 75/117 and Art. 6 of Directive 76/207 means that it is likely that the jurisprudence on Art. 6 will be applied to Art. 2.

[394] Case C–185/97 *Coote* [1998] ECR I–5199 makes clear that the principle of effective judicial protection derived from Art. 6 gives protection from other kinds of victimization apart from dismissal. Cf. COM(99) 565 where the Commission defines victimization as 'any adverse treatment or adverse consequence motivated directly or indirectly as a reaction to a complaint'. See below, n. 405.

[395] Case 222/84 [1986] ECR 1651.

including Articles 6 and 13 of the European Convention on Human Rights'.[396]

The second area in which the Court has limited Member States' discretion is that it has insisted that any sanction provided for by the national system must be such as to 'guarantee real and effective judicial protection ... it must also have a real deterrent effect on the employer'.[397] Therefore, if the Member State chooses to penalize the discrimination by the award of compensation that compensation must be adequate in relation to the damage sustained.[398] In both *Von Colson* and *Harz*[399] the compensation was limited to a purely nominal amount, the reimbursement of the travelling expenses incurred. The Court considered that this would not satisfy the requirements of Article 6.[400] Similarly, the Court held in *Marshall (No. 2)*[401] that the imposition of an upper limit on the amount of compensation received and the exclusion of an award of interest did not constitute proper implementation of Article 6. It reasoned that such limits restricted the amount of compensation 'a priori to a level which is not necessarily consistent with the requirement of ensuring real equality of opportunity through adequate reparation for the loss and damage sustained as a result of discriminatory dismissal'.[402] In addition, the Court said that excluding an award of interest to compensate for the loss sustained by the recipient of the compensation, as a result of the effluxion of time, until the capital sum awarded is actually paid breached Article 6.

The Court adopted a similarly broad, purposive interpretation of Article 6

---

[396] See also Case C–185/97 *Coote* [1998] ECR I–5199 where the Court said the requirement laid down by Art. 6 that recourse be available to the courts reflects a general principle of law which underlies the constitutional traditions common to the Member States and which is also enshrined in Art. 6 of the European Convention for the Protection of Human Rights and Fundamental Freedoms of 4 Nov. 1950. It added that by virtue of Art. 6 of the Directive, interpreted in the light of the general principle, all persons have the right to obtain an effective remedy in a competent court against measures which they consider to interfere with the equal treatment for men and women laid down in the Directive.

[397] Case 14/83 *Von Colson* [1984] ECR 1891, para. 23.

[398] Case 14/83 *Von Colson* [1984] ECR 1891, para. 23; Case C–271/91 *Marshall v. Southampton and South West Hampshire Area Health Authority (Teaching)(No. 2)* [1993] ECR I–4367, para. 26; McCrudden, 'The Effectiveness of European Equality Law: National Mechanisms for Enforcing Gender Equality Law in the Light of European Requirements' (1993) 13 *OJLS* 320. See also Fitzpatrick, 'Towards Strategic Litigation? Innovations in Sex Equality Litigation Procedures in the Member States of the European Community' (1992) 8 *IJCLLIR* 8.

[399] Case 79/83 [1984] ECR 1921. See also Case C–180/95 *Draehmpaehl* [1997] ECR I–2195, and Fitzpatrick, 'The Effectiveness of Equality Law Remedies: A European Community Law Perspective', in Hepple and Szyszczak, above n. 306.

[400] See further Curtin, 'Effective Sanctions and the Equal Treatment Directive: the *Von Colson* and *Harz* Cases' (1985) 22 *CMLRev.* 505.

[401] Case C–271/91 [1993] ECR I–4367. See Art. 6(2) in Com (2000) 334 final.

[402] English law now complies with the *Marshall (No. 2)* decision as a result of SI 1993/2798, The Sex Discrimination and Equal Pay (Remedies) Regulations 1993.

in *Draehmpaehl*,[403] a case concerning the measure of damages for an individual involved in a discriminatory recruitment process. Having noted that the Directive precluded provisions of domestic law making reparation of damage suffered as a result of discrimination on the grounds of sex subject to the requirement of fault,[404] the Court then considered the question of the adequacy of compensation. It drew a distinction between, on the one hand, less qualified applicants who would not have got the job even if there had been no discrimination in the recruitment process, and on the other, those applicants who would have got the job but for the discrimination.

As far as the latter group was concerned, the Court, basing its ruling on the principle of non-discrimination, said that the Directive precluded provisions of domestic law which, unlike other provisions of domestic civil and labour law, prescribed an upper limit of three months' salary for the amount of compensation which could be claimed. As far as the former category was concerned, the Court said that although reparation had to be adequate in relation to the damage sustained, the reparation could take into account the fact that even if there had been no discrimination in the process some applicants would not have obtained the position because the applicant appointed had superior qualifications. It said, therefore, that given that the only damage suffered by less qualified applicants was that resulting from the failure, because of the sex discrimination, to take their applications into consideration, it was not unreasonable for a Member State to lay down a statutory presumption that the damage suffered could not exceed a ceiling of three months' salary. However, the burden of proof rested with the employer, who had all the applications submitted, to show that the applicant would not have obtained the vacant position even if there had been no discrimination.

While most cases on effective remedies concern compensation, *Coote*[405] is authority for the fact that the obligation to provide an effective remedy includes protection against victimization. In that case the Court said that the principle of effective judicial control laid down in Article 6 would be deprived of an essential part of its effectiveness if the protection which it provided did not cover measures which an employer might take as a reaction to legal proceedings brought by an employee to enforce compliance with the principle of equal treatment. Therefore, it ruled that Article 6 required Member States to introduce into their national legal systems measures necessary to ensure

---

[403] Case C–180/95 [1997] ECR I–2195 (noted Steindorff (1997) 34 *CMLRev.* 1259). *Marshall (No. 2)* was not, however, referred to. Cf. the Court's robust approach to remedies with its attitude in Case C–66/95 *R v. Secretary of State for Social Security, ex parte Sutton* [1997] ECR I–2163, considered in Ch. 5.

[404] See also Case C–177/88 *Dekker* [1990] ECR I–3941, para. 22.

[405] Case C–185/97 [1998] ECR I–5199. See Dougan, 'The Equal Treatment Directive: Retaliation, Remedies and Direct Effect' (1999) 24 *ELRev.* 664.

judicial protection for workers whose employer refused to provide them with a reference as a result of victimization.

As the case law on effective judicial protection has developed, the Court has been forced to address a major issue, particularly in the light of its developing case law on pensions,[406] of claims brought after the expiry of national time limits, for arrears of pay which predate national limits on backdating of claims.[407] The Court has had to strike a balance between, on the one hand, legal certainty (and the cost to an individual pension scheme, government or employer) and the principle of effective judicial protection, on the other. In two social security cases, *Johnson*[408] and *Steenhorst-Neerings*[409] the Court held that a restriction on backdating was valid under Community law. However, in the context of equal pay this might have the effect of denying the individual the benefit of the entitlement. The interplay of these two issues can be seen in the cases of *Magorrian*[410] and *Levez*.[411]

In *Magorrian* the applicants began employment as full-time workers and then became part-time workers when they had children. When they retired they were not entitled to the more favourable pension benefits available to full-time workers. They brought a claim under Article 119 [new Article 141] in 1992. In response, it was argued that, under the relevant statute, no award of arrears of pay could be made relating to a period earlier than two years before the date on which the proceedings had been instituted (i.e. 1990). The Court said the fact that the right to be admitted to a scheme might have effect from a date no earlier than two years before the institution of proceedings would deprive the applicants of the additional benefits under the scheme to which they were entitled to be affiliated, since those benefits could be calculated only by reference to periods of service completed by them two years prior to the commencement of proceedings. The Court then distinguished *Magorrian* from *Johnson*. It said that in *Magorrian* the claim was not for the retroactive award of certain additional benefits but for recognition of entitlement to full membership of an occupational scheme. Whereas the rules at issue in *Johnson* merely limited the period, prior to commencement of proceedings, in respect of which backdated benefits could be obtained, the rule at issue in *Magorrian* prevented the entire record of service completed by those concerned after 8 April 1976 (the date of the judgment in *Defrenne (No. 2)*) until 1990 (two years prior to the start of proceedings) from being taken into account for the

---

[406] See further Ch. 5.

[407] These issues will be examined further in respect of social security claims under Directive 79/7, considered in Ch. 5.

[408] Case C–410/92 *Johnson v. Chief Adjudication Officer* [1994] ECR I–5483.

[409] Case C–338/91 *Steenhorst-Neerings v. Bestuur van de Bedrijfsvereniging* [1993] ECR I–5475.

[410] Case C–246/96 *Magorrian and Cunningham v. Eastern Health and Social Services Board and Department of Health and Social Services* [1997] ECR I–7153. See also Case C–70/98 *Preston v. Wolverhampton Health Care NHS Trust*, judgment of 16 May 2000, considered further in Ch. 5.

[411] Case C–326/96 *Levez v. TH Jennings (Harlow Pools) Ltd* [1998] ECR I–7835.

purposes of calculating the additional benefits which would be payable even after the date of the claim. Consequently, the Court said that the two-year rule rendered any action by individuals relying on Community law impossible in practice.

The Court also emphasized the principle of effectiveness in *Levez*.[412] Mrs Levez was appointed manager of a betting shop owned by Jennings in February 1991 at a salary of £10,800 *per annum*. The employer falsely declared to her that this had been her male predecessor's salary. In fact, Mrs Levez's salary did not reach that of the predecessor (£11,400 *per annum*) until April 1992. Mrs Levez did not find this out until September 1993, whereupon she brought a claim for equal pay. The UK Industrial Tribunal which heard the case in the first instance decided that Mrs Levez was entitled to a salary of £11,400 from the date on which she had taken up the job, and ordered Jennings to pay her arrears. Jennings appealed this decision, arguing that, in view of the national law concerning damages for failure to comply with the equal pay principle, the Industrial Tribunal had no power to award arrears of remuneration in respect of a time earlier than two years before the date on which the proceedings were instituted before the tribunal.[413] Thus, as Mrs Levez's application to the Industrial Tribunal was dated 17 September 1993, arrears could not be awarded in respect of the period before 17 September 1991.

The Court, having reviewed its jurisprudence on effective judicial protection, concluded that in principle it was compatible with Community law for national rules to prescribe reasonable limitation periods for bringing proceedings, in the interests of legal certainty. Therefore, a national procedural rule such as that at issue in *Levez*, would not in itself be incompatible with Community law.[414] However, the Court went on to consider the circumstances of Mrs Levez's case, and in particular the fact that the employer had concealed from Mrs Levez the pay of her predecessor. The Court pointed out that in such circumstances, an employee would have no means of determining whether she was being discriminated against. Thus the employer would effectively be able to deprive the employee of the entitlement to enforce the principle of equal pay before the courts.[415] To allow an employer in such a situation to rely on a procedural rule of national law would make it virtually impossible or excessively difficult for the employee to obtain arrears of remuneration in respect of sex discrimination in pay. In these circumstances, there existed no

---

[412] Case C–326/96 [1998] ECR I–7835.
[413] UK Equal Pay Act 1970, s 2(5).
[414] Para. 20.
[415] Cf. the Court's approach in respect of transparency and the burden of proof in Case 109/88 *Danfoss* [1989] ECR 3199.

justification for the application of the national rules in terms of legal certainty or the proper conduct of proceedings.[416]

Levez also concerned the principle of non-discrimination or equivalence as an exception to national procedural autonomy. It was argued by the employer and the United Kingdom government that Mrs Levez did have an adequate remedy in national law, in that she could bring proceedings not before the Industrial Tribunal, but before the county court on the basis of breach of contract pursuant to the UK Equal Pay Act 1970 and the tort of deceit committed by the employer. The national court asked the Court what would constitute a 'similar domestic action', in the context of the principle of equivalence, in the case of an equal pay claim, where national law made different provision for equal pay from that made for other employment rights. The Court essentially said that it was for the national court to determine this issue. Where the alternative remedy in the county court was likely to entail procedural rules or other conditions which were less favourable than those appertaining before an Industrial Tribunal, then the principle of equivalence would be breached. In making this determination, the national court would need to take into account matters such as the relative costs and delays involved in each proceedings.[417]

The Court in *Levez* showed some sensitivity to the practicalities of bringing an equal pay claim.[418] The reality of such claims is often that the employer is in a much stronger position than the employee, in terms of holding relevant information on comparative pay of men and women employees. In the absence of any duties of transparency, the remedial effect of equal pay law would be significantly reduced if an employer, particularly a deliberately deceitful employer, could hide behind technical procedural rules to escape an equal pay claim. What seems certain is that the Court is not going anywhere near so far as to impose on employers a duty to disclose sufficient information to allow women employees to ensure that they are paid equally with male comparators. Although to do so would no doubt improve the position of those seeking to bring an equal pay claim, it would also go a long way beyond the requirements of Article 141 and the Equal Pay Directive and, in the absence of legislation requiring such disclosure, would constitute too great an infringement of national procedural autonomy.

---

[416] Paras. 31–34. In *Levez (No. 2)* [1999] IRLR 764 the British EAT ruled that the two-year limitation on arrears of remuneration in s. 2(5) EqPA 1970 breached Community law in that it was less favourable than those governing similar claims, such as for unlawful deduction from wages and unlawful discrimination on the grounds of race. It ruled that the six-year limit in the Limitation Act 1980 would apply.

[417] See further on this issue Hervey and Rostant, 'After *Francovich*: State Liability and British Employment Law' (1996) 25 *ILJ* 259. See also Case C–70/98 *Preston v. Wolverhampton Health Care NHS Trust*, judgment of 16 May 2000, considered further in Ch. 5.

[418] See Barnard and Hervey, 'European Union Employment and Social Policy Survey 1998' (1998) 18 *Yearbook of European Law*, 613, 638–40.

3.2 Levelling Up or Down?

It might be expected that the realization of equality necessarily equates with a levelling up of entitlement. In *Defrenne (No. 2)*[419] the Court accepted this. It said that in view of the connection between Article 119 [new Article 141] and the harmonization of working conditions while the improvement is being maintained,[420] it was not possible to comply with Article 119 in ways other than by raising the lowest salaries.[421] However, levelling up will not always be the result, if there is no background requirement of distributive justice, since formal equality is satisfied whether the two parties are treated equally well or equally badly.[422] This can be seen in *Smith*[423] where the Court said that where the employer had decided to achieve equality by levelling down of entitlement (so that women received their pension at 65, the age at which the men had received it, rather than men receiving their pension at 60, as women had previously), this was compatible with Community law.

E. PREGNANCY, MATERNITY, AND LEAVE FOR FAMILY REASONS

With women taking primary responsibility for childcare in most Western societies, their flexibility to participate fully in work is limited. Since the first equality action programme the Commission has recognized that full equality of opportunity can only be achieved by taking measures which will 'enable men and women to reconcile their occupational and family obligations'.[424] The Community's policy has three strands. First, pregnant women must be provided with adequate protection. The case law of the Court and now Directive 92/85 on Pregnant Workers make an important contribution in this respect. Secondly, Directive 96/34 on Parental Leave, Directive 97/81 on Part-time Work and Directive 99/70 on Fixed-term Work[425] negotiated by the Social Partners make an important contribution towards providing rights for both men and women; and, thirdly, specific provision needs to be made for childcare. The adoption of a Council Recommendation on childcare

---

[419] Case 43/75 [1976] ECR 455. See also Case C–102/88 *Ruzius Wilbrink* [1989] ECR 4311.

[420] See Art. 117 [new Art. 136] and Case 126/86 *Zaera* [1987] ECR 3697.

[421] See also Case C–102/88 *Ruzius-Wilbrink* [1989] ECR I–4311 where the Court stated that part-timers are entitled to have the same system applied to them as other workers in proportion to their working hours, and the application of this in the case of collective agreements: Case 33/89 *Kowalska* [1990] ECR I–2591. See above n. 94.

[422] Fredman, above n. 61, 350.

[423] Case C–408/92 [1994] ECR I–4435.

[424] Third para. of point 16 of the Social Charter of 1989. See also the Resolution of the Council and the Ministers for Employment and Social Policy on Balanced Participation of Women and Men in Family and Working Life, agreed 6 June 2000.

[426] 92/241/EEC [1992] OJ L123/16.

represents one step in this direction.[426] This aspect of 'the equality package' is particularly important yet is confined at present to a soft law measure.

The importance of these three policy strands has been recognized in the equal opportunities pillar of the Luxembourg Employment Guidelines.[427] Under the heading 'Reconciling work and family life' the Council agreed:

Policies on career breaks, parental leave and part-time work, as well as flexible working arrangements which serve the interests of both employers and employees, are of particular importance to women and men. Implementation of the various Directives and social partner agreements in this area should be accelerated and monitored regularly. There must be an adequate provision of good quality care for children and other dependants in order to support women's and men's entry and continued participation in the labour market. An equal sharing of family responsibilities is crucial in this respect.

In order to strengthen equal opportunities the Member States and the Social Partners will 'design, implement and promote family-friendly policies, including affordable, accessible and high quality care services for children and other dependants, as well as parental and other leave schemes'.

1. Pregnancy

1.1 Case Law

The Court has shown considerable imagination in addressing discrimination faced by women on the grounds of their pregnancy.[428] In the first case, *Dekker*,[429] the employer decided not to appoint the applicant who was pregnant, even though she was considered the best person for the job, on the ground that the employer's insurers refused to cover the costs of her maternity leave. Despite the fact that all the other candidates for the job were women, the Court ruled that as employment can be refused because of pregnancy only to a woman, refusal to appoint a woman on the ground of her pregnancy constitutes direct discrimination on the ground of sex, contrary to Articles 2(1) and 3(1) of the Equal Treatment Directive. Unlike the English courts, the Court refused to undertake the exercise of finding a male

---

[426] 92/241/EEC [1992] OJ L123/16.

[427] Council Resolution of 15 Dec. 1997 on the 1998 Employment Guidelines [1998] OJ C30/1, as amended by Council Resolution of 22 Feb. 1999 on the 1999 Employment Guidelines [1999] OJ C69/2.

[428] See further Vegter and Prechal, *Report of the Network of Experts on the Implementation of the Equality Directives on Indirect Discrimination and Discrimination on Grounds of Pregnancy and Maternity* (Commission, Brussels, 1993) V/6008/93–EN. Also, see More, 'Reflections on Pregnancy Discrimination under European Community Law' (1992) 5 *JSWL* 48.

[429] Case C–177/88 [1990] ECR I–3941.

comparator 'suffering from an equivalent problem'.[430] Instead, it removed the need for a comparator by saying that since only women can become pregnant, less favourable treatment on the grounds of pregnancy automatically constitutes direct discrimination.[431]

While *Dekker* concerned the refusal to appoint a woman on the ground of her pregnancy, in *Hertz*[432] the Court ruled that the *dismissal* of a female worker on account of pregnancy also constituted direct discrimination on the grounds of sex contrary to Articles 1(1), 2(1), and 5(1) of the Equal Treatment Directive.[433] The Court adopted a similar approach in the more difficult case of *Webb*.[434] Mrs Webb was appointed by EMO Air Cargo Ltd initially to replace another employee, Mrs Stewart, who was about to go on maternity leave, but then to continue working on Mrs Stewart's return. Shortly after starting work Mrs Webb announced that she too was pregnant. When she was dismissed she claimed that she had been discriminated against on the grounds of sex. The employers, however, argued that she was dismissed because she was unavailable, at least at first, to work during the period for which she was needed. Emphasizing the fact that Mrs Webb was not employed on a fixed-term contract, the Court ruled that 'dismissal of a pregnant woman recruited for an *indefinite period* cannot be justified on grounds relating to her inability to fulfil a fundamental condition of her employment contract' (emphasis added). It therefore concluded that 'the dismissal of an employee who is recruited for an unlimited term with a view, initially, to replacing another employee during the latter's maternity leave' and 'who cannot do so because she is pregnant' was contrary to Articles 2(1) and 5(1) of the Directive. Therefore, *Hertz* and *Webb* make clear that dismissal for the reason of pregnancy or from the consequences of pregnancy, such as absence, is automatically sex discriminatory.

The Court extended the approach adopted in *Dekker* to the terms and conditions of employment. In *Thibault*[435] the Court ruled that the principle of non-discrimination requires that a woman who continues to be bound to her employer by her contract of employment during maternity leave should not be deprived of the benefit of working conditions which apply to both men and

[430] See e.g. the approach of the Court of Appeal in the English case of *Webb* v. *EMO Air Cargo* [1992] 1 CMLR 793. The Court in Case C–32/93 *Webb* [1994] ECR I–3567 said 'pregnancy is not in any way comparable with a pathological condition'. See above, nn. 196–197.

[431] Cf. Wintemute, 'When is Pregnancy Discrimination Indirect Discrimination' (1998) 27 *ILJ* 23. Honeyball, 'Pregnancy and Sex Discrimination' (2000) 29 *ILJ* 43, who emphasizes the lack of suitability of using the discrimination model to address pregnancy issues.

[432] Case C–179/88 *Handels- og Kontorfunktionærernes Forbund i Danmark (Hertz)* v. *Dansk Arbejdsgiverforening* [1990] ECR I–3979.

[433] This view was confirmed in Case C–421/92 *Habermann-Beltermann* [1994] ECR I–1657. See also Art. 10 of Directive 92/85/EC [1992] OJ L348/1.

[434] Case C–32/93 [1994] ECR I–3567. See also Case C–207/98 *Mahlburg*, judgment of 3 Feb. 2000.

[435] Case C–136/95 *Thibault* [1998] ECR I–2011.

women and were the result of that employment relationship. Therefore, the Court said, to deny a female employee the right to have her performance assessed annually would discriminate against her merely in her capacity as a worker because, if she had not been pregnant and had not taken the maternity leave to which she was entitled, she would have been assessed for the year in question and could therefore have qualified for promotion. Such conduct constituted discrimination based directly on grounds of sex within the meaning of the Directive.[436] Similarly in *Høj Pedersen*[437] the Court ruled that the fact that a woman was deprived, before the beginning of her maternity leave, of her full pay when her incapacity for work was the result of a pathological condition connected with her pregnancy had to be regarded as treatment based essentially on the pregnancy and thus as discriminatory. The only exception to this rule was where the sums received by employees by way of state benefits were equal to the amount of their pay. It would then be for the national court to ascertain whether the circumstance that the benefits were paid by a local authority was such as to bring about discrimination in breach of Article 119 [new Article 141].

In other respects, once a woman goes on maternity leave her situation changes. This was made clear by the Court in *Gillespie*.[438] The Court said that since the case concerned women taking maternity leave provided for by the national legislation they were in a special position requiring them to be afforded special protection.[439] This situation was not comparable either with that of a man or with a woman actually at work.[440] In respect of the payment during maternity leave, the Court said that, although maternity benefit constituted pay within the meaning of Article 119 [new Article 141], neither Article 119 nor Article 1 of Directive 75/117 required that women should continue to receive full pay during maternity leave, nor did those provisions lay down any specific criteria for determining the amount of benefit to be paid to them during that period. The Court did add, however, that the amount payable could not be so low as to undermine the purpose of the maternity leave, namely the protection of women before and after giving birth. In order to assess the adequacy of the amount payable, the national court had to take into account not only the length of the maternity leave but also the other forms of social protection afforded by the national law in the case of justified

---

[436] See also Case C–333/97 *Lewen* [2000] All ER(EC) 261, para. 48, discussed below, n. 486, where the Court ruled that Art. 119 [new Art. 141] precludes an employer from taking periods of maternity leave into account when granting a Christmas bonus so as to reduce the benefit *pro rata*.

[437] Case C–66/96 *Høj Pedersen v. Kvickly Skive* [1998] ECR I–7327.

[438] Case C–342/93 [1996] ECR I–475. See Conaghan, 'Pregnancy, Equality and the European Court of Justice: Interrogating *Gillespie*' (1998) 3 *IJLD* 115.

[439] It said that 'discrimination involves the application of different rules to comparable situations or the application of the same rule to different situations'.

[440] See above, nn. 196–197, and Case C–218/98 *Abdoulaye*, judgment of 16 Sept. 1999 (women could be paid a maternity bonus not payable to new fathers).

absence from work. On the facts of the case there was nothing to suggest that the amount of benefit granted was such as to undermine the objective of protecting maternity leave.

The Court also said in *Gillespie* that a woman on maternity leave should receive a pay rise awarded before or during that period. It said that the benefit paid during maternity leave was equivalent to a weekly payment calculated on the basis of the average pay received by the worker at the time when she was actually working and which was paid to her week by week, just like any other worker. The principle of non-discrimination therefore required that a woman who was still linked to her employer by a contract of employment or by an employment relationship during maternity leave had to benefit from any pay rise, even if backdated. To deny her such an increase would discriminate against her purely in her capacity as a worker since, had she not been pregnant, she would have received the pay rise.

Despite this long line of case law, the Court has not provided women suffering from the problems of pregnancy or childbirth with absolute protection. This was shown by the case of *Hertz*.[441] Hertz suffered from a complicated pregnancy, causing her to take a lot of sick leave. When the maternity leave came to an end she returned to work but shortly afterwards had to take a further 100 days' sick leave due to an illness resulting from her pregnancy. As a result, she was dismissed. The Court distinguished between two situations: first, the period of maternity leave and, secondly, the period after the maternity leave. During the first period the Court said that a woman was protected against dismissal due to absence; during the second period the Court said it saw no reason to distinguish an illness attributable to pregnancy or confinement from any other illness. It therefore applied a comparative test. It reasoned that although certain disorders were specific to one or other sex, the only question was whether a woman was dismissed on account of absence due to illness in the same circumstances as a man. If this was so, then there was no direct or indirect discrimination on the grounds of sex.

While this decision can be justified by reference to practical and economic necessity,[442] it cannot be defended in terms of logic: if the dismissal of a female worker on account of pregnancy constitutes direct discrimination, the dismissal of a woman on account of a pregnancy-related illness which only women can suffer should also constitute direct discrimination. Nevertheless, the Court reaffirmed this ruling in *Larsson*[443] and developed it further. It said

---

[441] Case C–179/88 [1990] ECR I–3979.

[442] See esp. Advocate General Darmon's discussion in his Joined Opinion in Cases C–177/88 *Dekker* ECR I–3941 and C–179/88 *Hertz* [1990] ECR I–3979, para. 43.

[443] Case C–400/95 *Larsson v. Føtex Supermarked* [1997] ECR I–2757. See Caracciolo di Torella, 'Maternity and Equal Treatment' (1998) 23 *ELRev.* 164.

that the Directive did not preclude dismissals which were the result of absences due to an illness attributable to pregnancy or confinement even where that illness arose during pregnancy and continued during and after maternity leave. This decision was much criticized and the Court reconsidered it in *Brown*.[444]

In *Brown* the employer had a policy of dismissing any employee who took more than 26 weeks sick leave. Mrs. Brown, who suffered from pregnancy-related disorders, was dismissed after 26 weeks absence in line with the policy. The Court said that although pregnancy was not in any way comparable to a pathological condition, pregnancy was a period during which disorders and complications might arise compelling a woman to undergo strict medical supervision and, in some cases, to rest absolutely for all or part of her pregnancy. Those disorders and complications, which might cause incapacity for work, formed part of the risks inherent in the condition of pregnancy and were thus a specific feature of that condition. The Court then said that the principle of non-discrimination required protection against dismissal 'throughout the period of pregnancy'. It therefore ruled that 'dismissal of a female worker during pregnancy for absences due to incapacity for work resulting from her pregnancy is linked to the occurrence of risks inherent in pregnancy and must therefore be regarded as essentially based on the fact of pregnancy. Such a dismissal can affect only women and therefore constitutes direct discrimination on grounds of sex'. The Court then said:

It is also clear from all the foregoing considerations that, contrary to the Court's ruling in Case C–400/95 *Larsson*, where a woman is absent owing to illness resulting from pregnancy or childbirth, and that illness arose during pregnancy and persisted during and after maternity leave, her absence not only during maternity leave but also during the period extending from the start of her pregnancy to the start of her maternity leave cannot be taken into account for computation of the period justifying her dismissal under national law. As to her absence after maternity leave, this may be taken into account under the same conditions as a man's absence, of the same duration, through incapacity for work.

Thus the entire period from the beginning of the pregnancy to the end of the maternity leave must now be regarded as a protected period, during which any pregnancy-related absence must be discounted. Therefore, the twenty-six-week period could only start to run once the maternity leave had ended (*Brown*), but the comparative test applies to pregnancy-related illnesses which manifest themselves or continue after the maternity leave comes to an end (*Hertz*).

---

[444] Case C–394/96 [1998] ECR I–4185. See Boch, 'Official: During Pregnancy, Females are Pregnant' (1998) 23 *ELRev.* 488.

The Court has, however, said that differential treatment on the grounds of pregnancy may be lawful in two situations. First, direct discrimination may be lawful if the employer's actions are caught within the derogation contained in Article 2(3) of Directive 76/207 (protection of women, particularly on the grounds of pregnancy and maternity).[445] In *Habermann-Beltermann*[446] the Court held that the prohibition on night-time work by pregnant women is 'unquestionably compatible with Article 2(3)'. However, since the prohibition on night-time work by pregnant women takes effect only for a limited period in relation to the total length of an indefinite contract 'the termination of a contract without a fixed term on account of the woman's pregnancy . . . cannot be justified on the ground that a statutory prohibition, imposed because of pregnancy, temporarily prevents the employee from performing night-work'.[447]

Secondly, the Court hinted in *Webb*[448] at the possibility that direct discrimination due to pregnancy may in some circumstances be justified in situations beyond those listed in Article 2(3) of the Directive. Although this runs contrary to the orthodox jurisprudence that direct discrimination can never be justified,[449] the Court said that 'dismissal of a pregnant woman recruited for an indefinite period cannot be justified on grounds relating to her inability to fulfil a fundamental condition of her employment contract'. By implication, the dismissal of a woman employed on a fixed-term contract—for example, a shop assistant employed over the Christmas period—may be justified if, on the ground of pregnancy, she is unable to fulfil the purpose of her contract.

1.2 Directive 92/85 on Pregnant Workers

The significance of the decisions of the Court will be reduced in the light of Directive 92/85/EC[450] which is designed to protect pregnant workers and workers who have recently given birth or who are breastfeeding.[451] The Directive is intended to provide minimum requirements for encouraging

---

[445] See text attached to nn. 291–302.
[446] Case C–421/92 [1994] ECR I–1657.
[447] See also Art. 7 of Directive 92/85 [1992] OJ L348/1.
[448] Case C–32/93 [1994] ECR I–3567.
[449] See text attached to nn. 150–162.
[450] Council Directive 92/85/EEC [1925] OJ L348/1 (tenth individual Directive adopted within the meaning of Art. 16(1) of Directive 89/391, considered further in Ch. 6) on the introduction of measures to encourage improvements in the safety and health at work of pregnant workers who have recently given birth or are breastfeeding. The Directive was based on Art. 118a [new Art. 137]. See further Cromack, 'The EC Pregnancy Directive Principle or Pragmatism?' (1993) 6 *JSWL* 261; Commission Report on Implementation: COM(99)100 final.
[451] These three terms are defined by reference to national law and practice and are dependent on the worker informing her employer of her condition (Art. 2). The term 'pregnant worker' will be used to apply to the three situations unless otherwise stated.

improvements,[452] especially in the working environment, to protect the health and safety of pregnant workers. The Directive provides three pillars of protection to pregnant workers, which, with one exception, exist from the first day of employment. First, pregnant workers are entitled to time off, without loss of pay, in order to attend ante-natal examinations, if such examinations have to take place within work hours.[453] Secondly, pregnant workers are entitled to a continuous period of at least fourteen weeks maternity leave, of which at least two weeks must be allocated before and/or after confinement.[454] During this period the pregnant workers' rights connected with the contract of employment, with the exception of pay, must be maintained.[455] The maintenance of pay or an (unspecified) 'adequate' allowance[456] must also be ensured, but Member States may make entitlement to pay conditional upon the worker fulfilling the conditions of eligibility for such benefits laid down by national legislation. These conditions may not, however, provide for periods of previous employment in excess of twelve months immediately prior to the presumed date of confinement.[457] As far as the level of maternity pay is concerned, the Court ruled in *Gillespie*[458] that the allowance must not be paid at such a derisory level as to undermine the purpose of the maternity leave.

Thirdly, Article 10(1) provides that pregnant workers cannot be dismissed during the period from the beginning of their pregnancy to the end of their maternity leave, save in exceptional cases not connected with their condition which are permitted under national law or practice. Employers must provide pregnant workers who are dismissed within this period with duly substantiated written grounds for dismissal[459] and Member States must provide a remedy for pregnant workers who are dismissed.[460] As a result of Article 10, the

---

[452] Art. 1(3) provides that the Directive may not have the effect of reducing the level of protection afforded to pregnant workers.

[453] Art. 9. This Art. applies only to pregnant workers.

[454] Art. 8(1) and (2).

[455] Art. 11(2)(a). See now Case C–342/93 Gillespie [1996] ECR I–475, above n. 440.

[456] Art. 11(2)(b). An allowance is adequate (Art. 11(3)) if it guarantees income at least equivalent to that which the worker concerned would receive in the event of a break in her activities on grounds connected with her state of health, subject to any ceiling laid down by national legislation, in other words sick pay. However, a statement of the Council and the Commission added to the Directive [1992] OJ L348/8 states that the reference to the state of health is not 'intended in any way to imply that pregnancy and childbirth be equated with sickness'. The link with such allowance is intended to serve as a concrete fixed reference in all Member States for the determination of the minimum amount of maternity allowance. In Case C–66/96 *Høj Pedersen* [1998] ECR I–7327 the Court said that Art. 11(3) applied only to pay or benefits received in the context of *maternity* leave and did not apply to allowances which a woman could claim when pregnant.

[457] Art. 11(2)(b) and (4).

[458] Case C–342/93 [1996] ECR I–475.

[459] Art. 10(2).

[460] Art. 10(3). In addition, Art. 12 provides more generally that Member States must allow those who consider themselves wronged by the failure to comply with the obligations of the Directive to pursue their claims by judicial process.

Court's case law on pregnancy-related dismissals under the Equal Treatment Directive, developed against the backcloth of Article 10,[461] has become redundant. However, given the limited scope of Directive 92/85, the case law on other forms of discrimination during pregnancy continues to be important.

The Directive also provides more specific rights to protect the health and safety of the pregnant worker. The Directive makes a distinction between the risks contained in Annex I (certain physical, biological, and chemical agents, certain industrial processes, and underground mining) and those contained in Annex II (a more limited list of physical, biological, and chemical agents and underground mining). In the case of the Annex I risks the employer is obliged to examine the nature, degree, and duration of exposure of the pregnant worker to these risks.[462] The pregnant worker and/or the workers' representatives are to be informed of any risks and of the measures to be taken. These measures may include a temporary adjustment to the working conditions or working hours of the pregnant worker. If this is not technically or objectively feasible, or cannot reasonably be required on duly substantiated grounds, the employer must take the necessary measures to move the worker to another job. If this is not possible the worker concerned must be granted leave in accordance with the national legislation for the whole of the period necessary to protect her health and safety.[463] These rules apply equally to Annex II risks. In addition, Article 6 provides that neither pregnant workers nor workers who are breastfeeding may be obliged to perform duties for which the assessment has revealed a risk of exposure to the agents and working conditions listed in Annex II, section A, in the case of pregnant workers, and Annex II, section B, in the case of workers who are breastfeeding.[464]

Article 7 recognizes that pregnant workers have the right not to have to work at night during their pregnancy and for a period to be determined by

---

[461] As the Court said in Case C–394/96 *Brown* [1998] ECR I–2757, it was 'precisely in view of the harmful effects which the risk of dismissal may have on the physical and mental state of women who are pregnant, women who have recently given birth or women who are breastfeeding, including the particularly serious risk that pregnant women may be prompted voluntarily to terminate their pregnancy, that the Community legislature, pursuant to Article 10 of Council Directive 92/85/EEC of 19 October 1992 ... provided for special protection to be given to women, by prohibiting dismissal during the period from the beginning of their pregnancy to the end of their maternity leave'. Therefore the Court took this 'general context' into account in construing the relevant provisions in *Brown*.

[462] Art. 4(1). Technical adjustments to Annex 1 can be made according to the provisions in Art. 12. Art. 3 obliges the Commission to draw up guidelines in conjunction with the Advisory Committee on Safety, Hygiene, and Health Protection at work, on the assessment of the chemical, physical, and biological agents and industrial processes considered hazardous for the health and safety of pregnant workers.

[463] Art. 5.

[464] Art. 6. Annex II may be amended only in accordance with the Art. 118a [new Art. 137] procedure.

the national authorities following childbirth. These rights are dependent on the production of a medical certificate stating that these arrangements are necessary for the safety or health of the worker. If this is the case then the pregnant worker must be transferred to daywork or be granted leave from work or an extension of maternity leave where such a transfer is not possible.

In *Boyle*[465] the Court had its first opportunity to consider Directive 92/85 in detail. It provided detailed and specific answers to technical questions raised. First, it said that Article 119 [new Article 141], Article 1 of Directive 75/117, and Article 11 of Directive 92/85 did not preclude a clause in an employment contract which made the payment, during the period of maternity leave referred to by Article 8 of Directive 92/85, of pay higher than the statutory payments in respect of maternity leave conditional on the worker's undertaking to return to work after the birth of the child for at least one month, failing which she was required to repay the difference between the amount of the pay she would have received during the period of maternity leave, on the one hand, and the amount of those payments, on the other.

Secondly, the Court said that Article 8 of Directive 92/85 and Article 5(1) of Directive 76/207 did not preclude a clause in an employment contract from requiring an employee who had expressed her intention to commence her maternity leave during the six weeks preceding the expected week of childbirth, and was on sick leave with a pregnancy-related illness immediately before that date and gave birth during the period of sick leave, to bring forward the date on which her paid maternity leave commenced either to the beginning of the sixth week preceding the expected week of childbirth or to the beginning of the period of sick leave, whichever was the later.

Thirdly, the Court said that a clause in an employment contract which prohibited a woman from taking sick leave during the minimum period of fourteen weeks' maternity leave to which a female worker was entitled pursuant to Article 8(1) of Directive 92/85, unless she elected to return to work and thus terminated her maternity leave, was not compatible with Directive 92/85. By contrast, a clause in an employment contract which prohibited a woman from taking sick leave during a period of supplementary maternity leave granted to her by the employer, unless she elected to return to work and thus terminated her maternity leave, was compatible with Directives 76/207 and 92/85.

Fourthly, the Court said that Directives 92/85 and 76/207 did not preclude a clause in an employment contract from limiting the period during which annual leave accrued to the minimum period of fourteen weeks' maternity

---

[465] Case C–411/96 *Boyle* v. *EOC* [1998] ECR I–6401.

leave to which female workers were entitled under Article 8 of Directive 92/85 and from providing that annual leave ceased to accrue during any period of supplementary maternity leave granted by the employer.

Fifthly, the Court said that Directive 92/85 precluded a clause in an employment contract from limiting, in the context of an occupational scheme wholly financed by the employer, the accrual of pension rights during the period of maternity leave referred to by Article 8 to the period during which the woman received the pay provided for by that contract or national legislation.

2. Parental Leave

The first collective agreement concluded by the Social Partners under the SPA was the Framework Agreement on Parental Leave.[466] It was extended to all workers by Directive 96/34/EC[467] which lays down minimum requirements designed to facilitate the reconciliation of parental and professional responsibilities for working parents.[468] It provides all workers, both men and women, who have an employment contract or an employment relationship,[469] with a non-transferable right to parental leave.[470]

The collective agreement envisages two main rights. First, the agreement entitles men and women workers to parental leave on the birth or adoption of a child to enable them to take care of that child, for at least three months, until a given age up to eight years, to be defined by the Member States or the Social Partners.[471] In order to ensure that workers can exercise their right to parental leave, they must be protected against dismissal on the grounds of applying for or taking parental leave in accordance with national legislation, collective agreements, or practice.[472] At the end of the parental leave workers have the right to return to the same job, or, if that is not possible, to an equivalent or similar job consistent with their employment contract or employment relationship.[473] In addition, rights acquired by the worker or in the process of being acquired on the date on which parental leave starts must be maintained

---

[466] The draft agreement was concluded on 6 Nov. 1995 by ETUC, CEEP, and UNICE and formally agreed on 14 Dec. 1995.

[467] [1996] OJ L145/4, amended by Council Directive 97/75/EC [1998] OJ L10/24, consolidated 16 Jan. 1998. A question has been referred to the ECJ as to whether the right to parental leave should apply to all parents after 15 December 1999 or only to those whose children were born or adopted after 15 December 1999: *L v. Secretary of State, ex parte TUC*, 23 May 2000.

[468] Clause 1(1).
[469] Clause 1(2).
[470] Clause 2(2).
[471] Clause 2(1).
[472] Clause 2(4).
[473] Clause 2(5).

as they stand until the end of the parental leave. These rights, including any changes arising from national law, agreements, or practice, will apply.[474]

Secondly, the agreement provides that workers are entitled to time off on the grounds of *force majeure* for urgent family reasons in cases of sickness or accident, making the immediate presence of the worker indispensable.[475] Member States and/or Social Partners may specify 'the conditions of access and modalities of application of this clause'.

The Directive leaves a large number of issues to be resolved by the Member State and/or Social Partners. In respect of parental leave, the Member States and/or the Social Partners may decide whether parental leave is granted on a full-time or part-time basis, in a fragmented way or in the form of a time credit system; whether entitlement to parental leave be subject to a period of work qualification and/or length of service qualification (which cannot exceed one year); whether to adjust conditions for access and modalities of application of parental leave to the special circumstances of adoption; and whether notice periods be given by the worker to the employer specifying the beginning or the end of the parental leave.[476] In addition, the Member States and the Social Partners can define the circumstances in which the employer is allowed to postpone the granting of parental leave for justifiable reasons relating to the operation of the undertaking[477] and can authorize that special arrangements be made for small undertakings.[478] Member States and the Social Partners must define the status of the employment contract or employment relationship for the period of the parental leave.[479] All matters relating to social security in relation to the agreement are left to be determined by the Member States according to national law,[480] and there is no reference to pay during the parental leave.

As we have seen, the rights provided here are minima and Member States can maintain or introduce more favourable provisions than those set out in Agreement.[481] Further, the implementation of the provisions of the collective agreement 'shall not constitute valid grounds for reducing the general level of protection afforded to workers in the field of this agreement'.[482] However, the agreement continues that this does not prejudice the right of the Member States and/or Social Partners to develop different legislative, regulatory or contractual provisions, in the light of changing circumstances (including the

---

[474] Clause 2(6).

[475] Clause 3(1).

[476] Art. 2(3)(a)–(d).

[477] e.g. where the work is of a seasonal nature, where a replacement cannot be found within the notice period, where a significant proportion of the workforce applies for parental leave at the same time, and where a specific function is of strategic importance.

[478] Clause 2(3)(e)–(f).

[479] Clause 2(7).

[480] Clause 2(8).

[481] Clause 3(1).

[482] Clause 4(2): the standard non-regression clause.

introduction of non-transferability), as long as the minimum requirements provided for in this agreement are complied with.

Insufficient time has elapsed to assess the effectiveness of the agreement which was implemented by the Directive. Nevertheless, experience from the Nordic countries where parental leave already exists indicates that it is usually the woman who takes the parental leave.[483] This fact was recognized by the Court in *Lewen*[484] where it said that failure to pay a Christmas bonus to employees on parental leave was *prima facie* indirectly discriminatory against women. Such discrimination contravened Article 119 [new Article 141] if the bonus was awarded retroactively for work performed in the course of the year and the woman did not receive an amount proportionate to the time worked. If, on the other hand, the bonus was paid as a way of encouraging those in active employment to work hard and to reward *future* loyalty to an employer then failure to pay such a bonus was not discriminatory since a woman on parental leave was in a 'special situation' which could not be 'assimilated to that of a man or woman at work since such leave involves suspension of the contract of employment and, therefore, of the respective obligations of the employer and the worker'.

Therefore, in respect of a *retrospective* payment the Court has used the principle of indirect discrimination contrary to Article 141 to provide women (but not men) with some protection, subject to the possibility of objective justification. If, on the other hand, the payment is made *prospectively* the Court treats those on parental leave, just like those on maternity leave,[485] as being in a 'special situation' and so Article 141 offers no protection. It also offers no protection against employers taking periods of parental leave (but not maternity leave) into account to reduce the benefit *pro rata*.[486]

3. Childcare

According to the Commission, the rationale for Recommendation 92/241 on Childcare Services[487] is both economic and social. Despite increasing numbers of women entering the labour force there has not been a correlative decrease in women's share of family responsibilities. According to the Commission, women will only be able to take advantage of the new jobs due to be

---

[483] Bruning and Plontenga, 'Parental Leave and Equal Opportunities' (1999) 9 *JESP* 195.
[484] Case C–333/97 [2000] All ER(EC) 261, para. 35.
[485] See above, nn. 438–440.
[486] Case C–333/97 *Lewen* [2000] All ER(EC) 261, paras. 48–49.
[487] Council Recommendation 92/241/EEC of 31 Mar. 1992 on childcare [1992] OJ L123/16.

created by the advent of the Single European Market if affordable support measures—including childcare—are available, enabling them time to train or retrain in order to be able to meet the demands of a restructured labour market.

According to Article 1, Member States, possibly in co-operation with national, regional, or local authorities, management and labour, and other relevant organizations and private individuals, should take and encourage initiatives in four areas:

- the provision of childcare services while parents are working, following a course of education or training in order to obtain employment, or are seeking a job or a course of education or training in order to obtain employment;
- special leave for employed parents with responsibility for the care and upbringing of children;[488]
- adapting the environment, structure, and organization of work to make them responsive to the needs of workers with children;[489]
- sharing of occupational, family, and upbringing responsibilities arising from the care of children between women and men. This includes, according to Article 6, encouraging increased participation by men in order to achieve a more equal sharing of parental responsibilities.

Childcare services, defined as any type of childcare, whether public or private, individual or collective, should be affordable, flexible, and diverse. They should combine reliable care, from the point of view of health and safety, with a general upbringing and a pedagogical approach. They should be available in all areas and regions of the Member States, and be accessible to parents and children, including children with special needs.[490]

This measure, being a recommendation, lacks the legal force of a Directive.[491] Furthermore, the broad strategic nature of the policy—and the complexities created by the recognition of subsidiarity in the provision of the services—means that it will be very difficult for an individual to raise provisions of the Recommendation before a national court. Nevertheless, the Recommendation has a symbolic value in demonstrating the EC's

---

[488] These special leave initiatives apply to both men and women. They are intended to combine some flexibility as to how leave may be taken (Art. 4).

[489] This includes action, esp. within the framework of a collective agreement to create an environment which takes into account the needs of all working parents with childcare responsibilities, ensures that due recognition is given to persons engaged in childcare services and the social value of their work; and promotes action, especially in the public sector, which can serve as an example in developing initiatives in this area (Art. 5).

[490] Art. 3.

[491] The Court has not been prepared to extend Art. 141 to reinforce this Recommendation: Case C–249/97 *Gruber*, judgment of 14 Sept. 1999.

commitment to childcare and Member States are obliged to inform the Commission of the measures taken to give effect to the Recommendation.[492]

F. SEXUAL HARASSMENT

Despite the considerable weight of evidence concerning the serious consequences of sexual harassment a Commission report found that in most countries there was no effective legal remedy against sexual harassment.[493] It therefore proposed that a specific directive should be passed with the aim of protecting workers from the risk of sexual harassment.[494] This suggestion was not followed. Instead, the Council passed a non-legally binding Resolution on the protection of the dignity of women and men at work.[495] This was followed by a Commission Recommendation and a Code of Conduct[496] which was approved by a Council Declaration.[497] While the Recommendation and the Code are not legally binding the Court held in *Grimaldi*,[498] in the context of a Recommendation on compensation for persons with occupational diseases, that national courts are bound to take Recommendations into account in order to decide disputes before them, in particular where they clarify the interpretation of national rules adopted in order to implement them or when they are designed to supplement binding Community measures, such as the Equal Treatment Directive.[499]

The definition of sexual harassment contained in the Council Resolution is useful. It is 'conduct of a sexual nature, or other conduct based on sex affecting the dignity of women and men at work, including conduct of superiors and colleagues'. This conduct is deemed to constitute an 'intolerable violation of the dignity of workers or trainees' and is unacceptable if:

[492] The Commission intends to follow up the Childcare Recommendation by assessing the implementation of the Recommendation and establishing baseline data on childcare infrastructure and services in the Member States (COM(94)333, 43).

[493] Rubinstein, *The Dignity of Women at Work: a Report on the Problem of Sexual Harassment in the Member States of the European Communities* (OPEC, Luxembourg, Oct. 1987).

[494] In June 1986 the European Parliament passed a resolution on violence against women which also called for a specific EEC Directive on sexual harassment [1986] OJ C176/79. The Social Partners started to negotiate an agreement on the prevention of sexual harassment at work with a view to concluding a Directive. UNICE pulled out of the negotiations: COM(96)373 and SEC(97)568.

[495] Resolution of the 29 May 1990 [1990] OJ C157/3.

[496] Commission Recommendation 92/131/EEC of 27 Nov. 1991 on the protection and dignity of men and women at work [1992] OJ L49/1. See generally Bakirci, 'Sexual Harassment in the Workplace in Relation to EC Legislation' (1998) 3 *IJLD* 3.

[497] Council Declaration of 19 Dec. 1991 on the Implementation of the Commission Recommendation on the Protection of the Dignity of Women and Men at Work including the Code of Practice to Combat Sexual Harassment (92/C27/01).

[498] Case 322/88 *Grimaldi* v. *Fonds des Maladies Professionnelles* [1989] ECR 4407.

[499] The Code and Recommendation were invoked by the Employment Appeal Tribunal in *Wadman* v. *Carpenter Farrer Partnership* [1993] IRLR 374.

(a) such conduct is unwanted, unreasonable, and offensive to the recipient;
(b) a person's rejection of or submission to such conduct on the part of employers or workers (including superiors or colleagues) is used explicitly or implicitly as a basis for a decision which affects that person's access to vocational training, access to employment, promotion, salary or any other employment decisions; and/or
(c) such conduct creates an intimidating, hostile, or humiliating work environment for the recipient.[500]

Thus, the definition of what constitutes sexual harassment is subjective, not objective: account is taken of the effect of the conduct upon the particular individual concerned rather than examining the effect of equivalent conduct on a 'reasonable person'. The motive of the perpetrator is largely irrelevant.

The Code suggests that conduct constituting sexual harassment may take the form of physical conduct of a sexual nature, ranging from unnecessary touching to assault, verbal conduct of a sexual nature, including unwelcome sexual advances, suggestive remarks and innuendoes, non-verbal conduct of a sexual nature, including the display of pornographic or sexually explicit pictures, leering, whistling, or making sexually suggestive gestures, and sex-based conduct, such as sex-based comments about appearance or dress. The essence of the definition is that the conduct is unwanted by the recipient. In the words of the Code, 'sexual attention becomes sexual harassment *if it is persisted in once it has been made clear that it is regarded by the recipient as offensive*, although one incident of harassment may constitute sexual harassment if sufficiently serious' (emphasis added).[501]

The definition of sexual harassment also distinguishes between conduct which damages the employee's working environment, creating a 'hostile work environment'[502] using US terminology (Article 1(c)), and conduct which is used as a basis for employment decisions affecting the victim (Article 1(b)). Legal effect is given to the prohibition of sexual harassment through Directive 76/207. The Council Resolution and the Commission Recommendation make clear that sexual harassment '*may* be, in certain circumstances, contrary to the principle of equal treatment within the meaning of Articles 3, 4 and 5 of Council Directive 76/207/EEC' (emphasis added). This is the approach

[500] Art. 1 of the Council's Resolution on the Dignity of Women and Men at Work [1990] OJ C157/3. For further definitions see the American EEOC's Guidelines on Sexual Harassment, 1980, 29 CFR, s. 1604. 11(f) and the discussion in Ellis, above n. 4, 215ff.

[501] See, in the British context, *Bracebridge Engineering* v. *Darby* [1990] IRLR 3 where the EAT accepted that a single serious sexual assault constituted unlawful sexual discrimination.

[502] In *Meritor Savings Bank* v. *Vinson* 477 US 57, 65 the US Supreme Court distinguished between hostile work environment and *quid pro quo* claims. Both are cognizable under Title VII though a hostile environment claim requires harassment that is severe or perverse. In *Burlington Industries* v. *Ellerth*, 26 June 1998, the Supreme Court doubted the utility of these terms and it is not proposed to adopt this distinction here.

adopted in the UK and Ireland where there has been judicial acceptance that sexual harassment may constitute unlawful discrimination:[503] usually the victim of the sexual harassment would not have been harassed or treated in that way had she been a man. She is thus a victim of discrimination. The link with the Equal Treatment Directive does, however, impose certain constraints on the development of a framework which would successfully eliminate all forms of sexual harassment. First, it imposes the requirement that there should be a comparator who is more favourably treated and, secondly, that the comparator and the victim should be of opposite sexes. Therefore, those who work in a single sex environment who find, for example, the display by their colleagues of pornographic photographs offensive might be left without a remedy. Similarly, those who discover that their comparators would be treated equally badly are also unable to claim that they are the victims of discrimination.[504] In addition, those who face harassment as a result of their sexual orientation, a situation envisaged by the Code of Conduct,[505] are unable to bring their claims within the confines of the Directive after the decision in *Grant*.[506] Further, neither the Equal Treatment Directive nor the Council Resolution on Dignity of Women and Men at work, despite its title, provide a general legally enforceable right to dignity in the workplace nor any legal protection against a hostile work environment.

Employers also stand to suffer from this rather unnatural link between sexual harassment and the Equal Treatment Directive. Faced by a claim of direct discrimination they may find themselves vicariously and strictly liable. Unless the Court introduces the possibility that direct discrimination can be objectively justified,[507] the employer can only resort to the defences contained

---

[503] See e.g. *Strathclyde Regional Council* v. *Poricelli* [1986] IRLR 134.

[504] See, in the British context, *Stewart* v. *Cleveland Guest (Engineering) Ltd* [1994] IRLR 440 where the Industrial Tribunal accepted that the display by male employees of pictures of nude women was detrimental to the applicant but no discrimination had occurred because a hypothetical man might also have complained so that the applicant had not shown that she had been treated less favourably. Cf. *British Telecommunications* v. *Williams* [1997] IRLR 668 where the EAT held that because the conduct which constitutes sexual harassment is itself gender-specific there is no need to look for a male comparator. Cf proposed amendment to Article 1 in Com (2000) 334 that sexual harassment is deemed to be discrimination on the grounds of sex.

[505] See discussion of para. 3.3 of the Code of Conduct. On the question whether less favourable treatment on the grounds of homosexuality may constitute direct discrimination, see Byre, 'Equality and Non-discrimination', in *Homosexuality: A European Community Issue Essays on Lesbian and Gay Rights in European Law and Policy*, eds. Waaldijk and Clapham (Martinus Nijhoff, The Hague, 1993). She suggests that the refusal to hire gay men may be directly discriminatory because it involves gender-based assumptions that homosexual men are unreliable, which do not take an individual's suitability for a job into account. These assumptions may not apply to female applicants. See also the European Parliament's Resolution on equal rights for homosexuals and lesbians in the EC [1994] OJ C61/40.

[506] Case C–249/96 [1998] ECR I–621. The US Supreme Court decided in *Oncale*, judgment of 4 Mar. 1998, that same sex sexual harassment was actionable as sex discrimination under Title VII. Cf. COM(99)565 concerning the proposed directives on discrimination considered below, n. 558.

[507] See text attached to nn. 150–162.

in the Equal Treatment Directive which cover very limited situations and, being derogations, are narrowly construed, and perhaps a more general argument that it took all reasonably practicable steps to prevent the harassment[508] which must be read into the Directive on the basis of the principle of proportionality.

Although the Resolution, Recommendation, and Code suggest that the Equal Treatment Directive may provide a remedy, their real emphasis is on means of preventing sexual harassment by changing attitudes and behaviour. The Code recommends that employers, in both the public and private sectors, should issue a policy statement, preferably linked to a broader policy of promoting equal opportunities, which expressly states that all employees have a right to be treated with dignity, that sexual harassment will not be permitted and that all employees have a right to complain about any sexual harassment. Furthermore, the policy should state that employees' complaints will be taken seriously, will be dealt with expeditiously, and that employees will not suffer victimization or retaliation as a result of making the complaint. The Code further recommends that the policy statement should leave no doubt about what is considered inappropriate behaviour and it should also specify that appropriate disciplinary measures will be taken against employees found guilty of sexual harassment. This statement must be communicated to all concerned to ensure maximum awareness.

The Code also expects that provision is made for both informal and formal means of resolving disputes. Employers should designate a specially trained officer to provide advice and assistance to employees subjected to sexual harassment and identify to whom a victim can make a complaint. Developing this idea, the European Parliament adopted a resolution calling for Member States to adopt legislation obliging employers to appoint an in-house confidential counsellor to deal with cases of sexual harassment.[509] Normally, formal proceedings should be commenced only after an unsuccessful informal approach to the alleged harasser has been made. This informal approach should make clear that particular behaviour is not welcome. Any investigations must be independent, objective, and handled with sensitivity, with due respect for the rights of both the complainant and the alleged harasser. Employers should monitor and review these procedures to ensure they are working effectively. Finally, the Code emphasizes that both trade unions and employees have a key role to play: trade unions by encouraging employers to develop policies on sexual harassment and advising their members of their rights not to be sexually harassed and supporting them when complaints arise; employees by

---

[508] Cf. s. 41 of the British Sex Discrimination Act 1975 where employers are liable for 'anything done by a person in the course of his employment . . . whether or not it was done with the employer's knowledge or approval' subject to the defence that the employer 'took such steps as were reasonably practicable to prevent the employee from doing that act'.

[509] B3–1735/91 [1994] OJ C61/246.

discouraging any form of reprehensible behaviour and making it clear that it is unacceptable.

G. OTHER AREAS OF DISCRIMINATION

1. Article 13

Perhaps one of the most significant changes introduced by the Treaty of Amsterdam in the field of social policy is the new non-discrimination legal basis found in Article 13 [ex Article 6a].[510] This provides:

Without prejudice to the other provisions of this Treaty and within the limits of the powers conferred by it on the Community, the Council, acting unanimously on a proposal from the Commission and after consulting the European Parliament, may take appropriate action to combat discrimination based on sex, racial or ethnic origin, religion or belief, disability, age or sexual orientation.[511]

A declaration adds that 'The conference agrees that, in drawing up measures under Article 100a [new Article 95], the institutions of the Community shall take account of the needs of persons with a disability'. The grounds listed in Article 13 on which discrimination is to be excluded are far-reaching (and more extensive than the list which appeared in an earlier version of the draft treaty). However, Presidential comments on an earlier draft of the text[512] indicate that Article 13 is merely an enabling measure, making it clear that action under this provision can only be taken within the sphere of Community competence, respecting the principles of subsidiarity and proportionality. The Presidential comments also indicate that the new Article 13 is not intended to have direct effect, although this will ultimately be a matter for the Court to decide.[513]

---

[510] See previously Recital 8 of the Community Social Charter 1989 does refer to the fact that 'in order to ensure equal treatment it is important to combat every form of discrimination, including discrimination on the grounds of sex, colour, race, opinions and beliefs, and, whereas, in the spirit of solidarity, it is important to combat social exclusion'.

[511] Only 'social origin' was lost from the original list proposed by the Irish Presidency, *The European Union Today and Tomorrow. Adapting the European Union for the Benefit of its Peoples and Preparing it for the Future. A General Outline for a Draft Revision of the Treaties*, Brussels, 5 Dec. 1996, CONF/2500/96. See Bell and Waddington, 'The 1996 Intergovernmental Conference and the Prospects of a Non-Discrimination Treaty Article' (1996) 25 *ILJ* 320; Bell, 'The New Article 13 EC Treaty: a Sound Basis for European Anti-discrimination Law?' (1999) 6 *Maastricht Journal of European and Comparative Law* 5; Waddington, 'Article 13 EC: Mere Rhetoric or a Harbinger of Change' (1999) 1 *CYELS* 175 and 'Testing the Limits of the EC Treaty Article on Non-discrimination' (1999) 28 *ILJ* 133; and Flynn, 'The Implications of Article 13 EC—After Amsterdam, will Some Forms of Discrimination be more Equal than Others?' (1999) 36 *CML-Rev.* 1127.

[512] CONF/3827/97.

[513] See generally Barnard, 'Article 13 through the Looking Glass of Citizenship', in *Legal Issues of the Amsterdam Treaty*, eds. O'Keeffe and Twomey (Hart, Oxford, 1999).

Article 13 has finally raised the profile of groups of citizens which had, hitherto, been largely overlooked and has given the Commission what it has long called for—the competence to act and a specific Treaty base on which to propose anti-discrimination legislation.[514] Further, its inclusion in the Treaty, unlike the origins of Article 141 [ex Article 119],[515] was not primarily prompted by the desire to combat discrimination for economic reasons or to complement the Single Market, but formed part of a trend 'reflected more in rhetoric than reality' to bring Europe 'closer to the citizens'.[516] The utility of Article 13 will depend in part on political commitment to achieving its goals. The requirement of unanimous voting in Council may impose a significant barrier to progress,[517] and the restricted role given to the European Parliament, through the use of the consultation procedure, has weakened an actor which has, in the past, pressurized the other institutions to take more ambitious steps to combat discrimination.[518]

The effectiveness of Article 13 will also depend on the meaning of the phrase 'Without prejudice to the other provisions of this Treaty and within the limits of the powers conferred by it on the Community'. The first limb of the phrase suggests that Article 13 will not apply where more specific legal bases are available (such as the new Article 141(3)).[519] The second limb may impose more of a restriction. The wording 'within the limits of the powers' contained in Article 13 can be compared to the wording of Article 12 [old Article 6] on non-discrimination on the grounds of nationality and the Dublin draft of what became Article 13. Both provide 'Within the scope of application of this Treaty'. The use of different wording in Article 13 and Article 12 tends to suggest that they bear different meanings and that the language of Article 13 is narrower than that of Article 12.[520] If this analysis is correct, this means that Article 13 may be relied on to prohibit discrimination only in

[514] See e.g. the Commission's White Paper on Social Policy, COM(94)333, Ch. VI, para. 27.

[515] See above nn. 7–9.

[516] Waddington, 'Article 13 EC: Mere Rhetoric or a Harbinger of Change' (1999) 1 *CYELS* 175 citing the Commission's Report of 10 May 1995 on the Operation of the Treaty on European Union which identifies as one of 'the major challenges for Europe . . . to make Europe the business of every citizen' included in *White Paper on the 1996 Intergovernmental Conference*, Vol. 1, Official Texts of the European Union Institutions (European Parliament, 1996).

[517] As Shaw notes ('European Union Citizenship: the IGC and Beyond' (1997) 3 *European Public Law* 413, 429), it becomes immediately apparent that Art. 13 was 'modelled on a relatively intergovernmental vision of Union legislative action'.

[518] See Waddington, above n. 516. E.g. only the Parliament has issued any soft law measures on sexual orientation (see e.g. Resolution by Parliament on equal rights for homosexuals and lesbians in the EC [1994] OJ C61/40, albeit that there is reference to sexual orientation in the Council Declaration on sexual harassment, above n. 505.

[519] This is significant for Art. 141(3) provides for the Art. 251 [ex Art. 189b] co-decision procedure, Art. 13 simple consultation and unanimous voting.

[520] Case C–152/82 *Forcheri v. Belgian State* [1983] ECR 2323 supports this view. At para. 13 the Court said that whereas 'educational and vocational training policy is not as such part of the areas which the Treaty has allotted to the *competence* of the Community institutions, the opportunity for such kinds of instruction falls within the *scope* of the Treaty' (emphasis added).

those areas in which the Community already has competence.[521] While it seems reasonably clear that the Community has competence to act in the field of work-related matters,[522] as narrowly construed,[523] the position in relation to education, particularly primary education, housing, and other services is far less clear. If any anti-discrimination legislation was confined to the more conventional area of employment issues, this would assist some but would continue to concentrate Community protection on 'market citizens' who are economically active,[524] rather than on those who may have a greater need for the rights but are excluded from protection.

The Commission has assuaged, and also confirmed, some of the concerns about the scope of Article 13 in its discrimination 'package' proposals. The 'package' consists of four instruments:

1. A Communication on certain Community measures to combat discrimination;[525]
2. A proposal for a directive to establish a general framework for equal treatment in employment and occupation (the 'horizontal' labour market Directive);[526]
3. A proposal for a directive to implement the principle of equal treatment between persons irrespective of racial or ethnic origin;[527]
4. A proposal for a decision to establish an Action Plan to combat discrimination 2001–6.[528]

The proposed horizontal Directive, which applies to all the groups identified in Article 13, including race and ethnic origin but excluding sex and nationality, concerns employment and occupation. The race Directive is, however, more ambitious and applies the principles of non-discrimination to:[529]

(a) the conditions for access to employment, to self-employment, and to occupation, including selection criteria and recruitment conditions, whatever the sector or branch of activity and at all levels of the professional hierarchy, including promotion;

---

[521] See Bell, above n. 511, and Whittle, 'Disability Discrimination and the Amsterdam Treaty' (1998) 23 *ELRev*. 50, 53.

[522] See e.g. Directive 76/207/EEC [1976] OJ L39/40.

[523] See e.g. Case 184/83 *Hofmann* [1984] ECR 3047, considered above, n. 70 and n. 292.

[524] See Everson, 'The Legacy of the Market Citizen' in *New Legal Dynamics of the European Union*, eds. Shaw and More (Clarendon, Oxford, 1995).

[525] COM(99)564.

[526] COM(99)565.

[527] COM(99)566. Now Council Directive 2000/43/EC [2000] OJ L180/22.

[528] COM(99)567.

[529] Art. 3(1). Art. 11(2) requires Member States to encourage the two sides of the industry to conclude at the appropriate level, including at undertaking level, agreements laying down anti-discrimination rules in these fields which fall within the scope of collective bargaining. These agreements must respect the minimum requirements laid down by this Directive and the relevant national implementing measures.

(b) access to all types and to all levels of vocational guidance, vocational training, advanced vocational training, and retraining including practical work experience;

(c) employment and working conditions, including dismissals and pay;

(d) membership of and involvement in an organization of workers or employers, or any other organization whose members carry on a particular profession, including the benefits provided for by such organizations;

(e) social protection including social security and healthcare;

(f) social advantages;[530]

(g) education;

(h) access to and supply of goods and services which are available to the public, including housing.

The European Parliament had already argued that the Directive should cover 'the fields of employment, education, health care, social security, housing and public and private services'.[531] The Commission justified the broad material scope of the Directive in order 'to make a serious contribution to curbing racism and xenophobia in Europe'.[532] It argues that 'participation in economic life is often a pre-requisite for successful social integration more widely'.[533] It says that 'Equally, social protection systems play a fundamental role in ensuring social cohesion, and in maintaining political stability and economic progress across the Union'.[534] It also recognizes that 'discrimination in access to benefits and other forms of support from the social protection system contributes to and compounds the marginalization of individuals from ethnic minority and immigrant backgrounds'.[535] It says that the same is true of social advantages 'which are often discretionary, with a character or purpose similar to social protection'.[536] It continues that high quality education is a prerequisite for successful integration into society and that discrimination in access to goods and services also limits social and economic integration, especially in access to finance, but also more widely.

---

[530] See further Ch. 3.

[531] Resolution of 29 Jan. 1998 [1998] OJ C56/35.

[532] COM(99)566, 5. The Directive does not apply to difference of treatment based on nationality and is without prejudice to provisions and conditions relating to entry and residence of TCNs and to any treatment which arises from the legal status of TCNs and stateless persons.

[533] Ibid.

[534] Ibid.

[535] Ibid.

[536] Ibid.

2. Discrimination on the Grounds of Race and Ethnic Minority

The European Council[537] and Council, Commission,[538] and Parliament[539] have long been concerned about racism and xenophobia but, in the absence of an express legal basis until now, have doubted the Community's competence to act. The Community institutions therefore limited their activities to issuing non-legally-binding declarations and resolutions.[540] For example, the Joint Declaration on Racism and Xenophobia of 11 June 1986[541] obliged the institutions, and also the individual Member States to take appropriate measures to combat all forms of intolerance, hostility, and use of force against people on the grounds of their racial, religious, cultural, social, or national differences. The Council Resolution on the Fight Against Racism and Xenophobia of 29 May 1990[542] encouraged Member States to take action including ratifying international conventions on racism, enacting national laws restraining discriminatory acts, and providing recourse to the legal system, and developing an effective policy of education[543] and information. This resolution received much criticism because references to protection for third country nationals were dropped.[544] However, the Declaration of the European Council on Racism and Xenophobia attached to the Treaty on European

---

[537] See e.g. Conclusions of Meetings of the European Council in Cannes in June 1995, Madrid in Dec. 1995, Florence in June 1996, and Dublin in Dec. 1996.

[538] See also COM(94)333, 52, and COM(98)183 An Action Plan against Racism.

[539] See also the Parliament's resolutions of 27 Oct. 1994 [1995] OJ C126/75, and 27 Apr. 1995 [1995] OJ C126/75.

[540] For a full list see Annex II of the Commission's Communication on certain Community measures to combat discrimination (COM(99)564). See also Gearty, 'The Internal and External "Other" in the Union Legal Order: Racism, Religious Intolerance and Xenophobia in Europe', in *The EU and Human Rights*, ed. Alston (OUP, Oxford, 1999) and Hervey, 'Putting Europe's House in Order: Racism, Race Discrimination and Xenophobia after the Treaty of Amsterdam', in *Legal Issues of the Amsterdam Treaty*, eds. O'Keeffe and Twomey (Hart, Oxford, 1999). Some anti-racist provisions have been included in legally binding instruments. For example, Art. 12 of Directive 89/552 [1989] OJ L298/23 provides that television advertising must not include any discrimination on grounds of race, sex, or nationality nor offend any religious or political beliefs and Art. 22 provides that Member States shall ensure that broadcasts do not contain any incitement to racial hatred on the grounds of race, sex, religion, or nationality. See also the Commission's Communication on racism, xenophobia, and anti-semitism (COM(95)653 final) where the Commission promised to propose the insertion of anti-discrimination clauses in new legislation.

[541] [1986] OJ C176/162. This Declaration was prompted in part by the European Parliament's Committee of Inquiry's Report into Racism and Xenophobia (The Evrigenis Report PE 97.547). See also the European Parliament's Committee of Inquiry on Racism and Xenophobia (the Ford Report) (OPEC, Luxembourg, 1991); Commission, *Moyens Juridiques Pour Combattre le Racisme et la Xénophobie*, 1993 (OPEC, Luxembourg, 1993) and The European Parliament's *Resolution on the Resurgence of Racism and Xenophobia in Europe and the Danger of Right-wing Extremist Violence* [1993] OJ C150/127.

[542] [1990] OJ C157/4.

[543] See also the Resolution of the Council and the representatives of Member States' governments of 23 Oct. 1995 on the response of educational systems to the problems of racism and xenophobia [1995] OJ C312/1.

[544] The Commission refused to associate itself with the Resolution and withdrew.

Union did include reference to the need to strengthen legal protection for third country immigrants and again endorsed the importance of the fight against discrimination in all its forms. The 1995 Resolution on the fight against racism and xenophobia, in the fields of employment and social affairs produced by the Council and the representatives of the Member States' governments[545] condemned racism, xenophobia, and anti-semitism, flagrant breaches of individual rights, and religious intolerance, particularly in the fields of employment and social affairs. It also recognized the great importance of implementing, in the field of social policy, policies based on the principles of non-discrimination and equal opportunities at Union and Member State level.[546] As a result, 1997 was designated European Year against Racism and a European Monitoring Centre on racism and xenophobia was set up.[547]

The Commission's proposal for a Directive implementing the principle of equal treatment between persons irrespective of racial or ethnic origin was introduced against this background. In its explanatory memorandum[548] the Commission says:

Europe's experiences of wars and conflicts throughout the 20th century—and even at its close—have brought to the fore the dangers of racism and the dramatic attacks on human dignity that have ensued. Yet, at the end of the century, racial discrimination is still not eradicated from everyday life in Europe.

It is widely acknowledged that legal measures are of paramount importance for combating racism and intolerance. The law not only protects victims and gives them a remedy, but also demonstrates society's firm opposition to racism and the genuine commitment of the authorities to curb discrimination. The enforcement of anti-racist laws can have a significant effect on the shaping of attitudes.

The Directive lays down 'broad objectives to ensure that discrimination is prohibited and that the victims of discrimination enjoy a basic minimum entitlement to redress'. In doing so the Directive will reinforce the 'fundamental values on which the Union in founded—liberty, democracy, the respect for human rights and fundamental freedoms and the rule of law—and contribute to the development of the Union as an area of freedom, security and justice. And it will help to strengthen economic and social cohesion'.[549]

The Directive implements the principle of equal treatment by prohibiting both direct and indirect discrimination based on racial or ethnic origin (but not nationality).[550] While racial and ethnic origin are not defined,[551] the

---

[545] Resolution 95/110 of 5 Oct. 1995 [1995] OJ C296/13.

[546] See also third pillar measures such as Joint Action 96/443/JHA [1996] OJ L185/5 concerning action to combat racism and xenophobia, discussed further in Ch. 3.

[547] Council Regulation 1035/97 [1997] OJ L151/2.

[548] COM(99)566, 2.

[549] COM(99)566, 4.

[550] According to the Commission, this is covered by Arts. 12 and 39 and the secondary legislation discussed further in Ch. 3.

[551] Cf. the decision of the House of Lords in the UK in *Mandla v. Lee* [1983] IRLR 209.

definitions of direct and indirect discrimination are intended to mirror those found in the context of sex equality.[552] Direct discrimination 'shall be taken to occur where one person is treated less favourably than another is, has been or would be treated in a comparable situation on grounds of racial or ethnic origin'. Indirect discrimination, by contrast, shall be taken to occur 'where an apparently neutral provision, criterion or practice would put persons of a racial or ethnic origin at a particular disadvantage compared with other persons, unless that provision, criterion or practice is objectively justified by a legitimate aim and the means of achieving that aim are appropriate and necessary'.[553] The Directive extends the principles contained in Articles 3 and 4 of the Burden of Proof Directive 97/80/EC[554] to race. Thus, 'when persons who consider themselves wronged because the principle of equal treatment has not been applied to them establish, before a court or other competent authority, facts from which it may be presumed that there has been direct or indirect discrimination, it shall be for the respondent to prove that there has been no breach of the principle of equal treatment'.[555]

Following the sex discrimination model, direct discrimination on the grounds of race or ethnic origin can be saved only by reference to an express defence, described in the Directive originally using the British terminology as a 'Genuine Occupational Qualification' (GOQ) and now described as a 'Genuine and determining occupational requirement'. Article 4 provides that 'Member States may provide that a difference of treatment which is based on a characteristic related to racial or ethnic origin shall not constitute discrimination where, by reason of the nature of the particular occupational activities concerned or of the context in which they are carried out, such a characteristic constitutes a genuine and determining occupational requirement, provided that the objective is legitimate and the requirement is proportionate'. The Commission noted that examples of such differences might, for example, be found where a person of a particular racial or ethnic origin is required for reasons of authenticity in a dramatic performance or where the holder of a particular job provides persons of a particular ethnic group with personal services promoting their welfare and those services can most effectively be provided by a person of that ethnic group. The Commission does, however, note that these GOQ situations will be highly exceptional. In addition, positive action is permitted. Following the wording of Article 141(4),[556] Article 5 provides that 'With a view to ensuring full equality in practice,

---

[552] Art. 2.

[553] Art. 2(2)(b), drawing on Case C–237/94 *O'Flynn v. Adjudication Officer* [1996] ECR I–2617, para. 18. The surprising feature of this definition is the emphasis on the effect on the individual rather than its impact on the group.

[554] [1998] OJ L14/16, amended by Council Directive 98/52 [1998] OJ L205/66.

[555] Art. 8(1).

[556] See above, text attached to n. 336.

the principle of equal treatment shall not prevent any member state from maintaining or adopting specific measures to prevent or compensate for disadvantages related to racial or ethnic origin'. Indirect discrimination can be objectively justified to which the *Bilka-Kaufhaus*[557] test is applied.

The Directive also introduces the innovation that 'Harassment shall be deemed to be discrimination' when an 'unwanted conduct unrelated to racial or ethnic origin takes place with the purpose or effect of violating the dignity of a person and of creating an intimidating, hostile, degrading, humiliating or offensive environment'. This provision circumvents the weakness identified above[558] with the existing Harassment Code of Conduct and attaches the force of the remedial provisions in the Directive to the anti-harassment provision.

The remedies provisions are found in Chapter II. They envisage two rights: the right of victims to a personal remedy against the discriminator (Article 7) as well as the duty on each Member State to lay down rules on penalties for breach of the Directive (Article 15). As far as the first right is concerned, Member States must ensure that 'judicial and/or administrative procedures, including where they deem it appropriate conciliation procedures, for the enforcement of obligations under this Directive are available to all persons who consider themselves wronged by failure to apply the principle of equal treatment to them, even after the relationship in which the discrimination is alleged to have occurred has ended' (Article 7(1)). While this reflects Article 6 of Directive 76/207,[559] a new requirement has been added by Article 7(2), obliging the Member States to ensure that 'associations, organisations or other legal entities, which have in accordance with the criteria laid down by their national law, a legitimate interest in ensuring that the provisions of this Directive are complied with, may engage, either on behalf or in support of the complainant, with his or her approval, in any judicial and/or administrative procedure provided for the enforcement of obligations under this Directive'.[559A] National time limits will apply (Article 7(3)).

To reinforce the effective legal protection the proposal contains a provision on victimization. Article 9 provides that 'Member States shall introduce in to their national legal systems such measures as are necessary to protect individuals from any adverse treatment or adverse consequence as a reaction to a complaint or to proceedings aimed at enforcing compliance with the principle of equal treatment'. In addition, as with the Burden of Proof Directive, Member States are obliged to ensure that adequate information on the provisions adopted pursuant to this Directive is brought to the attention of relevant persons by all appropriate means (Article 10). Member States must also

---

[557] Case 170/84 [1986] ECR 1607.

[558] Art. 2(3). See above, text attached to nn. 503–508.

[559] See above, nn. 395–405.

[559A] Provision is also made for Member States to encourage dialogue with appropriate NGOs (Art. 12).

ensure, following the model of Articles 3, 4, and 5 of Directive 76/207, the elimination of discrimination from any legal or administrative provisions, as well as from collective agreements or individual contracts of employment, rules of profit-making and non-profit-making associations and workers' and employers' associations (Article 14).

Article 11 requires the Member States to take 'adequate measures to promote the social dialogue between the two sides of industry with a view to fostering equal treatment, including through the monitoring of workplace practices, collective agreements, codes of conduct, research or exchange of experiences and good practices'. The European Social Partners have already concluded a Joint Declaration on Racism and Xenophobia in the Workplace adopted in Florence in 1995 and, at national level in certain states, have adopted framework agreements and codes of conduct on combating racial and ethnic discrimination in companies.

Perhaps the most striking feature of the race proposal is the obligation contained in Article 13 for Member States to 'designate a body or bodies for the promotion of equal treatment of all persons without discrimination on the grounds of racial or ethnic origin. These bodies may form part of agencies charged at national level with the defence of human rights or the safeguard of individuals' rights.' Not only must an agency be set up but, following the model of the British Commission for Racial Equality, these bodies must have among their functions: providing independent assistance to victims of discrimination in pursuing complaints about discrimination on grounds of racial or ethnic origin; conducting independent surveys concerning discrimination based on racial or ethnic origin; and publishing independent reports and making recommendations on issues relating to discrimination based on racial or ethnic origin. The Commission is now proposing the establishment of a similar body to promote equal treatment for men and women.[560A]

3. Discrimination on Other Grounds

The Community had begun to address the needs of some of the other groups identified in Article 13 through soft law measures. In the case of older people the Community Social Charter 1989 provided that 'every worker of the European Community must, at the time of retirement, be able to enjoy resources affording him or her a decent standard of living'. It adds that any person who has reached retirement age but who is not entitled to a pension must be entitled to sufficient resources and to medical and social assistance specifically suited to his needs. The Commission issued a Communication on the

---

[560A] Com (2000) 334 final.

elderly[560] and drafted an Action Programme providing for pilot projects, exchanges of experience, and improved information between groups representing the elderly. In a similar vein, the Council issued a Decision[561] on Community Action for the elderly which included designating 1993 as the European Year of the Elderly and of Solidarity between Generations.[562] This year was intended to raise awareness of the challenges resulting from an ageing population and the changes required to help the elderly identify with the process of Community integration. In addition the Council and Representatives of the governments of the Member States adopted a Resolution on the employment of older workers[563] based on the principle that increased efforts are needed to adjust the conditions in which workers in the latter part of their working lives work and are vocationally trained and that older workers must benefit from adequate resources and from measures to prevent their exclusion from the labour market.

As far as people with disabilities are concerned, the Commission has said that their social and economic integration is an important element of the social dimension of the Single Market.[564] According to Commission figures, more than 37 million Community nationals (10 per cent) are suffering from long-term physical or mental disabilities of varying degrees and they represent one of the most disadvantaged sections of the population.[565] The Community Social Charter 1989 therefore provided that all disabled persons, whatever the origin and nature of their disablement, must be entitled to additional concrete measures aimed at improving their social and professional integration. These measures must concern vocational training,[566] ergonomics, accessibility, mobility, means of transport,[567] and housing.

[560] Council Recommendation of 10 Dec. 1982 on the principles of a Community policy with regard to retirement age [1982] OJ L357/27 and Sergeant, *Age Discrimination in Employment* (IER, London, 1999).

[561] Council Decision 91/49/EEC [1991] OJ L28. See also Commission Decision 91/544/EEC on the Liaison Group on the Elderly [1991] OJ L296/42, amended most recently by Decision 99/141/EC [1999] OJ L45/54.

[562] Council Decision 92/440/EEC [1992] OJ L245. See now COM(99)221 final: 'Towards a Europe for all ages—promoting prosperity and intergenerational solidarity'.

[563] Resolution of the Council and of the Representatives of the Governments of the Member States meeting within the Council on the employment of older workers [1995] OJ C228/1. See also the Resolution of the European Parliament of 24 Feb. 1994 on measures for the elderly in the EC [1994] OJ C77/24.

[564] See esp. the three Helios programmes, most recently the Third Helios Programme, and the TIDE (technology initiative for disabled and elderly people). For earlier initiatives see Council Resolution of 21 Jan. 1974 [1994] OJ C13/1; and Council Resolution of 21 Dec. 1981 on the Social Integration of the Handicapped [1981] OJ C347/1.

[565] See Commission Communication on equality of opportunity for people with disabilities: a new European Community Disability strategy (COM(96)406 final).

[566] See also Resolution 90/703 of the Council and Ministers for Education Meeting with the Council of 31 May 1990, concerning the integration of children and young people with disabilities into ordinary systems of education [1990] OJ C162/2.

[567] See e.g. the proposal for a Council Directive on Transport for Workers with Reduced Mobility designed to improve disabled workers' mobility and to provide them with safe transport to work, COM(90)588 [1992] OJ C15/21.

The Council has also adopted a Recommendation on the Employment of Disabled People in the Community.[568] The Preamble contains the assertion that 'disabled people have the same right as all other workers to *equal* opportunity in training and employment'. The text of the Recommendation then talks in terms of '*fair* opportunities for disabled people'.[569] The Recommendation provides that Member States should establish policies designed, first, to eliminate negative discrimination by, for example, reviewing laws and regulations to ensure that they are not contrary to the principle of fair opportunity, and taking measures to avoid dismissals linked to disability; and secondly, to encourage 'positive action' for disabled people. This second head of policy describes positive action as the fixing by Member States, where appropriate and after consultation, 'of realistic percentage *targets* for the employment of disabled people in public or private enterprises having a minimum number of employees'.[570] This is very similar to the definition of positive *discrimination* which the Commission and some of the Member States will not countenance in the context of sex equality.[571] The Annex to the Recommendation contains guidelines for positive action to promote the employment and vocational training of disabled people, including policies relating to sheltered employment, vocational rehabilitation and training, and providing incentives to employers to assist with the special costs incurred to an employer of employing a disabled worker.[572] More recently, a Council Resolution on equal employment opportunities for people with disabilities has been adopted.[573] The Resolution reflects the shift from a welfare approach to a human rights-based approach focusing on prevention and removal of barriers that deny equality of access to people with disabilities to, *inter alia*, the labour market.[574] The Resolution underlines that disability employment policies should be strengthened within the National Action Plans; [575] that full use should be made of the European Structural funds, in particular the Social Fund, to promote equal employment opportunities; and that the Commission and the Member States should promote the principle of mainstreaming.[576]

The most significant step to protect other groups of people (with the exception of sex) from discrimination comes with the Commission's proposals for a 'horizontal' anti-discrimination Directive under Article 13. The proposal for a

---

[568] Council Recommendation 86/379/EEC of 24 July 1986 [1986] OJ L225/43.

[569] Art. 1.

[570] Art. 2(b). The minimum *might* be set at between 15 and 50.

[571] See text attached to nn. 336–337, above.

[572] Considerable help has been given from the European Social Fund.

[573] Council Resolution 99/702 [1999] OJ C186/3. See also the Resolution of the Council and Representatives of the governments meeting within Council of 20 Dec. 1996 on equality of opportunity for people with disabilities [1997] OJ C12/1.

[574] COM(99)565, 4.

[575] See further Ch. 9

[576] See also DGV, 'Mainstreaming Disability within EU Employment and Social Policy', http://europa.eu.int/comm/dg05/soc-prot/disable/dresden/workpaper_en.pdf.

Council Directive establishing a general framework for equal treatment in employment and occupation[577] applies to all 'persons irrespective of racial or ethnic origin, religion or belief, disability, age or sexual orientation' (Article 1). None of these categories is defined.

The material scope of the Directive is significantly narrower than the proposed race Directive. According to Article 3, the principle of equal treatment applies only to employment issues, namely:

(a) conditions for access to employment, self-employment, and occupation, including selection criteria and recruitment conditions, whatever the sector or branch of activity and at all levels of the professional hierarchy, including promotion;
(b) access to all types and to all levels of vocational guidance, vocational training, advanced vocational training, and retraining;
(c) employment and working conditions, including dismissals and pay;[578]
(d) membership of and involvement in an organization of workers or employers, or any other organization whose members carry on a particular profession, as well as the benefits provided for by such organizations.

The principle of equal treatment is defined in much the same way as for the Race Directive. Both direct and indirect discrimination are prohibited and harassment on any one of the grounds is deemed to be discrimination (Article 2(1)–(3)). Member States may also permit positive action (Article 6). In addition, in the case of people with a disability, employers are required to make 'reasonable accommodation' to enable such people 'to have access to, participate in, or advance in employment, unless this requirement creates an undue hardship'.[579] This is a core element of the new human rights-based approach to the elimination of discrimination against people with a disability on the labour market and a key feature of recent national legislation.

As with race, GOQs are available to justify directly discriminatory conduct and positive action is available,[580] but the list of derogations from this Directive is longer than in the race proposal. First, according to Article 4(1), Member States may allow for derogations based on a characteristic related to any of the discriminatory grounds where such a characteristic constitutes a GOQ. Secondly, special provision is made for '*entreprises de tendences*', organizations which promote certain religious values where the jobs need to be performed by employees who share the relevant religious opinion. Therefore,

---

[577] COM(99)565. See now 2000/C 177 E/07 [2000] OJ C 177 E/42.

[578] The Commission argues that the exclusion of Community competence in respect of pay by Art. 137(6) applies only to directives adopted under Art. 137 and does not apply to Community action under Art. 13: COM(99)565, 10.

[579] Art. 2(4). This would supplement the employer's obligation to adapt the workplace to disabled workers required by the Framework Directive 89/391 on health and safety [1989] OJ L183/1, considered further in Ch. 6.

[580] Art. 4.

Article 4(2) says that Member States may provide that, 'in the case of public or private organisations which pursue directly and essentially the aim of ideological guidance in the field of religion or belief with respect to education, information and the expression of opinions, and for the particular occupational activities within these organizations which are directly and essentially related to this aim, a difference of treatment based on a relevant characteristic related to religion or belief shall not constitute discrimination where, by reason of the nature of these activities, the characteristic constitutes a genuine occupational qualification'. Thirdly, special provision is made for age discrimination. Article 5 provides that the 'following differences of treatment, in particular, shall not constitute direct discrimination on grounds of age, *if they are objectively and reasonably justified by a legitimate aim and are appropriate and necessary* to the achievement of that aim' (emphasis added):

(a) the prohibition on access to employment or the provision of special working conditions to ensure the protection of young people and older workers;
(b) the fixing of a minimum age as a condition of eligibility for retirement or invalidity benefits;
(c) the fixing of different ages for employees or groups or categories of employees for entitlement to retirement or invalidity benefits on grounds of physical or mental occupational requirements;
(d) the fixing of a maximum age for recruitment which is based on the training requirements of the post in question or the need for a reasonable period of employment before retirement;
(e) the establishment of requirements concerning the length of professional experience;
(f) the establishment of age limits which are appropriate and necessary for the pursuit of legitimate labour market objectives.

The remedies provisions also mirror those in the race Directive: individuals or associations acting for them should have access to the judicial process (Article 8); the Burden of Proof Directive applies (Article 9); there is protection against victimization (Article 10); States are under an obligation to disseminate information (Article 11); and States should encourage the social dialogue to foster equal treatment (Article 12). States are, however, under no obligation to set up an independent agency to promote and enforce these rights.

The two proposed Directives are supported by an action programme[581] based on the premise that legislation alone is not enough to change attitudes. Given that, in the Commission's view, the 'added value' of a Community programme lies in 'the improving of knowledge, the strengthening of the capacity of actors and the raising of awareness',[582] the Action Programme is intended to:

---

[581] COM(99)567.   [582] Ibid., para. 7.

- improve the understanding of issues related to discrimination through improved knowledge and measurement and through the evaluation of the effectiveness of policies and practice;
- develop the capacity of 'target actors' (Member States, local and regional authorities, independent bodies responsible for the fight against discrimination, the Social Partners, and NGOs) to address discrimination effectively, in particular through support for the exchange of information and good practice and networking at European level;
- promote and disseminate the values and practices underlying the fight against discrimination.

To meet these objectives the Action Programme divides its activities into three strands: first, analysis of factors related to discrimination, collection of statistics, benchmarking, and evaluation; secondly, transnational co-operation between target actors and the promotion of networking at European level between NGOs concerned with discrimination; and, thirdly, awareness raising, in particular to emphasize the European dimension of the fight against discrimination and to publicize the results of the programme. These three strands are intended to underpin the legislation by facilitating 'changes in practices and attitudes and the mobilisation of all the actors concerned'.[583] In particular, they aim at enabling people to 'learn from the successes and failures of others and to build those lessons into their own actions to tackle discrimination at local level'.[584]

The discrimination 'package' is complemented by the Community's activities in other fields, especially in respect of employment. Not only do the Employment Guidelines[585] commit Member States to make the fight against discrimination against women a priority for all their actions in the labour market but they also require States to give special attention to the needs of the disabled, ethnic minorities, and other groups and individuals who may be disadvantaged in the labour market, including by discrimination.[586] This, as the discrimination package recognizes, is particularly important where certain groups suffer from double and treble discrimination: one of the consequences of the 20 per cent gap in the employment of men and women is that women are over-represented among the unemployed ethnic and religious minorities, among disabled people and the elderly.[587]

---

[583] Ibid., 2.

[584] COM(99)564, 7 and COM(99)567, 2.

[585] See above, n. 49–50.

[586] See esp. the EQUAL programme dealing with 'transnational cooperation to promote new means of combating all forms of discrimination and inequalities in connection with the labour market'. The Community Action Programme to combat discrimination (COM(99)567) will concentrate on areas where EQUAL does not provide support.

[587] COM(99)565, para. 3.1.2; Vousden, 'Gender Exclusion and Governance by Guideline' (1998) 4 *JSWFL* 468; and Mazey, 'EC Action on Behalf of Women: the Limits of Legislation' (1998) 27 *JCMS* 63.

The European Commission sees the discrimination package as an important pillar in the creation of 'civil society'[588] where, at the level of economic activity, all citizens have an occupation,[589] but also at the political level where interest groups play an

essential part as intermediaries in the exchange of information and opinion between governments and citizens, providing citizens with the means with which they may critically examine government action or proposals, and public authorities in their turn with expert advice, guidance on popular views, and essential feedback on the effects of their policies.[590]

In this way 'voluntary organisations and foundations make a profound and indispensable contribution to the democratic life of Europe'.[591] There are many hurdles to be overcome before the Commission's vision is realized, especially the principles of subsidiarity and proportionality and the unanimous vote in Council, but the Commission is sending a strong message that equality is the cornerstone of citizenship.

[588] See COM(99)567, para. 1, and COM(99)566, 2.

[589] Aron, 'Classe sociale, classe politique, classe dirigeante', in *Sociologie Politique*, eds. Birnbaum and Chauzel (1971), 134, cited in Decaux, 'Human Rights and Civil Society', in *The EU and Human Rights*, ed. Alston (OUP, Oxford, 1999), 903.

[590] COM(98)241 final, para. 9.1.

[591] Ibid.

5

Social Security and Pensions

The EU does not have a comprehensive package of social security legislation intended to harmonize the diverse national legislation. Instead, the legislative measures that do exist are piecemeal and are intended to address specific issues. On the one hand, Regulation 1408/71[1] is intended to encourage the *co-ordination* of national social security schemes to ensure that those wishing to exercise their rights of free movement do not suffer detriment in terms of their social security benefits. There is some overlap between the provisions of this Regulation and Article 7(2) of Regulation 1612/68[2] which requires that migrant workers and their families enjoy the same social and tax advantages as nationals. On the other hand, Directive 79/7[3] on equal treatment in State social security is intended to complement the two sex equality Directives, Directive 75/117 on equal pay[4] and Directive 76/207 on equal treatment.[5] In addition, Directive 86/378/EEC[6] was adopted to ensure equal treatment in respect of *occupational* social security. The contents of this Directive were largely superseded by the Court's case law on sex equality in respect of occupational pensions and survivors' benefits under Article 141 [ex Article 119] and was subsequently amended. This chapter therefore considers the two main social security measures, Regulation 1408/71 and Directive 79/7 as well as various soft law measures designed to assist in the process of convergence. It also examines the Court's case law on retirement and pensions which demonstrates the complex interplay between Article 141, Directive 79/7, Directive 86/378, and Directive 76/207.

A. REGULATION 1408/71 ON SOCIAL SECURITY

It was argued in Chapter 3 that the Community has taken extensive steps to ensure that the mobility of workers is not hindered in any way. One of the

---

[1] [1971] JO L149/2.
[2] [1968] OJ Spec. Ed. L257/2. Considered further in Ch. 3.
[3] [1979] OJ L6/24.
[4] [1975] OJ L45/19.
[5] [1976] OJ L39/40. In addition, Directive 92/85/EEC [1992] OJ L348/1 makes specific provision for entitlement to maternity leave and maternity benefits. These three Directives are considered in Ch. 4.
[6] [1986] OJ L225/40 as amended by Council Directive 96/97 [1997] OJ L46/20.

biggest potential barriers to freedom of movement is the absence of a common European Community-wide social security system—so long as each Member State continues to regulate its own social security the risk remains that workers leaving one State may lose their entitlement to any benefits which have accrued while they worked in that State when they enter another State.

To overcome such problems Article 42 [ex Article 51 as amended] provides:

The Council shall, acting in accordance with the procedure referred to in Article 251, adopt such measures in the field of social security as are necessary to provide freedom of movement for workers; to this end it shall make arrangements to secure for migrant workers and their dependants:

(a) aggregation, for the purpose of acquiring and retaining the right to benefit and of calculating the amount of benefit, of all periods taken into account under the laws of the several countries; [the aggregation principle]

(b) payment of benefits to persons resident in the territories of Member States. [the exportability principle]

The Council shall act unanimously throughout the procedure referred to in Article 251.[7]

Enacting such legislation was clearly seen as a priority: Regulations 3/58[8] and 4/58[9] came into force on 1 January 1959. These were revised and replaced on 1 October 1972 by Regulations 1408/71[10] and 574/72[11] containing substantive and procedural provisions respectively. These Regulations, in turn, have been substantially and regularly amended. The most important

---

[7] CONFER 4708/00 proposes a shift to qualified majority voting because the matter is closely linked to the achievement of the internal market; that measures adopted on the basis of Art. 42 have to be adopted frequently which is made more difficult by the unanimity rule; and the use of the unanimity procedure during the co-decision procedure is illogical. See also Art. 144 [ex Art. 121] which allows the Council, acting unanimously (CONFER 4708/00 suggests qualified majority voting), after consulting the ECOSOC, to assign to the Commission tasks in connection with the implementation of common measures, 'particularly as regards social security for the migrant workers referred to in Articles 39 to 42'.

[8] [1958] JO 561.

[9] [1958] JO 597.

[10] On the question of the overlap between the two Regulations see Case 32/76 *Alfonsa Saieva* v. *Caisse allocations familiales* [1976] ECR 1523, para. 15, where the Court ruled that benefits awarded under Regulation No. 3 which are more favourable than those payable under the new Regulation 1408/71 must not be reduced.

[11] [1971] JO L149/2 and [1972] JO L74/1, respectively. There is a version codified by Regulation (EEC) 2001/83 [1983] OJ L230/6. The Regulation has been reissued in a consolidated form as an annex to Regulation 118/97 [1997] OJ L28/1. This includes all amendments up to and including Regulation 7290/97 and replaces the consolidation which appeared in [1992] OJ C325/1. See also European Commission, *Your Social Security Rights when Moving within the European Union. A Practical Guide* (OPEC, Luxembourg, 1997). There is also a proposal pending to extend Regulation 1408/71 to third country nationals [1998] OJ C6/15 as well as a general proposal to recast the social security rules [1999] OJ C38/10.

amendment was contained in Regulation 1390/81[12] which extended the scope of Regulation 1408/71 to the self-employed. These two Regulations are vast and complex and it is beyond the scope of this book to provide a detailed analysis of each substantive provision.[13] Instead, this section is intended to offer an overview of the personal scope of Regulation 1408/71, the type of benefits it covers, especially as they affect workers who are moving between States. In particular, it focuses on the principles underpinning the Community approach to social security. The Court interprets questions referred to it[14] in the light of these principles, read in conjunction with the guidance provided by the Preamble to the Regulation,[15] and it is to these principles which we now turn.

1. The Principles of Co-ordination

Given the very different nature of the social security systems in the Member States of the EU (and the EEA), the different priorities in terms of national spending and the highly complex and technical nature of national social security law, no attempt has been made to *harmonize* social security law at Community level.[16] Instead the EU has, from its foundation, focused on the *co-ordination* of the diverse national legislation:[17] the national legislative systems remain distinct. The Court emphasized this in *Pinna*:[18]

Article 51 [new Article 42] of the Treaty provides for the co-ordination, not the harmonisation, of the legislation of the Member States. As a result, Article 51 leaves in being differences between the Member States' social security systems and, consequently, in the rights of persons working in the Member States. It follows that

---

[12] [1981] OJ L143/1. It does not apply to periods prior to 1 July 1982.

[13] For a more detailed analysis, see Watson, *Social Security Law in the European Communities* (Mansell, London, 1980); White, *EC Social Security Law* (Longman, Harlow, 1999); Hervey, *European Social Law and Policy* (Longman, Harlow, 1999); Luckhaus, 'European Social Security Law', in *The Law of Social Security*, eds. Ogus and Wikeley (Butterworths, London, 1995). See also Watson, 'Social Security for Migrants', in *European Community Law*, eds. Wyatt and Dashwood (3rd edn, Sweet and Maxwell, London, 1993).

[14] For a survey of the ECJ's case law on social security see reviews by: Knorpel (1981) 18 *CMLRev.* 579, (1982) 19 *CMLRev.* 105, (1983) 20 *CMLRev.* 97, (1984) 21 *CMLRev.* 241, (1985) 22 *CMLRev.* 43, (1986) 23 *CMLRev.* 359; Morgan (1987) 24 *CMLRev.* 483, (1988) 25 *CMLRev.* 391; Monroe (1990) 27 *CMLRev.* 547; Eichenhofer (1993) 30 *CMLRev.* 1021; Moore, 'Freedom of Movement and Migrant Workers' Social Security' (1998) 35 *CMLRev.* 409–57.

[15] See e.g. Case 63/76 *Inzirillo v. Caisse d'allocations familiales de l'arrondissement de Lyon* [1976] ECR 2057.

[16] On the question of harmonization, see van Langendonck, 'Social Security Legislation in the EEC' (1973) 2 *ILJ* 17, 23–7.

[17] Cf. Art. 137(3) [ex Art. 2(3) SPA] gives the Community the power to issue minimum standards Directives on 'social security and social protection of workers'. This new Treaty base is not qualified by the need that the Directives relate to co-ordination only, although the requirement of unanimous voting will limit its utility.

[18] Case 41/84 *Pinna v. Caisse d'allocations familiales de la Savoie* [1986] ECR 1, 24–5.

substantive and procedural differences between the social security systems of individual Member States, and hence in the rights of persons working in the Member States, are unaffected by Article 51 of the Treaty.

Therefore, individual Member States remain responsible for determining the detailed rules concerning the right or duty to be insured[19] as well as the financing of the schemes,[20] the conditions for affiliation,[21] and entitlement to benefits, and the actual level and scheme of benefits.[22] However, any features of those systems which have adverse effects on workers crossing national frontiers must be rectified.[23] This can be seen in *Terhoeve*[24] where the Court ruled that national legislation requiring an employed person working in another Member State to pay higher social security contributions than if he continued to reside in the same Member State constituted an obstacle to the free movement of workers contrary to Article 48 [new Article 39]. The Court added that such a heavier contributions burden could not be justified either by the fact that it stemmed from legislation whose objective was to simplify and co-ordinate the levying of income tax and social security contributions or by difficulties of a technical nature preventing other methods of collection or by certain income tax advantages. Therefore, the individual was entitled to pay the same level of contributions payable by a worker who had continued to reside in the Member State.

Regulation 1408/71 is constructed on the basis of four co-ordinating principles: non-discrimination, the single State rule, aggregation, and exportability. These principles are designed to displace the *territorial* basis of social security rights, whereby entitlements are provided on condition that contributions have been made in that territory, and to substitute in its place a *personal* right. This ensures that rights follow the individual.[25] These principles, derived in part from the Preamble to the Regulation and from a

---

[19] Case C–120/95 *Decker* v. *Caisse de maladie des Employés Privés* [1998] ECR I–1831 and Case C–158/96 *Kohll* v. *Union des Caisses de maladie* [1998] ECR I–1931.

[20] See e.g. Case 238/82 *Duphar* v. *Netherlands State* [1984] ECR 523; Case C–70/95 *Sodemare* v. *Regione Lombardia* [1997] ECR I–3395.

[21] Joined Cases C–88, C–102 and C–103/95 *Martínez Losado* v. *INEM* [1997] ECR I–895.

[22] See e.g. Case 266/78 *Brunori* [1979] ECR 2705; Wyatt, 'Eligibility for National Social Security Schemes a Matter for National Law' (1981) 6 *ELRev.* 41; and Case 110/79 *Coonan* v. *Insurance Officer* [1980] ECR 1445. See Watson, 'Affiliation to a Social Security Scheme' (1980) 5 *ELRev.* 220, 'Scope of Community Regulations on Social Security: Discrimination between Men and Women'(1984) 9 *ELRev.* 428.

[23] See Case 100/63 *Van der Veen* v. *Bestuur der Sociale Verzekeringsbank* [1964] ECR 565, 574. This does not imply alteration of schemes but rather Regulation 1408/71, being directly applicable, operates by conferring additional rights which Member States will apply by virtue of the Regulation and not by changing their own schemes.

[24] Case C–18/95 *Terhoeve* v. *Inspecteur van de Belastingdienst Particulieren* [1999] ECR I–345.

[25] Luckhaus, 'The Role of the "Economic" and the "Social" in Social Security and Community Law', in *National and European Law on the Threshold to the Single Market*, ed. Weich (Peter Lang, Berlin, 1993).

purposive interpretation of Articles 48 to 51 EC [new Articles 39 to 42],[26] have, as their overriding goal, that migrant workers and their families should suffer no disadvantage as a result of moving within the Community—the so-called *Petroni*[27] principle, which is considered below.

1.1 Non-discrimination

The first and most important principle is equality of treatment or non-discrimination on the ground of nationality.[28] A further manifestation of the principle laid down by Article 12 [ex Article 7 EEC/Article 6 EC],[29] the principle of equality is spelt out specifically by Article 3(1) of Regulation 1408/71:

Subject to the special provisions of this Treaty, persons resident in the territory of one of the Member States to whom this Regulation applies shall be subject to the same obligations and enjoy the same benefits under the legislation of any Member State as the nationals of that State.

The principle of non-discrimination outlaws both direct discrimination (less favourable treatment on the grounds of nationality) and indirect discrimination (the application of a requirement or condition to all applicants which in fact disadvantages a greater number of migrants).[30] Both points are well illustrated by the case of *Toia*.[31] An Italian woman was denied a benefit paid by the French social security system to French women over 65 with insufficient means who had brought up five children of French nationality. The Court ruled that the French authorities were correct not to rely on the fact that the mother did not have French nationality in assessing her eligibility for the benefit since this would have constituted direct discrimination. However, it declared that the condition that the children must be French was indirectly discriminatory and breached Article 3 unless it could be justified by objective reasons on grounds other than nationality. This was not the case on the facts.[32]

It seems that the principle of non-discrimination in the context of social security, unlike the more general rules on the free movement of persons, also prevents reverse discrimination—that is discrimination by national authorities against their own nationals and in favour of migrants.[33] In *Kenny*[34] the Court ruled that:

---

[26] See e.g. Case 50/75 *Caisse de pension des Employées Privés v. Massonet* [1975] ECR 1473, para. 9.

[27] Case 24/75 *Petroni v. Office des Pensions pour Travailleurs Salariés* [1964] ECR 565, 574.

[28] See e.g. Case 1/78 *Kenny v. Insurance Officer* [1978] ECR 1489 and Case 110/79 *Coonan* [1980] ECR 1445.

[29] See further Ch. 3.

[30] Case C–27/91 *Ursaff* [1991] ECR I–5531, para. 10. See further Ch. 3.

[31] Case 237/78 *CRAM v. Toia* [1979] ECR 2645.

[32] See also Case 33/88 *Allué and Coonan v. Università Venezia* [1989] ECR 1591.

[33] See further Ch. 3.

[34] Case 1/78 *Kenny* [1978] ECR 1489. See also Wyatt, 'Social Security Benefits and Discrimination by a Member State against its own Nationals' (1978) 3 *ELRev.* 488.

it is for the national legislation to lay down the conditions for the acquisition, retention, loss or suspension of the right to social security benefits so long as those conditions apply without discrimination to the *nationals of the Member State concerned* and to those of other Member States [emphasis added].[35]

It has been argued that since freedom of movement includes the right *not* to migrate, as well as the right to do so, reverse discrimination in the administration of social security rules should be regarded as incompatible with the Treaty.[36]

Finally, the application of the principle of non-discrimination may result in migrant workers receiving benefits inferior to those they would have received had they not exercised their rights of free movement, since benefits in the host Member State may be lower than those provided by the State of origin. As discussed below, the Court has developed the principle of 'no disadvantage' to help address this situation.

1.2 Single State Rule

The second co-ordinating principle is that only one national system of legislation can apply to the migrant worker at any one time (the single State rule).[37] While the Regulation lays down detailed choice of law rules, the basic position, according to Article 13, is that the system applicable is that of the country where the worker or the self-employed person works (*lex laboris*), irrespective of his or her place of residence or the employer's place of residence.[38] It is also the State of employment which is the 'competent state' for administering the social security benefits. The main exception is laid down in Article 14(1)(a) (workers) and Article 14a(1)(a) (self-employed) which provides that where a self-employed person or a worker normally works for a company in one Member State (A) but is posted to another Member State (B) for up to a year but continues to work for the same company, the worker

---

[35] Para. 16. Cf. Case C–153/91 *Petit v. Office National des Pensions* [1992] ECR I–4973.

[36] Watson, above n. 13, 326.

[37] Art. 13(1). This, of course, says nothing about the content of the rules applied.

[38] Art. 13(2)(a). In Case 302/84 *Ten Holder v. Nieuwe Algemene Bedrijfsvereniging* [1986] ECR 1821, the Court said that a worker who has ceased to carry on an activity in the territory of a Member State and who has not gone to work in another Member State continues to be subject to the legislation of the Member State in which s/he was last employed, regardless of the length of time which has elapsed since the termination of the activity in question and the end of the employment relationship. This principle was reversed by Art. 13(2)(f) (added by Art. 1(2) of Regulation 2195/91 [1991] OJ L206/2, effective from 29 July 1991). This provided that a person to whom the legislation of a Member State ceases to be applicable, without the legislation of another Member State becoming applicable to him 'shall be subject to the legislation of the Member State in whose territory he resides'.

remains subject to the legislation of State A.[39] In *Manpower*[40] the Court held that the equivalent provision to Article 14(1) in Regulation No. 3 applied to 'a worker who is engaged by an undertaking pursuing its activity in a Member State, is paid by that undertaking, is answerable to it for misconduct, is able to be dismissed by it and who on behalf of that undertaking performs work temporarily in another undertaking in another Member State', even where the employer was an employment agency specializing in short-term placements.[41]

The application of the single State rule ensures that the worker is either not simultaneously insured in two Member States and has to pay double the contributions or not insured at all. It therefore avoids 'any plurality or purposeless confusion of contributions and liabilities which would result from the simultaneous or alternate application of several legislative systems'.[42] However, while Article 13 suggests that the single State rule is exclusive,[43] the Court has not ruled out the possibility of the concurrent application of other systems, providing that workers are entitled to additional benefits for any additional contributions they are required to make.[44] As the Court explained in *Nonnenmacher*,[45] while the single State rule is intended to avoid placing migrant workers in an unfavourable legal position as regards social security the Regulation is 'not opposed to legislation by Member States designed to

[39] See generally Case C–18/95 *Terhoeve* [1999] ECR I–345. This can be extended for a further 12 months: Arts. 14(1)(b) (workers) and 14a(1)(b) (self-employed). In both cases this is subject to the consent of the Member State where the work is being done. The definition of 'employed' and 'self-employed' should be understood to refer to activities which are regarded as such for the purposes of the social security legislation of the Member State in whose territory those activities are pursued: Case C–340/94 *de Jaeck v. Staatssecretaris van Financiën* [1997] ECR I–461.

[40] Case 35/70 *Manpower v. Caisse primaire d'assurance maladie de Strasbourg* [1970] ECR 1251. See also Case C–202/97 *Fitzwilliam Executive Search Ltd v. Bestuur van het Landelijk Instituut Sociale Verzekeringen* [2000] All ER (EC) 144. For the employment rights of posted workers see Council Directive 96/71/EC [1996] OJ L18/1, discussed further in Ch. 3.

[41] There are two further important exceptions: (i) where a worker is normally employed in several Member States Art. 14(2)(b) provides that s/he is subject to legislation of Member State where s/he resides if s/he does some work there; if not, then s/he will be subject to the social security legislation of the country where the employer's registered office is situated, see Case 13/73 *Angenieux v. Hackenberg* [1973] ECR 935; (ii) where a person is self-employed in several Member States Art. 14a(2) provides that s/he is subject to the legislation of the Member State where s/he resides if s/he does some work there; if not, then s/he is subject to legislation of the country where s/he pursues his or her main activity. (For principal activity see Art. 12a(5)(d) Regulation 574/72.)

[42] Case 19/67 *Soziale Verzekeringsbank v. Van der Vecht* [1967] ECR 345. See also Case 50/75 *Massonet* [1975] ECR 1473, para. 15.

[43] Case 19/67 *Van der Vecht* [1967] ECR 345.

[44] See Wyatt and Dashwood, above n. 13, 333, and Case 302/84 *Ten Holder* [1986] ECR 1821. Art. 17 provides that it is possible for the competent authorities of the Member States to agree to provide exceptions to the choice of law rules in the interest of certain workers or categories of workers. According to the spirit and scheme of Art. 17 such agreements can have retrospective effect. Case 101/83 *Brusse* [1984] ECR 2223, para. 21. See also Watson, 'Agreement between Member States Concluded under Article 17 of Regulation 1408/71' (1984) 9 *ELRev*. 437.

[45] Case 92/63 *Nonnenmacher v. Sociale Verzekeringsbank* [1964] ECR 281.

bring about additional protection by way of social security for the benefit of migrant workers'.[46]

1.3 The Principle of Aggregation

The third principle of co-ordination, the principle of aggregation, ensures that the host Member State must take account of periods of insurance completed in other Member States when calculating whether the claimant has satisfied the necessary qualifying period of work, residence, or period of contributions in order to be entitled to receive the benefit. Consequently, rights in the process of being acquired must be preserved. In Regulation 1408/71 the principle of aggregation relates to sickness and maternity,[47] invalidity,[48] old age and survivors' pensions,[49] death grants,[50] unemployment benefits,[51] and family benefits and family allowances.[52]

1.4 The Principle of Exportability

The fourth principle, the principle of exportability or deterritoriality, preserves rights which have already been acquired. Long-term benefits, such as pensions, must be paid to the migrant by the Member State of origin, irrespective of where that person now resides[53] in the Union. Article 10(1) of Regulation 1408/71 provides:

invalidity, old-age or survivors' cash benefits, pensions for accidents at work or occupational diseases and death grants acquired under the legislation of one or more Member States shall not be subject to any reduction, modification, suspension, withdrawal or confiscation by reason of the fact that the recipient resides in the territory of a Member State other than that in which the institution responsible for payment is situated.

As the Court explained in *Smieja*,[54] the aim of Article 10(1) is to guarantee the party concerned the right to have the benefit of such payments, even after taking up residence in a different Member State, including the individual's country of origin. If a person's rights are derived from the legislation of

---

[46] Ibid., 288.

[47] Art. 18(1) provides that the host Member State must 'take account of periods of insurance . . . completed under the legislation of any other Member State as if they were periods completed under the legislation which it administers'.

[48] Art. 38.

[49] Art. 45.

[50] Art. 64.

[51] Art. 67.

[52] Art. 72.

[53] 'Residence' according to Art. 1(7)(b) means 'habitual residence'. Therefore, Art. 10(1) does not apply to temporary residence.

[54] Case 51/73 *Sociale Verzekeringsbank* v. *Smieja* [1973] ECR 1213. See also Case 92/81 *Carraciolo* [1982] ECR 2213.

several Member States, payment is made according to the provisions of the Regulation, including the principle of non-discrimination on the grounds of nationality contained in Article 3.

However, the newly introduced Article 10a provides that, notwithstanding the provisions of Article 10, special non-contributory benefits[55] may be limited to persons resident in the territory of the State granting the benefit. As we shall see, the inclusion of a new category of special non-contributory benefits to a certain extent disrupts the 'purity' of the co-ordination system of Regulation 1408/71, and at least appears to undermine the underlying principle of freedom of movement.[56]

1.5 Other Principles

The principles outlined above provide the four main pillars of co-ordination. Commentators have, however, identified three additional principles. The first is known as pro-raterization, the equitable distribution of the cost of the benefit between the Member States where the claimant has been insured. Each Member State pays in proportion to the length of time the claimant has been insured in that Member State. This is particularly important where benefits such as pensions are paid over a long period.[57]

The second principle prevents the overlapping of benefits. Article 12(1) provides that Regulation 1408/71 'can neither confer nor maintain the right to several benefits of the same kind for one and the same period of compulsory insurance'.[58] Nevertheless, as a result of the application of the single State principle, laid down by Article 13, Article 12 may result in claimants receiving less from the competent State than they would have received had they not moved. Consequently, as an application of the third principle identified, that workers should not suffer disadvantage as a result of exercising their rights of free movement, the Court has ruled that claimants should be entitled to receive the difference between the sum payable by the competent institution and the sum which would have been paid by the more generous State. This difference is payable by the more generous State.[59] Indeed, cases such as *Nonnenmacher*[60] suggest that not only should Community social security rules

---

[55] See below, n. 92.

[56] See Case C–132/96 *Stinco and Panfilo v. INPS* [1998] ECR I–5225, para. 16, in which the Court held that, as a derogation provision, Art. 10a must be interpreted strictly.

[57] Pro-raterization applies particularly in respect of long-term benefits, i.e. invalidity, old age, and death benefits by virtue of Arts. 40 and 46, and to a limited extent to occupational diseases (Art. 60). It does not apply to sickness and maternity benefits (Art. 18).

[58] This principle does not apply to benefits in respect of invalidity, old age, death (pensions), or occupational disease (Art. 12(1)).

[59] The competent State is the State where the person is insured (Art. 1(q)) which, according to Art. 13, is the State where the person works: see Case 128/88 *De Felice v. INASTI* [1989] ECR 923.

[60] Case 92/63 [1964] ECR 281.

not put the migrant worker at a disadvantage, they should improve his or her position.[61]

2. The Personal Scope of the Regulation

Article 2(1) provides that Regulation 1408/71[62] applies to 'employed or self-employed persons who are or have been subject to the legislation of one or more Member States[63] and who are nationals of one of the Member States . . . as well as to the members of their families[64] and their survivors'. Article 1(a)(i) explains that the employed and self-employed to whom the Regulation applies are defined as 'any person who is *insured*, compulsorily or on an optional continued basis, for one or more of the contingencies covered by branches of a social security scheme for employed or self-employed persons' (emphasis added).[65] Since this definition refers to people insured under the national legislation rather than by reference to Articles 39 and 43 [ex Articles 48 and 52], it seems that the reference to 'employed persons' is not synonymous with the definition of 'workers' developed by the Court in the context of Article 39 [ex Article 48]. In *Hoekstra*[66] the Court ruled that the term 'worker' has a Community meaning. It refers to 'all those who, as such and under whatever description, are covered by the different national systems of social security'. The Court then confirmed that the Regulation applies not only to workers in employment but also to 'the worker who, having left his job, is capable of taking another'.[67]

The Court has also given a broad interpretation to the term self-employed. In *Van Roosmalen*[68] the Court was asked to consider whether a Roman

[61] See also Case 24/75 *Petroni* [1975] ECR 1149.

[62] See, generally, Lasok, 'Employed and Self-Employed Persons in EEC Social Security Law' (1982) 4 *JSWL* 323.

[63] As a consequence of this wording, the Regulation applies to an employed or self-employed person who has only ever pursued his or her occupation in the country of origin, see Case 75/63 *Hoeckstra v. Bedrijfsvereniging Detailhandel* [1964] ECR 805.

[64] Defined in Art. 1(i) as any person defined or recognized as a member of the family or designated as a member of the household by the legislation under which benefits are provided. See also Case 139/82 *Piscitello v. INPS* [1983] ECR 1427. Members of the family are included irrespective of their nationality: Case 40/76 *Kermanschek v. Bundenstalt für Arbeit* [1976] ECR 1669.

[65] Stateless persons and refugees residing within the territory of one of the Member States are also covered by the Regulation but not by this book.

[66] Case 75/63 [1964] ECR 177.

[67] Ibid., 185. See also Case 99/80 *Galinsky v. Insurance Officer* [1981] ECR 941 where a person compulsorily insured as an employed person is a worker and Case 143/79 *Walsh v. Insurance Officer* [1980] ECR 1639 where a person entitled under legislation of a Member State to benefits covered by Regulation 1408/71 by virtue of contributions previously paid does not lose his status as a 'worker' within the meaning of Regulation 1408/71 by reason only of the fact that at the time when the contingency occurred he was no longer paying contributions and was not bound to do so. Part-time workers are also covered irrespective of the number of hours worked, see Case 2/89 *Bestuur van de Sociale Verzekeringsbank v. Kits van Heijningen* [1990] ECR 1753.

[68] Case 300/84 *Van Roosmalen v. Bestuur van de Bedrijfsvereniging* [1986] ECR 3095.

Catholic priest who served as a missionary in the Belgian Congo was a self-employed person within the meaning of Regulation 1408/71. It said that the expression 'self-employed person' applies to 'persons who are pursuing or have pursued, otherwise than under a contract of employment or by way of self-employment in a trade or profession, an occupation in respect of which they receive income permitting them to meet all or some of their needs, even if that income is supplied by third parties [parishioners] benefiting from the services of a missionary priest'.

As we have already seen, the Regulation applies not only to the employed and self-employed, who are nationals of one of the Member States, but also to their families and survivors who do not need to be nationals. However, while there was no nationality requirement for the application of the Regulation to the family members or survivors they had only derived rights (i.e. those rights acquired through their status as members of the worker's family) which meant they could not benefit from some provisions of the Regulation, such as the entitlement to claim unemployment benefit (Articles 67–71). This was the situation in *Kermaschek*[69] and subsequent judgments.[70] However, in *Cabanis-Issarte*[71] the Court changed its mind and ruled that members of the worker's family had personal rights to protection under the Regulation.

Under the applicable national law, Cabanis-Issarte, as a French national resident in the Netherlands, was required to pay higher voluntary contributions to supplement a period of compulsory insurance towards her State old-age pension than would have been payable by a Dutch national in her situation. The Court distinguished *Kermaschek* on the ground that the benefit at issue there was unemployment benefit, a benefit which was provided for workers and not for family members.[72] *Cabanis-Issarte* concerned the application of the non-discrimination principle in Article 3(1) which applied to 'persons resident in the territory of one of the Member States', without distinguishing between workers, family members, or surviving spouses.[73] Article 3(1) applied to Mrs Cabanis-Issarte. Any derogation from the equal treatment principle set out in Article 3(1) had therefore to be objectively justified.[74] The Court then reconsidered the established jurisprudence on family members, pointing out that:

the distinction between rights in person and derived rights . . . may undermine the fundamental Community law requirement that its rules should be applied uniformly, by making their applicability to individuals depend on whether the national law relating

---

[69] Case 40/76 [1976] ECR 1669.

[70] See e.g. Case 157/84 *Frascogna* v. *Caisse des dépôts et consignations* [1985] ECR 1739; Case 94/84 *ONEM* v. *Deak* [1985] ECR 1873; Case C–310/91 *Schmid* v. *Belgian State* [1993] ECR I–3011.

[71] Case C–308/93 *Bestuur van de Sociale Verzekeringsbank* v. *Cabanis-Issarte* [1996] ECR I–2097.

[72] Para. 23.

[73] Para. 26.

[74] Ibid.

to the benefits in question treats the rights concerned as rights in person or derived rights, in the light of the specific features of the domestic social security scheme.[75]

The Court said that such a distinction might undermine the spirit and pur-pose of the co-ordination rules, by introducing a disincentive to free move-ment of workers, if they might be concerned for the social security protection of their spouses, in the event of the migrant worker predeceasing his or her spouse.

The ruling in *Cabanis-Issarte* produces consistent treatment for family members who are citizens of the EU with that granted to family members of a worker from a non-Member State with which the Community has concluded a Co-operation Agreement.[76] The Court also seems to recognize that the solution found appropriate in many of the earlier cases—the application of Article 7(2), the 'social advantages' non-discrimination provision in Regula-tion 1612/68—will not always provide a solution consistent with promoting free movement of persons.[77] In view of the fundamental change of approach introduced, the Court limited the temporal scope of the judgment to claims relating to periods subsequent to the date of the judgment.[78]

Regulation 1408/71 also applies to survivors[79] of the employed or self-employed who have been subject to the legislation of the Member States, irrespective of the nationality of the employed or self-employed person, where the survivors are nationals of one of the Member States, and to civil servants or people who have been treated as civil servants according to the laws of the Member States. Most significantly, the Regulation does not apply to the non-employed (i.e. those who are not capable of taking another job), since the focus of this Regulation is to buttress the rules on free movement of *workers*.[80] Nor does it apply to third country nationals whatever their employed or non-employed status, unless a specific agreement provides otherwise.[81]

Finally, although an individual may fall within the personal scope of the Regulation in general terms, it may not assist individuals in respect of particu-

---

[75] Para. 31.

[76] Case C–18/90 *Office national de l'emploi* v. *Kziber* [1991] ECR 199; Case C–103/94 *Krid* v. *Caisse nationale d'assurance vieillesse* [1995] ECR I–719; see Moore, 'Case C–308/93 *Cabanis-Issarte*' (1997) 34 *CMLRev.* 727–39, 731.

[77] See futher Ch. 3. Moore (1997) 34 *CMLRev.* 727, 735–9. See Barnard and Hervey, 'European Union Employment and Social Policy Survey 1996 and 1997' (1997) 17 *YEL* 435, 479–480.

[78] Paras. 46–48.

[79] Defined in Art. 1(g) as any person defined or recognized as a survivor by the legislation under which the benefits are granted.

[80] Luckhaus, 'The Role of the "Economic" and the "Social" in Social Security and Community Law' in Weich (ed.), *National and European Law on the Threshold to the Single Market* (Peter Lang, Berlin, 1993).

[81] See Art. 39 of the EC Turkey Association Agreement [1977] OJ L361/29 and Decision 3/80 of the Association Council [1983] OJ L110/60.

lar benefits. For example, for the purpose of Article 73 on family benefits it is necessary not only to have past employment or self-employment but to be currently engaged in employment or self-employment.[82]

3. The Material Scope of the Regulation

3.1 Introduction

Community legislation makes a distinction between social security, social assistance, and mixed benefits.[83] Originally social security was based on ideas of social insurance against the occurrence of risks facing those in work—sickness, unemployment, and accidents at work. In addition, such insurance covered the 'risks' in life which were likely to occur—the birth of children, retirement, and the needs of survivors on the death of the bread-winner. Having paid insurance contributions (in the UK through national insurance) the individual would become entitled to the benefit on the occurrence of the particular risk, without the application of any means test. By contrast, social assistance looked to need, and was more likely to be discretionary, requiring a decision of some authority on the suitability of the applicant for support. The distinction between social security and social assistance became blurred, first, because entitlement to social assistance has tended to become a matter of right rather than discretion, and, secondly, because the burden of funding social insurance has resulted in moves to require a test of means even for some insurance-based benefits.[84] More recently, a third type of benefit has emerged: mixed benefits which display aspects of both social insurance and social assistance. The face of social insurance is presented by the recognition of a social risk (for example, suffering an injury or illness which results in permanent disability), and the benefit may be paid as of right to those meeting tightly defined conditions of entitlement without any means test. On the other hand, the benefit is not dependent on the payment of contributions, and for many recipients, the benefit represents their means of subsistence.[85]

Regulation 1408/71 applies to all legislation[86] relating to *social security*

---

[82] Case C–15/90 *Middleburgh* v. *Chief Adjudication Officer* [1991] ECR I–4655.

[83] White, above, n. 13, 5–6.

[84] Ibid., 6.

[85] Ibid.

[86] Legislation is defined by Art. 1(j) to include statutes, regulations, and other provisions and all other implementing measures, present or future, relating to the branches and schemes of social security. See also Case 61/65 *Vassen-Goebbels* v. *Beambtenfonds voor het Mijnbedrijf* [1966] ECR 377.

benefits. Article 4(1) provides that the following exhaustive[87] list of branches of social security[88] are covered by the Regulation:

- sickness and maternity benefits;
- invalidity benefits, including those intended for the maintenance or improvement of wage earning capacity;
- old-age benefits;
- survivors' benefits;
- benefits in respect of accidents at work or occupational diseases;
- death grants;
- unemployment benefits;
- family benefits.

The Regulation applies irrespective of whether the benefits are derived from general or special social security schemes, whether contributory or non-contributory.[89] In *Hughes* and *Newton*,[90] two important decisions concerning the UK benefits, family credit and mobility allowance, the Court recognized that non-contributory benefits of a mixed type—combining elements of both social security and social assistance—were also caught by Regulation 1408/71.[91] These decisions precipitated an amendment to Regulation 1408/71 which introduced the concept of special non-contributory benefits into Article 4(2)(a).[92] These special non-contributory benefits are provided under legislation or schemes other than those referred to in paragraph 1[93] or excluded by virtue of paragraph 4[94] where such benefits are intended either to provide supplementary, substitute or ancillary cover against the risks covered by the branches of social security referred to in paragraph 1 (a) to (h), or solely as specific protection for the disabled.

[87] Case 249/83 *Hoeckx* v. *Openbaar Centrum voor Maatschappelijk Welzijn Kalmthout* [1985] ECR 973.

[88] This is based on ILO Convention No. 102 of 1952. According to Art. 5, it is for the Member States to specify the schemes which are caught by Art. 4. Such declarations are only indicative in scope and are not legislative in character (Case 100/63 *Van der Veen* [1964] ECR 565) but they are conclusive proof that the benefits are considered social security benefits (Case 35/77 *Beerens* v. *Rijksdienst voor Arbeidsvoorziening* [1977] ECR 2249 and Case 237/78 *Toia* [1979] ECR 2645).

[89] Art. 4(2).

[90] Case C–78/91 *Hughes* v. *Chief Adjudication Officer* [1991] ECR I–4839 and Case C–356/89 *Newton* v. *Chief Adjudication Officer* [1991] ECR I–3107.

[91] For a comprehensive list of the relevant cases see *Social Europe* 3/92, 21. They include allowances for handicapped people (Case 63/76 *Inzirillo* [1976] ECR 2057), guaranteed income for old people in Belgium (Case 1/72 *Frilli* v. *Belgian State* [1972] ECR 457 and Case 261/83 *Castelli* v. *ONTFS* [1984] ECR 3199), benefits of a remedial nature (Case 14/72 *Heinze* v. *Landesversicherungsanstalt* [1972] ECR 1105). See also Wyatt, ' "Social Security" and "Social Assistance" under Regulation 1408/71' (1975–6) 1 *ELRev.* 127 and Watson, 'Minimum Income Benefits: Social Security or Social Assistance' (1985) 10 *ELRev.* 335.

[92] Regulation 1247/92 [1992] OJ L136/1.

[93] The 'traditional risks' of sickness, maternity, invalidity, old-age, death (including survivors' benefits), accidents at work, and industrial diseases, unemployment, and family benefits.

[94] Art. 4(4) provides that Regulation 1408/71 'shall not apply to social and medical assistance, to benefit schemes for victims of war or its consequences, or to special schemes for civil servants and persons treated as such'.

This formally brought these mixed benefits within the material scope of the Regulation but Article 10a provided that they were non-exportable.[95] This reduced the protection provided by the Regulation.

The Regulation does not apply, according to Article 4(4), to *social assistance* and medical assistance, to benefit schemes for victims of war or its consequences,[96] or to special schemes for civil servants.[97] Such cases of social assistance may, however, be caught by the principle of equal treatment in Article 7(2) of Regulation 1612/68[98] which, as the Court pointed out in *Inzirillo*[99] 'must be defined in such a way as to include *every* social and tax advantage, whether or not linked to a contract of employment' (emphasis added), such as an allowance for handicapped adults which was awarded by a Member State to its own nationals.[100]

Regulation 1408/71 provides no criteria for distinguishing between social security schemes, which fall within the material scope of Regulation 1408/71 and thus may be exportable, social assistance which is not, and the new special non-contributory benefits. Distinguishing between the three categories of benefit has been a matter for the Court which examines 'the factors relating to each benefit, in particular its purpose and the conditions of its grant'.[101] It does not depend on whether a benefit is classified as a social security benefit by national legislation.[102]

Social security is used to describe 'legislation which confers on the beneficiaries a legally defined position which involves no individual and discretionary assessment of need or personal circumstances'.[103] Social assistance, on the other hand, describes legislation designed to provide benefits to those in need, where eligibility is not dependent on periods of employment, affiliation, or insurance, but there is some element of individual assessment (means-testing).[104] In *Piscitello*[105] the Court found a *pensione sociale* to be a measure of social security because no provision was made for individual assessment and

[95] See above, nn. 53–56.

[96] See Case 9/78 *Directeur Régional de la Securité Sociale de Nancy* v. *Gillard* [1978] ECR 1661.

[97] It also seems not to apply to occupational social security schemes. This is certainly the view that the Commission has taken in its Communication to the Council on supplementary social security schemes: SEC(91)1332 final.

[98] See Ch. 3.

[99] Case 63/76 [1976] ECR 2057.

[100] Case 63/76 *Inzirillo* [1976] ECR 2057, para. 21. See Wyatt, 'The Social Security of Migrant Workers and their Families' (1977) 14 *CMLRev.* 411.

[101] Case 249/83 *Hoeckx* [1985] ECR 973. The Court ruled that a Member State's designation that a benefit is social assistance is not conclusive. See also Case 9/78 *Gillard* [1978] ECR 1661, para. 12.

[102] Case C–78/91 *Hughes* [1992] ECR I–4839, para. 14.

[103] Case 79/76 *Fossi* v. *Bundesknappschaft* [1977] ECR 667, para. 6. See also Case 249/83 *Hoeckx* [1985] ECR 973, para. 12, and Case 139/82 *Piscitello* [1983] ECR 1427.

[104] Case 139/82 *Piscitello* [1983] ECR 1427, para. 11. See also Council Recommendation of 24 June 1992 on common criteria concerning sufficient resources and social assistance in social protection: 92/441/EEC [1992] OJ L245/46.

[105] Case 139/82 [1983] ECR 1427.

the legislation conferred a legally defined status on recipients entitling them to a benefit analogous to an old-age pension.[106] On the other hand, in *Hoeckx*[107] the Belgian minimex (minimum means of subsistence) was considered to be a measure of social assistance. It was a benefit providing assistance to those without means, irrespective of periods of work or contributions or affiliation to any social security body. Need was the criterion for entitlement.

It used to be thought that social security benefits were granted on the occurrence of a specific risk.[108] Therefore, for the benefit to be considered as social security the legislation at issue must, in any event, satisfy one of the risks specified in Article 4(1).[109] More recently, the Court has relaxed the requirement, recognizing that Regulation 1408/71 applies to benefits where a *link* exists between the benefit and one of the contingencies listed in Article 4(1).[110] The Court has therefore ruled that Regulation 1408/71 covers preventive health care,[111] assistance for vocational training,[112] benefits for the disabled,[113] and certain measures of national recognition relating to acts of war or reparation for suffering or injury caused by the national socialist regime, supplementing or implementing the general provisions on social insurance.[114]

At times it is also difficult to distinguish between social assistance (which is totally excluded from the Regulation) and special non-contributory benefits referred to in Article 4(2a). Entitlement to the latter, by definition, does not arise through membership or contribution to a social security or insurance scheme, and, in some cases, some elements of means-testing may attach to the grant of special non-contributory benefits. These difficulties arose in respect of disability benefits in *Snares*[115] and *Partridge*.[116] Snares worked in the UK until the age of 39, when he suffered a serious accident which left him with severely impaired mobility. He received a Disability Living Allowance (DLA), a UK social security benefit which is non-contributory, not linked to incapacity for work, and non-means-tested. In November 1993, Snares

---

[106] The benefit was paid by reference to lack of means and did not prescribe any requirements as to periods of employment, affiliation, or insurance. This might indicate social assistance.

[107] Case 249/83 [1985] ECR 973.

[108] Case 33/65 *Dekker* [1965] ECR 901.

[109] The Court is moving in the same direction in the context of Directive 79/7: see below, nn. 207–211, and Joined Cases C–63 and C–64/91 *Jackson and Cresswell v. Chief Adjudication Officer* [1992] ECR I–4737.

[110] Case C–249/83 *Hoeckx* [1985] ECR 973.

[111] Case 14/72 *Heinze* [1972] ECR 1127 and Case 818/79 *Allgemeine Ortskrankasse Mittelfranken v. Landesversicherungsanstalt Schleswig-Holstein* [1980] ECR 2729.

[112] Case 375/85 *Camapana v. Bundesanstalt für Arbeit* [1987] ECR 2387.

[113] Case 39/74 *Costa v. Belgium* [1974] ECR 1251 and Case 63/76 *Inzirillo* [1976] ECR 2057.

[114] Case 79/76 *Fossi* [1977] ECR 667; Case 144/78 *Tinelli* [1979] ECR 757; Case 9/78 *Gillard* [1978] ECR 1661; Case 207/78 *Ministère public v. Even* [1979] ECR 2019; and Case 70/80 *Vigier* [1981] ECR 229.

[115] Case C–20/96 *Snares v. Chief Adjudication Officer* [1997] ECR I–6057.

[116] Case C–297/96 *Partridge v. The Adjudication Officer* [1998] ECR I–3467.

moved from the UK to Tenerife, where his mother lived, so that she could care for him. The relevant British legislation provides that DLA was available only to claimants who were resident in the UK.[117] Accordingly, the UK social security authorities decided that Snares' entitlement to DLA would cease, relying on Article 4(2a) and Article 10a. Snares challenged this decision, on the ground that the effect of the amendment was to remove from the scope of Article 4(1) a benefit which would have been granted irrespective of the place of residence. The question of the validity of the amending Regulation thus arose and was referred to the Court.

The Court noted that the principle of exportability, as found in Article 10(1) of the Regulation, was subject to the express exemption 'save as otherwise provided in this Regulation'. For example, the exportability of unemployment benefits was restricted in Article 69 of the Regulation to a period of three months. The validity of this particular restriction was tested in *Testa*,[118] where the Court held that it was not contrary to Article 51 [new Article 42] EC. Likewise, the Court said that derogations from the principle of exportability applicable to special non-contributory benefits, such as DLA, were lawful.[119] In practice, for Snares, the applicability of Articles 4(2a) and 10a of the Regulation to his situation meant that his benefit entitlement would be significantly reduced if he moved to Tenerife, a fact likely to deter free movement. His position was aggravated by the fact that the Spanish authorities could, in accordance with Directive 90/365/EEC,[120] refuse to grant Snares a right of residence, as he would not be in receipt of sufficient benefits from his 'home State' to avoid becoming a burden on the social security system of the host State. Thus, in making detailed provision for the system of co-ordination of social security benefits under Regulation 1408/71, the Court has confirmed that the EU legislature may lawfully enact measures which have the effect of *reducing* the mobility of persons within the EU. This conclusion was supported by the Court's rulings in *Partridge*,[121] concerning attendance allowance, and also by the ruling in *Swaddling*,[122] concerning income support. *Swaddling* confirms that the principles established in *Snares* and *Partridge* applied not only in the case of disability benefits, but also to the more general category of 'benefits . . . intended either to provide supplementary, substitute or ancillary cover against the risks covered by the branches of social security referred to in paragraph 1 (a) to (h)' of Article 4 of Regulation 1408/71.

---

[117] Social Security Contributions and Benefits Act 1992, s. 71 (6); Disability Living Allowance Regulations, Regulation 2(1) and (2). See Barnard and Hervey, 'European Union Employment and Social Policy Survey 1998' (1998) 18 *YEL* 613, 644–9.

[118] Joined Cases 41, 121, and 796/79 *Testa and Others* v. *Bundesanstalt für Arbeit* [1980] ECR 1979.

[119] Case C–20/96 *Snares* [1997] ECR I–6057, paras. 44–51, 54.

[120] [1990] OJ L180/28.

[121] Case C–297/96 [1998] ECR I–3467.

[122] Case C–90/97 *Swaddling* v. *The Adjudication Officer* [1999] ECR I–1075.

Robin Swaddling was a UK national. He worked in France from 1980 to 1988, but paid UK national insurance contributions. In 1988 he worked for six months in the UK; then he held fixed-term jobs in France until 1994. In 1994 he was made redundant when his employer's business failed. In January 1995, Swaddling returned to the UK. He applied for income support. The UK Regulations governing entitlement to income support provided that the applicable amount of the benefit was nil where the claimant was a 'person from abroad'.[123] A 'person from abroad' was defined as someone 'not habitually resident in the UK', except in the case of a 'worker' in the terms of Regulation 1612/68/EEC.[124] In practice, habitual residence for these terms was defined as an intention to remain in the UK *plus* at least eight weeks' actual residence. Thus a 'person from abroad' could not claim income support for the first eight weeks of his residence in the UK. Mr Swaddling was refused income support on the grounds that he did not meet the habitual residence test.

The Court followed its Advocate General by maintaining that income support was a 'special non-contributory benefit' in terms of Article 4(2a) of the Regulation.[125] Such benefits were only for persons resident in the territory of the State granting the benefit. Residence was a Community law concept, referring to the habitual centre of a person's interests.[126] However, the length of actual residence 'cannot be regarded as an intrinsic element of the concept of residence within the meaning of Article 10a'.[127] The habitual residence test, as applied to income support by the UK authorities, was inconsistent with Regulation 1408/71.[128] Thus the Court concluded that there was no need to consider Article 39 [ex Article 48] EC. The co-ordination provisions of Regulation 1408/71 were applicable.

The conclusions of the Court in cases such as *Swaddling*, *Snares*, and *Partridge* sit uneasily with the Court's ruling in *Martínez Sala*[129] in which the Court apparently regarded the primary Treaty rights of citizenship as prior to the provisions of regulatory co-ordination of social security law as set out in Regulation 1408/71. Martínez Sala was a Spanish national who had lived in Germany since 1968. She worked from 1976 to 1986 and for a brief period in 1989. After that, she was in receipt of social assistance benefits from the

---

[123] Social Security Contributions and Benefits Act 1992; Income Support (General) Regulations 1987, regulation 21.

[124] Further exceptions are given for workers in terms of Regulation 1251/70/EEC [1970] OJ Spec. Ed. II/402, on the right of workers to remain in the host State; for persons with the right to reside under Directive 68/360/EEC [1968] OJ Spec. Ed. II/485, on the abolition of restrictions on movement and residence within the Community for EU citizen workers and their families; or Directive 73/148/EEC [1973] OJ L172/14, on the abolition of such restrictions with regard to establishment and the provision of services for refugees; and for persons with exceptional leave to remain in the UK.

[125] Ibid., para. 24.

[126] Ibid., para. 29.

[127] Ibid., para. 30.

[128] Ibid., para. 33.

[129] Case C–85/96 *Martínez Sala v. Freistaat Bayern* [1998] ECR I–2691.

Germany authorities. In 1984, her residence permit expired. Thereafter, she was given a series of documents simply certifying that she had applied for an extension of her residence permit. A further residence permit was granted for one year in 1994, and extended for one year on its expiry. In January 1993, Ms Martínez Sala gave birth to a child. She applied for a child raising allowance (*Erzeihungsgeld*), but her application was rejected on the grounds that she was neither a German national nor in possession of a valid residence permit.

The national court referred to the Court various questions on the interpretation of Regulation 1408/71 and Regulation 1612/68. In terms of the material scope of these provisions, the Court held that the child raising allowance constituted both a 'family benefit' in the sense of Article 4(1) of Regulation 1408/71[130] and a 'social advantage' in the sense of Article 7(2) of Regulation 1612/68. The more difficult question concerned the personal scope of these provisions. On the question whether Ms Martínez Sala was a 'worker' in the sense of Article 48 [new Article 39] EC and Regulation 1612/68, the Court referred to its earlier case law to the effect that 'worker' was a Community law concept in this context,[131] and held that this was a question for the national court to decide. The question whether Martínez Sala was an 'employed person' in the sense of Regulation 1408/71 was more difficult. The German government argued that, for the purposes of entitlement to family benefits, only a person compulsorily insured against unemployment constitutes an 'employed person'. In this respect, the German government relied on the Court's earlier ruling in *Stöber and Pereira*[132] and on the provisions in the Annex to Regulation 1408/71 covering German family benefits. However, the Court said that the provisions of the Annex did not apply to Martínez Sala in respect of the benefits she was claiming, and hence held that her status was to be determined (by the national court) solely on the basis of Article 1(a) of Regulation 1408/71.

The Court then considered whether the residence requirement in respect of the child raising allowance was contrary to Community law. The Court had no difficulty in finding that, should the national court find that Martínez Sala fell within the personal scope of Community law, the residence requirement would be discriminatory on grounds of nationality in breach of Article 6 EC. As Martínez Sala was lawfully resident in Germany, there was no need to consider the Commission's argument to the effect that Article 8a [new Article 18] EC granted a new right of residence to citizens of the EU. Martínez Sala could rely on Article 6 [new Article 12] EC:

---

[130] Following Joined Cases C–245 and C–312/94 *Hoever and Zachow v. Land Nordrhein Westfalen* [1996] ECR I–4895.

[131] See e.g. Case 66/85 *Lawrie-Blum v. Land Baden-Württemberg* [1986] ECR 2121; Case 39/86 *Lair v. Universität Hannover* [1988] ECR 3161; and Case C–292/89 *The Queen v. Immigration Appeal Tribunal, ex parte Antonissen* [1991] ECR I–745, considered further in Ch. 3.

[132] Joined Cases C–4 and 5/95 *Stöber and Piosa Pereira v. Bundesanstalt für Arbeit* [1997] ECR I–511.

in all situations which fall within the scope *ratione materiae* of Community law, including the situation where a Member State delays or refuses to grant to that claimant a benefit that is provided to all persons lawfully resident in the territory of that state on the ground that the claimant is not in possession of a document which nationals of that same state are not required to have. . . .

Nothing would justify that discrimination on grounds of nationality in a case such as this.[133]

3.2 Specific Benefits

The content of Article 4(1) is fleshed out by eight chapters containing detailed provisions about various categories of benefit. For the purposes of this book five benefits most closely related to those in or who have been in employment[134] will be examined in outline: the so-called 'short-term' benefits—sickness and maternity benefits, unemployment benefits, and death grants; and the 'long-term' benefits—benefits for accidents at work, occupational diseases, and pension.

(a) Sickness and Maternity Benefits for Migrant Workers

Chapter 1 of Title III deals with sickness[135] and maternity benefits. The Regulations are particularly detailed because the basic rule that the competent State is the State where the worker is employed may present difficulties if the worker and his or her family are resident elsewhere. Two situations shall be considered. First, if a migrant worker residing and working in Member State A becomes ill in Member State A and claims in Member State A (the competent State)[136] he or she will, under the principle of equality, receive the same benefits as nationals under the same terms as nationals.[137] According to Article 18, the principle of aggregation applies where entitlement is conditional on the completion of a period of insurance, so that the competent institution (in State A) takes into account any periods of insurance, employment, or residence completed under the legislation of any other Member State as if they were periods completed under the legislation which it administers.[138]

The second situation is where the migrant worker habitually resides in Member State B and becomes ill there but works in Member State A, the

---

[133] See further Barnard and Hervey, 'European Union Employment and Social Policy Survey 1998' [1998] *YEL* 613, 644–9 and Ch. 3 above.

[134] For details of other benefits, esp. family benefits and invalidity benefits, see White, above n. 13.

[135] This includes insurance to pay for the costs of long-term care: Case C–160/96 *Molenaar v. Allgemeine Ortskrankenkasse Baden-Württemberg* [1998] ECR I–843.

[136] The competent State (Art. 1(q)) is the State where the person is insured which, according to Art. 13, is the State where the person works. The competent institution (Art. 1(o)) is the social security institution with which the worker is insured.

[137] Case 1/78 *Kenny* [1978] ECR 1489.

[138] Art. 18(1).

competent State.[139] For practical reasons Article 19 provides that *benefits in kind* (health services) are to be provided in the country of residence (State B), even if the recipient is affiliated to another Member State's social security system. These benefits in kind are provided on behalf of the competent institution in State A by the institution in the place of residence (State B), 'in accordance with the provisions of the legislation administered by that institution as though he were insured with it'. By contrast, cash benefits[140] are provided by the competent institution in State A but may be provided by the institution of the place of residence on behalf of the competent institution if they so agree. The Court has said that *benefits in kind* include health and welfare services as well as cash payments to reimburse the cost of those services for which the claimant has already been charged.[141] *Cash benefits*, on the other hand, are benefits to compensate for loss of earnings.[142] These rules apply to those who habitually reside in State B but who are temporarily working and living in State A, and those who have left State A to become habitually resident in State B but who remain subject to State A's legislation.[143]

Special rules apply to frontier workers. The term 'frontier worker' means any employed or self-employed person who pursues his occupation in the territory of a Member State and resides in the territory of another Member State to which he returns, as a rule, daily or at least once a week.[144] He can rely on Article 19 and can also obtain benefits in the territory of the competent State, State A. Members of his or her family may also receive benefits under the same conditions but receipt of such benefits must, except in urgent cases, be conditional on an agreement between the States concerned.

(b) Unemployment Benefits

As we have seen, the Community is keen to encourage people to move between Member States to look for work and this has been facilitated by Regulation 1408/71.[145] The need to invoke the Regulation may apply in three circumstances. First, if the migrant worker resides, *last* worked, and was insured in State A where he becomes unemployed and claims in State A (the competent State) the principle of aggregation applies. Thus, if its legislation makes entitlement conditional on periods of *insurance*, the competent

---

[139] The same rules apply to a worker's family (Art. 19(2)).

[140] This includes a benefit such as a care allowance: Case C–160/96 *Molenaar* [1998] ECR I–843.

[141] Wyatt and Dashwood, above n. 13, 338.

[142] See Case 61/65 *Vaassen* [1966] ECR 261.

[143] Case C–215/90 *Chief Adjudication Officer* v. *Twomey* [1992] ECR I–1823.

[144] Art. 1(7)(b).

[145] Ch. 6 of Title III (Arts. 67–71). See also Wikeley, 'Migrant Workers and Unemployment Benefit in the European Community' (1988) 10 *JSWL* 300.

institution in Member State A must take into account periods of insurance in any other Member State which would have counted as periods of insurance had they been completed under its own legislation; or, if its legislation makes entitlement conditional on periods of employment, periods of employment or insurance in any other Member State are counted as though they were periods of employment under its own legislation.[146]

The principle of aggregation is limited to the country in which the person claiming 'lastly' completed periods of insurance or unemployment. Thus, as White points out, a British national living and working in Germany who becomes unemployed in Germany cannot return to the UK to seek Job Seekers' Allowance (JSA) on the basis of contributions to the German scheme because he or she will not have last completed a period of insurance in the UK.[147]

If State A bases its calculation of benefit on the amount of previous earnings, Article 68 provides that account must be taken of the earnings of the unemployed person during his or her last employment in the territory of State A. If this employment lasted less than four weeks the figure to be used is the normal earnings in State A for employment equivalent or similar to the individual's last employment in the Member State from which he has come. In addition, Article 68(2) provides that Member States whose legislation provides that the amount of benefits varies with the number of members of the family shall take account of the members of the family of the person concerned who are residing in the territory of another State as if they were residing in the territory of the competent State.

The second situation is where the worker becomes unemployed in State A (competent State) and goes to look for work in State B where he or she has never been employed. It will be recalled that in *ex parte Antonissen* a work seeker enjoys some, if not all, the rights of a worker for at least three months.[148] Those people looking for work enjoy a limited right of exportability of unemployment benefit under Articles 69 and 70 of Regulation 1408/71. These provisions entitle work seekers to receive unemployment benefit during their stay provided they satisfy certain conditions: before leaving the competent State, Member State A, they must be registered with the employment services there; they must have remained available for work in Member State A for at least four weeks after becoming unemployed (unless waived under Article 69(1)(a)) in order to exhaust all the employment possibilities in Member State A, and they must register, within seven days of ceasing to be available to the employment services of State A, with the employment services of Member State B. They are then entitled to benefits paid by the authorities of State B, payable on behalf of State A and at State A's rates but reimbursed by the State

---

[146] Art. 67. See also Wyatt and Dashwood, above n. 13, 346.

[147] White, above n. 13, 86.

[148] Case C–292/88 *ex parte Antonissen* [1991] ECR I–745, see further Ch. 3.

of last employment, State A, unless State A waives this.[149] These benefits must be reimbursed by the authorities of the State where the unemployed person last worked (State A), unless the paying State, State B, waives this.[150] The unemployed are entitled to receive benefits for three months[151] from the date when they leave Member State A, provided they do not receive benefits for longer than they would be entitled to if they had stayed in State A.[152] If they return to the competent State (State A) within three months they maintain their entitlement in that State.[153] Failure to do so leads to the loss of all entitlement to benefit.

Article 69 can be invoked for only *one* period of three months between two periods of employment.[154] Therefore, X, who is British and has lost his job in the UK, can leave the UK and go to France to look for work. At the end of the three-month period X cannot leave France and go to look for employment in Spain without first having worked. Alternatively, X can go to France for two months and to Spain for the remaining month. According to Article 70, the unemployment benefits are provided by the institution of State B. Therefore, if Y went to France for one month and then returned to the UK he also could not seek a further authorization to go abroad again for the balance of the three months. These rules do not apply if the unemployed person has never been employed or never treated as an unemployed person under national law.[155]

The third situation covered by the Regulations is where the worker who, during his or her last employment, was employed in State A (the competent State) before becoming unemployed, but was resident in State B. Article 71 deals with this situation.[156] As far as frontier workers[157] are concerned, if they are 'partially or intermittently' unemployed they must remain available to the employment services in the competent State (State A) and claim unemployment benefit there, as though they were residing there.[158] By contrast, 'wholly unemployed' frontier workers are entitled to benefits in the State of residence, as though they had been subject to that State's legislation while working

[149] Art. 70.

[150] Art. 70(1) and (3).

[151] Host Member States are entitled to insist on the three-month limit: Case C–272/90 *van Noorden* v. *ASSEDIC* [1991] ECR I–2543 and Case C–62/91 *Gray* v. *Adjudication Officer* [1992] ECR I–2737. The Commission proposed an amendment to Art. 69 to address the situation of those most affected by the operation of Art. 69 wanting to return to a country with which they have close links [1980] OJ C169/22. However, the three-month limit may be extended in 'exceptional cases': see Art. 69(2), Case 139/78 *Coccioli* v. *Bundesanstalt für Arbeit* [1979] ECR 991 and Case 41/79 *Testa* v. *Bundesanstalt für Arbeit* [1980] ECR 1979. Cf. Case 24/75 *Petroni* [1975] ECR 1149.

[152] Art. 69(1)(c).

[153] Art. 69(2).

[154] Art. 69(3).

[155] See Case 66/77 *Kuyken* v. *Rijksdienst voor Arbeidsvoorziening* [1977] ECR 2311.

[156] These provisions as derogations to the basic rule must be interpreted strictly: see Case 76/76 *Di Paolo* v. *Office de l'Emploi* [1977] ECR 315.

[157] See above, n. 144.

[158] Art. 71(1)(a)(i).

there.[159] As far as other workers are concerned, wholly unemployed workers can choose whether unemployment benefits are paid in the country of last employment (State A) or in the country of residence (State B).[160] Partially or intermittently unemployed workers, by contrast, who remain available for work in the territory of the competent State (State A) receive unemployment benefits in accordance with the provisions of the legislation of the competent State as though they resided there. If the individual has the right to receive benefit in the competent State (State A) the individual's rights to benefit in the State of residence (State B) is suspended under Article 71(2).

(c) Death Grants

Death grants are covered by Articles 64–66. Article 64 provides for aggregation of periods of insurance necessary to give rise to entitlement. Article 65 removes territorial limitations by providing that if an employed or self-employed person, a pensioner, or member of his or her family dies in a Member State other than the competent State (State A), the Regulation deems that the death occurred in the competent State. Consequently, the competent institution must award death grants even if the person resided in a Member State other than the competent State.[161] These rules also apply when death is a result of an accident at work or occupational disease.

(d) Accidents at Work and Occupational Diseases

Articles 52–63 contain provisions covering accidents at work and occupational diseases.[162] Again, three situations will be considered. First, if the worker resides and works in State A under the principle of equal treatment, he or she is entitled to the same social security benefits as nationals in the same situation.[163] Secondly, if the worker habitually resides in State B but works in State A, the competent State, Article 52 modifies the basic rule concerning the competent State. It provides that if the worker sustains an accident at work or contracts an occupational disease he or she will receive benefits in kind from the State of residence (State B) provided on behalf of the competent institutions in State A, as if he or she were insured in State B. Cash benefits, on the other hand, are provided by the competent institution in State A unless State A has reached an agreement that State B will provide them on its behalf.[164] According to Article 53, a frontier worker may also obtain

---

[159] Art. 71(1)(a)(ii); Case C–131/95 *Huijbrechts* v. *Commissie voor de Behandeling van Administratieve Geschillen* [1997] ECR I–1409.

[160] Art. 71(1)(b).

[161] See also Case C–237/94 *O'Flynn* v. *Adjudication Officer* [1996] ECR I–2617 on funeral benefits, discussed in Ch. 3.

[162] Ch. 4 of Title III (Arts. 52–63).

[163] See also Art. 54. Art. 58 lays down detailed rules about the calculation of cash benefits.

[164] Art. 58(3) makes provision for increases in cash benefits for dependants where the competent State's legislation so provides.

benefits in the territory of the competent State. The benefits are provided by the competent institution in accordance with the provision of the legislation of that State, as if the person concerned were residing there.

Thirdly, if the worker has been exposed to the risk of an occupational disease in several Member States, Article 57 provides that the benefits that the worker and his or her family may claim are to be awarded exclusively under the legislation of the last State where the worker was employed in an activity likely to cause that disease. If there is no entitlement under the legislation of that State, entitlement may arise in the penultimate State and so on. If the law of that State requires that the disease must be diagnosed in that Member State for the benefit to be granted, this condition is satisfied if the disease was first diagnosed in the territory of another Member State. If, under the law of the paying Member State, the disease must be diagnosed within a certain time of the activity ceasing, the competent institution must take into account similar activities in other Member States as if they had been pursued in its State.

(e) Old Age and Death Pensions

The chapter of the Regulation concerning old age and death pensions[165] is particularly complex. This section aims only to outline the main principles: aggregation and apportionment or pro-raterization (so that the cost of the pensions is borne proportionately to contributions received). Consequently, the institution of each Member State in which a person has a record of insurance or residence which is reckonable for old age pensions is a competent institution.

Article 45 contains the basic aggregation rule requiring the competent institution to take account of periods of insurance, employment, or self-employment completed in another State, as if they had been completed there. If the employed or self-employed person is not entitled to a pension under the legislation of any one Member State in which he or she has been insured without the aid of Regulation 1408/71 then, according to Article 46(2)(a), the pension is calculated with reference to a theoretical amount. Each competent institution calculates the amount of benefit to which the claimant would have been entitled under its scheme if all the insurance periods or periods of residence completed by the worker had been completed in its State. On the basis of this theoretical amount each institution then establishes the actual amount of the benefit due from it by reference to the ratio which the periods of insurance or residence served in its State bear to the total insurance or residence completed in all States.

If, on the other hand, entitlement to benefit is on the basis of insurance periods completed in more than one Member State and the worker is entitled to a pension under the law of one of those Member States the competent

---

[165] Ch. 3 of Title III (Arts. 44–51).

institution of that State first decides the rate of the pension to which the worker would be entitled under that legislation alone. It then takes account of the claimant's insurance record in all Member States and applies the process of aggregation and apportionment described above to arrive at the actual amount to which he would be entitled by virtue of the regulation. The competent institution then compares this actual amount with the amount due under its legislation and awards whichever is the higher. Article 50 does, however, make provision for a guaranteed minimum pension. The country of residence must pay at least the minimum level of benefit paid in that country, as if all the periods of insurance completed by the claimant had been completed on its territory.

As we have seen, the system of co-ordination provided for in Regulation 1408/71 concerns only statutory pension schemes. It does not extend to supplementary pension schemes[166] intended to supplement benefits received under state schemes, such as occupational schemes, organized at the level of a company or industry and managed by employers and unions, or personal pension plans drawn up by, for example, life assurance companies. The Social Charter Action Programme expressed concern that the absence of co-ordination of supplementary or occupational social security schemes placed 'a brake on free movement'. In 1991 the Commission produced a Communication[167] which said that the Community should recognize the principle that each worker should be able to move to a job in another Member State without loss of rights to future retirement benefits. In particular, it argued that workers and others holding entitlement should have certain guarantees for equal treatment regarding the preservation of their vested pension rights deriving from supplementary pension schemes. Some of these objectives were achieved with the enactment of Directive 98/49/EC.[168] This is intended to protect the rights of members of supplementary pension schemes who move from one Member State to another. The protection refers to pension rights under both voluntary and compulsory supplementary pension schemes, with the exception of schemes covered by Regulation 1408/71.[169] It applies to members of supplementary pension schemes and others holding entitlement under such schemes who have acquired or are in the process of acquiring rights in one or more Member States.[170] Supplementary pensions are defined as 'retirement pensions and, where provided for by the rules of a supplementary pension

---

[166] Except for schemes which are covered by the term 'legislation' as defined by the first subpara. of Art. 1(j) of Regulation 1408/71 or in respect of which a Member State makes a declaration under that Art.

[167] SEC(91)1332 final, Brussels 22 July 1991, *Supplementary Social Security Schemes: the role of occupational pensions schemes in the social protection of workers and their implication for freedom of movement.*

[168] Council Directive 98/49/EC on safeguarding the supplementary pension rights of employed and self-employed persons moving within the Community [1998] OJ L209/46.

[169] Art. 1.

[170] Art. 2.

scheme[171] established in conformity with national legislation and practice, invalidity and survivors' benefits, intended to supplement or replace those provided in respect of the same contingencies by statutory social security schemes'.[172]

The nub of the Directive is found in Article 4. It applies the principle of equal treatment to migrant workers in respect of pensions to which contributions are no longer being made. This provides that:

Member States shall take the necessary measures to ensure the preservation of vested pension rights for members of a supplementary pension scheme in respect of whom contributions are no longer being made to that scheme as a consequence of their moving from one Member State to another, to the same extent as for members in respect of whom contributions are no longer being made but who remain within the same Member State. This Article shall also apply to other persons holding entitlement under the rules of the supplementary pension scheme in question.

In addition, Member States must ensure that, in respect of members of supplementary pension schemes and others holding entitlement under such schemes, supplementary pension schemes make payment in other Member States, net of any taxes and transaction charges which may be applicable, of all benefits due under such schemes.[173]

Article 6 deals with the position of posted workers. This provides that Member States must take measures to enable contributions to continue to be made to a supplementary pension scheme established in a Member State by or on behalf of a posted worker who is a member of such a scheme during the period of his or her posting in another Member State. If such contributions are made in one Member State then the posted worker and, where applicable, his employer are exempted from making contributions to a supplementary pension scheme in another Member State.[174]

Finally, Article 7 requires Member States to take measures to ensure that employers, trustees, or others responsible for the management of supplementary pension schemes provide adequate information to scheme members, when they move to another Member State, as to their pension rights and the choices which are available to them under the scheme. Such information must at least correspond to information given to scheme members in respect of whom contributions cease to be made but who remain within the same Member State.

---

[171] Art. 3(b) says a 'supplementary pension scheme' means any occupational pension scheme established in conformity with national legislation and practice such as a group insurance contract or pay-as-you-go scheme agreed by one or more branches or sectors, funded scheme or pension promise backed by book reserves, or any collective or other comparable arrangement intended to provide a supplementary pension for employed or self-employed persons.

[172] Art. 3(a).

[173] Art. 5.

[174] Art. 8 provides that this provision can apply to postings that commence on or after 25 July 2001.

This measure forms part of a wider series of initiatives designed to enable supplementary pension schemes to benefit from the Single Market and the euro. The proposals revolve around three main principles: better protection of scheme members coupled with more efficient investment by pension funds; gradual removal of obstacles to labour mobility; and continued co-ordination of Member States' tax systems so as to reduce the tax distortions affecting the provision of supplementary pensions products on a cross-border basis.[175]

4. Social Protection

As we have seen, Regulation 1408/71 emphasizes co-ordination of national social security schemes but does not aim to harmonize the benefits available or provide any details about their content. However, the Community Social Charter 1989 provides:

10. Every worker of the European Community shall have a right to adequate social protection and shall, whatever his status and whatever the size of the undertaking in which he is employed, enjoy an adequate level of social security benefits.

Persons who have been unable either to enter or re-enter the labour market and have no means of subsistence must be able to receive sufficient resources and social assistance in keeping with their particular situation.

24. Every worker of the European Community must, at the time of retirement, be able to enjoy resources affording him or her a decent standard of living.

25. Any person who has reached retirement age but who is not entitled to a pension or who does not have other means of subsistence, must be entitled to sufficient resources and to medical and social assistance specifically suited to his needs.

Thus, the Charter advocates the need for social assistance programmes, designed to provide a minimum level of protection to meet the basic living requirement of those unable to provide for themselves, in order to alleviate poverty and social exclusion.[176] Two soft law measures, Council Recommendation 92/441/EEC[177] on common criteria concerning sufficient resources and social assistance in social protection systems and Council Recommendation 92/442/EEC[178] on the convergence of social policy objectives, take a small step towards realizing these objectives. Both recommendations are intended to reinforce social cohesion within the Community by encouraging 'solidarity with regard to the least privileged and vulnerable people' and respecting 'human dignity [which] is one of the fundamental rights underlying Community law'.[179]

---

[175] Commission Communication on Supplementary Pension Schemes (http://europa.ue.int/comm/dg15).

[176] Hervey, *European Social Law and Policy* (Longman, Harlow, 1998), 158.

[177] [1992] OJ L245/46.

[178] Ibid.

[179] Preamble to Recommendation 92/441.

Recommendation 92/441 concentrates on the level of the resources available. It recommends that Member States 'recognise the basic right of a person to sufficient resources and social assistance to live in a manner compatible with human dignity as part of a comprehensive and consistent drive to combat social exclusion, and to adapt their social protection systems'.[180] It then lays down principles according to which this right must be assured. In particular, the resources should be provided on an individual basis,[181] should not be time limited,[182] and should be fixed at a level considered 'sufficient to cover essential needs with regard to respect for human dignity, taking account of living standards and price levels in the Member State concerned, for different types and sizes of household'.[183] Thus, the Recommendation guidance is carefully circumscribed by respect for the principle of subsidiarity and the divergence of national systems.[184]

Recommendation 92/442, by contrast, provides guidance on the coordination of national policies. Although still hemmed in by the principle of subsidiarity and respect for the autonomy of the national systems, it is more ambitious. It begins with four basic principles for social protection policies. First, it recommends that Member States give any person legally resident in their territory, regardless of resources, access to their health services.[185] It also recommends that States provide employed workers who retire or interrupt their careers with replacement income to maintain their standard of living.[186] Secondly, social benefits must be provided on a non-discriminatory basis without regard to 'nationality, race, sex, religion, customs or political opinion'[187] and must be granted according to the principles of fairness,[188] so that beneficiaries of social benefits receive their share from the improvements in the standard of living of the population as a whole. Thirdly, it recommends that social policies should adapt to the development of behaviour and of family structures responsive to changes in the labour market; and, fourthly, that social protection should be administered with maximum efficiency. The Recommendation then makes specific suggestions in respect of six policy areas—sickness, maternity, unemployment, and incapacity for work, the elderly, and the family.

The subsequent Council Resolution on the role of social protection systems in the fight against unemployment[189] marked a shift away from rights for those without work towards focusing on getting them back to work which

---

[180] Para. I.A.
[181] Para. I.B.2.
[182] Para. I.B.4.
[183] Para. I.C.1(a).
[184] See also the emphasis on subsidiarity in COM(97)102.
[185] Para. I.A.1(b).
[186] Para. I.A.1(d).
[187] Para. I.A.2(a).
[188] Para. I.A.2(b).
[189] [1996] OJ C386/3.

should provide sufficient and secure income.[190] It called on the Member States to incorporate into their social protection policies the objectives of combating unemployment and of integrating and reintegrating unemployed men and women into economic and social life.[191] The White Paper on Growth, Competitiveness, and Employment[192] said that there was insufficient motivation to work due to inappropriate social protection schemes and employment services. It also expressed concerns about the funding of these schemes by high non-wage costs, particularly in the form of statutory levies and charges, through which an equivalent of 40 per cent of the Community's GDP is channelled. It says that this imposes a heavy burden on business and impedes employment creation. It therefore recommended a reduction in non-wage labour costs ranging from 1–2 per cent of GDP for the EU as a whole.

These concerns were picked up in the Commission's Communication on 'Modernising and Improving Social Protection in the European Union'.[193] While recognizing that publicly funded social protection systems (social security and social assistance) established decades ago have played a 'fundamental role in ensuring income redistribution and cohesion, and in maintaining political stability and economic progress over the life of the Union', it notes that the systems account for 28 per cent of total EU GDP and are in need of modernization to ensure their continued effectiveness. Although it recognizes that social protection can be a productive factor, it expresses concern about the level of non-wage costs and the need for policies designed to improve flexibility and to provide security. This is reflected in the Entrepreneurship pillar of the Employment Guidelines which envisages setting a target for gradually reducing the overall tax burden and, where appropriate, a target for gradually reducing the fiscal pressure on labour and non-wage labour costs, in particular on relatively unskilled and low-paid labour.[194] The tenor of these developments seems to be that the results of future co-ordination of social protection may lead to the reduction in the level of benefits rather than their improvement, especially for those Member States participating in EMU which have agreed to limit public deficit to 3 per cent and have a maximum of 60 per cent of GDP in public debt.[195]

---

[190] See the Commission Communication, 'A Concerted Strategy for Modernising Social Protection' COM(2000)134. See also the Council Conclusions on the 'Strengthening of Cooperation for Modernising and Improving Social Protection' 2000/C8/05 [2000] OJ L8/7. The Lisbon Employment summit in Mar. 2000 encouraged the Council to strengthen co-operation between States by exchanging experiences and best practice (Presidency Conclusions, para. 31).

[191] Para. I.1.

[192] Bull. Supp 6/93, 124, 136ff.

[193] COM(97)102.

[194] Council Resolution 98/128 on the 1998 Employment Guidelines [1998] OJ 30/1, as amended.

[195] See Guild, 'How Can Social Protection Survive EMU? A United Kingdom Perspective' (1999) 24 *ELRev.* 22, citing Pakaslahti, *Does EMU Threaten European Welfare?*, Working Paper No. 17 (Observatoire Social Européen, June 1997).

B. DIRECTIVE 79/7: EQUAL TREATMENT IN SOCIAL SECURITY

Directive 79/7,[196] adopted alongside Directive 75/117[197] on equal pay for men and women and Directive 76/207[198] on equal treatment, formed a package of measures put forward under the 1974 Social Action Programme designed to eliminate discrimination between men and women both in the workplace and in respect of social security schemes.[199] Unlike Regulation 1408/71, Directive 79/7 does not require the beneficiaries to have exercised their rights of free movement but it insures only against the main employment risks of sickness, invalidity, unemployment, accidents at work, and old age.

1. The Material and Personal Scope of the Directive

According to Article 1, the purpose of Directive 79/7 is the *progressive implementation*[200] of the principle of equal treatment in matters of social security and other areas of social protection provided for in Article 3(1). These areas are:

(a) statutory schemes which provide protection against:

- sickness;
- invalidity;
- old age;
- accidents at work and occupational diseases;
- unemployment;[201] and

(b) social assistance, in so far as it is intended to supplement or replace schemes referred to in (a).

In *Drake*[202] the Court expanded the scope of Article 3(1) to include benefits

---

[196] Council Directive 79/7 of 19 Dec. 1978 on the progressive implementation of the principle of equal treatment for men and women in matters of social security [1979] OJ L6/1. It has been in force since 23 Dec. 1984. Member States therefore had six years to implement the Directive, the longest period ever set for a Directive (see Hoskyns, *Interpreting Gender: Women, Law and Politics in the European Union* (Verso, London, 1996), 111). Art. 5 requires Member States to take the measures necessary to abolish any laws, regulations, and administrative provisions, contrary to the principle of equal treatment. See Luckhaus, 'Changing Rules Enduring Structures' (1990) 53 *MLR* 655.

[197] [1975] OJ L45/19. See further Ch. 4.

[198] [1976] OJ L39/40. See further Ch. 4.

[199] The original draft of Directive 79/7 referred to both statutory and occupational social security schemes. During the negotiations the occupational dimension was postponed to a further directive: Directive 86/378/EEC [1986] OJ L225/40, as amended by Council Directive 96/97 [1997] OJ L46/20.

[200] The significance of this point was reiterated by the Court in Case 150/85 *Drake* v. *Chief Adjudication Officer* [1986] ECR 1995.

[201] Cf. the eight risks covered by Art. 4(1) of Regulation 1408/71.

[202] Case 150/85 [1986] ECR 1995.

which constitute 'the whole *or part*' of a statutory scheme providing protection against one of the specified risks, such as invalidity. The Court developed this idea in *ex parte Richardson*.[203] It said that in order to fall within the scope of the Directive, a benefit must constitute the whole or part of a statutory scheme providing protection against one of the specified risks, or a form of social assistance having the same objective. It added that although the way in which a benefit was granted was not decisive for the purposes of the Directive, in order to fall within its scope the benefit must be directly and effectively linked to the protection provided against one of the risks specified in Article 3(1).

However, as we shall see, *Drake* was a rather exceptional case and the Court has shown signs of retrenchment since then.[204] In *ex parte Smithson*,[205] a case concerning housing benefit which was paid to people on a low income, the Court said that since Article 3(1)(a) did not refer to statutory schemes relating to housing costs, the British legislation fell outside the scope of the Directive because it was not 'directly and effectively linked to the protection provided against one of the risks specified in Article 3(1)',[206] even though the recipient of the benefit was in one of the circumstances listed in Article 3(1). Similarly, in *Jackson and Cresswell*[207] the Court said that benefits designed to supplement the income of claimants (supplementary allowance and income support) were excluded from the scope of Directive 79/7. The Court pointed out that the national schemes exempted claimants from the obligation of being available for work which showed that 'the benefits in question cannot be regarded as being directly and effectively linked to protection against the risk of unemployment'.[208] The Court then recognized that despite the wording of Article 1(2) of Directive 76/207 'a scheme of benefits cannot be excluded from the scope of the Directive solely because, formally, it is part of a national social security system'.[209] However, the assertion that 'the method of calculating claimants' actual earnings . . . might affect sole mothers' ability to take up access to vocational training or part-time employment, is not sufficient to bring such schemes within the scope of Directive 76/207'.[210]

Thus, the stress now appears to be on whether the benefit provides direct and effective protection against one of the risks specified in Article 3(1) rather

---

[203] Case C–137/94 *R* v. *Secretary of State for Health, ex parte Richardson* [1995] ECR I–3407.

[204] Cousins, 'Equal Treatment and Social Security' (1994) 19 *ELRev.* 123. See further below, n. 217.

[205] Case C–243/90 *R* v. *Secretary of State for Social Security, ex parte Smithson* [1992] ECR I–467.

[206] Para. 12.

[207] Joined Cases C–63 and 64/91 [1992] ECR I–4737. This case concerned a challenge to the national legislation which prevented child-minding expenses to be taken into account in assessing entitlement to various means-tested payments on the ground that it indirectly discriminated against women.

[208] Para. 21.

[209] Para. 27.

[210] Para. 30. See also Case C–116/94 *Meyers* v. *Adjudication Officer* [1995] ECR I–2131.

than 'incidental' protection.[211] This helps to explain the decision in *Jackson and Cresswell* since it could be argued that most forms of cash benefit offer protection against unemployment, and the later decision in *Hoever and Zachow*[212] where the Court said a child-raising allowance was outside the scope of the Directive.[213] The emphasis on direct and effective protection can also be seen in *Atkins*[214] concerning a concessionary travel scheme which allowed men over the age of 65 and women aged over 60 reduced fares on public transport. The Court said that the benefit in *Atkins* was not directly and effectively linked to the protection provided against one of the risks specified in Article 3(1). The purpose of concessionary travel was to facilitate access to public transport for certain classes of persons who, for various reasons, were recognized as having a particular need for public transport and who were, for the same reasons, less well-off financially and materially. It said that although old age and invalidity were among the categories covered by Directive 79/7 they were only two of the criteria which might be applied to define the classes of beneficiaries of such a scheme of concessionary fares. The fact that the recipient of the benefit happened to fall within one of the categories envisaged by Article 3(1) was not sufficient to bring the benefit within the scope of EC law. By contrast, in *ex parte Richardson*[215] the Court ruled that prescription charges fell within the scope of Article 3(1) because they provided direct and effective protection against sickness; and in *ex parte Taylor*[216] the Court ruled that a winter fuel payment protected directly and effectively against the risk of old age.

The potential beneficiaries of the Directive are widely drawn by Article 2. It applies to the 'working population' which covers 'self-employed persons, workers and self-employed persons whose activity is interrupted by illness, accident or involuntary unemployment and persons seeking employment— and to retired or invalided workers and self-employed persons'. A person is still a member of the working population even if one of the risks mentioned in Article 3 materializes in relation to an ascendant, forcing the worker to interrupt his or her occupational activity. This was the situation in *Drake*.[217] Mrs Drake, who had given up work to care for her invalid mother, was regarded as a member of the working population, because her employment had been interrupted, albeit by the invalidity of another. The Court justified this conclusion by reference to the objectives of the Treaty and the Directive. It emphasized that 'there is a *clear economic link* between the benefit and the

---

[211] White, *EC Social Security Law* (Longman, Harlow, 1999), 121.

[212] Joined Cases C–245 and C–312/94 *Hoever and Zachow* [1996] ECR I–4895.

[213] Cf. Case C–139/95 *Livia Balestra v. Istituto Nazionale della Presidenza Sociale* [1997] ECR I–549 where early retirement benefits fell within Art. 3(1) because they provide protection against the 'risk' of old-age.

[214] Case C–228/94 *Atkins v. Wrekin DC and Department of Transport* [1996] ECR I–3633.

[215] Case C–137/94 [1995] ECR I–3633.

[216] Case C–382/98 *R v. Secretary of State for Social Security, ex parte Taylor*, judgment of 16 Dec. 1999, para. 23.

[217] Case 150/85 [1986] ECR 1995.

disabled person, since the disabled person derives an advantage from the fact that an allowance is paid to the person caring for him . . . the fact that a benefit . . . is paid to a third party and not directly to the disabled person does not place it outside the scope of Directive 79/7'.[218]

A person is also a member of the working population where the risk materializes while the person concerned is seeking employment immediately after a period without occupational activity;[219] or where the employment in question is regarded as minor since it consists of less than fifteen hours' work a week and attracts remuneration of less than one-seventh of the average monthly salary;[220] or where, as in *Verholen*,[221] the individual who is not within the Article (the husband) 'bears the effect' of the discriminatory treatment directed at another, his wife who is not a party to the proceedings but does fall within the scope of Article 2.

On the other hand, the Court has said that the Directive does not apply to people who are not working and are not seeking work or to people whose occupation or efforts to find work are not interrupted by one of the risks referred to in Article 3 of the Directive.[222] Therefore, in *Achterberg-te Riele* the Court held that a person who has given up his or her occupational activity in order to attend to the upbringing of his or her children did not fall within the scope of the Directive.[223] This point was confirmed in *Züchner*[224] where the Court ruled that Article 2 of Directive 79/7/EEC 'must be interpreted as not covering a person who undertakes, as an unremunerated activity, the care of his or her handicapped spouse, whatever the extent of that activity and the competence required in order to perform it, where the person in question did not, in order to do so, abandon an occupational activity or interrupt efforts to find employment'. Therefore, the Court was not prepared to extend the per-

---

[218] Ibid. This case was the subject of a well-orchestrated campaign led by the Invalid Care Allowance (ICA) campaign. See further Luckhaus, 'Payment for Caring: A European Solution' [1986] *PL* 526, who suggests that the Court was motivated by its desire to condemn such unabashed discrimination and so engaged in 'some well meaning subterfuge' in order to extend the reach of Community law into the realm of domestic unpaid work. See also Case C–343/92 *De Weerd, née Roks and Others* v. *Bestuur van de Bedrijfsvereniging voor de Gezondheid* [1994] ECR I–571.

[219] Case C–31/90 *Johnson* v. *Chief Adjudication Officer (No. 1)* [1991] ECR I–3723. The onus of proof is on the applicant to show that he or she was seeking work in these circumstances. This is a matter for the national court to decide, taking into account such factors as whether a person was registered with an employment organization, whether he or she had sent out job applications, and whether he or she could produce certificates to show that he or she had attended interviews.

[220] Case C–317/93 *Nolte* v. *Landesversicherungsanstalt Hannover* [1995] ECR I–4625 and Case C–444/93 *Megner and Scheffel* v. *Innungskrankenkasse Vorderpfalz* [1995] ECR I–4741. See also Case C–280/94 *Posthuma-van Damme* v. *Bestuur van de Bedrijfsvereniging voor Detailhandel* [1996] ECR I–179.

[221] Joined Cases C–87, 88/90 and 89/90 *Verholen* v. *Verzekeringsbank Amsterdam* [1991] ECR I–3757. Cf Case C–77/95 *Bruna-Alessandra Züchner* v. *Handelskrankenkasse (Ersatzkasse) Bremen* [1996] ECR I–5689, below n. 224, and Waddington, 'The Court of Justice Fails to Show its Caring Face' (1997) 22 *ELRev.* 587.

[222] Case 48/88 *Achterberg-te Riele and Others* v. *Sociale Verzekeringsbank* [1989] ECR 1963.

[223] Case C–31/90 *Johnson (No. 1)* [1991] ECR I–3723.

[224] Case C–77/95 [1996] ECR I–5689.

sonal scope of the Directive to a woman who is not 'economically active' (neither in paid employment, nor seeking work, nor whose employment was interrupted by one of the risks listed in Article 3 of the Directive) who gives special care to her invalid husband, even though she has to undertake special training to care for him properly. In the light of *Verholen*, this decision seems particularly harsh for unpaid carers. It also takes no account of the social circumstances in which a woman's relationship with the paid employment market and social security systems is constituted.[225] If Züchner's husband had had no relation to care for him, the caring work carried out by his carer would have been remunerated, either privately or by the State through its social security provision. However, caring work carried out by women on a private basis is not characterized by EC law as 'work' and therefore falls outside the scope of EC sex equality provisions. The Court seems to be concerned with delimiting the scope of application of Directive 79/7. To extend its scope to women such as Ms Züchner would, as the Court put it, 'have the effect of infinitely extending the scope of the directive'.[226] Such an extension might threaten severe disruption of national social security systems whose conceptual (and financial) basis is protection for economically active persons, whose employment is interrupted by a risk against which the social security system provides protection.

2. The Principle of Equal Treatment

Article 4(1) gives practical expression to the principle of equal treatment set out in Article 1.[227] It provides that:

there shall be no discrimination whatsoever on the ground of sex either directly, or indirectly, by reference in particular to marital or family status,[228] in particular, as concerns:

— the scope of the schemes and the conditions of access thereto,
— the obligation to contribute and the calculation of the contributions,
— the calculations of benefits including increases[229] due in respect of a spouse[230] and

---

[225] Sohrab, *Sexing the Benefit: Women, Social Security and Financial Independence in EC Sex Equality Law* (Dartmouth, Aldershot, 1996).

[226] Para. 15.

[227] Case 150/85 *Drake* [1986] ECR 1995.

[228] This definition closely mirrors that found in the Equal Treatment Directive. The reference to 'marital status' is particularly important because the national social security systems of the Member States are in general based on the model of the family unit, consisting of one breadwinner (male), one adult dependant (female), and dependent children. This model is highly prone to discrimination against the female sex.

[229] Member States are entitled to stipulate whatever increases they wish for entitlement to increases in social security benefits, provided they require fully with the principle of equal treatment laid down in Art. 4(1): Case C–377/89 *Cotter and Others* v. *Minister for Social Welfare* [1991] ECR I–1155.

[230] Spouses do not need to be dependent: Case C–377/89 *Cotter and Others* [1991] ECR I–1155.

for dependants[231] and the conditions governing the duration and retention of entitlements to benefits.[232]

The principle of equal treatment even applies where indivisible social security contributions relate to social security benefits which only partly come within the scope *rationae materiae* of Directive 79/7.[233]

The 'fundamental' principle of equal treatment was recognized in *Drake*.[234] In the United Kingdom an Invalid Care Allowance (ICA) was not payable to a married woman who lived with her husband although it was payable in corresponding circumstances to a man. The Court found that this legislation was directly discriminatory and contravened Articles 1 and 4(1).[235] In *FNV*[236] the Court said that Article 4(1) was sufficiently precise and unconditional to be directly effective.[237] These decisions paved the way to challenging a wide variety of national legislation which discriminated either directly or indirectly, usually against women. For example, in *Borrie Clarke*[238] the Court held that Article 4(1) did not permit Member States to make conditional or to limit the application of the principle of equal treatment, nor did it allow Member States to maintain beyond 22 December 1984 (the date for implementing the Directive) any inequalities of treatment which had their origin in the fact that conditions of entitlement to the benefit were those which applied before that date. *Borrie Clarke* concerned Severe Disablement Allowance (SDA), introduced to replace the discriminatory Non-Contributory Invalidity Pension (NCIP). In order to receive NCIP the household duties test was applied to women but not men. This asked whether the woman was capable of performing normal household duties. Under the transitional provisions, automatic entitlement to the SDA was subject to the same discriminatory criteria as for

---

[231] No proof of their dependency is actually required under the Directive as a prior condition of the application of the principle of equal treatment: Case C–377/89 *Cotter and Others* [1991] ECR I–1155.

[232] Art. 4(1). Art. 4(2) contains an exclusion for provisions relating to the protection of women on the grounds of maternity.

[233] Case C–373/89 *Caisse d'Assurances Sociales pour Travailleurs Indépendants 'Integrity'* v. *Rouvroy* [1990] ECR 1243.

[234] Case 150/85 [1986] ECR 1995.

[235] e.g. Case C–337/91 *A. M. van Gemert-Derks* v. *Bestuur van de Nieuwe Industriële Bedrijfsvereniging* [1993] ECR I–5435.

[236] Case 71/85 *Netherlands* v. *Federatie Nederlandse Vakbeweging* [1986] ECR 3855.

[237] The derogations contained in Arts. 5 and 7 of the Directive do not confer on the Member States the power to make conditional or limit the application of the principle of equal treatment and thus do not prevent Art. 4(1) from having direct effect. See Arnull, 'Equal Treatment and Social Security' (1987) 12 *ELRev.* 276. The fact that Art. 4(1) is directly effective has been endorsed by the Court in numerous cases including Case 150/85 *Drake* [1986] ECR 1995; Case 286/85 *McDermott and Cotter* v. *Minister for Social Welfare and Attorney General* [1987] ECR 1453; and Case 384/85 *J. B. Clarke* v. *Chief Adjudication Officer* [1987] ECR 2865. Member States can belatedly introduce legislation and make it retroactive to the date when implementation was required: see Case 80/87 *Dik and Mencutos-Demirci* v. *College van Burgermeester en Wethouders Arnhem and Winterswijk* [1988] ECR 1601.

[238] Case 384/85 [1987] ECR 2865.

NCIP (the 'household duties test'). The Court found that women were entitled to be treated in the same manner and to have the same rules applied to them as men.[239] Therefore, since a man was automatically entitled to the new SDA, a woman should also receive the new benefit automatically.

Relying on the decision in *Borrie Clarke* Mrs Johnson also claimed SDA.[240] She gave up work to look after her daughter in 1970. By 1980 she wished to return to work but, since she was unable to do so due to a back condition, she received NCIP. However, this payment was stopped when Mrs Johnson began to cohabit because she was considered capable of performing normal household duties. Mrs Johnson applied for SDA on the basis that she would have been entitled to the NCIP immediately prior to the abolition of the benefit, had the discriminatory household duties test not been applied to her in 1980. The Court supported her arguments, concluding that national legislation making entitlement to a benefit, such as the SDA, subject to an earlier claim for a benefit which incorporated a discriminatory requirement was incompatible with Article 4(1) of Directive 79/7. The national legislation therefore had to be set aside. Similarly, in *Cotter and Others*[241] the Court ruled that if married men have automatically received increases in social security benefits in respect of a spouse and children deemed to be dependants without having to prove actual dependency, married women without actual dependants were also entitled to those increases, even if in some circumstances that would result in double payment of the increases.

The cases considered so far concern legislation which was directly discriminatory. *Teuling*[242] confirms that Article 4(1) also outlaws indirectly discriminatory measures—that is, measures which, although formulated in neutral terms, work to the disadvantage of far more women than men[243]— unless they can be objectively justified. *Teuling* concerned a system of benefits where supplements were provided which, although not directly based on the sex of the beneficiaries, took account of their marital status or family situation. It became apparent that a considerably smaller number of women than men

---

[239] The Court applied *Borrie Clark* in another case concerning discriminatory transitional provisions, Case 80/87 *Dik and Mencutos-Demirci* [1988] ECR 1601, which in turn was applied in Case C–377/89 *Cotter and Others* [1991] ECR I–1155. See also Case 286/85 *McDermott and Cotter* [1987] ECR 1453 and Case C–154/92 *Van Cant* v. *Rijksdienst voor Pensioenen* [1993] ECR I–3811.

[240] Case C–31/90 *Johnson (No. 1)* [1991] ECR I–3723, noted by Laske (1992) 29 *CMLRev.* 101. See also below, n. 298.

[241] Case C–377/89 [1991] ECR I–1155. See also Case C–338/91 *Steenhorst-Neerings* v. *Bestuur van de Bedrijfsvereniging* [1993] ECR I–5475 where a national law deprived women of benefits which men continued to receive, even though the national court applied the law in a non-discriminatory manner.

[242] Case 30/85 *Teuling* v. *Bedrijfsvereniging voor de Chemische Industrie* [1987] ECR 2497.

[243] Case C–343/92 *De Weerd* [1994] ECR I–571, para. 33, and Case C–229/89 *Commission* v. *Belgium* [1991] ECR I–2205, para. 13. See generally Ch. 4 and Steiner, 'The Principle of Equal Treatment for Men and Women in Social Security', in *Sex Equality Law in the European Union*, eds. Hervey and O'Keeffe (Wiley, Chichester, 1996).

were entitled to such supplements and that the scheme was therefore indirectly discriminatory and contrary to Article 4(1), unless the system could be justified on grounds other than sex. The Court did accept the justification that the system sought to ensure an adequate minimum subsistence income for beneficiaries who had a dependent spouse or dependent children, by means of a supplement to the social security benefit which compensated for the greater burdens they had to bear in comparison with single people.

This approach was confirmed in *Ruzius-Wilbrink.*[244] This case concerned Dutch legislation providing disability allowances to workers which were lower for part-time workers than full-time workers. The Court found, first, that such a provision was indirectly discriminatory against female workers and, secondly, that the discrimination could not be objectively justified. The Court therefore concluded that since in the case of direct discrimination women were entitled to be treated in the same manner as men, so part-time workers had to be treated in the same way as full-timers in the case of indirect discrimination (a levelling up of benefit), because such rules relating to full-timers remained the only valid point of reference so long as the Directive had not been implemented correctly.[245]

The question of objective justification was considered further in *De Weerd.*[246] The case concerned national legislation making receipt of a benefit for incapacity for work subject to the requirement of having received a certain income from or in connection with work in the year preceding the commencement of the incapacity. That requirement was indirectly discriminatory because it affected more women than men and therefore breached Article 4(1) 'unless that measure is based on objectively justified factors unrelated to any discrimination on grounds of sex' (paragraph 33).[247] The Court continued, 'That is the case where the measures chosen reflect a legitimate social policy aim of the Member State whose legislation is at issue, are appropriate to achieve that aim and are necessary in order to do so' (paragraph 34).[248] Budgetary considerations did not, however, justify a difference in treatment. As the Court said '[A]lthough budgetary considerations may influence a Member State's choice of social policy and affect the nature or scope of the social protection measures it wishes to adopt, they cannot themselves consti-

---

[244] Case C–102/88 *Ruzius-Wilbrink* v. *Bedrijfsvereniging voor Overheidsdiensten* [1989] ECR 4311.

[245] Para. 16.

[246] Case C–343/92 [1994] ECR I–571.

[247] Para. 33, citing Case C–229/89 *Commission* v. *Belgium* [1991] ECR I–2205.

[248] This follows Case 171/88 *Rinner-Kühn* v. *FWW Spezial-Gebäudereinigung GmbH* [1989] ECR 2743, para. 14, concerning legislation which was *prima facie* indirectly discriminatory contrary to Art. 119 [new Art. 141]. In Case C–226/91 *Molenbroeck* v. *Sociale Verzekeringsbank* [1992] ECR I–5943 the Court emphasized 'the reasonable margin of discretion' allowed to Member States as to the nature of the social protection measures and the detailed arrangements for their implementation.

tute the aim pursued by that policy and cannot therefore justify discrimination against one of the sexes'. However, the Court did say that Community law did not prevent budgetary constraints being taken into account when making the continuance of entitlement to social security benefit dependent on certain conditions, the effect of which was to withdraw benefits from certain categories of people, provided that when the Member State did so they did not infringe the rule of equal treatment laid down in Article 4(1).[249]

In *Nolte*[250] and *Megner and Scheffel*[251] the Court relaxed the rigorous test for objective justification laid down in *De Weerd*. These cases concerned a German social security law under which individuals working fewer than fifteen hours per week and whose income did not exceed one-seventh of the monthly reference wage[252] ('minor' or 'marginal' part-time workers) were not subject to the statutory old-age insurance scheme and were also exempt from paying contributions for unemployment benefit. Although the legislation affected considerably more women than men, the German government argued that the exclusion of persons in minor employment corresponded to a structural principle of the German social security scheme. Having cited the test contained in paragraphs 33 and 34 of the judgment in *De Weerd* (see above), the Court then said that in the current state of Community law, social policy was a matter for the Member States.[253] Consequently, it was for the Member States to choose the measures capable of achieving the aim of their social and employment policy. In exercising that competence Member States had a broad margin of discretion. It then said:

It should be noted that the social and employment policy aim relied on by the German government is objectively unrelated to any discrimination on the grounds of sex and that, in exercising its competence, the national legislature was *reasonably entitled* to consider that the legislation in question was necessary in order to achieve that aim [emphasis added].

It therefore said that the legislation could not be described as indirectly discriminatory within the meaning of Article 4(1).[254] Thus, in the context of

[249] Para. 29.
[250] Case C–317/93 [1995] ECR I–4625. See generally Hervey, 'Sex Equality in Social Protection: New Institutional Perspectives on Allocation of Competence' (1998) 4 *ELJ* 196.
[251] Case C–444/93 [1995] ECR I–4741.
[252] The average monthly salary of persons insured under the statutory old-age insurance scheme during the previous calendar year.
[253] This point was made clearly by the Court in Case C–343/92 *De Weerd* [1994] ECR I–571, para. 28: 'Directive 79/7 leaves intact, however, the powers reserved by Articles 117 and 118 [new Arts. 136 and 140] of the Treaty to the Member States to define their social policy within the framework of close co-operation organised by the Commission, and consequently the nature and extent of the measures of social protection, including those relating to social security and the way in which they are implemented', citing Case C–229/89 *Commission v. Belgium* [1991] ECR I–2205. The point was again repeated in Case C–280/94 *Posthuma-van Damme* [1996] ECR I–179, para. 26.
[254] Case C–317/93 *Nolte* [1995] ECR I–4625, paras. 34 and 35; Case C–444/93 *Megner and Scheffel* [1995] ECR I–571, paras. 30 and 31.

social security at least, a weaker test of objective justification applies.[255] It was applied again in *Laperre*.[256] The case concerned the conditions of access (previous employment, age, and incapacity) to a non-means-tested social security benefit, the IOAW, which Mrs Laperre argued gave rise to indirect sex discrimination. Another scheme, the RWW, also provided a minimum income but was subject to a means test. The Netherlands government said that while the RWW aimed to bring the unemployed back to work by providing income for those of 'modest assets', the IOAW was not means-tested because the legislature sought to protect potential beneficiaries from having to break into their life savings given that they had little chance of rebuilding their assets by resuming gainful employment. The Court said that the aim relied on by the Dutch government was a matter of social policy, that it was objectively unrelated to any discrimination on the grounds of sex and that, in exercising its competence, the national legislature was reasonably entitled to consider that the legislation in question was necessary in order to achieve that aim.[257]

The Court also showed the same deference to the national system in *Posthuma-van Damme*.[258] In that case the Court was asked to consider whether its judgment in *De Weerd* meant that the national law could not be justified at all or only that it could not be justified on budgetary grounds. The Court confirmed the latter interpretation. It also accepted the Dutch government's arguments that guaranteeing a minimum income to people who had given up work on the grounds of incapacity satisfied a legitimate aim of social policy. It also agreed that imposing conditions on access to the benefit constituted a measure appropriate to achieving the objective which the national legislature, in the exercise of its competence, was reasonably entitled to consider necessary. The fact that the scheme replaced a scheme of pure national insurance and that the number of people who actually benefited was further reduced did not affect the finding. This case, more than any other, sounded the death knell to the rigorous approach adopted in *De Weerd*.

---

[255] See also the discussion of this subject in Ch. 4.

[256] Case C–8/94 *Laperre v. Bestuurcommissie beroepszaken in de provincie Zuid-Holland* [1996] ECR I–273.

[257] Although the Court was not provided with a detailed explanation of the employment conditions at issue, Advocate General Lenz was prepared to assume that the condition relating to employment operated to the disadvantage of women whose employment histories often had long gaps because of their need to fulfil their family obligations. Nevertheless, he accepted that the provisions were not contrary to Community law because Dutch law was entitled to offer specific protection to those who had maintained themselves from earned income over a long period.

[258] Case C–280/94 [1996] ECR I–179.

3. Exceptions and Derogations

Directive 79/7 contains permanent exceptions and temporary, 'permissive' derogations. Into the first category fall survivors' benefits, family benefits,[259] occupational pension schemes,[260] and provisions relating to the protection of women on the grounds of maternity.[261] Into the second category fall the derogations found in Article 7. Member States have the right to exclude from the scope of the Directive a long list of benefits,[262] the most significant of which is Article 7(1)(a), the determination of pensionable age for the purposes of granting old-age and retirement benefits, and the possible consequences for other benefits.[263]

3.1 Article 7(1)(a) on the Determination of Pensionable Age for Granting Old-age and Retirement Benefits

Article 7(1)(a) was at issue in *ex parte EOC*[264] where it was argued that the British state pension scheme, which allowed women to receive their state pension at 60 while men had to wait until 65, unlawfully discriminated against men in two ways. First, it required men to pay contributions for forty-four years to qualify for the same basic retirement pension as women who had contributed for only thirty-nine years. The corollary of this was that a man who had made contributions for thirty-nine years received a lower basic pension than a women who had contributed for thirty-nine years. Secondly, men working between the ages of 60 and 64 had to pay contributions but women in the same situation did not.

---

[259] Art. 3(2).

[260] Art. 3(3). See now Directive 86/378 [1986] OJ L225/40 on equal treatment in occupational social security as amended by Council Directive 96/97/EC [1997] OJ L46/20.

[261] Art. 4(2).

[262] The other exclusions relate to entitlements granted to those who have brought up children, derived entitlements of a wife, and the exercise of a right of option not to acquire rights or incur obligations under a statutory scheme. See further Atkins, 'The EEC Directive on Equal Treatment in Social Security Benefits' (1978–9) 1 *JSWL* 244.

[263] Art. 7(1), discussed further below. Member States must periodically examine matters excluded under Art. 7(1) in order to ascertain whether there is justification for maintaining the particular exclusion (Art. 7(2)). Art. 8(2) obliges the Member State to notify the Commission of the reasons for maintaining the derogation under Art. 7(2). A Directive on the Implementation of the Principle of Equal Treatment for Men and Women in Statutory and Occupational Social Security Schemes was proposed ([1988] OJ C95/4), designed to fill the gaps left by Directives 79/7 and 86/378, although its purpose may have been overtaken in part by decisions of the Court. It extends the principle of equal treatment to the areas previously excluded by the earlier Directives, esp. pensionable age in both statutory and occupational schemes. Art. 9 proposes two alternatives for achieving this objective: the first involves selecting a uniform age for men and women but with safeguards for those who have already reached a certain age close to retirement; the second envisages flexible retirement, allowing workers to choose their retirement age during a specified period, provided that the conditions, esp. with regard to the number of contribution years, are identical for both sexes.

[264] Case C–9/91 *R v. Secretary of State for Social Security, ex parte Equal Opportunities Commission* [1992] ECR I–4297.

According to the Court, the purpose of the Directive was to achieve *progressive* implementation of the principle of equal treatment in social security. The progressive nature of the implementation was reflected in the number of derogations. The purpose of the derogations, allowing Member States to maintain temporarily advantageous treatment of women in the field of state pensions, was to enable Member States 'progressively to adapt their pension systems [towards equality] without disrupting the complex financial equilibrium of those systems'. Therefore, any derogation under Article 7(1)(a) would be rendered nugatory if it did not apply to contribution periods, otherwise Member States would be obliged to alter the existing financial equilibrium substantially.

A similar approach can be found in *Graham*.[265] The case concerned two benefits, an invalidity pension and an invalidity allowance. Three women, who had to stop working before reaching pensionable age due to ill health, initially received sickness benefit and then invalidity pension at the full retirement pension rate. When they reached pensionable age (65 for men, 60 for women) they all opted to continue receiving their invalidity pension rather than a retirement pension which, unlike an invalidity pension, was taxable. As none of the women fulfilled the contribution conditions for the grant of a full retirement pension, the amount of their invalidity pension was reduced to the rate of the retirement pension which would have been paid to them. Had the claimants been men, they would have continued to receive the invalidity pension at the full retirement pension rate until they were 65 and only then would a reduction have been made to reflect the number of years that they had paid contributions.

Graham also complained about the discriminatory effect of the invalidity allowance which was paid in addition to an invalidity pension to a person who was more than five years below pensionable age on the first day of incapacity for work. Graham, who was aged over 55 when she became incapacitated for work, was refused the invalidity allowance. Had she been a man she would have received the payment.

The Court found that the forms of discrimination at issue were objectively linked to the setting of different pensionable ages for men and women. It said that since invalidity benefit was designed to replace income from an occupational activity there was nothing to prevent a Member State from providing for its cessation and replacement by a retirement pension at the time when the recipients would have stopped work because they had reached pensionable age. Consequently, the Court ruled that the derogation in Article 7(1)(a) applied to differences between the rates of invalidity pension payable to men and women from the time when they reached pensionable age. The Court added that, due to the link between invalidity pension and invalidity allow-

---

[265] Case C–92/94 *Secretary of State for Social Security v. Graham* [1995] ECR I–2521.

ance, the same conclusion applied with regard to the difference between the qualifying dates for the grant of invalidity allowance.

In other cases the Court has limited the use of the Article 7(1)(a) derogation. In *Thomas*[266] the Court said that in view of the fundamental importance of the principle of equal treatment the exception to the prohibition of discrimination on the grounds of sex had to be interpreted strictly. Therefore, forms of discrimination provided for in benefit schemes other than old-age and retirement pensions could be justified as being the consequence of determining a different retirement age according to sex 'only if such discrimination is objectively necessary in order to avoid disrupting the complex financial equilibrium of the social security system *or* to ensure consistency between retirement pension schemes and other benefit schemes' (emphasis added).[267] The case concerned the refusal under British law to grant severe disablement allowance and invalid care allowance to those who had reached state pensionable age. The Court suggested that discrimination between men and women under *non-contributory* schemes such as those was unnecessary to preserve the financial equilibrium of the entire social security system.

The decision in *Thomas* led to the significant ruling in *ex parte Richardson*.[268] Richardson, a retired man of 64, claimed that he was discriminated against on the grounds of his sex by national legislation which exempted women aged between 60 and 64 from paying prescription charges but not men of the same age. The Court agreed. It said that Article 7(1)(a) did not apply to the rules on prescription charges since the removal of the discrimination would not affect the financial equilibrium of the pension scheme and that the discrimination was not objectively necessary to ensure coherence between the retirement pension system and regulations concerning prescription charges.[269] In *ex parte Taylor*[270] the Court said that arguments concerning financial equilibrium also did not apply to non-contributory benefits, such as a winter fuel payment, and consequently eliminating discrimination had no impact on the

---

[266] Case C–328/91 *Secretary of State for Social Security* v. *Thomas and Others* [1993] ECR I–1247.

[267] Para. 12. While most subsequent cases concerned the first part of the formula, Case C–196/98 *Hepple* v. *Adjudication Officer*, judgment of 23 May 2000, emphasized the second part to justify excluding Reduced Earnings Allowance from the scope of 4(1) under the Art. 7(1)(a) derogation.

[268] Case C–137/94 [1995] ECR I–3633.

[269] In Case C–228/94 *Atkins* [1996] ECR I–3633 (reduced fares on public transport) the Advocate General urged the Court to follow *ex parte Richardson* rather than *Graham*. He said that the scheme fell within the material scope of the Directive, and that the derogation contained in Art. 7(1)(a) did not apply since the travel concessions had no connection with the extent of entitlement to an old-age pension nor with the overall financing of the pensions system. To remove the discrimination would not, he said, affect the financial equilibrium of the pensions scheme. However, as we saw above, the Court decided that the case fell outside the material scope of the Directive.

[270] Case C–382/98, judgment of 16 Dec. 1999, paras. 30–31; see also Case C–104/98 *Buchner* v. *Sozialversicherungsanstalt der Bauern*, judgment of 23 May 2000.

financial equilibrium of the social security scheme as a whole and so was not covered by the Article 7(1)(a) derogation.

A similarly restrictive approach to Article 7(1)(a) can be found in *Van Cant*.[271] From 1991 Belgian law allowed both men and women to receive their state pension from the age of 60, but it maintained a different method of calculating the pension for each sex. The Court ruled that this was discriminatory contrary to Article 4(1) of the Directive and could not be justified under Article 7(1)(a). It argued that once the national system took the step of abolishing the difference in state pensionable ages Article 7(1)(a) could no longer be relied on to justify maintaining a difference in the method of calculating the retirement pension which was linked to the difference in retirement ages.

This decision in *Van Cant* seemed to allow no scope for (necessary) transitional arrangements which may incorporate the discriminatory features of the earlier scheme. Paradoxically, had the Belgian government maintained different state pension ages it could have continued to rely on Article 7(1)(a) in respect of the method of calculating the pension.[272] There was some dispute in *Van Cant* whether the national law had maintained different pensionable ages. The Court ruled that this was a matter for the national court to decide. However, because different Belgian courts had reached different conclusions on this question, an interpretative law was passed which indicated that the different pensionable ages had not been removed.[273] The consequences of these developments were at issue in *De Vriendt*[274] and *Wolfs*.[275] The references in these cases concerned the new Belgian law establishing a flexible retirement age for men and women, which allows all workers to retire 'early' at the age of 60 during a transitional period. The amount of pension paid was accrued on an annual basis and calculated based on a proportion of the worker's remuneration for that year. For men the highest number of years taken into account to determine the pension was forty-five, but only forty for women. If a worker worked longer than this, the most advantageous forty-five or forty years were used as the basis for the calculation of the pension. Even under the new system, for men the relevant proportion of salary was one forty-fifth, but for women it was one-fortieth of salary. A number of Belgian men applied for their pensions to be calculated on the basis of fortieths of salary, rather than forty-fifths. Subsequent amendments to and implementations of Belgian law were to the effect that, for men, pensionable age was to be 65 and pension calculated in forty-fifths; for women, pensionable age was to be progressively raised to 65 over a transitional period of thirteen years, and the rate of pension was to be progressively raised over that period. The flexible

[271] Case C–154/92 [1993] ECR I–3811.

[272] Rubinstein, 'Comment' [1994] IRLR 1.

[273] White, above n. 13, 125.

[274] Joined Cases C–377–384/96 *De Vriendt and Others v. Rijksdienst voor Pensioen* [1998] ECR I–2105.

[275] Case C–154/96 *Wolfs v. Office national des pensions* [1998] ECR I–6173.

retirement age was to be maintained, allowing both men and women to take their pensions 'early' at 60, if they met an employment-record entitlement. The employment-record entitlement was to be twenty years in 1997, and to be progressively raised to thirty-five years in 2005. The question arose whether these provisions were compatible with Community law.

This time the Court held that the test was whether the rules in question were 'necessarily and objectively linked' to the difference in state pensionable age. The national court was to determine, as an issue of fact, whether the national legislation maintained a different pensionable age for men and women. If there was a difference, then 'the specification of the age for the award of a retirement pension effectively determines the length of the period during which persons can contribute to the pension scheme'.[276] In such a case, the method of calculating pensions would be necessarily and objectively linked to the pensionable age difference. Thus, if national legislation had maintained a different pensionable age for male and female workers, the Member State could calculate the amount of pension differently depending on the worker's sex. Differences in state pensionable ages could lawfully be maintained under Article 7(1)(a) to 'enable [Member States] progressively to adapt their pension systems in this respect without disrupting the complex financial equilibrium of those systems'.[277] Thus the principle established in *Van Cant* did not apply to transitional arrangements. The effect of these rulings was to leave it to the national court to decide whether the net effect of the Belgian legislation was to equalize state pensionable age. If it was not, then the different mechanisms for calculation were lawful within Article 7(1)(a).

The litigation raises a variation on the long-standing debate on whether Community sex equality law requires 'levelling up' of benefits, or pay, or treatment, to the level of the better treated sex, or whether it is permissible to achieve formal equality between men and women by 'levelling down' benefits to those enjoyed by the worse treated sex.[278] The Court's case law makes it absolutely clear that nothing in Directive 79/7 requires equalization of state pensionable ages by levelling up. This of course leaves maximum discretion for Member States in this sensitive area of national social policy. The Court's rulings also make clear that Community law implies no specific duty on Member States to undertake the equalization process in any particular way. This conclusion is problematic, as the economics of the situation mean that any equalization is bound to take time. Provision must be made for interim or transitional periods, often of several years or even decades. On the Court's interpretation in *De Vriendt* and *Wolfs*, Directive 79/7 seems to leave Member

---

[276] Joined Cases C–377–384/96 *De Vriendt* [1998] ECR I–2105, para. 29.
[277] Case C–154/96 *Wolfs* [1998] ECR I–6173, para. 25.
[278] See below, nn. 386–391.

States with full discretion even during that period. This is, at the least, a rather minimalist approach to the duties imposed by Directive 79/7.[279]

3.2 Other Derogations

Article 7(1) provides other grounds for derogating from the Directive. For example, Article 7(1)(c) allows Member States to exclude from the scope of the Directive the granting of entitlement to old-age benefits by virtue of the derived entitlement of a spouse. Therefore, in *Van Munster*[280] the Court said Directive 79/7 permitted a Member State not to apply to a retired person's pension the 'household rate', which took account of the position of both the retired person and his dependent spouse, where the spouse was entitled to a retirement pension in his or her own right.[281]

Article 7(1)(d) allows Member States to exclude from the scope of the Directive the granting of increases in long-term invalidity benefits, old-age benefits, accidents at work and occupational disease benefits for a dependent wife. This exception was successfully relied on by the UK in *Bramhill*.[282] The UK had abolished discrimination in relation to the rules relating to increases in long-term old-age benefits only for certain categories of women. The Court said that the retention of the discriminatory rules in respect of the women not benefiting from the changed rules fell within Article 7(1)(d).

4. Remedies

Article 6 of Directive 79/7 repeats almost verbatim the requirement laid down in Article 6 of the Equal Treatment Directive 76/207 for complainants to have the right to pursue their claims by judicial process.[283] The parallels between the two Directives indicated that it was likely that the Court would interpret Article 6 similarly in both cases. Therefore, the decision in *ex parte Sutton*,[284] delivered on the same day as *Draehmpaehl*,[285] came as a surprise and marked a departure from the emphasis on effective protection laid down in *Von Colson*[286] and *Marshall (No. 2)*[287] in the context of Directive 76/207. In *Sutton* a

[279] Barnard and Hervey, 'European Union Employment and Social Policy Survey 1998' (1998) 18 *YEL* 613, 649–51.

[280] Case C–165/91 *Van Munster* v. *Rijksdienst voor Pensionen* [1994] ECR I–4661.

[281] Para. 17.

[282] Case C–420/92 *Bramhill* v. *Chief Adjudication Officer* [1994] ECR I–3191.

[283] The Burden of Proof Directive also applies to Directive 79/7. See further Ch. 4.

[284] Case C–66/95 *The Queen* v. *Secretary of State for Social Security, ex parte Eunice Sutton* [1997] ECR I–2163.

[285] Case C–180/95 *Draehmpaehl* v. *Urania Immobilien Service* [1997] ECR I–2195, considered in Ch. 4.

[286] Case 14/83 *Von Colson and Kamann* v. *Land Nordrhein-Westfalen* [1984] ECR 1891.

[287] Case C–271/91 *Marshall (No. 2)* v. *Southampton and South West Area Health Authority* [1993] ECR I–4367.

question was raised concerning the payment of interest on arrears of a social security benefit, invalid care allowance (ICA), when the delay in payment of the benefit was the result of discrimination prohibited by Directive 79/7 which had been declared unlawful by the Court in *Thomas*.[288] In the light of the Court's ruling in *Marshall (No. 2)* that interest was payable for an award under Directive 76/207, Mrs Sutton and the Commission argued that interest should also be paid under Directive 79/7. They pointed out, first, that the wording of Article 6 of Directive 79/7 was practically identical to that of Article 6 of Directive 76/207. Secondly, they said both Directives pursued the same object-ive, namely real equality of treatment for men and women. Thirdly, they reasoned that Directive 79/7 gave effect to the legislative programme initiated by the adoption of Directive 76/207, which provided that subsequent instru-ments would be adopted with a view to ensuring the progressive implementa-tion of the principle of equal treatment in matters of social security.

The Court, however, rejected these submissions. It said that the judgment in *Marshall (No. 2)* concerned the award of interest on amounts payable by way of reparation for loss and damage sustained as a result of a discriminatory dismissal where full compensation for the loss and damage sustained could not leave out of account factors such as the effluxion of time, which might have reduced its value. Therefore, in accordance with the applicable national rules, the award of interest had to be regarded as an essential component of compensation for the purposes of restoring real equality of treatment. By contrast, *Sutton* concerned the right to receive interest on amounts payable by way of social security benefits. Those benefits were paid to the person con-cerned by the competent bodies which had to examine whether the conditions laid down in the relevant legislation were fulfilled. Consequently, the Court said the amounts paid by way of social security benefit were not compensa-tory in nature and in no way constituted reparation for loss or damage sus-tained. Therefore, it said, its reasoning in *Marshall (No. 2)* could not be applied; and Article 6 of Directive 79/7 merely required that the Member States adopt the measures necessary to enable all persons who consider them-selves to have been wronged by discrimination prohibited under the Directive to establish the unlawfulness of such discrimination and to obtain the benefits to which they would have been entitled in the absence of discrimination. The payment of interest on arrears of benefits could not be regarded as an essen-tial component of the right. These arguments are not convincing: the purpose of any remedy by way of arrears of payment is to place the complainant in the position they would have been in but for the discrimination. That must include interest on the money they would have otherwise received.[289]

The Court did not, however, leave Mrs Sutton entirely without a remedy, albeit in a different forum. It said (without having received a question on

[288] Case C–328/91 [1993] ECR I–1247; above, n. 266.
[289] Rubinstein, 'Comment' [1997] IRLR 487.

the point) that the State might be liable, following the cases of *Francovich (No. 1)*[290] and *ex parte Factortame (No. 3)*,[291] for loss and damage caused to individuals as a result of breaches of Community law for which the State can be held responsible. It said that a Member State's obligation to make reparation for the loss and damage was, however, subject to three conditions: the rule of law infringed must be intended to confer rights on individuals; the breach must be sufficiently serious; and there must be a direct causal link between the breach of the obligation resting on the State and the damage sustained by the injured parties. It then added that, while the right to reparation was founded directly on Community law where the three conditions set out above are fulfilled, the national law on liability provided the framework within which the State had to make reparation for the consequences of the loss and damage caused (the principle of national procedural autonomy),[292] provided always that the conditions laid down by national law relating to reparation of loss and damage were not less favourable than those relating to similar domestic claims (non-discrimination) and were not framed so as to make it virtually impossible or excessively difficult to obtain reparation (effectiveness). It therefore said that it was for the national court to assess, in the light of this principle, whether Mrs Sutton was entitled to reparation for the loss which she claimed to have suffered as a result of the breach of Community law by the UK, and, if appropriate, to determine the amount of such reparation.

Time limits for bringing a claim for equal treatment in respect of social security have also been controversial. In *Emmott*[293] the Court appeared to interfere with the principle of national procedural autonomy outlined above by saying that a Member State was precluded from relying on national procedural rules relating to time-limits for bringing proceedings so long as the Member State had not properly transposed the Directive into its domestic legal system. The facts of the case were striking. The applicant had relied on the Court's judgment in *McDermott and Cotter*[294] to claim entitlement to invalidity benefit under Article 4(1) of Directive 79/7. The administrative authorities declined to adjudicate on her claim since Directive 79/7 was the subject of proceedings before the national court. They then alleged that her claim was out of time, even though Directive 79/7 had still not been correctly transposed into national law. The Court ruled that:[295]

until such time as a directive has been properly transposed, a defaulting Member State may not rely on an individual's delay in initiating proceedings against it in order to

---

[290] Joined Cases C–6 and C–9/90 *Francovich (No. 1)* v. *Italy* [1990] ECR I–5357.

[291] Joined Cases C–46/93 *Brasserie du Pêcheur* v. *Bundesrepublik Deutschland* and C–48/95 R v. *Secretary of State for Transport, ex parte Factortame (No. 3)* [1996] ECR I–1029.

[292] Case 199/82 *Amministrazione delle Finanze dello Stato* v. *San Giorgio* [1983] ECR 3595 and see further Ch. 4.

[293] Case C–208/90 *Emmott* v. *Minister for Social Welfare* [1991] ECR I–4269.

[294] Case 286/85 [1987] ECR 1453.

[295] Para. 23.

protect rights conferred upon him by the provisions of the directive and that a period laid down by national law within which proceedings must be initiated cannot begin to run before that time.

Given the potential implications of the ruling in *Emmott* it is not surprising that the Court began to backtrack. In *Steenhorst-Neerings*,[296] for example, the Court said that *Emmott* did not establish an automatic entitlement to *damages* backdated to the date on which an EC Directive should have been implemented into domestic law. This case concerned a national procedural rule limiting the retroactive effect of claims made for the purpose of obtaining a particular benefit to one year. The Court distinguished *Steenhorst-Neerings* from *Emmott* on the ground that while *Emmott* concerned a domestic rule fixing time-limits for bringing actions, which had the effect of denying the right to rely on the Directive in order to claim, the rule in *Steenhorst* concerned only the amount of benefit. The limit in *Steenhorst* also served 'to ensure sound administration, most importantly so that it may be ascertained whether the claimant satisfied the conditions for eligibility, and so that the degree of incapacity which may vary over time, can be fixed'. The case also reflected 'the need to preserve financial balance in a scheme'.[297] Similarly, in *Johnson (No. 2)*,[298] Mrs Johnson, who had been discriminated against in respect of her claim for NCIP and SDA,[299] was given SDA for a period of twelve months prior to her claim but was refused payments in respect of any period prior to that date. The Court said that the decision in *Emmott* was justified by the particular circumstances of the case. The national rule in *Johnson (No. 2)*, on the other hand, was similar to that in *Steenhorst-Neerings* where 'Neither rule constitutes a bar to proceedings; they merely limit the period prior to the bringing of the claim in respect of which arrears of benefit are payable'.[300]

In *Fantask*[301] the Court confirmed the limits to the ruling in *Emmott*. Having reasserted the principle of national procedural autonomy the Court pointed out that, in the interests of legal certainty, the setting of reasonable limitation periods for bringing proceedings was compatible with Community law. It said that such periods could not be regarded as rendering virtually impossible or excessively difficult the exercise of rights conferred by Community law, even if expiry of those periods necessarily entailed the dismissal, in whole or in part, of the action brought. The Court therefore ruled that the five-year limitation period at issue in *Fantask* had to be considered reasonable, especially since the period applied without distinction to actions based on Community law and those based on national law. The Court then referred to its decisions in

---

[296] Case C–338/91 [1993] ECR I–5475.
[297] Para. 23.
[298] Case C–410/92 *Johnson (No. 2)* v. *Chief Adjudication Officer* [1994] ECR I–5483.
[299] Case C–31/90 *Johnson (No. 1)* [1991] ECR I–3723. See above, n. 240.
[300] Para. 30.
[301] Case C–188/95 *Fantask and Others* v. *Industriministeriet* [1997] ECR I–6783.

Johnson (No. 2) and *Steenhorst-Neerings* and said that the solution adopted in *Emmott* was justified by the particular circumstances of the case, in which the time bar had the result of depriving the applicant of any opportunity whatever to rely on her right to equal treatment under a Community directive. Where the time bar did not have that effect, as in *Fantask* itself, Member States could rely on national time limits, provided that they were was not less favourable for actions based on Community law than for actions based on national law, and did not render virtually impossible or excessively difficult the exercise of rights conferred by Community law (as was the case in *Emmott*),[302] even where a Member State had not properly transposed the Directive.

C. EQUALITY, RETIREMENT, AND PENSIONS

The application of the principle of equality to the highly controversial field of retirement and pensions demonstrates both the interface between Article 141 [ex Article 119] and the equality Directives, and the potential cost to employers and to the State of granting equality to men and women. Some Member States have directly discriminated between men and women in respect of state pension age, allowing men to receive their state pension at 65, but women at 60. Retirement age and occupational pension age have mirrored the state pension age. 'Retirement age' relates solely to the age at which a worker retires—the upper age at which the worker stops working. Pension age is the age at which a worker is entitled to receive a pension, from the State (state pension age) or the employer (occupational pension age). The application of the sex equality rules will be considered in respect of each in turn.

1. Retirement Age

Although the Court has now decided in *Marshall (No. 1)*[303] that men and women must not suffer discrimination in respect of retirement age, the Court had some difficulty reaching this conclusion. In the earliest case on this point, *Defrenne (No. 3)*,[304] the Court held that Article 119 [new Article 141] did not apply to discriminatory retirement ages. In that case air hostesses, but not cabin stewards, had to retire when they reached the age of 40. The Court said that since retirement age related to working conditions, Article 119 could not

---

[302] Coppel, 'Domestic Law Limitations on Recovery for Breach of EC Law' (1998) 27 *ILJ* 259, 260.
[303] Case 152/84 *Marshall v. Southampton and South West Hampshire Area Health Authority (Teaching) (No. 1)* [1986] ECR 723. See also Art. 6(f) of Directive 86/378/EEC [1986] OJ L225/40 as amended by Directive 96/97 [1997] OJ L46/20.
[304] Case 149/77 *Defrenne v. SABENA (No. 3)* [1978] ECR 1365.

be stretched to apply to this situation. The next decision, *Burton*,[305] arose after the enactment of the Equal Treatment Directive 76/207.[306] This case concerned a voluntary redundancy scheme under which male employees could take voluntary redundancy at 60, women at 55—five years earlier than the British state pension age in each case. Burton, a man of 58 who was refused redundancy on the ground that he was too young, claimed that he was a victim of discrimination. The Court argued that the case concerned not the benefit itself—the same amount was paid to men and women—but *the conditions of access to the benefit*.[307] The matter therefore fell to be considered under the Equal Treatment Directive and not under Article 119 [new Article 141]. It then decided that although the term 'dismissal' in Article 5(1) had to be broadly construed to include the termination of an employment relationship even as part of a voluntary redundancy scheme, it concluded that British Rail's redundancy scheme was not discriminatory because the only difference in treatment stemmed from the fact that the state pension age was not the same for both sexes. This difference in ages did not amount to discrimination prohibited by Community law because Article 7(1) of Directive 79/7 expressly excluded the determination of pensionable age from the application of the equality principle.[308] To borrow the derogations from one Directive and apply them to another was an extraordinary step to take and one the Court has not since repeated.

The issue was finally resolved in *Marshall (No. 1)*.[309] Helen Marshall worked for an area health authority whose policy was that women should retire at 60 but men could carry on working until 65, ages which coincided with the state pension age. Marshall wanted to work until she was 65 but was forced to retire at 62. She claimed that she had been discriminated against, contrary to Article 5 of Directive 76/207. Her case was referred to the Court at the same time as *Roberts v. Tate & Lyle*.[310] Tate & Lyle's occupational pension scheme provided for compulsory retirement with a pension at 65 for men and 60 for women. When Tate & Lyle closed down one of its depots employees up to five years away from normal retirement age (60 for men and 55 for women)

---

[305] Case 19/81 *Burton v. British Railways Board* [1982] ECR 555. For criticism of this decision, see Lester, 'The Uncertain Trumpet, References to the Court of Justice from the United Kingdom: Equal Pay and Equal Treatment without Sex Discrimination', in *Article 177 EEC: Experiences and Problems*, eds. Schermers, Timmermans, Kellermann, Watson (The Asser Institute, The Hague, 1987).

[306] See above, Ch. 4.

[307] It is widely thought that *Burton* has been *sotto voce* overruled on this point. The distinction between access to payment as opposed to the amount of benefit was not maintained in Case 170/84 *Bilka-Kaufhaus v. Weber von Hartz* [1986] ECR 1607 where the Court recognized that access to benefits for part-timers fell within Art. 119 [new Art. 141]: see Curtin, 'Scalping the Community Legislator: Occupational Pensions and "Barber"' (1990) 27 *CMLRev.* 475, 482.

[308] It now seems that the exceptions to Directive 79/7 are confined exclusively to the field of social security benefits: see Case 152/84 *Marshall (No. 1)* [1986] ECR 723, 746.

[309] Case 152/84 [1986] ECR 723.

[310] Case 151/84 *Roberts v. Tate & Lyle* [1986] ECR 703.

received an early pension. The men complained that this was discriminatory and so the company agreed that both men and women would receive the pension at 55. Miss Roberts, who was 53, then argued that the revised plan was also discriminatory since a male employee was entitled to receive a pension ten years before the normal retirement age whereas women could receive the pension only five years before the normal retirement age.

These two cases, *Marshall* and *Roberts*, and a third, *Beets Proper*,[311] the facts of which were very similar to those in *Marshall*, presented the Court with a menu of options, forcing it to examine whether to require equality in respect of retirement ages and, if so, how. The Court opted for the formal equality model offered by *Marshall*. However, in order to achieve this the Court had to address the problems caused by *Burton*. Its solution was to sever the link between retirement age and state pension age. It argued that *Marshall* did not concern the conditions for payment of an old age pension but concerned the fixing of an age limit with regard to the termination of employment pursuant to a general policy concerning dismissal, which was covered by Article 5 of Directive 76/207/EEC. Consequently, Article 7(1)(a) of Directive 79/7 did not apply since it covered only the determination of pensionable age for the purpose of granting old age and retirement pensions. Therefore, since Article 5 was directly effective it could be invoked by Miss Marshall against her state employer to insist on equal treatment.[312] Similarly, in *Roberts* the Court concluded that the case concerned dismissal as a result of mass redundancy and not the granting of old-age or retirement pensions and so Article 5 of Directive 76/207 again applied. It then ruled that it was compatible with Article 5 to lay down a single age for the dismissal of men and women and the grant of an early retirement pension.

As a consequence of these decisions the Court has ensured formal equality in respect of retirement age but in so doing it has created an artificial distinction between retirement age and pension age. This is particularly a problem for men. While it may now be possible for men to retire at 60, with their female colleagues, the right to retire is of limited value if the men are dependent on a state pension which is not payable until they are 65. These inconsistencies are due to the maintenance of discriminatory state pension ages which, as we shall now see, are compatible with Community law.

---

[311] Case 262/84 *Beets Proper v. F. van Landschot Bankers NV* [1986] ECR 773. See also Millett, 'European Community Law: Sex Equality and Retirement Age' (1987) 36 *ICLQ* 616.

[312] In Case 262/84 *Beets Proper* [1986] ECR 773 the Court reiterated the principle laid down in *Marshall* but this time applied it to discriminatory retirement ages contained in a contract of employment based on a collective agreement. No reference to direct effect was made in that case.

2. State Pension Age

In *Defrenne (No. 1)*[313] the Court made it clear that differences in state pension age would not fall within the ambit of Article 119 [new Article 141]. In the words of the Court:

Although payment in the nature of social security benefits is not excluded in principle from the concept of pay it is not possible to include in this concept as defined in Article 119 [new Article 141] social security schemes and benefits especially retirement pensions which are directly settled by law without any reference to any element of consultation within the undertaking or industry concerned and which cover without exception all workers in general.

The case concerned a pension scheme which applied to all flight personnel of civil airlines with the exception of air hostesses. Miss Defrenne, an air hostess, argued that the scheme was discriminatory, contrary to Article 119 [new Article 141]. The Court disagreed. Its argument had two elements. First, it said that the scheme was determined less by the employment relationship between the employer and the worker than by considerations of social policy. Secondly, it said that the worker would receive the benefits not by reason of the employer's contributions but solely because the worker fulfilled the legal conditions for the grant of the benefits. Therefore, it said that the retirement pension did not constitute consideration which the workers received indirectly from their employer within the meaning of Article 119 [new Article 141].

Since Article 141 cannot be used to eliminate a discriminatory state pension age then it is compatible with Community law to maintain this discrimination. As we saw in *Burton*,[314] this is confirmed by Article 7(1)(a) of Directive 79/7 which provides a derogation from the principle of equal treatment in respect of social security in the case of the determination of pensionable age for the purposes of granting old age and retirement pensions, and accepted by the Court in *ex parte EOC*.[315]

Measures taken by an employer to mitigate the consequences of a discriminatory pension age are compatible with Community law. In *Roberts*[316] the employer reduced a woman's bridging pension by the amount of the state pension from the age of 60 but made no such reduction in respect of a man until the age of 65. While acknowledging that bridging pensions are 'pay' within the meaning of Article 119 [new Article 141], the Court ruled that the difference in the 'objective premise'—that women receive a state pension

---

[313] Case 80/70 *Defrenne v. Belgian State (No. 1)* [1971] ECR 445.

[314] Case 19/87 [1982] ECR 555.

[315] Case C–9/91 [1992] ECR I–4297. In the UK from 2020 men and women will both receive their state pensions at 65, which represents a levelling down of benefit for women, with the changes being introduced over a 10-year period from 2010.

[316] Case C–132/92 *Birds Eye Walls v. Roberts* [1993] ECR I–5579. See now Art. 2(3) of Directive 86/378.

at 60 but men do not—leading to differences in the amount of the bridging pension paid to men and women 'cannot be considered discriminatory'. This view can be contrasted with the approach adopted by the British House of Lords in *James*[317] where the Court ruled that gender-based criteria are discriminatory, *per se*, regardless of their purpose or justification.

3. Occupational Pensions

Occupational pensions are offered by employers to their employees in connection with their employment. In defined contribution or money purchase schemes the employer and employee agree to a level of contributions, usually a fixed percentage of salary, and the resulting lump sum saved is used to purchase a pension at the time of retirement. In defined benefit or final salary schemes there is usually a fixed employee contribution (although in some schemes the employer funds the total cost) but the employer undertakes to provide a level of benefits according to a formula. Consequently the employer's contribution to the scheme will vary from year to year.[318] These occupational pensions can be a substitute for a state pension (such as a pension contracted-out from the state scheme) or a supplement to a state pension. Following the model of state schemes the occupational pension age for many schemes was also discriminatory. For this reason Directive 86/378,[319] introduced to implement the principle of equal treatment in occupational social security schemes, allowed for derogations in respect of, *inter alia*, occupational pension age.

Directive 86/378 was intended to complement Directive 79/7,[320] and the beneficiaries of the principle of equal treatment[321] were almost identical in both. Occupational social security schemes are defined as those schemes not covered by Directive 79/7 whose purpose is to provide workers, including the self-employed, in an 'undertaking or group of undertakings, area of economic activity, occupational sector or group of sectors with benefits intended to supplement the benefits provided by the statutory social schemes or to replace them'.[322] It applies to occupational schemes which provide protection against sickness, invalidity, old-age, including early retirement, industrial accidents, occupational diseases, and unemployment. It also applies to occupational schemes which provide for other social benefits, in cash or in kind, and in particular survivors' benefits and family allowances, if such benefits

---

[317] *James v. Eastleigh Borough Council* [1990] 3 WLR 55.

[318] Nobles, *Pensions, Employment and the Law* (Clarendon Press, Oxford, 1993), 8.

[319] [1986] OJ L225/40.

[320] Art. 3(3) of Directive 79/7 said that the Council will adopt provisions defining the principle of equal treatment in occupational pension schemes.

[321] Art. 3.

[322] Art. 2(1).

constitute consideration paid by the employer to the worker in connection with the worker's employment.[323]

Article 5 spells out that:

1. Under the conditions laid down in the following provisions, the principle of equal treatment implies that there shall be no discrimination on the basis of sex, either directly or indirectly, by reference in particular to marital or family status, especially as regards:

— the scope of the schemes and the conditions of access to them;
— the obligation to contribute and the calculation of contributions;
— the calculation of benefits, including supplementary benefits due in respect of a spouse or dependants, and the conditions governing the duration and retention of entitlement to benefits.

2. The principle of equal treatment shall not prejudice the provisions relating to the protection of women by reason of maternity.

Article 6 gave examples of provisions which contravened the principle of equal treatment. The list included determining people who could participate in occupational schemes, laying down different rules as regards the age of entry into the scheme or minimum periods of employment, setting different conditions for granting the benefits, fixing different retirement ages, setting different levels of benefit, except in so far as it may be necessary to take account of actuarial factors, and setting different levels of worker contribution.[324]

As already mentioned, the Directive did, however, contain an extensive list of derogations in Article 9. In particular, Member States could defer compulsory application of the principle of equal treatment with regard to (a) the determination of pensionable age for the purposes of granting old-age and retirement pensions, and the possible implications for other benefits, either until the date on which such equality is achieved in statutory schemes, or at the latest until such equality is required by a Directive; (b) survivors' pensions until a Directive requires the application of the principle of equal treatment; and (c) to setting the levels of worker contributions to take account of the different actuarial calculations factors, at least until the expiry of a thirteen-year period as from 30 July 1986. As we shall see, considerable doubt was cast on the legality of most of these derogations, with the exception of the derogation relating to actuarial factors, by the Court's case law, in particular *Ten Oever*[325] (survivors' benefits) and *Barber*[326] (occupational pensions age) which 'automatically invalidates certain provisions of Directive 86/378'.[327] In each

---

[323] Art. 4.
[324] See also Art. 9(c).
[325] Case C–109/91 *Ten Oever* v. *Stichting Bedrijfspensionenfonds voor het Glazenwassers- en Schoomaakbedrijf* [1993] ECR I–4879.
[326] Case C–262/88 *Barber* v. *Guardian Royal Exchange Assurance Group* [1990] ECR I–1889.
[327] Preamble to Council Directive 96/97/EC [1997] OJ L46/20.

case the benefit concerned was deemed to fall within the definition of 'pay' in Article 119 [new Article 141] of the Treaty which took precedence over the Directive. As the Court said in *Moroni*,[328] the 'effects of the Directive do not matter, for its provisions cannot in any way restrict the scope of Article 119'.[329] This led to the adoption of a new Directive 96/97/EC[330] amending Directive 86/378 to 'adapt the provisions affected by the *Barber* case law'.[331] The derogations from the Directive now apply largely to the self-employed.[332]

3.1 Occupational Pensions, 'Pay', and Article 141

There had been hints in the early case law that occupational pensions could fall within the definition of pay in Article 141. For example, in *Garland*[333] the Court said that the concept of pay embraced both 'immediate and *future* benefits',[334] which in that case included free travel after retirement. Consequently, occupational pensions, although received after employment, could be construed as a type of remuneration received directly or indirectly from the employer. Advocate General Dutheillet de Lamothe in *Defrenne (No. 1)*[335] had also taken this view. He considered that pensions payable directly by the employer came within the scope of Article 119 [new Article 141] since they could be regarded as a form of deferred pay. He also regarded *supplementary* pensions as falling within the scope of Article 119 if they could be regarded as being independent of the state scheme. On the facts of *Defrenne (No. 1)* the Court found that this was not the case.

Advocate General Dutheillet de Lamothe's approach in *Defrenne (No. 1)* was endorsed by the Court in *Bilka-Kaufhaus*.[336] The case concerned an occupational pension scheme which, although adopted in accordance with German legislation, was voluntary in origin and arose from an agreement between the employer and the works council.[337] It *supplemented* the social security legislation with benefits financed entirely by the employer. In the words of the Court the scheme was contractual rather than statutory and formed an integral part of the contracts of employment. The scheme

---

[328] Case C–110/91 *Moroni v. Collo* [1993] ECR I–6591, para. 24.

[329] Approved in Case C–7/93 *Bestuur van het Algemeen burgerlijk Pensioenfonds v. Beune* [1994] ECR I–4471 where the Court said that the same interpretation applied with regard to Art. 8(2).

[330] [1996] OJ L46/20.

[331] Preamble to Directive 96/97.

[332] e.g. new Art. 2(2)(a) and (b); Art. 9.

[333] Case 12/81 *Garland v. British Rail Engineering* [1982] ECR 359.

[334] Para. 5.

[335] Case 80/70 [1971] ECR 445. See above, Ch.4.

[336] Case 170/84 [1986] ECR 1607.

[337] The emphasis on agreement is important. It takes precedence over the criterion of statutory origin. However, the negotiations between the employer's and the employees' representatives must result in a formal agreement and not just consultation: Case C–7/93 *Beune* [1994] ECR I–4471, para. 32.

therefore offered the necessary link between pay and the employment relationship which was absent from the scheme in *Defrenne (No. 1)*.[338]

Advocate General Warner in *Worringham*,[339] however, did not feel the distinctions made by Advocate General Dutheillet de Lamothe in *Defrenne (No. 1)* were so easy to apply in the context of the British system of contracted-out schemes which were a *substitute for* the state scheme and not a *supplement to* the state scheme. Because he was worried that an unbalanced result would arise if equalization was required in the context of occupational schemes and not in the case of the state scheme, he argued that such contracted-out occupational schemes had to fall outside Article 119 [new Article 141]. *Worringham* concerned a pension scheme under which men were required to contribute to the bank's pension scheme from the date on which they started work but women could start to make contributions only when they reached the age of 25. The contributions amounted to 5 per cent of an employee's salary. In order to make up for this difference men under 25 received a 5 per cent addition to their gross pay. If a man left the bank before he was 25 he was entitled to a refund on his contributions but women leaving before the age of 25 received nothing. Women also suffered other disadvantages: any redundancy pay, unemployment benefit, and credit facilities were calculated by reference to gross earnings which would be less for women than for men.

The bank argued that the case concerned a contracted-out scheme and so Article 119 [new Article 141] did not apply; the women argued that the scheme was a supplementary scheme to which Article 119 did apply. The Court, by examining the discriminatory effects rather than the legal nature of the scheme, noted the way in which the contributions affected the calculation of gross pay. It concluded that contributions to a retirement benefits scheme, which were paid by the employer in the name of the employees by means of an addition to the gross salary, were 'pay' within the meaning of Article 119[340] and therefore no discrimination was permitted.

In *Newstead*,[341] by contrast, the Court found that the deduction in question resulted in a reduction in *net* pay because of a contribution paid to a social security scheme, and in no way affected gross pay. It therefore said that Article 119 [new Article 141] did not apply. Newstead was a civil servant employed by the Department of Transport. He was required to contribute to an occupational pension scheme which made provision for a widow's pension

---

[338] Case 80/70 [1971] ECR 445.

[339] Case 69/80 *Worringham* v. *Lloyd's Bank* [1981] ECR 767. See Ellis and Morrell, 'Sex Discrimination in Pension Schemes: Has Community Law Changed the Rules?' (1992) 21 *ILJ* 16.

[340] Cf. Case 23/83 *Liefting* v. *Academisch Zieckenhuis bij de Universiteit van Amsterdam* [1984] ECR 3225. Curtin, above n. 307, concludes that the Court is prepared to look squarely at the nature of the pension scheme when confronted with questions relating to the payment of benefits (*Defrenne (No. 1)* and *Bilka-Kaufhaus*) but not when the questions can be confined to the effect of contributions to pension schemes on gross pay (*Worringham* and *Liefting*). See also old Art. 6(c) of Directive 86/378.

[341] Case 192/85 *Newstead* v. *Department of Transport* [1987] ECR 4753.

fund. All male civil servants were obliged to contribute to this scheme at a rate of 1.5 per cent of their gross salary, irrespective of their marital status; female civil servants had the choice whether to contribute to the scheme. Civil servants who remained unmarried throughout the period during which they were covered by the scheme were entitled to a refund of their contributions plus interest at 4 per cent when they left the service. Newstead, a confirmed bachelor in his fifties, objected to making this payment, albeit temporarily, and claimed that he was the victim of unlawful discrimination. The Court decided that the pension scheme was a substitute for a social security scheme and consequently any contribution to such a scheme was 'considered to fall within the scope of Article 118 [new Article 140] of the Treaty and not Article 119 [new Article 141]'.

This decision has been the subject of much criticism and it is difficult to reconcile it with the earlier cases.[342] It took the momentous decision by the Court in *Barber* to cut through this muddle and state authoritatively that occupational pensions, including contracted-out pension schemes,[343] constituted 'pay' within the meaning of Article 141.[344] Barber belonged to a non-contributory pension scheme (a scheme wholly financed by the employer). Since the scheme was contracted-out from the state pension scheme it was a substitute for the state scheme. Under the terms of the scheme the normal pensionable age was fixed at 62 for men and 57 for women—three years prior to the state pension age. In the event of redundancy, members of the pension fund were entitled to an immediate pension at 55 for men and 50 for women, seven years before the scheme's normal pensionable age. Staff who did not fulfil these conditions but who had been made redundant received cash benefits calculated on the basis of their years of service and a deferred pension payable at the normal pensionable age. Barber found himself in this position. Made redundant at 52, he received the cash benefits, statutory redundancy pay, and an *ex gratia* payment but he was not entitled to his occupational pension until he was 62. A woman of 52 would have received the pension immediately, as well as the statutory redundancy payment, and the total value of those benefits would have been greater than the amount paid to him. Barber claimed that he had been discriminated against on the grounds of his sex.[345]

The Court began by distinguishing contracted-out private occupational

---

[342] See e.g. Arnull, 'Widow's Mite' (1988) 13 *ELRev.* 136.

[343] In Case C–7/93 *Beune* [1994] ECR I–4471, para. 37, the Court said that benefits awarded under an occupational scheme which *partly or entirely* take the place of the benefits paid by a statutory social security scheme may also fall within the scope of Art. 119 [new Art. 141].

[344] Case C–262/88 *Barber* [1990] ECR I–1887. On the effect of *Barber* on the pensions industry see Moffat and Luckhaus, 'Occupational Pension Schemes, Equality and Europe: a Decade of Change' (1998) 20 *JSWL* 1.

[345] A comparator is necessary. In Case C–200/91 *Coloroll Pension Trustees* v. *Russell* [1994] ECR I–4389 the Court ruled that Art. 119 [new Art. 141] did not apply to schemes whose members were all of one sex (para. 104).

schemes from the state social security scheme in *Defrenne (No. 1)*.[346] First, it noted that contracted-out schemes resulted from either an agreement between workers and employers or a unilateral decision by the employer. The schemes were funded by the employer or by the employer and the workers with no contribution from the public authorities. The Court therefore concluded that such occupational pension schemes formed part of the consideration offered to the workers by the employer. Secondly, the Court said that such schemes were not compulsorily applicable to general categories of workers: they applied only to workers employed in certain undertakings, with the result that affiliation to those schemes derived from the employment relationship with a given employer. In addition, such schemes were governed by their own rules, even if they were established in conformity with national legislation. Thirdly, the Court reasoned that even if such occupational schemes were substitutes for the general statutory scheme these schemes might grant their members benefits greater than those paid under the statutory scheme, with the result that their economic function was similar to that of supplementary schemes, which, as the Court had held in *Bilka-Kaufhaus*,[347] fell within the concept of pay within the meaning of Article 119 [new Article 141]. Therefore, a pension paid under a contracted-out scheme constituted consideration paid by an employer in respect of his employment and consequently fell within the scope of Article 119.

3.2 The Application of the Equality Principle to Occupational Pension Schemes

It is clear that the principle of non-discrimination laid down by Article 141 relates to the *quantum* of benefit[348] so that men and women receive the same amount. In *Barber*[349] the Court established that *each* benefit received under an occupational pension scheme was to be paid on a non-discriminatory basis:[350] it was not sufficient to make a comprehensive assessment of the total consideration paid to workers. The Court's justification for reaching this conclusion was pragmatic: it referred to the fundamental principle of transparency which would enable national courts to review schemes with a view to eliminating discrimination based on sex. The Court argued that such judicial review would be difficult and the

---

[346] Case 80/70 [1971] ECR 445.

[347] Case 170/84 [1986] ECR 1607.

[348] Curtin suggests that *Barber* does not require that the total amount of a particular benefit be mathematically equal since neither the costs nor the value of the total pension benefits will ever be known in advance. She argues that *Barber* requires that the *rate* at which the benefit is enjoyed be equal: (1990) 27 *CMLRev.* 475, 484–5.

[349] Case C–262/88 [1990] ECR I–1889.

[350] This is also the approach which had been adopted by the House of Lords in *Haywards* v. *Cammell Laird* [1988] 2 WLR 1134 concerning the interpretation of the English Equal Pay Act 1970.

effectiveness of Article 119 [new Article 141] would be diminished if the national courts were required to make a comparative assessment of the package of consideration granted.

Article 141 applies not only to the quantum of benefits, as Article 6 of Directive 86/378 indicated,[351] but also to access and conditions of access to the scheme.[352] The question of *access* was first raised in *Bilka-Kaufhaus*[353] where the Court ruled that Article 119 [new Article 141] covered not only entitlement to benefits paid by an occupational pensions scheme but also the right to be a member of such a scheme. In *Bilka-Kaufhaus* the employers refused to pay Mrs Weber, a part-time worker, an occupational pension since she had not worked full time for the minimum period of fifteen years. She alleged that the exclusion of part-time workers from the occupational pension scheme constituted indirect discrimination, contrary to Article 119. As the Court had explained in *Jenkins*,[354] if a pay policy set a lower hourly rate for part-time work than for full-time work entailed discrimination between men and women, the same applied where part-time workers were refused access to a company pension. Since a pension fell within the definition of pay, it followed that hour for hour the total remuneration paid by the employer to full-time workers was higher than that paid to part-time workers. The Court followed this approach in *Vroege*.[355] It said that an occupational pension scheme which excluded part-time workers from membership contravened Article 119 [new Article 141] if the exclusion affected a much greater number of women than men, and which the employer could not explain by objectively justified factors unrelated to any discrimination on grounds of sex. In *Vroege* the Court also recognized that the exclusion of married women from membership of an occupational pension scheme did entail discrimination directly based on sex and was contrary to Article 119.[356]

As far as *conditions of access* are concerned, the principle of equality in Article 141 also applies. As the Court ruled in *Barber*,[357] Article 119 [new Article 141] prohibited any discrimination with regard to pay as between men and women, *whatever the system which gives rise to such inequality.* Thus, the Court said it was contrary to Article 119 to impose an age condition which differed according to sex in respect of pensions paid under a contracted-out scheme, even if the difference between the pensionable ages for men and women was based on the age laid down by the national statutory

---

[351] See above, n. 324.
[352] See also Arts. 5(1) and 6(a) of Directive 86/378.
[353] Case 170/84 [1986] ECR 1607.
[354] Case 96/80 *Jenkins* v. *Kingsgate* [1981] ECR 911.
[355] Case C–57/93 *Vroege* v. *NCIV* [1994] ECR I–4541.
[356] See also Case C–128/93 *Fisscher* v. *Voorhuis Hengelo BV* [1994] ECR I–4583.
[357] Case C–262/88 [1990] ECR I–1889. See also Art. 6(e) of Directive 86/378.

scheme. The Court extended this ruling to supplementary (non-contracted-out) occupational pension schemes in *Moroni*[358] and *Coloroll*.[359]

Earlier cases, such as *Burton*,[360] *Marshall (No. 1)*,[361] and *Roberts*,[362] had, however, suggested that fixing pensionable ages related to the *conditions of access* to the pension and consequently was governed by the Equal Treatment Directives, despite the consequences that such discrimination might have for the worker's pay.[363] On the other hand, Article 1 of the Equal Pay Directive, which is designed to facilitate the application of Article 119 [new Article 141],[364] makes clear that 'the principle of equal pay . . . means the elimination of all discrimination on the grounds of sex with regard to all aspects and *conditions of remuneration*' (emphasis added) and so the *Barber* judgment serves only to clarify the law.[365] Nevertheless, the *Barber* judgment has blurred the distinction between the Equal Treatment Directive and Article 119 [new Article 141],[366] but by bringing conditions of access to the benefit within the ambit of Article 141 the Court has ensured that more employees will be able to take advantage of the principle of equal pay, since Article 141 has both horizontal and vertical direct effect.

3.3 The Non-retrospective Effect of the *Barber* Judgment

The Court, aware of the potential financial consequences of any decision on equalization of benefits under an occupational pension scheme, decided to limit the retrospective effect of its judgment. It had already restricted the retrospective effect of its judgment in *Defrenne (No. 2)*[367] 'by way of exception, taking account of the serious difficulties which its judgment may create as regards events in the past'. Thus, the direct effect of Article 119 [new Article 141] which was established in that case for the first time could not be invoked in respect of periods of service prior to 8 April 1976, the date of the judgment in *Defrenne (No. 2)*. In *Barber* the Court considered that, in the light of the exclusion of pensionable age from the scope of Directive 79/7 and the formal extension of this derogation by Article 9(a) of Directive 86/378/EEC to occupational pension schemes, Member States were reasonably entitled to consider that Article 119 did not apply to pensions paid under contracted-out

---

[358] Case C–110/91 [1993] ECR I–6591.
[359] Case C–200/91 [1994] ECR I–4389.
[360] Case 19/81 [1982] ECR 555.
[361] Case 152/84 [1986] ECR 723.
[362] Case 151/84 [1986] ECR 703.
[363] Art. 5 of Directive 76/207 and Art. 6(f) of Directive 86/378.
[364] Case 96/80 *Jenkins* [1981] ECR 911.
[365] See also Arts. 5(1) and 6(e) of Directive 86/378.
[366] The Court has never expressly ruled on the relationship between Art. 119 [new Art. 141] and the Equal Treatment Directive but Advocate General van Gerven in *Barber* [1990] ECR I–1889 did suggest that the two were not mutually exclusive.
[367] Case 43/75 [1976] ECR 455.

schemes. Therefore, in the interests of legal certainty and out of a wish to avoid upsetting the financial balance of many contracted-out pension schemes, the Court concluded that:

the direct effect of Article 119 [new Article 141] of the Treaty may not be relied upon in order to claim entitlement to a pension with effect from a date prior to that of this judgment (17 May 1990), except in the case of workers or those claiming under them who have before that date initiated proceedings or raised an equivalent claim under the applicable national law.

The Court then added that 'no restriction on the effects of the aforesaid interpretation can be permitted as regards the acquisition of entitlement to a pension as from the date of this judgment'.

Such statements caused considerable uncertainty about the precise meaning of the scope of the non-retrospectivity ruling. Advocate General van Gerven discussed four possible interpretations:[368]

A *first interpretation* would be to apply the principle of equal treatment only to workers who became members of, and began to pay contributions to, an occupational pension scheme as from 17 May 1990. This view would deprive the *Barber* judgment of almost all retroactive effect. In practical terms, it would mean that the full effect of the judgment would be felt only after a period of about 40 years.

A *second interpretation* is that the principle of equal treatment should only be applied to benefits payable in respect of periods of service after 17 May 1990. Periods of service prior to that date would not be affected by the direct effect of Article 119 [new Article 141].

According to a *third interpretation*, the principle of equal treatment must be applied to all pensions which are payable or paid for the first time after 17 May 1990, irrespective of the fact that all or some of the pension accrued during, and on the basis of, periods of service completed or contributions paid prior to that date. In other words, it is not the periods of service (before or after the judgment in *Barber*) which are decisive, but the date on which the pension falls to be paid.

A *fourth interpretation* would be to apply equal treatment to all pension payments made after 17 May 1990, including benefits or pensions which had already fallen due and, here again, as in the previous interpretation, irrespective of the date of the periods of service during which the pension accrued. This interpretation undoubtedly has the most far-reaching effect.

At the Intergovernmental Conference at Maastricht the Heads of State added Protocol No. 2 to 'clarify' the temporal limitation of *Barber*. This provides:

For the purposes of Article 119 [Article 141] of the Treaty establishing the European Community, benefits under occupational social security schemes shall not be

---

[368] Cases C–109, C–110, C–152, and C–200/91 *Ten Oever, Moroni, Neath,* and *Coloroll* [1993] ECR I–4879. See also Honeyball and Shaw, 'Sex and the Retiring Man' (1991) 16 *ELRev.* 56 and Curtin, above n. 307, 487.

considered as remuneration if and insofar as they are attributable to periods of employment prior to 17 May 1990, except in the case of workers or those claiming under them who have before that date initiated legal proceedings or introduced an equivalent claim under the applicable national law.

The Protocol favours the second approach identified by Advocate General van Gerven that benefits need to be equal only in respect of periods of employment after 17 May 1990. This view was then followed by the Court in *Ten Oever*.[369] The Court said that account had to be taken of the fact that in the case of pensions 'there is a time lag between the accrual of entitlement to the pension, which occurred gradually throughout the employee's working life and its actual payment, which is deferred until a particular age'.[370] It noted the way in which occupational pension funds are financed and the accounting links existing in each individual case between the periodic contributions and the future amounts paid. It then continued that 'equality of treatment in the matter of occupational pensions may be claimed only in relation to benefits payable in respect of periods of employment subsequent to 17 May 1990, the date of the *Barber* judgment, subject to the exception prescribed therein for workers or those claiming under them who have, before that date, initiated legal proceedings or raised an equivalent claim under the applicable national law'. The Court therefore followed Protocol No. 2[371] and avoided a constitutional conflict with the Council.

Protocol No. 2 makes no distinction between contracted-out and supplementary occupational schemes, talking only in general terms of 'benefits under occupational social security schemes'. This suggested that the *Barber* time limit also applied to supplementary schemes. This was confirmed by *Moroni*[372] and *Coloroll*,[373] despite the fact that in the earlier case of *Bilka-Kaufhaus*,[374] which also concerned supplementary occupational schemes, no temporal limitation was imposed.

It is now quite clear that Article 141 [ex Article 119] does not apply to any benefit or part of any benefit relating to service before 17 May 1990 (except for legal claims started before that date)[375] and true equality of pension *benefits* will not be achieved under Community law until all those employed prior to 17 May 1990 have retired. However, *Barber* does require all occupational schemes to allow men and women to receive the occupational pensions at the

---

[369] Case C–109/91 [1993] ECR I–4879 and applied in Case C–152/91 *Neath v. Steeper* [1993] ECR I–6935 and Case C–200/91 *Coloroll* [1994] ECR I–4389.

[370] See further Advocate General van Gerven in Case C–109/91 *Ten Oever* [1993] ECR I–4879. The same justification was given by the Court to justify the application of the *Barber* limitation to transfer benefits and lump-sum options in Case C–152/91 *Neath* [1993] ECR I–6953.

[371] See also Art. 2 of Directive 96/97.

[372] Case C–110/91 [1993] ECR I–6591, para. 33.

[373] Case C–200/91 [1994] ECR I–4389, para. 71.

[374] Case 170/84 [1986] ECR 1607.

[375] This was confirmed by Advocate General Ruiz-Jarabo Colomer in Case C–166/99 *Defreyne v. SABENA*, 16 Mar. 2000 and the ECJ, 13 July 2000.

same age, as from 17 May 1990, albeit that the payments which relate to service prior to 17 May 1990 are of different amounts.

A simple example may serve to illustrate the application of the *Barber* principles.[376] In May 1984 ABC Ltd employs Mrs X and Mr Y, both aged 50. ABC Ltd runs an occupational pension scheme with a normal pension age of 60 for women and 65 for men. An actuarial reduction of 4 per cent *per annum* is made for each year by which retirement precedes the normal pension age. Mrs X and Mr Y both retire in May 1994 aged 60. Mr Y's pension is subject to a 20 per cent actuarial reduction (4% x 5 years). Therefore, if Mrs X receives £1,000 per month, Mr Y will receive only £800 due to the 20 per cent actuarial reduction. As a result of the decision in *Barber* he will be able to claim an additional £80 per month (total £880 per month) calculated as follows:

May 1984–May 1990 (period of service between date of commencement of employment and date of *Barber* judgment)

6/10 of service	£600
Minus 20% actuarial reduction	£120
	£480

May 1990–May 1994 (period of service between date of *Barber* judgment and date of retirement when no deduction can be made)

4/10 of service	£400
	£400
Total	£880

The temporal limitation in *Barber* also applies to survivors' benefits[377] and to benefits not linked to actual service, such as a lump sum payment in the event of an employee's death, where the operative event (the death) occurred before 17 May 1990.[378] However, according to the Court in *Vroege*[379] and *Fisscher*,[380] it does not apply to conditions of membership of occupational schemes which is governed by the judgment in *Bilka-Kaufhaus*[381] where no temporal limitation was prescribed. This serves to emphasize the Court's

---

[376] I am grateful for Lorraine Fletcher's help in this area.

[377] Case C–109/91 *Ten Oever* [1993] ECR I–4879, considered below at n. 393.

[378] Case C–200/91 *Coloroll* [1994] ECR I–4389.

[379] Case C–57/93 [1994] ECR I–4541, para. 32. In *Vroege* the Court pointed out that a limitation of the effects in time of an interpretative preliminary ruling can only be in the actual judgment ruling upon the interpretation sought. Consequently, if the Court had considered it necessary to impose a limit in time, it would have done so in *Bilka-Kaufhaus*. See also Case C–7/93 *Beune* [1994] ECR I–4471, paras. 61–62, and Case C–128/93 *Fisscher* [1994] ECR I–4583, para. 28.

[380] Case C–128/93 [1994] ECR I–4583.

[381] Case 170/84 [1986] ECR 1607. The Court has repeated this in Joined Cases C–270 and C–271/97 *Deutsche Post AG v. Sievers and Schrage*, judgment of 10 Feb. 2000, paras. 34 and 35; Joined Cases C–234 and C–235/96 *Deutsche Telekom AG v. Vick and Conze*, judgment of 10 Feb. 2000, para. 40; and Case C–50/96 *Deutsche Telekom v. Schröder*, judgment of 10 Feb. 2000, para. 38.

ambivalence towards financial costs. While accepting that retrospective rights to equality in *benefits* might upset the financial balance of pension schemes, it did not seem aware of the costs of granting retrospective *access* to those benefits. Consequently, the direct effect of Article 119 [new Article 141] can be relied on in order to claim equal treatment retroactively in relation to the right to join an occupational pension scheme and this may apply from 8 April 1976,[382] the date of *Defrenne (No. 2)*.[383] This may mean that both the employer and the employee have to make contributions from 8 April 1976, although national time limits may preclude such extensive retrospective claims.[384] In the case of part-timers claiming access to a pension scheme the employers may attempt to show that any indirect discrimination that occurred from 1976 could at any given moment be objectively justified and so no discrimination occurred, hence no contribution needed to be paid for that period. If national law allows retrospective claims before 8 April 1976, this is compatible with Community law, despite the risk of competition being distorted between economic operators in the different Member States.[385]

3.4 Levelling Up or Down?

The *Barber* judgment did not, however, make clear whether the equalization demanded by Article 119 [new Article 141] required levelling the man's terms up to the more favourable terms enjoyed by the women or whether it permitted levelling the woman's terms down to the man's terms. A question was referred to the Court on this point in *Smith*.[386] In that case the employer, in order to give effect to the *Barber* judgment in its own occupational pension scheme, decided that as from 1 July 1991 both men and women would receive their occupational pensions at 65 (levelling down of the women's conditions) rather than providing that the men would receive their occupational pensions at 60 at the same age as the women (levelling up). The Court was faced with a difficult choice: levelling down was more affordable for the pension schemes, particularly in the light of an ageing population, but levelling up was more consistent with the Treaty's aspiration of an improvement in working conditions and its earlier jurisprudence. In *Defrenne (No. 2)*[387], for example, the

---

[382] Case C–57/93 *Vroege* [1994] ECR I–4541.

[383] Case 43/75 [1976] ECR 455.

[384] Case C–128/93 *Fisscher* [1994] ECR I–4583, but cf. Case C–246/96 *Mary Teresa Magorrian and Irene Patricia Cunningham* v. *Eastern Health and Social Services Board and Department of Health and Social Services* [1997] ECR I–7153.

[385] Case C–50/96 *Schröder*, judgment of 10 Feb. 2000, paras. 50 and 59; Joined Cases C–234 and C–235/96 *Vick and Conze*, judgment of 10 Feb. 2000, para. 50; and Joined Cases C–270 and C–271/97 *Sievers and Schrage*, judgment of 10 Feb. 2000, para. 59.

[386] Case C–408/92 *Smith* v. *Avdel Systems* [1994] ECR I–4435. The Court reached similar conclusions in Case C–28/93 *Van den Akker* v. *Stichting Shell Pensioenfonds* [1994] ECR I–4527 and Case C–200/91 *Coloroll* [1994] ECR I–4389, para. 36.

[387] Case 43/75 [1976] ECR 455.

Court said that in view of the connection between Article 119 [new Article 141] and the harmonization of working conditions while the improvement is being maintained,[388] compliance with Article 119 could not be achieved in ways other than by raising the lowest salaries.[389] Similarly, in *Nimz*[390] the Court ruled that the national court was obliged to apply to the members who had been victims of discrimination 'the same arrangements as are applied to other employees, arrangements which, *failing the correct application of Article 119 [new Article 141] of the EEC Treaty in national law*, remain the only valid system of reference' (emphasis added).

In *Smith* the Court reached a compromise solution. It identified three separate points of time: first, the period before 17 May 1990, the date of the *Barber* judgment;[391] secondly, after 17 May 1990 but before any remedial action had been taken by the employer; and, thirdly, once remedial action had been taken. In respect of the first period (service prior to 17 May 1990), the *Barber* judgment excluded the application of Article 119 [new Article 141] to pension benefits payable in respect of those periods so that employers and trustees were not required to ensure equal treatment as far as those benefits were concerned. However, in respect of the second period (periods after 17 May 1990), when the Court found that discrimination in relation to pay existed, and so long as measures bringing about equal treatment had not been adopted by the scheme, the Court ruled that the only proper way of complying with Article 119 [new Article 141] was to grant those in the disadvantaged class, the men, the same advantages as those enjoyed by the people in the favoured class, the women (levelling up).

Table 5.1 *The Effect of the Decision in* Smith v. Avdel Systems

no equality required	levelling up	choice of employer whether to level up or down
17 May 1990 (date of *Barber* judgment)	1 July 1991 (date on which pension scheme adopted measures to achieve equality)	

---

[388] See Art. 117 [new Art. 136] and Case 126/86 *Giménez Zaera* v. *Instituto Nacional de la Seguridad Social* [1987] ECR 3697.

[389] Case 43/75 [1976] ECR 455. See also Case C–102/88 *Ruzius-Wilbrink* [1989] ECR 4311 where the Court stated that part-timers were entitled to have the same system applied to them as other workers in proportion to their working hours, and the application of this in the case of collective agreements: Case 33/89 *Kowalska* v. *Freie und Hansestadt Hamburg* [1990] ECR I–2591.

[390] Case C–184/89 [1991] ECR I–297.

[391] See above, n. 368.

As regards the third period (periods of service completed after the entry into force of rules designed to eliminate discrimination (1 July 1991)), the Court said that Article 119 [new Article 141] did not preclude measures which achieve equal treatment by reducing the advantages of persons previously favoured (levelling down) since Article 119 merely required that men and women should receive the same pay for the same work without imposing any specific level of pay.[392] The Court added that since equal treatment was a fundamental principle of Community law its application by employers must be 'immediate and full'. As a result, 'the achievement of equality cannot be made progressive on a basis that still maintains discrimination, even if only temporarily'. Therefore, it was not possible to phase in the process of levelling down.

If the principles laid down in *Smith* v. *Avdel* are applied to the example outlined above, with the modification that the employer equalized the occupational pension age to 65 for both men and women in May 1991, Mrs X will receive £940 a month, and Mr Y £820. This is calculated as shown in Table 5.2. on the following page.

3.5 *Barber* and Beyond

In the light of the decision in *Barber* a series of other pension practices have been examined for unlawful discrimination.

(a) Survivors' Benefits

In *Ten Oever*[393] the Court established that the concept of pay in Article 119 [new Article 141] included survivors' benefits. Mr Ten Oever's wife belonged to an occupational pension scheme which provided for a survivor's pension for widows only. It was not until 1 January 1989 that this entitlement extended to widowers. Mrs Ten Oever died on 13 October 1988 and Mr Ten Oever unsuccessfully claimed entitlement to a survivor's pension. The Court ruled that since this scheme was a result of an agreement between both sides of industry and was funded wholly by the employees and the employers, without any financial contribution from the public purse,[394] this survivor's pension fell within the scope of Article 119 [new Article 141]. The Court added that it was not relevant that a survivor's pension was paid, by definition, not to the employee but to the employee's survivor.[395] Entitlement to such a benefit was consideration deriving from the survivor's spouse's membership of the scheme, the pension being vested in the survivor by reason of the employment relationship that had existed between the

---

[392] See also Preamble to amended Directive 86/378.

[393] Case C–109/91 [1993] ECR I–4879. See also Case C–147/95 *DEI* v. *Evrenopoulos* [1997] ECR I–2057; and Case C–50/99 *Podesta* v. *CRICA*, judgment of 25 May 2000.

[394] Cf. Case 80/70 *Defrenne (No. 1)* [1971] ECR 445.

[395] This is now recognized in Art. 3 of Directive 86/378 as amended by Directive 96/97.

Table 5.2 Application of the Principles in Smith v. Avdel Systems

---

Mrs X's position

| *1984–1990* | 6/10 of service | £600 | ——— |
| | | | £600 |

| *1990–1991* | 1/10 of service | £100 | ——— |
| | | | £100 |

1991–1994	(period of service for which levelling down is permitted)		
	3/10 of service	£300	
	Minus 20% actuarial reduction for early retirement	£60	———
			£240
			———
	Total		£940

Mr Y's position

1984–1990	(no equality required)		
	6/10 of service	£600	
	Minus 20% actuarial reduction for early retirement	£120	———
			£480

1990–1991	(period of service between date of *Barber* judgment and date on which pension scheme adopts measures to achieve equality: levelling up required and no actuarial reduction can be made)		
	1/10 of service	£100	———
			£100

1991–1994	(period of service for which levelling down is permitted)		
	3/10 of service	£300	
	Minus 20% actuarial reduction for early retirement	£60	———
			£240
			———
	Total		£820

---

employer and the survivor's spouse and being paid to him or her by reason of the spouse's employment.[396] In *Coloroll*[397] the Court confirmed that the survivor could rely on Article 119 [new Article 141] to assert his rights since the right to payment of a survivor's pension arose at the time of the death of an

---

[396] Since survivors' pensions now fall in principle within Art. 119 [new Art. 141]. The exclusion of survivors' pensions from the application of the principle of equal treatment in Art. 9(b) of Directive 86/378 was *ultra vires*.

[397] Case C–200/91 [1994] ECR I–4389.

employee affiliated to the scheme and the survivor was the only person in a position to assert the right. The Court also confirmed in *Coloroll* that the temporal limitation laid down in *Barber* applied to survivors' pensions.

(b) Actuarial Factors

In *Neath*[398] the Court drew the line at expanding the definition of 'pay' in Article 119 [new Article 141] to include the use of actuarial factors differing according to sex in funded and defined-benefit schemes. Mr Neath belonged to a contributory defined-benefit/final salary scheme where male and female employees' contributions were identical[399] but the employer's contributions varied over time to ensure that the pension scheme was properly funded to cover the cost of pensions promised. The employer's contributions were higher for female than for male employees, due to a variety of actuarial factors in the mechanism for funding the scheme, including the fact that women live, on average, longer than men. This meant that when part of the pension was converted into capital, the male employees received lower sums than the female employees.

While recognizing that the commitment by the employer to pay a periodic pension to the employees fell within the definition of pay in Article 119, the Court ruled that that 'commitment does not necessarily have to do with the funding arrangements (including the selection of actuarial factors) chosen to secure the periodic payment of the pension' which remained outside the scope of Article 119. Consequently, since the use of sex-based actuarial factors in funded defined-benefit schemes did not fall within Article 119, inequalities in the amounts of capital benefits 'whose value can only be determined on the basis of the arrangements chosen for funding the scheme are likewise not struck at by Article 119 [new Article 141]'.[400]

However, sex-based actuarial factors run directly contrary to the essence of anti-discrimination laws which require that workers be regarded on the basis of their individual characteristics and not on the basis of gender-stereotypes. As Advocate General van Gerven recognized, health, race, occupation, and social class provide better indicators of life expectancy, and other Community countries manage their occupation pension schemes without reference to sex-based actuarial factors. However, in the UK sex-based actuarial assumptions are used not only by employers but also by pension providers to whom it would be difficult to extend the application of Article 119 [new Article 141].[401]

---

[398] Case C–152/91 [1993] ECR I–6935 affirmed in Case C–200/91 *Coloroll* [1994] ECR I–4389, para. 85.

[399] The employees' contributions are an element of pay since they are deducted directly from an employee's salary which, according to the Court in Case 69/80 *Worringham* [1981] ECR 767, is pay. In Case C–200/91 *Coloroll* [1994] ECR I–4389 the Court added that whether contributions are payable by the employer or the employees has no bearing on the concept of pay (para. 88).

[400] Case C–152/91 *Neath* [1993] ECR I–6935, para. 33, and Case C–200/91 *Coloroll* [1994] ECR I–4389, para. 85. See also new Art. 6(1)(h) and (i), para. 2, of Directive 86/378.

[401] Rubinstein, Editorial [1994] IRLR 51.

The rationale behind the decision in *Neath* focuses on the fact that the case concerns a defined-benefit scheme where the employer knows the extent of the commitment. The same considerations may not apply to money purchase schemes. The Court has yet to rule on this point.[402]

(c) Additional Voluntary Contributions

The Court also took a strict line in respect of Additional Voluntary Contributions (AVCs) paid by employees to secure additional benefits such as an additional tax-free lump sum.[403] Since the AVCs are paid into a separate fund merely administered by the occupational scheme, and since they secure benefits additional to those connected with their employment, the Court said in *Coloroll*[404] that AVCs were not pay within the meaning of Article 119 [new Article 141].

3.6. Remedies

The obligation to secure equality applies not only to employers but also to the trustees of a pension scheme. The Court made this clear in *Barber*.[405] The Court recognized that Article 119 [new Article 141] applied to an occupational pension scheme set up in the form of a trust and administered by trustees who were technically independent of the employer because Article 119 applied to 'consideration received indirectly from the employer'.[406] In *Coloroll*[407] the Court added that the trustees were bound to do everything within the scope of their powers to ensure compliance with the principle of equal treatment, especially when a worker changes job, transferring pension rights from one occupational scheme to another. When the worker reaches retirement age, the *second* scheme is obliged to increase the benefits it undertook to pay him when accepting the transfer so as to eliminate the effects, contrary to Article 119, suffered by the worker due to the inadequacy of the capital transferred because of discrimination suffered under the first scheme.[408]

If securing the principle of equality is beyond the powers of trustees, employers and trustees are bound to use all means available under domestic law to rectify this. This might include having recourse to the national courts, especially where the involvement of the courts is necessary to amend the provisions of the pension scheme or trust deed.[409] The courts are bound to

---

[402] But see new Art. 6(1)(h) and (i), para. 1.

[403] Case C–200/91 *Coloroll* [1994] ECR I–4389.

[404] Case C–200/91 [1994] ECR I–4389.

[405] Case C–262/88 [1990] ECR I–1889, paras. 28 and 29. See also new Art. 6(2) of Directive 86/378.

[406] The Court has also said that Art. 119 applies to administrators of a pension scheme (Case C–128/93 *Fisscher* [1994] ECR I–4583, para. 32).

[407] Case C–200/91 [1994] ECR I–4389.

[408] This only applies to benefits payable in periods of service subsequent to 17 May 1990.

[409] Case C–200/91 *Coloroll* [1994] ECR I–4389, para. 39.

provide the legal protection which individuals derive from the direct effect of provisions of the Treaty,[410] and where necessary they must disapply any incompatible domestic provisions.

Given the long-term investment involved in accumulating a pension, the question of backdating of pensionable service and national time limits has become a major issue, particularly in respect of access to occupational pensions. It will be recalled that the temporal limitation laid down in *Barber*[411] did not apply to the right of access to schemes, but only to benefits payable under those schemes. Consequently, the direct effect of Article 119 [new Article 141] could be relied on in order retroactively to claim equal treatment in relation to the right to join an occupational pension scheme and this may be done as from 8 April 1976. However, the Court said in *Vroege*[412] and *Fisscher*[413] that national time limits might preclude such extensive retrospective claims.

Doubt has been cast on this aspect of these decisions by *Magorrian*.[414] In that case the applicants began employment as full-time workers and then became part-time workers when they had children. When they retired they were not entitled to the more favourable pension benefits available to full-time workers. In response to their claim under Article 119, the UK government argued that under section 2(5) of the Equal Pay Act (EqPA) 1970 no award of arrears of pay could be made relating to a period earlier than two years before the date on which the proceedings were instituted. The Court, reaffirming its decisions in *Vroege* and *Fisscher*, said that the direct effect of Article 119 [new Article 141] could be relied on, as from 8 April 1976, in order retroactively to claim equal treatment in relation to the *right to join* (access to) an occupational pension scheme. The UK, however, argued that this case concerned the amount of *benefits* payable under the scheme (to which the *Barber* temporal limitation would apply) and not the right to belong to the scheme. The Court, however, referring to its decision in *Dietz*,[415] said that membership of a scheme would be of no interest to employees if it did not confer entitlement to the benefits provided by the scheme in question. Therefore, entitlement to a retirement pension under an occupational scheme was indissolubly linked to the right to join such a scheme. It continued that the same was true in *Magorrian* where the discrimination suffered by part-time workers stemmed from discrimination concerning access to a special scheme which conferred entitlement to additional benefits.

As far as the backdating was concerned, the Court said the fact that the

---

[410] Case C–213/89 *R v. Secreatary of State for Transport, ex parte Factortame* [1990] ECR I–2433, para. 19.
[411] Case C–262/88 [1990] ECR I–1889.
[412] Case C–57/93 [1994] ECR I–4541.
[413] Case C–128/93 [1994] ECR I–4583.
[414] Case C–246/96 [1997] ECR I–7153.
[415] Case C–435/93 *Dietz v. Stichting Thuiszorg Rotterdam* [1996] ECR I–5223.

right to be admitted to a scheme could take place no earlier than two years before the institution of proceedings deprived the applicants of the additional benefits under the scheme to which they were entitled to be affiliated. However, the UK argued that following *Johnson (No. 2)*[416] and *Steenhorst-Neerings*[417] a restriction on backdating was valid under Community law. The Court disagreed. It said that in *Magorrian* the claim was not for the retroactive award of certain additional benefits but for recognition of entitlement to full membership of an occupational scheme. Whereas the rules at issue in *Johnson* merely limited the period, prior to commencement of proceedings, in respect of which backdated benefits could be obtained, the rule at issue in *Magorrian* prevented the entire record of service from 8 April 1976 until 1990 from being taken into account for the purposes of calculating the additional benefits which would be payable even after the date of the claim. Consequently, the Court said that the UK rule rendered any action by individuals relying on Community law impossible in practice and limited the direct effect of Article 119 [new Article 141] of the Treaty in cases in which no such limitation had been laid down either in the Court's case law or in Protocol No. 2.

The scope of this aspect of the ruling is not clear and sits unhappily with the earlier rulings in *Fisscher* and *Fantask*.[418] It seems that in the ordinary case of a limitation on the retroactive effect of such claims, the claim is limited in terms of periods which are prior to the date of institution of proceedings but the claimant is able to vindicate her rights for the future. On the Court's view of the effect of the rule in *Magorrian* it prevented the applicants from claiming access to the scheme for the future as well: if each woman could count only two years of past part-time service towards the twenty-year requirement, both would have to come out of retirement and seek to work for some considerable time into the future to vindicate their rights of access under Article 119 [new Article 141].[419] However, the Court has created a problematic distinction between access and benefits payable because benefit claims can usually be defined in terms of claims for full access to that benefit and access claims can usually be described in terms of a claim for benefit which flows from the access.[420]

Nevertheless, in *Preston*[421] the Court reaffirmed its ruling in *Magorrian* and maintained the distinction between the arrears of benefit and the right to retroactive access. In *Preston* the aim of the proceedings was to obtain basic

[416] Case C–410/92 [1994] ECR I–5483.
[417] Case C–338/91 [1993] ECR I–5475.
[418] Case C–188/95 [1997] ECR I–6783.
[419] Coppel, 'Domestic Law Limitations on Recovery for Breach of EC Law' (1998) 27 *ILJ* 259, 261.
[420] Rubinstein, 'Editorial' [1998] IRLR 55.
[421] Case C–78/98 *Preston and Others* v. *Wolverhampton Healthcare NHS Trust and Others*, judgment of 16 May 2000.

retirement pensions for the individual applicants. In *Magorrian* the individuals had sought recognition of their right to retroactive membership of a pension scheme in order to receive *additional* benefits. Therefore, in *Preston* the Court said that this reinforced its view in *Magorrian* that Community law precluded a national rule under which a claim for recognition of entitlement to join an occupational pension scheme was limited to a period which started to run two years prior to commencement of proceedings.[422] However, the Court did remind the claimants that 'the fact that a worker can claim retroactively to join an occupational pension scheme does not allow him to avoid paying the contributions relating to the period of membership concerned.[423]

In *Preston* the Court also had to consider the time limits for actually making a claim. Under section 2(4) of the EqPA a claim for membership of an occupational scheme had to be lodged within a period of six months following the end of the employment to which the claim related. Having reasserted the principle of national procedural autonomy,[424] the Court ruled[425] that the setting of a six-month time limit could not be regarded as 'constituting an obstacle to obtaining the payment of sums to which, albeit not yet payable, the claimants are entitled under Article 119 of the Treaty. Such a limitation period does not render impossible or excessively difficult the exercise of rights conferred by the Community legal order and is not therefore liable to strike at the very essence of those rights'.[426] Thus, the six-month time limit did not fall foul of the principle of effectiveness, the second limitation on the principle of national procedural autonomy. The Court then considered the position of those claimants who worked regularly, but periodically or intermittently, for the same employer under successive legally separate short-term contracts. It said that as far as these workers were concerned, setting the starting point of the six-month limitation period at the end of *each* contract did render the exercise of the right conferred by Article 119 excessively difficult.

The Court then considered whether the six-month limit failed the principle of equivalence, the first limitation to the principle of national procedural autonomy. This requires 'that the rule at issue be applied without distinction, whether the infringement alleged is of Community law or national law, where the purpose and cause of action are similar'.[427] Citing *Levez*,[428] the Court said that an action alleging infringement of a statute such as the EqPA did not constitute a domestic action similar to an action alleging infringement of Article 119 of the Treaty. It said that the fact that 'the same procedural rules

---

[422] Para. 42.
[423] Para. 39, citing Case C–18/93 *Fisscher* [1994] ECR I–4583, para. 37.
[424] Para. 31, above, n. 292.
[425] Case C–188/95 *Fantask* [1997] ECR I–6783, above n. 301.
[426] Para. 34.
[427] Para. 55.
[428] Case C–326/96 *Levez* v. *TH Jennings (Harlow Pools) Ltd* [1998] ECR I–7835 considered further in Ch. 4.

applied to two comparable claims, one relying on a right conferred by Community law, the other on a right acquired under domestic law, was not enough to ensure compliance with the principle of equivalence, since one and the same form of action was involved'.[429] The Court then gave some guidance on determining similarity. It said that the national court had to consider whether the actions were similar as regards their purpose, cause of action, and essential characteristics. National courts also had to examine whether the rules were similar taking into account the role they played in the procedure as a whole, as well as the operation of that procedure and any special features of those rules.

[429] Para. 51.

6

Health, Safety, and Working Conditions

This chapter examines the measures adopted by the Community under the broad spectrum of health and safety and working conditions. First, it looks at the measures traditionally regarded—certainly from a common law perspective—as health and safety matters: the Framework Directive 89/391 on health and safety and, in outline only, its daughters. It then examines those measures which fall within a rather broader—and more Scandinavian—definition of health and safety which encompasses references to the working environment. In particular, it examines the Working Time Directive 93/104 and Directives designed to protect those facing specific risks—pregnant workers, young workers, and atypical workers. Finally, it looks at two measures which are traditionally considered labour law matters—proof of the contract of employment, and pay.

A. THE DEVELOPMENT OF A POLICY IN RESPECT OF HEALTH AND SAFETY

1. Introduction

The desire to set minimum standards to protect workers and harmonize costs has produced an extensive European legislative framework in the field of health and safety.[1] The need for worker protection is recognized implicitly by Article 136 [ex Article 117] on the improvement in working conditions and standards of living of workers[2] and confirmed by Article 140 [ex Article 118], which empowers the Commission to promote close co-operation between Member States in the field of occupational hygiene. It is estimated that 6,000 fatal accidents occur at work each year and 4.8 million occupational accidents. Industrial accidents and work-related ill health not only represent a cost in terms of human suffering but also cost national economies between 1.5 and 4 per cent of GDP.[3] The Commission argues that higher health and

---

[1] For full details of all legislation see http://europa.eu.int/comm/dg05/h&s/intro/referenc.htm and for related texts see http://www.eu-osha.es/legislation. See generally Neal, 'Regulating Health and Safety at Work: Developing European Policy for the Millennium' (1998) 14 *IJCLLIR* 217.

[2] See also Art. 3 ECSC; Art. 2 Euratom refers to the establishment of uniform safety standards to protect the health of workers.

[3] See http://europa.eu.int/comm/dg05/h&s/intro/prog2000.htm.

safety standards, while initially imposing increased costs, should guarantee in the long term a reduction in the number of accidents and occupational diseases, thereby reducing costs to business, and increasing competitiveness without reducing the number of jobs.[4] The Commission also says that more efficient and safer work practices also lead to an increase in productivity and better industrial relations.

The costs argument also manifests itself in terms of the creation of a level playing field: Community rules on health and safety are binding on all Member States, allowing equal conditions of competition to prevail. Without such Community legislation, it is believed that those countries with low health and safety standards gain a competitive advantage over those countries with higher standards and thus greater costs. This argument has particular resonance within the UK, which has always guaranteed relatively high levels of health and safety protection for its workforce, for which British industry has incurred a heavier financial burden.

Despite British concerns, all Member States have traditionally regulated the health and safety of workers, through constitutional provisions (Greece, Portugal, Italy, and Luxembourg), codes, or statutes (for example France, Netherlands, Germany, and Spain) or through implied terms in the contract of employment (for example, UK and Ireland).[5] Moreover, in all States a general duty is imposed on employers to provide safe and healthy working conditions. This is variously described as the duty to ensure 'with the diligence of a good father' that work takes place in suitable conditions for health and safety and to observe the requirements of the law (Belgium), 'to take measures necessary in relation to the type of work and the state of technology to protect the physical and mental welfare for employees' and to observe the requirements of the law (Italy) and to ensure so far as reasonably practicable the health, safety, and welfare of all employees (UK). Individual Member States have also evolved a common pattern to the legislative control of occupational health and safety. This involves, first, a basic framework of primary legislation establishing general principles and some specific requirements.[6] This framework may provide the basis for more detailed and specific secondary legislation. Next, secondary legislation, such as regulations, decrees, orders, and so forth, sets out detailed requirements based on general principles established in the primary legislation. Finally, codes of practice and technical guidance provide a third tier in some Member States. While breaches of codes and guidelines are not generally offences, evidence of compliance or non-compliance may be

---

[4] COM(88)74, Commission's Memorandum to the Framework Directive 89/391/EEC.

[5] See generally *The Regulation of Working Conditions in the Member States of the European Community*, Vol. I, *Social Europe* 4/92, 108–11.

[6] See e.g. Denmark, the Working Environment Act 1975; Greece, Health and Safety of Workers Act 1985; Ireland, the Safety, Health and Welfare at Work Act 1989; Netherlands, the Working Environment Act 1980; UK, Health and Safety at Work Act 1974.

used in legal proceedings.[7] In recent years this approach has influenced the Commission's strategy to legislation. It has adopted framework directives prescribing general duties and more specific daughter directives.

2. Historical Perspective

2.1 The Early Days

Within the framework of the ECSC Treaty[8] various research programmes were carried out in the field of health and safety and various attempts were made to reduce the number of explosions and fires in coal mines. Similarly, in the early stages of the evolution of a Community policy on health and safety under the Treaty of Rome the emphasis was on 'mapping' the area and identifying the problems.[9] This was followed by the 1974 Social Action Pro-gramme[10] which talked of establishing a programme for workers 'aimed at the humanisation of their living and working conditions . . . with particular reference to: . . . improvement in safety and health conditions at work'. This precipitated the establishment of the Advisory Committee for Safety, Hygiene, and Health Protection at Work,[11] designed to assist the Commission in prepar-ing and implementing activities in the fields of health, safety, and hygiene and the adoption of the first two health and safety directives, concerning signs at the workplace and protection against vinyl chloride monomers (VCMs). The safety signs Directive 77/576 was introduced in the face of increasing free-dom of movement of persons to reduce both the risk of accidents at work and occupational diseases due to language problems. The Directive provided a comprehensive set of colour co-ordinated signs to draw the workers' attention to specific hazards in the workplace.[12] This Directive was replaced by Directive

---

[7] See above, n. 6, 109.

[8] Art. 55(2) ECSC.

[9] For a detailed discussion of the development of a Community policy on health and safety, see Neal and Wright (eds.), *The European Communities' Health and Safety Legislation* (Chapman & Hall, London, 1992), Preface.

[10] Council Resolution 74/C 13/1 of 21 Jan. 1974.

[11] Council Decision 74/325/EEC [1975] OJ C185/15. A year later the European Foundation for the Improvement of Living and Working Conditions (the Dublin Foundation) was established (Regulation 1365/75 [1975] OJ C139/1), a body engaged in applied research in areas of social policy, including the improvement and protection of the environment. As a result of the Com-munity Social Charter 1989 there is now a European Agency for Safety and Health at Work Council Regulation (EC) 2062/94 [1994] OJ L216/1 amended by Council Regulation (EC) 1643/95 [1995] OJ L156/1, COM(90)564 final [1991] OJ C27/3 which is intended to provide support for the implementation of programmes relating to the workplace, including technical and scientific assistance and co-ordination as well as assistance in the field of training.

[12] Art. 1(1): red means stop or prohibition and is also used to identify fire-fighting equipment; yellow, caution or possible danger and can be used to identify particular dangers, such as fire, radiation and chemical hazards, as well as to identify steps and dangerous obstacles; green, no danger or first aid and can be used to identify emergency routes and exits, first aid stations, and rescue points; and blue, a mandatory sign or a sign that conveys information and is used to demonstrate the obligation to wear individual safety equipment and the location of a telephone.

92/58[13] which builds on the principles and colour scheme laid down by Directive 77/576.

The VCM Directive 78/610/EEC[14] provided an early example of the model which was to be applied in subsequent Directives. The protection offered by the Directive includes technical preventive measures designed to reduce the concentration of VCM to which workers are exposed to the lowest possible levels,[15] setting limits on the atmospheric concentration of VCM in the working area,[16] making provisions for monitoring the atmospheric concentration of VCM,[17] and making, where necessary, provision for personal protection measures.[18] It also requires the employer, first, to provide adequate information to the workers on the risks to which they are exposed and the precautions to be taken;[19] secondly, to keep a register of workers with particulars of the type and duration of their work and the exposure to which they have been subjected;[20] and thirdly, to provide medical surveillance, ensuring that workers are examined by a competent doctor, both on recruitment or prior to taking up the activities and subsequently.

This period also saw the first action programme on safety and health at work, covering the period 1978–82,[21] followed by the second action programme 1982–6. The first action programme resulted in the enactment of the first Framework Directive on hazardous agents, 80/1107/EEC,[22] which

---

[13] Council Directive 92/58/EEC of 24 June 1992 on the minimum requirements for the provision of safety and/or health signs at work [1992] OJ L245/23 (ninth individual Directive within the meaning of Art. 16(1) of Directive 89/391) COM(90)664 final. It came into force on 24 June 1994. The principles relating to Directive 89/391 (see below nn. 49–129), including information and consultation of workers, apply equally to this Directive.

[14] Council Directive 78/610/EEC on the approximation of laws, regulations, and administrative provisions of the Member States on the protection of the health of workers exposed to VCM [1978] OJ L197/12.

[15] Art. 3(1).

[16] Arts. 2(b) and 4 and Annex I.

[17] Arts. 5 and 6.

[18] Art. 7.

[19] Art. 8.

[20] Art. 9.

[21] Council Resolution of 29 June 1978 [1978] OJ C165/1, supplemented and revised by the Second Action Programme—Council Resolution of 27 Feb. 1984 [1984] OJ C67/02. The first action programme focused principally on the causes of occupational accidents and diseases, protection against dangerous substances, prevention of the hazards and harmful effects associated with machinery, and the improvement of human behaviour. The second action programme added training, information, statistics, and research, and co-operation with other international bodies such as the ILO and WHO.

[22] Council Directive 80/1107/EEC of 27 Nov. 1980 on the protection of workers from the risks related to exposure to chemical, physical, and biological agents at work [1980] OJ L327/8. This Directive was modified by Council Directive 88/642/EEC [1988] OJ L356/74; Commission Directive 91/322/EEC [1991] OJ L177/22 and Commission Directive 96/94/EC [1996] OJ L338/86. See also Council Directive 89/694/EEC of 21 Dec. 1989 on vocational training for certain drivers of vehicles carrying dangerous goods by road [1989] OJ L398/33. Drivers of vehicles carrying dangerous goods must be in possession of a vocational training certificate as from 1 July 1992 for the carriage of dangerous goods in tanks and the carriage of explosive substances, and as from

was intended to protect workers against risks to their health and safety, including the prevention of such risks, arising from exposure to harmful chemical, physical, and biological agents.[23] The Directive said that exposure of workers to agents must be avoided or kept at as low a level *as is reasonably practicable.*[24] This provided a margin of discretion in the application of the Directive, particularly for small companies, which has been removed in the directives adopted under the subsequent framework Directive, Directive 89/391/EEC, despite strong arguments made to the contrary by the UK and the Commission.

The 1980 Directive was followed by directives concerning the chemical agents lead,[25] and asbestos,[26] and the physical agent noise.[27] All three Directives have as their aim the protection of workers against risks to their health (or hearing), including the prevention of such risks, arising or likely to arise at

1 Jan. 1995 (1 Jan. 1996 in the case of Portugal) for all other types of carriage. The Commission has also proposed a directive on uniform procedures for checks on the transport of dangerous goods by road (94/C26/08 COM(93)665 final—SYN 487) and amended proposal (94/C238/04 COM(94)340 final—SYN 487). It has also proposed a directive on the approximation of the laws of the Member States with regard to the transport of dangerous goods by road (94/C17/05 COM(93)548 final—SYN 477). See also Directive 93/75/EEC [1993] OJ L247/19 concerning minimum requirements for vessels bound for or leaving Community ports and carrying dangerous or polluting goods. This has raised the question of the importance of a common system of marking dangerous substances. Council Directive 67/548/EEC on the approximation of the laws, regulations, and administrative provisions relating to the classification, packaging and labelling of dangerous substances on the market [1967] JO L196/1. Council Directive 88/379/EEC on the approximation of laws, regulations, and administrative provisions of the Member States relating to the classification, packaging, and labelling of dangerous preparations to man and the environment [1988] OJ L187/14 as adapted to technical progress by Commission Directive 93/18/EEC [1993] OJ L104/46. Directive 88/379 requires Member States to introduce a system of safety sheets which led to Commission Directive 91/155/EEC of 5 Mar. 1991 defining and laying down the detailed arrangements for the system of specific information relating to the dangerous preparations in implementation of Art. 10 of Directive 88/379 [1991] OJ L76/35. This Directive has been amended by Commission Directive 93/112/EEC [1993] OJ 104/46. Finally, see also Directive 82/501/EEC on the major-accident hazards of certain industrial activities [1982] OJ L230/1, amended by Council Directive 87/216/EEC [1987] OJ L85/36, Council Directive 86/610/EEC [1988] OJ L336/14 and Council Directive 91/692/EEC [1991] OJ L377/48. See also Council Directive 96/82/EC [1997] OJ L10/13 on the control of major-accident hazards involving dangerous substances.

[23] Art. 1(1).

[24] Art. 3(1).

[25] Council Directive 82/605/EEC on the protection of workers from the risks related to the exposure to metallic lead and its ionic compounds at work [1982] OJ L247/12. See now Directive 98/24 [1998] OJ L131/11.

[26] Council Directive 83/477/EEC of 19 September 1983 on the protection of workers from the risks relating to exposure to asbestos at work [1983] OJ L263/25 due to be implemented by 1 Jan. 1987. This Directive was amended by Council Directive 91/382/EEC [1991] OJ L206/16, due to be implemented by 1 Jan. 1993 or 1 Jan. 1996 in the case of asbestos mining industries, and 1 Jan. 1996 and 1 Jan. 1999 in the case of Greece, and by Directive 98/24/EC [1998] OJ L131/11 and Council Conclusions of 7 Apr. 1998 [1998] OJ C142/1.

[27] Council Directive 86/188/EEC on the protection of workers from the risks relating to exposure to noise at work [1983] OJ L137/28. This Directive has been amended by Directive 98/24/EC [1998] OJ L131/11.

work from exposure to these agents. The Directives lay down limit values on the exposure to the agents and other specific requirements relating to risk assessment, risk reduction, medical surveillance, and the provision of workers with information, following the pattern of the parent Directive. The fourth daughter Directive bans the use of certain specified substances altogether,[28] on the ground that these products represented a serious risk to the health and safety of workers and that precautions were not sufficient to ensure a satisfactory level of health and safety protection. The parent Directive, as amended, and Directive 82/605/EEC on lead and Directive 88/364/EEC banning certain agents, have been reviewed and are now included in Directive 98/24/EC on chemical agents.[29]

2.2 The Single European Act 1986 and Beyond

The Single European Act, passed to facilitate the completion of the internal market in goods, persons, services, and capital by 31 December 1992,[30] also contained limited recognition of the role of a social dimension to the internal market programme, by means of the new Article 118a [new Article 137].[31] Article 118a(1) contained the commitment that:

Member States shall pay particular attention to encouraging improvements, especially in the working environment, as regards the health and safety of workers, and shall set as their objective the harmonisation of conditions in this area, while maintaining the improvements made.

In order to achieve this objective a new legal basis was introduced. Article 118a(2) provided that:

the Council, acting by a qualified majority on a proposal from the Commission, in co-operation with the European Parliament, . . . shall adopt, by means of directives, minimum requirements[32] for gradual implementation, having regard to the conditions and technical rules obtaining in each of the Member States.[33]

---

[28] Council Directive 88/364/EEC on the protection of workers by the banning of certain specified agents and/or certain work activities [1988] OJ L179/44.

[29] [1998] OJ L131/11.

[30] Art. 8a EEC/Art. 7a EC [now Art. 14].

[31] Art. 21 SEA.

[32] The reference to minimum standards does not imply lowest common denominator standards. Instead it refers to the power granted by Art. 118a(3), introduced at the behest of the Danes in an attempt to avoid downward harmonization, enabling Member States to maintain or introduce more stringent conditions. This view was confirmed in Case C–84/96 *UK v. Council* [1996] ECR I–5755, para. 17, and again in Case C–2/97 *IP v. Borsana* [1998] ECR I–8597, para. 35. See further Ch. 2.

[33] Art. G(33) TEU replaced the reference to qualified majority voting and the co-operation procedure with the requirement 'acting in accordance with the procedure laid down by Art. 189c'. The Treaty of Amsterdam changed the co-operation procedure to the co-decision procedure.

The introduction of qualified majority voting marked a significant departure from the unanimous vote required by Article 100 [new Article 94] for measures directly affecting the establishment or functioning of the Common Market. For the Commission this represented an ideal opportunity to push through social measures on the basis that they were health and safety matters, thereby circumventing the UK's veto. The only constraint imposed upon the Commission was that the Directives must avoid imposing 'administrative, financial and legal constraints in a way which would hold back the creation and development of small and medium sized undertakings'.[34]

In addition to the new legal basis on health and safety in Article 118a, the Single European Act also introduced Article 100a(2) [new Article 95(2)] which provided that measures relating to 'the rights and interests of employed persons' could not be adopted by qualified majority voting, as provided by Article 100a(1) [new Article 95]. This meant that the unanimous voting rules laid down by Article 100 [new Article 94] applied.[35] As the UK government discovered in *Working Time*,[36] there is no clear line which distinguishes Article 100a(2) from Article 118a.

The Treaty of Amsterdam revised the wording of Article 118a [new Article 137]. Article 137(1) provides that 'the Community shall support and complement the activities of the Member States' in the fields of, *inter alia*, 'improvement in particular of the working environment to protect workers' health and safety' and 'working conditions'. The inclusion of working conditions is significant for it recognizes that there is a blurring of the distinction between health and safety matters which required qualified majority voting and other issues affecting working conditions which, prior to Amsterdam, may have required unanimous voting under Article 100 [new Article 94] and Article 100a(2) [new Article 95(2)]. Previously, it had taken a broad construction by the Court in the *Working Time* case[37] to ensure that measures which had as their 'principal aim' the protection of health and safety, albeit with ancillary objectives such as employment rights, could be adopted under Article 118a. The Treaty of Amsterdam also introduced the co-decision procedure (Article 251 [ex Article 189b]) for the adoption of measures listed in Article 137(1).

Article 100a(1) [new Article 95(1)] gave the Community competence to enact, by qualified majority vote (and after Maastricht the Article 189b [new Article 251] procedure), measures for the harmonization of national rules which have as their objective the 'establishment and functioning of the

---

[34] Art. 118a(2) [new Art. 137(2)], para. 2.

[35] It also might mean that the nature of the Directive might differ since Art. 100 [new Art. 94] makes no reference to setting minimum standards, although Directives 75/129 [1975] OJ L48/29 and 77/187 [1977] OJ L 61/126 on collective redundancies and transfers of undertakings respectively adopted under Art. 100 [new Art. 94] do allow Member States to set minimum standards.

[36] Case C–84/94 *UK v. Council* [1996] ECR I–5755. See further Ch. 2.

[37] Ibid.

internal market' which includes encouraging free movement of goods. This
was also relevant for health and safety at work because directives adopted
under Article 100a [new Article 95] are intended to ensure the placing on the
market of safe products including machines and personal protective equipment (the so-called 'product' or 'trading' directives), the professional use of
which is addressed by directives based on Article 118a [new Article 137].
This is made clear by Article 100a(3) [new Article 95(3)] which requires the
Commission, in its proposals under Article 100a(1) [new Article 95(1)] concerning health and safety,[38] environmental protection, and consumer protection to 'take as a base a high level of protection, *taking account in particular of
any new development based on scientific facts*'.[39] Article 100a(4) [new Article
95(5)] provides that Member States can derogate from a harmonization
measure if they deem it necessary to apply national provisions on grounds
relating to the protection of the environment or the working environment.
The Treaty of Amsterdam tightened up the procedure for Member States to
make such derogations.[40]

Equipped with the new Article 118a [new Article 137] the Commission
drew up a third action programme[41] to outline ideas for applying Article
118a, and this formed the basis of the 1989 Social Charter[42] and its related
Action Programme.[43] Article 19(1) of the Social Charter provides that:

Every worker must enjoy satisfactory health and safety conditions in his working
environment. Appropriate measures must be taken in order to achieve further harmonisation of conditions in this area while maintaining the improvements made.

Article 19(3) adds, in recognition of the role of Article 100a(3) and (4) [new
Articles 95(3) and (4)], that 'the provisions regarding implementation of the
internal market shall help to ensure such protection'. Thus, the Social Charter Action Programme identified a two-pronged approach: the adoption of
'product' or 'trading' directives based on Article 100a(1) [new Article 95(1)]
and provisions concerning worker protection in the working environment,
often complementary to the technical provisions and based on Article 118a
[new Article 137], including a new Framework Directive 89/391/EEC[44] and
its daughter directives laying down minimum health and safety requirements
for the workplace, the use of work equipment, personal protective equipment,
and chemical and biological agents. The Commission also emphasized that
priority would be given to new initiatives in areas where safety causes

[38] See Council Directives 89/392/EEC [1989] OJ L183/9 and 89/686/EEC [1989] OJ L399/19
as amended.
[39] Wording added by the Treaty of Amsterdam.
[40] Art. 95(5)–(10).
[41] COM(87)520 final and Council Resolution on Safety, Hygiene, and Health at Work of
21 Dec. 1987 [1987] OJ C28/88.
[42] COM(89)471 final.
[43] COM(89)568 final.
[44] [1989] OJ L183/1.

significant problems, such as the building industry, and fisheries. In addition, the Commission urged Member States to put forward ideas for a schedule of industrial diseases, which has led to a Commission Recommendation[45] suggesting that Member States introduce into their national laws provisions concerning scientifically recognized occupational diseases liable to compensation and subject to preventive measures. Although this Recommendation is only soft law, the Court in *Grimaldi v. Fonds des Maladies Professionnelles*[46] ruled that recommendations must be taken into account by national courts in order to decide disputes before them, in particular when recommendations clarify the interpretation of national rules adopted in order to implement them or when they are designed to supplement binding Community measures.

The fourth Community action programme[47] was designed to support the implementation and the application of the existing legislation. It also put increased emphasis on non-legislative measures.[48] In particular, the Commission focused on making legislation more effective, preparing for enlargement, and strengthening the link with employability, especially after the Amsterdam and Luxembourg summits. The Commission is also examining the new health and safety risks faced by the changing structure of the working population and employment patterns: an ageing workforce; a steady increase in the proportion of female workers; an increase in casual and part-time work; and, in economic sectors other than agriculture, self-employment, with a continuing increase in jobs in the service sector.

B. FRAMEWORK DIRECTIVE 89/391

The Framework Directive, Directive 89/391/EEC,[49] marked the advent of a new approach to health and safety. While building on the principles laid down in the parent Directive 80/1107, Directive 89/391/EEC and its more specific daughter directives[50] lack the detailed technical requirements found in the earlier directives, relying instead on broad general principles which lack the precision found in the earlier directives. Article 1(1) makes clear that the object of the Directive is to introduce measures to encourage improvements in

---

[45] Commission Recommendation 90/326/EEC of 22 May 1990 to the Member States concerning the adoption of a European Schedule of Occupational Diseases [1990] OJ L160/90. See also the Commission's earlier Recommendations 2188/62 of 23 July 1962 and 66/462/CEE of 20 July 1966.

[46] Case C–322/88 [1989] ECR I–4407.

[47] COM(95)282 final [1995] OJ C262/18.

[48] See esp. the proposed SAFE programme designed to finance guidance and information to help small and medium sized enterprises apply Community legislation correctly (COM(95)282 and COM(96)652). This remains unadopted.

[49] [1989] OJ L183/1.

[50] The enactment of these daughter directives is provided for under Art. 16(1) of Directive 89/391.

the health and safety of workers at work. To that end, it contains 'general principles concerning the prevention of occupational risks, the protection of safety and health, the elimination of risk and accident factors, the informing, consultation [and] balanced participation of workers and their representatives'.[51] The exclusion of detailed technical requirements has obviated the need for lengthy technical debates.[52] Instead, the specification of any relevant technical standards is left to be resolved later through a Technical Adaptation Procedure.[53]

Directive 89/391 lays down minimum standards: it does not justify any reduction in the levels of protection already achieved in Member States, since the States are committed to encouraging improvements in working conditions and harmonizing conditions while maintaining the improvements made.[54] This is specifically recognized in Article 1(3) which provides that the Directive shall be without prejudice to 'existing or future national and Community provisions which are more favourable to protection of safety and health of workers at work'. The Directive therefore provides a social element to complement the economic objectives of the completion of the internal market.[55]

1. The Personal Scope of the Directive

The Directive applies to all sectors of activity, both public and private. This includes, in a non-exhaustive list, industrial activity, agricultural, commercial, administrative, service, educational and cultural activities, and leisure.[56] There are limited derogations in the case of 'certain specific *public sector* activities' (emphasis added), such as the armed forces or police,[57] and 'certain specific activities in the civil protection services'.[58] The Directive recognizes that these occupations inevitably conflict with the principle of health and safety. Nevertheless, even in these situations, the health and safety of workers must be 'ensured as far as possible in the light of the objectives of the Directive'.[59] 'Workers' means any persons employed by an employer, including

---

[51] Art. 1(2).

[52] See James, *The European Community: A Positive Force in UK Health and Safety Law* (Institute of Employment Rights, London, 1993) 6.

[53] See e.g. Art. 17 of Directive 89/391/EEC.

[54] Para. 5 of the Preamble.

[55] COM(88)0073 final. For a discussion of this Directive and others in the EC context see Weiss, 'The Industrial Relations of Occupational Health: The Impact of the Framework Directive on FRG' (1990) 6 *IJCLLIR* 119; Mialon, 'Safety at Work in French Firms' (1990) 6 *IJCLLIR* 129; Montuschi, 'Health and Safety Provision in Italy' (1990) 6 *IJCLLIR* 146; Martinez, 'Health and Safety at Work in the EEC and the Impact on Spain' (1990) 6 *IJCLLIR* 159.

[56] Art. 2(1).

[57] Art. 2(2).

[58] e.g. the fire service would be included in this category.

[59] Art. 2(2).

trainees and apprentices but excluding domestic servants.[60] Thus, by implication, the self-employed are excluded from the benefit of the Directives unless otherwise provided. 'Employers' means natural or legal persons having an employment relationship with the worker and having responsibility for the undertaking and/or the establishment.

2. Employers' Obligations

Article 5(1) contains the demanding obligation that the employer has the duty 'to ensure the health and safety of workers in *every aspect* related to the work' (emphasis added). This duty extends to taking responsibility for services provided by third parties[61] and is not diminished by the fact that workers themselves also have obligations in the field of health and safety.[62] Such a definitive statement, when read in conjunction with Article 1(1), clearly sets the tenor of the Directive: worker protection. Member States may, however,

provide for the exclusion or the limitation of employers' responsibility where occurrences are due to unusual *and* unforeseeable circumstances, beyond the employers' control, or to *exceptional* events, the consequence of which could not have been avoided despite the exercise of *all due care* [emphasis added].[63]

This derogation, being an exception to the basic principle of the Directive, will be narrowly construed[64] and is unlikely to permit broad defences based on financial considerations[65] or arguments related to lack of time or effort to deal with the risk. The emphasis on the exceptional nature of the events also suggests that, on its face, a defence that the employer took all reasonably practicable steps to avoid the risk would not be acceptable. On the other hand, since the general principle of proportionality applies to the Directive as a whole, it may well be that a more general defence based on proportionality, applies to all the provisions in the Directive.

Article 6 fleshes out the general obligations on employers. The obligations imposed are wide reaching: not only must employers take the measures *necessary* for safety and health protection of workers, but they must also prevent the occurrence of occupational risks, provide information and training, and establish the necessary organization and means.[66] These measures must be

---

[60] Art. 3(a).

[61] Arts. 5(2) and 7(3).

[62] Art. 5(3).

[63] Art. 5(4).

[64] To see the application of two principles in the context of the free movement of workers, see Case 41/74 *Van Duyn* v. *Home Office* [1974] ECR 1337, para. 18.

[65] Although see above, n. 34.

[66] Art. 6(1).

adjusted to take account of changing circumstances combined with the aim of improving the existing situation.[67]

Article 6(2) then details the following general principles of prevention[68] designed to guide the employer when implementing health and safety measures:

(a) avoiding risks;
(b) evaluating the risks which cannot be avoided;
(c) combating the risks at source;
(d) adapting the work to the individual, especially as regards the design of work places, the choice of work equipment, and the choice of working and production methods, with a view, in particular, to alleviating monotonous work and work at a predetermined work rate, thus reducing the effects on health. This provision probably goes further than legislation in all Member States. It is a key requirement which addresses the well-being of workers in a comprehensive way rather than focusing on specific hazards;[69]
(e) adapting to technical progress;
(f) replacing the dangerous by the non-dangerous or the less dangerous (the principle of substitution);
(g) developing a coherent prevention policy which covers technology, organization of work, working conditions, social relationships, and the influence of factors related to the working environment;
(h) giving collective protective measures priority over individual protective measures;
(i) giving appropriate instructions to the workers.

The only qualification found in the Directive to the application of this demanding guidance is that the principles operate in conjunction with a consideration of the nature of the activities of the enterprise or establishment.[70]

The employers' duties can be subdivided into the following five categories:[71] duty of awareness and evaluation, duty to plan and take action, duty to train and direct the workforce, duty to inform and consult workers and their representatives, and duty to report. These will be considered in turn.

2.1 Duty of Awareness and Evaluation

Article 9(1)(a) requires the employer to have conducted an assessment of the risks to the health and safety at work and be aware of the situation of groups

---

[67] Ibid.

[68] Defined in Art. 3(d) to mean all steps or measures taken or planned at all stages of work in the undertaking to prevent or reduce occupational risks.

[69] See above n. 6, 112. For a similar idea see the principal of the humanization of work contained in Art. 13 of the Working Time Directive 93/104/EC [1993] OJ L307/18.

[70] Art. 6(3).

[71] See Neal and Wright, above, n. 9, 18, and Neal, 'The European Framework Directive on the Health and Safety of Workers: Challenges for the UK' (1990) 6 *IJCLLIR* 80, 82.

of workers who are exposed to particular risks. Respecting the principle of subsidiarity, the Directive prescribes the objectives to be achieved but allows Member States to decide how these objectives are to be achieved. This means that the Directive provides no guidance as to how this risk assessment is to be carried out nor indications of the minimum enquiry necessary to satisfy the requirements of the Directive.

Having completed the assessment, employers must then evaluate the risks to the safety and health of workers, *inter alia*, in the choice of work equipment, the chemical substances or preparations used and the fitting out of the workplace,[72] and decide on the protective measures to be taken and, if necessary, the protective equipment to be used.[73] As part of this assessment the employer, when entrusting tasks to a worker, must take account of the capabilities of the individual workers as regards health and safety.[74] This is particularly relevant in the case of pregnant women or women who have recently given birth or who are breastfeeding.[75] Further, Article 14 requires that workers receive health surveillance appropriate to the health and safety risks they incur at work. These health checks may be provided as part of the national health system. According to the Preamble, employers must also keep themselves informed of the latest advances in technology and scientific findings concerning workplace design.[76] This suggests that the review of health and safety measures should be a continuous process, requiring constant reassessment and evaluation.

2.2 Duty to Plan and Take Action

Having completed the assessment the employer must, where necessary, introduce preventive measures and changes to working and production to improve the health and safety of workers. Any steps taken must form part of a coherent prevention policy[77] and be integrated into all the activities of the undertaking and at all hierarchical levels.[78] In addition, particularly sensitive risk groups must be protected against the dangers which specifically affect them.[79]

The Framework Directive, when read in conjunction with the various daughter Directives, envisages a hierarchy of control measures as follows:[80]

— Elimination of risk from the workplace. While this is clearly advantageous from a health and safety perspective it may not be feasible in practice.

---

[72] Art. 6(3)(a).
[73] Art. 9(1)(b).
[74] Art. 6(3)(b).
[75] See also Directive 92/85/EEC [1992] OJ L348/1.
[76] See also Art. 6(2)(e).
[77] Art. 6(2)(g).
[78] Art. 6(3)(a), para. 2.
[79] Art. 15.
[80] HSIB 200, 5.

Consequently, employers must consider means by which those risks can be reduced.

— The principle of substitution. This may involve replacing one chemical with another one which is less dangerous but is still capable of working as effectively. It may also involve the substitution of another form of the same substance which is likely to be less hazardous, for example, by replacing powdered ingredients with a less dusty form.[81]

— Engineering control. This may involve introducing ventilation, enclosing dangerous processes,[82] using mechanical handling aids,[83] or automating parts of the process.

— Personal protective equipment (PPE).[84] From a health and safety perspective this is the least advantageous because much PPE is not 100 per cent effective[85] and its success is largely dependent on the correct selection of the most appropriate type of PPE. It also protects only the individual rather than the workforce collectively. The disadvantages of this approach are reflected in Article 6(2)(h) of the Framework Directive which requires employers to give collective protective measures priority over individual protective measures.

Where several undertakings share a workplace it is possible that the different employers may co-operate in implementing the health and safety provisions and co-ordinate their action in protecting and preventing occupational risks.[86] Nevertheless, whatever action is taken 'may in no circumstances involve the worker in financial cost'.[87] This refrain also appears in various daughter directives.[88]

In order to carry out activities related to the protection and prevention of occupational risks, including the risks faced by young workers,[89] the employer can designate one or more workers to fulfil the tasks.[90] Where no appropriate workers exist the employer can enlist 'competent external services or persons' who must be fully informed by the employer of the factors which may affect the health and safety of workers.[91] Delegating the tasks does not mean, however, that the employer is able to delegate responsibility for health and safety.[92]

---

[81] See further HSIB 200, 5.

[82] See Art. 5 of Directive 90/394/EEC [1990] OJ L196/1 discussed at nn. 191–209.

[83] See Art. 3(1) of Directive 90/269/EEC [1990] OJ L156/9, discussed at nn. 172–175.

[84] See Directive 89/656/EEC [1989] OJ L393/181 discussed at nn. 166–171.

[85] e.g. the effectiveness of respiratory protective equipment can be reduced if the user wears glasses or has a beard.

[86] Art. 6(4).

[87] Art. 6(5).

[88] e.g. Directive 90/270 on VDUs and Directive 89/656 on PPE, discussed below, nn. 176–190 and 166–171, respectively.

[89] Arts. 6(4) and 7(3) of Directive 94/33/EEC [1994] OJ L216/12.

[90] Art. 7(1).

[91] Art. 7(3) and (4).

[92] Art. 5(2).

Both the internal and external health and safety staff must have the necessary skills and be sufficient in number to deal with the organization of the health and safety measures, taking into account the size of the undertaking, the hazards to which the workers are exposed and their distribution throughout the entire undertaking or establishment.[93] This provision does allow a certain degree of flexibility, particularly for SMEs, as to the appointment of health and safety personnel. Finally, Article 7(2) provides that those workers to whom responsibility for health and safety has been designated must be given adequate time to enable them to fulfil their obligations[94] and must not be placed at a disadvantage in respect of their careers because of their activities in relation to health and safety.[95]

In the specific context of first-aid, fire-fighting, and the evacuation of workers Article 8(2) provides that again the employer can designate workers who are required to implement such measures.[96] However, the most significant feature of Article 8 is the right to stop work. Article 8(3) provides that the employer must also give instructions to enable workers in the event of serious, imminent, and unavoidable danger to stop work and/or immediately leave the workplace and proceed to a place of safety. If, in these circumstances, workers do leave their workplace under instruction from the employer, or at their own initiative when an immediate supervisor cannot be contacted, they must not be placed at 'any disadvantage because of their action and must be protected against any harmful and unjustified conduct'.[97] Therefore, they should be protected from dismissal or any lesser disciplinary measure. Furthermore, where workers have acted on their own initiative because a superior cannot be contacted and have taken appropriate steps in the face of serious and imminent danger, a subjective test is applied and account is taken of their knowledge and the technical means at their disposal. They are only liable to censure if they acted carelessly or there was negligence on their part.[98]

The employer must also refrain from asking workers to resume work in a situation where serious and imminent danger still exists, save in exceptional cases for reasons duly substantiated.[99] This provision is principally designed to apply to safety and repair workers.

---

[93] Art. 7(5). Member States may specify the appropriate numbers, see Art. 7(8).

[94] There is no provision for time off without loss of pay in the case of designated workers. Cf. Art. 11(5) which does, expressly, provide for this. This might be explained by the fact that responsibility for health and safety may be part of a designated worker's job and therefore they will be paid for it.

[95] Art. 7(2).

[96] Art. 8(1) and (2).

[97] Art. 8(4) and (5).

[98] Art. 8(5).

[99] Art. 8(3)(c).

2.3 Duty to Train and Direct the Workforce

Article 12 provides that all workers must receive adequate health and safety training, particularly relating to the operation of their work stations. This training must be given on recruitment, if and when workers change jobs, if the work equipment is changed, or if new technology is introduced. The training must be adapted to take account of new or changed risks and repeated periodically where necessary.[100] Special training must be provided for workers' representatives with a specific role in the health and safety protection of workers.[101] In either case, training must not be at the workers' or workers' representatives' expense and must take place during working hours.[102]

In addition, the Directive recognizes the role of the responsible exercise of managerial prerogative. Article 6(2)(i) talks of an employer giving 'appropriate instructions to the workers' and where there are specific danger areas the employer must ensure that only workers who have received adequate instructions may have access to them.[103]

2.4 Duty to Inform Workers and Workers' Representatives, to Consult, and to Encourage the Participation of the Workforce

As part of its general desire to include the Social Partners in decision-making,[104] the Community has long had ambitions of incorporating contributions of both management and labour in decisions and initiatives in the field of health and safety.[105] This was given further impetus by Article 118(b) [now Article 138] providing for a social dialogue, and the Community Social Charter 1989 which requires that health and safety measures must take account of the need for 'the training, information, consultation and balanced participation of workers as regards the risks incurred and the steps taken to eliminate or reduce them'.[106]

It is possible to identify three distinct approaches to workplace organization on health and safety.[107] In the first system, found in Germany, Luxembourg, Italy, and the Netherlands, works councils elected by employees occupy a

---

[100] Art. 12(1).

[101] Art. 12(3).

[102] Art. 12(4).

[103] Art. 6(3)(d). This provision may be read in conjunction with Art. 8(3)(c).

[104] See further Chs. 2 and 8.

[105] See the Preambles to the 1978 and 1984 Action Programmes and the 1988 Action Programme which envisaged that the Advisory Committee on Safety, Health, and Hygiene as a 'highly appropriate forum for consultation between two sides of industry'. See Neal and Wright, above, n. 9, 19–20.

[106] COM(89)471 final, para. 19(2).

[107] See above, n. 6, 114, and COM(88)073 final. See also Korostoff, Zimmermann and Ryan, 'Rethinking the OSHA Approach to Workplace Safety: A Look at Worker Participation in the Enforcement of Safety Regulations in Sweden, France and Great Britain' (1991) 13 *Comparative Labour Law Journal* 45.

central position, and safety delegates or committees play only a secondary role. Works councils have the right to approve or reject measures proposed by the employer, assist in planning, monitor compliance with the legislation, be informed of relevant information, and accompany inspectors on visits and consult with them. The second approach sees joint safety committees as the main channel of participation. In Belgium a special committee must be established to act as a forum for consultation between the employer and employee in all undertakings with more than fifty employees. Similarly, health and safety committees must be set up in all establishments which employ over fifty people in France and Portugal. In Spain committees are compulsory for certain companies, depending on the number of employees and the nature of the risk. The third system, found in Denmark and the UK, involves the workers electing safety representatives. These representatives become members of safety committees and are entitled to be informed of all relevant information and to consult the relevant inspectorates.

Directive 89/391/EEC does impose onerous requirements on employers in respect of the provision of information to the workers themselves and/or to their representatives.[108] The duty to inform extends to temporary and hired workers currently working in the enterprise or establishment[109] and workers from any outside undertakings working in the employer's establishment.[110] Depending on the size of the undertaking and in accordance with national laws and/or practices, the employer must, according to Article 10, provide all necessary information concerning:

(a) the safety and health risks and protective and preventive measures and activities in respect of both of the undertakings and/or establishments in general, and each type of work station and job;
(b) the measures taken to deal with first-aid, fire-fighting and evacuation.[111]

In order to help workers or workers' representatives with specific responsibility for health and safety in their task, they must be provided with the results of the risk assessment conducted by the employer and details of the necessary protective measures to be taken, as well as details about occupational accidents and illnesses and any reports made to national authorities concerning health and safety.[112]

---

[108] The term 'workers' representatives with specific responsibility for the safety and health of workers' is defined by Art. 3(c) as any person elected, chosen, or designated in accordance with national laws and/or practices to represent workers where problems arise relating to safety and health protection of workers at work.

[109] Art. 10(1)(c). See also Arts. 3 and 7 of Directive 91/383/EEC [1991] OJ L206/19 on atypical workers.

[110] Art. 10(2).

[111] Art. 10(1). According to Art. 10(2) the employer must take appropriate measures so that employers of workers from any outside undertaking receive adequate information on the matters listed in Art. 10(1).

[112] Art. 10(3).

Article 11(1) provides that employers must also consult workers and/or their representatives and allow them to take part in discussions on all questions relating to safety and health at work, including working conditions and the working environment, the planning and introduction of new technology,[113] and the consequences of the choice of equipment on the safety and health of workers.[114] The Article pre-supposes:[115]

— the consultation of workers;
— the right of workers and/or their representatives to make proposals, including making proposals which mitigate hazards for workers and/or remove sources of danger;[116]
— balanced participation in accordance with national laws and/or practices.[117]

The phrase 'balanced participation' is not defined. It may presuppose the existence of a completely unionized workforce, a situation which is increasingly rare, and one which sits uncomfortably with the right provided for in the Social Charter both to be and *not to be* a trade union member.[118] Furthermore, it has been suggested that the qualification 'in accordance with national laws and practices' has caused particular problems of interpretation,[119] allowing a diversity of potentially inadequate implementation.

Workers or workers' representatives must be consulted in advance *and in good time*[120] with regard to any measure which may substantially affect health and safety, the appointment of designated workers, risk assessment, and the provision of information, the enlistment of services or personnel, and the planning and organization of training.[121] If they consider that the measures taken and the means employed by the employer are inadequate for the purposes of ensuring health and safety they are entitled to appeal to the national authority responsible for health and safety protection.[122] They must also be given the opportunity to submit their observations during inspection visits by the competent authorities.[123]

---

[113] A study found that only 60 per cent of firms in Europe satisfied this requirement: see Krieger, 'Employee Participation in Health and Safety Protection' (1990) 6 *IJCLLIR* 217.

[114] Art. 6(3)(c).

[115] Art. 11(1).

[116] Art. 11(3).

[117] Art. 11(1).

[118] Nielsen and Szyszczak, *The Social Dimension of the European Community* (2nd edn, Handelshøjskolens Forlag, Copenhagen, 1997), 211.

[119] Walters and Freeman, 'Employee Representation in Health and Safety in the Workplace: a Comparative Study in Five European Countries', OPEC, cited in *HSIB* 201, 6. See also Walters, *Worker Participation in Health and Safety: A European Comparison* (Institute of Employment Rights, London, 1990).

[120] Cf. Directive 75/129 on collective redundancies [1975] OJ L48/29, discussed in Ch. 7.

[121] Art. 11(2).

[122] Art. 11(6).

[123] Ibid.

As with designated workers, workers and their representatives entitled to be consulted about health and safety matters must be given adequate time off work without loss of pay to fulfil their duties. They must also be provided with the necessary means to enable them to exercise their rights and functions[124] and must not be placed at a disadvantage because of their activities in respect of health and safety.[125] In other words, they cannot be dismissed or suffer any other detriment. The full requirements of the information and consultation provisions have been incorporated into the daughter directives.

Research conducted on behalf of the European Commission has revealed a picture of only partial implementation in the Member States of the provisions relating to worker representation. This is particularly so in the case of small workplaces and those in the tertiary sector. The same report criticized the Directive's provisions on worker involvement and consultation in that they allow Member States to continue to exempt small workplaces from participative arrangements, they do little to stimulate the development of more general institutions of workforce representation, and they fail to encourage state enforcement agencies to adopt a more interventionist role where such institutions are absent.[126]

2.5 Duty to Report

The employer must draw up a list of accidents which resulted in the worker being unfit for work for more than three working days[127] and provide these reports to the responsible national authorities.[128] The detail and scope of the reports may be determined by the Member States, taking into account the size of the undertaking and the nature of its activities.[129]

3. Workers' Responsibilities

Complementing the duties imposed on the employer, the Directive also places significant and detailed obligations on workers. Article 13(1) lays down the general principle that:

It shall be the responsibility of each worker to take care as far as possible of his own safety and health and that of other persons affected by his acts or commissions at work in accordance with his training and the instructions given by his employer.

Article 13(2) fleshes out this obligation, with examples of three specific

---

[124] Art. 11(5).
[125] Art. 11(4).
[126] Walters and Freeman, above n. 119.
[127] Art. 9(1)(b).
[128] Art. 9(1)(d).
[129] Art. 9(2).

duties. The first requires the worker to make correct use of personal protective equipment,[130] machinery, apparatus, tools, dangerous substances, transport equipment, and other means of production.[131] This includes refraining from disconnecting, changing, or arbitrarily removing safety devices fitted to the machinery and equipment.[132]

The second obligation is that the worker should immediately inform the employer or workers with responsibility for health and safety of any work situation they have reasonable grounds for considering represents a serious and immediate danger to health and safety and of any shortcomings in the protection arrangements.[133] Thirdly, workers must co-operate with the employer or workers with specific responsibility for health and safety to implement health and safety measures[134] and to ensure that the working environment and working conditions are safe.[135] Nevertheless, the final responsibility for health and safety matters rests with the employer.[136]

4. Remedies

Article 4 of the Directive provides that Member States must take the necessary steps 'to ensure that the employers, workers and workers' representatives are subject to the legal provisions necessary for the implementation of [the] Directive' but the final responsibility rests with the Member States who must ensure 'adequate controls and supervision'. Although the Directive does not expressly state that Member States must provide workers with recourse to the judicial process if they are denied the rights conferred by the Directive, as a general principle of Community law[137] some remedy must be provided to secure full implementation of the Directive. In *Commission v. Greece*[138] the Court made clear that an infringement of Community law must be 'penalised under conditions, both procedural and substantive, which are analogous to those applicable to infringements of national law of similar nature and importance' and that the penalty must be 'effective, proportionate and dissuasive'.

---

[130] Art. 13(2)(b).
[131] Art. 13(2)(a).
[132] Art. 13(2)(c).
[133] Art. 13(2)(d).
[134] Art. 13(2)(e).
[135] Art. 13(2)(f).
[136] Art. 5(3).
[137] See e.g. Case C–326/88 *Hansen* [1990] ECR I–2911.
[138] Case 68/88 *Commission v. Greece* [1989] ECR 2965.

C. THE DAUGHTER DIRECTIVES

The Framework Directive provides that a series of individual directives will be passed to cover specific risks.[139] The general principles contained in the parent Directive apply to the daughter Directives, without prejudice to the more specific provisions of the daughter Directives.[140] These daughter Directives can loosely be divided into three categories: those affecting the workplace, those laying down requirements relating to work equipment, and those relating to chemical, physical, and biological agents. They will be considered in outline under these headings.

1. The Workplace Directives

Community legislation on the workplace has adopted a twin-track approach: a general directive covering most industries running parallel with a number of complementary measures targeting specific sectors.

1.1 Directive 89/654/EEC on the Minimum Safety and Health Requirements for the Workplace

The principal aim of this Directive[141] is to protect the health and safety of workers through the proper layout of the workplace. A workplace is defined as 'the place intended to house workstations on the premises of undertakings and/or establishments and any other place within the area of the undertaking to which the worker has access in the course of his employment'.[142] Article 6 imposes general requirements on the employer to safeguard the health and safety of workers by ensuring that:

(a) traffic routes to emergency exits and the exits themselves are kept clear at all times;
(b) technical maintenance of the workplace and of the equipment and devices is carried out, and that any faults are rectified as quickly as possible;
(c) the workplace, the equipment and any devices are regularly cleaned to an adequate level of hygiene;
(d) safety equipment and devices intended to prevent or eliminate hazards are regularly maintained and checked.

---

[139] Art. 16(1).

[140] See e.g. Art. 1(3) of Directive 89/654.

[141] Council Directive 89/654/EEC on the minimum health and safety requirements for the workplace (first individual Directive within the meaning of Art. 16(1) of Directive 89/391/EEC) [1989] OJ L393/1. See also COM(88)74 final.

[142] Art. 2.

Workers must be informed and consulted about any measures to be taken concerning health and safety at the workplace.[143] More detailed obligations imposed on employers in connection with their workplaces are found in the Annexes to the Directive. The nature of the obligations depends on whether the workplace is used for the first time after 31 December 1992 or whether it is already in use. The obligations do not, however, apply to specific risk sectors, where there is a particularly high incidence of accidents[144] which are covered by specific directives.

1.2 Specific Risk Sectors

Developing and expanding the principles in Directive 89/654, specific directives are intended to address the special problems relating to industries identified as creating a particular risk. To date, five directives have been passed.[145] Directive 92/57 concerns the health and safety requirements at temporary or mobile construction sites.[146] It acknowledges that the work site[147] brings together the self-employed and a number of different undertakings working at the site simultaneously or in succession, and that the self-employed, as well as employed workers, must be bound by certain obligations to avoid exposing other workers to various risks.[148] The Directive aims at a 'global approach to accident prevention':[149] by establishing a chain of responsibility linking all the parties concerned—the clients, the project supervisors, the employers, the co-ordinators, and the self-employed—and by integrating health and safety requirements at all stages of the project, in particular by strengthening co-ordination between the parties.[150]

Two Directives concern the mineral-extracting industry: Directive 92/91/EEC concerns the safety and health protection of workers in the mineral-extracting industries through drilling,[151] which takes into account the

---

[143] Arts. 7 and 8.

[144] Art. 1(2).

[145] In addition, there are other proposals: amended proposal for a Council Directive on the minimum safety and health requirements for transport activities and workplaces on means of transport, COM(93)421 final SYN 420 [1993] OJ C294/4, and a proposal for a Council Directive on the minimum safety and health requirements for transport activities and workplaces on means of transport (COM(92)234 final SYN 420 [1993] OJ C25/17.

[146] Council Directive 92/57/EEC on the implementation of minimum health and safety requirements at temporary or mobile construction sites (eighth individual Directive) [1992] OJ L245/6 and corrections [1993] OJ L15/34, [1993] OJ L33/18, OJ [1993] L41/50. See also COM(90)275 final.

[147] Defined to include any construction site at which building or civil engineering works are carried out (Art. 2(a)). A non-exhaustive list of building and civil engineering works is contained in Annex I.

[148] COM(90)275 final.

[149] Ibid.

[150] See esp. Art. 3.

[151] Council Directive 92/91/EEC on the minimum requirements for improving the safety and health protection of workers in the mineral-extracting industries through drilling (eleventh individual Directive) [1992] OJ L348/9.

findings of the Cullen inquiry into the Piper Alpha oil platform disaster,[152] and Directive 92/104/EEC[153] concerns the health and safety protection of workers in surface and underground mineral-extracting industries. Both Directives follow a common format. They impose the following general obligations on employers to ensure that:[154]

— workplaces are designed, constructed, equipped, commissioned, operated, and maintained in such a way that workers can perform the work assigned to them without endangering their safety and/or health and/or those of other workers;
— the operation of workplaces when workers are present takes place under the supervision of a person in charge;
— work involving special risk is entrusted only to competent staff and carried out in accordance with instructions given;
— safety instructions are comprehensible to all the workers concerned;
— appropriate first-aid facilities are provided;
— any relevant safety drills are performed at regular intervals.

Directive 93/103/EC[155] concerns the minimum health and safety requirement on board fishing vessels. The Directive imposes general duties relating to all vessels and specific obligations on vessels depending on their age and size. Owners must ensure that their boats are used without endangering the health and safety of workers, in particular in foreseeable meteorological conditions, without prejudice to the responsibility of the skipper.[156] Owners also have responsibility in respect of equipment and maintenance: they must ensure that the vessels and their fittings and equipment are technically maintained, that any defects are rectified as quickly as possible, and that the equipment is hygienic.[157] In addition, the vessel must be supplied with an adequate quantity of suitable emergency and survival equipment, including life-saving equipment and personal protective equipment.[158]

Finally, Directive 99/92/EC on explosive atmospheres has been adopted.[159]

---

[152] HSIB 196, 12, and HSIB 181, 2.

[153] Council Directive 92/104/EEC on the minimum requirements for improving the safety and health protection of workers in surface and underground mineral-extracting industries (twelfth individual Directive) [1992] OJ L404/10). See also COM(92)14 final/2.

[154] Art. 3.

[155] Council Directive 93/103/EEC [1993] OJ L307/1. See also Council Directive 92/29/EEC [1992] OJ L113/19 on minimum health and safety requirements for improved medical treatment on board vessels.

[156] Art. 3(1)(a). The skipper is the person commanding the vessel or having responsibility for it (Art. 2(g)).

[157] Art. 7.

[158] Ibid.

[159] European Parliament and Council Directive 99/52/EC on minimum requirements for improving safety and health protection of workers potentially at risk form explosive atmospheres (15th individual Directive) [2000] OJ L23/57 (Corrigendum [2000] OJ L134/36). See also European Parliament and Council Directive 94/9/EC [1994] OJ L100/1 on equipment and protective systems in potentially explosive atmospheres.

This requires the establishment of a coherent strategy for the prevention of explosions.

2. Equipment Used at Work

The directives examined so far address the health and safety problems arising from the layout of the workplace. The next group of directives concerns the rules relating to the equipment used by workers. The principal Directive 89/655/EEC,[160] concerning the minimum health and safety requirements for the use of work equipment by workers, obliges employers to ensure that the work equipment made available to workers is suitable for the work to be carried out, or properly adapted for that purpose, and may be used by workers without impairment to their health and safety.[161] Work equipment, defined to include any machine, apparatus, tool, or installation used at work,[162] must be selected to take account of the specific working conditions and hazards existing in the workplace.[163] The equipment provided must satisfy the minimum requirements laid down in the Annex.[164]

Three directives supplement Directive 89/655 providing individual, as opposed to collective,[165] protection. First, Directive 89/656/EEC concerns the use by workers of personal protective equipment (PPE) in the workplace.[166] PPE can be used only when the risks cannot be avoided or sufficiently limited by technical means of collective protection or by measures, methods of procedures, or work organization. PPE means all equipment designed to be worn or held by workers to protect them against one or more hazards likely to

---

[160] Council Directive 89/655/EEC (second individual Directive) [1989] OJ L393/13. See also COM(88)75. This has been amended by Council Directive 95/63/EC [1995] OJ L335/28. It is due to be amended again to address the problems of working at a height.

[161] Art. 3.

[162] Art. 2(a). This is much broader than the original draft which envisaged minimum requirements for machinery only.

[163] Art. 3(1).

[164] Art. 4(1)(a)(ii). The equipment must satisfy these requirements by 31 Dec. 1992 in the case of equipment provided for the first time after that date or within four years in the case of existing equipment. This delay in implementation is designed to lessen the immediate financial burden, particularly on small businesses. Member States can set a shorter time limit provided that the time limit is not so short that it does not enable employers to make the changes or entail a cost that is excessive compared with what they would have to meet if the time limit had been longer: see Case C–2/97 *Borsana* [1998] ECR I–8597, para. 53.

[165] Collective protection is considered more favourable: Art. 6(2)(b) of Directive 89/391/EEC [1989] OJ L183/1. See also Art. 4 of Directive 80/1107 [1980] OJ L327/7.

[166] Directive 89/656/EEC on the minimum health and safety requirements for the use by workers of personal protective equipment at the workplace (third individual Directive) [1989] OJ L393/18. COM(88)76 final. See also the Commission Communication of 30 Dec. 1989 (89/C 328/02) on the implementation of Council Directive 89/656/EEC.

endanger their health and safety.[167] PPE must comply with the relevant Community provisions in the design and manufacture of the equipment,[168] and must:[169]

— be appropriate for the risks involved, without itself leading to any increased risk;
— correspond to existing conditions in the workplace;
— take account of ergonomic requirements and the worker's state of health;
— fit the wearer correctly after any necessary adjustment.

Any PPE which is chosen must be provided free of charge by the employer,[170] who must ensure that it is in good working order and in a satisfactory and hygienic condition. The employer must also inform workers of the purpose of the PPE and arrange appropriate training and demonstrations.[171]

The second Directive, Directive 90/269/EEC, addresses the health and safety requirements involved in the manual handling of heavy loads.[172] Manual handling is defined to mean 'any transporting or supporting of a load, by one or more workers, including lifting, putting down, pushing, pulling, carrying or moving of a load, which by reason of its characteristics or of unfavourable ergonomic conditions involves a risk particularly of back injury to workers'.[173] The Directive envisages a hierarchy of measures which employers must consider. Primarily, they are obliged to take appropriate organizational measures, in particular by providing for the use of mechanical equipment, to avoid the need for manual handling of loads by workers.[174] Other steps might include redesigning the job to eliminate manual handling altogether or automating the process. If this is not possible, employers must strive to reduce the risk involved.[175]

The third Directive 90/270/EEC lays down minimum health and safety

---

[167] Art. 2(1).
[168] Both Directive 89/655/EEC on work equipment and Directive 89/656/EEC on PPE provide a social supplement to two specific, technical 'product' directives setting minimum safety standards in respect of machinery, Council Directive 89/392/EEC on the approximation of the laws of the Member States relating to machinery [1989] OJ L183/9, Council Directive 89/686/EEC on the approximation of the laws of the Member States relating to PPE [1989] OJ L399/19 as amended by Council Directive 93/68/EEC [1993] OJ L220/1 and by Council Directive 93/95/EEC [1993] OJ L276/11, and European Parliament and Council Directive 96/58/EC [1996] OJ L236/44. See also Commission Communication 2000/C 76/03 [2000] OJ C76/3 and 2000/C 159/03 [2000] OJ C 159/3.
[169] Art. 4(1).
[170] Art. 4(b). The worker can be asked to make a contribution towards the cost of the PPE where its use is not exclusive to the workplace.
[171] Art. 4(7)–(8).
[172] Council Directive 90/269/EEC on the minimum health and safety requirements for the manual handling of loads where there is a risk particularly of back injury to workers (fourth individual Directive) [1990] OJ L156/9. See also COM(88)78 final.
[173] Art. 2.
[174] Art. 3(1).
[175] Art. 3(2).

requirements for work with display screen equipment (VDUs).[176] The Directive applies to any worker, as defined in Article 3(a) of Directive 89/391/EEC, 'who habitually uses display screen equipment as a significant part of his normal work'.[177] Neither the term 'habitual' nor the term 'significant' is defined. In X[178] the Court ruled that Article 3(a) could not be defined in the abstract and that it was for the Member States who, given the vagueness of the phrase, had a broad discretion to specify its meaning when adopting national implementing measures.

The specific obligations imposed on employers are fivefold. First, they must analyse the workstations[179] to evaluate the health and safety conditions affecting their workers, particularly as regards possible risks to eyesight, physical problems, and mental stress, and to take measures to remedy the risks found.[180] Secondly, they must ensure that workstations comply with the minimum requirements set out in the Annex.[181] Thirdly, the worker must receive training on the use of the workstation before commencing work and further training whenever the organization of the workstation is substantially modified.[182] Fourthly, employers are obliged to keep themselves informed of the latest advances in technology and scientific findings concerning workstation design so that they can make any changes necessary to guarantee better levels of health and safety protection.[183] Fifthly, the employer must plan the worker's activities in such a way that daily work on a display screen is periodically interrupted by breaks or changes of activity reducing the workload at the display screen.[184] In addition, workers are entitled[185] to an appropriate eye and eyesight test carried out by a person with the necessary capabilities before commencing display screen work, at regular intervals thereafter, and whenever they experience visual difficulties which may be due to display screen work.[186] If, as a result of this examination, workers need further assistance

---

[176] Council Directive 90/270/EEC (fifth individual Directive) [1990] OJ L156/14, COM(88)77.

[177] Art. 2(c).

[178] Joined Cases C–74 and C–129/95 *Criminal Proceedings v. X* [1996] ECR I–6609, para. 30. See also Case C–11/99 *Dietrich v. Westdeutscher Rundfunk*, judgment of 6 July 2000.

[179] Work station is defined to mean an assembly comprising display screen equipment, which may be provided with a keyboard or input device and/or software determining the operator/ machine interface, optional accessories, peripherals including the disketted drive, telephone, modem, printer, document holder, work chair, and work desk or work surface, and the immediate work environment (Art. 2(b)).

[180] Art. 3.

[181] Arts. 4 and 5 respectively. These requirements apply to all workstations and not just those used by 'habitual users' (Case C–74/95 *X* [1996] ECR I–6609, para. 41).

[182] Art. 6(2).

[183] Preamble to the Directive.

[184] Art. 7.

[185] Art. 9. Earlier drafts talked of workers being obliged to have an appropriate eyesight test, but this was considered an invasion of workers' privacy.

[186] Art. 9(1). According to Case C–74/95 *X* [1996] ECR I-6609, para. 36, regular eye tests must be carried out on all workers to whom the Directive applies and not just to certain categories of workers.

they are entitled to an ophthalmological examination[187] and, if need be, they must be provided with 'special corrective appliances appropriate for the work concerned' if normal appliances cannot be used.[188] Protection of workers' eyes and eyesight may be provided as part of the national health system,[189] but, in any case, measures taken pursuant to this Article may 'in no circumstances involve workers in additional financial cost'.[190]

3. Carcinogens, Chemical, Physical, and Biological Agents

As we have already seen, the four daughters under the first Parent Directive 80/1107/EEC concerned specific agents (for example asbestos and lead). The new approach adopted under the Second Framework Directive 89/391 is to address the problems of classes of agents—biological, physical, and chemical agents and carcinogens. The first of these new directives, Directive 90/394/EEC,[191] originally one of the daughter directives under Directive 80/1107/EEC, introduces general and specific measures for a list of occupational carcinogens[192] and reputedly carcinogenic processes.[193] This Directive was modified by Council Directive 97/42/EC.[194] The latest Directive clarifies certain provisions of the former Directive. Further, it fixes limit values for professional exposure for benzene. As the Court confirmed in *Borsana*,[195] this is a minimum standards Directive and Member States are free to impose more stringent measures for the protection of working conditions, authorized by Article 118a(3) [new Article 137(5)] and Directive 90/394, provided they do not

---

[187] Art. 9(2). The *X* case makes clear that this applies only to those for whom an Art. 9(1) test reveals that they need further assistance.

[188] Art. 9(3).

[189] Art. 9(5).

[190] Art. 9(4).

[191] Directive 90/394/EEC on the protection of workers from the risks relating to exposure to carcinogens at work (sixth individual Directive) [1990] OJ L196/1. Its adoption was also inspired by the 'Europe Against Cancer' campaign, see Decisions 88/351/EEC [1988] OJ L160/52 and 90/238/Euratom, EEC, and ECSC [1990] OJ L137/31.

[192] Defined as a process which may cause cancer and with reference to Directive 67/548/EEC [1967] OJ L196/1, Directive 88/379/EEC [1988] OJ L187/14 and Annex I to this Directive. An IARC (International Agreement for Research on Cancer) survey found that of 107 chemical substances examined, 38 were carcinogens and 68 were probably carcinogens COM(87)641 final.

[193] The Directive does not apply to workers exposed to radiation (Art. 1(2)). This is covered by the Euratom Treaty and directives adopted under that Treaty, in particular Directive 80/836/Euratom [1980] OJ L246/1 laying down the fundamental principles governing operational protection of exposed workers and Directive 90/641/Euratom [1990] OJ L349/21 on the operational protection of outside workers exposed to the risk of ionizing radiation during their activities in a controlled area. Council Directive 96/29/Euratom lays down basic safety standards for the protection of the health of workers and the general public against the dangers arising from ionizing radiation [1996] OJ L159/1.

[194] [1997] OJ L179/4. It was amended again by Council Directive 99/38/EC [1999] OJ L138/66.

[195] Case C-2/97 *Borsana* [1998] ECR I-8597.

undermine the coherence of Community action in the area of workers' health and safety.[196]

The Directive provides that where workers are, or are likely to be, exposed to carcinogens, employers must determine the nature, degree, and duration of workers' exposure in order to assess the risk posed to their health and safety.[197] Article 4 applies the principle of substitution, requiring employers to use non-carcinogenic substitutes which are not dangerous or are less dangerous to a worker's health and safety. Where that is technically unfeasible employers must ensure that production is carried out in a closed system and must take appropriate measures to protect workers[198]—by limiting the quantities of carcinogen in the workplace,[199] reducing the number of workers likely to be exposed,[200] providing individual protective equipment and appropriate washing facilities,[201] laying emergency plans,[202] providing for safe storage and disposal of the waste,[203] organizing continuous *ad hoc* training,[204] providing information to workers and/or their representatives,[205] and arranging medical surveillance.[206] Whatever the cost of these measures, it must not be imposed on the workers.[207] Finally, the list of the persons exposed in the firm must always be accessible to the workers themselves and to their medical representatives.[208] Details of the preventive steps taken must be made available to the competent national authority on request.[209]

The scope of this Directive is potentially very broad, for Article 11 expressly recognizes that employers must inform workers of 'the potential risks to health, including the additional risk due to tobacco consumption'. Since there is a recognized link between cigarettes and cancer, the obligations imposed by this Directive on all employers are far reaching. The Commission recognizes that this Directive will impose a financial burden particularly on industries such as those producing chemicals, fibre, sterilizing agents, crystal glass, and wood preservatives. It argues, however, that enterprises will benefit in the long term through reduced sickness absence and rehabilitation costs, and fewer retirements due to ill-health.

---

[196] Paras. 37 and 39.

[197] Art. 3.

[198] Art. 5. This is contingent on the outcome of the assessment of risks under Art. 3: Case C–2/97 *Borsana* [1998] ECR I–8597, para. 41.

[199] Art. 4. This is not contingent on the outcome of the risk assessment under Art. 3: Case C–2/97 *Borsana* [1998] ECR I–8597, para. 41.

[200] Art. 5(4)(b).

[201] Art. 10.

[202] Art. 5(4)(k).

[203] Art. 5(4)(m).

[204] Art. 11.

[205] Art. 12.

[206] Art. 14.

[207] Art. 10(l).

[208] Art. 12(c) and (d).

[209] Art. 6.

The structure and approach adopted in Directive 90/394/EEC on carcino-gens is mirrored in Directive 90/679/EEC on biological agents.[210] This Direct-ive relates to those who work in laboratories, hospitals, and veterinary clinics[211] and those who are employed in the manufacturing industries, par-ticularly those manufacturing vaccines, and those dealing with sewage and breweries. The Directive classes biological agents, defined as micro-organisms, including those which have been genetically modified,[212] cell cultures and human endo-parasites, which may be able to provoke any infection, allergy, or toxicity,[213] into four categories according to their intrinsic danger,[214] and defines appropriate confinement measures. Once again the Directive requires the employer to assess the risks posed by the exposure to the biological agent,[215] replace the harmful agent where possible,[216] and, if not, reduce the risks connected with the exposure to the agents.[217] Detailed requirements on worker training, information, and consultation[218] and medical surveil-lance,[219] including the availability of vaccines,[220] also apply.

Directive 98/24/EC on chemical agents[221] replaces in a single Directive the first parent Directive 80/1107/EEC, as amended, the lead Directive 82/605/EEC, and Directive 88/364/EEC banning specific agents at work. A chemical

---

[210] Council Directive 90/679/EEC of 26 Nov. 1990 on the protection of workers from the risks related to exposure to biological agents at work (seventh individual Directive) [1990] OJ L374/1, amended by Council Directive 93/88/EEC of 12 Oct. 1993 [1993] OJ L268/71, corrected [1994] OJ L217/18; Council Directive 95/30/EEC of 30 June 1995 [1995] OJ L155/410; Commission Directive 97/59/EC [1997] OJ L282/33 and Commission Directive 97/65/EC [1997] OJ L335/17, which took particular account of the risks concerning the transmissibility of the BSE agent at work.

[211] Arts. 15 and 16.

[212] Two further Directives have been passed concerning genetically modified organisms (GMOs). The first, Directive 90/219/EEC of 23 Apr. 1990 [1990] OJ L117/1, amended by Commission Directive 94/51/EC [1994] OJ L297/29, concerns the contained use of GMOs which refers to any work in conditions which are intended to prevent the escape of GMOs into the environment with a view to protecting human health and the environment. The Directive requires risk assessment, minimizing the level of risk and drawing up emergency plans. The second, Directive 90/220/EEC [1990] OJ L117/15, concerns the deliberate release of GMOs into the environment for research purposes and the marketing of products involving GMOs. Those enterprises proposing to undertake either of these activities must notify the competent author-ities, assess and provide information on the risks, and may make specified information available to the public.

[213] Art. 2(a).

[214] Art. 2(d).

[215] Arts. 3 and 4.

[216] Art. 5.

[217] Art. 6.

[218] Arts. 7, 9, 10, and 12.

[219] Art. 14.

[220] See esp. Directive 93/88/EEC [1993] OJ L268/71.

[221] Council Directive 98/24/EC of 7 Apr. 1998 on the protection of the health and safety of workers from the risks related to chemical agents at work (fourteenth individual Directive within the meaning of Art. 16(1) of Directive 89/391/EEC) [1998] OJ L131/11. The earlier documents can be found in COM(93)155 final—SYN 459 and amended proposal (94/C191/04), COM(94)230 final—SYN 459.

agent is defined as any chemical element or compound, on its own or admixed, as it occurs in the natural state or as produced by any work activity, whether or not produced intentionally and whether or not placed on the market. The Directive follows the pattern of its sister directives: it requires a risk assessment to be made, it lays down occupational exposure levels, and it provides for worker consultation, information, and medical surveillance. Similarly, the current proposal for a directive on physical agents also follows this pattern.[222] It aims to harmonize the minimum health and safety requirements regarding exposure of workers to the risks arising from physical agents. The physical agents to be covered include noise, vibration, non-ionizing electromagnetic radiation (ultra-violet and infra-red light). The Directive establishes threshold action and ceiling levels for exposure to the agents. In addition, employers are required to conduct exposure risk assessments, reduce any risks, provide personal protective equipment, conduct health surveillance depending on levels of exposure, and engage in worker consultation, information, and training.

D. WORKING TIME

The Working Time Directive clearly demonstrates the emerging grey area between traditional health and safety measures and the rights of employed persons.

1. Background

The Working Time Directive 93/104/EEC[223] and the Young Workers Directive 94/33/EC[224] were both adopted under Article 118a EC [new Article 137] and formed key pillars of the EC's Social Charter Action Programme. Previously there existed certain sectoral legislation[225] and some soft law measures on working time: a Council Recommendation of 1975 on the principle of the forty-hour week and four weeks' annual paid holiday,[226] and a Resolution of

---

[222] Proposed Directive 93/C77/02 [1993] OJ C77/12, COM(92)560 final and the amended proposal 94/C230/03 COM(94) 284—SYN 449.

[223] [1993] OJ L307/18.

[224] [1994] OJ L216/12.

[225] Regulations limiting the working hours of drivers of larger passenger vehicles and most goods vehicles over 3.5 tonnes. Regulation (EEC) 3820/85 [1985] OJ L3701 on the harmonization of certain social legislation relating to road transport; Regulation (EEC) 3821/85 [1985] OJ L371/8 on recording equipment in road transport; Directive 88/599/EEC [1988] OJ L325/55 on standard checking procedures on recording equipment in road transport. These Regulations led to tachographs being installed in lorry cabs and coaches.

[226] Recommendation 75/457/EEC [1975] OJ L199/32.

1979 on the adaptation of working time,[227] aimed primarily at the reduction in working time for the purposes of job creation.[228] The Community Social Charter 1989 marked a change in emphasis. Articles 7 and 8 advocated action on the duration and organization of working time so that the completion of the internal market led to an improvement in the living and working conditions of workers in the EC. This enabled the Commission to conceive a directive on working time, not as a job creation measure but a health and safety matter, enabling it to select Article 118a [new Article 137] as the appropriate legal basis. To support its choice the Commission cited a variety of studies which variously showed that weekly working time of more than fifty hours could, in the long run, be harmful to health and safety, that working weeks of more than six days showed some correlation with health problems including fatigue and disturbed sleep, and that longer working hours substantially increased the probability of accidents at work.[229] This evidence was, however, disputed[230] and the UK challenged, albeit unsuccessfully, the choice of legal basis.[231]

2. Personal and Material Scope of Directive 93/104

Directive 93/104 concerns all sectors of activity, both public and private, as defined by Article 2 of the Framework Directive 89/391 on health and safety (industrial, agricultural, commercial, administrative, service, educational, cultural, leisure, etc.).[232] It does not apply to:[233]

— (mobile and non-mobile) workers in the transport industry, namely, air, rail, road, sea, inland waterway, and lake transport, sea fishing, other work at sea;
— the activities of doctors in training (Article 1(3));[234]
— certain specific activities such as the armed forces or the police, or certain specific activities in the civil protection services, but only where the characteristics of those activities inevitably conflict with the require-

---

[227] [1982] OJ L357/27.

[228] See also Council Recommendation 82/857/EEC on the principles of a Community policy with regard to retirement age [1982] OJ L357/27 which also has the objective of lower activity levels.

[229] COM(90)317.

[230] See Bercusson, *Working Time in Britain: Towards a European Model*, Part I (Institute of Employment Rights, London, 1993) 4.

[231] Case C–84/94 *UK v. Council* [1996] ECR I–5755, considered further in Ch. 2.

[232] [1989] OJ L183/1. See above, n. 56.

[233] The Commission has made proposals to address the excluded sectors: see below nn. 293–299.

[234] Accepted by Advocate General Saggio in Case C–303/98 *Sindicato de Médicos de Asistencia Pública (SIMAP) v. Conselleria de Sanidad y Consumo de la Generalidad Valencia*, Opinion delivered 16 Dec. 1999.

ments of the Framework Directive 89/391 (Article 2(2) of Directive 89/391).[235]

The Directive applies to 'workers' which are defined in Article 3 of Directive 89/391[236] as 'any person employed by an employer, including trainees and apprentices but excluding domestic servants'. It does not apply to those normally regarded as self-employed.

3. Derogations

The Directive contains a complex series of derogations (see Table 6.1) which Member States can choose to apply but they can take advantage of them only if they have actually passed legislation to implement them.[237] In summary, they fall into four categories.

3.1 Unmeasured Working Time

With due regard for the general principles of the protection of the safety and health of workers, Member States may derogate from Articles 3, 4, 5, 6, 8,

Table 6.1 Summary of the Derogations from the Directive

Derogations	Art. 3 daily rest	Art. 4 in-work rest breaks	Art. 5 weekly rest	Art. 6 max. weekly working time	Art. 7 annual leave	Art. 8 length of night	Art. 16 reference periods
Category A: unmeasured working time	√	√	√	√	×	√	√
Category B: other special cases	√	√	√	×	×	√	√
Category C: shift work	√	×	√	×	×	×	×
Category D: collective agreements	√	√	√	×	×	√	√

[235] This exclusion is included due to the reference in Art. 1(3) of Directive 93/104 to Art. 2(2) of Directive 89/391.

[236] Art. 1(3) and (4).

[237] Case C–303/98 *SIMAP*, Opinion of 16 Dec. 1999.

and 16 of the Directive when 'on account of the specific characteristics of the activity concerned, the duration of the working time is not measured and/or predetermined or can be determined by the workers themselves', particularly in the case of managing executives, family workers, and 'religious' workers.[238] As the guidance notes accompanying the British implementation of the Directive explain,[239] this derogation essentially applies to workers who have complete control over the hours they work and whose time is not monitored or determined by their employer. Such a situation may occur if workers can decide when the work is to be done, or may adjust the time worked as they see fit. An indicator may be if workers have discretion over whether to work on a given day without needing to consult their employer.

3.2 Other Special Cases

In the case of industries requiring 'continuity of service or production' (for example security, prisons, hospitals, the utilities, and the press),[240] or industries where there is a foreseeable surge of activity (for example, tourism and agriculture),[241] or where the worker's home and work are distant,[242] or where there is a dangerous situation,[243] derogations can be adopted from Articles 3, 4, 5, 8, and 16 of the Directive by laws, regulations, administrative provisions, collective agreements, or agreements between the two sides of industry. These derogations are subject to the requirement that the workers concerned are afforded equivalent periods of compensatory rest or that, in exceptional cases in which it is not possible for objective reasons to grant such rest, the workers concerned are afforded appropriate protection. As far as the option to derogate from Article 16(2) is concerned (reference period of four months for calculating average weekly working time), the reference period may not exceed six months, or twelve months where there are objective, technical, or work organization reasons and a collective agreement or agreement between the two sides of industry has been concluded.[244]

3.3 Shift Work

Shift work is defined as any method of organizing work in shifts, whereby workers succeed each other, at the same workstations, according to a *certain*

---

[238] Art. 17(1).
[239] Para. 2.2.2. of DTI, *Regulatory Guidance on the Working Time Regulations* (DTI, London, 28 Aug. 1998).
[240] Art. 17(2)(2.1)(b)–(c).
[241] Art. 17(2)(2.1)(d).
[242] Art. 17(2)(2.1)(a).
[243] Defined as circumstances described in Art. 5(4) of Directive 89/391 and in cases of accident or imminent risk of accident (Art. 17(2)(2.2)).
[244] Art. 17(4).

pattern, including a rotating pattern, which may be continuous or discontinuous, entailing the need for workers to work at different times over a given period of days or weeks.[245] This period is not defined by the Directive. Articles 3 and 5 do not apply in relation to shift workers when they change shift and cannot take a daily and/or weekly rest period between the end of one shift and the start of the next one or in the case of activities involving periods of work split up over the day, as may be the case for cleaning staff. Again, this is subject to the principle of compensatory rest.

3.4 Collective Agreements or Agreements between the Two Sides of Industry

Derogations may be made from Articles 3, 4, 5, 8, and 16[246] by means of collective agreements or agreements between the two sides of industry at national or regional level.[247] These derogations are allowed on condition that equivalent compensating rest periods are granted to the workers concerned or, in exceptional cases where it is not possible for objective reasons to grant such periods, the workers concerned are afforded appropriate protection.[248] Therefore, collective agreements are permitted to lower the standard of protection provided by the legislation.[249]

4. Minimum Standards, Health and Safety, and the Principle of Humanization of Work

The provisions of Framework Directive 89/391 on health and safety are fully applicable to the Working Time Directive, without prejudice to the more stringent and/or specific provisions contained in the Working Time Directive.[250] Similarly, the provisions of the Working Time Directive do not apply where other Community instruments exist relating to specific occupations.[251] The Directive also does not affect the right of Member States or the

---

[245] Art. 2(5).

[246] As far as derogations from Art. 16(2) are concerned, the same periods apply as for other special cases (Category 3.2 workers) (see above, nn. 240–242, and Art. 17(4)).

[247] Art. 17(3), para. 1. Where collective agreements permit it, derogations can be made by means of collective agreements or agreements between the two sides of industry at a lower level (Art. 17(3), para. 1). Member States where there is no system for ensuring the conclusion of collective agreements or agreements between the two sides of industry or Member States where there is a specific legislative framework may allow derogations by collective agreement or agreement between the two sides of industry at the appropriate collective level (Art. 17(3), para. 2).

[248] Art. 17(3), para. 3.

[249] Art. 17(3).

[250] Art. 1(4).

[251] Art. 14. See e.g. Council Regulation 3820/85 relating to road transport [1985] OJ L370/1.

two sides of industry to conclude agreements which are more favourable to the health and safety protection of workers.[252] The Directive is, therefore, following the Framework Directive 89/391, a minimum standards Directive.[253]

The general organizing principle of the Directive, found in Article 13, is 'humanization of work'.[254] This provides that an employer intending to organize work according to a certain pattern must take account of the:

general principle of adapting work to the worker, with a view, in particular, to alleviating monotonous work and work at a pre-determined work rate, depending on the type of activity, *and* of health and safety requirements, especially as regards breaks during working time [emphasis added].

This provision envisages not only implementing health and safety measures but also respecting the general principle of adapting the work to the worker, an idea which is not directly related to health and safety requirements as narrowly construed. This principle is entirely consistent with the broader duty imposed on employers by some Continental systems. In Italy, for example, Article 1087 of the Civil Code provides that the employer must adopt in the organization of the enterprise all measures which, according to the nature of the work, experience, and technical possibilities, are required to protect the physical integrity and moral personality of the employees. From the common law perspective, this breaks down the distinction between the duty of mutual trust and confidence and the duty to protect the worker's health and safety, and may lie at the heart of the debate about the choice of legal basis.

5. Limits and Entitlements

The Directive makes a distinction between limits and entitlements. The provisions concerning working time and night work are *limits*. This means employers must not allow workers to exceed those limits, subject to derogations and, where appropriate, the individual opt-out (see below). By contrast, the rest provisions all concern worker *entitlements*. This means that the employer cannot lawfully require the worker to work during any such period. On the other hand, if workers choose to work in a way which means foregoing a rest period to which they are entitled this is not unlawful and

---

[252] Art. 15.

[253] See further above, n. 32.

[254] See Bercusson, above, n. 230. Although Art. 13 is located at the end of Section III on night work there is no evidence that it is confined to this section, particularly since the Art. makes express reference to breaks during working time which is found in Section II. Indeed, it appears from the breadth of Art. 13 that all provisions must be interpreted in the light of the principle of humanization of work.

workers are free to do so. In the UK the distinction between limits and entitlements is reflected in the way in which the provisions are enforced. Limits are enforced through criminal sanctions against the employer as well as civil action brought by the worker, whereas, entitlements are enforced only through civil action in an Employment Tribunal.

5.1 Entitlements: Daily and Weekly Rest Periods and Annual Leave

(a) Daily Rest and In-work Rest Breaks

Every worker is entitled to a minimum daily rest period of eleven consecutive hours per twenty-four-hour period.[255] Although this implies a thirteen-hour working day the principle of the 'humanization of work' would prevent an employer from requiring a worker to work such long hours regularly. Derogations are possible for workers listed in sections 3.1–3.4 above.

If the working day is longer than six hours every worker is entitled to an in-work rest break, the details of which, including the duration of the break and the terms on which it is taken, must, by preference, be laid down by collective agreement between the two sides of industry or, failing that, by national legislation.[256] Once again, derogations are possible, this time for the workers in sections 3.1, 3.2, and 3.4 above.

(b) Weekly Rest Period

In addition to the daily rest period, workers are also entitled to weekly rest. Article 5 provides for a minimum uninterrupted rest period of twenty-four hours for each seven-day period worked plus the eleven hours' daily rest. Therefore, workers are entitled to thirty-five consecutive hours of rest (eleven hours' daily rest plus twenty-four hours' weekly rest) at least once a week averaged over fourteen days.[257] However, if objective, technical, or work organization conditions justify it,[258] a minimum rest period of twenty-four hours (instead of thirty-five hours) may be applied.[259] Derogations are possible for workers in sections 3.1–3.4 above.

Article 5(2) provided that the minimum weekly rest period 'shall in principle include Sunday'. This provision was consistent with the Court's jurisprudence on Sunday trading.[260] However, the UK government successfully challenged the validity of this provision in the *Working Time Directive* case. The Court said that the 'Council has failed to explain why Sunday as a weekly rest day, is more closely connected with health and safety of workers than any

---

[255] Art. 3.
[256] Art. 4.
[257] Art. 16(1).
[258] Cf. this language with Art. 4 of Directive 77/187/EEC [1977] OJ L61/26 on transfer of undertakings.
[259] Art. 5(3).
[260] See e.g. Case C–169/91 *Stoke-on-Trent City Council v. B & Q* [1992] ECR I–6457.

other day of the week'. As a result, the provision 'which is severable from the other provisions of the Directive' had to be annulled.

(c) Annual Leave

According to the Directive, every worker is entitled to *paid* annual leave of at least four weeks,[261] in accordance with conditions for entitlement to, and granting of, such leave laid down by national legislation and/or practice.[262] Thus, pre-existing national rules permitting workers to qualify for the minimum entitlement to annual leave after twelve months' service would continue to apply.[263] The minimum period of paid annual leave cannot be replaced by an allowance in lieu, except where the employment relationship is terminated.[264]

There are no derogations from this provision. It therefore appears that the right to four weeks' paid annual leave applies to all workers falling within the scope of the Directive, including part-timers and those on other atypical contracts for whom, presumably, the entitlement will be provided on a *pro rata* basis, although this is not expressly provided for in the Directive. Member States did, however, have the option under Article 18(1)(b)(ii) of 'making use' of a transitional period of not more than three years from 23 November 1996 (i.e. until 23 November 1999), during which every worker could receive three weeks' paid annual leave.[265]

5.2 Limits: Working Time

Article 6 provides that although working hours should be regulated by laws, regulations, or administrative provisions or by collective agreements or agreements between the two sides of industry, the average working time for each seven-day period, *including overtime*, must not exceed forty-eight hours over a reference period of four months. Periods of paid annual leave under

---

[261] It is not clear whether the public holidays are included in this entitlement.

[262] Art. 7(1).

[263] The introduction of a service requirement where none existed previously might breach the non-regression clause found in Art. 18(3).

[264] Art. 7(2).

[265] Prior to the UK's implementation of the Directive, the EAT found in *Gibson* v. *East Riding of Yorkshire Council* [1999] IRLR 358 that, notwithstanding the derogations, Art. 7 was sufficiently clear and precise to have direct effect so that during the period from 23 Nov. 1996 to 1 Oct. 1998 an employee of an emanation of the State (such as Ms Gibson, a swimming instructor at a leisure centre) could take advantage of four weeks' paid leave and not three, since the UK had not enacted legislation to take advantage of the period of delayed implementation. The tribunal left the question open whether an individual in private sector employment would have an action for *Francovich* damages. However, in *R* v. *Attorney General for Northern Ireland, ex parte Burns* [1999] IRLR 315 Kerr J seemed to think that the UK's delayed implementation of the Directive in Northern Ireland was an actionable breach of Community law: it constituted a sufficiently serious breach and therefore the Member State was liable for an injury suffered by an individual who suffered loss and damage as a result.

Table 6.2 Statutory and Collective Regulation of Daily and Weekly Working Hours and Rest Periods in the Member States (Hours Unless Otherwise Stated)

Member State	Working week	Maximum daily number of hours	Daily rest	Weekly rest statutory/CA[1]
Belgium	40	12 with CA	—	24/48
Denmark	no legislation	—	11	24/48
Germany	48	10	—	24/48
Greece	5 day-week	12	—	24/36–48
Spain	40	9	12	36/48
France	39	12 with CA	—	24/48
Ireland	48	12	—	24/48
Italy	48	10	—	24/48
Luxembourg	40	10	—	44/48
Netherlands	48	10	9 to 11	24/48
Portugal	48	10	—	24/36–48
United Kingdom		no general statutory provisions		/48

Source: Commission explanatory memorandum accompanying the Draft Working Time Directive and the Regulation of Working Conditions in the Member States of the European Community, Vol. I, *Social Europe* 4/92.

[1] CA means collective agreements covering most workers.

Article 7 or sick leave must not be included or must be neutral in the calculation.[266] As Table 6.2 demonstrates, of those Member States which regulate working hours five States adopt a forty-eight-hour maximum while the other Member States, with the exception of Greece, set a maximum of forty hours or less. Indeed, since the Table was prepared both France and Italy have been moving towards a thirty-five-hour week in the name of job creation. On the other hand, Table 6.3 shows that statutory regulation of overtime varies enormously between States. The Directive does not try to reconcile these differing provisions but simply requires overtime to be included in the calculation of the maximum forty-eight-hour week.[267] This does raise the question of how to reduce the dependency of certain sections of industry and services on systematic overtime.[268]

Working time is defined in Article 2(1) as 'any period during which the worker is working, at the employer's disposal and carrying out his activities or

---

[266] Art. 16(2). By virtue of Art. 17 it is possible to derogate from this provision, but any derogations must not result in the establishment of a reference period exceeding six months. However, Member States have the option, subject to compliance with the general principles relating to the protection of health and safety of workers, and allowing for objective or technical reasons or reasons concerning the organization of work, to allow collective agreements to set reference periods which do not exceed 12 months (Art. 17(4)).

[267] Art. 6(2).

[268] See further *Working Time: An LRD Guide to the New Directive* (Labour Research Department, London, Mar. 1994) 11.

Table 6.3 Statutory Regulation of Maximum Periods of Overtime and Night Working Hours During Which Work is not Permitted in the Member States

Member State	Maximum periods of overtime	Hours when night work prohibited
Belgium	65 hours per three months	20.00–06.00
Denmark	governed by CA	no legislation
FR Germany	2 hours per day up to 30 days on basis of 48-hour week	20.00–06.00
Greece	3 hours per day, 18 hours in a week, 150 hours a year in private sector	22.00–07.00
Spain	80 hours per year	22.00–06.00
France	9 hours a week, 130 p.a. more when authorized	22.00–05.00
Ireland	2 hours per day, 12 hours per week, 240 hours p.a.	22.00–06.00
Italy	no legislation	22.00–08.00
Luxembourg	2 hours per day	no general legislation [1]
Netherlands	between 0.5 and 3.5 hours a day	22.00–06.00
Portugal	2 hours a day, 160 p.a.	22.00–07.00
United Kingdom	no legislation	no legislation

Source: *The Regulation of Working Conditions in the Member States of the European Community*, Vol. I, *Social Europe* 4/92.

[1] Nursing mothers and pregnant women cannot work between 22.00 and 06.00.

duties, in accordance with national laws and/or practices'. It is not clear whether this definition is to be read cumulatively or disjunctively. This is of particular significance to 'on-call workers'. If read disjunctively, then for on-call workers waiting at home, this time constitutes working time. If read cumulatively, then this time may not represent working time since the worker is not 'working' or 'carrying out his activities'.[269] In *SIMAP*[270] the Advocate General considered this question. He suggested that periods during which doctors were available and physically present at the health centre constituted working time, as did periods during which doctors had to be available to come into work, even though they were not at the medical centre.

A complex set of derogations apply to this provision. In the case of workers covered by the unmeasured working time derogation (section 3.1 above) Member States can derogate both from Article 6 (forty-eight-hour week) *and* Article 16 (the reference period) provided due regard is paid to the general principles of the protection of the safety and health of workers. In the case of workers listed in sections 3.2 and 3.4 above (other special cases and collective

[269] A question has been referred to the Court on this point in Case C–303/98 *SIMAP*.
[270] Ibid., Opinion 16 Dec. 1999.

agreements) Member States can derogate only from Article 16 (reference period) but, according to Article 17(4), the option to derogate may not result in the establishment of a reference period exceeding six months. However, Member States have the option, subject to compliance with general principles relating to the protection of health and safety of workers, of allowing for objective or technical reasons concerning the organization of work, collective agreements or agreements concluded between the two sides of industry to set longer reference periods but in no event exceeding twelve months.

Further, Article 18(1)(b)(i) provides that Member States need not apply Article 6 on the maximum forty-eight-hour week (the individual opt-out) provided certain conditions are satisfied. Member States must ensure that:

— the general principle of the protection of health and safety of workers is respected;
— no employer requires a worker to work more than forty-eight hours over a seven-day period unless the worker's consent has been obtained previously;
— any worker refusing to give this consent must not be subjected to any detriment by the employer as a result;
— the employer must keep up-to-date records of all workers who work more than forty-eight hours a week;
— records must be placed at the disposal of the competent authorities, who may, for reasons connected with the health and safety of workers, prohibit or restrict the possibility of exceeding the maximum weekly working hours;
— the employer provides the competent authorities at their request with information on cases in which agreement has been given by workers to perform work exceeding forty-eight hours over a period of seven days (calculated as an average for any reference period set down under the option available in Article 16(2)).

It is not clear whether Article 18(1)(b)(i) represents a further permanent derogation from the principle laid down in the Working Time Directive, subject to review before 2003, or, more likely, a temporary derogation facility, lasting seven years and subject to review.[271]

5.3 Limits: Night Work

Night time is defined as any period of not less than seven hours, as defined by national law, and which must include, in any case, the period between midnight and 5 a.m.[272] This gives the national systems a possible range of the hours between 10 p.m. and 7 a.m. to designate as night time. Night workers are defined in two ways by the Directive. First, 'night workers' are those who, during night time, work at least three hours of their daily working time as a

---

[271] Bercusson, above n. 230, 17.   [272] Art. 2(3).

normal course.[273] Secondly, the Directive defines night workers as those who are likely to work a certain proportion of their working time during night time, as defined by national legislation *or* collective agreements concluded by the two sides of industry at national or regional level.[274] The definition of night worker was considered by the High Court in Northern Ireland in *ex parte Burns*.[275] The applicant worked a rotating shift pattern during which she worked, one week in three, from 9 p.m. to 7 a.m. The government argued that she was not a night worker since night workers are those who work night shifts exclusively or predominantly. Kerr J rejected this, arguing that night working should be a 'regular feature' of the employment. In *SIMAP*[276] Advocate General Saggio said that doctors working at night or who were contactable at night constituted night workers.

Normal working hours for night work must not exceed an average of eight hours in any twenty-four-hour period.[277] The reference period is to be determined after consulting the two sides of industry or by collective agreements or agreements concluded between the two sides of industry at national or regional level.[278] Night workers whose work involves special hazards or mental strain—to be defined by national legislation or collective agreements or agreements concluded between the two sides of industry—must not work more than eight hours in any period of twenty-four hours during which they work at night.[279] Thus, no reference period exists in the case of such workers.

In addition, night workers are entitled to a free and confidential health assessment, possibly conducted within the national health system before their assignment and then at regular intervals thereafter.[280] If night workers are found to suffer from health problems connected with the fact that they work at night they must be transferred wherever possible to suitable day work.[281] In addition, Member States can make the work of 'certain categories of night workers subject to certain guarantees, under the conditions laid down by national law and practice, in the case of workers who incur risks to their safety or health linked to night time working'.[282] However, any guarantees made must be careful not to offend the principle of equal treatment of men and women.[283] Employers who *regularly* use night workers must inform the

---

[273] Art. 2(4)(a).
[274] Art. 2(4)(b).
[275] [1999] IRLR 315.
[276] Case C–303/98, Opinion 16 Dec. 1999.
[277] Art. 8(1).
[278] Art. 16(3).
[279] Art. 8(2).
[280] Art. 9(1)(a), (2) and (3).
[281] Art. 9(1)(b).
[282] Art. 10.
[283] See Case 312/86 *Commission v. France* [1988] ECR 3559; Case 345/89 *Criminal Proceedings Against Stoeckel* [1991] ECR I–4047 and Case C–158/91 *Ministère public and Direction du travail et de l'emploi v. Levy* [1993] ECR I–4287, discussed in Ch. 4.

competent authorities on request.[284] Finally, Article 12 provides that both night workers and shift workers must enjoy health and safety protection appropriate to the nature of their work, and that such protection is equivalent to that applicable to other workers and is available at all times.

6. Collective Agreements

A key feature of this Directive is the important role envisaged for the Social Partners, not only in implementing the Directive,[285] but in setting substantive standards in relation to night work, daily rest breaks, maximum weekly working hours, including overtime, and annual holidays.[286] Derogations at enterprise level are to be shaped by framework agreements at national or regional level.[287] This prompts the conclusion that while the Working Time Directive breaks new ground in the development of European collective labour law[288] it raises questions about the degree of union representation of the workforce and the extent of the coverage of such agreements.[289]

In the UK, the collective dimension of the Directive has posed considerable problems for a traditionally single channel system.[290] With the decline in trade union membership and recognition, the Working Time Regulations 1998 which implement the Directive have also recognized a role for elected worker representatives in the absence of a recognized trade union. In addition, they have also recognized that individual workers may negotiate for themselves in certain contexts. The Regulations therefore permit three types of agreement:

— collective agreements;
— workforce agreements; and
— relevant agreements.

Collective agreements are agreements defined in section 178 of the Trade Union and Labour Relations (Consolidation) Act (TULR(C)A) 1992 where the trade unions are recognized and independent.[291] 'Workforce agreements' are designed to provide a mechanism for employers to agree working time

---

[284] Art. 11.

[285] This is not new, see e.g. Directive 91/533 on Proof of the Employment Contract [1991] OJ L288/32.

[286] The formula 'Collective agreements or agreements between the two sides of industry' appears in all the Directive's provisions incorporating collective bargaining: Arts. 2(4)(b)(ii), 4, 6(1), 8(2), 15, 16(3), 17(2)–(4).

[287] Bercusson, above, n. 230, 47.

[288] Ibid., n. 230, 48. See further Bercusson, *Working Time in Britain: Towards a European Model: Part II Collective Bargaining in Europe and the UK* (Institute of Employment Rights, London, 1994).

[289] See further Ch. 1.

[290] See further Ch. 8.

[291] As defined by s. 5 TULR(C)A 1992.

arrangements with workers who do not have *any terms and conditions set by collective agreement* (Schedule 1, paragraph 2), thereby acknowledging the primacy of collective agreements. To be valid a 'workforce agreement' must:

— be in writing;
— have effect for a specified period not exceeding five years;
— apply either to all of the relevant members of the workforce (other than those covered by collective agreement—thus employers cannot by-pass a recognized trade union), or to all of the relevant members of the work-force who belong to a particular group;
— be signed by the representatives of the workforce[292] or the representatives of the group where appropriate (excluding in either case any representative not a relevant member of the workforce on the date on which the agreement was first made available for signature). If the employer employed twenty or fewer workers on the date on which the agreement was first made available for signature it must be signed either by the appropriate representatives *or* by the majority of workers.

In addition copies of the agreement and such guidance as workers may reasonably require to understand it fully must be made available by the employer to all the workers for whom it is intended before the agreement is signed. The Regulations also introduce the concept of 'relevant agreement' to specify dates from which reference periods start to run and to determine the meaning of the terms working time and night time. A relevant agreement is defined as (Regulation 2(1)):

— any provision of a collective agreement which forms *part of a contract* between him and his employer (i.e. only those collectively agreed terms which have been incorporated into the contract);
— a workforce agreement (see above);
— or any other agreement in writing which is legally enforceable as between the worker and the employer.

The last limb in the definition of a relevant agreement removes any collective component to the negotiation.

---

[292] Para. 2 of Sch. 1 provides that 'representatives of the workforce' are workers duly elected to represent the relevant members of the workforce; 'representatives of the group' are workers duly elected to represent the members of a particular group; and representatives are 'duly elected' if their election satisfies the requirements of para. 3 of the Schedule. The Working Time Regulations provide some details of the method of carrying out elections (Sch. 1, para. 3). The Working Time Regulations are, however, far less prescriptive than those contained in TULR(C)A 1992 for the election of trade union officials and, as the TUC has pointed out, employers have too much power in deciding how the representatives are to be elected and there are no controls on ballot-rigging (Research paper 98/82, 25). This has prompted concern whether the elected worker representatives will pass the test of representativity laid down by the Court in Case T–135/96 *UEAPME v. Council of the European Union* [1998] ECR II–2335.

7. The Excluded Sectors

On 15 July 1997 the Commission adopted a White Paper[293] examining the nature and extent of the sectors excluded from the Directive, the scale of the problem, the legal and contractual situation in the Member States, and the initiatives taken. The Commission opted for a differentiated approach:

— extending all the provisions of Directive 93/104/EC to non-mobile workers, i.e. all those working in the transport sector but whose work is primarily office-based (the 'horizontal' directive);
— extending to all mobile workers (including sea-going fishermen) and to those involved in 'other work at sea' (offshore workers involving the exploration, extraction, or exploitation of mineral resources and diving in connection with such activities) the provisions of Directive 93/104/EC on the four weeks' paid annual holiday, health checks for night workers, guarantee of adequate rest, and capping the number of working hours per year;
— adopting for each sector or activity specific legislation on working time and rest periods for mobile workers and *mutatis mutandis* those involved in 'sea fishing' and 'other work at sea'.

In the light of the sectoral social dialogue which has been highly influential in this area, the Commission has modified its approach. For example, mobile railway workers will be fully covered by Directive 93/104 but mobile workers in sea transport will be covered only by a specific Directive implementing the agreement between the Social Partners.[294]

7.1 The Horizontal Directive

Under this proposal the scope of Directive 93/104/EEC is to be extended to cover all non-mobile workers, including doctors in training. It will also apply to offshore workers and mobile railway workers. In addition, a number of provisions are to be introduced with regard to other mobile workers (road transport, inland waterway, air transport, sea fishing).[295] It has also been agreed that for doctors in training there is to be at least a five-year transition period before the forty-eight hour limit to the working week applies. The transition period would be broken down into three stages:

— fifty-eight hours for the first three years;
— fifty-six hours for the following two years;
— fifty-two hours for any remaining period.

---

[293] COM(97)334.
[294] Communication from the Commission to the Council, the European Parliament, the Economic and Social Committee on the organization of working time in the sectors and activities excluded from Directive 93/104/EC of 23 Nov. 1998 on which the following draws heavily.
[295] Agreement was reached on this Directive by the Social Affairs Council on 25 May 1999.

This transition period was considered necessary to enable Member States to train sufficient numbers of doctors to allow for the implementation of the Directive.

7.2 Sectoral Measures

(a) Road Transport

Despite intensive negotiations held in the joint committee on road transport, the Social Partners did not manage to reach agreement on working time but did identify the main elements to be considered as the basis for the Commission's two proposals for directives covering the road transport sector. The first proposal is an extension of the scope of Directive 93/104/EC to all non-mobile workers and the provision of certain rights to mobile workers in the road transport sector in general. The second proposal is for a separate directive, applicable to all mobile workers carrying out road transport work, including mobile workers employed by enterprises carrying out transport work on their own account. Self-employed drivers, when driving a bus, coach, or heavy goods vehicle, are also included in this draft, which supplements the provisions of Regulation (EEC) 3820/85 on driving rest periods. The Commission says that this will also improve road safety and reduce the distortions of competition arising from the extreme fragmentation of road transport companies into very small units. The new draft Council Directive is without prejudice to this Regulation, which remains applicable in its entirety.

This second proposal has three key objectives: first, to guarantee a level of social protection equivalent to that currently applied to mobile workers in other transport sectors; secondly, to protect the health and safety of all road users; and, thirdly, to remove unfair competition in the Single Market. The specific proposal for a Directive on mobile workers in road transport lays down, in particular:

— a broader definition of working time to cover driving time *and* rest periods;
— forty-eight hours maximum average working week over a four-month reference period and maximum weekly working time of sixty hours;
— a break of at least thirty minutes when the total working time is between six and nine hours and at least forty-five minutes when total daily working time is more than nine hours;
— daily rest of at least eleven hours, which may be reduced to ten hours provided there is compensatory rest of at least twelve hours within the following four weeks;
— weekly rest of thirty-five hours;
— a ban on night workers working more than eight hours per day, or more than ten hours as long as a daily average of eight hours is not exceeded over a two-month reference period;

— a tighter definition of night work than in the general Working Time Directive.

The Commission also provides for derogations to Directive 93/104/EC:

— article 3 (maximum weekly working time), article 5 (rest periods), and article 6 (night workers) by means of national legislation or through collective agreements or other agreements between the Social Partners, on condition that the workers concerned are provided with equivalent periods of compensatory rest;
— article 3 (maximum weekly working time) to extend the reference period for calculating the average maximum weekly working time of forty-eight hours from four to six months, unless the average weekly working time is reduced to thirty-nine hours and thirty-five hours respectively.

(b) Sea Transport

The Commission made two proposals for directives and a recommendation in the maritime sector. These have all now been adopted. The first Directive[296] implements the sectoral agreement on the organization of working time of seafarers concluded by the European Community Shipowners' Association (ECSA) and the Federation of Transport Workers in the European Union (FST). This agreement reflects the provision of the ILO Convention 180 on seafarers' hours of work. It provides for either a maximum number of working hours (fourteen hours in any twenty-four-hour period and seventy-two hours in any seven-day period) or a minimum rest period regime (ten hours in any twenty-four-hour period and seventy-seven hours in any seven-day period). The second Directive concerns enforcement of seafarers' hours of work on board ships using Community ports.[297] The Recommendation[298] is for the ratification of ILO Convention 180 (1996) and the 1996 protocol to ILO Convention 147 (1976).

(c) Other Sectors

— Rail transport: the Social Partners meeting in the joint committee on rail transport reached agreements on 18 September 1996 on including all railway workers—whether non-mobile or mobile—under Directive 93/ 104/EC, subject to specific derogation for 'drivers and railway staff on board trains'.

---

[296] Council Directive 99/63/EC concerning the Agreement on the Organization of Working time of Seafarers concluded by the European Community Shipowners' Association (ECSA) and the Federation of Transport Workers' Unions in the European Union (FST) [1999] OJ L167/33, corrected [1999] OJ L244/64.

[297] European Parliament and Council Directive 99/95/EC [2000] OJ L14/29.

[298] Commission Recommendation 99/130/EC on ratification of ILO Convention 180 concerning seafarers' hours of work and the manning of ships, and ratification of the 1996 Protocol to the 1976 Merchant Shipping (minimum standards) Convention.

— Air transport: with the agreement of the Social Partners non-mobile workers in the sector will be covered by Directive 93/104/EC. As far as mobile workers are concerned, the social partners[298A] signed a working time agreement on 22 March 2000 covering pilots and cabin crew. This is the second European sectoral agreement.[298B] The Commission is going to make a proposal to the Council to extend the agreement to all workers as a Directive. The agreement limits annual working time to 2,000 hours but includes 'some elements of standby for duty assignment as determined by the applicable law'. It restricts flying time to 900 hours and contains a provision on a monthly and yearly minimum number of rest days. The agreement also requires 'appropriate' health and safety protection for all mobile personnel.

— Inland waterway: serious negotiations between Social Partners in the joint committee on inland waterway transport have not been held and so no agreement is being reached in the sector. As well as including mobile workers in this sector in the horizontal directive (even though the provisions of Article 3 (daily rest), Article 4 (in-work rest breaks), Article 5 (weekly rest), and Article 8 (duration of night work) do not apply), the Commission is preparing an additional sector-specific proposal.

— Sea fishing: the Social Partners have not managed to reach agreement in the joint committee on fisheries. As a result, the Commission has proposed extending Directive 93/104/EC to cover mobile workers in this sector. However, under the new Article 17b the provisions of Article 3 (daily rest), Article 4 (rest period), Article 5 (weekly rest), and Article 8 (duration of night work) do not apply. Member States must, however, take the necessary measures to ensure that workers have a right to rest. The Social Affairs Council agreed on a sector-specific Directive on fishermen inspired by the Social Partners' agreement on seafarers.[299]

— Other activities at sea ('offshore' workers): the Commission intends to extend Directive 93/104/EC to workers carrying out 'other activities at sea'. The draft Directive amending Council Directive 93/104/EC takes account of special shift work arrangements required by the sector. The reference period for calculating average working time is to be extended from four to twelve months in respect of workers in performing offshore work. Share fishermen are excluded from the right to four weeks' paid leave but the Commission will propose a specific directive on working time and rest periods for sea fishermen which will also provide adequate alternative arrangements for paid leave for share fishermen.

[298A] Association of the European Airlines, the European Regional Airlines Association, the International Association of Charter Airlines, the European Transport Workers' Federation (ETF, for the cabin crew) and the European Cockpit Association (ECA, for the pilots).

[298B] See above n. 296.

[299] See above, n. 296.

8. Conclusions

The Luxembourg employment strategy includes a pillar on adaptability. This pillar has provided the main focus for demand-side flexibility. According to the 1998 Employment Guidelines the Social Partners are invited to negotiate, at the appropriate levels, agreements to 'modernise the organisation of work, including flexible working arrangements, with the aim of making undertakings productive and competitive and achieving the required balance between flexibility and security'. While the sectoral-specific Directives negotiated by the Social Partners represent a step in this direction, many businesses view the original Directive 93/104 as a significant constraint on their ability to introduce flexible working arrangements.

E. SPECIFIC RISK GROUPS

The Court's decision in *UK* v. *Council* to uphold the choice of Article 118a [new Article 137] as the legal basis for the Working Time Directive 93/104 saved three other directives designed to protect specific groups of workers adopted in the same period—pregnant workers, young workers, and atypical workers[300]—all adopted under Article 118a but combining a mixture of health and safety with working conditions and employment rights. This combination can be seen in the Pregnant Workers Directive 92/85/EEC.[301] On the one hand, the Directive contains elements of health and safety protection: it is designated the tenth daughter directive within the framework of the Health and Safety Directive 89/391,[302] and so the principles contained in the parent Directive apply.[303] Thus the employer must assess the nature, degree, and duration of exposure to physical, chemical, and biological agents in order to determine the risks to the health and safety of the pregnant worker and so decide what measures to take.[304] If necessary the employer must take steps to ensure that the risks of exposure are avoided[305] and the worker must be informed both of the risks and the steps to be taken.[306] On the other hand, the Directive also provides that pregnant workers should not be obliged to work at

---

[300] See also Commission Recommendation 98/370/EC on the ratification of ILO Convention 177 on homework of 20 June 1996 (notified under Doc. No. C(1998)764) [1998] OJ L165/32.

[301] Council Directive 92/85/EEC on the introduction of measures to encourage improvements in the safety and health at work of pregnant workers and workers who have recently given birth or are breastfeeding (tenth individual Directive) [1992] OJ L348/1.

[302] Art. 1(1).

[303] Art. 1(2).

[304] Art. 4.

[305] Art. 5(1).

[306] Art. 4(2).

night,[307] should be allowed time off for ante-natal examinations,[308] and be entitled to fourteen weeks' maternity leave,[309] during which time they must be protected from dismissal. These provisions, when read in the light of the 'employment rights' contained in Article 11, point to 'rights and interests of employed persons' under Article 100a(2) [now Article 95(2)] and not just health and safety measures. This Directive is considered in more detail in Chapter 4. This section will consider the Young Workers' Directive and the Directives concerning atypical workers.

1. Young Workers Directive 94/33/EC

The Young Workers Directive[310] is intended to prevent abuse of young people's labour while allowing sufficient flexibility in schemes providing both work experience and training. Member States must ensure that employers guarantee that young people (any person under 18 'having an employment contract or employment relationship')[311] have working conditions which suit their age, and are protected against 'economic exploitation and against any work likely to harm their safety, health or physical, mental, moral or social development or to jeopardise their education'.[312] Since this is the purpose of the Directive any subsequent provisions must be interpreted in the light of this objective.

Member States do, however, have the option not to apply the Directive to occasional work or short-term work involving either domestic service in a private household or work in family undertakings provided the work is not regarded as being harmful, damaging, or dangerous to young people.[313] The memorandum accompanying the Directive explains that the Directive is not intended to apply to occasional or limited work in the family context, for example, work in the household or in the family business, whether agriculture (for example, grape picking or crop harvesting) or in a distributive or craft trade (for example, shelf filling or other light shop work).[314]

The Directive envisages two categories of young workers: first, children, defined as any young person less than 15 years old or who is still subject to

---

[307] Art. 7(1).
[308] Art. 9.
[309] Art. 8.
[310] Council Directive 94/33/EC [1994] OJ L216/12. See also Commission Recommendation 67/125/EEC [1967] OJ 25/405. See COM(91)543 final—SYN 383, Brussels 17 Mar. 1992. Inspiration for the Directive came, in particular, from ILO Conventions 5, 6, 7, 10, 13, 15, 16, 33, 58, 59, 60, 77, 78, 79, 90, 112, 123, 124, 138, the European Social Charter 1961 Art. 7, and Art. 32 of the UN Convention on the Rights of the Child.
[311] Arts. 3(a) and 2(1).
[312] Art. 1(3).
[313] Art. 2(2).
[314] COM(91)543, 10.

compulsory full-time schooling under national law,[315] and, secondly, adolescents, defined as any young person who is at least 15 years old but younger than 18, who is no longer subject to compulsory full-time schooling.[316] The basic premise of the Directive is that while work by adolescents must be strictly regulated under the conditions laid down by the Directive work by children is prohibited.[317]

In the case of children Member States do, however, have the option to derogate from this basic prohibition in three circumstances. First, children can perform cultural, artistic, sports, or advertising work, subject to prior authorization by a competent authority,[318] provided that the activities are not harmful either to the safety, health, and development of children or to their attendance at school or their participation in vocational training programmes.[319] The Member States must also prescribe the working conditions for children taking advantage of this exception. Secondly, children over 14 can work under a combined work/training scheme or an 'in-plant work experience scheme'.[320] Thirdly, children over 14 can perform light work, defined to mean all work, taking into account the inherent nature of the tasks involved and the particular conditions under which they are to be performed, which is not likely to harm the health and safety or development of young people nor harm their attendance at school, their participation in vocational guidance and training or their capacity to benefit from the instruction received.[321] This exception appears to allow children over 14 to continue to do newspaper rounds and babysitting, provided in both cases the time taken does not jeopardize their health, safety and schooling. Member States can also permit 13-year-olds to perform designated types of light work provided that the Member States specify the conditions in which the work is to be performed.[322]

As with the Framework Directive 89/391 on health and safety, the Young Workers' Directive also imposes general obligations on employers to take the necessary measures to protect the safety and health of all young workers permitted to work by the Directive. This requires the employer to conduct a risk assessment before young people begin work and when there is any major change in their working conditions. In particular, employers must pay

---

[315] Art. 3(b).

[316] Art. 3(c). Member States must ensure that the minimum working or employment age is not lower than the minimum age at which compulsory full-time schooling as imposed by national law ends or 15 years in any event.

[317] Arts. 1(1) and 4(1).

[318] However, in the case of children over 13 Member States can authorize the employment of children in cultural, artistic, sports, or advertising agencies (Art. 5(3)). Member States with a specific authorization system for modelling agencies can retain that system (Art. 5(4)).

[319] Art. 5(2)(ii).

[320] Art. 4(2)(b).

[321] Art. 3(d).

[322] Art. 4(3).

particular regard to the fitting-out and layout of the workplace, the nature, degree, and duration of exposure to physical, biological, and chemical agents, the form, range, and use of work equipment, the arrangement of the work process and the level of training and instruction given to young workers.[323] If this assessment reveals a risk to the physical or mental health, safety or development of young people 'an appropriate free assessment and monitoring of their health must be provided',[324] possibly as part of the national health system, and involving the protective and preventive services referred to in Article 7 of Directive 89/391/EEC.[325] In addition, employers must inform both the young workers and their legal representatives of possible risks and measures adopted to protect their health and safety.[326]

Given the 'vulnerability of young people' due to their 'absence of awareness of existing or potential risks' or because 'young people have not yet fully matured', Member States must ensure that young people are protected from any specific risks[327] to their health, safety, and development. Young workers are also prohibited from being employed in work which is beyond their physical or psychological capacity, work involving harmful radiation or exposure to agents which are toxic, carcinogenic, cause heritable genetic damage, or chronically affect human health in any other way; work which puts them at risk of accidents; or work where their health may suffer from extreme cold, heat, noise, vibration, or from handling heavy loads. Exceptionally, derogations from these provisions can be made in the case of adolescents, where it is indispensable for their vocational training, providing that their work is performed under the supervision of a 'designated worker'.[328]

In the case of children permitted to perform light work or engage in a training scheme, the Directive limits their working time to:[329]

— eight hours a day and forty hours a week for work performed under a combined work/training scheme or work experience scheme;[330]
— two hours on a school day and twelve hours a week for work performed outside the hours fixed for school attendance if this is permitted by national law; daily working time must not exceed seven hours, or eight hours in the case of children over the age of 15;
— seven hours a day and thirty-five hours a week for work performed during

---

[323] Art. 6(1) and (2).

[324] Art. 6(2).

[325] [1989] OJ L183/1.

[326] Art. 6(3).

[327] Art. 7(2). This includes work involving harmful exposure to the physical, biological, and chemical agents referred to in point I of the Annex to the Young Workers' Directive and to the processes and work referred to in point II of the Annex. Changes to the Annex can be made in accordance with the procedure in Art. 17 of Directive 89/391/EEC.

[328] See Art. 7 of Directive 89/391/EEC.

[329] Art. 8(1).

[330] Art. 8(1)(a). Time spent training counts as working time (Art. 8(3)). Member States can derogate from Art. 8(1)(a) but must determine the conditions for such derogation (Art. 8(5)).

the school holiday period; eight hours a day and forty hours a week in the case of the over 15s;

— seven hours a day and thirty-five hours a week for light work performed by children no longer subject to compulsory full-time schooling.

Adolescents can work up to eight hours a day and forty hours a week.[331] Where daily working time is more than four and a half hours, young people are entitled to a break of at least thirty minutes.[332]

Children cannot work between 20.00 and 06.00[333] and adolescents between 22.00 and 06.00 or between 23.00 and 07.00,[334] although adolescents may work at night under the supervision of an adult if Member States so provide, but not between midnight and 04.00.[335] However, Member States may authorize adolescents to work between midnight and 04.00 in the shipping or fisheries sector, the armed forces and the police, hospitals and similar establishments, cultural, artistic, sports, or advertising activities, where there are objective grounds for doing so, and provided that adolescents are allowed suitable compensatory rest.[336] In addition, for each twenty-four-hour period, children are entitled to a minimum rest period of fourteen consecutive hours and adolescents to twelve consecutive hours.[337] Although it appears that children can therefore work ten hours a day and adolescents fourteen hours a day such an interpretation directly contradicts the requirements of Article 8 on working time. Further, for each seven-day period worked, both children and adolescents are entitled to a minimum rest period of two days, consecutive if possible, including in principle a Sunday.[338] Where justified by technical or organizational reasons the minimum rest period may be reduced, but may in no circumstances be less than thirty-six consecutive hours.[339] However, extensive derogations are permitted to this rule, in the case of the shipping and fisheries sectors, the armed forces or the police, work performed in hospitals or similar establishments, agriculture, tourism, hotels and catering, and activities involving periods of work split up over the day.[340] It is also possible, in the

---

[331] Art. 8(2). Member States can derogate from this provision either by way of exception or where there are objective grounds for so doing provided the Member State determines the conditions, limits, and procedure for implementing such derogations (Art. 8(5)).

[332] Art. 12.

[333] Art. 9(1)(a).

[334] Art. 9(1)(b).

[335] Art. 9(2).

[336] Art. 9(2). Adolescents are also entitled to a free health assessment prior to any assignment to night work and at regular intervals thereafter, unless their work is of 'an exceptional nature' (Art. 9(3)).

[337] Art. 10(1).

[338] Art. 10(2). The equivalent provision in the Working Time Directive 93/104 was annulled. See above, n. 260.

[339] Ibid.

[340] Art. 10(4). There must be objective grounds for derogation, workers must be granted compensatory rest time, and the objectives set out in Art. 1 of the Directive must not be called into question.

case of adolescents, to derogate from the provisions on working time, night work, and rest periods in the case of *force majeure*, provided that the work is temporary, must be performed immediately, that adult workers are not available, and that the adolescents are allowed equivalent compensatory rest time in the following three weeks.[341] Finally, children who are permitted to work on a combined work/training scheme or doing light work must have a period free from work including, as far as possible, in the school holidays.[342] No minimum period of leave is specified, nor is the situation of adolescents addressed. Presumably, the Working Time Directive 93/104/EEC[343] applies in these circumstances.

Member States are required either to implement the Directive by 22 June 1996 or to ensure that the two sides of industry introduce the requisite provisions by means of collective agreements.[344] The UK, however, did not need to implement certain provisions[345] of the Directive until the year 2000.[346] This was the first time in the social field that a named Member State secured at least a significant delay in implementing a Directive. When implementing the Directive Member States must also prescribe measures to be applied in the event of failure to comply with the provisions adopted to implement the Directive.

The parallels between the Young Workers Directive and Directive 93/104 on Working Time are obvious, and concerns about lack of flexibility and the burdens on small business apply to both. The Directive applies to all types of business regardless of size, in both the public and private sectors.[347] Certain sectors of the economy will be particularly affected, including the distributive trades, hotels and catering, services, and events for the young. On the other hand, the ILO has criticized the Directive for not being compatible with the international conventions (a point strongly denied by the Commission).[348] Yet the Directive does not go as far as the Community Social Charter 1989 intended: Article 21 requires that young people who are in gainful employment must receive equitable remuneration in accordance with national practice, and Article 23 provides that following the end of compulsory education, young people must be entitled to receive initial vocational training of a sufficient duration to enable them to adapt to the requirements of their future working life. Perhaps the choice of Article 118a [new Article 138] as the appropriate legal basis has prevented the development of a more ambitious

---

[341] Art. 13.

[342] Art. 11.

[343] [1993] OJ L307/18.

[344] Art. 17(1)(a).

[345] Art. 8(1)(b) limiting the working time of children to two hours a day on a school day and 12 hours a week; Art. 8(2), limiting the working time of adolescents to eight hours a day and 40 hours a week; and Art. 9(1)(b) and (2), relating to the night work of adolescents.

[346] Art. 17(1)(b).

[347] COM(91)543 final—SYN 383, 51.

[348] WE/2/94, 20 Jan. 1994.

programme for young workers. Certainly the Commission has been constrained from drawing up a broad catalogue of rights to benefit young people
and future Community citizens: in particular, the right to education, training
and even the right to social assistance.[349]

2. Atypical Workers

2.1 Background

The Community Social Charter 1989 identified the need for action to ensure
the improvement in living and working conditions as regards 'forms of
employment other than open-ended contracts, such as fixed-term contracts,
part-time working, temporary work and seasonal work'. The Action Programme noted that atypical workers constitute an 'important component in
the organisation of the labour market', and said that the growth of atypical
work, 'often in a quite anarchical manner' raised a 'danger of seeing the
development of terms of employment such as to cause problems of social
dumping, or even distortion of competition, at Community level' unless safeguards were introduced.[350]

Although Directive 91/533/EEC on proof of the employment contract[351]
provided some transparency in contracts of employment, the Commission
proposed three specific directives concerning atypical workers, intended to
improve the operation of the internal market and introduce greater transparency into the labour market, to improve living and working conditions of
workers; and protecting the health and safety of workers at the workplace.
The three Directives were proposed on three different legal bases. The first,
and least radical, Directive 91/383/EEC, proposed on the basis of Article
118a [new Article 137], concerned health and safety and was the only measure successfully adopted. The second, proposed on the basis of Article 100
[new Article 94],[352] applied the principle of non-discrimination to atypical
workers,[353] in a limited set of circumstances, subject to the principle of

---

[349] See further Castillo, 'La Protection des Enfants dans la Communaute Européenne' [1990]
Revue du Marché Commun 361.

[350] For a review of the legislation in the Member States, see 282 *EIRR* 17, 284 *EIRR*12, and
285 *EIRR* 13. See also Meulders, Plasman and Meulders, *Atypical Employment in the EC*
(Dartmouth, Aldershot, 1994).

[351] [1991] OJ L288/32. See below, nn. 400–426. This is not the case in France where national
law already obliges employers to provide atypical workers with a written contract (see Rodière,
Droit Social de l'Union Européenne (LGDJ, Paris, 1998)326).

[352] COM(90)228 final [1990] OJ C224/90.

[353] Atypical work was defined in both the Arts. 100 and 100a Directives as including: (i) part-
time employment involving shorter working hours than statutory, collectively agreed, or usual
working hours; (ii) temporary employment relationships in the form of: (a) fixed-term contracts,
including seasonal work, concluded directly between the employer and the employee, where the
end of the contract is established by objective conditions such as reaching a specific date,

objective justification. The third Directive, proposed on the basis of Article 100a [new Article 95], contained the more ambitious aim of creating a level playing field of indirect costs for employing atypical workers. As the Commission explained,[354] variations in wage costs relating to atypical employment are often due to factors unrelated to productivity—principally to national laws and collectively agreed regulations. Cost differences 'not justified by the workers' performance over time unit' are mainly related to costs arising from social protection and indirect costs associated with the duration of the contract, such as seniority. For example, costs to employers in some Member States arising from statutory social protection schemes, such as sickness, unemployment, insurance, and pensions, vary according to whether the worker concerned is employed full-time or part-time. As a result some States can produce goods and services with lower labour costs than others for reasons unrelated to productivity, thus placing them at a competitive advantage.[355]

The proposed Article 100a Directive imposed three obligations on the Member States. First, Member States had to ensure that atypical employees were afforded, *vis-à-vis* full-time employees, social protection under statutory and occupational social security schemes underpinned by the same groundwork and the same criteria, taking into account the duration of work and/or pay.[356] Therefore, those employees working more than eight hours a week would be entitled to maternity protection, protection against unfair dismissal, redundancy payments, occupational pensions, sickness benefits, and survivors' benefits. Secondly, Member States had to ensure that part-time workers (but not the other classes of atypical worker) received the same entitlements to annual holidays, dismissal allowances, and seniority allowances as full-time employees, in proportion to the total hours worked.[357] Thirdly, Member States had to ensure that national laws provided a limit on the renewal of temporary employment relationships of twelve months or less,

completing a specific task or the occurrence of a specific event; and (b) temporary employment which covers any relationship between the temporary employment business (a temp agency), which is the employer, and its employees (the temps), where the employees have no contract with the user undertaking where they perform their activities. In other words, the employees have a contract with the temp agency which sends them to work as a temp for a user company needing additional staff.

[354] Proposal for a Council Directive on the Approximation of Laws of the Member States Relating to Certain Employment Relationships with Regard to Distortions of Competition COM(90)228 final [1990] OJ C224/90; amended proposal in COM(90)533 final [1990] OJ C305/90.

[355] In Denmark e.g., complementary pension scheme contributions amounting to about 2.5 per cent of the gross wages of the employees concerned are not paid by employers in respect of employment of less than 10 hours per week. In Ireland, main social security contributions amounting to 15.95 per cent of gross wages are not paid in respect of employment for less than 18 hours a week, 200 *EIRR* 13 (Sept. 1990).

[356] Art. 2.

[357] Art. 3.

so that the total period of employment did not exceed thirty-six months.[358] In addition, an equitable allowance had to be paid in the event of an unjustified break in the employment relationship before the end of the fixed term.[359] Neither this Directive nor the Article 100 Directive was adopted. It took two agreements by the Social Partners to apply the principle of non-discrimination (similar to the Article 100 Directive) to part-time and fixed-term workers and to limit the renewal of fixed-term contracts.[360]

No attempt is made in any of the directives to challenge the need for these new forms of employment. The Commission recognizes that the marked increase in the more flexible forms of work contract is 'not only because management wants to increase flexibility but also because the workers involved quite often prefer alternative work patterns'. Nevertheless, it also recognizes that if these flexible forms of work are to be generally accepted there is a need to ensure that such workers are given broadly equivalent working conditions to standard workers.[361] The three Directives adopted on atypical workers will now be considered.

2.2 Directive 91/383/EEC on Health and Safety

Council Directive 91/383/EEC[362] encourages improvement in the health and safety of atypical workers who are defined as those on fixed-term contracts and those in temporary employment relationships.[363] By applying the principle of equal treatment, the Directive requires atypical workers to be given the same level of health and safety protection as other workers in the user undertaking.[364] The Directive warns that the existence of an atypical employment relationship does not justify different treatment in respect of health and safety, especially as regards access to personal protective equipment.[365] Consequently, as a bare minimum,[366] the Framework Directive 89/391/EEC[367] on health and safety and all the individual daughter directives apply equally to atypical workers.[368]

In addition, all atypical workers must be informed of the risks they face before taking up a particular activity, including any special occupational

---

[358] Art. 4(a).

[359] Art. 4(b).

[360] See now Directive 97/81/EC [1998] OJ L14/9 on part-time work and Directive 99/70/EC on fixed-term work [1999] OJ L175/43. See further Ch. 4 and below nn. 375–390.

[361] COM(94)333, 30.

[362] [1991] OJ L206/19. See also COM(90)228 final.

[363] Art. 1. No reference is made to part-time workers.

[364] Art. 2(1).

[365] Art. 2(2).

[366] Art. 9 provides that the Directive is without prejudice to existing or future national or Community legislation which is more favourable to the health and safety protection of atypical workers.

[367] [1989] OJ L183/1.

[368] Art. 2(3).

qualifications or skills or special medical surveillance required.[369] In the case of temporary employment relationships (temps), the user undertaking must also specify to the temp agency, possibly in a contract of assignment, the occupational qualifications required and the specific features of the job to be filled, and these details must be conveyed by the temp agency to the workers concerned.[370] It is, however, the user undertaking which is responsible for the conditions in which the temp's work is performed. This is without prejudice to any responsibility imposed on the temp agency by national law.[371] This is perhaps the most controversial feature of the Directive. Although it is useful to identify one individual as being responsible for the temp, at times it may be preferable for the employer, usually the temp agency, to take responsibility, for it is the agency which has the ongoing relationship with the temp and it is the agency which can monitor the individual's long-term exposure to, for example, radiation, over a variety of temporary jobs.

Atypical workers must also receive sufficient training appropriate to the job, taking into account the qualifications and experience[372] of the worker, who must be provided with special medical surveillance where the nature of the work demands it.[373] Member States have the option to extend that medical surveillance beyond the end of the employment relationship or to exclude atypical workers from work which is particularly dangerous to their health and safety.[374]

2.3 Directive 97/81/EC on Part-time Work

Given that the other two proposals for Directives on 'certain employment relationships' were blocked in Council (the Article 100 and 100a Directives) the Commission decided to initiate the procedure under Article 3 [new Article 138] of the SPA. In June 1996 the Social Partners (UNICE, ETUC, and CEEP) announced their intention to begin negotiations. On 6 June 1997 they agreed the 'European Framework Agreement on Part-time Work', which, following the procedure under Article 4(2), SPA [new Article 139(2)] was subsequently implemented by Council Directive 97/81/EC[375] and extended to the UK by Council Directive 98/23/EC.[376] The drafting of the Agreement was much

---

[369] Art. 3.

[370] Art. 7.

[371] Art. 8.

[372] Art. 4.

[373] Art. 5. The existence of atypical workers at an undertaking must be notified to workers designated to protect and prevent occupational risks in accordance with Art. 7 of Directive 89/391 (Art. 6).

[374] Art. 5.

[375] [1998] OJ L14/9.

[376] [1998] OJ L131/10. Consolidated legislation [1998] OJ L131/13. On the background to the legislation, see Jeffery, 'Not Really Going to Work? Of the Directive on Part-time Work, "Atypical Work" and Attempts to Regulate It' (1998) 3 *ILJ* 193.

influenced by the 1994 ILO Convention No. 175 establishing minimum standards on part-time work and the supplementary Recommendation 182.[377]

The purpose of the framework agreement is, first, 'to provide for the removal of discrimination against part-time workers and to improve the quality of part-time work'; and secondly, 'to facilitate the development of part-time work on a voluntary basis and to contribute to the flexible organisation of working time in a manner which takes into account the needs of employers and workers'.[378] As the Preamble makes clear, the Directive applies the principle of non-discrimination to employment conditions and not to social security. Thus, an important aspect of the Article 100a proposal has disappeared.

The Directive applies to part-time workers who have an employment contract or employment relationship as defined by the law, collective agreement, or practice in force in each Member State,[379] but not to the self-employed. Further, Member States can, after consultation with the Social Partners in accordance with national law, collective agreements, or practice, and/or the Social Partners at the appropriate level in conformity with national industrial relations practice, for (unspecified) objective reasons, exclude wholly or partly from the terms of this agreement part-time workers who work on a casual basis. Such exclusions should be reviewed periodically to establish whether the objective reasons for making them remain valid. The term 'part-time worker' refers to an employee whose normal hours of work, calculated on a weekly basis or on average over a period of employment of up to one year, are less than the normal hours of work of a comparable full-time worker.[380] Clause 3(2) explains that the term 'comparable full-time worker' means a 'full-time worker in the same establishment having the same type of employment contract or relationship, who is engaged in the same or a similar work/occupation, due regard being given to other considerations which may include seniority, and qualification/skills'. Where there is no comparable full-time worker in the same establishment, the comparison shall be made by reference to the applicable collective agreement or, where there is no applicable collective agreement, in accordance with national law, collective agreements, or practice.

The essence of the Directive can be found in Clause 4(1). This provides that 'in respect of employment conditions, part-time workers shall not be treated in a less favourable manner than comparable full-time workers solely because they work part-time unless different treatment is justified on objective grounds. Where appropriate, the principle of *pro rata temporis* shall apply.'

---

[377] See further ibid., 200, and Murray, 'Social Justice for Women? The ILO's Convention on Part-time Work' (1999) 15 *IJCLLIR* 3.

[378] Clause 1.

[379] Clause 2.

[380] Clause 3.

Clause 4 concludes that 'The modalities of application of this clause shall be defined by the Member States and/or Social Partners, having regard to European legislation, national law, collective agreements and practice'. The principle of non-discrimination is, however, subject to a defence where the difference in treatment is justifiable on (unspecified) objective grounds.[381] Clause 4(4) provides that:

When justified by objective reasons, Member States, after consultation of the Social Partners in accordance, with national law or practice and/or Social Partners may, where appropriate, make access to particular conditions of employment subject to a period of service, time worked or earnings qualification. Qualifications relating to access by part-time workers to particular conditions of employment should be reviewed periodically having regard to the principle of non-discrimination as expressed in clause 4.1.

In addition, Member States and, within their spheres of responsibility, the Social Partners are charged with the responsibility of identifying and, where possible, removing obstacles to part-time work.[382] This particular provision could be read as inviting the removal of protective legislation which, according to deregulatory thinking, may hinder opportunities for part-time work. Although it is too broadly phrased to amount to an instruction to deregulate, it could be prayed in aid by a Member State to justify the exclusion of part-time workers from protective measures.[383] However, the obligation to remove such obstacles is subject to the principle of non-discrimination and to the non-regression provision found in Clause 6(2).

The Directive also considers the question of the movement of workers from full-time to part-time work, and vice versa. A worker's refusal to transfer from the one form of work to the other is not to constitute, of itself, a valid ground for dismissal (clause 5(2)); conversely, the employer must give consideration to requests by workers to transfer between full-time and part-time work and must provide information about opportunities for transfers, but is not required to accede to workers' requests (clause 5(3)).

The Part-time Workers Directive in effect places on a legislative footing the case law of the Court in relation to part-time workers. Under Article 141 [ex Article 119] on equal pay and Directive 76/207 the Court has been willing to find that less favourable treatment of part-time workers is indirectly discriminatory on the ground of sex since the majority of those working part-time are women. In practical terms, it seems that the Part-time Workers Directive will take away two stages from indirect discrimination cases involving part-time workers. First, the Directive removes the obligation to show that

---

[381] See Case 170/84 *Bilka-Kaufhaus v. Weber von Hartz* [1986] ECR 1607. See further Ch. 4.
[382] Clause 5.
[383] See Deakin and Barnard, 'European Community Social Law and Policy: Evolution or Regression' (1999) 4 *IRJ* 355.

a full-time work requirement has an adverse impact on women in a particular pool in order to force the employer to justify: merely discriminating against the part-timer will be unlawful *per se* unless it can be justified. Secondly, it seems that a worker will not have to show that she cannot comply with a full-time work requirement to seek to challenge it: treating full-time and part-time staff differently requires justification of itself. Further, the Directive gives rights to male part-timers who, prior to the Directive, would have had difficulty in arguing that they were disproportionately affected.

2.4 Directive 99/70 Fixed-Term Work

In the Preamble to the Part-time Work Agreement the Social Partners announced their intention to consider the need for similar agreements relating to other forms of flexible work. At much the same time a ground-breaking tripartite collective agreement on flexibility and security was entered into in the Netherlands in 1996. This agreement provided for greater flexibility in temporary work, but at the same time offered new guarantees to the workers. Thus the maximum length of one or more fixed-term contracts was increased to two years. Beyond three years the contract was to be reclassified as an indefinite contract. It also ended the regime of *a priori* authorization of temping agencies and their exclusion from certain sectors. At the same time the agreement also normalized the situation of temps: their temping contract becomes a fixed-term contract which, if extended for more than three years, becomes an indefinite contract. On 23 March 1998 the European Social Partners announced their intention of starting negotiations on fixed-term work. They concluded a framework agreement on 18 March 1999 which the Council put into effect by Directive 99/70 on 28 June 1999.[384] They intend to 'consider the need' for a similar agreement relating to temporary agency work.

The purpose of the 1999 agreement is to 'improve the quality of fixed-term work by ensuring the application of the principle of non-discrimination; and to establish a framework to prevent abuse arising from the use of successive fixed term employment contracts or relationships'.[385] It applies to 'fixed-term workers who have an employment contract or employment relationship as defined in law, collective agreements or practice in each Member State'.[386] Clause 3 provides that 'fixed-term worker' means a person having an employment contract or relationship entered into directly between an employer and a worker where the end of the employment contract or

---

[384] [1999] OJ L175/143. For the original proposal, see COM(99)203 final. The Member States have until 10 July 2001 to comply with the Directive (see Corrigendum [1999] OJ L244/64). For a discussion of the potential impact of the Directive, see the contributions to the special issue of the (1999) 15/2 *IJCLLIR (International Journal of Comparative Labour Law and Industrial Relations)*.

[385] Clause 1.

[386] Clause 2.

relationship is determined by objective conditions such as reaching a specific date, completing a specific task, or the occurrence of a specific event. The Preamble to the agreement makes clear that the 'agreement applies to fixed-term workers with the exception of those placed by a temporary work agency at the disposition of a user enterprise'. In addition, Member States, after consultation with the Social Partners, may provide that this agreement does not apply to:[387]

(a) initial vocational training relationships and apprenticeship schemes;
(b) employment contracts and relationships which have been concluded within the framework of a specific public or publicly-supported training, integration, and vocational retraining programme.

The agreement contains three main rights for fixed-term workers. First, as with the part-time work agreement, the principle of non-discrimination applies. Clause 4 provides that in respect of the (limited) field of employment conditions, fixed-term workers shall not be treated in a less favourable manner than comparable permanent workers solely because they have a fixed-term contract or relationship unless justified on objective grounds. Where appropriate, the principle of *pro rata temporis* applies. The term 'comparable permanent worker' means a worker with an employment contract or relationship of an indefinite duration, in the same establishment, engaged in the same or similar work/occupation, due regard being given to qualifications/skills.[388] Where there is no comparable permanent worker in the same establishment, the comparison must be made by reference to the applicable collective agreement, or where there is no applicable collective agreement, in accordance with national law, collective agreements, or practice. The arrangements for the application of this Clause are to be defined by the Member States after consultation with the Social Partners, having regard to Community law, national law, collective agreements, and practice. Further, Clause 4(4) provides that period of service qualifications relating to particular conditions of employment must be the same for fixed-term workers as for permanent workers except where different length of service qualifications are justified on objective grounds.

The second pillar of protection found in the Directive is prevention of abuse of fixed-term contracts. In some countries such as the UK there are, at present, no limits on the number of occasions on which fixed-term contracts can be renewed. As a result, Clause 5(1) provides that:

Member States, after consultation with social partners in accordance with national law, collective agreements or practice, and/or the social partners, shall, where there are no equivalent legal measures to prevent abuse, introduce in a manner which takes

---

[387] Clause 2(2).
[388] Clause 3(2).

account of the needs of specific sectors and/or categories of workers, one or more of the following measures:

(a) objective reasons justifying the renewal of such contracts or relationships;
(b) the maximum total duration of successive fixed-term employment contracts or relationships;[389]
(c) the number of renewals of such contracts or relationships.'

The third right in the Directive relates to information. Clause 6 requires employers to inform fixed-term workers about vacancies which become available in the undertaking or establishment by, for example, displaying a general announcement at a suitable place in the undertaking, to ensure that fixed-term workers have the same opportunity to secure permanent positions as other workers. Further, as far as possible, employers must facilitate access by fixed-term workers to appropriate training opportunities to enhance their skills, career development, and occupational mobility. Clause 7 requires that fixed-term workers be taken into consideration in calculating the threshold above which workers' representative bodies provided for in national and Community law may be constituted in the undertaking, as required by national provisions.[390] In addition, employers are, as far as possible, to give consideration to the provision of appropriate information to existing workers' representative bodies about fixed-term work in the undertaking.

3. Conclusions

During the 1980s the Commission attempted to circumscribe the use of temporary work.[391] In a proposed Directive of 1982[392] the Commission listed limited grounds on which fixed term and temporary work provided by employment agencies could be used. In the intervening fifteen years attitudes have changed. The EU has identified flexibility in employment as an important part of an EU employment strategy. As we have seen, under the pillar of 'Encouraging Adaptability' the 1998 Employment Guidelines[393] provide that the Social Partners are invited to negotiate, at the appropriate levels, agreements 'to modernise the organisation of work, including flexible working

---

[389] Member States after consultation with the Social Partners and/or the Social Partners, shall, where appropriate, determine under what conditions fixed term employment contracts or relationships: (a) shall be regarded as 'successive'; (b) shall be deemed to be contracts or relationships of an indefinite duration (Clause 5(2)).

[390] The arrangements for the application of Clause 7.1 are to be defined by Member States after consultation with the Social Partners and/or the Social Partners in accordance with national law, collective agreements or practice and having regard to Clause 4.1.

[391] See Murray, 'Normalising Temporary Work' (1999) 28 *ILJ* 269.

[392] [1982] OJ C128/2.

[393] Council Resolution of 15 Dec. 1997 on the 1998 Employment Guidelines [1998] OJ C30/1. See also the Supiot Report, *Transformation of Labour Law in Europe* (CEC, Brussels, June 1998), para. 755.

arrangements, with the aim of making undertakings productive and competitive and achieving the required balance between flexibility and security'. Under the Equal Opportunities Pillar the 1999 Employment Guidelines[394] emphasized the importance of ensuring that 'women are able to benefit positively from flexible forms of work organisation'.

The two agreements attempt to reconcile on the one hand demand side needs for numerical flexibility, allowing the firm to modulate the numbers employed, and on the other the supply side needs for family friendly policies.[395] In respect of the 24 million people working part-time in the EU there may be a degree of coalescence of interests: from the employer's point of view part-time work provides the flexibility necessary to meet changing consumer demands. From the worker's point of view it provides the flexibility to make it easier to combine work with other family responsibilities.[396] Through the principle of non-discrimination the agreement provides a degree of protection for these workers. However, while part-time work may well represent a positive 'choice' for many workers, those engaged under fixed-term contracts would usually choose, given the chance, contracts of indefinite duration,[397] since fixed-term contracts by their very nature are insecure and precarious. It is therefore somewhat surprising that both the part-time work and fixed-term work agreements are drafted in a similar manner and are based on the principle of non-discrimination.

To a limited extent the difference between the two types of work is recognized. The fixed-term work agreement does not contain a clause requiring Member States and the Social Partners to remove obstacles to fixed-term work. Further, the Preamble to the fixed-term work agreement expressly states that 'contracts of an indefinite duration are, and will continue to be, the general form of employment relationship'. Given the differences between the nature of fixed-term and part-time work, Murray argues,[398] the protection that temporary workers need is a full-fledged scheme of portability of entitlements which recognizes all relevant working experience, even if undertaken with different employers and with breaks in between, to qualify for employment rights. This, rather than the principle of non-discrimination, would provide security for fixed-term workers which would balance the flexibility offered by fixed-term contracts to employers.

---

[394] Council Resolution on the 1999 Employment Guidelines.

[395] See, generally, Deakin and Reed, 'Between Social Policy and EMU: the New Employment Title of the EC Treaty', in *Social Law and Policy in an Evolving European Union*, ed. Shaw (Hart, Oxford, 2000, forthcoming).

[396] Green Paper, *Partnership for a New Organisation of Work*, COM(97)127 final, para. 52.

[397] See Delsen, 'Atypical Employment Relations and Government Policy in Europe' (1991) 5 *Labour* 123 and Murray above n. 391.

[398] Murray, above n. 391, 269.

F. WORKING CONDITIONS

Finally, this chapter considers two further measures adopted under the Social Charter Action Programme concerning working conditions: a Directive on the Proof of the Employment Contract 91/533/EEC which is intended to harmonize the diverse national laws concerning the provision of information about working conditions,[399] and an Opinion on an Equitable Wage.

1. Directive 91/533/EEC on Proof of Employment Contract

The Social Charter Action Programme recognized that the great diversity of terms of recruitment and multiplicity of types of employment contract might hinder the mobility of workers. It concluded that Community workers, particularly those covered by atypical contracts, must have their working conditions set out in writing, to ensure greater transparency in the respective rights and obligations of employers and employees throughout the Community market. As Rodière points out, the final text of Directive 91/533/EEC,[400] inspired by British law, was rapidly adopted and is richer, more precise, and more demanding than the Commission's original proposal.[401] In essence, the Directive obliges employers to provide all employees with a document containing information about the essential elements of their contract or employment relationship.

1.1 Material and Personal Scope of the Directive

The Directive applies to every paid employee having a contract *or* an employment relationship defined by the law in force in a Member State and/or governed by the law in force in a Member State.[402] Under German law the contract of employment (*Arbeitsvertrag*) is a contract of service by which the employee undertakes to perform work in accordance with instructions.[403] The contract of employment establishes an employment relationship (*Arbeitsverhältnis*). While the contract of employment consists only of the specific arrangements relating to work that are agreed between the employer and

---

[399] See also e.g. Directive 96/71/EC concerning the posting of workers [1997] OJ L18/1 adopted on the basis of Arts. 57(2) and 66 [new Arts. 47(2) and 55], discussed further in Ch. 3.

[400] Council Directive 91/533/EEC [1991] OJ L288/32 on an employer's obligation to inform employees of the conditions applicable to the contract or employment relationship. See also COM(90)563 final. Although the UK and Ireland were the only countries with pre-existing rules providing that most employess are entitled to a written statement of their terms and conditions, the UK abstained in the final vote.

[401] Rodière, above n. 351.

[402] Art. 1(1). It would appear that this definition does not apply to the self-employed.

[403] Civil Code 611.

employee, the employment relationship encompasses the entire legal relationship between the contracting parties. The rights and obligations concerned may be laid down either by the individual contract or by collective agreement or by law. If the contract of employment is invalid but the employee has already entered into employment there still exists a valid employment relationship with retrospective effect, including all the rights and obligations between employer and employee in the form of a *de facto* employment relationship.[404] Italian law also recognizes a distinction between these two terms. An employment relationship (*rapporto di lavoro*) is the legal relationship in which the worker is obliged to work and the employer to remunerate this work. In addition, ancillary duties (and ancillary rights) exist, including the duty to obey, loyalty, annual holidays. The employment relationship is brought about by the conclusion of a contract of employment (*contratto di lavoro*) between the worker and the employer.[405]

In considering the term 'employment relationship' the Commission, in its memorandum accompanying the draft Directive envisaged both wholly new forms of employment and variations on traditional forms, including distance work, training schemes, work/training contracts, work outside the traditional workplace, job-sharing, and on-call work. However, in order to 'maintain a certain degree of flexibility in employment relationships'[406] Member States can exclude two categories of employees from the Directive's scope. The first relates to those employees who have a contract or employment relationship not exceeding one month and/or with a working week not exceeding eight hours. It has been suggested[407] that such an exclusion may be indirectly discriminatory against women since a higher proportion of women than men work part-time. However, if the Court's reasoning in *Kirshammer*[408] is accepted, such discrimination may be objectively justified to secure flexibility. The second category of employees who may be excluded from the scope of the Directive are those employees of a casual and/or specific nature, provided, in these cases, that the non-application is justified by objective considerations.[409] The second category may apply to casual workers or seasonal workers such as fruit pickers, cleaners, hotel staff, and others on very short-term contracts for occasional days or for a fixed purpose. The burden of proof would rest on the employer to justify the failure to provide the employee with the relevant information.

---

[404] Weiss, *European Employment and Industrial Relations Glossary, Germany* (Sweet & Maxwell, London, 1992), paras. 82 and 85.

[405] Treu, *European Employment and Industrial Relations Glossary* (Sweet & Maxwell, London, 1991), paras. 188 and 561.

[406] Preamble to Directive 91/533/EEC.

[407] See Clark and Hall, 'The Cinderella Directive? Employee Rights to Information about Conditions Applicable to their Contract or Employment Relationship' (1992) 21 *ILJ* 106, 111.

[408] Case C–189/91 *Petra Kirshammer-Hack v. Sidal* [1993] ECR I–6185.

[409] Art. 1(2).

1.2 Employer's Obligations

The employer is obliged to notify the employees of the essential aspects of the contract or employment relationship.[410] This must include at least:[411]

(a) the identity of the parties;
(b) the place of work or, if there is no fixed or main place of work, a statement to that effect and details of the registered place of business or, where appropriate, the domicile of the employer;
(c) the title, grade, nature, or category of work and a brief description of the work;
(d) the date of commencement of the contract; and,
(e) in the case of a temporary contract, its duration;
(f) the amount of paid leave;[412]
(g) the length of the notice periods;
(h) the initial basic amount, the other component elements and the frequency of payment of the employee's remuneration;
(i) the length of the employee's normal working day or working week;
(j) where necessary the collective agreements governing the employee's conditions of work.

As Rodière points out,[413] the obligation to inform the employee of these essential aspects conceals another rule: that all these aspects must have been agreed for the relationship to have been formed correctly. However, the position under English law is different. As Parker LJ said in *Eagland*[414] where no terms exist relating to, for example, holiday pay and sick pay, English law on written statements does not empower or require the tribunal to impose on the parties terms which had not been agreed.[415]

Article 3(1) provides that this information must be given to the employee 'not later than two months[416] after the commencement of employment' in the form of a written contract of employment and/or a letter of engagement and/or one or more other written documents, where one of these documents contains at least all the information required by (a)–(d), (h), and (i). Alternatively, the employer can provide the employee with a written declaration signed by the employer containing the information listed in (a)–(j). The

---

[410] Art. 2(1). 'Contract' will be used to refer to both contracts and employment relationships.
[411] Art. 2(2). The Court ruled in Case C–253/96 *Kampelmann and Others* v. *Landschaftsverband Westfalen-Lippe and Others* [1997] ECR I–6907 that Art. 2(2)(c) is sufficiently precise and unconditional to have direct effect.
[412] This information may be given by reference to the laws, regulations, administrative, or statutory provisions or collective agreements governing those particular points.
[413] See above, n. 401, 328.
[414] *Eagland* v. *British Telecommunications* [1992] IRLR 323.
[415] See further below, nn. 418–419.
[416] If the work comes to an end before the period of two months expires, then the information must be provided by the end of the contract at the latest.

written declaration can either take the place of the written documents or can supplement these documents. Employees going to work abroad for more than a month must be provided with additional information, including details of the duration of the period abroad, the currency to be used for the payment of remuneration, benefits in cash or kind, and details of their repatriation.[417]

Article 5 provides that if the terms and conditions of employment are changed in the course of the contract, the employee must be notified in writing at the earliest opportunity, and not later than one month after the date of entry into force of the change. This rule does not apply if the contractual terms are altered as a result of a change in the laws, regulations, and administrative or statutory provisions or collective agreements.

According to Article 6, the rules laid down by the Directive do not prejudice national rules and practice concerning the form of the contract, proof of the existence and the content of the contract, and any relevant procedural rules. In the UK the written statement of terms is merely evidence of the terms of the contract but does not constitute the contract itself. However, as Browne-Wilkinson J said in *Systems Floors* v. *Daniel*[418] the written particulars represent 'strong prima facie evidence' of the contract terms. The written terms do, however, place a 'heavy burden on the employer to show that the actual terms of the contract are different from those which he has set out in the statutory statement'. This 'heavy burden' does not apply to the employee who wishes to show that the contract terms are different from those in the statement.[419]

The probative value of the written statement of terms was considered by the Court in *Kampelmann*.[420] The Court said that although under Article 6 of the Directive national rules concerning the burden of proof are not to be affected, as such, by the Directive, the employer's obligation to notify an employee of the essential aspects of the contract or employment relationship must be given some meaning. The Court said that objective would not be achieved if the employee were unable in any way to use the information contained in the notification referred to in Article 2(1) as evidence before the national courts, particularly in disputes concerning essential aspects of the contract or employment relationship. The Court therefore ruled that national courts must apply and interpret their national rules on the burden of proof in the light of the purpose of the Directive, giving the notification referred to in Article 2(1) such evidential weight as to allow it to serve as factual proof of the essential aspects of the contract of employment or employment relationship, and enjoying such presumption as to its correctness as would attach, in domestic law, to any similar document drawn up by the employer and

---

[417] Art. 4.
[418] [1982] ICR 54, 58.
[419] *Robertson v. British Gas Corporation* [1983] ICR 351.
[420] Case C–253/96 [1997] ECR I–6907.

communicated to the employee.[421] Since, however, the Directive does not itself lay down any rules of evidence, proof of the essential aspects of the contract or employment relationship cannot depend solely on the employer's notification under Article 2(1). The employer must therefore be allowed to bring any evidence to the contrary, by showing that the information in the notification is either inherently incorrect or has been shown to be so in fact.[422] Thus, the judgment in *Kampelmann* is compatible with the approach adopted by the English courts outlined above. Nevertheless, as Kenner concludes,[423] while the central thrust of *Kampelmann* has fortified Directive 91/533 as a means of transmitting contractual information in a transparent form, it has also helped to reveal its most serious limitation. Article 6 ensures that the employer retains a large measure of control over the contractual bargain. The precise content of the contract remains a matter for the parties. The Directive is concerned with how that information is conveyed. Where the framework of regulation at national level is stripped away and no longer offers a minimum level of protection in the enumerated areas there is no compulsion on the employer to include them in the contractual terms and the Directive offers no protection.

Member States may, of course, introduce rules which are more favourable to employees.[424] They must also ensure that employees who consider themselves wronged by failure to comply with the obligations arising from the Directive can pursue their claims by judicial process.[425] Thus, as usual, remedies are a matter for the Member States. The most effective remedy in the circumstances would be an order that the employer produce a written statement compatible with the provisions of the Directive. The Directive does not require this but clearly envisages it as a possibility: Article 8(2) provides that, with the exception of expatriate employees, employees on temporary contracts and employees not covered by collective agreements, prior to seeking a judicial remedy must notify the employer who has fifteen days to reply.

The Directive was due to be implemented by 30 June 1993, either by the enactment of laws, regulations, or administrative provisions, or by way of agreement between employers' and workers' representatives.[426] Member States must also ensure that the employer, on request, provides those employees already in employment with any of the documents listed in (a)–(i) within two months and, in the case of expatriate employees, any documents laid down by Article 4(1).

---

[421] Para. 33.

[422] Para. 34.

[423] Kenner, 'Statement or Contract—Some reflections on the EC Employee Information (Contract or Employment Relationship) Directive after *Kampelmann*' (1999) 28 *ILJ* 205.

[424] Art. 7.

[425] Art. 8(1).

[426] The Commission sent formal letters of notice to Belgium, France, Germany, Greece, Ireland, Italy, Luxembourg, the Netherlands, Portugal, and the UK for their failure to notify national implementing provisions.

2. Pay

Article 5 of the Social Charter 1989 provides that 'all employment shall be fairly remunerated; to this effect, in accordance with arrangements applying in each country, 'workers shall be assured of an equitable wage, i.e. a wage sufficient to enable them to have a decent standard of living'. The term 'equitable' wage is carefully selected. No reference is made to a 'minimum' wage. Respecting the principle of subsidiarity, the Commission states in its Action Programme that wage setting is a matter for the Member States and the two sides of industry alone. It recognizes that the majority of the Member States, either through their constitutions, legislation, or by means of international agreements to which they are party, guarantee the right of workers to sufficient remuneration to provide them and their families with a decent standard of living. As a result it recognizes that it is not the Community's task to set a decent reference wage. It argued that low pay gives a competitive advantage: minimum wage provision means that richer countries would deprive poorer countries of their competitive advantage.[427] Although the link between low pay and competitiveness has been disputed,[428] and the evidence suggesting that the introduction of a minimum wage would cause large-scale unemployment is not conclusive,[429] the Commission has exercised extreme caution, being prepared only to 'outline certain basic principles on equitable wages' in a non-legally binding opinion.[430] Article 1 of the Opinion defines an equitable wage as meaning 'that all workers should receive a reward for work done which in the context of the society in which they live and work is fair and sufficient to enable them to have a decent standard of living'. Four principles underpin the Commission's approach: the first involves the recognition of the role of investment and training in order to achieve high productivity and high quality employment; the second restates the proposition that the pursuit of equitable wages is to be seen as part of the Community's basic objectives of greater economic and social cohesion and more harmonious development; the third recognizes that discriminatory wage practices should be eliminated; and the fourth recommends that attitudes to traditionally low-paid groups should be reassessed. In the context of discrimination, the commitment to pay an equitable wage to all workers, 'irrespective of gender, disability, race, religion, ethnic origin or nationality', was an important step forward because it goes further than the commitment contained elsewhere

---

[427] House of Lords Evidence 1989, 16.
[428] Deakin and Wilkinson, *The Economics of Employment Rights* (Institute of Employment Rights, London, 1991), esp. at 32–3.
[429] For a summary of the available research see 225 *EIRR*, Oct. 1992, 21.
[430] COM(93)388 final.

in Community law to equal pay without discrimination on the grounds of sex[431] or nationality.[432]

The Commission envisaged a three-pronged plan of action: first, improving transparency of the labour market by better collection and dissemination of comparable statistical information about wage structures in the Community; secondly, ensuring that the right to an equitable wage is respected, in particular by prohibiting discrimination, ensuring fair treatment for workers in all age groups and for home workers, and establishing the mechanisms for negotiated minima and the strengthening of collective bargaining arrangements. Member States should also ensure that 'the measures taken do not force low-paid workers into the informal economy and do not encourage unlawful employment practices'. They should also ensure that wages agreed under the contract of employment are paid in full and that employees are 'correctly paid in respect of periods of leave and sickness'. Thirdly, action should be taken to improve the long-term productivity and earnings potential of the workforce. Finally, the Social Partners are invited to address all the issues raised in the Opinion, in particular to examine what contribution they can make to ensuring the right of every worker to an equitable wage. Indeed, the Social Partners have already considered questions relating to the adaptation of remuneration systems as part of the social dialogue.[433] However, little further action can be expected at Community level on matters relating to pay. Article 137(6) [ex Article 2(6) SPA] provides that the provisions of Article 137 will not apply to pay.

Accompanying the Commission's opinion on an equitable wage is the Council Recommendation 92/441/EEC on common criteria concerning sufficient resources and social assistance in the social protection systems.[434] While the former concentrates on fair remuneration for work performed with particular attention paid to the more vulnerable members of the labour force, the latter concerns guaranteed minimum income from all sources, and contains a far more resounding commitment to respect for human rights. Article 1 contains the important recommendation for Member States to:

recognise the basic right of a person to sufficient resources and social assistance to live in a manner compatible with human dignity as part of a comprehensive and consistent drive to combat social exclusion.

Member States are encouraged to fix the amount of resources considered sufficient to cover essential needs, taking account of living standards and price levels in the Member State concerned, and grant to people whose resources fall below this level the sums necessary to supplement their income, while safeguarding an incentive to seek employment.

---

[431] Art. 141 EC [ex Art. 119 EC]. See further Ch. 4.
[432] Art. 7 (1) of Regulation 1612/68. See further Ch. 3.
[433] Commission, *Adaptation of Remuneration Systems* (EC Commission, Luxembourg, 1993).
[434] COM(91)161 final [1992] OJ L245/46. See further Ch. 5.

G. CONCLUSION

The Commission has recognized that with the completion of the existing Social Action Programme a substantial base of labour standards has been consolidated into European law.[435] However, the Community needs now to consider the direction in which it wishes to go. As a result of the Green Paper on Social Policy, a variety of proposals were put forward for legislative action at Union level, to extend the floor of binding rights and enforce the minimum standards. These proposals include protection against individual dismissal, the prohibition of discrimination against workers who wish to enforce their rights or who refuse to perform unlawful tasks, the right to payment of wages on public holidays and during illness and the right of the worker to be heard in internal company matters which concern him or her personally. In addition the Commission has suggested that there are a number of other areas— for example, home working and teleworking—where new approaches might be developed with a view to possible Union action.[436]

Although these plans might form part of the so-called European social model, as we have seen,[437] this grand vision is not attainable in the medium term, if at all. If European social policy will for the foreseeable future be made in a two-tier polity, the Community will need to occupy a new 'social regulatory space' and not simply try to replicate national attainments at Community level. One way forward would be for the Community to specialize, concentrating its efforts in certain areas rather than trying to spread itself too thinly. As we saw in Chapter 4, the pursuit of sex equality is one area which is clearly identified as the Community's own.[438] This chapter demonstrates the EU's expertise in the field of health and safety. It could also, given its experience with part-time and fixed-term work—explore issues of accommodating employment rights with new forms of work[439] and employment relationships due to downsizing, outsourcing, subcontracting, teleworking, and networking. Its experience in the field of equal opportunities might help to ensure that women—and ultimately ethnic minorities—are not prejudiced by these developments and that those traditionally excluded from the labour market, such as the disabled, can benefit from them. Conversely, there is little justification for the Community moving to occupy a field which is already exhaustively regulated by national law and where the Community could provide little

---

[435] COM(94)333, 31.

[436] Ibid., 32.

[437] See further Ch. 1.

[438] Ibid., 44. See also COM(95)381, A–13, where the Commission says it has been 'a prime mover in changing the status of women in society'.

[439] See the Commission Green Paper, *Partnership for a New Organisation of Work*, COM(97)127, para. 42. See further Bercusson *et al.*, 'A Manifesto for Social Europe' (1997) 3 *ELJ* 189.

added value. Unfair dismissal laws[440] which 'depend on the organic relation-ships in each country between managerial power, workers' participation, judicial supervision and administrative intervention by public authorities' provide one such example.[441]

---

[440] Miguel Rodriguez-Pinero y Bravo-Ferrer, *Individual Dismissals in the Member States of the European Community: The Advantages and Difficulties of Community Action*, Report for the Commission of the EC, DGV, V/5767/93 EN.

[441] Hepple, 'European Rules on Dismissal Law' (1997) 18 *Comparative Labour Law Journal* 204.

7

Employment Rights on the Restructuring of Enterprises

Three important directives, concerning employees' rights on the transfer of undertakings (Directive 77/187), collective redundancies (Directive 75/129), and insolvency (Directive 80/987), were adopted as part of the 1974–6 Social Action Programme. Drafted against the backcloth of restructuring of enterprises, due in part to the gradual realization of the Common Market, the Directives were passed to secure two objectives. On the one hand, they were designed to assist in this process of restructuring, in order to facilitate the emergence of more competitive and efficient undertakings.[1] The Directives therefore did not question the managerial prerogative to restructure and to dismiss employees. On the other hand, the Directives were intended to address the social consequences of these managerial decisions and mitigate their effects. In this respect the Directives were intended both to encourage a greater degree of industrial democracy and to provide an element of social protection.[2]

With the advent of the internal market programme in 1986 the Community focused its attention on the social consequences of *transnational* corporate restructuring, caused by the need of a market economy to establish, on the most appropriate sites, 'businesses capable of implementing the large-scale economic operations which a large market is likely to require'.[3] As a result, the Community revised the Directive on Collective Redundancies to give it a transnational dimension[4] and revised Directive 77/187 on Transfers, by Directive 98/50,[5] in the light of the Court's now extensive jurisprudence.[6]

---

[1] As a result, Art. 100 [new Art. 94], concerning the approximation of measures which directly affect the establishment and functioning of the Common Market, was chosen as the legal base for all three directives.

[2] Blanpain, recalling the discussions held in a group of labour law experts from different Member States, *Labour Law and Industrial Relations of the European Community* (Kluwer, Deventer, 1991), 153.

[3] COM(94)300, 3.

[4] Council Directive 92/56/EEC [1992] OJ L245/3.

[5] [1998] OJ L201/88.

[6] Preambular para. 5 says that 'considerations of legal security and transparency require that the legal concept of transfer be clarified in the light of the case law of the Court', but that 'such clarification does not alter the scope of Directive 77/187 as interpreted by the Court of Justice'.

A. TRANSFERS OF UNDERTAKINGS

1. Introduction

Since 1928 French law has required that if there is a change in the juridical situation of an employer, for example, as a result of succession, sale, or fusion, all contracts of employment existing on the date of the transfer will continue between the new employer and the employees of the enterprise.[7] This provision was introduced at the behest of employers to ensure that, on the date of the transfer, not only were the assets of the business transferred but also the workforce. This provided the new employer with the necessary skills and knowledge to operate the equipment. In other countries, most notably the UK, the employment contract was considered to be a personal contract and therefore could not be transferred to another employer. The new employer could therefore not expect to receive a trained workforce in the event of a transfer, but neither could employees be guaranteed any job security.

Directive 77/187/EEC[8] altered the common law position.[9] The Preamble recognizes that 'economic trends are bringing in their wake, at both national and Community level, changes in the structure of undertakings, through transfers of undertakings'. The Preamble continues that it is 'necessary to provide for the protection of employees in the event of a change of employer, in particular, to ensure that their rights are safeguarded'.[10] The Court has been particularly influenced by this wording,[11] and has, at times, been

[7] L122–12, al 2 *Code du Travail* (previously Art. 23, al 7 puis 8 of Livre 1) from a law of 18 July 1928. See Couturier, *Droit du Travail, I/Les Relations Individuelles de Travail* (PUF, Paris, 1993), 373.

[8] Council Directive 77/187/EEC on the approximation of the laws of the Member States relating to the safeguarding of employees' rights in the event of transfers of undertakings, businesses or parts of businesses [1977] OJ L61/126, as amended by Directive 98/50/EC [1998] OJ L201/88. The Directive will continue to be known as Directive 77/187, although Arts. 1–7 are to be replaced by the provisions of Directive 98/50. This chapter will contain references to the old and new numbers. Directive 98/50 is due to be implemented by 17 July 2001. This Directive cannot be relied on before that date: see Case C–336/95 *Trevejo v. Fondo de Garantía Salarial* [1997] ECR I–2115, although, as we shall see, the Court has drawn inspiration from it. The new numbers introduced by this Directive shall be used throughout, with indications where the substance of the provision has been changed. See Hunt, 'Success at Last? The Amendment of the Acquired Rights Directive' (1999) 24 *ELRev.* 215; Painter and Hardy, 'Acquiring "Revised" Rights? Council Proposal to Revise the Acquired Rights Directive' (1996) 3 *Maastricht Journal of European and Comparative Law* 35.

[9] The Directive was significantly watered down from earlier drafts: Elias, 'The Transfer of Undertakings: A Reluctantly Acquired Right' (1982) 3 *Company Lawyer* 147, 156, described the 'protections afforded to employees are now but a pale shadow of what might once have been anticipated'.

[10] For the interface between the need to transfer ownership and to save jobs in the context of Small and Medium Enterprises, see Commission, *Communication from the Commission on the Transfer of Businesses* [1994] OJ C204/1.

[11] Case 135/83 *Abels v. Bedrijfsvereniging voor de Metaalindustrie en de Electrotechnische Industrie* [1985] ECR 469, para. 6; Case 179/83 *Industrie Bond FNV v. Netherlands* [1985] ECR 511, para. 4; Case 186/83 *Botzen v. Rotterdamse Drbogdok Maatschappij* [1985] ECR 519, para. 6; Case 19/83 *Wendelboe v. L J Music* [1985] ECR 457, para. 8; Case 105/84 *Foreningen af Arbejdsledere i*

prepared to give a purposive interpretation to the Directive to ensure that employees' rights are safeguarded which,[12] as the Court pointed out in *Schmidt*, constitutes the subject matter of the Directive.[13]

The Directive provides three pillars of protection for employees. First, it provides for the automatic transfer of the employment relationship with all of its rights and obligations from the transferor to the transferee in the event of a transfer (see Figure 7. 1).[14] Secondly, it protects workers against dismissal[15] by the transferor (the natural or legal person who, by reason of the transfer, ceases to be the employer in the undertaking) or transferee (the natural or legal person who becomes the employer).[16] This is, however, subject to the

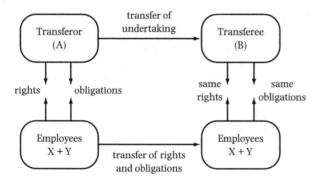

Figure 7.1 Consequences of a Transfer of an Undertaking

Danmark v. Danmols Inventar [1985] ECR 2639, para. 15; Case 24/85 *Spijkers v. Benedik* [1986] ECR 1119, para. 6; Case 237/84 *Commission v. Belgium* [1986] ECR 1247; Case 235/84 *Commission v. Italy* [1986] ECR 2291, para. 2; Case 287/86 *Landsorganisationen i Danmark for Tjenerforbundet i Danmark v. Ny Mølle Kro* [1987] ECR 5465, para. 11; Case 324/86 *Foreningen af Arbejdsledere i Danmark v. Daddy's Dance Hall* [1988] ECR 739, para. 9; Joined Cases 144 and 145/87 *Berg v. Besselsen* [1988] ECR 2559; Case 101/87 *Bork International v. Foreningen af Arbejdsledere i Danmark* [1988] ECR 3057, para. 13; Case C–362/89 *d'Urso v. Ercole Marelli Elettromeccanica Generale* [1991] ECR I–4105; Case C–29/91 *Sophie Redmond Stichting v. Bartol* [1992] ECR I–3189; Joined Cases C–132, 138, and 139/91 *Katsikas v. Konstantinidis and Skreb and Schroll v. PCO Stavereibetrieb Paetz & Co. Nachfolger GmbH* [1992] ECR I–6577, and Case C–209/91 *Watson Rask and Christensen v. ISS Kantineservice A/S* [1992] ECR I–5755; Case C–392/92 *Schmidt v. Spar und Leihkasse* [1994] ECR I–1311, para. 15; Case C–399/96 *Europièces v. Wilfried Sanders and Automotive Industries Holding Company SA* [1998] ECR I–6965, para. 37.

[12] To provide some guidance on this complex case law, the Commission has issued a memorandum on Acquired Rights of Workers in Cases of Transfers of Undertakings (http://europa.eu.int/comm/dg05/soc-dial/labour/memo/memoen.htm). This memo provides guidelines on the application of Directive 77/187 based on the Court's case law. See generally Hunt, 'The Court of Justice as a Policy Actor: the Acquired Rights Directive' (1998) 18 *Legal Studies* 336.

[13] Case C–392/92 [1994] ECR I–1311, para. 16. See also the Title of the Directive and Hardy and Adnett, '"Entrepreneurial Freedom versus Employee Rights": The Acquired Rights Directive and EU Social Policy Post Amsterdam' (1999) 9 *JESP* 127.

[14] Art. 3(1).

[15] Art. 4(1).

[16] Art. 2(1)(a) and (b) [ex Art. 2(a) and (b)].

employer's right to dismiss employees for 'economic, technical or organizational reasons entailing changes in the workforce'. Thirdly, the Directive requires the transferor and the transferee to inform and consult the representatives of the employees affected by the transfer.[17] These three pillars of protection are minimum requirements. Consequently, Member States are free either to apply laws, regulations, or administrative provisions which are more favourable to employees[18] or, following Directive 98/50, to promote or permit more favourable collective agreements or agreements between the Social Partners.

Further, the Directive is intended only as a means of 'partial harmonization',[19] extending the protection guaranteed to workers by the laws of the individual Member States to cover the case where an undertaking is transferred. It is not, according to the Court in *Danmols Inventar*, intended to 'establish a uniform level of protection throughout the Community on the basis of common criteria'.[20] For this reason the Court has been prepared to allow national courts a considerable degree of discretion in applying the Directive.[21] For example, it has permitted national traditions to inform the meaning of key terms, such as the definition of 'employee'.[22] National law also prescribes the consequences of a refusal to be transferred[23] and the sanction in the case of the failure to inform and consult worker representatives and the dismissal of a worker in the event of a transfer. This has the effect of allowing a divergence in the level of employee protection across the Community.

The Directive is not without its critics, who argue that it interferes with free enterprise. They say that it severely restricts contractors in their ability to restructure their workforces, or to devise new, performance-related arrangements, or to introduce innovative ways of doing the work, thus interfering with any anticipated increase in efficiency and possibly dissuading a potential transferee from acquiring the undertaking.[24] Not surprisingly, the Commission makes a different assessment. It says:

Generally speaking, as far as legislation is concerned, the effectiveness in social terms of the protection afforded by the Directive is beyond dispute. The Directive has proved

---

[17] Art. 6.

[18] Art. 7.

[19] Case 105/84 *Danmols Inventar* [1985] ECR 2639, para. 26.

[20] Case 105/84 [1985] ECR 2639, para. 26.

[21] See e.g. Case 24/85 *Spijkers* [1986] ECR 1119, para. 14.

[22] Case 105/84 *Danmols Inventar* [1985] ECR 2639, para. 16, and now Art. 2(2) of Directive 77/187 introduced by Directive 98/50.

[23] Joined Cases C–132, 138 and 139/91 *Katsikas* [1992] ECR I–6577.

[24] Earl Howe, *Hansard*, HL Debs. vol. 533, col. 148, in the context of a discussion on whether the British rules which implement the Directive should be extended to all transfers of work from a local authority direct service organization to an external contractor, discussed in Napier, *CCT, Marketing Testing and Employment Rights, The Effects of TUPE and the Acquired Rights Directive* (Institute of Employment Rights, London, 1993) 12. See also the arguments of the Italian government in Case C–362/89 *d'Urso* [1991] ECR I–4105.

to be an invaluable instrument for the protection of workers in the event of the reorganization of an undertaking, by ensuring peaceful and consensual economic and technological restructuring and providing minimum standards for promoting fair competition in the context of such changes.[25]

2. The Personal Scope of the Directive

The rights laid down by the Directive are conferred, in the English language version, on 'employees' who are defined by Directive 98/50 as 'any person who, in the Member State concerned, is protected as an employee under national employment law'.[26] Thus, while the Court has insisted on a Community definition of the term 'worker' for the purpose of Article 39 [ex Article 48],[27] it has not imposed the same requirement in the context of Directive 77/187[28] because, as we have seen, the Court explained in *Danmols Inventar*[29] that the Directive is only 'intended to achieve partial harmonisation . . . its aim is therefore to ensure, as far as possible, that the contract of employment or the employment relationship[30] continues unchanged with the transferee'.

It is also a matter for national law whether a contract of employment exists.[31] This has now been reflected in new Article 2(2) of Directive 77/187 introduced by Directive 98/50, which provides that the Directive shall be 'without prejudice to national law as regards the definition of the contract of employment or employment relationship'. However, new Article 2(2) continues that Member States shall not exclude contracts of employment or employment relationships from the Directive solely because:

---

[25] Memorandum on the acquired rights of workers, above n. 12.

[26] Art. 2(1)(d). Case C–29/91 *Bartol* [1992] ECR I–3189, para. 18, affirming Case 105/84 *Danmols Inventar* [1985] ECR 2639, para. 27, and Case 237/84 *Commission v. Belgium* [1986] ECR 1247, para. 13. Thus, public service employees are not covered by the Directive in so far as they are not subject to the labour law in force in the Member States. Although the English version of the Directive uses the term 'employee', other language versions use 'worker' and the Court uses the terms interchangeably. See e.g. para. 15 in Case 19/83 *Wendelboe* [1985] ECR 457. See translator's note in Case 105/84 *Danmols Inventar* [1985] ECR 2639.

[27] See e.g. Case 53/81 *Levin* [1982] ECR 1035. This is considered further in Ch. 3.

[28] Advocate General Slynn in Case 105/84 *Danmols Inventar* [1985] ECR 2639 agreed that the Directive did not envisage a Community definition of the term 'worker'. However, any definition would be based on the following—'an employee is one who, in return for remuneration, agrees to work for another and who can, as a matter of law, be directed as to what he does and how he does it, whether pursuant to a contract of employment or an employment relationship': Hepple, 'Community Measures for the Protection of Workers on Dismissal' (1977) 14 *CMLRev.* 489, 494.

[29] Case 105/84 [1985] ECR 2639.

[30] The reference to the 'contract of employment or employment relationship' may embrace the German *Arbeitsvertrag* and *Arbeitsverhältnis* and the Italian *contratto di lavoro* and *rapporto di lavoro* where the employment relationship arises out of the contract of employment, considered further in Ch. 6.

[31] Case 19/83 *Wendelboe* [1985] ECR 457, para. 16.

— of the number of working hours performed or to be performed;
— they are workers employed on a fixed-term contract as defined by Article 1(1) of Directive 91/383;[32]
— they are 'temps' within the meaning of Article 1(2) of Directive 91/383 and the undertaking transferred is or is part of the temp agency which is the employer.

The Directive confers rights only on those employees who, during their working hours, are *wholly* engaged in the part of the business transferred.[33] Advocate General Slynn in *Botzen* suggested that in order to determine whether a worker is 'wholly engaged' in the part of the organization transferred it is necessary to consider whether the worker would have been employed by the owners of that part or by the owners of the remaining part, if that part of the business had been separately owned before the transfer.[34] The only exception made by Advocate General Slynn to the requirement of being 'wholly engaged' is where an employee was required to perform other duties to an extent which could be described as *de minimis*. If, however, a worker is in fact engaged in the activities of the whole business or in several parts then he cannot be regarded for the purpose of the Directive as an employee of the part of the business transferred. Thus, a person who works for several parts of a company, including the part transferred—for example, a sales representative or a personnel officer—could not claim to be transferred to the new employer, for his or her job may be different in scope, a position which is not envisaged by the Directive.

This view was taken by the Court which found that an employment relationship was essentially characterized by the link existing between the employee and the part of the undertaking or business to which he was assigned to carry out his duties.[35] Therefore, the Directive would not apply to those employees who, although not employees in the transferred part of the undertaking, performed certain duties which involved the use of assets assigned to the part transferred or who, while being employed in an administration department of the undertaking which was not transferred, carried out certain duties for the benefit of the part transferred.

The employees must be employed by the transferor undertaking on the date of transfer. The transferee is therefore not liable in respect of obligations concerning holiday pay and compensation to employees who were not employed in the undertaking on the date of transfer.[36] Subsequent employees

---

[32] [1991] OJ L206/19, see further Ch. 6.
[33] This will cover full-time and part-time workers: Advocate General Slynn in Case 186/83 *Botzen* [1985] ECR 519.
[34] Case 186/83 [1985] ECR 519.
[35] Case 186/83 *Botzen* [1985] ECR 519 and Case C–392/92 *Schmidt* [1994] ECR I–1311.
[36] Case 19/83 *Wendelboe* [1985] ECR 457. The Court reached this conclusion after examining the various language versions of the Directive. In the Dutch, French, German, Greek, and Italian versions the phrase 'existing on the date of the transfer' relates unequivocally to the expression

also cannot enjoy the benefits of the Directive;[37] nor can employees who have decided *of their own volition*[38] that they do not wish to continue the employment relationship with the new employer after transfer.[39]

The Directive also confers rights on employees' representatives. These are defined in Article 2(1)(c) as the representatives of the employees provided for by the laws or practice of the Member States.[40] These representatives may be trade unionists or works councillors. The continental European tradition has typically provided for this 'dual channel' approach. In the UK, however, the information and consultation procedures laid down by the Directive originally applied only to recognized trade unions—the British 'single channel' approach through which all worker representation has traditionally been directed. Nevertheless, the Court ruled in enforcement proceedings[41] that the UK had failed to transpose the Directive fully, since it did not provide a mechanism for the designation of workers' representatives where an employer refused to recognize a trade union. The UK government argued that, as a Directive of partial harmonization, the term 'workers' representatives' referred to those representatives provided for by the laws and practices of the Member States. The Court, however, said that the Directive was not simply a *renvoi* to the rules in force in the Member States.[42] Instead, Member States had the task of determining the arrangements for designating the workers' representatives who must be informed and consulted: although the Directive achieved only partial harmonization, the limited character of such harmonization could not deprive the provisions of the Directive of their effectiveness.

As Davies pointed out, for the first time the Court effectively required a Member State to amend collective representation structures to bring them into line with Community norms, raising complex issues about trade union recognition.[43] However, since the Directive did not require 'full harmonisation of national systems for the representation of employees in an undertaking'[44] the UK government had considerable discretion as to how to bring UK law

---

'contract of employment . . . or employment relationship' and the English and Danish versions are capable of bearing the same interpretation. Furthermore, Art. 3(3) distinguishes between 'employees' and 'persons no longer employed'. Art. 3(1) does not make that distinction.

[37] Case 287/86 *Ny Mølle Kro* [1987] ECR 5465, para. 26.

[38] Advocate General Slynn in Case 105/84 *Danmols Inventar* [1985] ECR 2639, however, stressed that it was crucial for the national courts to ensure that any such agreement is 'genuine and not tainted by duress on the part of the transferor or the transferee'.

[39] Case 105/84 *Danmols Inventar* [1985] ECR 2639, para. 26.

[40] Art. 2(1)(c) [ex Art. 2(1)].

[41] Case C–382/92 *Commission v. UK* [1994] ECR I–2435.

[42] The Court cited Case 61/81 *Commission v. UK* [1982] ECR 2601 which held that national legislation making it possible to impede protection unconditionally granted to employees by a directive is contrary to Community law.

[43] Davies, 'A Challenge to Single Channel' (1994) 23 *ILJ* 272.

[44] Case C–382/92 *Commission v. UK* [1994] ECR I–2435, para. 28, and Case C–383/92 *Commission v. UK* [1994] ECR I–2435, para. 25.

into line. The UK's initial response can be found in SI 1995/2587[45] requiring an employer, from 1 March 1996, to consult with 'appropriate representatives' of any 'affected employees'. These 'appropriate representatives' are:

(a) employee representatives elected by them, *or*
(b) if the employees are of a description in respect of which an independent trade union is recognized by the employer, representatives of the trade union.[46]

Originally the employer could choose which group to consult,[47] although concerns about inadequate implementation led the Labour government to provide that only where a recognized trade union does not exist can consultation take place with worker representatives.[48] This new legislation is reinforced by the statutory recognition procedure introduced by the Employment Relations Act 1999, albeit that this procedure was not itself introduced at the behest of the EC. The creation of 'worker representatives' marked the first substantial inroad into the single channel. However, the legislation ensures that consultation with employee representatives is considered very much a secondary channel or, as Davies describes it, 'a modified single channel'.[49]

3. The Material and Territorial Scope of the Directive

According to Article 1(1)(a) [ex Article 1(1)], the Directive applies 'to the transfer of an undertaking, business or part[50] of a business to another employer as a result of a legal transfer or merger'.[51] Because this is the

---

[45] The Collective Redundancies and Transfer of Undertakings (Protection of Employment) (Amendment) Regulations 1995, amending SI 1981/1794 Transfer of Undertakings (Protection of Employment) Regulations 1981, Regulation 10.

[46] Regulation 3(1), Regulation 9(4).

[47] For criticism, see Hall, 'Beyond Recognition? Employee Representation and EU Law' (1996) 25 *ILJ* 15, 17.

[48] Unsuccessful judicial review proceedings were brought in *R v. Secretary of State for Trade and Industry, ex parte Unison* [1996] IRLR 438, challenging the implementation; the DTI issued a consultation paper, *Employees' Information and Consultation Rights on Transfers of Undertakings and Collective Redundancies*, URN 97/988. The new Regulations are found in SI 1999/1925 The Collective Redundancies and Transfer of Undertakings Regulations (Protection of Employment) (Amendment) Regulations 1999. The new Regulations also make some provision for the election of worker representatives.

[49] Davies, above n. 43, 279.

[50] The Court has also refused to define comprehensively what is meant by 'part of' a business. In Case 186/83 *Botzen* [1985] ECR 519, Advocate General Slynn suggested that this was a question of fact but that 'it will usually involve the transfer of a department or a factory or facet of the business' or the sale of 'a fraction or a single unit of business'.

[51] The Directive does not apply to sea-going vessels (Art. 1(3)). The Commission proposed that the rights conferred by the Directive, with the exception of rights relating to consultation, should also apply to seagoing vessels (Art. 1(4) of 94/C274/08) but this was not adopted in the final draft.

threshold requirement—the gateway to the protection conferred by the Directive—this provision has been the subject of considerable litigation, particularly regarding the meaning of the terms 'transfer of an undertaking' and 'legal transfer'. At first it seemed that the transfer of an undertaking had to occur as a direct consequence of a legal transfer or merger. This view was taken by the Court in *Abels*.[52] However, in subsequent cases a distinction seems to have emerged between the terms 'transfer of an undertaking' and 'legal transfer'.[53] Although the Court has not adopted a consistent stance on this point the decision in *Bartol*[54] suggests that the two concepts are distinct and require the answer to two sequential questions: first, is the transfer a legal transfer within the meaning of the Directive (for example, sale, contracting-out, leasing, etc.)?[55] If so, then the second question asks whether there is a transfer of an undertaking on the facts, applying the criteria laid down by the Court in *Spijkers*.[55A] These two questions will be considered in turn below (sections 3.1–3.3).

It is not entirely clear why in some cases the Court has developed a distinction between a legal transfer and a transfer of an undertaking. Much seems to turn on the nature of the questions posed by the national courts. If the national court has asked only whether a transfer of an undertaking has occurred, then the Court will refer the national court to the *Spijkers* tests.[56] If, on the other hand, the national court asks specifically about the concept of a 'legal transfer', then the Court itself will provide assistance as to its meaning.[57] This will often occur when an unusual situation arises—a lease-purchase arrangement, a retransfer, or a withdrawal of subsidy.[58]

Once the Court has established whether the particular transfer may, in principle, constitute a legal transfer it then becomes a matter for the national court to decide whether a transfer has actually occurred on the facts of the case. An example of this approach can be found in *Daddy's Dance Hall*.[59] Here the Court said:

The fact that in such a case the transfer is effected in two stages . . . *does not prevent the Directive from applying* [the question of a legal transfer] provided that the economic unit in question retains its identity; that is so in particular when, as in this case, the business is carried on without interruption by the new lessee with the same staff as

---

[52] Case 135/83 [1985] ECR 469.

[53] De Groot, 'The Council Directive on the Safeguarding of Employees' Rights in the Event of Transfers of Undertakings: An Overview of the Case Law' (1993) 30 *CMLRev*. 331.

[54] Case C–29/91 [1992] ECR I–3189, para. 9.

[55] See below, text attached to nn. 62–98.

[55A] Case 24/85 [1986] ECR 1119 below nn. 103–111.

[56] See e.g. Case 24/85 [1986] ECR 1119 itself.

[57] See e.g. Case 287/86 *Ny Mølle Kro* [1987] ECR 5465.

[58] Joined Cases 144 and 145/87 *Berg* [1988] ECR 2559; Case 287/86 *Ny Mølle Kro* [1987] ECR 5465; and Case C–29/91 *Bartol* [1992] ECR I–3189, respectively.

[59] Case 324/86 [1988] ECR 739.

were employed in the business before the transfer [the *Spijkers criteria*][60] [emphasis added].[61]

By delimiting responsibilities in this way the Court has achieved a workable solution. Having provided a detailed framework in *Spijkers* it has delegated decision-making in this area to the national court. The Court itself will, however, continue to give rulings on the legal situations to which the Directive will, in principle, apply.

3.1 Legal Transfer

The notion of 'legal' transfer relates to the method of the transfer. At first the cases concerned contractual relations—the sale of a business being the paradigm example[62]—and subsequently more complex contractual transactions, including leasing arrangements and contracting out of services (section (*a*) below). However, due to the textual discrepancies between the different language versions of the Directive, initially it was not clear from the earlier cases whether the Directive covered only transfers arising from a contract, as the Dutch, German, French, Greek, Italian, Spanish, and Portuguese versions suggest,[63] or whether it was wide enough to cover other transfers in addition to those resulting from a contract, as the English version ('legal transfer') and the Danish version (*overdragelse*)[64] suggest. The Court has, however, adopted a broad purposive interpretation of the notion of a legal transfer[65] and it is now clear that the Directive applies, in principle, to all transfers resulting not only from a contract but also from an administrative or legislative act (section (*b*) below),[66] or a court decision (section 4 below).[67] As the Court said in *Allen*,[68] it is clear that the Directive is intended to cover 'any legal change in the person of the employer'. Therefore, it can apply to a transfer between two subsidiary companies in the same group, which are distinct legal persons each with

---

[60] Case 24/85 [1986] ECR 1119.

[61] Similarly, see para. 14 of Case 101/87 *Bork* [1988] ECR 3057 and para. 21 of Case C–209/81 *Rask* [1992] ECR I–5755.

[62] See Case 287/86 *Ny Mølle Kro* [1987] ECR 5465, para. 12, discussed below.

[63] *Overdracht krachtens overeen kommst, verträgliche Überträgung, cession conventionnelle, sumbatkij exphoorijsij, cessione contrattuale, cesion contractual, cesio contractual.*

[64] The Danish version includes transfers by way of gift as well as by contract, but not by court order or inheritance.

[65] Case 135/83 *Abels* [1985] ECR 469.

[66] See below, nn. 89–91.

[67] See e.g. Case 135/83 *Abels* [1985] ECR 469 (*surséance van betaling* proceedings); Case C–362/89 *d'Urso* [1991] ECR I–4105 (special administration for large companies in critical difficulties); Case –319/94 *Déthier Equipement* v. *Dassy* [1998] ECR I–1061 (winding up by the Court where the undertaking continues to trade); and Case C–399/96 *Europièces* [1998] ECR I–6965 (voluntary liquidation of a company), discussed further in text accompanying nn. 148–180, below.

[68] Case C–234/98 *Allen* v. *Amalgamated Construction Co. Ltd*, judgment of 2 Dec. 1999, para. 17.

specific employment relationships with their employees.[69] It even made no difference that the companies had the same ownership, management, and premises and were engaged in the same work.

(a) Transfers by Contract

Leasing arrangements

Several cases have concerned leasing arrangements and the rescission of leases (see Figure 7.2). *Ny Mølle Kro*[70] provides a good example. A leased a restaurant to B. When B failed to comply with the terms of the agreement A rescinded the lease and ran the restaurant herself. The Court reasoned that 'employees of an undertaking whose employer changes without any change in ownership are in a situation *comparable to that of employees of an undertaking which is sold* and require equivalent protection'[71] (emphasis added). Consequently, it said that the Directive would apply to this type of situation. Similarly, in *Daddy's Dance Hall*[72] A leased a restaurant to B. A subsequently terminated the lease with effect from 25 February 1983 and agreed that C should take the lease from that date. Once again the Court found that this could constitute a legal transfer and so the Directive applied. Finally, in *Bork*[73] the Court held that the Directive would also apply in the case of a two-stage

Case 324/86 *Daddy's Dance Hall*

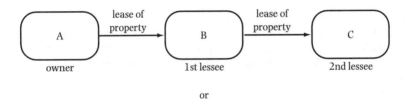

or

Case 287/86 *Ny Mølle Kro*

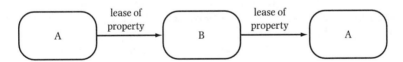

Figure 7.2 Leasing Arrangements

[69] The Court expressly did not apply its case law on competition (Art. 81 [ex Art. 85]), esp. Case C–73/95P *Viho v. Commission* [1996] ECR I–5457.

[70] Case 287/86 [1987] ECR 5465. See also Joined Cases 144 and 145/87 *Berg* [1988] ECR 2559 where the Court found that the transfer of a bar-discotheque by means of a lease-purchase agreement and the restoration of the undertaking to its owner as a result of a judicial decision constituted a legal transfer.

[71] Para. 12.

[72] Case 324/86 [1988] ECR 739.

[73] Case 101/87 [1988] ECR 3057.

transfer. In that case A leased a veneer factory to B. In the autumn of 1981 B gave notice terminating the lease with effect from 22 December 1981 and dismissed the factory's employees with the appropriate period of notice (stage 1). On 30 December 1981 A then sold the factory to C (stage 2), who took on more than half of B's staff. The Court held that the Directive would apply to this situation provided that the undertaking retained its identity (the transfer of undertaking question: see below in section 3.3).[74]

Contracting-out

Contracting-out is the process by which services previously provided in-house, and often ancillary to the main activity of the transferor, are offered out to tender to be performed by contractors.[75] The question is whether the transfer constitutes a legal transfer within the meaning of the Directive, thereby obliging the transferee to employ the transferor's staff on the same terms and conditions as before. The Court first considered this question in *Rask*.[76] Philips agreed with ISS that ISS would assume full responsibility for the running of Philips' canteens. In particular, it would be responsible for menu planning, purchasing and preparation of the food, and for the recruitment and training of staff. In return, Philips agreed to pay ISS a fixed monthly sum and allowed ISS to use Philip's premises, free of charge, including the canteens, equipment, and utilities.

The Court ruled that the Directive 'may apply to a situation in which the owner of an undertaking entrusts to the owner of another undertaking by means of a contract, the responsibility of providing a service for employees, previously operated directly, for a fee and various other benefits the terms of which are determined by the agreement made between them'. Therefore, the Directive applies, in principle, to the contracting out of services both in the private sector, as in *Rask* itself, and, according to *Sánchez Hidalgo*,[77] in the public sector. The Court said in *Rask* that it was irrelevant both that the activity transferred was only an ancillary[78] activity of the transferor undertaking, not necessarily related to its main activities, and that the agreement between the transferor and the transferee related to the provision of services exclusively for the benefit of the transferor. The Court repeated this conclusion in *Schmidt*[79] where it held that the fact that the activity concerned (cleaning) was performed, prior to the transfer, by a single employee was not sufficient to preclude the application of the Directive. The Court explained

---

[74] The Directive would also apply to the transfer from B to A: this can be inferred from para. 19 of Joined Cases 144 and 145/87 *Berg* [1988] ECR 2559.

[75] See More, 'The Acquired Rights Directive: Frustrating or Facilitating Labour Market Flexibility', in *New Legal Dynamics of European Union*, eds. Shaw and More (Clarendon, Oxford, 1995).

[76] Case C–209/91 [1992] ECR I–5755.

[77] Joined Cases C–173 and C–247/96 *Sánchez Hidalgo and Others* [1998] ECR I–8237.

[78] This is confirmed by new Art. 1(b) introduced by Directive 98/50.

[79] Case C–392/92 [1994] ECR I–1311, para. 15.

that the application of the Directive did not depend on the number of employees assigned to the part of the undertaking which was the subject of the transfer.

The cases considered so far concern 'first-round' contracting-out. The leasing cases, such as *Bork*[80] and *Ny Mølle Kro*,[81] suggested that the Directive would also apply, in principle, to second-round contracting-out and contracting back in. This was confirmed by *Süzen*[82] and *Sánchez Hidalgo*,[83] concerning second round contracting-out, and *Hernández Vidal*,[84] which concerned contracting back in (see Figure 7.3). Since the Directive applies to successive transfers, there is no need for any direct contractual relationship between the transferor and transferee;[85] and the transfer may take place in two stages, through the intermediary of a third party, such as the owner, or the person putting up the capital.[86] Therefore, in *Merckx*[87] where a motor vehicle dealership concluded with one undertaking was terminated and a new dealership was awarded to another undertaking pursuing the same activities, the transfer of undertaking was the result of a legal transfer for the purposes of the Directive.

(b) Transfer as a Result of a Legislative or Administrative Decision

As we have seen, for a long time it was assumed that the Directive applied only where, in the context of *contractual relations*,[88] there was a change in the legal or natural person who is responsible for carrying on the business. However, the decision in *Bartol*[89] cast doubt on the orthodoxy. The Dr Sophie Redmond Foundation provided assistance to drug addicts in the Netherlands,

---

[80] Case 101/87 [1988] ECR 3057.

[81] Case 287/86 [1987] ECR 5456.

[82] Case C–13/95 *Ayse Süzen v. Zehnacker Gebäudereinigung GmbH Krankenhausservice* [1997] ECR I–1259, considered further below n. 125.

[83] Joined Cases C–127, C–229/96, and C–74/97 *Hernández Vidal and Others* [1998] ECR I–8179. The Court said that 'the presence of a sufficiently structured and autonomous entity within the undertaking awarded the contract is, in principle, not affected by the circumstance, which occurs quite frequently, that the undertaking is subject to observance of precise obligations imposed on it by the contract-awarding body'. It said that although the influence which the contract-awarding body has on the service provided by the undertaking concerned may be extensive, the service-providing undertaking nevertheless normally retains a certain degree of freedom, albeit reduced, in organizing and performing the service in question, without its task being capable of being interpreted as simply one of making personnel available to the contract-awarding body (para. 27).

[84] Joined Cases C–173 and C–247/96 [1998] ECR I–8237.

[85] Ibid., para. 23. See also Joined Cases C–171 and C–172/94 *Merckx v. Ford Motors Company and Neuhuys* [1996] ECR I–1253. See also Case C–13/95 *Süzen* [1997] ECR I–1259 and Case E-21/95 *Eidesund* [1996] IRLR 684.

[86] Joined Cases C–173 and C–247/96 *Sánchez Hidalgo* [1998] ECR I–8237, para. 23.

[87] Joined Cases C–171 and C–172/94 [1996] ECR I–1253.

[88] Joined Cases 144 and 145/87 *Berg* [1988] ECR 2559 as approved in para. 13 of Case 101/87 *Bork* [1988] ECR 3057.

[89] Case C–29/91 [1992] ECR I–3189.

First Round Contracting Out: *Rask, Schmidt*

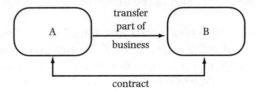

Second Round Contracting Out

1) Contracting out to Third Parties: *Süzen, Sánchez Hidalgo*

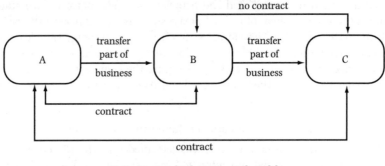

2) Contracting back in: *Hernández Vidal*

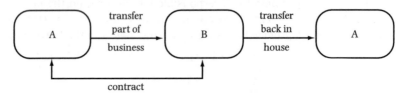

Figure 7.3 First and Second Round Contracting Out and Contracting Back In

with funding provided by grants from the local authority. When the local authority decided to terminate the grant to the Redmond Foundation the staff were dismissed and the Foundation was closed. The local authority then switched the grant to another organization concerned with drug dependency, Sigma, which decided not to take on all of the former Redmond staff. The Court ruled that such a situation was capable of constituting a legal transfer and so the Directive, in principle, applied. Further, the Court said that it was irrelevant that the decision was taken unilaterally by the local authority.

The Court did not expressly rule that the Directive would apply even where the change in employer occurred without any contractual involvement. However, if this is the logical conclusion based on the facts in *Bartol* the Directive will apply to other dispositions, such as gifts, transfers of ownership on the basis of succession, and the case where, as a result of an administrative measure or a judicial decision, one business person succeeds another.[90] However, Advocate General van Gerven in *Bartol* presumed that a contract was an essential prerequisite to a transfer but he insisted that 'contract' be given an extremely broad interpretation, describing the situation where there is an element of consensus between the parties—an interpretation so broad as significantly to undermine the concept of a contract. In order to clarify the situation the Commission proposed that all language versions of the Directive be revised so as to include any transfer effected by contract or by some other disposition or operation of law, judicial decision, or administrative measure.[91] This was not, however, adopted in the final version but does indicate how the Court has nearly defined the requirement of a 'legal transfer' out of being a serious impediment to the applicability of the Directive.

3.2 Mergers

Article 1(1)(a) [ex Article 1(1)] refers to a second mode of transfer of an undertaking as resulting from a merger. The concept of a merger is not defined in Directive 77/187/EEC, although it has always been assumed that the term refers to a merger within the meaning of Articles 3(1) and 4(1) of Council Directive 78/855/EEC.[92] Article 12 of this Directive makes express reference to the fact that employees' rights are to be protected in accordance with Directive 77/187 in the event of a merger. Similarly, Article 1(4) of the proposed tenth Council Directive[93] provides that the rights of employees of companies involved in a cross-border merger will be regulated in accordance with Directive 77/187/EEC. Article 11 of Council Directive 82/891/EEC[94] contains similar wording in the context of a division[95] of a public limited company. However, although the thirty-first recital to Council Regulation

---

[90] This last category was suggested by Advocate General Mancini in Case 287/86 *Ny Mølle Kro* [1987] ECR 5465. He argues that such an interpretation puts emphasis on the non-technical term transfer and regards the case of a legal transfer and merger as examples of this. See further nn. 148–180 below.

[91] Art. 1(1), para. 1, 94/C274/08.

[92] Third Council Directive concerning mergers of public limited companies [1978] OJ L295/36. For an additional discussion of the definition of mergers in the context of taxation, see Art. 2(1)(a) of Council Directive 90/434/EEC [1990] OJ L225/1.

[93] Proposal for a tenth Council directive concerning cross-border mergers of public limited companies COM(84)727 final, 85/C23/08.

[94] [1982] OJ L378/47.

[95] A division, or rather, using the language of the Directive, a 'division by acquisition', is defined in Art. 2(1) to mean the operation whereby, after being wound up without going into liquidation, a company transfers to more than one company all its assets and liabilities in exchange for the allocation to the shareholders of the company being divided of shares in the companies receiving contributions as a result of the division (hereinafter referred to as 'recipient companies') and possibly a cash payment not exceeding 10 per cent of the nominal value of the shares allocated or, where they have no nominal value, of their accounting par value.

4064/89 on the control of concentrations between undertakings[96] expressly states that it does not detract from 'the collective rights of employees as recognized in the undertakings concerned' it provides no machinery for ensuring these rights.

The crucial point is that the merger for the purposes of Directive 77/187/EEC must involve a change of identity of the employer. Consequently, the operation of the Directive is said to be confined to 'assets-mergers', for example by the sale of an undertaking by private contract, provided that the original employer is not retained in some nominal capacity, in which case the Directive does not apply. 'Share mergers' or takeovers by the acquisition of share capital—where one company acquires the control of another without any change in the identity of the employer—are excluded from the scope of the Directive[97] because the rules relating to transfers are intended to deal with legal problems arising when the identity of the *employer* is changed. When a change of share ownership occurs legal theory considers that there is only a change in the identity of the proprietor of the share capital and not a change in the legal identity of the employer, albeit that, in reality, this change may be just as important to an employee as the change in identity of the employer following the transfer of the undertaking as recognized by the Directive. The majority shareholder may have plans for a major restructuring of the enterprise with a significant impact on the employees who are denied protection under the Directive. Earlier drafts of the original Directive 77/187 did extend its provisions to takeovers by acquisition of share capital, but this was omitted from the final draft. This omission may be attributed to the difficult interface between labour law and company law and the corresponding overlap between the responsibilities of DG V and DG XV of the Commission.[98] Nevertheless, it is a serious omission for many employees because in States such as the UK transfer by the sale of share capital is the most common form of transfer.

---

[96] [1989] OJ L395/1, as corrected by corrigendum published in [1990] OJ L257/1, and amended by [1994] OJ C241/57, Decision 95/1 [1995] OJ L1/1 and Regulation 1310/97 [1997] OJ L180/1.

[97] Hepple, above n. 28, 493. However, doubt has been cast on this view by Advocate General van Gerven in Case C–29/91 *Bartol* [1992] ECR I–3189. He argues that since the term merger has not been defined it should be given the usual commercial definition. In other words, it refers to a case where two or more undertakings which were formerly independent of each other unite or amalgamate, giving rise to a merger in the broader sense of the term. He therefore invokes Art. 3(1) of Council Regulation (EEC) 4064/89 as amended ([1989] OJ L395/1), which provides that a merger occurs where: '(a) two or more previously independent undertakings merge, or (b) one or more persons already controlling at least one undertaking, or one or more undertakings acquire, *whether by purchase of securities or assets*, by contract or other means direct or indirect control of the whole or parts of one or more other undertakings' (emphasis added). The Court has yet to rule on this point.

[98] Analogous problems have arisen in the context of the proposals for Societas Europea (Bull. Supp. 4/75 and [1991] OJ C176/1), the fifth Company Law Directive ([1975] OJ C240/75 and [1983] OJ C240/2) and the tenth Directive on Cross Border Mergers (85/C23/08), considered further in Ch. 8.

3.3 A Transfer of an Undertaking

Having established that the legal nature of the transfer falls, in principle, within the scope of the Directive, the next question is whether there is a transfer of the undertaking on the facts. According to the Court in *Ny Mølle Kro*:[99]

The Directive is therefore applicable where, following a legal transfer or a merger, there is a change in the legal or natural person who is responsible for carrying on the business and who by virtue of that fact incurs the obligations of an employer *vis-à-vis* employees of the undertaking, regardless of whether or not the ownership of the undertaking is transferred.[100]

Therefore the Court, when deciding whether a transfer has occurred, has rejected the stance of the property lawyer, refusing to consider questions of ownership,[101] and has favoured instead an employment test, looking to see whether one employer has replaced another.[102] This is clearly illustrated by the leading case of *Spijkers*.[103] Spijkers was employed as an assistant manager of a slaughterhouse by Colaris. By December 1982, when the business activities of Colaris had ceased and no goodwill remained, Benedik Abbatoir purchased the entire slaughterhouse, various rooms and offices, the land, and certain specified goods. From February 1983 Benedik Abbatoir operated the slaughterhouse, having taken on all of Colaris' employees except Spijkers and one other. Spijkers contended that there had been a transfer of an undertaking within the meaning of the Directive.

The Court ruled that the decisive criterion for establishing whether there was a transfer for the purposes of the Directive was whether:

the business in question *retains its identity inasmuch as it is transferred as a going concern*, which may be indicated in particular by the fact that its operation is actually continued or resumed by the new employer with the same or similar activities [emphasis added].[104]

In order to decide whether the business was transferred as a going concern the Court ruled that 'it is necessary to consider all the facts characterising the transaction', including:

---

[99] Case 287/86 [1987] ECR 5465.

[100] Para. 12. For similar wording see para. 13 of Case 101/87 *Bork* [1988] ECR 3057 approving the decision in Joined Cases 144 and 145/87 *Berg* [1988] ECR 2559.

[101] See also Joined Cases 144 and 145/87 *Berg* [1988] ECR 2559 'regardless of whether or not *ownership* is transferred' (emphasis added).

[102] See also Case 101/87 *Bork* [1988] ECR 3057 and Joined Cases 144 and 145/87 *Berg* [1988] ECR 2559.

[103] Case 24/85 [1986] ECR 1119.

[104] Wording from para. 18 of Case 287/86 *Ny Mølle Kro* [1987] ECR 5465 referring to Case 24/85 *Spijkers* [1986] ECR 1119, and Case C–29/91 *Dr Sophie Redmond* v. *Bartol* [1992] ECR I–3189, para. 23. e.g. in Case C–392/92 *Schmidt* [1994] ECR I–1311 the Court noted the similarity in the cleaning work performed before and after transfer.

— the type of undertaking or business;
— whether the business' tangible assets,[105] such as buildings and movable property, and intangible assets[106] were transferred;[107]
— the value of intangible assets at the time of transfer;
— whether the majority of its employees are taken over by the new employer;
— whether its customers are transferred;
— the degree of similarity between the activities carried on before and after the transfer;[108]
— the period, if any, for which those activities were suspended.[109]

No single factor is decisive.[110] Armed with these criteria, it is the task of the national court to decide whether the business retains its identity inasmuch as it has been transferred as a going concern, making an overall assessment of the overall position.[111]

Although the Court has reaffirmed the *Spijkers* criteria in a number of cases,[112] in subsequent judgments it has focused on—and vacillated

---

[105] It is clear that a transfer does *not* occur merely because the assets of a business are disposed of: Case 24/85 *Spijkers* [1986] ECR 1119, para. 12. However, as Advocate General Slynn pointed out, the Courts will identify any sham agreements for the disposal of assets designed to avoid the provisions of the Directive.

[106] Added by Case 101/87 *Bork* [1988] ECR 305. See also Case C–29/91 *Bartol* [1992] ECR I–3189.

[107] Advocate General Slynn in Case 24/85 *Spijkers* [1986] ECR 1119 suggested that the fact that at the date of transfer trading has ceased or had been substantially reduced did not prevent there being a transfer of a business if the wherewithal to carry on the business, such as plant, was available to be transferred. He also suggested that the fact that goodwill or existing contracts had not been transferred was not conclusive against there being a transfer because the transferee may want to take over the activities of the business to supply the transferee's existing customers, or to search out different types of consumer.

[108] Similarly, the fact that the business was carried on in a different way was not conclusive against there being a transfer—new methods, new types of machinery and new customers were relevant factors but they did not prevent there being a transfer *in reality*. The activities before and after the transfer did not need to be the same, for this would undermine the broad scope of the Directive (per Advocate General van Gerven in Case C–29/91 *Bartol* [1992] ECR I–3189).

[109] Advocate General Slynn in Case 24/85 *Spijkers* [1986] ECR 1119 suggested that the transferee might want to spend time reorganizing or renovating the premises before reopening. If the employees were kept on and trading was resumed a national court was entitled to find that there was a transfer. In Case 287/86 *Ny Mølle Kro* [1987] ECR 5465 the undertaking, a restaurant, was regularly closed for part of the year. The transfer occurred when the undertaking was temporarily closed and the staff were absent. The Court decided that while this was a relevant factor it did not preclude the application of the Directive. The seasonal closure of a business did not mean that the undertaking had ceased to be a going concern. It was, however, for the national court to make the relevant factual appraisal. See also Case 101/87 *Bork* [1988] ECR 3057 where the closure coincided with the Christmas and New Year holiday.

[110] Case C–392/92 *Schmidt* [1994] ECR I–1311, para. 16; Case C–13/95 *Süzen* [1997] ECR I–1259, para. 14.

[111] Advocate General Slynn in Case 24/85 *Spijkers* [1986] ECR 1119 argued for a 'realistic and robust view' to be taken of the facts. 'Technical rules are to be avoided and the substance matters more than the form.'

[112] See e.g. Case 287/86 *Ny Mølle Kro* [1987] ECR 5465; Case 101/87 *Bork* [1988] ECR 3057; and Case C–29/91 *Bartol* [1992] ECR I–3189; Case C–13/95 *Süzen* [1997] ECR I–1259; Joined Cases C–173 and 247/96 *Sánchez Hidalgo* [1998] ECR I–8237.

between—two elements of the *Spijkers* formula: 'activity' on the one hand 'retains its identity' (now more usually rephrased) as a 'stable economic entity' on the other. Pre-*Süzen*[113] it tended to look at a primarily labour law test focusing on 'activity': has the new employer taken over the running of the same or similar business activities as its predecessor? Post-*Süzen* the Court emphasized the application of the more commercial test, focusing on whether the business had been transferred as a 'stable economic entity'. The labour law test was more likely to produce the result that there had been a transfer of an undertaking, which is consistent with the often expressed[114] employment protection objectives of the Directive.

The application of the labour law approach can be seen most clearly in *Schmidt*,[115] the case of the contracting out of cleaning services where the work was performed by a single employee. The Court emphasized that the decisive criterion for establishing whether there was a transfer was whether the business in question retained its identity, which was indicated by actual continuation or resumption by the new employer of the same or similar activities (namely, cleaning work performed by the same employee). The Court therefore rejected the arguments made by the German and UK governments that the absence of any transfer of tangible assets precluded the existence of a transfer.

This decision attracted a considerable amount of adverse comment, especially in Germany. As Rubinstein pointed out, the *reductio ad absurdum* of the decision is that the Directive and its national implementing legislation would apply 'when I changed the contractor who cut my lawn. Absurd or not, there is nothing in *Schmidt* which provides a basis for concluding that that is not the law'.[116]

The decision in *Rygaard*[117] might have suggested that the Court was considering a change of approach. Rygaard was employed by A, a firm of carpenters, building C's canteen. A told C that it wanted part of the work to be carried out by company B. B and C agreed that B would perform the contract, that some of A's workers would continue working for B, and that B would take over materials on the building site to complete the contracted work. A then wrote to Rygaard informing him that he would be dismissed on 30 April 1992, explaining that the firm was to be wound up and that the work would be taken over by B. The letter added that from 1 February 1992 Rygaard would be transferred to B. Following *Schmidt*, Rygaard argued that a transfer of an undertaking had

---

[113] Case C–13/95 [1997] ECR I–1259.

[114] See above, n. 11.

[115] Case C–392/92 [1994] ECR I–1311, para. 16.

[116] Rubinstein, 'Editorial' [1994] IRLR 257. See also De Groot, 'The Council Directive on the Safeguarding of Employees' Rights in the Event of Transfers of Undertakings: an Overview of Recent Case Law' (1998) 35 CMLRev. 707, 714.

[117] Case C–48/94 *Ledernes Hovedorganisation, acting for Rygaard v. Dansk Arbejdsgiverforening, acting for Strø Mølle Akustik* [1995] ECR I–2745.

occurred because the works taken over by B were the same as those entrusted to A, and that the duration of the works could not be decisive in determining whether a transfer of an undertaking had taken place. The Court rejected his arguments and focused instead on the commercial test. It said:

the authorities cited above presuppose that the transfer relates to a *stable economic entity* whose activity is not limited to performing one specific works contract. That is not the case of an undertaking which transfers to another undertaking one of its building works with a view to completion of that work. Such a transfer could come within the terms of the Directive only if it included the transfer of a body of assets enabling the activities or certain activities of the transferor undertaking to be carried on in a stable way [emphasis added].

That is not so where the transferor undertaking merely makes available to the new contractor certain workers and material. Thus, in *Allen*[118] the Court distinguished *Rygaard* on its facts, because in *Allen* a complete works project was transferred, probably along with some assets.

Rygaard serves to remind national courts of the relevance of the existence of a body of assets (even though it is not of paramount importance) and the requirement of a stable economic entity confirms that there is a distinction between a one-off project of limited duration and contracting out of a continuing function.[119] However, *Rygaard* did not sound the death knell to the *Schmidt* 'same activity' approach which can still be detected in *Merckx*.[120] M and N were employed as salesmen by Anfo Motors, a Ford dealership in which Ford was the major shareholder. When Anfo Motors ceased its activities, the dealership was transferred to Novorabel which employed fourteen of the sixty-four Anfo Motors employees on the same terms and conditions. Anfo Motors informed its customers of the situation and recommended the services of the new dealer. The Court, having cited the *Spijkers* criteria, considered that the transfer of the dealership was a transfer of an undertaking.[121] It reached this conclusion even though, as in *Schmidt*, there was no transfer of tangible assets, the business was carried on under a different name, from different premises with different facilities, and was situated in a different area of the same conurbation. The Court insisted only that the contract territory remain the same.[122] The fact that a majority of the staff had been dismissed when the transfer occurred did not preclude the application of the Directive. The

---

[118] Case C–234/98, judgment of 2 Dec. 1999, para. 37.

[119] Rubinstein [1996] IRLR 1. This was the view adopted by the British Employment Appeal Tribunal in *BSG Property Services v. Tuck* [1996] IRLR 134. The EAT considered that *Rygaard* did not alter the decision of the Court and that 'the requirement of "the stable economic entity" has to be read in the context of that case [*Rygaard*] and is apt to exclude economic activities under a short-term, one-off contract'. Continuing and recurrent maintenance activities in the present case could constitute a transfer of an undertaking.

[120] Joined Cases C–171 and C–172/94 [1996] ECR I–1253, esp. paras. 18, 23, and 30.

[121] Para. 19.

[122] Para. 21.

dismissals might have taken place for economic, technical, or organizational reasons, in compliance with Article 4(1),[123] but failure to comply with Article 4(1) did not preclude the application of the Directive. The Court concluded that 'where a motor vehicle dealership concluded with one undertaking is terminated and a new dealership is awarded to another undertaking *pursuing the same activities*, the transfer of the undertaking is the result of a legal transfer' (emphasis added).[124]

The question of the transfer of staff and assets was the crucial issue in the important case of *Süzen* which seemed to change the emphasis in the test for a transfer of an undertaking.[125] The national court asked whether the Directive applied to a situation in which a person (A) who had entrusted the cleaning of his premises to a first undertaking (B) terminated his contract with (B) and, for the performance of similar work, entered into a new contract with a second undertaking (C) without any concomitant transfer of tangible or intangible business assets from one undertaking to the other (see Figure 7.3). The Court observed that the aim of the Directive was to ensure continuity of employment relationships within an economic entity, irrespective of any change of ownership. It said that the decisive criterion for establishing the existence of a transfer within the meaning of the Directive was whether the entity in question retained its identity, as indicated, *inter alia*, by the fact that its operation was actually continued or resumed. However, the Court said, following the approach in *Rygaard*, for the Directive to be applicable the transfer had to relate to a stable economic entity whose activity was not limited to performing one specific works contract. The term entity thus referred to an 'organised grouping of persons and assets facilitating the exercise of an economic activity which pursues a specific objective'.[126] Having emphasized the importance of the 'economic entity' test, it then seemed to reject the labour law test accepted in *Schmidt*. It said:

the mere fact that the service provided by the old and the new awardees of a contract is similar does not support the conclusion that an economic entity has been transferred. An entity cannot be reduced to the activity entrusted to it. Its identity also emerged from other factors, such as its workforce, its management staff, the way in which its work is organised, its operating methods or indeed, where appropriate, the operational resources available to it.[127]

The Court said that the mere loss of a service contract to a competitor could not, therefore, by itself indicate the existence of a transfer within the meaning of the Directive. In those circumstances, the service undertaking previously entrusted with the contract (B) did not, on losing a customer, thereby cease

[123] See text attached to nn. 213–229.
[124] Para. 30.
[125] Case C–13/95 [1997] ECR I–1259 (noted Davies (1997) 26 *ILJ* 193).
[126] Para. 13.
[127] Para. 15.

fully to exist, and a business or part of a business belonging to it could not be considered to have been transferred to the new awardee of the contract (C). The Court's approach on this point *de facto* implemented the Commission's proposed definition of 'transfer of an undertaking' as a 'transfer of an economic activity which retains its identity' but the 'transfer only of an activity of an undertaking . . . does not itself constitute a transfer'.[128] This proposal had been successfully blocked by the European Parliament.

In applying the 'economic entity' test the Court considered the activity carried on and the production or operating methods employed in the relevant undertaking. Where, on the one hand, a particular business requires tangible or intangible assets, there is a transfer of an undertaking only where there is a transfer of 'significant tangible or intangible assets'.[129] Where, on the other hand, an economic entity is able, in certain sectors, 'to function without any significant tangible or intangible assets, the maintenance of its identity following the transaction affecting it cannot, logically, depend on the transfer of such assets'.[130] Therefore, the Court said in certain labour-intensive sectors (such as services) a group of workers engaged in a joint activity on a permanent basis may themselves constitute an economic entity. The Court said it must be recognized that such an entity is capable of maintaining its identity after it has been transferred where the new employer (C) does not merely pursue the activity in question 'but also takes over a major part, in terms of their numbers and skills, of the employees specially assigned by his predecessor' (B) to that task. In those circumstances, the new employer takes over a body of assets enabling him to carry on the activities or certain activities of the transferor undertaking on a regular basis. It is for the national court to establish, in the light of this interpretative guidance, whether a transfer has occurred in this case.[131]

Thus, the Court seems to be making a distinction between assets transfers, which constitute a transfer of an undertaking, and non-assets transfers.[132] In the latter case there is only a transfer where the transferee takes over a majority of the transfers staff. As Davies points out, this test has a peculiar 'boot strap' quality to it. Since an advisor may need to know whether the Directive applies in order to determine whether the transferee ought to take the employees of the transferor into its employ, it is unhelpful to try to answer that question by the application of the test whether the transferee has in fact

---

[128] COM(97)60 final [1997] OJ C124J.

[129] Para. 23.

[130] Para. 18.

[131] Para. 21. See also Case E–3/96 *Tor Angeir Ask and Others* v. *ABD Offshore Technology AS and Aker Offshore Partner AS* [1997] OJ C136/7.

[132] The Commission suggested that in determining whether the entity has maintained its identity, situations can be categorized as three types: where the means of production are transferred, where non-material assets, such as knowledge and expertise, are transferred, and situations where no knowledge or expertise is required to do the job.

done that very thing (though the test may be workable where the question is confined to ascertaining the terms to which the transferred employees are entitled).[133] This test also enables transferees to avoid their obligations under the Directive: if few assets are transferred the transferee could avoid the Directive by refusing to employ the 'major part' of the workforce. This test renders the Directive in many cases a 'voluntary obligation', which is contrary to the spirit of a directive designed to give employment protection.

It is not at all clear whether the decision in *Süzen* is confined to second-round contracting out or could apply equally to first-round contracting out.[134] It is also not clear whether the *Süzen* 'economic entity' focus has effectively replaced the 'same activity' test in *Schmidt*.[135] There are indications that this may be the case. First, the emphasis on 'economic entity' has now been picked up in the definition of 'transfer' introduced by Directive 98/50. It defines transfer as 'the transfer of an economic entity which retains its identity, meaning an organised grouping of resources which has the objective of pursuing an economic activity whether or not that activity is central or ancillary'.[136] Secondly, two judgments delivered on the same day—*Hernández Vidal*[137] and *Sánchez Hidalgo*[138]—have also re-emphasized the 'economic entity' test.[139] *Hernández Vidal* concerned contracting back in (see Figure 7.3) where A, having employed B to clean its premises, decided to end the contract and carry out the work itself. The Court made it clear that in order for the Directive to be applicable it must relate to a 'stable economic entity', as defined in *Süzen*. The Court added that while such an entity must be sufficiently structured and autonomous, it need not necessarily have significant assets, tangible or intangible. Indeed, in certain sectors, such as cleaning, these assets are often reduced to their most basic and the activity is essentially based on manpower. So, the Court continued, 'an organised grouping of wage earners who are specifically and permanently assigned to a common task may, in the absence of other factors of production, amount to an economic entity'.[140]

The questions referred in *Sánchez Hidalgo* concerned public bodies (A) which had contracted out a home-help service and a surveillance contract to two private undertakings (B) and decided, on expiry of the contracts, not to

---

[133] Davies, above, n. 125, 196.
[134] See Davies, above, n. 125, 194–5, and *Süzen*, paras. 8 and 9.
[135] The English Court of Appeal in *Betts v. Brintel Helicopters* [1997] IRLR 361 recognized that *Süzen* represented 'a shift of emphasis'. However, the Court of Appeal in *ECM v. Cox* [1999] IRLR 559 said that *Süzen* did not overrule *Schmidt* and *Spijkers* and required the Court to make an appraisal based on the *Spijkers*' criteria. Mummery LJ said that the importance of *Süzen* had been 'overstated'.
[136] Art. 1(b).
[137] Joined Cases C–127, C–229/96, and C–74/97 [1998] ECR I–8179.
[138] Joined Cases C–173 and C–247/96 [1998] ECR I–8237. See also now Case C–234/98 *Allen*, judgment of 2 Dec. 1999, para. 29.
[139] Para. 30 in both judgments.
[140] Para. 27.

renew them with B but to conclude contracts with other undertakings (C) (see Figure 7.3). The Court concluded that the Directive applied to the facts of this case provided that 'the operation is accompanied by the transfer of an "economic entity" between the two undertakings'. The reference to transfer of an 'economic entity' rather than 'a major part of the workforce' perhaps suggests a change in emphasis from *Süzen*, although the heavy reliance on *Süzen* in the judgments means that it is difficult to predict this with confidence.

Advocate General Damasco Ruiz-Jarbo Colomer provided a helpful summary of this labyrinthine case law in *Allen*.[141] He said:

the criteria identified hitherto by the Court for determining whether there has been a transfer within the meaning of Article 1(1) of Directive 77/187 are the following: there must be an economic entity, defined as an organized grouping of persons and assets for the exercise of an economic activity which pursues a specific objective; that entity must be organised in a stable manner and not limited to performing one specific works contract; there must be a change, in terms of contractual relations, in the legal or natural person who is responsible for carrying on the business and who incurs the obligations of an employer towards employees of the entity; the economic entity must retain its identity, which is marked both by the continuation by the new employer of the same activities and by the continuity of its workforce, its management staff, the way in which its work is organized, its operating methods or the operational resources available to it.

With the exception of *Bartol*, the cases considered so far have all concerned the private sector. The Court has, however, developed some different rules in respect of the public sector. In *Hencke*[142] the Court ruled that the reorganization of structures of the public administration or the transfer of administrative functions between public administrative authorities did not constitute a 'transfer of an undertaking' within the meaning of the Directive. In an extremely terse judgment, the Court said that the purpose of a number of municipalities grouping together was to improve the performance of those municipalities' administrative tasks. The transfer carried out between the municipality and the administrative collectivity related only to activities involving 'the exercise of public authority'. The Court said that even if it was assumed that those activities had aspects of an economic nature, they could only be ancillary.

In *Hencke* the Court, therefore, focused on the fact that the authority was not a business exercising an economic activity, as required by the EC Treaty, but was involved with public administration exercising public law powers. The Court, however, made no reference to its earlier decision in *Bartol*[143] where the Court considered that the term 'legal transfer' covered the situation

---

[141] Case C–234/98, judgment of 2 Dec. 1999.
[142] Case C–298/94 *Annette Henke v. Gemeinde Schierke and Verwaltungsgemeinschaft* [1996] ECR I–4989.
[143] Case C–29/91 [1992] ECR I–1311.

where a public authority decided to terminate the subsidy paid to one legal person, as a result of which the activities of that person were fully and definitively terminated, and to transfer it to another legal person with a similar aim. It also did not refer to *Commission v. UK*[144] where the Court found that the 'non-commercial venture' exclusion from the UK Regulations implementing the Directive breached the Directive. Nevertheless, the Council of Ministers has followed the Court's approach. New Article 1(1)(c) introduced by Directive 98/50 now provides that 'An administrative reorganization of public administrative authorities, or the transfer of administrative functions between public administrative authorities, is not a transfer within the meaning of this Directive'.[145] However, as the Court pointed out in *Sánchez Hidalgo*,[146] where a public body contracts out a service which does not involve the exercise of public authority, the Directive will still apply.

3.4 Territorial Scope

Article 1(2) provides that the Directive applies 'where and in so far as the undertaking, business or part of [the undertaking or] business to be transferred is situated in the territorial scope of the Treaty'.[147] It is the physical location of the business and not the location of the ownership that is the determinative feature. This may lead to a significant gap in the protection of workers within the Community since, if the business is transferred from outside the Community to a Community undertaking, workers in the acquiring Community enterprise may be adversely affected by the transfer. The Directive also does not apply to transfers of businesses located outside the Community but which belong to a company whose head office is in the territory of a Member State.

4. Insolvency and Measures Falling Short of a Declaration of Insolvency

Transfers on insolvency are considered to be a special type of transfer to which the provisions of the Directive do not apply. Originally, Directive 77/187/EEC did not expressly exclude transfers on insolvency from its scope, but the Court said in *Abels*[148] that the Directive did not apply to transfers of

[144] Case C–382/92 [1994] ECR I–2435.
[145] This prompts De Groot, above, n. 116, 722, to observe that there exists a 'presumption of non-applicability of the Directive' as far as public administrative authorities are concerned.
[146] Joined Cases C–173 and C–247/96 [1998] ECR I–8237, para. 24.
[147] This includes a Member State of the EEA (Norway, Iceland, and Liechtenstein).
[148] The Court repeated its decision in Case 135/83 [1985] ECR 469 in three cases decided on the same day as *Abels*: Case 186/83 *Botzen* [1985] ECR 519, Case 19/83 *Wendelboe* [1985] ECR 457, and Case 179/83 *Industrie Bond FNV* [1985] ECR 511.

undertakings 'taking place in the context of insolvency proceedings instituted with a view to the liquidation of assets of the transferor under the supervision of the competent judicial authority'.[149] According to the Court, the rationale behind this decision related to the special nature of the laws on insolvency[150] which are designed to weigh up the various interests involved, in particular those of the creditors. Consequently, insolvency rules derogate, at least in part, from the provisions of social law, both at national and Community level.[151] Therefore, the Court concluded, an express provision in Directive 77/ 187 would be required before it applied to an insolvency situation. In *Abels* the plaintiff was employed by Thole when, by successive decisions of the District Court, Thole was granted *surséance van betaling* (judicial leave to suspend payment of debts) in 1981 and then went into liquidation in 1982. During the liquidation proceedings Thole's business was transferred to TPP which continued to operate the undertaking and took over most of the workforce, including the plaintiff. The plaintiff, however, complained that he had not received his wages or various other payments as required by the Directive.

It was argued by the Danish government that the transfer rules should apply to employees whose employer has become insolvent because this was the time when the workers were in most need of protection. By contrast, the Dutch government and the Commission argued that if the Directive applied this might dissuade a potential transferee from acquiring an undertaking on conditions acceptable to the creditors, who might then prefer instead to sell the assets of the undertaking separately, thereby avoiding the scope of the Directive.[152] This, they argued, would entail the loss of all the jobs in the enterprise which would detract from the utility of the Directive. As the Commission has subsequently recognized, the underlying problem here is the conflict between the acquired rights of employees and those of other creditors upon insolvency. If the employees of the insolvent transferor undertaking and all their rights and entitlements are transferred to the new solvent transferee, the effect is to treat those employees more favourably than other creditors of the insolvent undertaking. The creditors will assert that the transferee will pay less for the transferred undertaking, as a result of having to take over all liabilities to the new employees, and hence the pool of assets

---

[149] This was deemed important by Advocate General van Gerven in Case C–362/89 *d'Urso* [1991] ECR I–4105. He said it was insufficient that the preconditions to insolvency have been fulfilled.

[150] In the Community context, see Council Directive 80/987/EEC [1980] OJ L283/23 considered in section C below. The Council did not take the opportunity of the enactment of Directive 80/987 to apply Directive 77/187/EEC to an insolvency situation.

[151] In the Community context, see Art. 1(2)(d) of Directive 75/129/EEC [1995] OJ L48/29 on collective redundancies which expressly excludes from its scope workers affected by termination of an establishment's activities 'where that is a result of a judicial decision'.

[152] Assets only sales fall outside the scope of the Directive: see Case 24/85 *Spijkers* [1986] ECR 1119.

against which the creditors of the insolvent undertaking can claim will be reduced.[153]

The Court, while acknowledging that 'considerable uncertainty exists regarding the impact on the labour market of transfer of undertakings in the case of employer's insolvency', seemed to accept the Dutch government's view. It therefore decided that the interests of employees would be better served if the Directive did *not* apply 'otherwise a serious risk of general deterioration in living and working conditions of workers, contrary to the social objectives of the Treaty', could not be ruled out.

The Court has, however, refused to extend the scope of its ruling in *Abels*. In *Bartol*,[154] for example, the Court refused to countenance arguments that the Directive did not apply to situations comparable with insolvency, such as the closure of a foundation due to the withdrawal of its subsidy by the local authority. In *Merckx*,[155] the Court ruled that the application of the Directive could not be excluded merely because the transferor discontinued its activities when the transfer was made and was then put into liquidation. It added that if the business of that undertaking was carried on by another undertaking this tended to confirm that there had been a transfer for the purposes of the Directive. Even in *Abels*[156] the Court imposed two limits to its own ruling. First, it said that Member States could, if they wished, apply the provisions of the Directive to a transfer arising in the event of insolvency.[157] Secondly, it said that the Directive did apply to situations where an undertaking was transferred to another employer in the course of a procedure, such as the Dutch '*surséance van betaling*'.[158] This procedure allows a company, with the leave of the court, to suspend payment of its debts with a view to reaching a settlement. Such a settlement is intended to ensure that the undertaking is able to continue operating in the future.

This raises the question how to distinguish between insolvency proceedings, to which the Directive will not apply, and pre-insolvency proceedings, to which the Directive will apply. Advocate General van Gerven in *d'Urso*[159] offered some guidance. First, he distinguished between the two proceedings by reference to their purpose. He suggested that an inherent characteristic of *surséance* proceedings is that they are intended to resolve temporary cash-flow problems and not to liquidate the assets of the debtor—in other words, to

[153] Explanatory memorandum, COM(94)300, para. 23.
[154] Case C–29/91 [1992] ECR I–3189.
[155] Joined Cases C–171 and C–172/94 [1996] ECR I–1253.
[156] Case 135/83 [1985] ECR 469.
[157] See Art. 7 of Directive 77/187/EEC. This has been done by Spain, France, Germany, Denmark, and the UK.
[158] This point was confirmed in three cases decided on the same day as Case 135/83 *Abels* [1985] ECR 469: Case 186/83 *Botzen* [1985] ECR 519, Case 19/83 *Wendelboe* [1985] ECR 457, Case 179/83 *Industrie Bond FNV* [1985] ECR 511, and Case 105/84 *Danmols Inventar* [1985] ECR 2639.
[159] Case C–362/89 [1991] ECR I–4105.

prevent insolvency. Insolvency proceedings, by contrast, are fundamentally different: their purpose is the liquidation of property by selling the assets with a view to off-setting the liabilities. Secondly, Advocate General van Gerven distinguished between the two proceedings, by reference to judicial control. In the case of *surséance* proceedings the supervision of the Court over the commencement and the course of the proceedings is much more limited than in the case of insolvency. The judge's control extends only to ensuring that the debtor respects the obligations he has entered into. On the other hand, in insolvency the judge has more extensive control. This may be accompanied by the creation of an administration or a trust with special powers to determine the value of the undertaking, to sell off the assets and to meet the liabilities, which in turn is accompanied by the creation of a compulsory trust of the affairs of the debtor, who is deprived of any power to manage or to dispose of the assets. In *surséance* proceedings, there will be one or more designated receivers or administrators who will exercise control over the debtor, to whom they must give assistance or authorization before the debtor can carry out certain acts, but without ever depriving the debtor of the rights to manage or dispose of this property.

In *Abels*[160] the Court also emphasized the importance of judicial supervision in the insolvency or liquidation proceedings[161] as the distinguishing criteria between insolvency and pre-insolvency proceedings. However, in *d'Urso*[162] it recognized that the nature of the supervision (e.g. judicial or administrative) was not conclusive, the only determining criterion being the objective to be attained by the proceedings. If the procedure was akin to insolvency, involving the liquidation of the debtor's assets in order to pay off the collective creditors,[163] then the transfers effected in this context were excluded from the scope of the Directive. If, on the other hand, the procedure was designed to save those parts of the business which were healthy, allowing the business to continue or resume trading, the provisions of the Directive did apply.

In *d'Urso* the applicants were employed by EMG which was put into 'special administration' in May 1981. In September 1985 the functional part of EMG was transferred to a specially formed company. Two-thirds of the employees were transferred but the others, including the applicants, remained in employment with the transferor, EMG, although their contracts were suspended and they received compensation instead from the wages guarantee fund (*cassa integrazione guadagni straordinaria*). The applicants sought a declaration that their contracts had been transferred to the new company. The Court ruled that the Directive did not apply to transfers of an undertaking

---

[160] Case 135/83 [1985] ECR 469.

[161] These terms are used interchangeably by the Court, see e.g. paras. 23 and 28. See also Case C–362/89 *d'Urso* [1991] ECR I–4105, para. 23.

[162] Ibid.

[163] Ibid., para. 31.

made as part of a creditor's settlement of the kind provided for in Italian legislation on 'compulsory administrative liquidation as referred to in the law of 3 April 1979 on special administration for large companies in difficulty'. However, the Directive did apply when it had been decided that the undertaking was to continue trading.[164]

The Court reaffirmed its *d'Urso* decision in *Spano*[165] where it held that the Directive applied to the transfer of an undertaking declared to be in critical difficulties pursuant to Italian Law No. 675 of 12 August 1977. It pointed out that the purpose of such a declaration was to enable the undertaking to retrieve its economic and financial situation and above all to preserve jobs, that the procedure in question was designed to promote the continuation of its business with a view to its subsequent recovery and that, by contrast with insolvency proceedings, it did not involve any judicial supervision or any measure whereby the assets of the undertaking were put under administration and did not provide for any suspension of payments.

The Court was obliged to give more detailed guidance about the nature of the distinction between the two types of insolvency proceedings in *Déthier*.[166] In May 1991 the Tribunal de Commerce made an order putting Sovam into liquidation and appointed a liquidator. Three weeks later the liquidator dismissed Dassy and shortly afterwards transferred the assets of Sovam to Déthier under an agreement approved by the Tribunal de Commerce. The question was whether this winding up procedure constituted an insolvency procedure. In deciding whether the Directive applied the Court said that the determining factor to be taken into consideration was the *purpose* of the procedure in question, but that account also had to be taken of the *form* of the procedure, in particular, in so far as it means that the undertaking continues or ceases trading, and also of the Directive's objectives. On the facts of the case, the Court said that it was apparent that although the objective of the Belgian procedure could sometimes be similar to those of insolvency proceedings, this was not necessarily the case, since liquidation proceedings could be used whenever it was wished to bring a company's activities to an end and whatever the reasons for that decision.[167] Since the criterion relating to the *purpose* of the procedure for winding up was not conclusive, the Court examined the procedure in detail. It pointed out that the liquidator, although appointed by the court, was an organ of the company who sold the assets under the supervision of the general meeting; that there was no special procedure for establishing liabilities under the supervision of the court; and that a creditor could enforce his debt against the company and obtain judgment against it. By

---

[164] It has been suggested that the Court in this case confused *amministrazione controllata* (the Italian equivalent of the Dutch *surséance van betaling*) and *amministrazione straordinaria* (the Italian equivalent of liquidation). *Amministrazione straordinaria* was at issue here.

[165] Case C–472/93 *Spano and Others* v. *Fiat Geotech and Fiat Hitachi* [1995] ECR I–4321.

[166] Case C–319/94 [1998] ECR I–1061.

[167] Para. 27.

contrast, in the case of an insolvency, the administrator was a third party *vis-à-vis* the company and realized the assets under the supervision of the court; that the liabilities of the company were established in accordance with a special procedure and individual enforcement actions were prohibited. Therefore, the Court concluded that where an undertaking continues to trade while it is being wound up by the court this is not an insolvency procedure.

In *Europièces*[168] the Court applied its ruling in *Déthier* to the case of voluntary liquidation which, it noted, is 'essentially similar to winding up by the court, save for the fact that it falls to the shareholders in general meeting, and not to the court, to take the decision to wind up the company, appoint the liquidators and determine their powers'.[169] Since, at least in some procedural respects, voluntary liquidation has even less in common with insolvency than winding up by the court, the Directive applied.

The distinction drawn by the Court between insolvency and pre-insolvency proceedings may be based on a false premise. Although it has acknowledged that the two types of proceedings share many common characteristics,[170] the Court has failed to recognize that the reason many companies go into pre-insolvent procedures is that there is a greater chance of selling off at least part of the company's business as a going concern, thereby securing at least some of the workers' jobs. This is precisely the situation which justified excluding insolvent companies from the operation of the Directive.[171] Nevertheless, the distinction between liquidation of insolvent companies and other ways of dealing with them has now been incorporated in the new Directive 98/50/EEC.[172] Article 4a(1) provides that unless Member States provide otherwise, Articles 3 and 4 of the Directive (concerning transfer of the contract of employment and dismissals) do not apply to a transfer where the transferor is 'the subject of bankruptcy proceedings or any analogous insolvency proceedings which have been instituted with a view to the liquidation of the assets of the transferor and are under the supervision of a competent public authority'.[173] If Member States decide that Articles 3 and 4 do apply to a transfer during insolvency proceedings which have been opened in relation to a transferor (whether or not those proceedings have been instituted with a

---

[168] Case C–399/96 [1998] ECR I–6965.

[169] Only where a majority of the shareholders cannot be assembled must the company apply to the court for a declaration putting it into liquidation. The court then designates the liquidators in accordance with the company's articles of association or pursuant to the decision of the shareholders in general meeting, unless it is clear that disagreement between the shareholders will prevent them from taking a decision in general meeting, in which case the court itself appoints a liquidator.

[170] See e.g. Case C–362/89 *d'Urso* [1991] ECR I–4105, para. 24.

[171] Davies, 'Acquired Rights, Creditors' Rights, Freedom of Contract, and Industrial Democracy' (1989) 9 *Yearbook of European Law* 21, 47.

[172] [1998] OJ L201/88.

[173] Art. 4a(1). The supervision of a competent public authority may be an insolvency practitioner authorized by a competent public authority.

view to the liquidation of the assets of the transferor), a Member State may provide that:[174]

— the transferor's debts arising from any contracts of employment or employment relationships and payable before the transfer or before the opening of the insolvency proceedings are not transferred to the transferee, provided that the proceedings give rise to protection at least equivalent to that provided for by Council Directive 80/987/EEC on the protection of employees in the event of the insolvency of their employer; and/or

— the transferee or transferor on the one hand, and the representatives of the employees on the other hand may agree alterations, in so far as current law and practice permit,[175] to the employees' terms and conditions of employment designed to safeguard employment opportunities by ensuring the survival of the economic entity being transferred.[176] Further, a Member State may apply this provision to *any* transfers where the transferor is in a situation of 'serious economic crisis'[177] and open to judicial supervision, on condition that such provisions already exist in national law by 17 July 1998.[178] Therefore worker representatives can agree collectively to the modification of terms and conditions of employment. Thus, Directive 98/50, like the Working Time Directive 93/104, permits derogations from the legislative minima *in pejus*.[179] In addition, new Article 5(1) paragraph 3 provides that where the transferor is the subject of bankruptcy proceedings or analogous proceedings, as described in Article 4a(1), Member States 'may take the necessary measures to ensure that the transferred employees are properly represented until the new election or designation of representatives of the employees'. These new provisions are striking for their 'pick-and-mix' quality.[180] Member States are given a great deal of discretion which provisions to apply.

Finally, Article 4a(4) requires Member States to take appropriate measures with a view to preventing misuse of insolvency proceedings in such a way as to deprive employees of their rights in the event of a transfer.

[174] Art. 4a(2).
[175] Thus, the representatives cannot agree to anything which the individual employee could not have negotiated him- or herself.
[176] Cf. Case C–362/89 *d'Urso* [1991] ECR I–4105. As Davies notes in 'Amendments to the Aquired Rights Directive' (1998) 27 *ILJ* 365, 369, the Directive 'strikes a blow for collective contractual freedom'.
[177] A situation of 'serious economic crisis' is to be defined by public law and declared by a competent public authority. In Italy an enterprise in crisis can go into *amministrazione controllata*, a procedure similar to the Dutch *surséance van betaling*, which allows the trade unions, as a derogation from Art. 2112 of the Civil Code, to agree to the reduction in protection for those workers transferred to the solvent transferee.
[178] Art. 4a(3). The Commission must report on the effects of this provision before 17 July 2003.
[179] Barnard, 'The Working Time Regulations 1998' (1999) 28 *ILJ* 61.
[180] Hunt described these provisions as having an 'open-textured, framework nature' (above n. 8, 228).

5. Safeguarding Individual Employees' Rights

If the transfer is a transfer of an undertaking within the meaning of Directive 77/187, then, according to the Court in *Wendelboe*,[181]

the scheme and purposes of the Directive, . . . [are] intended to ensure, as far as possible, that the employment relationship continues unchanged with the transferee and by protecting workers against dismissals motivated solely by the fact of the transfer. . . .[182]

In other words, the Directive is intended to protect those employees who are performing an identical job but under the orders of a different employer. The protection conferred has two pillars: first, the transfer of rights and obligations arising from the contract of employment and collective agreements (Article 3) and, secondly, the protection against dismissal (Article 4).

5.1 Rights Arising from the Contract of Employment or Employment Relationship

(a) General Rule

Article 3(1) paragraph 1, as amended, requires the transferee to respect the transferor's rights and obligations towards the employees, thereby limiting the managerial autonomy of the transferee. It provides that:

The transferor's rights and obligations arising from a contract of employment or from an employment relationship[183] existing on the date of a transfer shall, by reason of such transfer, be transferred to the transferee.

Therefore, the transferor's rights and obligations, existing at the time of transfer, the details of which are determined by national law,[184] are *automatically* transferred to the transferee.[185]

The Court takes Article 3(1) at face value. This is clearly demonstrated by the decision in *Rask*.[186] In that case the transferee changed the date of payment of the employee's salary from the last Thursday in the month to the last

---

[181] Case 19/83 [1985] ECR 457.

[182] Para. 15. Similar sentiments are expressed in Joined Cases C–132, 138, and 139/91 *Katsikas* [1992] ECR I–6577, para. 21, and Case C–362/89 *d'Urso* [1991] ECR I–4105, para. 9.

[183] For the ease of reference 'contract of employment' will be used and should be interpreted as including 'employment relationship'.

[184] As the Court pointed out in Case 324/86 *Daddy's Dance Hall* [1988] ECR 739, the Directive was intended to achieve only partial harmonization. Consequently, it was not intended to establish a uniform level of protection throughout the Community on the basis of common criteria. Thus, it could only be relied upon to ensure that the employee concerned was protected in his relations with the transferee to the same extent as he was in his relations with the transferor under the legal rules of the Member State concerned.

[185] See e.g. Joined Cases 144 and 145/87 *Berg* [1988] ECR 2559, para. 13. In technical terms this means subrogating the rights and obligations of the transferor to the transferee.

[186] Case C–209/91 [1992] ECR I–5755.

day in the month. The transferee also changed the composition of the payment: the plaintiffs no longer received allowances for laundry or for shoes, although the total amount of their pay remained unchanged. The Court ruled that Article 3(1) required that the terms of the contract of employment could not be varied on the transfer, notwithstanding that the total amount of pay remained unchanged. However, as the Court pointed out in both *Rask*[187] and subsequently in *Schmidt*,[188] the Directive does not preclude an amendment to the employment relationship with the new employer, in so far as national law allows such an amendment otherwise than through a transfer of the undertaking.

For the transferor, Article 3(1) means a discharge from all obligations arising under the contract of employment[189] from the date of transfer,[190] as the Court made clear in *Berg*.[191] In that case some employees objected to the transfer of certain contractual obligations which the transferor had, prior to the transfer, contracted with them to observe although they did not object to the transfer of their contract of employment. Nevertheless, the Court said that the transferor was released from his obligations as an employer solely by reason of the transfer and irrespective of the consent of the employees concerned. The Court re-emphasized this point in *Rotsart*.[192] It said that in the event of the transfer of an undertaking the contract of employment between the staff employed by the undertaking transferred could not be maintained with the transferor and was automatically continued with the transferee by the mere fact of the transfer. The Court added that the transfer of the contracts of employment could not be made subject to the intention of the transferor or the transferee, and that the transferee could not obstruct the transfer by refusing to fulfil his obligations.

Although the basic principle is that the transferor is discharged from all obligations at the date of transfer, Member States can provide for joint liability for both the transferor and transferee after the date of the transfer in respect

---

[187] Ibid.

[188] Ibid, para. 19. On the facts, although the transferee offered to employ the transferred employee for a higher wage than she had received previously, she was not prepared to work on those terms because she thought that her hourly wage would, in fact, be lower due to the increase in the surface area to be cleaned.

[189] The British EAT ruled in *Kerry Foods Ltd* v. *Kreber* [2000] IRLR 10 that the duty to consult was a right which arose from the individual contract between each employee and the employer and therefore fell within Art. 3(1).

[190] According to the Court in Case C–305/94 *Claude Rotsart de Hertaing* v. *J. Benoidt SA, in liquidation and Others* [1996] ECR I–5927, the transfer of the contracts of employment and employment relationships pursuant to Art. 3(1) of the Directive necessarily takes place on the date of the transfer of the undertaking and cannot be postponed to another date at the will of the transferor or the transferee since to allow the transferor or transferee the possibility of choosing the date from which the contract of employment or employment relationship is transferred would amount to allowing employers to derogate, at least temporarily, from the provisions of the Directive. This was not possible since the provisions are mandatory.

[191] Joined Cases 144 and 145/87 [1988] ECR 2559.

[192] Case C–305/94 [1996] ECR I–5927.

of obligations which arose before the transfer from a contract of employment existing on the date of transfer.[193] Various Member States (for example, Spain, France, Greece, Italy, the Netherlands, Portugal, and Germany) have adopted some form of a co-liability rule so that the transferor continues to be liable for pre-transfer debts with the transferee. The period during which the transferor remains liable varies from six months (Portugal) to three years (Spain), while no time limit is fixed in France and Greece. Other Member States have adopted no co-liability rule so only the transferee is liable.[194]

New Article 3(2), added at the last minute by Directive 98/50, provides, in the interests of transparency, that Member States *may* adopt appropriate measures to ensure that the transferor notifies the transferee of all the rights and obligations which will be transferred to the transferee under Article 3, in so far as the transferor knew or ought to have known of the existence of those rights and obligations. However, a failure to notify will not affect the transfer of any of the rights or obligations.[195]

(b) Consent to Transfer

The protection provided by the Directive is a matter of public policy and, as we have seen, operates independently of the will of the parties.[196] This approach contradicts the deep seated, particularly common law, notion that contract is based on a voluntary agreement between the parties. Thus, it is a principle of English law that contracts can be transferred only by novation, which requires the consent of both parties to the contract and of the substituting party. In a similar vein is the rule in the law of obligations that a debt may only be transferred with the creditor's consent. Nevertheless, the Court expressly rejected such arguments in *Berg*, maintaining that the Directive overrides these principles[197] and does not permit derogations which are unfavourable to employees. Therefore, the Court has said that employees are not entitled to waive the rights conferred on them by the Directive, nor can these rights be restricted even with their consent. This position is not altered by the fact that the employees obtain new benefits in compensation for the disadvantages resulting from the amendments to their contract of employment so that, taking the matter as a whole, they are not placed in a worse position than before.[198]

---

[193] Art. 3(1), para. 2, as amended.

[194] COM(94)300.

[195] See further Davies, above n. 176, 371.

[196] Case 324/86 *Daddy's Dance Hall* [1988] ECR 739.

[197] Joined Cases 144 and 145/87 *Berg* [1988] ECR 2559, para. 13.

[198] Case 324/86 *Daddy's Dance Hall* [1988] ECR 739, para. 13. See also Case C–362/89 *d'Urso* [1991] ECR I–4105 where the Court said that the implementation of rights laid down by the Directive could not be made dependent on the agreement of the transferor, transferee, employees' representative, or employees themselves. For the problems experienced by the House of Lords in addressing this issue, see *Wilson v. St Helens B.C., British Fuels v. Meade* [1999] IRLR 706. The Commission proposed that the Directive should contain a declaratory provision that, with the

Given that, after *Berg*, employees cannot give their consent to changes in terms and conditions of employment or whether certain terms be transferred, it was also thought that their consent whether their contract as a whole be transferred was not relevant,[199] since it has always been assumed that continued employment by the transferor would be the more attractive proposition for the employee. This may not always be the case. If the transferor is a public sector undertaking and the transferee a small private company of uncertain financial stability, with a doubtful commercial strategy or less favourable employment policies (including, perhaps, the policy relating to preservation and payment of pensions),[200] the employee may be well advised not to transfer. The Court opened up this option in *Katsikas* and *Skreb*[201] where it made clear that employees could refuse to be transferred. In the first case, Katsikas, an employee in a restaurant run by Konstantinidis, refused to work for Mitossis to whom Konstantinidis had sub-let the restaurant. As a result, Konstantinidis dismissed Katsikas. In the second case, two employees were dismissed by their employers when they refused to accept the transfer of their employment relationship to another company to whom their employers had transferred their section of the business. The employees relied on Article 613a(1) BGB which, according to the case law of the Bundesarbeitsgericht, does not oblige employees to accept the automatic transfer of their contracts of employment in the event of a transfer.[202]

The Court reasoned that although the Directive permitted an employee to remain in employment with the new employer on the same terms and conditions as those agreed with the transferor, the Directive did not impose an obligation on the employee to continue the employment relationship with the transferee. Such an obligation would undermine the fundamental rights of employees who had to be free to choose their employer and could not be obliged to work for an employer whom they had not freely chosen.[203] This

exception of insolvency situations, the transferee and the employees cannot by consent restrict any of the rights contained in the Directive, and that no provision should be made for waiver by collective agreements. This was not adopted in the final version.

[199] See para. 11 of Joined Cases 144 and 145/87 *Berg* [1988] ECR 2559; Case C–362/89 *d'Urso* [1991] ECR I–4105, para. 12; and Case 101/87 *Bork* [1988] ECR 3057, para. 17.

[200] See further Advocate General van Gerven's Opinion in Joined Cases C–132, 138, and 139/91 *Katsikas* [1992] ECR I–6577.

[201] Ibid.

[202] See further Advocate General van Gerven's Opinion in ibid., where he cited the judgment of the Bundesarbeitsgericht of 2 Oct. 1974, BAG AP, Art. 613a of the BGB No. 1, judgment of 21 July 1977, BAG AP, Art. 613a of the BGB No. 8; judgment of 17 Nov. 1977, BAG AP, Art. 613a of the BGB, No. 10; judgment of 6 Feb. 1980, BAG AP, Art. 613a of the BGB, No. 21; judgment of 15 Feb. 1984, BAG AP, Art. 613a of the BGB No. 37; finally, judgment of 30 Oct. 1986, BAG AP, Art. 613a of the BGB, No. 55. He suggested that such judicial interpretation could be deemed to fall within the meaning of Art. 7 of the Directive (right of Member States to apply more favourable rules to employees).

[203] The decision accords with the English common law position, stated by Lord Atkin in *Noakes* v. *Doncaster Amalgamated Collieries* [1940] AC 1014, 1026: 'I had fancied that ingrained in the personal status of a citizen under our laws was the right to choose for himself whom he would

means that although employees cannot agree to waive their rights under the Directive nor contract for different terms since the provisions of the Directive are mandatory, the employee can decide of his or her own accord not to be transferred.[204] This decision seems to give precedence to the employment protection aspect of the Directive over the needs of the transferor to have a workforce, the original objectives of the French law in 1928. However, the judgment comes with a sting in the tail: if the employee did voluntarily decide not to transfer then it was for the Member States to determine the fate of the contract of employment. The Court made clear that the Directive did not oblige Member States to provide that the contract of employment or employment relationship be continued with the transferor. In Germany the contract of employment does generally continue with the transferor while in the UK and France the contract of employment is considered as terminated with no protection from the law of dismissal.[205] This is a significant practical limitation to the fundamental rights recognized in the judgment.

(c) Rights Arising from a Collective Agreement

Article 3(3) [ex Article 3(2)] provides that following the transfer the transferee is obliged to observe the terms and conditions of any collective agreement on the same terms as the transferor.[206] In many Member States this is merely a corollary of contractual subrogation, since in most systems the conditions of employment established by collective agreements are automatically incorporated in individual contracts.[207] This may well mean that different collective agreements regulate the employment conditions of different sections of the transferee's workforce which may interfere with the '*unité du personnel*'. Consequently, in some States, such as Spain, the law provides that if the terms of the collective agreements enjoyed by the transferee's workers are superior to those of the transferor's workers, the transferor's workers enjoy the better terms. The obligation on the transferee to respect the terms of pre-existing collective agreements lasts until the date of termination or expiry of the collective agreement or the entry into force or application of

---

serve and that this right of choice constituted the main difference between a servant and a serf'. See also Art. 4(2) of the European Convention on Human Rights concerning the prohibition of forced or compulsory labour and in the UK; s. 236 Trade Union and Labour Relations (Consolidation) Act (TULR(C)A) 1992.

[204] The Court confirmed this ruling in Joined Cases C–171 and 172/94 *Merckx* [1996] ECR I–1253; Case C–399/96 *Europièces* [1998] ECR I–6965, para. 38.

[205] This was inserted into Regulation 5(4B) Transfer of Undertakings (Protection of Employment) Regulations (TUPE) 1981 by s. 33(4)(c) Trade Union Reform and Employment Rights Act (TURERA) 1993.

[206] The requirement that the transferee must respect 'customary industrial practice', which would include rules and practices governing the working environment which are not contractually binding, was removed from the final draft of the Directive (Hepple, above, n. 28, 495).

[207] Commission report to Council on progress with regard to the implementation of Directive 77/187/EEC, SEC(92)857 final, 2 June 1992, 29.

another collective agreement. However, Member States may limit the period for observing the agreement to one year.[208]

(d) Pension Rights, Invalidity and Survivors' Benefits

The final draft of the Directive 77/187 excluded the protection conferred by the Directive on employees' rights to 'old age, invalidity or survivor's benefits under supplementary company or inter-company schemes outside the statutory social security schemes',[209] unless Member States provide otherwise.[210] The EFTA Court confirmed in *Eidesund*[211] that the new contractor was not obliged to maintain contributions to the employee's occupational pension scheme. From an employee's perspective, this is a grave omission from the Directive. Since an occupational pension scheme may constitute an integral part of any remuneration package its loss would make any transfer considerably less attractive. The transferor, who may be insolvent, remains responsible under the terms of the scheme for any liabilities but the transferred employee nor the transferor would continue to make contributions. The Directive does provide, in Article 3(4)(a), second paragraph [ex Article 3(3)], that if the Directive does not apply to these benefits, the Member States must adopt the measures necessary to protect the interests of employees and persons no longer employed in the transferor's business at the time of transfer in respect of rights conferring on them immediate or retrospective entitlement to these benefits. Thus, the obligation falls on the Member State[212] and not the transferee, and it extends to persons no longer employed, as well as to employees.

5.2 Rights Relating to Dismissal

The second pillar of employment protection offered by the Directive relates to rights on dismissal. The first sentence of Article 4(1) provides that the transfer of the undertaking shall not *in itself* constitute grounds for dismissal by the transferor or the transferee. Article 4(2) applies to constructive dismissal. This provides that if the contract of employment is terminated because the transfer involves a substantial change in working conditions[213] to the detriment of

---

[208] Art. 3(3), para. 2.

[209] Art. 3(4)(a) [ex Art. 3(3)]. The British Employment Appeal Tribunal confirmed in *Walden Engineering* v. *Warrener* [1993] IRLR 420 that contracted out occupational pension schemes fell within the definition of 'supplementary schemes' and consequently are excluded from the Directive.

[210] Added by Directive 98/50. See further Hepple and Mumgaard, 'Pension Rights in Business Transfers' (1998) 27 *ILJ* 309.

[211] Case E–2/95 [1996] IRLR 684. See also the English Court of Appeal's ruling to the same effect in *Adams* v. *Lancashire County Council* [1997] IRLR 436.

[212] Failure to implement may result in enforcement proceedings. See Case 235/84 *Commission* v. *Italy* [1986] ECR 2291, but the provision is unlikely to be directly effective, see e.g. the views of the English EAT in *Warrener* [1993] IRLR 420.

[213] This is a matter for the national court to decide: see Case C–399/96 *Europièces* [1998] ECR I–6965.

the employee, the employer shall be regarded as having been responsible for termination of the contract. In *Merckx*[214] the Court ruled that a change in the level of remuneration awarded to an employee constituted a substantial change in working conditions, even where the remuneration depended on the turnover achieved. In the UK such dismissals are automatically unfair.[215]

The Court has refused to allow a wedge to be driven between the two pillars of employment protection contained in Articles 3 and 4. As has already been seen, the employment protection provision only applies to those workers who have a contract of employment at the date of transfer,[216] which must be decided on the basis of national law.[217] In an attempt to avoid the provisions of the Directive, transferors, usually at the behest of the transferee, have dismissed the workforce shortly before the transfer and then the transferee has re-engaged the workforce after the transfer, usually with inferior terms and conditions. The Court in *Bork*[218] has tried to eliminate such practices. It said that it was for the national court to decide whether the only reason for dismissal was the transfer itself. In reaching its decision the national court must take account of the objective circumstances in which the dismissal occurred, noting, in particular the fact that the dismissal took place on a date close to that of the transfer and that the workers concerned were re-engaged by the transferee.[219] If the national court decides that the dismissal occurred because of the transfer then those employees 'dismissed' in breach of Article 4(1) must be considered as still employed by the undertaking on the date of the transfer, with the result that the transferor's obligations towards the employees are automatically transferred to the transferee.

Does this mean that an employee, dismissed by the transferor for a transfer-related reason before the transfer or the transferee after the transfer, can enforce the primary obligation to continued employment? Recent case law suggests that the answer is no. In *Déthier*[220] the Court said that the contract of employment of a person unlawfully dismissed shortly before the transfer must be regarded as still extant as against the transferee even if the dismissed employee was not taken on by him after the undertaking was transferred.[221]

---

[214] Joined Cases C-171 and C–172/94 [1996] ECR I-1253.

[215] Unlike in other categories of unfair dismissal, the employee is required to satisfy the normal qualifying period to claim for unfair dismissal (one year), see TUPE Reg. 8(5)(b) inserted by SI 1995/2587 reversing *Milligan* v. *Securicor* [1995] IRLR 288. Such dismissals are, however, legally effective, according to the House of Lords in *Wilson* [1998] IRLR 706, and not a legal nullity, as the Court of Appeal had thought [1997] IRLR 505.

[216] Case 19/83 *Wendelboe* [1985] ECR 457, para. 13.

[217] Case 101/87 *Bork* [1988] ECR 3057, para. 17.

[218] Ibid. See also the decision of the House of Lords in *Litster* v. *Forth Dry Dock & Engineering Co. Ltd* [1990] 1 AC 546 where it said that the Directive applied both to those who were employed immediately before the transfer and those who would have been so employed had they not been unfairly dismissed.

[219] Case 101/87 *Bork* [1988] ECR 3057, paras. 18 and 19.

[220] Case C–319/94 [1998] ECR I–1061.

[221] Para. 41.

This employee can then claim that their dismissal was unlawful against the transferee. This suggests that the transferee is liable for all secondary contractual obligations, such as the right to claim unfair dismissal, but not the primary obligation to continued employment. This approach was recently adopted in the United Kingdom by the House of Lords in *British Fuels* and *Wilson*[222] where Lord Slynn said the transferee must meet all of the transferor's contractual and statutory obligations unless either the employee objects to being employed by the transferee or the reason or principal reason for dismissal was ETOR.[223]

The general rule contained in Article 4(1) that the transfer shall not constitute grounds for dismissal is subject to two limitations. First, Member States may exclude certain specific categories of employees who are not covered by the dismissal laws or practice of the Member States from the protection conferred by the first sentence of Article 4(1). However, in *Commission* v. *Belgium*[224] the Court ruled that Member States cannot use this exception as a means of depriving workers of their rights in the event of a transfer who already enjoy some protection, albeit limited, against dismissal under national law. Secondly, Article 4(1), second sentence, provides that:

This provision shall not stand in the way of dismissals that may take place for economic, technical or organizational reasons [ETOR] entailing changes in the workforce.[225]

The Court has offered surprisingly little guidance on the meaning of ETOR but seems merely, as in *Merckx*,[226] to pay lip service to the existence of the provision. The English courts, by contrast, have given the matter some attention. They have found that an 'economic' reason has to relate to the conduct of the business. Therefore, dismissals for reasons of redundancy fall within the ETOR[227] exception and the transferee must make a redundancy payment. On the other hand, broader economic reasons, such as the desire on the part of the transferor to achieve a higher sale price or achieve a sale at all, did not constitute an economic reason.[228] Flexibility and cost-cutting measures also do not constitute ETOR because the 'reason itself does not involve any change either in the number or the functions of the workforce'.[229]

---

[222] *British Fuels Ltd* v. *Baxendale; Wilson* v. *St Helens Borough Council* [1998] 4 All ER 609.
[223] See below, n. 225.
[224] Case 237/84 [1986] ECR 1247.
[225] This exception has received substantial criticism (Elias, above, n. 9, 153). Elias has questioned the need for an exception in that form. He argues that Art. 4 risks creating a bigger exception than some national laws would have permitted. From the Court's perspective it reduces the impact of the decision in Case C–392/92 *Schmidt* [1994] ECR I–1311, para. 18.
[226] Case C–171/94 [1996] ECR I–1253.
[227] It was confirmed in Case C–319/94 *Déthier* [1998] ECR I–1061 that the ETOR exception applies to both the transferor and the transferee.
[228] *Wheeler* v. *Patel* [1987] IRLR 631.
[229] *Berriman* v. *Delabole Slate* [1990] ICR 85.

The employer must be motivated by a genuine economic, technical reason and that reason must result in the dismissals. Therefore, any attempt by a transferee to rely on this provision to dismiss employees who are later re-engaged by the same transferee, usually on inferior terms, must be regarded with suspicion. This view receives some support from Advocate General van Gerven in *d'Urso*. He refused to countenance the argument that the Directive permits *any* dismissal for economic, technical, or organizational reasons. In fact, he says, the Directive expressly prohibits such dismissals when they occur as a result of the transfer of the undertaking. Only dismissals which would have been made in any case, for instance if the decision was taken before there was any question of transferring the undertaking, fall within the exclusion. He therefore concludes that Article 4 cannot be relied on as justification for dismissing some employees because the undertaking has been transferred.

6. Collective Rights

The Directive envisages an important role for representatives of the employees.[230] Consequently, the aim of Article 5 is to safeguard and preserve the status and function of the 'representatives' or of the representation of the employees 'affected by the transfer', as laid down by the laws, regulations, or administrative provisions of the Member States, in the event of a transfer. This protection is subject to two conditions. First, the business must preserve its autonomy.[231] Therefore, it must continue to be a unit capable of operating independently and not be absorbed into a larger unit. Secondly, if 'the conditions necessary for the re-appointment of the representatives of the employees or for the reconstitution of the representation of the employees are fulfilled the status and function of the original representatives will not be preserved'.[232] This may occur where the transfer results in an increase in the workforce necessitating a change in the number of representatives or in the structure of the representation.[233] Workers' representatives whose term of office expires as a result of the transfer continue to enjoy the protection afforded by legislation in the Member States against action taken by employers which may be detrimental to workers' representatives.[234]

In order to advise the employees of what is happening, Article 6 requires

---

[230] Defined in Art. 2(1)(c) and discussed in the text accompanying nn. 40–49.

[231] If the business does not preserve its autonomy, the Member States must take the necessary measures to ensure that the employees transferred, who were represented before the transfer, continue to be properly represented during the period prior to the reconstitution or reappointment of the representatives of the employees (Art. 5(1), para. 4).

[232] Art. 5(1), para. 2.

[233] See Art. 5(1), para. 2, Commission Report to the Council, SEC(92)857 final, Brussels, 2 June 1992.

[234] Art. 5(2).

that the representatives of the employees be informed and consulted. As far as information is concerned, Article 6(1) requires the transferor *and* the transferee to *inform* the representatives of their respective employees affected by a transfer of the following:

— the date or proposed date of the transfer;[235]
— the reasons for the transfer;
— the legal, economic, and social implications of the transfer for the employees;
— the measures envisaged in relation to the employees.

Both the transferor and the transferee are obliged to give the information to the employees' representatives in 'good time' before the transfer is carried out, but no specific time limit is set. The transferee is under an additional obligation to provide its own employees' representatives with information as regards the employees' conditions of work and employment before the transferees' employees are directly affected by the transfer.[236]

Employees' representatives have direct input only concerning 'measures' envisaged in relation to the employees, such as a reduction in the workforce, or the introduction of new working methods:[237] under Article 6(2) they have a right to be *consulted*,[238] again in good time, with a *view to seeking their agreement*. Thus, the Directive does provide for an element of employee participation, at least through their representatives, in commercial decisions but neither the employees nor their representatives have the right to veto any such decisions.

In Germany Article 112(1) of the Law on Labour Relations at the Workplace provides that the works council and the head of the undertaking may agree on a social plan intended to compensate for or mitigate the detrimental economic consequences which the worker might suffer as a result of the envisaged change. In the event of disagreement on the social plan, either of the two sides may bring the matter before the conciliation committee, an arbitration body comprising an equal number of members appointed by the head of the firm and the works council, with a Chair acceptable to both sides whose decision is binding.[239] This procedure can continue. Article 6(3) provides that if the national system permits employees' representatives to have recourse to an arbitration board to obtain a decision on the 'measures to be

---

[235] Added by Directive 98/50 [1998] OJ L201/88.

[236] Art. 6(1), para. 3.

[237] European Works Councils may also have to be consulted in respect of these matters as well as transfers of production and mergers; see para. 2 of the Annex to Directive 94/45/EC [1994] OJ L254/64.

[238] The first draft envisaged negotiations by the employees' representatives with the transferor or transferee with a view to seeking agreement and in default the matter could be referred to arbitration.

[239] Commission Report to the Council, SEC(92)857 final, 93.

taken in relation to employees', the duties of information and consultation may be limited to cases where the transfer is likely to entail 'serious disadvantages for a considerable number of employees'. Nevertheless, the information and consultations must concern the measures envisaged in relation to employees and must take place in good time before the transfer is effected.[240]

New Article 6(4) addresses the situation of transnational companies where decisions may be taken by the parent in one State which affects a subsidiary in another State. In line with the amendments to the Directive on Collective Redundancies,[241] Directive 98/50 provides that it is no 'excuse' for an employer in breach of the information and consultation provisions to argue that the information was not provided by the undertaking which took the decision.[242] Article 6 applies irrespective of whether the decision resulting in the transfer is taken by the employer or an undertaking controlling the employer.

Finally, Member States have the option of limiting the information and consultation rights to those businesses which in terms of the number of employees meet 'the conditions for the election or nomination of a collegiate body representing the employees'.[243] This provision addresses a situation such as that in the Netherlands where the statutory requirement of information and consultation of representatives of workers applies only to works councils,[244] and consequently to undertakings employing at least 100 people, or at least thirty-five people for more than one-third of the normal working hours, where the election of a works council is mandatory.[245] In the case of smaller undertakings where there are no employee representatives Article 6(6) provides that the employees themselves must be given the same information 'in advance' (not in good time) as would have been given to the employee representatives.[246]

7. Implementation and Remedies

While Article 8 of Directive 77/187 required Member States to bring into force laws, regulations, and administrative provisions to comply with the Directive, Article 2(1) of Directive 98/50 also permits the employers and the

---

[240] Art. 6(3), paras. 2 and 3.

[241] Council Directive 92/56/EEC [1992] OJ L245/3. See below, n. 264.

[242] Art. 6(4), para. 2.

[243] Art. 6(5).

[244] Art. 25 of the Law on Works Councils.

[245] The proposed Directive (94/C274/08) provides that the Member States can limit the information and consultation requirements to undertakings or businesses which normally employ 50 or more employees. This was not included in the final version but reflects the Commission's thinking in the more general information and consultation proposal discussed in Ch. 8.

[246] Under Art. 6(5) of Directive 77/187 the employees had only very limited information rights about when a transfer was to take place.

employees' representatives to introduce the required provisions 'by means of agreement',[247] albeit that the Member States retain the responsibility to ensure that all workers are afforded the full protection provided for by the Directive.[248] In the words of the Court, 'the state guarantee must cover all cases where effective protection is not ensured by other means'. Thus, in *Commission* v. *Italy*, the Court accepted that collective agreements could be used as a means of laying down procedures for informing and consulting employees' representatives affected by a transfer.[249] However, since these agreements covered only specific economic sectors, the Italian government was obliged to enact appropriate laws, regulations, or administrative measures to ensure full compliance with Article 6(1) and (2) of the Directive.

While Directive 77/187 provides rights for employees and their representatives it makes no provision for remedies in the event of the failure by a transferor or transferee to recognize those rights.[250] However, in *Commission* v. *UK*[251] the Court said that where a Community Directive did not specifically provide any penalty for an infringement or referred to national laws, regulations, and administrative provisions, Article 5 [new Article 10] EC required the Member States to take all measures necessary to guarantee the application and effectiveness of Community law. While the choice of penalties remained within their discretion (the principle of national procedural autonomy),[252] Member States had to ensure, in particular, that infringements of Community law were penalized under conditions, both procedural and substantive, which were analogous to those applicable to infringements of national law of a similar nature and importance and which, in any event, made the penalty effective, proportionate, and dissuasive.[253] Under UK law, an employer who failed to consult employee representatives at the time of the transfer could be ordered to pay a penalty of up to a maximum of four weeks' pay to employees affected by the transfer. However, if the employer also dismisses employees on grounds of redundancy any protective award made against the employer for failing to consult employees' representatives in the event of collective redundancies could be set off against any penalty payment received by the employee which, when combined with the financial ceiling on

---

[247] As approved by the Court: Case 143/83 *Commission* v. *Denmark* [1985] ECR 427, as confirmed by Case 235/84 *Commission* v. *Italy* [1986] ECR 2291.

[248] See new Art. 2(1) of Directive 98/50/EC [1998] OJ L201/88.

[249] Cf. Advocate General Slynn, in Case 235/84 *Commission* v. *Italy* [1986] ECR 2291, who doubted whether collective agreements could be used as a means of implementing a directive.

[250] New Art. 7a does, however, require those employees who consider themselves wronged by failure to comply with obligations arising from the Directive to pursue their claims by judicial process after possible recourse to other competent authorities.

[251] Case C–382/92 [1994] ECR I–2435.

[252] Considered further in Ch. 4.

[253] With regard to Community regulations see the judgments in Case 68/88 *Commission* v. *Greece* [1989] ECR 2965, paras. 23 and 24, and in Case C–7/90 *Criminal Proceedings against Vandevenne and Others* [1991] ECR I–4371, para. 11.

the penalty, significantly weakened the initial financial penalty. In the eyes of the Court such a penalty was not a true deterrent and consequently the UK legislation did not comply with Article 5 [new Article 10] EC.

B. THE COLLECTIVE REDUNDANCIES DIRECTIVES

Council Directive 75/129/EEC[254] was passed as part of the 1974–6 Social Action Programme.[255] According to Blanpain, the Directive had its origins in the *AKZO* case. AKZO, a Dutch–German multi-national enterprise wanted to make 5,000 workers redundant as part of a programme of restructuring. AKZO compared the costs of dismissing workers in the various States where it had subsidiaries and chose to dismiss workers in the country where the costs were the lowest. This led to calls for action to be taken at European level to prevent this from happening again. The purpose of Directive 75/129/EEC is twofold:[256] first, 'that greater protection should be afforded to workers in the event of collective redundancies, while taking into account the need for balanced economic and social development within the Community';[257] and, secondly, to promote 'approximation . . . while the improvement (in living and working conditions) is being maintained within the meaning of Article 117 [new Article 136] of the Treaty'.[258]

In order to achieve these objectives the Directive sets minimum standards[259] to ensure both that major redundancies are subjected to proper consultation with worker representatives and that the competent public authority is notified prior to dismissal.[260] The Directive is not, however, designed to harmonize national practices and procedures for making redundancies.[261] Nor is it designed to affect the employer's freedom to effect or refrain from effecting collective dismissals.[262] This was confirmed in *Rockfon*[263] where the Court said

[254] Council Directive 75/129/EEC of 17 Feb. 1975 on the approximation of the laws of the Member States relating to collective redundancies [1975] OJ L48/29 and Council Directive 92/56/EEC of 24 June 1992 amending Directive 75/129/EEC on the approximation of the laws of the Member States relating to collective redundancies [1992] OJ L245/3.

[255] See, further, Blanpain, *Labour Law and Industrial Relations of the European Community* (Kluwer, Deventer, 1991) 153.

[256] Case 215/83 *Commission v. Belgium* [1985] ECR 103.

[257] This is confirmed by the Court in Case C–250/97 *Lauge v. Lønmodtagernes Garantifond* [1998] ECR I–8737.

[258] Case 215/83 *Commission v. Belgium* [1985] ECR 1039, para. 2.

[259] National laws, regulations, and administrative provisions can lay down laws more favourable to workers and, since Directive 92/56, Member States can promote or allow the application of collective agreements more favourable to workers (Art. 5).

[260] Case 284/83 *Dansk Metalarbeiderforbund and Special Arbeiderforbundet i Danmark v. Nielsen & Son Maskin-fabrik A/S in liquidation* [1985] ECR 553, para. 10.

[261] Case 284/83 *Nielsen* [1985] ECR 553 and Case C–383/92 *Commission v. UK* [1994] ECR I–2435.

[262] Case 284/83 *Nielsen* [1985] ECR 553, para. 10.

[263] Case C–449/93 *Rockfon A/S v. Specialarbejderforbundet i Danmark, acting for Nielsen* [1995] ECR I–4291.

that companies retained autonomy to manage their internal affairs. It said that 'the sole purpose of the Directive is the partial harmonisation of collective redundancy procedures and that its aim is not to restrict the freedom of undertakings to organise their activities and arrange their personnel departments in the way which they think best suits their needs'.

Directive 75/129 was amended by Directive 92/56/EEC[264] which was drafted against the backcloth of increasing transnationalization of companies with decisions being taken by controlling employers in other Member States. Directive 75/129 and Directive 92/56 were consolidated and repealed by Council Directive 98/59/EC[265] to which all subsequent references relate.

1. The Material and Personal Scope of the Directive

Article 1(1)(a) defines collective redundancies as 'dismissals effected by an employer for one or more reasons *not related to the individual* workers concerned' where the number of redundancies is:

(i)   either, over a period of thirty days:

  — at least ten redundancies in establishments normally employing more than twenty and fewer than 100 workers;
  — at least 10 per cent of the number of workers in establishments normally employing at least 100 but fewer than 300 workers;
  — at least thirty in establishments normally employing 300 workers or more;

(ii) or, over a period of ninety days, at least twenty, irrespective of the number of workers normally employed in the establishments in question.

The choice between these alternatives is left to the Member State (see Table 7.1). Directive 92/56 added that for the purpose of calculating the number of redundancies 'terminations of an employment contract which occur to the individual workers' are to be treated as redundancies provided at least five redundancies occur.[266] Thus, other forms of termination, such as voluntary early retirement, are included within the scope of the Directive, but these must be taken to be, like the redundancies themselves, for a reason not related to the individual worker.[267]

The definition of collective redundancies contains both an objective element concerning the scale of the redundancies (number or percentage of

---

[264] [1992] OJ L245/3.
[265] [1998] OJ L225/16.
[266] Art. 1(1).
[267] Bourn, 'Amending the Collective Dismissals Directive: a Case of Rearranging the Deck-chairs' (1993) 9 *Int. Jo. Comp. LLIR* 227, 234.

Table 7.1 Definition of Collective Dismissals in the Member States

	Minimum number of employees constituting a collective dismissal	Time period over which dismissals occur	Size of establishment
Belgium	10	60 days	20–100
	10%	60 days	100–200
	30	60 days	300
Denmark	10	30 days	20–100
	10%	30 days	100–300
	30	30 days	300
France	10	30 days	—
	30	6 months	—
Germany	5	30 days	20–59
	10% or at least 25 employees	30 days	60–500
	30	30 days	500+
Greece	5	—	20–50
	2–3%, with maximum of 30[1]	—	50+
Ireland	5	30 days	21–49
	10	30 days	50–99
	10%	30 days	100–299
	30	30 days	300+
Italy	No reference made to number of dismissals	—	—
Luxembourg	10	30 days	—
	20	60 days	—
Netherlands	20	simultaneously or up to a period of 3 months	—
Spain	No numerical thresholds	—	—
Portugal	2	3months	2–50
	5	3 months	51+
UK	100	90 days	—
	20	30 days	—

Source: *Social Europe* 4/92 and Report by the Commission to the Council on progress with regard to implementation of the Directive on the approximation of laws relating to collective redundancies SEC(91)1639.

[1] It is prohibited in Greece to dismiss more than 30 employees. The exact percentage is determined every semester by ministerial decision in accordance with developments in the labour market.

workers to be made redundant over a given period), and a subjective element concerning the reasons for the redundancies.[268] As far as the objective element is concerned, the Court gave some guidance in *Rockfon*.[269] Rockfon, part of

[268] See Commission Report to Council, SEC(91)1639 final, Brussels, 13 Sep. 1991, 11.
[269] Case C–449/93 [1995] ECR I–4291.

a multinational group, shared a joint personnel department responsible for recruitment and dismissals with three other companies in the group. Internal rules required that any dismissal decision had to be taken in consultation with the personnel department. Between 10 and 28 November 1989 Rockfon dismissed twenty-four or twenty-five employees from its workforce of 162. Rockfon, considering itself to be part of the multinational group and therefore falling under the threshold provided by the Directive, did not consult the employees, and did not inform the relevant public authority. The question for the Court was whether Rockfon by itself constituted an establishment. If so, then the dismissals were carried out in breach of the consultation requirements of the Directive since Danish law had chosen the first option provided by Article 1(1)(a) (over a period of thirty days, at least ten dismissals in establishments normally employing between twenty and 100 workers, 10 per cent of the number of workers in establishments normally employing between 100 and 300 workers) to implement the Directive.

Although 'establishment' is not defined in the Directive, the Court said that the term was to be given a Community meaning. The different language versions of the Directive use different terms:[270] 'establishment', 'undertaking', 'work centre', 'local unit', 'place of work'. The Court said that a broad interpretation of the term establishment would allow companies belonging to the same group to try to make it more difficult for the Directive to apply to them by conferring on a separate decision-making body the power to take decisions concerning redundancies. As a result, they would be able to escape the obligation to follow the procedures provided by the Directive. It therefore said that the term 'establishment' had to be interpreted as the unit to which the workers made redundant were assigned to carry out their duties.[271] It was not essential for the unit in question to be endowed with a management which could independently effect collective redundancies.[272] Since Danish law had chosen the first option provided for by Article 1(1)(a) the purposive construction set out in *Rockfon* defining 'establishment' narrowly was of benefit to Danish workers. Indeed, the Court expressly said that the purpose of the Directive was to afford workers greater protection in the event of collective redundancies. However, for countries such as the UK, which have chosen the second option provided for by Article 1(1)(a) (twenty employees at one establishment within a period of ninety days), the decision in *Rockfon* threatens to undermine the position of those employees,[273] since the more broadly defined

---

[270] Danish *virksomhed*, Dutch *plaatselijke eenheid*, English 'establishment', Finnish *yritys*, German *Betrieb*, Italian *stabilemento*, Portugese *estabelecimento*, Spanish *centro de trabajo*, Swedish *arbetsplats*.

[271] Citing Case 186/83 *Botzen* [1985] ECR 519, discussed in the text attached to n. 50, above.

[272] This approach is supported by the fact that the Commission's initial proposal for the Directive used the term 'undertaking' and that term was defined as 'local employment unit'.

[273] Rubinstein, 'Editorial' [1996] IRLR 113.

the establishment, the more likely the threshold of twenty employees will be met.

As far as the subjective element is concerned, the reasons for the redundancies must not be 'related to the individual workers concerned'. Therefore, dismissals for reasons relating to a worker's behaviour (e.g. disciplinary dismissals) are excluded from the scope of the Directive. In *Commission v. UK*[274] the Court found that the British definition of redundancy—the cessation of a business or cessation or diminution in the requirements of a business to carry out work of a particular kind[275]—was too narrow since it did not cover cases where workers were dismissed as a result of new working arrangements which were unconnected with the volume of business.[276]

The Directive applies only when the employer dismisses the employees. It does not apply to termination of employment by the employees themselves since this might be contrary to the employer's wishes and it would prevent the employer from discharging the obligations laid down by the Directive. This, according to the Court in *Nielsen*,[277] would lead to a result contrary to that sought by the Directive, namely to avoid or reduce collective redundancies.[278] The position may, however, be different if the employer, without seriously trying to stay in business, has forced the workers to give notice in order to escape the obligations imposed by the Directive.[279]

The Directive does not apply to:[280]

— collective redundancies resulting from the expiry of fixed-term contracts or the completion of a particular task in the case of a contract to perform a particular task;[281]
— workers employed by public administrative bodies or by establishments governed by public law (or, in Member States where this concept is unknown, by equivalent bodies);
— the crews of seagoing vessels.[282]

Since these instances are exceptions to the general rule they must be construed narrowly. Directive 75/129 also excluded workers affected by the

---

[274] Case C–383/92 [1994] ECR I–2435.

[275] S. 195 TULR(C)A 1992.

[276] S. 195 TULR(C)A 1992 was amended by s. 34 TURERA 1993 to bring British law into line with the Directive. This now provides that 'references to dismissal as redundant are references to dismissal for a reason not related to the individual concerned or for a number of reasons all of which are not so related'.

[277] Case 284/83 [1985] ECR 553.

[278] Ibid., para. 10.

[279] Advocate General Lenz, Case 284/83 *Nielsen* [1985] ECR 553.

[280] Art. 1(2). The Belgian government was condemned for failing to implement these provisions correctly in Case 215/83 *Commission v. Belgium* [1985] ECR 1039.

[281] The Directive does, however, apply to redundancies which take place prior to the date of expiry of fixed-term contracts or to the completion of the specific task.

[282] Cf. Art. 3(1) where Member States have the discretion whether to require dismissals arising in such circumstances to be notified to the public authority.

termination of an establishment's activities where this is the result of a judicial decision. Directive 92/56 removed this exception.[283]

The most notable omissions from this list of exceptions are cases of emergency or *force majeure*. The Court considered such a situation in *Nielsen*.[284] In February 1980 the employer, Nielsen, informed workers' representatives of its financial difficulties. On 14 March 1980 it informed the bankruptcy court that it was suspending payment of its debts, and, when it failed to provide a bank guarantee for the future payment of wages, the trade unions advised their members to stop work. On 25 March 1980 the employer was declared insolvent and the following day the workers were given notice of dismissal. The trade union argued that as soon as the employer experienced financial difficulties it ought to have contemplated collective redundancies, and thus the application of the Directive. The Court disagreed. It argued that this interpretation would cause employers to incur penalties for failing to have foreseen the collective redundancies and consequently failing to implement the procedure required by the Directive. This would run counter to the wording of Article 1(2)(d) which excluded from the scope of the Directive collective redundancies caused by 'the termination of an establishment's activities where that is the result of a judicial decision'.[285] The logic of these arguments is undermined now that Article 1(2)(d) has been deleted by Article 1 of Directive 92/56/EEC,[286] so the position in respect of *force majeure* is unclear.

2. The Employer's Obligations

2.1 Consultation of Workers' Representatives

Article 2(1) provides that 'where an employer is contemplating collective redundancies, he shall begin consultations with the workers' representatives in good time *with a view to reaching an agreement*' (emphasis added).[287] The reference to 'consultation' with a view to reaching an 'agreement'[288] blurs the distinction between consultation and collective bargaining. No specific time limit is prescribed for carrying out this process, although it seems that consultations must begin at an early stage in the decision-making process and

---

[283] This is subject to the possibility of recourse to the derogation provided for in Arts. 3(1), para. 2, and 4(4): see below, n. 311.

[284] Case 284/83 [1985] ECR 553.

[285] Para. 16.

[286] See above, n. 283.

[287] See also ILO Convention 158 and Art. 2(1)(b) of the Additional Protocol to the Social Charter.

[288] A concept absent from the UK legislation: see Case C–383/92 *Commission* v. *UK* [1994] ECR I–2479. Implemented by s. 34(2)(c) TURERA 1993 and included in s. 188 TULR(C)A 1992.

certainly before any decision has been taken,[289] to enable workers' representatives to participate in the decision-making process and in finding ways to deal with the associated social problems.

These consultations are with 'workers' representatives', defined as those representatives provided for by the laws or practices of the Member States.[290] This enables consultation to continue within established frameworks of the German and Dutch works councils, the French *comité d'entreprise*, and collective bargaining in the UK, Ireland, and Denmark.[291] The UK's implementation of this provision (along with the equivalent term in Directive 77/187) was, however, found by the Court to be defective since only recognized trade unions could be consulted.[292]

The substance of these consultations must cover, as a minimum, two matters: first, ways and means of avoiding collective redundancies or reducing the number of employees affected; and, secondly, ways of mitigating the consequences of the redundancies by recourse to 'social measures aimed, *inter alia*, at aid for redeploying or retraining workers made redundant'.[293] This is a pale reflection of the 'social plan' recognized by German law—a special form of redundancy programme drawn up by management and the works council in a legally binding agreement designed to 'compensate or reduce economic disadvantages for employees in the event of a substantial alteration to the establishment'.[294] The fact that ways of avoiding collective redundancies appear as the first item on the list suggests that the drafters of the Directive did not presume that redundancies would occur and considered that the avoidance of redundancies was at least as important as giving rights to those who will be made redundant.

Since the emphasis is on consultation and not just information the Directive also makes provision to ensure that the consultations are effective. To enable the workers' representatives to make constructive proposals the employer is obliged to supply the workers' representatives[295] in good time during the course of the consultations with all relevant information[296] *and the employer must 'in any event' give in writing:*[297]

---

[289] See the *obiter dicta* of Glidewell LJ in *R v. British Coal Corporation and Secretary of State for Trade and Industry, ex parte Vardy* [1993] IRLR 104 which envisage consultation at an early stage when the employer is first envisaging the possibility that he may have to make employees redundant.

[290] Art. 1(1)(b).   [291] Hepple, above, n. 28, 491.

[292] Case C–383/92 *Commission v. UK* [1994] ECR I–2479. See above, nn. 41–49.

[293] Art. 2(2). Furthermore, according to para. 2, Member States can provide that the workers' representatives can call upon the services of experts in accordance with national law or practice. Thus, there will still be a contrast between the position in France where employees may call upon the services of an accountant (*expert comptable*) and in Denmark and the UK where no such obligation exists (Bourn, above n. 267, 236).

[294] Weiss, *European Employment and Industrial Relations Glossary: Germany* (Sweet & Maxwell, London, 1992), para. 657.

[295] The European Works Council will also need to be consulted, see para. 2 of Annex to Directive 94/45/EC [1994] OJ L254/64 discussed in Ch. 8.

[296] Art. 2(3)(a).   [297] Art. 2(3)(b).

— the reasons for the projected redundancies;
— the number of categories of workers to be made redundant[298] (Directive 75/129/EEC talked of the number of workers to be made redundant);
— the number and categories of workers normally employed;
— the period over which the redundancies are to be effected;

Directive 92/56 added two further items to this list:

— the criteria proposed for the selection of workers to be made redundant in so far as national legislation and/or practice confers this power on the employer;
— the method for calculating any redundancy payments other than those arising out of national legislation and/or practice.

The most important addition made by Directive 92/56 is that the obligation to consult workers' representatives applies 'irrespective of whether the decision regarding collective redundancies is being taken by the employer *or by an undertaking controlling the employer*'.[299] It is therefore now no defence for an employer to argue that the parent or controlling undertaking had not provided the employer with the necessary information.[300] This provision was introduced in the light of the increasing 'transnationalization' of commercial ventures. As the Commission said, the dismantling of national barriers has led to major corporate reorganization, involving a significant increase in takeovers, mergers, and joint ventures.[301] As a result, decisions affecting the workforce might be taken by a controlling undertaking which might not be situated in one of the Member States. The obligation to acquire the information is, however, placed on the controlled undertaking to avoid the problem of extraterritoriality. The approach adopted by the Collective Redundancies Directive to complex corporate structures contrasts favourably with that adopted under the European Works Council Directive 94/45/EC[302] where rights are given against central management at a time when there is an increasing tendency towards decentralizing decision-making in corporate groups.

This entire consultation procedure is only triggered when the employer is *contemplating* redundancies or has drawn up a plan for collective redundancies. By implication the Directive does not apply when redundancies occur which have not been 'contemplated' since, as the Court recognized in

---

[298] The tone of this section does suggest that the fact that redundancies will occur is a *fait accompli* which contradicts the tenor of Art. 2(1) and (2).

[299] Art. 2(4), para. 1.

[300] Art. 2(4), para. 2.

[301] According to the Commission's figures, the number of mergers and acquisitions carried out by the top 1,000 European industrial enterprises doubled every three years during the 1980s, increasing from 208 in 1984–5 to 492 in 1988–9: Commission, *XXth Report on Competition Policy*, cited in COM(94)300, 2.

[302] [1994] OJ L254/64. See also Bourn, above n. 267, 237.

Nielsen,[303] there is no implied obligation under the Directive to foresee collective redundancies. The Court said that the Directive did not stipulate the circumstances in which employers must contemplate collective redundancies
and in no way affected their freedom to decide whether and when they must
formulate plans for collective dismissals. This ruling favours the disorganized
employer who would not have contemplated redundancies, to whom the Directive will not apply, to the detriment of the more far-sighted employer who
has been planning or contemplating redundancies, to whom the consultation
procedures laid down by the Directive will apply.

2.2 Notification of the 'Competent Public Authority'

In France and the Netherlands the competent authorities have long-
established powers to authorize or prohibit redundancies. In the Netherlands
the procedure involves a system whereby the Dutch labour office issues a
number of permits to dismiss.[304] Due to resistance from the UK, this principle
was not included in the Directive.[305] Instead, Article 3(1) imposes an administrative obligation on employers to notify 'the competent public authority' in
writing of any projected redundancies.[306] The notification must contain all
information relevant to the projected redundancies, the consultations with
the workers' representatives provided for in Article 2,[307] and particularly the
reasons for the redundancies, the number of workers to be made redundant,
the number of workers normally employed, and the period over which the
redundancies are to be effected.[308] In the case of planned collective redundancies arising from termination of the establishment's activities as a result of a
judicial decision, the Member States can provide that the employer is obliged
to notify the competent public authority on the request of the authority.[309]
The employer must also send a copy of the Article 3(1) notification to
the workers' representatives who may send any comments they have to the
competent authority.[310]

---

[303] Case 284/83 [1985] ECR 553.

[304] In the Netherlands the employer wishing to terminate employment contracts unilaterally
must apply to the District Labour Office for a permit. In 1980 98,387 permits were requested by
employers, of which 16 per cent concerned 20 employees or more. In 1993 107,998 permits
were requested, of which 15 per cent concerned 20 employees or more (based on figures for the
Dutch Ministry for Social Affairs and Employment).

[305] Freedland, 'Employment Protection: Redundancy Procedures and the EEC' (1976) 5–6 *ILJ*
24, 27.

[306] Advocate General Lenz argues that the employer must give notice to the competent authorities if he actually plans to make collective redundancies, whereas representatives of workers
must be consulted at an earlier stage (Case 284/83 *Nielsen* [1985] ECR 553, 557).

[307] Art. 2(3), para. 2, obliges the employer to forward to the competent authority all written
communications referred to in Art. 2(3)(b) except the method for calculating any redundancy
payments.

[308] Art. 3(1), para. 2.

[309] Added by Directive 92/56 as second sentence of para. 1 of Art. 3(1).

[310] Art. 3(2).

In principle, the proposed redundancies cannot take place until at least thirty days after the Article 3(1) notification. The purpose of this delay is to enable the competent authority to seek solutions to the problems raised by the projected redundancies.[311] It is not clear whether this means that the authority should intervene in an attempt to stave off the redundancies or rather that it should make provision for coping with those employees who will be unemployed as a result of the redundancies.

The Member State can grant the competent authority the power to reduce the thirty-day period.[312] If, however, the initial period of delay is for less than sixty days Member States can grant the competent authority the power to extend the initial period to sixty days or longer[313] following notification, where the problems raised by the projected collective redundancies are not likely to be solved within the initial period.[314] The employer (but not the workers' representatives) must be informed of the extension and the reason such an extension has been granted before the expiry of the initial thirty-day period.[315]

3. Final Provisions and Remedies

The Member States were obliged to implement both Directives 75/129 and 92/56 within two years of their notification.[316] The Court is strict about ensuring correct implementation, as the Belgian government found to its cost:

Member States must fulfil their obligations under Community Directives in every respect and may not plead provisions, practices or circumstances existing in their internal legal system in order to justify a failure to comply with those obligations.[317]

It said that the Belgian government could not plead that in practice very few workers were excluded from the benefits of the Directive, nor that the government's failure to comply fully with the Directive was justified by the fact that Belgian law provided the workers in question with other forms of security. The Italian government was equally unsuccessful in the arguments it

---

[311] Art. 4(2). Directive 92/56 added that Member States need not apply this provision to collective redundancies arising from the termination of the establishment's activities where this is the result of a judicial decision (Art. 4(4)). In Case C–250/97 *Lauge* [1998] ECR I–8737 the Court ruled that this derogation does not apply to collective redundancies occurring on the same day as that on which the employer files a winding up petition and terminates the undertaking's activities and the court issues a winding up order which takes effect from the date on which the petition was filed.

[312] Art. 4(1), para. 2.

[313] Art. 4(3), para. 2.

[314] Art. 4(3), para. 1.

[315] Art. 4(3), para. 3.

[316] Art. 6, 19 Feb. 1977 and 24 June 1994, respectively.

[317] Case 215/83 *Commission v. Belgium* [1985] ECR 1039.

raised in enforcement proceedings brought against it. Although it claimed that the Italian system as a whole created conditions and established procedures making it possible to attain the objectives of the Directive, it did concede that in certain sectors the legislation was not as comprehensive as the Directive required.[318]

Directive 75/129/EEC, like Directive 77/187, made no express provision for remedies in the event of employers' failure to comply with their obligations. However, in the case of the *Commission v. UK*[319] the Court insisted that Member States must ensure that infringements of Community law were penalized under conditions, both procedural and substantive, which are analogous to those applicable to infringements of national law and which make the penalty effective, proportionate, and dissuasive. Consequently the Court ruled that British law which allowed a protective award, payable by an employer who has failed to consult workers' representatives to a dismissed employees, could be set off in full or in part against any other amounts owed by the employer to the employees, deprived the sanction of its practical effect and deterrent value. In several Member States collective redundancies carried out in contravention of the Directive are null and void.[320] Originally this was also included in the new draft Directive but, faced with opposition from ECOSOC, the UK government, and employers, it was deleted from the final version. Instead, Article 6, introduced by Directive 92/56, requires Member States to ensure 'that judicial and/or administrative procedures for the enforcement of obligations under this Directive are available to the workers' representatives or to the workers'.

C. INSOLVENCY DIRECTIVE 80/987/EEC

The Insolvency Directive[321] is the third in the trilogy of measures designed to confer some protection on employees this time faced with their employers' insolvency due to increased competition caused by the advent of the Common Market. Also based on Article 100 [new Article 94], the Directive, as the preamble notes, has dual objectives—both to promote the approximation of laws and to improve the living and working conditions by protecting employees in the event of the insolvency of their employer.[322]

---

[318] Case 91/81 *Commission v. Italy* [1982] ECR 2133. Further enforcement proceedings were later brought for failing to implement the judgment in Case 91/81: see Case 131/84 *Commission v. Italy* [1985] ECR 3531.

[319] Case C–383/92 [1994] ECR I–2479.

[320] Bourn, above n. 267.

[321] Council Directive 80/987/EEC [1980] OJ L283/23 on the approximation of the laws of the Member States relating to the protection of employees in the event of insolvency of their employer, as amended by Directive 87/164 [1987] OJ L66/11. See COM(96)696 on the implementation of the Directive.

[322] See also Case 22/87 *Commission v. Italy* [1989] ECR 143.

1. The Material and Personal Scope of the Directive

According to Article 1(1), the Directive applies to employees' claims arising from contracts of employment or employment relationships[323] and existing against employers who are in a state of insolvency. According to Article 2, an employer is considered to be in a state of insolvency when 'a request has been made for the opening of proceedings involving the employer's assets ... to satisfy collectively the claims of creditors', and which make it possible to take into consideration employees' claims; and where the competent national authority has 'either decided to open proceedings, or established that the employer's undertaking or business has been definitively closed down and that the available assets are insufficient to warrant the opening of proceedings'.[324] This is the only definition provided by the Directive; other terms used—for example, employee, employer, pay, and rights conferring immediate or prospective entitlements—are defined by reference to national law.[325] Nevertheless, in *Francovich (No. 1)*[326] the Court ruled that Articles 1 and 2 were sufficiently precise and unconditional to be directly effective.

Member States may under Article 1(2) exclude two categories of employees from the scope of the Directive. First, employees can be excluded by virtue of the 'special nature' of the employees' contract of employment. The details are provided in the Annex to the Directive but it includes domestic servants in Spain and the Netherlands, out-workers, employees who are relatives of the employer, seasonal, casual, or part-time workers in Ireland, and crews of fishing vessels in Greece and the UK. In *Wagner-Miret*[327] the Court ruled that the Directive was intended to apply to all categories of employees defined as employees under national law, with the exception of those listed in the annex. Spain was successful in obtaining an exclusion for domestic servants employed by a natural person in the annex. However, Spanish legislation also excluded higher management staff, who were classified as employees, from protection under the Directive but did not request their inclusion in the annex. Consequently, the Court ruled that higher management staff could not be excluded from the scope of the Directive.

Secondly, employees can be excluded from the protection of the Directive because of the existence of other forms of guarantee which offer the employee protection equivalent to that conferred by the Directive. Again the Annex provides full details but the list includes the crews of seagoing vessels in Greece, Italy, and the UK and permanent and pensionable employees of

---

[323] The term 'contract of employment' will be now be used to describe both the contract of employment and the employment relationship unless otherwise stated.

[324] Art. 2(1).

[325] Art. 2(2).

[326] Joined Cases C–6 and C–9/90 *Francovich (No. 1) and Bonifaci v. Italy* [1991] ECR I–5357.

[327] Case C–334/92 *Wagner-Miret v. Fondo de Garantía Salarial* [1993] ECR I–6911.

local or other public authorities and certain groups of teachers in Ireland. However, as the Court pointed out in *Commission v. Greece*,[328] since the purpose of the Directive is to ensure a minimum degree of protection for all employees these exclusions are possible only by way of exception.

The interrelationship between Articles 1(1), (2), and 2 was considered in *Francovich (No. 1)* and *(No. 2)*. In *Francovich (No. 1)*[329] the applicants' employer went into liquidation, leaving them with arrears of salary outstanding at a time when the Italian government had failed to implement the Directive. The Court ruled that in order to determine whether a person should be regarded as intended to benefit under the Directive a national court must verify, first, whether the person concerned is an employed person under national law and whether he is excluded from the scope of the Directive in accordance with Article 1(2) and the Annex, and then ascertain whether a state of insolvency exists, as provided for in Article 2 of the Directive.

After the Court's decision in *Francovich (No. 1)* the Italian government adopted Decree–Law No. 80 (13 February 1992) transposing the Directive into national law. Under this law, several categories of employer were excluded from proceedings to satisfy the claims of creditors collectively. In *Francovich (No. 2)*[330] the national court asked whether this was compatible with Article 2 of the Directive. The Court said that it was clear from the terms of Article 2 that in order for an employer to be deemed to be in a state of insolvency, four conditions have to be satisfied:

1. that the laws, regulations, and administrative provisions of the Member States concerned provide for proceedings involving the employer's assets to satisfy collectively the claims of creditors;
2. that employees' claims resulting from contracts of employment or employment relationships may be taken into consideration in such proceedings;
3. that a request has been made for proceedings to be opened;
4. that the authority competent under the national provisions has either decided to open proceedings or established that the employer's undertaking or business has been definitively closed down and that the available assets are insufficient to warrant the opening of the proceedings.

Therefore the Directive could not be relied on by employees whose contract of employment or employment relationship was with an employer who could not, under national law, be subject to proceedings to satisfy collectively the claims of creditors. Such an employer could not be in a 'state of insolvency' within the specific meaning of that phrase as used in the Directive, even though this might mean that the protection afforded by the Directive varies

---

[328] Case C–53/88 *Commission v. Greece* [1990] ECR I–3931.
[329] Joined Cases C–6 and C–9/90 [1991] ECR I–5357. See further below nn. 340–343.
[330] Case C–479/93 *Francovich (No. 2) v. Italy* [1995] ECR I–3843.

from one Member State to another as a result of differences between the various national rules governing proceedings to satisfy collectively the claims of creditors.[331]

2. The Protection Conferred by the Directive

The Directive provides three tiers of protection for the worker: first, the payment of outstanding claims against the employer, including arrears of wages, by a specially established guarantee institution; secondly, the guarantee by the Member States that the insolvent employer's non-payment of state social security contributions does not adversely afffect employees' benefit entitlement; and thirdly, in the case of former employees, the protection of their entitlement to old-age benefits under supplementary company or intercompany pension schemes.

2.1 Payment by Guarantee Institutions of Employees' Claims

Article 3(1) obliges Member States to set up guarantee institutions to 'guarantee' the payment of employees' outstanding claims resulting from contracts of employment or employment relationships and relating to pay for a period prior to a given date. The onus is on the Member State to lay down the detailed rules for the organization, financing, and operation of the guarantee institution (Article 5).[332] The employees' claims, including pay, are guaranteed for a period prior to a given date.[333] Member States can select the date and the period for which to guarantee the payment.[334] They may also opt to limit the liability.[335] The Directive does, however, lay down minimum standards depending on the chosen period:

(1) if the chosen date is the 'onset of the employer's insolvency',[336] the

---

[331] This point was also recognized in the Preamble which provides that 'differences still remain between the Member States as regards the extent of the protection of employees in this respect; . . . efforts should be directed at reducing these differences, which can have a direct effect on the functioning of the common market'.

[332] The Member States must, however, take three principles into account: the assets of the guarantee institution must be independent of the employers' operating capital and be inaccessible to proceedings for insolvency; employers must contribute to the financing of the institution unless the costs are fully covered by the public authorities; and the guarantee institution's liabilities must not depend on whether obligations to contribute to the financing have been fulfilled.

[333] Art. 3(1) and Case 22/87 *Commission v. Italy* [1989] ECR 143.

[334] Art. 3(2).

[335] Art. 4(1).

[336] According to the Court in Case C–373/95 *Maso v. INPS* [1997] ECR I–4051, the phrase 'onset of the employer's insolvency', referred to in Arts. 3(2) and 4(2) of Directive 80/987, corresponds to the date of the request that proceedings to satisfy collectively the claims of creditors be opened, since the guarantee cannot be provided prior to a decision to open such proceedings or to a finding that the business has been definitively closed down where the assets are insufficient.

Member State must at least ensure the payment of outstanding claims relating to pay for the last three months[337] of the contract of employment occurring within a period of six months preceding the date of the onset of the employer's insolvency;

(2) if the chosen date is that of the notice of dismissal issued to the employee on account of the employer's insolvency, then the Member State must ensure the payment of outstanding claims relating to pay for the last three months of the contract of employment preceding the date of the notice of dismissal issued to the employee on account of the employer's insolvency;

(3) if the chosen date is the onset of the employer's insolvency or that on which the contract of employment was discontinued on account of the employer's insolvency, the Member State must ensure the payment of outstanding claims relating to pay for the last eighteen months of the contract of employment preceding the date of the onset of the employer's insolvency or the date on which the contract of employment with the employee was discontinued on account of the employer's insolvency. In this case Member States may limit the liability to make payment to pay corresponding to a period of eight weeks or to several shorter periods totalling eight weeks.[338]

Finally, in recognition that the Directive does not have solely welfarist objectives, Article 4(3) permits the Member States to set a ceiling for payment, so that the sums paid do not exceed 'the social objective of the Directive'. The Commission must be notified of the means of calculating this ceiling. Even if the Commission has not been informed, Member States are still free to set a ceiling.[339]

In *Francovich (No. 1)*[340] the Court considered Articles 3 and 4, concerning the content of the guarantee, to be sufficiently precise and unconditional to be directly effective. The fact that the Member States had a choice of date from which payment of the claims were to be guaranteed presented no obstacle[341]—the minimum guarantee was the date which imposed the least burden on the guarantee institution, i.e. the date of the onset of the employer's insolvency. However, the wide discretion conferred on the Member States by Article 5 in establishing the guarantee institution meant that it was not sufficiently precise to enable individuals to rely on it before the national court.[342] However, the Court did say that the State would be liable for failing to

---

[337] This means calendar months (Case C–373/95 *Maso* [1997] ECR I–4051).

[338] Arts. 3(2) and 4(2). See generally Case C–125/97 *Regeling v. Bestuur van de Bedrijfs–vereniging voor de Metaalnijverheid* [1998] ECR I–4493.

[339] Case C–235/95 *AGS Assedic Pas-de-Calais v. Dumon and Froment* [1998] ECR I–4531.

[340] Joined Cases C–6 and C–9/90 [1991] ECR I–5357.

[341] Case 71/85 *Netherlands v. FNV* [1986] ECR 3855 and Case 286/85 *McDermott and Cotter v. Minister for Social Welfare and Attorney-General* [1987] ECR 1453.

[342] Joined Cases C–6 and 9/90 *Francovich (No. 1)* [1991] ECR I–5357.

implement the Directive.[343] Similarly in *Wagner-Miret*,[344] the Court said that the discretion given to the Member States by Article 5 of the Directive with regard to the organization, operation, and financing of the guarantee institutions meant that higher management staff could not rely on the Directive to request payment of amounts owing by way of salary from the guarantee institution established for the other categories of employee. The Court then added that even when interpreted in the light of the Directive, in accordance with the principles laid down in *Marleasing*,[345] national law did not enable higher management staff to obtain the benefits provided by the guarantee institutions. However, such staff were entitled, as in *Francovich (No. 1)* itself, to request the State concerned to make good the loss and damage sustained as a result of the failure to implement the Directive (considered in section 3 below).

More recently the Court has had to consider the question of which State's guarantee institution has to pay where the employees work in one Member State but the employer becomes insolvent in another. In *Mosbæk*[346] the Court ruled the guarantee institution responsible for the payment of the employee's claims under Article 3 was the institution of the State in which, according to Article 2, either it was decided to open the proceedings to settle the creditors' claims or that the employer's undertaking has been closed down. However, in *Everson*[347] the Court distinguished *Mosbæk*. In *Mosbæk* the British insolvent company was not established or registered in Denmark: the employee merely acted as its agent there. She was paid directly and no tax or social security contributions were deducted under Danish law. The UK's guarantee institution was therefore obliged to meet the claim. In *Everson*, by contrast, an Irish company was established and registered in the UK and paid its workers through its branch, collecting the taxes and social security contributions under UK law. In this case the guarantee institution of the State of employment (the UK) was liable for payment of outstanding claims to the employees employed on that territory when the employer was placed in liquidation.

2.2 Provisions concerning Social Security and Old-age Benefits

Article 6 states that Member States have the option to provide that the guarantee institution is not responsible for the contributions owed by the insolvent employer either to the national statutory social security scheme or to supplementary company or inter-company pension schemes.[348] Nevertheless, Article 7 provides that Member States *must* ensure that the non-payment by

---

[343] See below, nn. 355–361.

[344] Case C–334/92 [1993] ECR I–6911.

[345] Case C–109/89 [1990] ECR I–4135.

[346] Case C–117/96 *Mosbæk v. Lønmodtagernes Garantifond* [1997] ECR I–5017.

[347] Case C–198/98 *Everson and Barrass v. Secretary of State for Trade and Industry*, judgment of 16 Dec. 1999, para. 19.

[348] Art. 6. This view was confirmed by Case 22/87 *Commission v. Italy* [1989] ECR 143, para. 32.

the insolvent employer of compulsory contributions to their insurance institutions under the state social security scheme does not adversely affect employees' benefit entitlement inasmuch as the employees' contributions were deducted at source from the remuneration paid.[349] In other words, as the Court explained in *Commission* v. *Italy*,[350] Member States must choose another system for guaranteeing employees' entitlement to social security benefits.

Not only does the Directive provide some protection to workers employed at the time of the employer's insolvency but it requires Member States to protect 'the interests of employees and of persons having already left the employer's undertaking or business at the date of the onset of the employer's insolvency' in respect of rights conferring on them immediate or prospective entitlement to old-age benefits, including survivors' benefits, under occupational or supplementary schemes which fall outside the national statutory social security system.[351] However, these protective provisions do not prevent Member States from either taking measures to avoid abuses or refusing or reducing the liability of the guarantee institution if it appears that 'fulfilment of the obligation is unjustifiable because of the existence of special links between the employee and the employer and of common interests resulting in collusion between them'.[352]

3. Final Provisions

The rules laid down are the minimum: Member States have the option of introducing laws, regulations, or administrative provisions which are more favourable to employees.[353] Nevertheless, Member States were obliged at least to implement the provisions of the Directive by 20 October 1983.[354] Directive 80/987/EEC differs from the Directives on Transfers and Collective Redundancies in that it envisages a particular role for the State which cannot be fulfilled by any other body. Consequently, as we saw above, the Court recognized in *Francovich (No. 1)*[355] that the key provision of the Directive—Article 5 on the establishment of a guarantee institution—could not be directly effective[356]

---

[349] Art. 7. This does not explain the fate of an insolvent employer's unpaid contributions to an occupational scheme.

[350] Case 22/87 [1989] ECR 143.

[351] Art. 8.

[352] Art. 10.

[353] Art. 9.

[354] Failure to implement the Directive has led to enforcement proceedings brought against Italy and Greece: see Case 22/87 *Commission* v. *Italy* [1989] ECR 143 and Case C–53/88 *Commission* v. *Greece* [1990] ECR I–3931.

[355] Joined Cases C–6 and C–9/90 *Francovich* v. *Italy (No. 1)* [1991] ECR I–5357.

[356] In Joined Cases C–140, C–141, C–278, and C–279/91 *Suffritti* v. *INPS* [1992] ECR I–6337 the Court, however, held that the plaintiffs could not rely on the provisions of the Directive since both the declarations of insolvency and the termination of the employment relationships took place before the expiry of the time limit for the implementation of the Directive. The Court reminded the parties that it is only where a Member State has not correctly implemented a Directive within the period of implementation laid down that individuals can rely on rights which derive directly from provisions of the Directive before their national courts.

and so could not be relied on by the applicants in the national court to claim arrears of salary. Instead, the Court ruled that Francovich and Bonifaci were obliged to sue the State for damages for the loss suffered due to the Italian government's failure to implement the Directive. Famously, it said that Member States were required to make good loss or damage caused to individuals by their failure to transpose a Directive since the principle of state liability was inherent in the system of the Treaty.[357] In *Francovich (No. 1)* the Court laid down three conditions for state liability, which it subsequently refined,[358] namely, that the rule of law infringed must have been intended to confer rights on individuals and the content of those rights must have been identifiable; the breach must be sufficiently serious (always satisfied in the case of total failure to implement a directive);[359] and there must be a direct causal link between the breach of the obligation resting on the State and the damage sustained by the injured parties.[360] In *Factortame (No. 3)*,[361] the Court established that the reparation must be commensurate with the loss or damage sustained, so as to ensure effective protection for the rights of the individuals harmed. Subject to this proviso, it is on the basis of the rules of national law on liability that the State must make reparation for the consequences of the loss or damage caused. However, the conditions for reparation of loss or damage laid down by national law must not be less favourable than those relating to similar domestic claims and must not be so framed as to make it virtually impossible or excessively difficult to obtain reparation.

In *Maso*[362] and *Bonifaci*[363] the Court considered the extent of the reparation for the loss or damage arising from such failure. The Court said that in making good the loss or damage sustained by employees as a result of the belated transposition of the Directive, a Member State was entitled to apply retroactively the belated implementing measures to such employees, including rules against aggregation or other limitations on the liability of the guarantee institution, provided that the Directive had been properly transposed.

---

[357] Joined Cases C–6 and C–9/90 *Francovich (No. 1)* [1991] ECR I–5357.

[358] Ibid., para. 35; Joined Cases C–46 and C–48/93 *Brasserie du Pêcheur and ex parte Factortame and Others* [1996] ECR I–1029, para. 31; Case C–392/93 *R v. Secretary of State for Trade and Industry, ex parte British Telecommunications* [1996] ECR I–1631, para. 38; and Case C–5/94 *R v. MAFF, ex parte Hedley Lomas* [1996] ECR I–2553, para. 24. See also Cases C–302/97 *Konle v. Austria* [1999] ECR I–3099 and Case C–424/97 *Haim (No. 2) v. KVN*, judgment of 4 July 2000 which make clear that damages need not necessarily be provided by the federal state but can also be payable by any other public law body legally distinct from the state.

[359] Joined Cases C–178, C–179, C–188, C–189, and C–190/94 *Dillenkofer and Others v. Bundesrepublik Deutschland* [1996] ECR I–4845, para. 20.

[360] Joined Cases C–46 and C–48/93 *ex parte Factortame (No. 3)* [1996] ECR I–1029, para. 51; Case C–392/93 *ex parte British Telecommunications* [1996] ECR I–1631, para. 39; Case C–5/94 *ex parte Hedley Lomas* [1996] ECR I–2553, para. 25; and Joined Cases C–178, C–179, C–188, C–189, and C–190/94 *Dillenkofer and Others* [1996] ECR I–4845, para. 21.

[361] Para. 82.

[362] Case C–373/95 [1997] ECR I–4051.

[363] Joined Cases C–94 and C–95/95 *Bonifaci v. INPS* [1997] ECR I–3969.

However, it was for the national court to ensure that reparation of the loss or damage sustained by the beneficiaries was adequate. Retroactive and proper application in full of the measures implementing the Directive would suffice unless the beneficiaries established the existence of complementary loss sustained on account of the fact that they were unable to benefit at the appropriate time from the financial advantages guaranteed by the Directive. If so, such loss also had to be made good.

Finally, in *Palmisani*[364] the Court ruled that Community law allowed Member States to require any action for reparation of the loss or damage sustained as a result of the belated transposition of Directive 80/987/EEC to be brought within a limitation period of one year from the date of its transposition into national law, provided that the limitation period was no less favourable than procedural requirements in respect of similar actions of a domestic nature.

D. CONCLUSIONS

Despite the overt recognition that the directives on transfers of undertakings, collective redundancies, and insolvency have a welfarist or market-correcting purpose (the protection of labour standards), it has become increasingly clear that the Court is also motivated by the desire to ensure a level playing field of costs so that the financial burden of restructuring an enterprise is the same in all Member States. Express acknowledgement of this can be found in the *Commission v. UK*[365] cases where the Court said:

By harmonising the rules applicable to collective redundancies,[366] the Community legislature intended both to ensure comparable protection of workers' rights in the different Member States and *to harmonise the costs which such protective rules entail for Community undertakings* [emphasis added].

However, the effectiveness of this level playing field of costs is significantly reduced by the degree to which key matters are dictated by national legislation or practice. As we have seen in *Katsikas*,[367] while the Court recognized the worker's right to refuse to be transferred it allowed national law to prescribe the consequences for the worker of his or her refusal. As a result some Member States have said that the worker's contract of employment is treated as terminated, while in others the contract with the transferor will usually continue. If the Court was genuinely committed to worker protection it could

---

[364] Case C–261/95 *Palmisani* v. *INPS* [1997] ECR I–4025.

[365] Case C–383/92 [1994] ECR I–2479.

[366] The Court used the same words in the context of the Directive on safeguarding employees' rights in the event of transfers of undertakings in Case C–382/92 *Commission* v. *UK* [1994] ECR I–2435.

[367] Joined Cases C–132, C–138, and C–139/91 [1992] ECR I–6577.

have provided that workers must not be prejudiced as a result of their decision not to be transferred.

It is perhaps concern about high levels of unemployment that has prompted the Court to re-orientate its case law, particularly in the context of transfers after *Süzen*,[368] in favour of the economic imperative to pursue the most cost-efficient forms of organization, such as contracting out. Concerns about unemployment are also reflected in the amendments to the Directives on Collective Redundancies and Transfers and show a shift towards an increasing flexibility and adaptability which, as we have seen,[369] forms one of the four key pillars of the Community's employment policy. Yet, the lack of clarity and consistency in the Court's rulings carry their own cost and it is in this context that the criticism of the Court is most deserved.

[368] Case C–13/95 [1997] ECR I–1259.
[369] See further Ch. 1. See also Hunt, above n. 8, 229.

8

Collective Labour Law

Collective labour law traditionally embraces the body of rules regulating the relationship between the collectivity of employees and employers or groups of employers. The diversity of collective labour law is reflected in the Community Social Charter 1989. It envisages rights of information, consultation, and participation for workers.[1] It also talks of employers and workers 'having the right of association to constitute professional organisations or trade unions of their choice for the defence of their economic and social interests' or not to do so if they do not wish,[2] the right to 'negotiate and conclude collective agreements',[3] and the right to resort to collective action including strikes.[4] With the exception of the right to join or not to join a trade union, reference is made in all cases to national legislation and practice to clarify the substance and exercise of the right. In reality, only the rights to information, consultation, and participation of workers' representatives and collective bargaining[5] have taken on any concrete form in the Community legal order. The Social Charter Action Programme made no concrete proposals to substantiate the other collective labour rights and Article 137(6)[6] expressly excludes 'pay, the right of association, the right to strike or the right to impose lock-outs' from the Community's competence under Article 137.

In recent years information and consultation requirements and the development of the social dialogue have attracted renewed interest as a key to modernizing the organization of work and improving levels of employment.[7] As the Report on *Managing Change* points out:

Regular, transparent, comprehensive dialogue creates trust. . . . The systematic development of social dialogue within companies, nationally and at European level is fundamental to managing change and preventing negative social consequences and deterioration of the social fabric. . . . Social dialogue ensures a balance is maintained between corporate flexibility and workers' safety [security].[8]

---

[1] Arts. 17–18.

[2] Art. 11.

[3] Art. 12.

[4] Art. 13. The internal legal order of the Member States is free to determine the conditions and the extent to which the rights laid down in Arts. 11–13 apply to the armed forces, police, and civil service (Art. 14).

[5] See further Chs. 1 and 2.

[6] Ex Art. 2(6) Social Policy Agreement (SPA).

[7] See COM(98)592 discussed further below, nn. 197–204.

[8] Final Report of the High Level Group on Economic and Social Implications of Industrial Change, Nov. 1998, 9.

The argument runs that workers who participate in decisions which affect them enjoy a greater degree of job satisfaction and should be more productive than those who simply accept orders.[9] Social dialogue, replacing the more traditional hierarchical management arrangements, is therefore seen as the cornerstone of corporate governance designed to create a high skill, high effort, high trust European labour market. These theories draw on the success of the German economy which has been attributed in part to its system of co-determination (*Mitbestimmung*) where workers are involved in decision-making not only at plant level through works councils but also at company level through the membership of workers' representatives on the supervisory board.[10]

Such participation brings costs as well as benefits. This has led to fears of social dumping[11]—that in the absence of Community regulation companies will incorporate in countries which take a low-cost approach to employment relations. In the EU this has not been a real problem since most countries operate the *siège réel* doctrine whereby a company's 'real seat' is the country where its central administration or principal place of business is located. Therefore, a company incorporated in the UK but with its plant and operations in Germany will be considered under German law to have its real seat in Germany. The decision of the Court in *Centros*[12] has, however, cast doubt on the compatibility of the real seat doctrine with Community law. This, in turn, may create further pressure for the enactment of Community legislation on worker representation to protect existing German worker participation structures from such challenges albeit that most labour law rights are applied to employers located within the territory and not to companies as such.

---

[9] Cheffins, *Company Law: Theory, Structure and Operation* (OUP, Oxford, 1997).

[10] See Adams, 'The Right to Participate' (1992) 5 *Employee Resp. and Rts J.* 91, 94, and 97; and Thelan, *Union of Parts: Labor Politics in Postwar Germany* (Cornell University Press, Ithaca, NY, 1991), 1–5, 25–32, cited and discussed in Cheffins, above, n. 9, 582. Cf. Kraft, 'Empirical Studies on Codetermination: A Selective Survey and Research Design', in *Co-determination: A Discussion of Different Approaches*, eds. Nutzinger and Backhaus (Springer-Verlag, Berlin, 1989).

[11] These arguments are considered further in Ch. 1.

[12] Case C–212/97 *Centros v. Erhvervs- og Selskabsstyrelsen* [1999] ECR I–1459. See also Barnard and Deakin, 'In Search of Coherence: Social Policy, the Single Market and Fundamental Rights'. [1999–2000] *IRJ European Annual Review*, forthcoming.

A. THE RIGHT TO INFORMATION, CONSULTATION, AND PARTICIPATION

1. Introduction

1.1 Terminology

While there is considerable overlap between the terms information, consultation, and participation, shades of meaning can be distinguished. The provision of information is unilateral: the information is provided by management to the workers' representatives. Consultation, on the other hand, is bilateral, allowing workers' representatives the possibility of making their views known. At times consultation, as conceived by the Community, approaches collective bargaining. This can be seen in the case of Article 2 of Directive 98/59/EC[13] on collective redundancies which requires the employer to consult with the workers' representatives 'with a view to reaching agreement'. Similarly, Article 2(1)(f) of the European Works Councils (EWCs) Directive 94/45,[14] defines consultation as 'the exchange of views and *establishment of dialogue* between employees' representatives and central management or any more appropriate level of management' (emphasis added).

Participation can be regarded as a generic term embracing all types of industrial democracy,[15] ranging from the provision of information, consultation, and collective bargaining to more extensive involvement in the employer's decision-making process. This participation can be direct or indirect.[16] Direct participation permits *individual* employees to take part directly in decision-making or other company processes. The most obvious example of this is employee participation in company finances through profit-related pay or equity sharing. It can also include involvement in decision-making, particularly at workplace level. Such participation is designed primarily to promote motivation in order to achieve company goals such as increased productivity, better quality control, and a greater sense of loyalty.

Indirect or representative participation, on the other hand, involves procedures through which workers are *collectively* represented in the company's decision-making processes. The purpose of such participation is primarily the representation of interests. This participation can loosely be divided into two categories: first, employee representatives who sit on the company's board

---

[13] [1999] OJ L225/16.

[14] [1994] OJ L354/64 as amended by Council Directive 97/74/EC [1997] OJ L10/20.

[15] See generally Kahn-Freund, 'Industrial Democracy' (1977) 6 *ILJ* 65; Davies and Wedderburn, 'The Land of Industrial Democracy' (1977) 6 *ILJ* 197.

[16] Gold and Hall, 'Legal Regulation and the Practice of Employee Participation in the European Community', European Foundation for the Improvement of Living and Working Conditions, EF/WP/90/41/EN, 26.

where their involvement is limited to structural matters at company level;[17] and, secondly, the establishment of works councils (or equivalent bodies) whose rights comprise the disclosure of information, consultation, and co-determination[18] over areas of concern at plant, company, or group level. These types of indirect participation are designed to improve worker representation in the decision-making process. This, it is believed, will improve operational efficiency because problems are identified and resolved at an earlier stage, and, as we have seen, workers feel a greater commitment to decisions in which they are involved or represented. The nature of such participation at national level will now be considered. This will provide the framework in which to understand the EU's legislation.

1.2 Worker Representation on the Company Board

The first type of indirect participation involves worker representation on the company board. Some Member States, notably the UK and Ireland, adopt a unitary or one-tiered system where the company is managed by a single administrative board which does not contain worker representation. Other Member States, notably Germany and the Netherlands, adopt a two-tier system to corporate structure under which the company is managed by a management board under the supervision of a supervisory board. Under German law elected employees or trade unionists are members of the supervisory organ (*Aufsichtsrat*) of the company.[19] While they constitute one-third of the members in companies employing between 500 and 2,000 employees,[20] in companies employing 2,000 employees or more a system of quasi-parity operates where there are as many members representing the employees as representing the shareholders.[21] The chair, however, is always a representative of the shareholders and has a casting vote in the case of deadlock.[22] While this method of worker participation, described as co-determination, ensures considerable influence from employees,[23] it also has wider implications for the relationship between management and labour. As Simitis points out, if co-determination is understood not only as a right to participate in the decision-making process but also as a duty to accept and defend the results of

---

[17] Ibid., 26.

[18] Co-determination means employee representatives sharing responsibility with management for making decisions in areas such as organization of working time, methods of remuneration, leave arrangements, health and safety, and bonus arrangements (ibid., 14).

[19] See generally Weiss, *Labour Law and Industrial Relations in the Federal Republic of Germany* (Kluwer, Deventer, 1989), 173–83.

[20] Works Constitution Law 1952.

[21] Co-determination Law (*Mitbestimmungsgesetz*) 1976.

[22] S. 29(2)of the Co-determination Law 1976.

[23] Although some commentators suggest that employee directors play only a peripheral role and that the supervisory board has only a small number of meetings annually which tend to be short and perfunctory. See Cheffins, above, n. 9, 592 and 594.

this process, strikes may prove increasingly questionable, at least as long as they are motivated by claims directly connected with the enterprise. He concludes that any effort aiming at the institutionalization of participation is clearly an attempt to modify the conflict structures. By attacking the privileges of employers, workers' representation also alters the position of employees. The freedom of bargaining and the right to strike rest on the dissociation of workers and enterprise policy.[24] With employee representatives on the board this can no longer be the case.

The Dutch system starts from a different premise to its German counterpart. It views the supervisory board as a genuinely non-executive body, reflecting as far as possible the views of the outside world and divorced from the internal power politics of the company; its role is to guide and supervise management on behalf of the shareholders and the employees.[25] Consequently, it considers that there is no place on the supervisory board for either trade union representatives or employees. Whenever a vacancy on the board arises the remaining members of the board co-opt a person from a list of candidates nominated separately by the shareholders, management, and the works council. The new member must be independent and so cannot be an employee or a trade unionist. If one of the groups objects to the appointment it can pronounce a veto, in which case the matter is decided by the Enterprise Chamber Court.

1.3 Other Types of Worker Representation

The second type of indirect worker participation involves worker representatives receiving information, being consulted, and sometimes engaging in collective bargaining. In the UK worker representation has traditionally been channelled through recognized unions.[26] The concept of works councils or their equivalents has been largely unfamiliar.[27] This is known as the single-channel approach. This approach to industrial relations, combined with the abstention of the State from involvement in industrial relations, has been a distinguishing characteristic of British industrial relations since the nineteenth century.[28] Indeed, in 1954 Kahn-Freund observed that British indus-

---

[24] Simitis, 'Workers' Participation in the Enterprise—Transcending Company Law?' (1975) 38 *MLR* 1.

[25] See, Welch, 'The Final Draft Directive—A False Dawn' (1983) 9 *ELRev.* 83, 86.

[26] Traditionally, recognition has been entirely a matter for employers. This position has been changed in part by s.1 and Schedule I to the Employment Relations Act 1999, introducing a new s. 70A to the Trade Union and Labour Relations (Consolidation) Act (TULR(C)A) 1992. See Wedderburn, 'Collective Bargaining or Legal Enactment: the 1999 Act and Union Recognition' (2000) 29 *ILJ* 1.

[27] Some UK companies have, however, set up joint consultative committees comprising both management and employee representatives.

[28] Clark and Winchester, 'Management and Trade Unions', in *Personnel Management: Comprehensive Guide to Theory and Practice in Britain*, ed. Sisson (Blackwell, Oxford, 1994), 714.

trial relations have, in the main, developed by way of industrial autonomy.[29] At the end of the 1970s he noted that although '[i]n many respects the law intervenes in the organisation of collective labour relations today in a decisive way ... [t]his intervention ... remains supplementary and is in no sense antagonistic to the principle of autonomy'.[30] This picture has, however, significantly altered in the recent past, due in part to increased government intervention in industrial relations and in part to external pressure from the EC. The pattern beginning to emerge is one of a significantly weakened union structure combined with the development of alternative methods of worker consultation mechanisms influenced by the 'dual channel' approach found on the Continent.

Closer inspection of three main 'Continental' systems—Germany, France, and Italy—shows, however, that there is no one 'Continental' approach. Germany has the most sophisticated dual model.[31] In essence unions and employers' associations are responsible for collective bargaining, usually at a sectoral or regional level, concerning quantitative matters (especially wages and hours); works councils and management are responsible for relations for essentially qualitative issues at company level. This dual system has an elaborate legal basis. The Works Constitution Act 1972 (*BetrVG*) requires the election of a works council (*Betriebsrat*) in all but the smallest private firms and defines precisely the questions on which councils possess rights of information, consultation, and co-determination.[32] Information and consultation rights apply to personnel planning and changes in work processes, the working environment, new technology, and job content. There is also a right to information in respect of financial matters.

The most famous aspect of the German system, co-determination (*Mitbestimmung*), has two limbs. On the one hand, it allows employee representation on company boards, outlined above.[33] On the other, it implies at least a provisional right of veto for works councils in respect of social matters, such as principles of remuneration and the introduction of new payment methods, bonus rates and performance related pay, daily and weekly work schedules,

---

[29] Kahn-Freund, 'Legal Framework', in *The System of Industrial Relations in Great Britain*, eds. Flanders and Clegg (Blackwell, Oxford, 1954), 43, cited in Simpson, *The Determination of Trade Union Representativeness in the United Kingdom*, Paper presented to the ILO, Oct. 1994, 1.

[30] Kahn-Freund, 'Labour Law', in *Selected Writings* (Stevens, London, 1978), 39.

[31] The following draws on Jacobi *et al.* 'Germany: Facing New Challenges', in Ferner and Hyman (eds.), *Industrial Relations in the New Europe* (Blackwell, Oxford, 1998).

[32] There is also provision for combined works councils (*Konzernbetriebsräte*) in multi-plant companies. There is parallel legislation in the public sector: the Federal Staff Representation Act with supplementary Acts in the various *Länder*.

[33] There are three different types of legal provision: the *BetrVG* 1952 provides for one-third employee representation on the supervisory boards of all companies with over 500 employees; the Co-determination Act 1976 provides notional parity in firms with more than 2,000 employees; and the 1951 Coal, Iron and Steel Industry Co-Determination Act allowing for parity co-determination. See also Weiss, *European Employment and Industrial Relations Glossary: Germany* (Sweet and Maxwell, London, 1992).

regulation of overtime and short-term working, holiday arrangements, and the use of technical devices to monitor employees' performance. It also covers such personnel matters as policies for recruitment, transfer, and regrading. In specific circumstances there is a right of veto over individual cases of hiring, grading, transfer, and dismissal. The participation rights are linked to the legal obligation to work with management 'in a spirit of mutual trust for the good of employees and of the establishment' and negotiation must be conducted 'with a serious desire to reach agreement'. However, despite these elaborate provisions in many small and medium-sized companies no works council exists. It has been estimated that only 24 per cent of all eligible private enterprises, covering 60 per cent of the private sector workforce, have a works council.[34]

A study conducted by Sadowski, Backes-Gellner, and Frick[35] of 2,392 private-sector firms in Germany during the period from May 1985 to April 1987 considered the organizational and institutional efficiency of works councils.[36] In respect of 'dismissals and quits' the authors discovered that German firms had an average turnover rate of 35 per cent. In firms with a works council the percentage was 26 per cent while in those without it was 38 per cent. The number of dismissals per 100 employees was 7.8 and voluntary resignations was 10.4 in firms with a works council and 14.6 (dismissals) and 15.7 (voluntary resignations) in firms without. Firms with a works council had a dismissal rate 2.9 per cent lower than that experienced by firms without plant level representation.[37] They also found that union density had no influence on the dismissal rate. This prompted the authors to conclude that since hiring and training costs are usually higher than firing costs, firms on average benefited from the presence of works councils with regard to their user costs of labour.[38]

The French system is characterized by a multitude of representative institutions, developed against a background of very low trade union density, whose functions relate largely to information and consultation but not collective bargaining.[39] Employee delegates (*délégués du personnel*) (compulsory in

---

[34] Jacobi *et al.*, above, n. 31, 211.

[35] 'Works Councils: Barriers or Boosts for the Competitiveness for German Firms?' (1995) 33 *BJIR* 493.

[36] In Germany the level of compliance with the Works Constitution Act is poor: only 24 per cent of firms with at least five permanent employees has a works council.

[37] In Germany prior consultation with the works council is a prerequisite for the validity of any dismissal (ss. 102–3 Works Constitution Act). The authors' findings indicate that works councils do not oppose dismissals *per se*. In only 6 per cent of all dismissals do works councils express their misgivings (arguing that the dismissal is socially unacceptable, that no social plan has been designed), while in 8 per cent of cases they lodge a formal contradiction. In the remaining 86 per cent of cases the works councils either explicitly agree with the employer (66 per cent) or remain silent (20 per cent).

[38] In SMES, if a works council actually exists, it is either ignored or completely isolated by authoritarian owners/managers. Cheffins, above, n. 9, 593, citing Lane, below, n. 206, 233–4.

[39] The courts do, however, accord certain legal force to agreements between the enterprise and the works council.

companies with ten or more workers) were introduced to deal with individual employee grievances and to ensure that labour laws and collective agreements were enforced. This is the most widespread form of worker representation in France.[40] Works councils (*Comités d'entreprise*), compulsory in companies of fifty or more employees, have information and consultation rights and are responsible for developing social and cultural activities. The head of the enterprise chairs the works council meetings.[41] Group committees (*comités de groupes*) enable works committees to intervene in corporate decision centres beyond their own establishment. Reforms in 1993 allowed firms with between fifty and 199 employees to opt for a single representative structure instead of two, with employee delegates taking over the works committee representative role. Workplace union branches (*sections syndicales*) and trade union delegates in companies (*délégués syndicaux*) carry out union activities and participate in plant level bargaining. *Délégués syndicaux* represent their union in dealings with the head of the enterprise but have the task of protecting the interests both of the union members and the enterprise's workforce as a whole. Provision is also made for a special trade union delegate who sits on the works council in a consultative capacity (*représentant syndical*).

This brief description of the French and German systems tends to suggest that the two channels (trade unions and worker representatives) are entirely separate and potentially in competition.[42] The true position is very different. Although by law in Germany there is a formal distinction between works councils and trade unions, the reality is that more than three-quarters of all works councillors are unionists.[43] Further, there is a relation of mutual dependence between trade unions and works councils: the union supplies the works council with information and expertise while works councillors sustain union organization by recruiting new members and functioning as the arm of

---

[40] Lyon-Caen, *European Employment and Industrial Relations Glossary: France* (Sweet and Maxwell, London, 1993), para. 262.

[41] The workplace health and safety committee (*comité d'hygiène, de sécurité et des conditions de travail*), compulsory in enterprises with more than 50 employees, has an important information and consultative role in respect of health and safety.

[42] In France it has been observed that the works council is a 'complement to union power, yet is also virtually its competitor': Lyon-Caen, *European Employment Industrial Relations Glossary: France, European Foundation for Living and Working Conditions* (Sweet and Maxwell, London, 1993), para. 153.

[43] In the 1995 works council elections the member-unions of the Deutsche Gewerkschaftsbund gained two-thirds of all council seats, a percentage comparable to 1990, with the non-unionized candidates gaining a quarter of all the seats. The predominance of union members on works councils is a pattern repeated elsewhere. In the 1994/5 works council elections in Spain the candidates of the trade union confederations constituted 82.8 per cent of all delegates elected (*European Industrial Relations Review* 267, 26). For the situation in the Netherlands, see Visser, 'Works Councils and Trade Unions: Rivals or Allies?' (1993) 29 *The Netherlands Journal of Social Sciences* 64. A survey in the Netherlands revealed that union members make up around 65 per cent of works councillors, where union density is only around 25 per cent (Rood, 'The Netherlands', in *International Encyclopedia of Labour Law and Industrial Relations*, ed. Blanpain (Kluwer, Deventer, 1993), 83).

the trade union in the workplace.[44] In France the link between trade unions and the other forms of worker representation has actually been supported by the State. Since union density is remarkably low the State has intervened to compensate for trade union weakness by granting special legal rights to enable unions to represent the interests of all employees and not only those of a limited membership.[45] In particular, the State has granted a quasi-monopoly to the five national confederations (CGT, CFDT, CGT-FO, CFTC, CGC) in collective bargaining at all levels. Employee delegates, works committee and safety committee representatives are elected by the whole workforce from a list of candidates proposed in the first instance by the five national trade union confederations. The aim of this is to strengthen national unions at enterprise level.

In Italy there is also an overlap between the role of trade unions and bodies representing the workforce as a whole. The reforms of 1993 led to the adoption of a single body of worker representation in all workplaces, the RSU (*rappresentanza sindicale unitaria*, unitary union representative structure), replacing the three overlapping forms of worker representation which had previously existed (a mixture of works councils (*Commissione interna*), workplace-based trade union representation by the most representative union (RSA) and factory councils). RSUs are bodies of both general and union representation, elected by the workforce as a whole but with unions having priority in nominating candidates.[46] The Italian system therefore reinforces the idea that the second channel is not an alternative to unionization but supportive of it.

In the UK trade unions are also familiar with acting in a dual capacity: collective bargaining is carried out on behalf of members and non-members alike. Yet in the UK any second channel is perceived as a threat to established trade unions and risks undermining collective bargaining. The explanation for this difference in perception may lie in the strong sense of the autonomy of trade unions. Unions pride themselves on their independence from the State and employers. Other forms of worker representatives are seen as dominated by the employers. Unions organize themselves and competition between them is regulated by themselves in the form of the Bridlington principles.

---

[44] See generally Gamillscheg, 'Trade Union Representativity in German Law', in *Labour Law at the Crossroads: Changing Employment Relationships. Studies in Honour of Benjamin Aaron*, eds. Bellace and Rood (Kluwer, Deventer, 1997).

[45] This section relies on Goetschy, 'France: the Limits of Reform', in Ferner and Hyman (eds.), above, n. 31.

[46] Regalia and Regini, 'Italy: the Dual Character of Industrial Relations', in Ferner and Hyman (eds.), above, n. 31. These arrangements are extremely complex: see Wedderburn, 'Consultation and Collective Bargaining in Europe: Success or Ideology?' (1997) 26 *ILJ* 1, 16.

2. Developments at Community Level

At Community level, the communiqué issued by the heads of state at the Paris summit in 1972 made reference to the importance of increasing the involvement of the Social Partners in the economic and social decisions of the Community,[47] a view endorsed by the 1974 Action Programme.[48] While the right to information and consultation had already been introduced without much controversy in specific areas, most notably health and safety,[49] collective redundancies,[50] and transfer of undertakings,[51] there was continued resistance to the introduction of a more general, systematic, and institutionalized right to employee participation in corporate decision-making. The long and tortuous legislative history of various proposals over the last twenty-five years bears testimony to this.[52]

2.1 European Company Statute

As early as 1970 the Commission made proposals for a European Company Statute,[53] referred to as an SE (*Societas Europea*), a free-standing cross-frontier European company which could be established independently of existing national laws, on the grounds that it was the only way that European industry and services could take full advantage of the internal market, and pool their resources to be able to compete with Japan and the USA. An essential element of this proposal was for worker participation in the company. The original Commission proposal was for a Regulation[54] which included provisions for an obligatory two-tier board with German-style worker participation. This combined one-third to one-half employee representation on the supervisory board, charged with overseeing and appointing the management board, and the mandatory establishment of a works council. The amended proposal strengthened the original version by proposing that the supervisory

---

[47] Final declaration, EC Bull. 10/1972, 15–24.

[48] [1974] OJ C13/1, EC Bull. 2/1974. The Commission has also taken the view that the structure and activities of Community enterprises, esp. transnational enterprises, must be sufficiently transparent for the benefit of shareholders, creditors, employees and the public interest in general. See Commission's Communication on *Multinational undertakings and the Community*, EC Bull. Supp. 15/1973.

[49] The Framework Directive 89/391/EEC on health and safety [1989] OJ L183/1 discussed in Ch. 6.

[50] Council Directive 75/129/EEC [1975] OJ L48/29, as amended by Council Directive 92/56/EC [1992] OJ L245/3 and consolidated in Council Directive 98/59/EC [1998] OJ L225/16 described in Ch. 7.

[51] See Council Directive 77/187/EEC [1977] OJ L61 as amended by Council Directive 98/50/EC [1998] OJ L201/88, discussed in Ch. 7.

[52] See, generally, Kolvenbach, 'EEC Company Law Harmonisation and Worker Participation' (1990) 11 *University of Pennsylvania Journal of International Business Law* 709.

[53] [1970] OJ C124/2, EC Bull. 8/1970 amended by COM(75)150 final.

[54] [1970] OJ C124/1, EC Bull. Supp. 8/1970.

board be made up of one-third employee representatives and one-third share-holder representatives, with the remainder being co-opted by these two groups.[55] The principal area for disagreement in Council related to worker participation and negotiations ceased in 1982.

The 1985 White Paper, 'Completing the Internal Market', provided for the preparation of a new European Company Statute. As a result, two legislative measures were proposed, a Regulation on the Statute for a European Company,[56] and a Directive complementing the statute[57] with regard to the involvement of employees in the European Company.[58] The proposed directive sets out measures to enable employees 'to participate in the supervision and strategic development' of SEs. As the Commission concludes, 'the inevitable restructuring of European industry will be more efficiently achieved and necessary change more readily accepted if all the interests concerned are involved in and fully committed to the one process. In particular the role of the social dialogue is a vital one; it is essential that the workers in the Community should be able to recognize the internal market as the one they have helped to create and as one in which their interests are appropriately safeguarded'.[59]

This worker involvement is, however, confined to the supervision and the strategic development of the SE and does not extend to day-to-day management.[60] The proposed directive proposes four models of worker participation, closely resembling those found in the draft Fifth Company Law Directive:[61]

(1) between one-half and one-third of the members of the supervisory or administrative board must be appointed by the employees of the SE or their representatives. The representatives of the employees of the SE must be elected according to the law and practice of the Member States;[62]

(2) the members of the supervisory or administrative board can be co-opted by the board but the general meeting of the shareholders or the representatives of the employees can propose candidates and may also, on specific grounds, object to the appointment of a particular candidate. If so, the appointment may not be made until an independent body established under public law has declared the objection inadmissible (the Dutch system);[63]

(3) a separate body representing the workers of the SE which must be informed by the board of management or the administrative board, at

---

[55] Bull. Supp. 4/75. See also *EIRR* 223, 25.

[56] [1989] OJ C263/41.

[57] COM (89)268 final—SYN 218 and 219, 1. Later (at 3) the Directive is described as an 'indispensable complement to the regulation'. Modified proposal COM(91)174 final—SYN 219.

[58] [1989] OJ C263/69.

[59] COM(88)320, 2.

[60] Art. 2.

[61] See below, nn. 78–103.

[62] Art. 4(1).

[63] Art. 4(2).

least every three months, of the progress of the company's business, including that of undertakings controlled by it which might have a significant effect on the operation of the SE. The boards must, however, inform the separate body without delay of any information which might have significant repercussions on the situation of the SE. The separate body can also demand information on all matters affecting working conditions and is entitled to receive the documents provided for the general meeting of shareholders. Finally, the separate body must be informed and consulted by management before any of the five strategic decisions discussed below can be taken;[64]

(4) Article 6 provides that the management board or the administrative board also has the option of entering into agreements with the employees or their representatives to establish other arrangements for worker participation. Once again, this freedom is substantially restricted by the minimum information and consultation requirements laid down by Article 6(2) which include the right to receive the same information as provided to the separate body and to receive the documents provided for the shareholders' meeting. Article 6 is the only provision which requires confidentiality on the part of the employee representatives and provides that information which might seriously jeopardize the interests of the SE or disrupt its projects may be withheld.[65]

In the case of the unitary board, the administrative board must have at least three members appointed by the general meeting and, where the model of participation in use requires it, by the employees.[66] The management board can only implement the following decisions following prior authorization of the supervisory board or of the administrative board as a whole:

(a) the closure or transfer of establishments or of substantial parts of establishments;
(b) substantial reduction, extension, or alteration of the activities of the SE;
(c) substantial organizational changes within the SE;
(d) the establishment of co-operation with other undertakings;
(e) the establishment of a subsidiary or holding company.[67]

Not only has the Commission proposed the statute for a European Company but it also has more recently proposed statutes for a European Association,[68] a European Co-operative Society,[69] and a European Mutual Society.[70] A

---

[64] Art. 5.
[65] Arts. 63–65.
[66] Arts. 66–67.
[67] Art. 72(1) of the draft regulation.
[68] [1992] OJ C99/2.
[69] [1992] OJ C99/4.
[70] [1992] OJ C99/6.

European Association (EA) would allow its members to pool their knowledge or their activities for a purpose in the general interest or to promote directly or indirectly the trade or professional interests of its members.[71] The profits from any economic activity carried out by the EA are to be devoted exclusively to the pursuit of its objects and cannot be divided among the members.[72] A European Cooperative Society, by contrast, is 'essentially groups of persons, operating in accordance with their principles, which are different from those applying to other businesses'.[73] A European Mutual Society (ME) will guarantee its members, in return for a subscription, full settlement of contractual undertakings entered into in the course of activities authorized by its statutes such as providence, insurance, health assistance, and credit.[74] All three proposed regulations are supplemented by directives permitting the involvement of employees.[75] However, this involvement is limited to informing and consulting employees and does not permit workers' representatives to participate in decision-making on the board of management either through a separate committee representing the employees or within any other structure agreed between the executive committees of the founder entities and the representatives of the employees. The information and consultation must occur 'in good time' and cover at least the following areas:[76]

- any proposals which might significantly affect the interests of the employees of the organisation, without prejudice to the Community provisions concerning information and consultation;[77]
- any question concerning conditions of employment, in particular changes affecting the organisation of the new body and the introduction of new working methods or new products and/or services;
- all documents submitted to the organisation's general meeting;
- certain other operations including closing or transferring a large establishment or a substantial part of such an establishment, substantially reducing, extending or altering the activities of the organisation and raising certain loans.

All of these proposals are currently stuck in Council.

---

[71] Art. 1 [1992] OJ C99/1, COM(91)273—SYN 386.

[72] Art. 1, para. 2.

[73] Preamble to the proposal for a Council Regulation on the Statute for a European Cooperative Society [1992] OJ C99/17.

[74] Art. 1(2) of the proposal for a Council Regulation on the Statute for a European Mutual Society [1992] OJ C99/40.

[75] 92/C 99/2 (European Association), 92/C 99/4 (European Cooperative Society), 92/C 99/6 (European Mutual Society).

[76] Art. 4(1).

[77] Directives 98/59/EC [1999] OJ L225/216, 77/187/EEC [1977] OJ L61/26 as amended by Directive 98/50/EC [1998] OJ L201/88, and 94/45/EC [1994] OJ L254/64.

2.2 Draft Fifth Company Directive

Companies operating in more than one Member State which have chosen not to adopt SE status may be affected by the proposal, known as the draft Fifth Company Directive, on the structure of public limited companies,[78] providing a menu of options for employee participation in undertakings employing at least 1,000 people, including on company boards. This draft directive forms part of a series of Directives proposed under Article 54(3)(g) [new Article 44(2)(g)] which aim to co-ordinate national legislation relating to public limited companies.[79] The draft directive has a chequered history. The 1972 version was based exclusively on a two-tier system,[80] which conflicted with the unitary board found in the new Member States, notably the UK and Ireland. Ten years later the Commission adopted an amended and more flexible proposal which, although trying to accommodate the diverse national traditions, remains blocked by the Council.[81] It is to apply to all public limited companies[82] with 1,000 or more employees.[83] The proposed directive requires that a two-tier system—run by a management organ, supervised by a supervisory organ[84] which appoints the members of the management organ[85]— must be provided in all Member States which companies are free to adopt if they wish.[86] The revised draft also envisages the possibility of a company operating under the unitary system being managed by the executive members of an administrative organ under the supervision of non-executive members who must appoint the executive members. The number of non-executive

---

[78] The proposal was originally published in 1972 and revised in 1975 and 1983 [1983] OJ C240/2. In 1988 the Commission prepared an amended text for consultation with the Member States.

[79] See generally Cheffins, above, n. 9, ch. 9.

[80] [1972] OJ C131/44. See Temple Lang, 'The Fifth EEC Directive on the Harmonisation of Company Law' (1975) 12 *CMLRev.* 155 and 345. See also Pipkorn, 'The Draft Directive on Procedures for Informing and Consulting Employees' (1983) 20 *CMLRev.* 725, 731. According to Pipkorn, the objective of the Directive was that the interests of shareholders should no longer be the sole motivation behind entrepreneurial decisions. Instead, through formalized co-operative discussions within a strategic decision-making body in the company, business policy should conform to the responsibility owed by public limited companies to their constituent elements of capital and labour and, more generally, to society as a whole.

[81] [1983] OJ C240/2.

[82] e.g. *Aktiengesellschaft* (Germany), *la societé anonyme/de naamloze vennootschap* (Belgium), *aktieselskabet* (Denmark), *la societé anonyme* (France and Luxembourg), the public company limited by shares or by guarantee (UK and Ireland), *la società per azioni* (Italy), *de naamloze vennootschap* (Netherlands) (Art. 1(1)).

[83] Arts. 4(1) and 21(b).

[84] The supervisory organ can receive a wide range of information including at least a quarterly written report on company affairs (Art. 11). It must also give its consent to decisions relating to the closure or transfer of the undertaking or substantial parts of the undertaking, substantial curtailment or extension of the activities of the undertaking, substantial organizational changes in the undertaking, and establishment of long-term co-operation with other undertakings or the termination of such co-operation (Art. 12).

[85] Art. 3(1).

[86] Art. 2(1).

members must be divisible by three and greater than the number of executive members. This is intended to make the unitary board genuinely equivalent to the two-tier board. Subject to the option of a two-tiered board being available, Member States can choose which of the following systems to apply:

(1) A two-tier structure of management and supervisory boards with employees electing between one-third and one-half of the supervisory board[87] (the 'German model'). Employee representatives must be appointed by a system of proportional representation, all employees must be able to participate in the election which must be by secret ballot, and free expression of opinion must be guaranteed.[88] If employee representatives constitute one-half of the board[89] the voting procedures of the supervisory organ must ensure that decisions are ultimately taken by the members appointed by the general meeting.[90]

(2) A two-tier structure of management and supervisory boards, with the employee representatives having the right to veto nominations for the supervisory board where the board co-opts its own members (the 'Dutch model'). If the nomination is vetoed the appointment cannot be made unless the objection is declared unfounded by an independent body existing under public law.[91] Unlike the Dutch system, however, the proposed directive does not give employee representatives or shareholders the right to nominate candidates, denying them their main opportunity to influence the composition of the board, nor does the proposal incorporate the central feature of the Dutch system—the ineligibility of employees of the company or trade union officials connected with the company for membership of the supervisory board.[92] Questions have also been raised whether this model is really equivalent to the other options provided by the proposed directive, and thus counts as a means of employee participation since the limited right to veto a particular candidate falls far short of the right to elect up to one-half of the members of the board.[93]

(3) A unitary board of directors with employees electing between one-third

---

[87] Art. 4b(1).

[88] Arts. 4i and 21j.

[89] Membership of the supervisory board also has its disadvantages: the proposed directive is silent on the standard of care and skill required of board members, but members of the board are personally liable without limit (although directors may exonerate themselves if they can show that no fault is attributable to them personally (Art. 10(2)) to the company for loss suffered by the company through breach of the law, memorandum, or articles, or for any other wrongful acts committed in the course of their duties (Art. 14(1)). See Boyle, 'Draft Fifth Directive: Implications for Directors' Duties, Board Structure and Employee Participation' (1992) 13 *Company Lawyer* 6.

[90] Art. 4b(2).

[91] Art. 4(c).

[92] Welch, above n. 25, 86.

[93] Ibid.

and one-half of the non-executive directors.[94] If the employees are permitted to appoint one-half of the non-executive members the board's voting procedure must ensure that decisions of the non-executive members may ultimately be taken by the members appointed by the general meeting. While some commentators viewed the prospect of employee directors on a unitary board in charge of day-to-day management with concern,[95] others have noted that this third option presupposes that all unitary boards are executive boards which do not delegate any of their powers to a managing director, management committee, or individual directors.[96] In the UK, delegation does occur, certainly in large companies[97] where professional management demands a degree of expertise which cannot be supplied by part-time directors. Managers of a company take day-to-day decisions and implement policy, and the board may meet only once a quarter when it takes important decisions and formulates policy. Its role in policy formulation is therefore not very different from that of a supervisory board in a two-tier system.[98]

(4) A consultative council combined with either a two-tier board or unitary board. This proposal is loosely based on the works council system found in continental Member States. It envisages a body—the consultative council—elected by all employees having the right to receive from the administrative or management bodies regular information and to be consulted on the administration, situation, progress, and prospects of the company, its competitive position, credit situation, and investment plans. The consultative council is also intended to have the same right to information as the non-executive directors or members of the supervisory organ.[99] This proposal risks conflict arising between the consultative council and the trade unions, particularly in the UK where, as we have seen, in the absence of any rival representative structure, the scope of collective bargaining has developed to a greater extent than in continental EC States.[100] The council is a purely consultative body which, in common with employee representatives in models one and three, has no power to veto management decisions. However, the employee representatives on a consultative council have one advantage over their colleagues in a minority position on a company board which may be hostile to their presence: their loyalty is not divided and they are free to defend employee interests with more vigour in a body composed exclusively of employees.[101]

---

[94] Art. 21d. On the acceptability of this see Turner, 'The Fifth Company Law Directive—A Saga of the Lawyer in the First Elected European Parliament' (1982) 3 *Business Law Review* 215.

[95] Ibid., for example.

[96] Welch, above n. 25, 93.

[97] See Table A, Art. 72.

[98] Welch, above n. 25, 93.

[99] Arts. 21e and 4d, respectively.

[100] Welch, above, n. 25, 92.

[101] Welch, above, n. 25, 95.

(5) Collective agreements guaranteeing a measure of employee participation with either a two-tier or unitary board (the 'Italian model').[102] Employee participation is to be regulated in accordance with collective agreements concluded between the company and organizations representing trade unions.[103] The flexibility and autonomy apparently provided by this option are undermined by the requirement that there must be employee participation on the supervisory board or administrative organ (model 1) or a consultative council (model 4).

These models of participation draw on existing practice in the Member States but the proposed directive provides that where a majority of employees have expressed their opposition to such participation employee participation shall not be implemented in a company. This proposal still continues to be stuck in Council.

2.3 The DG V (Employment and Social Affairs) Approach

The proposals considered in the previous sections have been the product of the 'company law' approach of DG XV (Internal Market) of the Commission. Striving towards harmonization of national laws relating to the structure of public limited companies, including employee participation in the decision-making process, its approach has been relatively detailed and prescriptive.[104] On the other hand, a different 'social affairs' approach can be detected in DG V's legislative proposals concerning the more limited ambition of informing and consulting the employees of undertakings with complex structures, in particular transnational undertakings.[105] Its approach has been more pragmatic, relying on Member States' existing employee representation arrangements instead of specifying particular models.[106] Its first attempt to put forward an information and consultation procedure (ICP) was the ill-fated and highly controversial 'Vredling' Directive in 1980,[107] which was substantially amended by the 'Richard' proposal in 1983.[108] These proposals were

---

[102] Welch, above n. 25.

[103] Arts. 4e and 21f.

[104] Hall, *Legislating for Employee Participation: A Case Study of the European Works Council Directive*, Warwick Papers in Industrial Relations, 1992. An expanded version of this can be found in Hall, 'Behind the European Works Councils Directive: The European Commission's Legislative Strategy' (1992) 30 *BJIR* 547.

[105] [1980] OJ L297/3, EC Bull. Supp. 3/80.

[106] Hall, above n. 104, 6.

[107] [1980] OJ C297/3, Bull. Supp. 3/80, discussed by Vandamme, 'L'Information et la Consultation des Travailleurs dans la proposition de directive sur les entreprises a structure complexe, en particulier transnationale' [1982] *Revue du Marché Commun* 368 and Blanpain *et al.*, *The Vredling Proposal. Information and Consultation of Employees in Multinational Enterprises* (Kluwer, Deventer, 1983).

[108] [1983] OJ C217/3, Bull. Supp. 2/83, 3. Discussed by Blanquet, 'Amended Proposal for a Directive on Procedures for Informing and Consulting Employees—From the "Vredling Proposal" to the "Richard Proposal" ', *Social Europe* 9/83, 19.

considered sisters to the directives on collective redundancies, transfers of undertakings, and the proposed Fifth Company Law Directive.[109]

The 'Vredling' proposal laid down procedures for informing and consulting the employees of a subsidiary in the Community when the parent and the subsidiary employed at least 1,000 workers. It required the management of the parent undertaking to forward to local management at least once a year 'general but explicit information giving a clear picture of the activities of the parent undertaking and its subsidiaries'.[110] The information related, in particular, to the structure of the company, its economic and financial situation, the probable development of the business and of production and sales, the employment situation, and probable trends and investment prospects. With the exception of confidential information, local management was required to forward this information to the employees' representatives. In addition, information about decisions taken by the parent company liable to have serious consequences for the interests of the employees of its subsidiaries, including the closure or transfer of an establishment and other major organizational changes, had to be forwarded to local management in good time before the final decision was taken. In these circumstances, local management was obliged to forward the information to the employees' representatives, who had thirty days to give their opinion, and then to hold consultations with a view to reaching agreement on the measures planned in respect of the employees.[111]

The proposed directive thus contained two key rights: the right to periodic information and the right to be consulted in advance of important decisions in the life of the undertaking. No interaction between central management and local representatives was prescribed, in order to preserve the autonomy of local management and to prevent it from being by-passed.[112] Nevertheless, both proposals prompted heated opposition and were accused first of being complicated and unfamiliar, secondly of interfering with information and consultation practices already in existence at national level (because the proposal covered large undertakings or groups of undertakings in a single State), and thirdly of disrupting voluntarist systems of industrial relations.[113] Allegations that the Commission was trying to harmonize diverse national industrial relations systems were not new,[114] but became an increasingly sensitive issue as the doctrine of subsidiarity gained in importance.

In 1986, the Council postponed further consideration of the directive until

[109] Pipkorn, 'The Draft Directive on Procedures for Informing and Consulting Employees' (1983) 20 *CMLRev.* 725, 726–7.

[110] Art. 3(1).

[111] Art. 4(3).

[112] Docksey, 'Information and Consultation of Employees: the United Kingdom and the Vredling Directive' (1986) 49 MLR 281, 285.

[113] Ibid., 281.

[114] See the Commission's concern expressed in its Green Paper on Employee Participation and Company Structures, EC Bull. Supp. 8/75.

1989. Discussions have still not resumed. However, the Council did adopt a resolution[115] relating to the Commission's 1983 proposals, which acknowledged the great political and economic importance of the problem and emphasized the importance of the social area in the context of the completion of the Community internal market and the need for greater convergence between the rights of employees in the Member States to be informed and consulted about the major decisions in the undertakings concerned. It also urged the Commission to continue its work on the subject and, where appropriate, to present another proposal.

In its Social Charter Action programme, the Commission proposed that, subject to the outcome of resumed discussions on the proposed Vredling Directive, there was to be an instrument on procedures for the information, consultation, and participation of workers in *European* scale undertakings and also an instrument—a Recommendation—on equity sharing and financial participation by workers. While the latter proposal has been adopted with relatively little opposition,[116] the former proposal to introduce European Works Councils (EWCs) was, once again, the subject of fierce opposition but a Directive was finally adopted under the Social Policy Agreement (SPA).[117]

2.4 European Works Councils

The increasing transnationalization of undertakings and groups of undertakings has highlighted the limits of national legislation on employee participation: national procedures for information and consultation have effect only within the legal framework of that country, benefit only the employees of that State, and generally relate only to activities carried out within the national boundaries, when key corporate decisions affecting a particular establishment are taken at a head office in another country. The Commission has identified a significant growth in the number of mergers carried out by Europe's largest industrial enterprises and, since 1987, the most rapid growth has been in acquisitions involving Community enterprises from two different Member States.[118] According to the Commission, while the Directives on Collective Redundancies[119] and Transfer of Undertakings[120] address some of the problems produced by market restructuring, the paucity of national provisions on consultation and information have been revealed. In response to this trend,

---

[115] V86/C203/1, Council Conclusions of 21 July 1986.

[116] Council Recommendation 92/443/EEC [1992] OJ L245/53.

[117] Council Directive 94/95/EC [1994] OJ L254/64. See below in section 3.

[118] Commission, 'The Impact of the Internal Market by Industrial Sector: the Challenge for the Member States' European Economy/Social Europe (special edn, OPEC, Luxembourg, 1992).

[119] Council Directive 75/129/EEC [1975] OJ L48/29. This Directive was amended by Council Directive 92/56/EEC [1992] OJ L245 to reflect the increasing transnationalization of companies and consolidated by Council Directive 98/59/EC [1998] OJ L225/16.

[120] Council Directive 77/187/EEC [1977] OJ L61/26.

a clutch of multinationals, mostly French and German (BSN, Bull, Elf-Aquitaine, Pechiney, Rhône-Poulenc, Saint Gobain, Thomson, Nestlé, Allainz, Volkswagen and Mercedes-Benz) established various types of jointly-agreed European level information and consultation arrangements.[121] These were influenced by the French basic model: a joint management/employee forum meets annually, at the employer's expense, to discuss information provided by management about group-level matters relating to corporate strategy, finances, and employment.[122]

Given the unfortunate history of its earlier legislative proposals in this area,[123] these precedents helped the Commission to identify a new legislative approach which would respect the principles of subsidiarity.[124] Community legislation could focus on the transnational dimension of employee information and consultation,[125] accommodating but not cutting across national practice in respect of employee representation,[126] in order to bridge the gap between increasingly transnational corporate decision-making and workers' nationally-defined and nationally-confined information and consultation rights.[127] At first, the Commission proposed, largely due to trade union pressure to encourage cross-border collective bargaining,[128] the establishment of an EWC,[129] the term used for a transnational, pan-European forum of employee representatives within multi-national corporate groups for the purposes of information disclosure and consultation with group-level management.[130] This marked a significant departure from the earlier Vredling Directive[131] where no single body had been proposed for employee representation but information and consultation procedures were to be channelled through the existing national representation structures. Despite this, the proposed European Works Council Directive was the political successor to the Vredling proposals and it also drew heavily on earlier proposals for the European Company Statute.

The initial proposal for a directive provided for the establishment of an EWC

---

[121] Marginson, 'European Integration and Trans-national Management—Union Relations in the Enterprise' (1992) 30 *BJIR* 529, 540. The operation of these bodies is considered in Gold and Hall, *European Level Information and Consultation in Multi-National Companies: An Evaluation of Practice*, European Foundation for the Improvement of Living and Working Conditions (OPEC, Luxembourg, 1992).

[122] Hall, above n. 104, 4.

[123] See text attached to nn. 104–115, above.

[124] COM(90)581, para. 17.

[125] See also the Opinion of the Economic and Social Committee on the social consequences of cross-frontier mergers [1989] OJ C329/10.

[126] Commission Social Charter Action Programme, *Social Europe* (Special Edn) 1/90, 66.

[127] Gold and Hall, 'Statutory European Works Councils: the Final Countdown?' (1994) 25 *IRJ* 177, 178.

[128] Hall, above n. 104, 3.

[129] COM(90)581 final [1990] OJ C39/10, amended proposal COM(91)345 final. See also, 206 *EIRR* 12.

[130] Gold and Hall, above n. 127, 177–8.

[131] See above, nn. 110–114.

in Community-scale undertakings or groups of undertakings with at least 1,000 employees in the EC, and at least two establishments in different Member States with a minimum of 100 employees in each, as a result of an agreement by a special negotiating body. If an agreement could not be reached, certain minimum requirements laid down in the annex were triggered relating to the composition and organization of the EWC and the information and consultation which had to occur.

Despite the emphasis on the transnational issues that would fall within the EWC's competence and the assertion that the EWC was not intended to interfere with existing information, consultation, or negotiation rights,[132] the UK remained implacably opposed to the principle of the directive. It argued, first, that the proposals would undermine existing successful arrangements for consultation, particularly at local levels; secondly, that it would impose new statutory restrictions on a company's freedom to implement decisions and consequently would cause costly delays; and thirdly, that the directive would deter inward investment, rendering firms more prone to settle in only one Member State[133] or discourage them from expanding above 1,000 employees. Finally, it said that the EWCs would impose a form of collective arrangement which would undermine the many successful local employee involvement practices currently in place and weaken the important role played in them by individual employees.[134] Since the proposal was based on Article 100 [new Article 94], the UK was able successfully to block its adoption by the Council.

In October 1993 the Commission abandoned its attempt to secure unanimous agreement on the directive and proposed to reintroduce the measure under the SPA, but this time providing for a choice between an EWC and an information and consultation procedure (ICP). The Social Partners were consulted, as required by Article 3(2) [new Article 138(2)],[135] and then the Commission produced a revised draft where the term 'European Works Council' was dropped and replaced by 'information and consultation structure', which remained very similar to the EWC of earlier drafts.[136] This draft formed the basis for unsuccessful negotiations between the Social Partners. UNICE, the employers' association, considered that employee participation measures should not be regulated or harmonized by the Community but should be allowed to evolve naturally, to reflect local circumstances. It also considered that too much emphasis was placed by the Commission on regulated collective relationships between employers and trade unions or workers' representatives and not enough on direct employee contact and involvement with

---

[132] See e.g. COM(90)581, para. 20(iii).

[133] Cf. Visser, 'Works Councils and Trade Unions in the Netherlands: Rivals or Allies?' (1993) 29 *The Netherlands Journal of Social Sciences* 64, esp. 86–7.

[134] Employment Department, *The United Kingdom in Europe: People, Jobs and Progress*, August 1993, 6–17.

[135] 241 *EIRR* 28.

[136] See further 242 *EIRR* 13.

management.[137] Meanwhile, ETUC, the trade union body, strongly favoured the introduction of measures encouraging employee participation and called for a basic European legal framework to guarantee the information, consult-ation, and participation rights of workers' representatives at all levels of decision-making within undertakings.[138]

With the breakdown of talks between the Social Partners, the Commission issued a further proposal for a Council Directive on 'the establishment of European Committees or procedures in Community-scale undertakings and Community-scale groups of undertakings for the purposes of informing and consulting employees'.[139] This proposal, based on Article 2(2) of the SPA, was designed to improve the right to information and consultation of employees in Community-scale undertakings and groups of undertakings[140] by establish-ing either a 'European Committee',[141] the term works council having been dropped, *or* a procedure for informing and consulting employees, the more flexible alternative emphasized by the Belgian presidency in 1993.[142] The term 'European Works Council' was reinstated in the final version of Directive 94/45/EC[143] adopted in September 1994. Since Directive 94/45 was adopted under the SPA the UK was initially excluded but with the Labour govern-ment's willingness to accede to the Social Chapter the Directive was extended to the UK in 1997.[144]

The requirement to establish an EWC or a procedure for informing and consulting (ICP) employees applies only to Community-scale under-takings and Community-scale groups of undertakings[145] with more than 1,000 employees across the eighteen Member States[146] and at least two

---

[137] UNICE Press Release, 24 Oct.1989, cited in Gold and Hall, *Legal Regulation and the Practice of Employee Participation in the European Community*, European Foundation for the Improvement of Living and Working Conditions, Working Paper No. EF/WP/90/41/EN.

[138] Gold and Hall, above, n. 127, 46. Despite these disagreements a working party set up as a result of the Val Duchesse social dialogue did manage to identify some common ground as to the need for information and consultation on the introduction of new technology (6 Mar. 1987).

[139] COM(94)134 final [1994] OJ C199/10.

[140] Art. 1(1).

[141] This term reflects the terminology used in voluntary information and consultation arrangements.

[142] Art. 1(2).

[143] [1994] OJ L254/64.

[144] Council Directive 97/74/EC [1997] OJ L10/20.

[145] Art. 1(1) and (2). A group of undertakings means a controlling undertaking, defined to mean an undertaking which can exercise a dominant influence over another undertaking by virtue of ownership, financial participation, or the rules which govern it (Art. 3(1) and (2)) and its controlled undertakings (Art. 2(1)(b)). These definitions are based on Council Directive 89/440/EEC [1989] OJ L210/1, amending Directive 71/305/EEC on the co-ordination of procedures for the award of public works contracts.

[146] Art. 2(1)(a). This includes the EEA States. The prescribed thresholds for the size of the workforce are to be based on the average number of employees, including part-time employees, employed during the previous two years calculated according to national legislation and/or practice (Art. 2(2)).

establishments[147] in different Member States each employing at least 150 people.[148] The Commission justified this dual threshold, first, on the ground that small businesses should not be burdened with additional obligations and, secondly, that the Directive should have no effect on existing ICPs in Member States based on national legislation and practices.[149] The Directive also applies where Community-scale undertakings or groups of undertakings have their headquarters outside the territory of the Member States but meet the threshold requirements in the eighteen Member States.[150] Legal responsibility for carrying out the Directive's requirements fall on either a representative agent of the undertaking or group of undertakings or the undertaking with the highest number of employees in the territory of the Member States.[151]

The Directive envisages a two-tier approach towards the establishment of an EWC or ICP (see Figure 8.1). The first stage involves voluntary negotiations. If there is no agreement, the mandatory ('subsidiary') provisions laid down in the annex to the Directive are triggered at the second stage. The procedure for the first stage is activated at the initiative of central management of the undertaking or the controlling undertaking in a group of undertakings[152] or at the written request of at least 100 employees or their representatives[153] in at least two undertakings in at least two Member States.[154] This prevents an EWC from being imposed from the outside. The onus is on central management to create the conditions and means necessary for the establishment of an EWC or ICP.[155]

When a request has been received, a 'special negotiating body' (SNB) of between three and seventeen members[156] must be set up. Individual Member States must determine the method to be used for the election or appointment of the members of the SNB.[157] The role of the SNB, possibly with the

---

[147] In the case of 'Community-scale group of undertakings', read 'group undertaking' in the place of 'establishment' (Art. 2(1)(c)).

[148] Art. 2(1)(a) and (c). Member States may provide that this Directive does not apply to merchant navy crews (Art. 1(5)).

[149] See also Art. 12(2). Member States do not have the option of introducing rules more favourable to employees.

[150] Art. 4(2).

[151] Art. 4(2).

[152] Art. 2(1)(e).

[153] Employees' representatives means the employees' representatives provided for by national law or practice (Art. 2(1)(d)), a definition drawn from Council Directives 75/129/EEC on collective redundancies and 77/187/EEC on transfers of undertakings.

[154] Art. 5(1).

[155] Art. 4(1).

[156] Art. 5(2)(b).

[157] Art. 5(2)(a). The right to elect or appoint members of the SNB must apply equally to employees in those undertakings 'in which there are no employees' representatives through no fault of their own'. Special rules apply to ensure an even representation of employees (Art. 5(2)(c)). Central management and local management must be informed of the composition of the SNB (Art. 5(2)(d)).

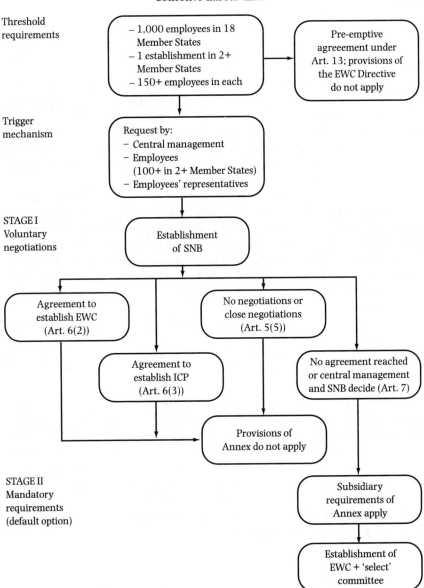

Threshold requirements

Trigger mechanism

STAGE I
Voluntary
negotiations

STAGE II
Mandatory
requirements
(default option)

Figure 8.1 The Consequences of the Negotiation Procedure prescribed by Council Directive 94/95/EC

assistance of experts,[158] is to determine by written agreement with central management the scope, composition, functions, and term of office of the EWC(s) or the arrangements for implementing an ICP.[159] Central management must convene a meeting with the SNB.[160] While respecting the autonomy of the parties, the Directive provides that the agreement to establish an EWC should include details of the undertakings covered by the agreement, the composition of the EWC, the number of members, the allocation of seats and the term of office, the function and procedure for informing and consulting the EWC, the venue, frequency and duration of meetings of the EWC, the financial and material resources to be allocated to the EWC, the duration of the agreement, and the procedure for its renegotiation.[161]

Alternatively, the central management and the special negotiating body may decide to establish an ICP, instead of an EWC. If so, the agreement must specify the methods by which the employees' representatives will have the right to meet to discuss the information conveyed to them.[162] The information supplied must relate, in particular, to transnational questions which significantly affect workers' interests.[163] Whether an EWC or ICP is established, the minimum requirements laid down in the annex do not need to be incorporated into the agreement.[164]

The SNB can also decide, by at least two-thirds of the votes, not to open negotiations or to terminate the negotiations already opened. In this case the provisions in the Annex do not apply and a new request to convene the SNB cannot be made for at least two years, unless the parties lay down a shorter period.[165]

If, after three years of negotiations, the parties cannot reach an agreement on the nature, function, or powers of the EWC, or if management fails to initiate negotiations within six months of the request being made, or if the two parties prefer, the second stage applies and the requirements laid down by the legislation of the Member State in which the central management is situated will apply, which must include the 'subsidiary' requirements set out in the Annex.[166] Thus negotiators are fully aware that failure will result in a mandatory procedure being imposed or, as Bercusson describes it, they are bargaining in the shadow of the law.[167]

---

[158] Art. 5(4), para. 2. Member States may limit funding to one expert only (Art. 5(6), para. 2).
[159] Art. 5(3).
[160] Art. 5(4). Expenses relating to the negotiations must be borne by the central management (Art. 5(6)).
[161] Art. 6(2).
[162] Art. 6(3), paras. 1 and 2.
[163] Art. 6(3), para. 3.
[164] Art. 6(4). 63 agreements have been concluded under Art.6 (http://www.eurofound.ie/ewc/).
[165] Art. 5(5).
[166] Art. 7(1) and (2).
[167] Bercusson, 'Maastricht: A Fundamental Change in European Labour Law' (1992) 23 *IRJ* 177.

The Annex lays down fairly modest requirements regarding the com-position[168] and operating methods of the EWC, requiring a minimum of one information and consultation meeting per year on the basis of a report drawn up by central management covering such issues as the structure, economic, and financial situation of the business; the probable development of the business and of production and sales; the employment situation and future trends; investments and substantial changes concerning the organization of the business; the introduction of new working methods or production processes; transfers of production; mergers and cut-backs or closures of undertakings or collective redundancies.[169]

In addition to the annual information and consultation meeting of the EWC, the annex requires that a 'select' committee,[170] a type of executive committee of the EWC, be informed of important decisions on matters such as relocation, closures, and collective redundancies. At its request, the select committee will have the right to meet central management or any other more appropriate level of management so as to be informed and consulted on measures significantly affecting employees' interests.[171]

The meeting with the select committee must take place as soon as possible. There must be a report drawn up by central management on which the select committee can give its opinion either at a meeting or within a reasonable time. However, the Annex provides that this meeting will not affect the prerogatives of the central management. This is a compromise between the employers, who were concerned about the disruptive effects of having too many consultation meetings every time an important decision was to be taken, and the Commission, which felt that the consultation of workers was an essential element in achieving the objectives of the proposed directive.

The operating expenses of the EWC must be borne by the Community-scale undertaking or group of undertakings. This approach reflects the current practice on the part of undertakings which have already set up groups of this kind. The Commission calculates that the costs of the Directive amount to a maximum of 10 ECU per year per worker. According to the Commission,[172] given the substantial advantages that such EWCs can bring for the

---

[168] The EWC shall be composed of employees of the Community-scale undertaking or group of undertakings or appointed from their number by the employees' representatives or in their absence the entire body of employees. The EWC will have between 3 and 30 members.

[169] Annex, para. 2. According to Art. 12(1), the Directive does not affect measures taken pursuant to the Directives on collective redundancies 75/129/EEC [1975] OJ L48/29 and transfer of undertakings 77/187/EEC [1997] OJ L61/26. In the event of collective redundancies both the EWC and the employees' representatives of the undertakings affected must be consulted. See further Ch. 7.

[170] Annex, para. 3. If there is no select committee the EWC must be informed.

[171] The members of the EWC who have been elected or appointed by undertakings which are directly affected have a right to participate in the meeting organized with the select committee.

[172] COM(94)134.

two parties, by contributing to a better mutual flow of information and a constructive dialogue, it seems reasonable to suppose that these subsidiary requirements will not impose a significant additional burden on central management.

The Directive also contains three provisions designed to ensure that the EWCs function smoothly. The first deals with confidentiality of the information received. While in principle the members of the EWC or ICP can inform the employees' representatives, or, in their absence, the employees themselves, of the content and outcome of the information and consultation procedure, Member States can provide that members of the SNBs or of the EWCs or employee representatives in the ICPs and any experts which assist them are not authorized to reveal any information which has been expressly given to them in confidence, even after the expiry of their terms of office.[173] In addition, Member States must provide that management can withhold any information which, according to objective criteria, would seriously harm the functioning of the undertakings concerned or would be prejudicial to them.[174] In response to a fear that these provisions could be abused by management, the Commission has said that the EWCs should be run by respecting the principles of transparency and mutual respect, particularly as prescribed by Article 9 (see below). The Directive also provides a practical solution to these concerns: Article 11(4) requires that complainants should have access to administrative or judicial appeal procedures where central management requires confidentiality or does not give information.

The second provision designed to ensure that the Directive functions smoothly can be found in Article 9. This requires that 'The central management and the European Works Council shall work in a spirit of cooperation with due regard to their reciprocal rights and obligations'.[175] The same shall apply to 'cooperation between the central management and employees' representatives in the framework of an information and consultation procedure'.[176] Such statements are designed to set the tenor of the Directive and it seems likely that the Directive will be interpreted in this light. Thus, the Directive does not provide for bypass procedures, nor does it lay down a fixed period within which decisions subject to consultation cannot be put into practice in the absence of an opinion on the part of the employees' representatives on the EWC.

The third step taken by the Directive to ensure the successful functioning of

---

[173] Art. 8(1). Special provisions apply to *'entreprises de tendences'* in Art. 8(3).

[174] Art. 8(2). Member States can make such dispensation subject to prior administrative or judicial authorization.

[175] This draws on the joint opinion adopted by the two sides of industry in Mar. 1987.

[176] See also Art. 6(1).

the information and consultation procedure is that the Directive requires employment protection for those employees involved in the SNBs, EWCs, or ICPs. Article 10 provides that these employees should enjoy the same protection and guarantees provided for employees' representatives under national law and/or practice, including the payment of wages.

Despite the complex legislative history of this Directive its substance has remained largely intact. Its provisions draw heavily on the structure of the French and German Works Councils but lack the sophisticated co-determination principles found in the German system. The Directive goes further than the information provisions found in existing EWCs. Perhaps the most striking feature of the Directive, when contrasted with the earlier Vredling proposal, is the flexibility conferred. In the past, the principal criticism of the various proposals has been that they were too rigid and bureaucratic and incompatible with decentralized management structures. However, the Directive now allows the Member States to determine practical matters, such as election methods, and encourages the Social Partners to negotiate the details of the operation of the agreement in order to accommodate local requirements. This allows what Streeck describes as convergence rather than harmonization.[177] The greatest flexibility was provided by the so-called Article 13 voluntary agreements. Article 13 provides that where on 22 September 1996, an agreement was already in existence[178] which covered the entire workforce, the obligations contained in the Directive did not apply; and when these agreements expire the parties can decide jointly to renew them, failing which the provisions of the Directive will apply. Three hundred and eighty-six such agreements were signed by the September 1996 deadline,[179] including fifty-eight signed by British companies. This highlights the spillover effect of the SPA from which the UK government thought it had secured an opt-out.

How important is this Directive? Ramsay argues that EWCs have a symbolic significance for industrial democracy.[180] Even with limited powers the assertion of the right of labour to information and consultation provides some fetter to rights of ownership and management. Schulten, on the other hand, argues that the establishment of a new transnational micro-corporatism will not be free from tensions and contradictions because the

---

[177] Streeck, 'Citizenship under Regime Competition: The Case of European Works Councils', MPIfG Working Paper 97/3.

[178] 15 Dec.1999 for the UK or earlier if the date of transposition in the UK is before then: Art. 3(1) of Directive 97/74/EC [1998] OJ L10/22.

[179] See Marginson, Gilman, Jacobi, and Krieger, *Negotiating European Works Councils: an Analysis of Agreements under Article 13*, European Foundation of Living and Working Conditions, EF9839. A particularly high incidence of such agreements can be found in Norway: see Knudsen and Bruun, 'European Works Councils in the Nordic Countries: An Opportunity and a Challenge for Trade Unionism' (1998) 4 *EJIR* 131.

[180] Ramsay 'Fool's Gold? European Works Council and Workplace Democracy' (1997) 28 *ILJ* 314, 320.

Euro-company will also continue regime shopping to take advantage of the different national and local social standards, thereby playing off its national personnel against each other.[181] He also suggests that the EWCs might exacerbate the trend towards decentralized, company-specific regulation by detaching MNC's national subsidiaries from their national or sectoral systems.

How successful are EWCs? Some commentators express concerns that the lack of co-determination leads to the danger that EWCs will become a vehicle for 'Europeanized human resource management strategy';[182] and that they will subside into hearing management reports and offering some 'desultory discussion on the information offered but remaining insignificant to employee relations still driven through local and national negotiations'.[183] Ramsay is also concerned that MNCs, if they choose to take the initiative, may be able to increase management control by selling their own message convincingly, and by increasing enterprise consciousness by squeezing out external union representation. He notes that voluntary agreements to date tend to shift the emphasis from employee-run meetings to management-run meetings, since only 18 per cent specify an employee chair, while 54 per cent specify a management chair.

The unions, on the other hand, have swiftly grasped the benefits of such EWCs,[184] aided by generous EU funding for preparatory EWC meetings.[185] They are especially keen on sharing information and strategy and on exchanging ideas. They also think that EWCs help in countering perceived management attempts to misinform national workforces or 'play them off' against one another. In the longer term, they think this might lead to a more co-ordinated approach to collective bargaining among national unions—albeit restricted in the first instance to issues such as health and safety. Management is far less keen: research by Gold and Hall found that management was implacably opposed to the development of European-level collective bargaining.[186]

---

[181] Schulten, 'European Works Councils: Prospects for a New System of European Industrial Relations' (1996) 2 *EJIR* 303.

[182] Lecher and Rüb, 'The Constitution of European Works Councils: from Information Forum to Social Actor' (1999) 5 *EJIR* 7, 8.

[183] Ramsay above n. 180.

[184] 246 *EIRR* 16, and Gold and Hall, above n. 121, 49.

[185] The budget was intended 'to finance transnational meetings of employees' representatives from undertakings operating on a transfrontier basis in the Community'. See 238 and 246 *EIRR*. See also Roberts, 'Where are European Works Councils?—an Update' (1993) 24 *IRJ* 178, 180. The budget was for 17 million ECU in 1993 and 1994, comprising about 30 per cent of the Commission's entire 'social dialogue and employment budget'. This prompted criticism from the employers who argued that their organizations did not receive similar financial assistance, contrary to the requirements of Art. 3(1) SPA [new Art. 138(1)] which obliged the Commission to provide 'balanced support' to management and labour at Community level.

[186] Gold and Hall (1992), above n. 121, 65.

TUC research has also reported some problems in tailoring meetings of representatives to the complex business structures of multinationals since decision-making may well occur, not centrally, but at product division level or lower. This view was supported by a study conducted by the Multi-national Business Forum[187] which argued that meaningful ICPs must follow company decision-making machinery: a statutory obligation to inform and consult at a level at which business decisions are not routinely taken is 'at best a waste of resources, and at worst necessitates the creation of a parallel and irrelevant organisation'.[188] Marginson also considers that the success of European industrial relations is dependent upon the structure of the multi-national enterprise. He argues that common management approaches across borders are less likely in companies which have expanded their access to markets in different European countries through licensing or franchise arrangements with local producers or joint ventures with enterprises based in other Member States. On the other hand, he suggests that in those trans-nationals that are organized to face the market on a European-wide basis, and where the primary axis of internal organization is around international product divisions, management is more likely to have an interest in develop-ing common, cross-border approaches to the management of its workforce. However, even in these companies a series of other factors are likely to condition the extent of managerial interest in a European-wide approach to labour relations. For example, Marginson considers a Community-wide approach more feasible where the organization has been established through greenfield operations rather than through acquisitions or mergers. He concludes that companies are more likely to have an interest in develop-ing common approaches to labour relations management on a European basis where production activities are integrated across borders, and where the same activity is carried out at different locations. Management phil-osophy still remains an important factor: while some companies may wish to limit the scope for the exercise of coercive comparisons by keeping their labour relations as decentralized as possible, others might judge a European-level forum useful in increasing trade union and employee aware-ness of comparative labour relations performance across locations, thereby influencing behaviour.[189]

Evidence from the small number of multinationals which do have informa-tion or, more rarely, consultation procedures—BSN, Bull, Elf-Aquitaine, Pech-iney, Rhône-Poulenc, Saint Gobain, Thomson, Nestlé, Allianz, Volkswagen,

---

[187] 'Thriving on Diversity: Informing and Consulting Employees in Multinational Enterprises', Sept. 1993, 238 *EIRR*.

[188] See also Marginson, Buitendam, Deutschmann, and Perulli, 'The Emergence of the Euro-company: Towards a European Industrial Relations' (1993) 24 *IRJ* 182.

[189] Marginson, 'European Integration and Transnational Management-Union Relations in the Enterprise' (1992) 30 *BJIR* 529.

and Mercedes-Benz[190]—tends to support Marginson's view. Production in the companies or divisions is organized on a European footing within a unified European management structure and the companies are engaged in similar types of activity in different countries.[191] A large number of the companies involved are French. Marginson suggests that this underlines the importance of the creation by statute of enterprise-level consultative arrangements within France and the influence of the broader political climate on French management.[192]

2.5 Dealing with the Backlog

The successful adoption of the EWC Directive 94/45 prompted the Commission to examine in its Medium Term Social Action Programme 1995–7 the volume of unadopted legislation relating to worker information and consultation.[193] First, in respect of the draft Fifth Company Directive the Commission was to consider the possibility of deleting the information and consultation provisions from the proposal. It also intended to initiate consultations with the Social Partners on the advisability and possible direction of Community action in the field of information and consultation of employees in national undertakings. This is considered below. Secondly, the Commission was to examine whether the European Works Council Directive could help the adoption of the proposals for regulations concerning the four statutes. Thirdly, the Commission proposed to withdraw the draft European Works Council Directive and the Vredling Directive 'which are now overtaken' by Directive 94/45. However, in its subsequent Communication,[194] the Commission changed its mind and argued that the Vredling draft should not be withdrawn until a 'comprehensive solution to the whole problem has been found'. In the light of these proposals the Commission issued a Communication on Information and Consultation[195] which aimed to 'take stock of the current situation ... and explore whether there might not be new ways of moving forward' without reopening the debate in a 'controversial way'. It proposed a new approach based around four ideas:

(a) *simplification*: if the nine sets of proposals in this area were all adopted they would create a complex and overlapping web of rules. Consequently, the Commission proposed a simpler approach involving possibly two general legal frameworks on information and consultation at European level:

---

[190] Gold and Hall, above, n. 121, and 288 *EIRR*.
[191] Marginson, above n. 189, 541.
[192] Ibid.
[193] COM(95)134 final 16–17.
[194] COM(95)547.
[195] COM(95)547 final, discussed at *EIRR* 263, Dec. 1995, 18.

one on transnational aspects (the EWC Directive), the other on national aspects to be created by a new legal instrument.

(b) *coherence*: noting that the EWC Directive provides general rules on transnational information and consultation while there are currently only specific rules on national information and consultation in the event of redundancies or transfers, the Commission argued that the new approach of general legal frameworks could be justified on the grounds of the coherence of Community legislation and, in particular, that the information and consultation provisions of the Directive on redundancies and transfers would be more effective in their preventive role against a background of stable and permanent information and consultation provisions.

(c) *pragmatism and balance*: recognizing that consensus on employee involvement on company boards was very hard to achieve, the Commission intended to focus on the information and consultation of employee representatives.

(d) *generality*: the Commission was keen to follow the success of the EWC Directive and apply it to national ICPs. It also stressed the importance of applying the rules throughout the EC: 'there seems to be little justification for one or more countries being granted an exemption in this area, which would give an unfair advantage to businesses that have their registered office there rather than in another Member State'.

The Commission then proposed three options: first, maintaining the status quo, although 'it seems to offer little hope of progress'; second, a global approach establishing general European level frameworks on informing and consulting employees and withdrawing both the Vredling and Fifth Company Directive and the participation provisions of the four proposals for statutes. This would pave the way for the third option—unblocking the four proposals for European statutes.[196] This is seen as urgent in order to provide businesses with instruments to help them adapt to the single market and global competition.

---

[196] This could be done in two ways: first, withdrawal of the proposals for the employee participation Directives accompanying the draft regulations on each of the four statutes, but with the proviso that no European company, association, co-operative, or mutual society could be set up in a Member State that had not transposed the EWC Directive; or, secondly, no conditions would be attached to withdrawal of the draft directives and European companies, etc. which decide to set up in the UK would not be subject to the same transnational information and consultation requirements as those registered elsewhere in the EU.

2.6 General Framework for Informing and Consulting Employees in the EC

(a) Background

As we have seen, the Commission now sees the successful conclusion of *national* information and consultation provisions as crucial to unblocking the gamut of unadopted legislation. Its more recent documents connected to the European Employment Strategy reveal a further justification for the enactment of such legislation: the Green Paper on Partnership identified the challenge for social policy as being 'how to reconcile security for workers with the flexibility which firms need'.[197] The answer lies in an 'improved organization of work' which, although unable 'of itself to solve the unemployment problem', may nevertheless 'make a valuable contribution, firstly, to the competitiveness of European firms, and secondly, to the improvement of the quality of working life and the employability of the workforce'.[198] Flexibility within organizations is to be encouraged, it suggests, by reinforcing mechanisms for employee participation at the level of the plant or enterprise; 'the role of workers in decision-making and the need to review and strengthen the existing arrangements for workers' involvement in their companies will . . . become essential issues'.[199] Thus, the role of the Social Partners is one of assisting the 'modernization' of working arrangements at enterprise level. This theme intersects with the idea that co-operation between labour and management can provide a basis for functional flexibility or adaptability (multi-skilling in return for greater job security) and hence for competitiveness at enterprise level.[200] In some accounts, an explicit link is made between the achievement of flexibility in work organization and the preservation of job security within a framework of employee representation. In particular, the Social Action Programme 1998–2000 recognizes that 'Social dialogue has a key role in achieving the right balance'[201] between flexibility and security. Further, in its Green Paper on Partnership for a New Organization of Work, the Commission concluded that:

Industrial relations will require, in a new organisation of work to be built on a basis of cooperation and common interest. Therefore new forms of industrial relations have to be developed, including, for example, greater participation by employees, since efficient production requires enhanced levels of both trust and commitment by firms.[202]

---

[197] COM(97)127 final, Executive Summary.
[198] Ibid., para. 4.
[199] Ibid., para. 44.
[200] Deakin and Reed, 'Between Social Policy, and EMU: The New Employment Title of the EC Treaty' in Shaw (ed.), *Social Law and Policy in an Evolving European Union* (Hart, Oxford, forthcoming).
[201] COM(98)259, III.2.
[202] COM(97)127, para. 23.

This has now been recognized in the Employment 2000 guidelines.[203] Under the adaptability pillar guideline 16 has been amended to 'take account of the publicly expressed willingness of the social partners to engage in a joint process for modernising the organisation of work'.[204]

Some have doubted the validity of these claims. Cheffins,[205] for example, argues that employees are often cynical about worker participation measures, and so employers have little to gain by keeping in place whatever participative measures they have introduced; that over time employees in high-effort work-places have an incentive to free-ride off the efforts of fellow members; that the *quid pro quo* for flexibility, job security, creates a cosy environment where there is little likelihood of being fired which might hurt production levels, and a low turnover of staff gives little chance for promotion. This, in turn, may have a negative impact on flexibility, as would any formalized, bureaucratic decision-making process[206] which might cause a company to postpone facing economic realities and defer changes which are required to foster the company's long-term growth and development.

Despite these concerns, the Community documents continue to emphasize the importance of flexibility and security. For example, the Final Report of the High Level Group on the economic and social implications of industrial change,[207] published late in 1998, concluded that 'top-performing companies have a good social dialogue with their employees because motivated people are the vital component for commercial success'. The Group considered 'necessary the initiatives taken by the European Union, corporations, the social partners and governments to create a broader, high quality system of information and consultation'. It added that the group agreed on 'the need to create a European framework for information and consultation with employees, whilst acknowledging the current situation at national level'.[208] The Davignon Report[209] and the Gyllenhammer Report[210] also suggested that information and consultation were factors for productivity as they contributed to the creation of a highly skilled and committed workforce.

---

[203] See further Ch. 1.

[204] Commission Proposal for Guidelines for Member States' Employment Policies 2000, 4. See now Council Decision 2000/228/EC [2000] OJ L72/15.

[205] Cheffins, above n. 9, 583–5, 588.

[206] Citing Lane, *Management and Labour in Europe: The Industrial Enterprise in Germany, Britain and France* (E. Elgar Ltd, Aldershot, 1989), 232 and 236; and Hopt, 'Labor Representation on Corporate Boards: Impacts and Problems for Corporate Governance and Integration in Europe' (1994) 14 *Int. Rev. of Law and Econ.*, 203, 207–8, 210–11, 214.

[207] Commission, *Managing Change*, Gyllenhammer Report, Nov. 1998, 5, http://europa.eu.int/comm/dg05/soc-dial/gyllenhamer/gyllen-en.pdf.

[208] Ibid.

[209] 'European System of Worker Involvement, with regard to the European Company Statute and other Pending proposals'. See also Council Conclusions of 27 June 1997 on further discussion of worker involvement in the European Company [1997] OJ C227/1.

[210] 'Interim Report of the High Level Expert Group on the Economic and Social Impact of Industrial Change'. See further above n. 207.

These arguments prompted the Commission to introduce a new proposal on information and consultation.

(b) The Proposal

The Commission hoped that the Social Partners would be able to negotiate a European level collective agreement to fulfil these objectives but, while the ETUC and CEEP were willing, UNICE refused, largely due to the British CBI's resistance. It argued, first, that any such agreement would not conform with the principle of subsidiarity; secondly, that there were adequate legal frameworks at national level; thirdly, that there was no link between employee information and consultation and job security; and, fourthly, that labour management should be the exclusive preserve of the company's internal organization. Regretting 'this lack of willingness to negotiate',[211] the Commission decided to present a proposal, even though faced with objections from the UK government.[212] It justified this on the grounds of adaptability and the weaknesses of Community and national provisions. As the Commission explained, 'Several events, which have given rise to enormous political and media attention (notably the Renault affair),[213] have illustrated the weakness of national and Community law. In fact, it has become clear that, even where information and consultation provisions existed, they were not effective as they were either only ritual in nature or effective only *a posteriori*'.[214] It has also argued that existing Community laws on informing and consulting workers are fragmented and that the current Community provisions do not contain adequate provisions for sanctioning decisions which are taken in contravention of workers' rights to information and consultation.

Article 1 of the Directive says that the Directive's objective is to establish a general framework for informing and consulting employees in the EC. Article 1(2) adds:

When defining or implementing information and consultation procedures, the employer and the employees' representatives shall work in a spirit of co-operation and with due regard for their reciprocal rights and obligations, taking into account the interests both of the undertaking and of the employees.

The proposed directive is to apply to 'public or private undertakings carrying out an economic activity, whether or not operating for gain, which are located within the territory of the Member States of the EC and have at least 50 employees, without prejudice to the provisions of Article 4(3)'.[215] This defin-

---

[211] COM(98)612, 2.

[212] Fairness at Work White Paper, Cm 3968 (1998), para. 4.5.

[213] Renault announced the closure of its Vilvoorde plant in Belgium with the loss of 3,100 jobs without respecting the rules on collective redundancies.

[214] See generally 'Employee Representatives in Europe and their Economic Prerogatives', Supp. *Social Europe* 3/96.

[215] Art. 2(1)(a).

ition draws on the revisions to Directive 77/187[216] and the case law of the Court. This definition also provides a threshold, in terms of fifty or more workers employed, for the application of the Directive. According to the Commission, this excludes 97 per cent of companies in the EU with salaried employees. Further, Member States will have the option of raising the threshold to 100 employed workers (Article 4(3)) and, according to Article 2(2), Member States may 'lay down particular provisions applicable to undertakings which pursue directly and essentially political, professional organisation, religious, charitable, educational, scientific or artistic aims, as well as aims involving information and the expression of opinions, on condition that, at the date of adoption of this Directive, such particular provisions already exist in national legislation'.[217]

In the interests of flexibility, Article 3(1) authorizes Member States to allow the Social Partners 'at the appropriate level, including at undertaking level', to determine the procedures for implementing the employee information and consultation requirements referred to in Articles 1, 2, and 4 of the Directive. This will probably mean that in many cases the Directive will probably be transposed into national law in such a way as to make use of existing provisions and instruments. Article 3(2) authorizes Social Partners, under conditions and within limits to be determined by the Member States, to enter arrangements which are different from those referred to in Article 2(1)(d) and (e) on the definition of information and consultation and Article 4.

Article 4(1) lays down the subjects to be covered by information and consultation in so far as the Social Partners have not entered into an agreement as referred to in Article 3. This provides:

'Without prejudice to any provisions and/or practices more favourable to employees in force in the Member States, employee information and consultation shall, if there is no agreement between the social partners as envisaged in Article 3, cover:

(a) information on the recent as well as the reasonably foreseeable development of the undertaking's activities and its economic and financial situation;
(b) information and consultation on the situation, structure and reasonably foreseeable developments of employment within the undertaking and, where the employer's evaluation suggests that employment within the undertaking may be under threat, the anticipatory measures envisaged, in particular for employee training and skill development, with a view to offsetting the potential negative developments or their consequences and increasing the employability of the employees likely to be affected'; given the novelty of these provisions, paragraph 3 allows Member States to limit the scope of information and consultation procedures concerning employment trends to undertakings with at least 100 employees;

---

[216] New Art. 1 of Directive 98/50 [1998] OJ L201/88.

[217] See also Art. 8(3) of European Works Council Directive 94/45/EC concerning these *'entreprises de tendences'*.

'(c) information and consultation on decisions likely to lead to substantial changes in work organisation or in contractual relations, including those covered by the Community provisions referred to in Article 8(1).'

Thus, the Directive covers three subject areas: economic or strategic matters (paragraph (a)), employment trends within the undertaking and associated measures (paragraph (b)), and specific decisions concerning work organization or contractual relations (paragraph (c)). Since the matters referred to in paragraph (a) are generally outside the control of the employer, these are subject only to information.

'Information' means 'transmission by the employer to the employees' representatives of information containing all relevant facts on the subjects set down in Article 4(1), ensuring that the timing, means of communication and content of the information are such as to ensure its effectiveness, particularly in enabling the employees' representatives to examine the information thoroughly and, where appropriate, prepare consultations'.[218]

'Consultation' means:

the organisation of a dialogue and exchange of views between the employer and the employees' representatives on the subjects set out in Article 4(1)(b) and (c),

— ensuring that the timing, method, and content are such that this step is effective;
— at the appropriate level of management and representation, depending on the subject under discussion;
— on the basis of the relevant information to be supplied by the employer and the opinion which the employees' representatives are entitled to formulate;
— including the employees' representatives' right to meet with the employer and obtain a response, and the reasons for that response, to any opinion they may formulate;
— including, in the case of decisions within the scope of the employer's management powers, an attempt to seek prior agreement on the decisions referred to in Article 4(1)(c).[219]

'Employees' representatives' means 'the employees' representatives provided for by national laws and/or practices'.[220] This formulation allows Member States, for the purposes of application of the Directive, to use not only collegiate forms of employee representation, but also individual representatives (workforce delegates, trade union delegates, and others).[221] Article 6

---

[218] Art. 2(1)(d).

[219] Art. 2(1)(e). Consultation might not be enough. As Gospel and Palmer point out in *British Industrial Relations* (2nd edn, Routledge, London, 1993), 195, it consists of listening, nodding, and going away without acting.

[220] Art. 2(1)(c). For the difficulty this definition creates see Case C–382/92 *Commission v. UK* [1994] ECR I–2435.

[221] For the problems associated with this formula see Ch. 7.

establishes the principle of protection of employees' representatives.[222] The general wording proposed by the Commission is justified by the fact that all Member States already have an adequate body of rules on this subject.

Article 4(2) allows the Member States to determine procedures for ensuring information and consultation of employees. This is, however, subject to the constraint that the useful effect of the procedures in question must be ensured. Article 5 deals with the confidentiality of the information provided, and the right to withhold certain information if it would seriously harm the functioning of the undertaking or would be prejudicial to it. The text is identical to that of Directive 94/45/EC. Article 7(1) then provides for procedures allowing the employees' representatives to challenge the confidential nature of such information, as well as allowing the employer to ensure respect for the obligation of confidentiality. More generally, Article 7 imposes a number of obligations on Member States regarding protection of the rights created by the proposed Directive. The wording of the provision is broadly based on current Community law and the case law of the Court.[223]

Article 7(1) relates to 'adequate administrative or judicial' enforcement procedures. Article 7(2) relates to the remedies themselves, which must be 'effective, proportionate and dissuasive'. Article 7(3) contains a provision which does not have a precedent in the Community directives on employee information and consultation. It says:

Member States shall provide that in case of serious breach by the employer of the information and consultation obligations in respect of the decisions referred to in Article 4(1)(c) of this Directive, where such decisions would have direct and immediate consequences in terms of substantial change or termination of the employment contracts or employment relations, these decisions shall *have no legal effect* on the employment contracts or employment relationships of the employees affected. The non production of legal effects will continue until such time as the employer has fulfilled his obligations or, if this is no longer possible, adequate redress has been established, in accordance with the arrangements and procedures to be determined by the Member States.

The provision of the previous paragraph also applies to corresponding obligations under the agreements referred to in Article 3.

Within the meaning of the previous paragraphs, serious breaches are:

(a) the total absence of information and/or consultation of the employees' representatives prior to a decision being taken or the public announcement of that decision; or

(b) the withholding of important information or provision of false information rendering ineffective the exercise of the right to information and consultation [emphasis added].

---

[222] This is based on the corresponding Art. of Directive 94/45/EC.
[223] See further esp. Ch. 4.

Thus, decisions taken in serious violation of obligations under the Directive do not give rise to legal effects in respect of the contracts or employment relationships of the employees concerned. This relates to the decisions referred to in Article 4(1)(c), where such decisions would have direct and immediate consequences in terms of substantial change or termination of the employment contracts or employment relationships. By its nature this suspension has no effects with respect to third parties. It is not a matter of rendering the decision null and void in itself, but of preventing it from having legal effects on the employment contracts of the employees concerned until the moment when the employer has fulfilled his obligations or, if this is no longer possible, adequate redress has been established.

Finally, Article 8 sets out the links between the proposed Directive and Directives 98/59/EC, 77/187/EEC, and 94/45/EC, as well as other national provisions in force in this field. As the proposed Directive applies to the subjects referred to by the first two directives mentioned, the more stringent and/or specific provisions remain applicable. This means that national arrangements relating to collective redundancies and transfers of undertakings will have to be consistent both with this framework Directive and the two individual Directives.

3. The Merger Regulation

Limited recognition of the collective interests of workers can also be found in other contexts, such as the Merger Regulation 4064/89.[224] According to this Regulation concentrations with a Community dimension, as defined by the Regulation,[225] must be notified to the Commission which then must consider whether the merger is compatible with the Common Market.[226] In making this appraisal the Commission may take into account considerations of a social nature. This is confirmed by the thirteenth recital of the Preamble which provides that:

---

[224] [1989] OJ L395/1 as corrected by Corrigendum published in [1990] OJ L257/1 and amended by [1994] OJ C241/57, Decision 95/1 [1995] OJ L1/1 and Regulation 1310/97 [1997] OJ L180/1. See also the proposed Tenth Company Law Directive which would allow Member States to withhold authorization for mergers that displace legislated employee-participation rights [1985] OJ C23/11. See also the draft Thirteenth Directive on Takeovers [1997] OJ C378/10. Concerns about the possibly lengthy and costly disruptions to bids led to the deletion of any references to employees' consultation rights. According to Article 6 of the current draft, as soon as the bid is made the employees' representatives or, if none exist, the employees' themselves must be informed.

[225] Arts. 1 and 3 of the Regulation.

[226] Art. 2.

The Commission must place its appraisal within the general framework of the achievement referred to in Article 2 of the Treaty, including that of strengthening the Community's economic and social cohesion, referred to in Article 130a.[227]

The Preamble also states that the 'Regulation in no way detracts from the collective rights of employees as recognised in the undertakings concerned'.[228] Article 18(4) entitles the Commission to hear the views of 'natural or legal persons showing a sufficient interest . . . the recognised representatives[229] of their employees shall be entitled, upon application, to be heard'.[230] As the Court of First Instance explained in the *Grandes Sources* case,[231] the primacy given in the Merger Regulation to the establishment of a system of free competition may in certain cases be reconciled, in the context of an assessment of whether a concentration is compatible with the Common Market, with the social effects of that operation if they are liable to affect adversely the social objectives referred to in Article 2 of the Treaty. The CFI continued that the Commission, therefore, might have to ascertain whether 'the concentration is liable to have consequences, even if only indirectly, for the position of the employees in the undertakings in question, such as to affect the level or conditions of employment in the Community or a substantial part of it'.

The *Grandes Sources* case concerned the *Nestlé/Perrier* merger.[232] Although the trade union representatives (CGT Perrier) had met with the Commission to express their concerns about the social consequences of the merger, the Commission allowed the merger to proceed, provided that Nestlé complied with certain conditions, including selling the brand names and *sources* Vichy, Thonon, Pierval, and Saint-Yorre. This led to two sets of legal challenges. First, the trade union and the Perrier works council sought judicial review under Article 173 [new Article 230] of the Commission's Decision allowing the merger.[233] Under Article 230 natural or legal persons can challenge a decision

---

[227] New Art. 158, considered further in Ch. 1.

[228] Para. 31.

[229] In Case T–96/92 *Comité Central d'Entreprise de la Société Generale des Grandes Sources v. Commission* [1995] ECR II–1213, para. 34, the Court said that it is for the Member States to define which organizations are competent to represent the collective interest of the employees and to determine their rights and prerogatives, subject to the adoption of harmonization measures such as the European Works Council Directive 94/45/EC [1994] OJ L254/64.

[230] See also para. 19 of the Preamble. For the difficulties involved in invoking these provisions see Case T–96/92R *Comité Central d'Entreprise v. Commission* [1992] ECR II–2579 and Case T–12/93R *Comité Central d'entreprise de la Société Anonyme Vittel and Comité d'établissement de Pierval v. Commission* [1993] ECR II–449, Order of the President of the Court of First Instance [1993] ECR II–449; Anderman, 'European Community Merger and Social Policy' (1993) 22 *ILJ* 318.

[231] Case T–96/92 *Comité Central d'Entreprise de la Société Generale des Grandes Sources v. Commission* [1995] ECR II–1213, para. 28. See also Case T–12/93 *Vittel v. Commission* [1995] ECR II–1247, para. 38.

[232] Case No. IV/M.190, *Nestlé/Perrier* [1992] OJ L356/1.

[233] They also made a separate application for interim relief under Arts. 185 and 186 [new Arts. 242 and 243] but this was dismissed: Case T–96/92R [1992] ECR I–2579.

addressed to another provided it is of direct and individual concern to them. In the *Perrier* case the Court ruled that while the employee representatives were individually concerned by the Commission's Decision they were not directly concerned because the Decision did not prejudice either the rights of the organizations or the employees affected. However, the Court did say that the employee representatives had standing to bring proceedings to ensure that the procedural guarantees which they were entitled to assert during the administrative procedure under the Merger Regulation were satisfied.

The second proceedings were brought by the Vittel and Pierval works councils, challenging the transfer of the Pierval spring which was operated by Vittel. Interim relief was initially granted,[234] suspending the operation of the Commission Decision until certain obstacles relating to the transfer of the rights to exploit Vichy and Thonon had been removed and the Court had been informed of that fact by the Commission.[235] In the subsequent judicial review proceedings, the applicants, now supported by the Perrier trade union and works council, sought annulment of either the Commission's Decision as a whole or the imposition of the conditions by the Commission.[236] Once again the Court found that since the applicants were the recognized representatives of the employees concerned by the concentration and they were expressly mentioned in Regulation 4064/89 they were individually concerned. However, they were not directly concerned and so had no *locus standi* because the transfer of the Pierval plant 'did not in itself entail any direct consequences for the rights which the employees derived from their contract of employment'.[237] These rights were protected by Directive 77/187 on transfers[238] and (now) Directive 98/59 on collective redundancies.[239]

By contrast, in the context of state aid there are no legislative provisions comparable to those in Regulation 4064/89 which expressly grant procedural prerogatives to the recognized representatives of employees. Therefore, the Court of First Instance said in *SFP*[240] that employees' representatives were not individually concerned for the purposes of having *locus standi* to challenge a Commission decision declaring state aid to the industry to be incompatible with the Common Market and ordering its recovery. The

---

[234] Case T–12/93R *Comité Central d'Entreprise de la Société Anonyme Vittel and Comité d'établissement de Pierval v. Commission* [1993] ECR II–449.

[235] Following the communication of that information the applications for interim measures were dismissed by order of the President of the CFI [1993] ECR II–785.

[236] Case T–12/93 *Vittel* [1995] ECR II–1247.

[237] Para. 58.

[238] [1977] OJ L61/26 as amended.

[239] [1998] OJ L225/16.

[240] Case T–189/97 *Comité d'entreprise de la société française de production v. Commission* [1998] ECR II–335.

Commission did, however, concede in that case that bodies representing employees of the undertaking in receipt of aid might *qua* parties concerned within the meaning of Article 93(2) [new Article 88(2)] submit comments to the Commission on considerations of a social nature which could be taken into account by the Commission.[241]

Worker participation provisions also do not exist in Regulation 2137/85 on European Economic Interest Groupings (EEIGs).[242] The Preamble, however, states that the laws of the Member States and Community apply to matters not covered by the Regulation, including social and labour law. The Regulation provides that an EEIG must employ not more than 500 workers,[243] a threshold inserted to avoid circumvention of the German employee participation provisions by German companies forming or joining an EEIG registered in another Member State with more lax worker participation rules.[244]

4. Financial Participation of Employees in a Company

The discussion so far has focused on industrial democracy: employee participation in the processes of management and decision-making within the firm. Economic democracy, on the other hand, has enjoyed a renaissance in recent years. It covers a variety of forms of participation in the ownership of the enterprise and in the distribution of economic rewards.[245] While in the case of a wholly-owned workers co-operative, economic democracy can go hand in hand with industrial democracy, more usually economic rewards are designed to encourage, in an indirect way, 'identification' of employees with employers and to produce incentives for employees to increase the profitability of their employing company by allowing them to reap some of the benefits of that increase (generally through share ownership or profit-sharing).[246] This form of 'financial flexibility' offers both macroeconomic and microeconomic benefits. The macroeconomic effects relate to the flexibility of the job market: if workers accept a substantial proportion of their remuneration as a profit-related element, either in cash or shares in the company, then the company's wage bill increases only as it becomes more profitable. Consequently, the dangers of wage inflation are reduced. Companies can also deal with fluctuations in the economic cycle by reducing the profit-related pay element rather than dismissing workers.[247] At the microeconomic level profit-sharing can lead to

[241] Para. 41.

[242] [1995] OJ L199/1.

[243] Art. 3(2)(c) of Regulation 2137/85 [1985] OJ L199/1.

[244] Nielsen and Szyszczak, *The Social Dimension of the European Community* (Handelshøjkolens Forlag, Copenhagen, 1997).

[245] McLean, *Fair Shares—The Future of Employee Financial Participation in the UK* (IER, London, 1994), 3.

[246] Ibid., 3.

[247] McLean, above n. 245, 3 and 4, for a critique of this view.

increased effort and efficiency because employees with a financial stake in a company have an incentive to work more productively and co-operate more willingly with management.[248] This in turn leads to improved competitiveness and better industrial relations.

The Community has made various attempts to encourage the development of such schemes. For example, the Capital Directive on the formation of public limited liability companies and the maintenance and alteration of capital[249] permits Member States to derogate from certain provisions of the Directive on the grounds of the need to adopt or apply provisions designed to encourage the participation of employees in the capital of companies.[250] In 1979 the Commission published a memorandum on employee participation on asset formation[251] but despite a resolution by the Parliament in 1983 calling on the Commission to draw up a recommendation and to consider whether a directive might be necessary, little progress was made. However, in the Social Charter Action Programme, the Commission said that employee participation in asset formation and productive capital formation helped bring about a fairer distribution of wealth and was a means of attaining an adequate level of non-inflationary growth. This, combined with the advantages of greater involvement of workers in the progress of their companies, precipitated the adoption of a non-legally binding Recommendation concerning the promotion of employee participation in profits and enterprise results, known by the acronym PEPPER.[252]

The PEPPER Recommendation invites the Member States to acknowledge the potential benefits of a wider use of schemes to increase the participation of employees in the profits of the enterprise and to take account of the role and the responsibility of management and labour in this context. It recommends that the Member States ensure that legal structures are adequate to allow the introduction of such schemes, and to consider the possibility of financial advantages to encourage their introduction. The Recommendation also lists key points in the preparation of such schemes or in reviewing existing schemes, including the regularity of bonus payments and the formula for

---

[248] This model still allows room for 'free-riders' where an individual employee calculates that if other workers continue to perform optimally and he does not, the firm's productivity should be only marginally affected; the value of his ownership stake should not change and he can retain the gains from his self-serving behaviour. If most employees think this way the viability of the enterprise is threatened. Therefore managers are necessary to monitor the staff's performance. See Cheffins, above, n. 9, 559.

[249] Directive 77/91/EEC [1977] OJ L26/1 as amended by Council Directive 92/101/EEC [1992] OJ L347/64.

[250] Art. 41(1). Moreover, Art. 41(2) provides that Member States may decide not to apply certain provisions of the Directive to companies incorporated under a special law which issue both capital shares and workers' shares, the latter being issued to the company's employees as a body, who are represented at general meetings of shareholders by delegates having the right to vote.

[251] Bull. Supp. 6/79.

[252] Council Recommendation 92/443/EEC [1992] OJ L243/53.

calculating the payment to each employee. The Commission suggests that the existence of financial participation schemes should not stand in the way of normal negotiations dealing with wages and conditions of employment. It also recommends that the risks inherent in participation schemes, particularly if their investments are relatively undiversified,[253] should be made clear to employees.

It seemed that the Commission was not at first totally convinced by the benefits of these schemes. In the Preamble to the Recommendation, it states that the body of empirical research into the effects of PEPPER schemes 'does not yet provide overwhelming evidence of strong overall advantages'. It has been argued that although companies with extensive financial participation schemes do perform better on average than companies without them, this is at least as likely to be because they are better managed overall and have progressive employment policies. Recent research suggests that employees tend to regard PEPPER schemes as a perk.[254] The Commission's view is now changing. In its Communication on Modernizing the Organization of Work[255] it considered that the financial participation of employees was an important way of promoting workers' motivation and adaptability. There is some evidence that a 'sense of ownership' is an important 'intervening variable' between actual ownership and attitudinal change, although it has been found that opportunities for participating in decision-making are more important than ownership *per se* in generating feelings of ownership.[256]

B. FREEDOM OF ASSOCIATION, COLLECTIVE BARGAINING, AND COLLECTIVE ACTION

So far this chapter has considered the Community rights given (or proposed to be given) to worker representatives. These representatives may well be trade unions, as in the UK, or elected worker representatives, such as works councils. The next section focuses on how the Community protects and promotes both trade union rights and the rights of employers and their associations.[257]

---

[253] For developments in France, see *EIRR* 243, 28.

[254] McLean, above n. 245, 4.

[255] COM(98)592, 5.

[256] Pendleton, Wilson, and Wright, 'The Perception and Effects of Share Ownership: Empirical Evidence from Employee Buy-outs' (1998) 36 *BJIR* 99 and Pendleton, 'Characteristics of Workplaces with Financial Participation: Evidence from the Workplace Industrial Relations Survey' (1997) 28 *IRJ* 103.

[257] See generally, Commission, *The Regulation of Working Conditions in the Member States of the European Community, Volume 2, Social Europe* Supp. 5/93.

1. Freedom of Association

Article 11 of the Community Social Charter 1989 provides:

Employers and workers of the European Community shall have the right of association in order to constitute professional organisations or trade unions of their choice for the defence of their economic and social interests. Every employer and every worker shall have the freedom to join or not to join such organisations without any personal or occupational damage being thereby suffered by him.

The Social Charter Action Programme talks only of responsibility for the implementation of such policies resting with the Member States 'in accordance with their national traditions and policies'. Certainly the right to freedom of association, that is 'to join, without interference by the state, in associations to attain various ends',[258] exists in all Member States of the Union. In most States (Belgium, Denmark, France, Germany, Greece, Italy, Luxembourg, Netherlands, Spain, and Portugal) the right of freedom of association is considered so fundamental that it is enshrined in the Constitution.

The right to freedom of association can also be found in various international instruments, in particular the International Labour Organization (ILO) Conventions 87 and 98, the United Nations Universal Declaration of Human Rights,[259] and the accompanying International Covenant on Economic, Social, and Cultural Rights[260] and the International Covenant on Civil and Political Rights.[261] Most importantly, for the Community's purposes,[262] freedom of association is recognized in the European Convention on Human Rights (ECHR)[263] and the complementary European Social Charter (ESC) 1961. Article 11(1) of the European Convention talks of workers having the rights of freedom of association with others, 'including the right to form and to join trade unions for the protection of their interests'. The contents of

---

[258] Application 6094/73 *Association X v. Sweden* Dec.6. July 1977, D.R. 9, 5, at 7 in the context of the European Convention on Human Rights.

[259] Art. 23(4): 'Everyone has the right to form and join trade unions for the protection of his interests' but it also provides that 'no one may be compelled to belong to any association' (Art. 20(2)).

[260] Art. 8(1). See generally Wedderburn, 'Freedom of Association or Right to Organise? The Common Law and International Sources', in Wedderburn, *Employment Rights in Britain and Europe: Selected Papers in Labour Law* (Lawrence and Wishart, London, 1991).

[261] Art. 22.

[262] The Preamble to the Single European Act 1986 recognized both the ECHR and the ESC 1961 as forming part of the foundations of the European Community. Art. 6 [ex Art. F(2)] of the Treaty on European Union also provides that the Union must respect fundamental rights as guaranteed by the ECHR and Art. 136 [ex Art. 117 as amended by the Treaty of Amsterdam] refers to 'fundamental social rights such as those set out in the European Social Charter 1961 . . . and in the 1989 Community Charter . . .'.

[263] See generally Boyle, Harris, and Warbrick, *Law of the European Convention on Human Rights* (Butterworths, London, 1995), ch. 12, and Jacobs and White, *The European Convention on Human Rights* (2nd edn, Clarendon, Oxford, 1996), ch. 13.

Article 11(1) are largely reiterated in Part I[264] of the European Social Charter 1961[265] but expanded in Part II, where Article 5 provides that 'with a view to ensuring or promoting the freedom of workers and employers to form local, national or international organisations for the protection of their economic and social interests and to join those organisations, the Contracting parties undertake that national law shall not be such as to impair, nor shall it be so applied as to impair, this freedom'.[266]

Article 11(2) ECHR lists the circumstances in which the exercise of freedom of association can be limited. It provides:

No restriction shall be placed on the exercise of these rights other than such as are prescribed by law and are necessary in a democratic society in the interests of national security or public safety, for the prevention of disorder or crime, for the protection of health or morals or for the protection of the rights and freedoms of others.[267] This article shall not prevent the imposition of lawful restrictions on the exercise of these rights by members of the armed forces, of the police or of the administration of the state.

The question of what constitutes 'lawful restrictions' was at issue in the *GCHQ* case.[268] Here the Commission considered a ban on unions and union membership at a government intelligence-gathering centre to be lawful. However, the case fell at the admissibility stage.

Both the ECHR and the European Community Social Charter 1989 recognize two components to freedom of association. The first is the right to establish *unions*, which should be free to 'draw up their own rules, to administer their own affairs and to establish and join trade union federations'.[269] The use of the noun 'union' in the plural is important, because, as the Court of Human Rights indicated in *Young, James and Webster*,[270] it precludes the establishment of union monopolies and envisages the freedom to establish rival unions. The second right, and the corollary of the first, is for people to join those unions.

---

[264] Part I of the Charter takes the form of a declaration which lists those social and economic rights which all Contracting Parties must accept as the aim of their policies. Part II consists of the breakdown of those rights into their component parts which it then elaborates. States are then obliged to consider themselves bound by such articles or paragraphs of articles as they choose subject to certain fundamental provisions and an overall minimum selection.

[265] A new Protocol to the Social Charter was concluded in 1991 designed to improve the machinery of the Charter.

[266] It has been suggested that while the Convention organs are prepared to look at the European Social Charter 1961 as an aid to interpretation, they have done so in a way that minimizes its impact on Art. 11: Lewis-Anthony, 'Case Law of Art. 11 of the European Convention on Human Rights', *Freedom of Association* (Martinus Nijhoff, Dordrecht, 1994), Council of Europe, citing *Swedish Engine Drivers v. Sweden*, Eur. Ct. H.R., judgment of 6 Feb.1976, Series A, No. 2.

[267] Art. 14 of the Community Social Charter merely states that 'the internal legal order of the Member States shall determine under which conditions and to what extent the rights provided for in Arts. 11–13 apply to the armed forces, the police and the civil service'.

[268] Application No. 11603/85 *Council of Civil Service Unions v. United Kingdom*, Dec. 20. Jan. 1987, D.R. 50, 228. Cf. this decision with the decision of the ILO's Freedom of Association Committee, 234th Report of the Committee on Freedom of Association, Case No. 1261.

[269] Application No. 10550/83 *Cheall v. United Kingdom*, Dec.13 May 1985, D.R. 42, 178.

[270] *Young, James and Webster v. United Kingdom*, Eur. Ct. H.R, Series B, No. 39.

The Community Charter also expressly recognizes the negative freedom, the right of an individual not to join a union. Consequently, a closed shop contravenes a worker's fundamental right.[271] There is evidence that when the ECHR was drafted the right not to join a trade union was expressly excluded.[272] Nevertheless, the organs of the ECHR have not been constrained by this, and in *Sigurjonsson*,[273] a case concerning a pre-entry closed shop, the Court of Human Rights pronounced conclusively that 'Article 11 must be viewed as encompassing a negative right of association'.

The Community Charter expressly states that workers (or employers) must not suffer any 'personal or occupational damage' as a result of exercising their freedom of association.[274] This might include dismissal or action short of dismissal, or pressure by an employer on an employee to give up a position in the union. While such action is not expressly proscribed by the ECHR, the Convention provides practical recourse: Article 13 says that 'everyone whose rights and freedoms as set forth in this Convention are violated shall have an effective remedy before a national authority'.

As far as Community law is concerned, Article 137(6) [ex Article 2(6) SPA] expressly excludes freedom of association from the Community's competence, at least under Article 137. On the other hand, the Court has recognized freedom of association to be a fundamental right. In a staff case, *Kortner*,[275] the Court said 'Under the general principles of labour law the freedom of trade union activity recognised under Article 24a of the Staff Regulations means not only that officials and servants have the right without hindrance to form associations of their own choosing, but also that these associations are free to do anything lawful to protect the interests of their members as employees'. Thus, as Advocate General Jacobs noted in *Albany*,[276] the Court arguably recognized, first, the individual right to form and join an association and, secondly, the collective right to take action. In his view the fundamental nature of those two rights was confirmed in *Bosman*[277] with respect to freedom of association in general and in *Maurissen* more specifically

---

[271] See generally von Prondzynski, *Freedom of Association and Industrial Relations: A Comparative Study* (Mansell, London, 1987), chs. 7 and 8.

[272] Report of 19 June 1950 of the Conference of Senior Officials, in Vol. 4 *Collected Edition of Travaux Préparatoires*, cited in Lewis-Anthony, above n. 266, 45. See also Beddard, *Human Rights in Europe* (3rd edn, Grotius, Cambridge, 1993), 113.

[273] *Sigurjonsson v. Ireland*, Eur. Ct. H.R, judgment of 30 June 1993, Series A, No. 264. See earlier *Young, James and Webster* (post-entry closed shop), Eur. Ct. H.R., judgment of 13 Aug. 1981, Series A, No. 44, 21, para. 52.

[274] No express prohibition is made by the Charter against unions exploiting their dominant position by e.g. expelling members contrary to union rules.

[275] Case 175/73 *Union Syndicale, Massa and Kortner v. Commission* [1974] ECR 917, para. 14.

[276] Case C–67/96 *Albany International BV v. Stichting Bedrijfspensioenfonds Textielindustrie*, judgment of 21 Sept. 1999.

[277] Case C–415/93 *Union Royale Belge des Sociétés de Football Association and Others v. Bosman and Others* [1995] ECR I–4921, paras. 79 and 80.

with regard to trade unions.[278] The recognition of freedom of association as a fundamental right is significant for two reasons. First, 'fundamental rights form an integral part of the general principles of law whose observation the Court ensures'.[279] These fundamental rights must be respected both by the Community institutions and the Member States, when acting in the Community law field.[280] Secondly, it is a recognition of the important role played by unions as part of the democratic process.[281] There is, however, a paradox in this recognition: the Community is increasingly recognizing, and giving greater powers and responsibilities to, the Social Partners[282] at a time when in most States, with the exception of the Scandinavian countries, trade union membership is declining.

Will these developments lead to the creation of a European-wide trade union movement? At present this seems unlikely. Industrial relations in the Member States are characterized by the diversity of trade unions. In some Member States, such as the UK, Germany, Ireland, and Denmark, unions are 'unified'. In others unions are politically-ideological and confessional (i.e. religiously orientated).[283] In the Netherlands, for example, the three main trade union confederations comprise, first, a confederation (FNV) created from a merger between the socialist and most of the Catholic organizations; secondly, a Protestant Union federation (CNV) which includes some Catholic civil service unions which refused to join the socialists; and, thirdly, a federation of white collar organizations (MHP).[284] Similarly, in Italy industrial relations reflect that country's divisions in politics and ideology: Catholic and anti-Catholic, Communist and anti-Communist, collectivist and individualist.[285] This pattern is echoed in Belgium where the three main ideological pillars of society— Catholicism, Protestantism, and socialism—are cross-cut in industrial relations by the differences: between employer and employee, Catholic and non-Catholic, and French-speaking and Flemish-speaking communities.[286]

---

[278] Joined Cases C–193 and C–194/87 *Maurissen and European Public Service Union v. Court of Auditors* [1990] ECR I–95, paras. 11–16 and 21.

[279] 'For that purpose the Court draws inspiration from the constitutional traditions common to the Member States and from the guidelines supplied by international treaties for the protection of human rights on which the Member States have collaborated or of which they are signatories' *Opinion 2/94* [1996] ECR I–1759, para. 33. 'The European Convention on Human Rights has special significance in that respect': Case C–260/89 *ERT v. DEP* [1991] ECR I–2925, para. 41.

[280] See further Ch. 1.

[281] Sciarra, 'Regulating European Unions: An Issue for 1992' (1990) 11 *Comp. Lab. LJ* 141, 162–3.

[282] See further below, nn. 344–349 and Ch. 2.

[283] See Zachert, 'Trade Unions in Europe: Dusk or a New Dawn?' (1993) 9 *Int. Jo. Compar. LLIR* 15, 16.

[284] Visser, 'The End of an Era and the End of a System', in *Industrial Relations in the New Europe*, eds. Ferner and Hyman, above n. 31, 328.

[285] Ferner and Hyman, 'Italy: Between Political Exchange and Micro-Corporatism', in *Industrial Relations in the New Europe*, eds. Ferner and Hyman (Blackwell, Oxford, 1992), 524.

[286] See Vilrokx and Van Leemput, 'Belgium: A New Ability in Industrial Relations?', in Ferner and Hyman eds., above, n. 31, 363 and 367.

The existence of such differences, combined with the lack of significant transnational power resources,[287] suggest that worker representation will continue to take place primarily within the national or subnational context but with co-operation through the European trade union confederation.

2. The Right to Engage in Collective Bargaining

As we have seen, Community legislation emphasizes information and consultation with worker representatives. This can be a far cry from collective bargaining since no agreement need be reached and ultimately the final decision rests with the employer. As Wedderburn points out, the guest missing from the European table is collective bargaining, which is 'for us [in the UK] the primary traditional method for the expression of workers' interests'.[288] In the original Treaty of Rome the Social Partners had only a discreet presence[289]—through the Economic and Social Committee (ECOSOC)[290] and collective bargaining was the subject of close co-operation which the Commission was obliged to promote between the Member States.[291] The situation has changed dramatically since 1957 and the Social Partners now have a potentially important role, both as legislators and as managers of change as part of the European Employment Strategy. The Commission's discourse now focuses on the need to develop 'a strong partnership at all appropriate levels: at European, national, sectoral and enterprise level' to 'negotiate agreements to modernise the organisation of work'.[292]

2.1 The Definition of Collective Bargaining and the Content of Collective Agreements

In its broad sense[293] collective bargaining is a process of interest accommodation which includes all sorts of bipartite or tripartite discussions relating to labour problems directly or indirectly affecting a group of workers. The

---

[287] Jensen, Madsen, and Due, 'A Role for a Pan-European Trade Union Movement?—Possibilities in European IR-Regulation' (1995) 26 *IRJ* 4.

[288] Lord Wedderburn, above, n. 46, 6.

[289] Rodière, *Droit Social de l'Union Européenne* (LGDJ, Paris, 1998), 77.

[290] Arts. 257–262 [ex Arts. 193–198].

[291] Art. 118 [new Art. 140] provides that subject matter of close co-operation includes 'the right of association, and collective bargaining between employers and workers'.

[292] COM(98)592, 2, and 1999 Employment Guidelines.

[293] See Cordova, 'Collective Bargaining', in *Comparative Labour Law and Industrial Relations*, ed. Blanpain (3rd edn, Kluwer, Deventer, 1987). See now Blanpain ed., *Comparative Labour Law and Industrial Relations in Industrialised Market Economies* (5th edn, Kluwer, Deventer, 1993). These definitions roughly correspond to what is called in France the informal and formal types of negotiation (*negociation officieuse* and *negociation officielle*).

discussions may take place in different fora, with or without the presence of governments, and aim at ascertaining the view of the other party, obtaining a concession, or reaching a compromise. A narrower but more precise meaning of collective bargaining views it only in connection with the bipartite discussions leading to the conclusion of agreements. Collective bargaining here involves a process of negotiations between individual employers or representatives of employers' organizations and trade union representatives. Collective bargaining offers a variety of benefits. As Advocate General Jacobs pointed out in *Albany*:[294]

It is widely accepted that collective agreements between management and labour prevent costly labour conflicts, reduce transaction costs through a collective and rule-based negotiation process and promote predictability and transparency. A measure of equilibrium between the bargaining power on both sides helps to ensure a balanced outcome for both sides and for society as a whole.

As a rule, any agreement concluded is regarded as binding not only on its signatories but on the groups they represent.

The content of collective agreements can be determined by the contracting parties but comprise principally normative clauses and contractual or obligatory clauses. The normative stipulations refer to the terms and conditions of work which must be observed in all the individual employment contracts in the enterprise concerned. These include all aspects of working conditions, wages, fringe benefits (for example, additional holiday pay and sickness benefits), job classifications, working hours, time off, training, job security, and non-contributory benefit schemes. The collective agreement can also contain collective normative stipulations relating to informing and consulting workers, worker participation, and procedural rules.[295]

The contractual or obligatory clauses include all provisions spelling out the rights and duties of the parties. Often the main duty is the peace obligation, which means that for the duration of the agreement neither of the parties is permitted to initiate industrial action against the other party with the intention of altering the conditions laid down in the collective agreement. Such an obligation is considered to be a natural consequence of collective bargaining, which is supposed to bring stability to labour relations, or, as the Germans see it, the peace obligation is derived from the function of the collective agreement as a 'peace convention'. This obligation may be absolute, in which case the parties are obliged to refrain from all industrial action,[296] or relative, in which case neither of the parties is, for the duration of the collective agreement, permitted to initiate industrial action against the other party with the

---

[294] Case C–67/96, judgment of 21 Sept. 1999, para. 181.

[295] Commission, *Comparative Study on Rules Governing Working Conditions in the Member States: a Synopsis*, SEC(89)1137.

[296] Birk, 'Industrial Conflict: The Law of Strikes and Lock-outs', in Blanpain ed., above n. 293, 413.

intention of altering conditions laid down in the agreement.[297] The relative peace obligation offers trade unions the advantage of safeguarding their right to formulate new demands if and when substantive changes in the socio-economic environment occur.[298]

The peace obligation is recognized in Belgium, Denmark, Germany, Greece, Luxembourg, the Netherlands, and Spain. In Spain the obligation is only absolute if agreed upon by the contracting parties. In France and Italy peace obligation clauses are seldom included in collective agreements as they are regarded as a limitation on the right to strike. In France, however, the Labour Code does provide that parties to a collective agreement are bound not to do anything which might compromise the faithful implementation of the agreement within the limits laid down by the agreement itself.[299]

Article 12(1) of the Community Social Charter 1989 provides that 'Employers or employers' organisations, on the one hand, and workers' organisations on the other, shall have the right to negotiate and conclude collective agreements under the conditions laid down by national legislation and practice'. In most Member States collective bargaining has been used as a means of setting standards or improving upon standards laid down by statute. At one end of the spectrum lies Denmark where collective agreements form the cornerstone of labour standards. At the other lies the UK where there is a statutory presumption that collective agreements are not legally binding[300] between the parties. Collective agreements do have legal effect if incorporated into the contract of employment, but equally, since collective agreements do not constitute a floor of rights, the individual contract can be used to derogate from its provisions. In between lie Romano-Germanic countries such as Belgium, France, Germany, and Greece where collectively agreed norms can be given by law an *erga omnes* or extended effect.[301] Thus, the law is used to ensure that the normative terms of collective agreements are applied more generally throughout the industry or sector. The original rationale for this procedure was the need to avoid unfair competition from non-unionized enterprises, but subsequently the extension mechanism has been justified by the need to promote collective bargaining and to pursue more egalitarian goals.[302]

---

[297] Commission, above n. 295, SEC(89)1137.

[298] Cordova, above n. 293, 28.

[299] Commission, above n. 295, SEC(89)1137.

[300] S. 179 TULR(C)A 1992.

[301] In Spain in branches with difficulties in reaching collective agreements, the Ministry of Labour may take the initiative for extension. This is also an option in France. In Greece an agreement which covers 60 per cent of the workforce is normally eligible for extension. In the Netherlands the same applies to an agreement covering an 'important majority' of the workforce and in Germany one of the criteria for extension is that 50 per cent of the employees in question are covered.

[302] Cordova, 'Collective Bargaining', in Blanpain ed., above n. 298, 329.

2.2 Development of Collective Bargaining at Community Level

The Commission has long aspired to develop European-level collective bargaining[303] from the weak legal basis provided by Article 118 [new Article 140]. This said that the Commission should have the task of promoting close co-operation between Member States in the social field, especially in matters relating to, *inter alia*, 'the right of association, and collective bargaining between employers and workers'. The Commission was given some support by the inclusion of new Article 118b [now heavily amended by Article 139] by the Single European Act 1986. This provided that 'The Commission shall endeavour to develop the dialogue between management and labour at European level which could, if the two sides consider it desirable, lead to relations based on agreement'. This was reinforced by Article 12(2) of the Community Social Charter 1989 which provides that 'The dialogue between the two sides of industry at European level which *must* be developed, may, if the parties deem it desirable, result in contractual relations in particular at inter-occupational and sectoral level' (emphasis added). The Commission's view was that there should be 'complementarity between legislative initiatives on the part of the institutions and independent action by the two sides of industry'. The establishment of a balance between these two approaches would make it possible to manage 'the diversity of social practices and traditions specific to each Member State'.[304]

The Commission's drive towards establishing a European industrial relations area has been frustrated by the fact that traditionally trade unions and employers' associations are national in scope, and collective bargaining is usually conducted within a national framework or even at regional or enterprise level rather than at a centralized European level. Despite this, the Social Partners have long co-operated at Community level, for example, by participating in both formal and informal consultation. Formal consultation occurs in the Economic and Social Committee (ECOSOC),[305] in cross-industry advisory committees such as the European Social Fund Committee, and in the Standing Committee on Employment, established in 1970,[306] for the purpose of consultation between the Council, the Commission, and the representatives of management and labour to advise on the co-ordination of labour market policies.[307] Consultation has also occurred informally, for example, where the Commission has sought the opinions of the EC-level Social Partners on its proposals for social legislation. This arrangement was placed on a

[303] See generally Bercusson, *European Labour Law* (Butterworths, London, 1996), ch. 35.
[304] *Social Europe* 1/88, 67.
[305] See further Ch. 2.
[306] Council Decision 70/532/EEC [1970] OJ L273/25 as repealed by Council Decision 99/207/EC [1999] OJ L72/33. This Committee must now be consulted by the Employment Committee under the Employment Title (Art. 2 of Decision 2000/98/EC [2000] OJ L217/34).
[307] In addition, there are special or consultative committees on subjects such as free movement of persons, social security, health and safety, and the social fund.

formal footing by the Social Policy Agreement of the Treaty on European Union.[308]

In addition, management and labour have been meeting at a sectoral level since the establishment of joint committees with the Commission's assistance in the 1960s. These committees, with equal numbers of employers and employee representatives, covered agriculture (1963), road transport (1965), transport by inland waterway (1967), sea fishing (1968), rail transport (1971), and more recently civil aviation and telecommunications (1990).[309] They produced a number of joint opinions and recommendations on employment, working conditions, and health and safety, but did not enter into European-wide collective agreements, largely due to opposition by the employers.[310] The Commission intended these bodies to 'contribute to the construction of a European system of industrial relations and foster free collective bargaining'[311] but the reality fell far short of these aspirations. Although some committees were successful, particularly those with Community-level issues to discuss (the agriculture, fisheries, and transport committees), many participants felt that the committees were formal and bureaucratic and doubted both the usefulness of their work and the Commission's real interest in their activities.[312] Consequently, the Commission initiated an informal dialogue between the sectoral Social Partners with the aim of encouraging exchanges of views, consultation on Community policies, and the organization of studies and seminars, designed to 'create a climate of confidence between employers and workers'.[313] In the late 1980s this led to a new form of sectoral dialogue: informal working groups with the role of carrying out studies on employment in their sector and providing the Commission with a forum to consult on specific proposals. These contacts were formalized with the establishment of new sectoral dialogue committees.[314]

Calls for increased dialogue between employers, trade unions, and the Community continued, not just at the sectoral level but at the intersectoral level, as a means of both dealing with economic recession and resolving the impasse which had been reached by the mid 1980s in passing social policy initiatives. Jacques Delors, then the Commission President, seized on the idea of the social dialogue as a vehicle for formulating social policy. He told the European Parliament: 'Collective bargaining must remain one of the cornerstones of our economy, and efforts must be made to secure some

---

[308] Art. 3(2) [new Art. 138]. See further Ch. 2.

[309] For more details see *Social Europe* 2/95, 30.

[310] See 'The Sectoral Social Dialogue' 224 *EIRR* 14 and Hepple, *European Social Dialogue—Alibi or Opportunity?* (Institute of Employment Rights, London, 1993), 13.

[311] *Social Europe* 2/85.

[312] 224 *EIRR* 16.

[313] Ibid.

[314] Commission Communication on Adapting and Promoting the Social Dialogue at Community Level COM(98)332 and Commission Decision 98/500/EC [1998] OJ L225/27.

harmonisation at Community level. That is why I raised the idea ... of European collective agreements to provide the framework which is essential for the achievement of a large market'.[315] This precipitated what has become known as the Val Duchesse interprofessional or intersectoral social dialogue between the European Trade Union Confederation (ETUC), representing employees, the Union of Industrial and Employers' Confederations of Europe (UNICE), representing private sector employers, and the European Centre of Public Enterprises[316] (CEEP), for public-sector employers. Two working parties were established, one looking at the implications of new technology and work, the other dealing with employment and macroeconomic policies. Both groups issued 'Joint Opinions',[317] so called because the employers refused to countenance the notion of European-level collective agreements. However the impetus was soon lost, in part because the exact purpose of the social dialogue had never been resolved.[318]

It was, however, against this backcloth that the new Article 118b [now heavily amended by Article 139] was introduced into the Treaty of Rome by the Single European Act 1986, requiring the Commission to develop the dialogue between management and labour at European level. However, since the Treaty prescribed no formal procedures for the organization of the dialogue and failed to specify the legal consequences of any such dialogue it was difficult to regard Article 118b as more than a political gesture, legitimating the talks which had already begun at Val Duchesse in January 1985.[319] It did lead to a relaunch of the Val Duchesse dialogue, focusing this time on education and training and the problems surrounding the emergence of a European labour market. The relaunched dialogue was more productive. The education and training group produced three joint opinions and the working party on the labour market one further opinion, but these opinions lacked specific application and there was no requirement for the signatory parties to apply them.[320]

These joint opinions did send out the message that the two sides of industry could work together, and this paved the way for consultation with the Social Partners in the drafting of the Community Social Charter 1989.[321] Their involvement is reflected in the numerous references to collective agreements, particularly as a means of guaranteeing the fundamental social rights in the Charter (Article 27) and 'the active involvement of the two sides of industry'

---

[315] Cited in 'The Social Dialogue—Euro-Bargaining in the Making?' 220 *EIRR* 25, 27.

[316] Now known as the European Centre of Enterprises with Public Participation.

[317] e.g. 6 Nov. 1986 for the macro-economic committee, 6 Mar. 1987 for the new technology committee.

[318] 220 *EIRR* 27.

[319] Hepple, above n. 310, 16.

[320] Ibid., 28.

[321] See generally, Guéry, 'European Collective Bargaining and the Maastricht Treaty' (1992) 131 *International Labour Review* 581.

(Preamble). However, the most significant contribution of the Val Duchesse talks was the formulation by the Social Partners of a joint approach to the role of the social dialogue after Maastricht. A joint agreement, concluded on 31 October 1991, was presented to the Maastricht intergovernmental conference and was transposed almost verbatim into Articles 3 and 4 [new Articles 138 and 139] of the SPA by the Treaty on European Union.[322] This Agreement entitles the Social Partners not only to be consulted about proposed legislation[323] but also to enter a dialogue which may lead to agreements[324] which can be implemented by a Council 'decision'—or in reality a directive—on a proposal from the Commission.[325] The agreement is annexed to the Directive and, out of respect for the autonomy of the Social Partners, cannot be amended by the Council in the process of adopting the measure.

The SPA and now, since Amsterdam, the Title on Social Policy has thus revitalized the transnational role of the Social Partners and European-level collective bargaining. The success of this approach has been mixed. The first attempt by the Social Partners to use their new powers—to negotiate an agreement on EWCs—ended in failure and, as we have seen, the Commission had to step in to push the proposal through the usual legislative route.[326] However, they have succeeded in negotiating three agreements: on parental leave,[327] part-time work,[328] and fixed-term work.[329]

In 1996 the Commission adopted a consultation document to gather views on the means to promote and develop the European social dialogue,[330] followed by a Communication in 1998.[331] According to this Communication, the Commission intends to adapt and promote the future social dialogue by taking action in four main fields:

- *Information*: the Commission is to set in place more efficient channels for the exchange of information with all the Social Partners and it will encourage the European Social Partners to follow up the outcome of the European social dialogue with their affiliates at national level;
- *Consultation*: the Commission has replaced the existing Joint Committees at

---

[322] See further Ch. 2 and Case C–67/96 *Albany*, judgment of 21 Sept. 1999, para. 54, considered below, nn. 374–395.

[323] Art. 138(2) [ex Art. 3(2)].

[324] Art. 139(1) [ex Art. 4(1)].

[325] Art. 139(2) [ex Art. 4(2)]. The English language version of the Treaty provides for a 'decision'. This has been interpreted to mean any legally binding instrument, including directives.

[326] European Works Council (EWC) Directive 94/95/EC [1994] OJ L254/64) as amended by Council Directive 97/74/EC [1998] OJ L10/22.

[327] The Directive on Parental Leave (Council Directive 96/34/EC on the framework agreement on parental leave concluded by UNICE, CEEP, and the ETUC [1996] OJ L145/4) as amended by Council Directive 97/75/EC [1998] OJ L10/24.

[328] Council Directive 97/81/EC [1998] OJ L14/9 as amended by Council Directive 98/23/EC [1998] OJ L131/10.

[329] Council Directive 99/70/EC [1999] OJ L175/43.

[330] COM(96)448 concerning the development of the social dialogue at Community level.

[331] COM(98)322 adapting and promoting the social dialogue.

sectoral level with the new more flexible sectoral dialogue committees. At cross-industry level the advisory committees are to be rationalized and the Commission is to ensure that all Social Partners are effectively consulted on ongoing policy developments;

- *Employment partnership*: the Commission has reformed the Standing Committee on Employment[332] in order to strengthen the exchange between the Commission, the Council, and the Social Partners, on the basis of the Council Resolution on the 1998 Employment Guidelines;[333]
- *Negotiation*: the Commission is to continue to encourage the further development of contractual relations both at cross-industry and sectoral levels.

With a view to promoting and improving the working of the social dialogue, the Communication continues that the Commission has set itself three objectives: a more open social dialogue, a more effective dialogue between the European institutions and the Social Partners, and the development of real collective bargaining at European level.

Allowing the Social Partners such a significant role can be seen as a form of subsidiarity—that decisions should be taken as close to the citizens as possible. Yet, herein lies a paradox: although the Social Partners are negotiating, they are doing so at transnational, European level, at a time when decentralized collective bargaining is the trend in many States (with the exception of smaller States, such as Finland and Norway).[334] In the UK, for example, most leading firms have abandoned industry-wide agreements and moved towards single-employer bargaining.[335] However, the European-level agreements which result from the social dialogue are inevitably framework agreements by their nature, which allows local level collective agreements and/or domestic legislation to flesh out the details.[336] Yet, as the European-level Social Partners gain confidence in their ability to negotiate successfully, greater emphasis will be placed on their legitimacy and accountability—on their representativeness. UEAPME, the organization for small and medium-sized enterprises, has already challenged, albeit unsuccessfully, its exclusion from the negotiations on parental leave before the Court of First Instance.[337]

---

[332] Council Decision 1999/207/EC [1999] OJ L72/33.

[333] See further Ch. 1.

[334] Hansen, Madsen, and Jensen, 'The Complex Reality of Convergence and Diversification in European Industrial Relations Systems' (1997) 3 *EJIR* 357; Brown, Deakin, and Ryan, 'The Effects of British Industrial Relations Legislation 1979–1997' (1997) 38 *National Institute Economic Review* 70. This is even starting to occur in Denmark: see Gill, Knudsen, and Lind, 'Are There Cracks in the Danish Model of Industrial Relations' (1998) 29 *IRJ* 30.

[335] Edwards *et al.*, above n. 31, 19.

[336] Traxler describes this as 'organized decentralization' in 'European Trade Union Policy and Collective Bargaining: Mechanisms and Levels of Labour Market Regulation in Comparison' (1996) 2 *Transfer* 287. This has operated in a number of Member States in the 1990s. See e.g. Visser, 'Two Cheers for Corporatism, One for the Market and Industrial Relations, Wage Moderation and Job Growth in the Netherlands' (1998) 36 *BJIR* 269.

[337] Case T–135/96 *UEAPME* v. *Council* [1998] ECR II–2335, considered further in Ch. 2.

Collective bargaining has also been strengthened, this time at national level, by the fact that social policy directives can now be implemented by collective bargaining. For example, the Directives on proof of the employment contract,[338] working time,[339] and young workers[340] contain a clause providing that the Member States must pass laws, regulations, or administrative provisions to adopt the Directive by a particular date or shall ensure 'that the employers' and workers' representatives introduce the required provisions by way of agreement'. This method of implementation has been confirmed by Article 139(2) [ex Article 4(2) SPA]. Collective agreements or their equivalents can also be used to flesh out substantive standards in the directives. For example, Article 4 of the Working Time Directive 93/104/EC[341] requires that rest breaks must be provided if the working day lasts longer than six hours but that details of breaks, 'including duration and the terms on which it is granted, shall be laid down in collective agreements or agreements between the two sides of industry or, *failing that*, by national legislation' (emphasis added). This is an example of what the Dutch and Germans call an opening clause, allowing greater flexibility of practices (notably over working time) at company level.[342] On the other hand, a more striking feature of the Working Time Directive is that it allows collectively agreed derogations from the legislative norms *in pejus*,[343] thereby allowing standards to deteriorate. For example, derogations may be made from the rights relating to daily rest, breaks, weekly rest, length of night work, and reference periods by 'collective agreements or agreements concluded between the two sides of industry'.

Thus, the Community has placed growing emphasis on the articulation of complementary modes of regulation, based on collective agreement, operating at different levels—supranational, national, and subnational—which together constitute a 'regulatory complex' combining both flexibility and devolution.[344] New impetus has been given to the social dialogue by the European Employment Strategy. The Council Resolution on the 1998 Employment Guidelines made specific appeals to the interprofessional and sectoral Social Partners at European and national level to take new initiatives, especially regarding adaptability and employability by:[345]

- promoting the modernization of work organization and working patterns

---

[338] Council Directive 91/533/EEC [1991] OJ L288/32.

[339] Council Directive 93/104/EC [1993] OJ L307/18. See Scheuer, 'The Impact of Collective Agreements on Working Time in Denmark' (1999) 37 *BJIR* 465.

[340] Council Directive 94/33/EC [1994] OJ L216/12. See generally Adinolfi, 'Implementation of Social Policy Directives through Collective Agreements' (1988) 25 *CMLRev.* 291.

[341] [1993] OJ L307/18.

[342] Ferner and Hyman, above, n. 31, p. xvi.

[343] See generally Lord Wedderburn, 'Collective Bargaining at European Level: the Inderogability Problem' (1992) 21 *ILJ* 245.

[344] Marginson and Sisson, 'European Collective Bargaining: A Virtual Prospect' (1998) 36 *JCMS* 505, 514.

[345] See further Ch. 1.

through negotiation at the appropriate levels, particularly in economic sectors undergoing structural change, agreements on work organization including working time and flexible working arrangements with the aim of making enterprises productive and competitive, and achieving the required balance between flexibility and security;

- developing the social dimension of the process of industrial restructuring, especially in the context of worker information and consultation;
- opening workplaces across Europe for training work practice, traineeships, and other forms of employability measures; and,
- promoting equal opportunities between women and men, both in a wide context and on specific initiatives, aimed at reconciling work and family life, for example, the development of further policies on career breaks, parental leave, and part-time work.

The National Action Plans have also offered the Social Partners the opportunity to contribute to employment policy.[346] For some Member States this approach is by no means new. It has long been a tradition in certain States to respond to persistent structural mass unemployment by entering into central agreements at national level. For example, in France the 1993 five-year employment law spawned a series of central agreements and in Italy a major tripartite pact was signed in 1996.[347]

The EMU process and economic convergence have also 'progressively made visible the importance of the role of the Social Partners, not only in influencing the local competitiveness and employment conditions, but also as a major player in the achievement of growth and an employment-friendly overall policy mix in the Euro zone and in the Community'.[348] The role of the Social Partners has also been underlined in Agenda 2000 and the opening of negotiations with the applicant Member States. The Commission is encouraging the political and administrative bodies in the applicant countries to associate the Social Partners closely on the pre-enlargement policy of the EU and to adapt the national legal frameworks so as to promote the development of the social dialogue, thereby enabling the Social Partners to play an effective role in the framework of the social dialogue after accession.[349]

In Continental Europe, where there is a significant Catholic tradition, the idea of the 'Social Partners' has implied a societal recognition of the different interests of workers and employers, an acceptance and encouragement of the collective representation of these interests, and an aspiration that their organized accommodation may provide an effective basis for the regulation of work

---

[346] Communication from the Commission 'From Guidelines to Action: The National Action Plans for Employment' COM(98)316.

[347] Ferner and Hyman, 'Introduction', in Ferner and Hyman eds., above, n. 31, p. xxi.

[348] Commission Communication, 'Adapting and Promoting the Social Dialogue at Community Level' COM(98)322, 4. See further Ch. 1.

[349] COM(98)322, 17.

and the labour market.[350] As we have seen, to an extent this is being replicated at EU level and a form of tripartite or bipartite concertation—or Euro-corporatism—is emerging. The role now envisaged for the Social Partners is one of partnership[351] and co-operation rather than adversarialism, a shift from industrial pluralism[352] to a more managerialist perspective, a shift from divergent objectives to shared objectives.[353] 'Partnership' in this sense con-notes having a share in an enterprise or relationship of some type, whether economic or social.[354] This, in turn, implies some degree of commitment to the enterprise over the medium or long term and some influence over its governance.[355] Haynes and Allen note four common elements in relationships based on partnership—mutual legitimization; commitment to co-operative processes; joint decision-making or consultation; and job security/employability exchanged for co-operation in implementing change and flexi-bility. As they point out, partnership is fraught with difficulty and highly vulnerable. The co-operative mode of engagement may conflict with the personal beliefs and attitudes of workers, union officials, and managers. This is likely to be exacerbated when the partnership occurs at European level, several stages removed from those represented, at a time when the legitimacy of the European Social Partners is being contested in some quarters.

Do these developments mean the advent of European collective bargaining resulting in collective agreements determining pay and other substantive conditions of the kind associated with sectoral agreements found in most countries? Marginson and Sisson argue that this is unlikely.[356] Instead they suggest that what will result is 'virtual collective bargaining'. This covers two processes: first the conclusion of framework agreements at European inter-professional, European sectoral, and European company levels, establishing

---

[350] Ferner and Hyman, 'Introduction', in Ferner and Hyman eds., above, n. 31, pp. xv–xvi.

[351] See e.g. the Commission's Green Paper *Partnership for a New Organisation of Work* COM(97)127. See also 'Developing a European Industrial Relations and Partnership Culture': COM(98)322, 17; 'a process, based on partnership, represents the most promising way of modernising working life': COM(98)592; 'a partnership-based working method aimed at identi-fying consistent solutions in all areas affected by the crisis': High Level Group, 'Managing Change', Nov. 1998. See also the British Fairness at Work White Paper (http://www.dti.gov.ui/IR/fairness/) where the government talks of the principles of fairness of work and competitiveness providing a 'blueprint for the development of partnership in the longer term' (para. 1.11). At para. 4.7 it talks of trade unions as being 'a force for fair treatment, and a means of driving towards innovation and partnerships'.

[352] For a classic exposition of pluralism in labour law, see Kahn-Freund's *Labour and the Law* by Davies and Freedland (3rd edn, Stevens, London, 1983).

[353] See the typology suggested in Terry, 'Systems of Collective Employee Representation in Non-union Firms in the UK' (1999) 30 *IRJ* 16, 17.

[354] Haynes and Allen, 'Partnership Unionism: A Viable Strategy', Paper prepared for presenta-tion to the British Universities Industrial Relations Association Conference, July 1999.

[355] Note the language of stakeholding in the High Level Group's Report, *Managing Change*, 6, http://europa.eu.int/comm/dg05/empl&esf/ees_en.htm.

[356] Marginson and Sisson, 'European Collective Bargaining: A Virtual Prospect' (1998) 36 *JCMS* 505.

parameters and objectives which negotiators at subsidiary levels in individual countries (national, sector, and enterprise) are expected or required to operate. Secondly, it will cover arm's length bargaining where employers and union representatives do not negotiate face to face at European level but the outcomes of sector and enterprise bargaining are increasingly anticipated and co-ordinated across countries by the use of comparisons, pattern setting, and the diffusion of best practice.[357]

2.3 Is There a Fundamental Right to Bargain Collectively?

As we have seen in *Albany*, Advocate General Jacobs considered freedom of association and the right to take collective action to be fundamental rights. However, he did not consider collective bargaining—the freedom most fully articulated in the Community legal order—to be a fundamental right. His argument ran as follows. First, he said that only Article 6 of the European Social Charter 1961 expressly recognized the existence of a fundamental right to bargain.[358] However, he said, the mere fact that a right is included in the Charter does not mean that it is generally recognized as a fundamental right. The structure of the Charter is such that the rights set out represent policy goals rather than enforceable rights, and the States parties to it are required only to select which of the rights specified they undertake to protect. He then pointed to Article 4 of 'the carefully drafted "Right to Organise and Collective Bargaining Convention" [which] imposes on the Contracting States an obligation to "encourage and promote" collective bargaining. No right is granted'.[359]

He then considered the case law of the European Court of Human Rights. He said that 'there is a telling absence of any reference to the right to bargain collectively'. First, he cited the *Swedish Engine Drivers*[360] case where the majority of the Commission of Human Rights had argued in favour of the recognition of trade unions' right to engage in collective bargaining. The Court held that it did not have to give a ruling on that question since, it said, such a right was not at issue and was granted to the applicant union under national law. Since then, the European Court of Human Rights has never expressly recognized the existence of that right. Advocate General Jacobs then noted that there was evidence that the Court was reluctant to do so.[361] On Article 6(1) of the European Social Charter 1961, which requires that the States 'promote joint consultation between workers and employers', the Court has said that '[t]he prudence of the terms used shows that the Charter does not provide for

---

[357] See e.g. Walsh, Zappalá, and Brown, 'European Integration and the Pay Policies of British Multinationals' (1995) 26 *IRJ* 84.

[358] Case C–67/96 *Albany*, judgment of 21 Sept. 1999, para. 146.

[359] Para. 147.

[360] *Swedish Engine Drivers' Union v. Sweden*, 6 Feb. 1976, Eur. Ct HR Rep., Series A, No. 20 (1976).

[361] Para. 149.

a real right to consultation'.[362] On Article 6(2), which requires the State 'to promote, where necessary and appropriate, machinery for voluntary negotiations between employers and employees', the Court has held that 'the prudence of the wording . . . demonstrates that the Charter does not provide for a real right to have any such agreement concluded'.[363] Secondly, Advocate General Jacobs said[364] that the Court has consistently stressed that 'trade union freedom is only one form or a special aspect of freedom of association' and that 'Article [11] does not secure any particular treatment of trade unions'.[365]

Thirdly, he considered the decision in *Gustafsson*[366] where the Court had to consider a conflict between a trade union which put pressure on an employer who did not want to take part in the collective bargaining process in his industry[367] through boycotts and other actions. The employer contended that compulsion to participate in the collective agreement would in practice amount to compulsion to join an employers' association. The majority of the Court said that with regard to trade union activities, '[I]n view of the sensitive character of the social and political issues involved in achieving a proper balance between the competing interests . . . and the wide degree of divergence between the domestic systems in the particular area under consideration, the Contracting States should enjoy a wide margin of appreciation in their choice of the means to be employed'.[368] Then it merely stressed that it saw 'no reason to doubt that the union action pursued legitimate interests consistent with Article 11 of the Convention'. It continued that '[I]t should also be recalled in this context that the legitimate character of collective bargaining is recognised by a number of international instruments'.

Thus, Advocate General Jacobs said that 'the Court appears to have been careful to avoid concluding that the Convention guarantees the right to collective bargaining'. He therefore concluded that:

it cannot be said that there is sufficient convergence of national legal orders and international legal instruments on the recognition of a specific fundamental right to bargain collectively.[369]

Moreover, the collective bargaining process, like any other negotiation between economic actors, is in my view sufficiently protected by the general principle of freedom of contract. Therefore, a more specific fundamental right to protection is not needed. In

---

[362] *National Union of Belgian Police v. Belgium*, 27 Oct. 1975, Eur. Ct HR Rep., Series A, No. 19 (1975), para. 38.

[363] *Swedish Engine Drivers' Union v. Sweden*, 6 Feb. 1976, Eur. Ct HR Rep., Series A, No. 20 (1976), para. 39.

[364] Para. 150.

[365] *Schmidt and Dahlström v. Sweden*, 6 Feb. 1976, Eur. Ct HR Rep., Series A, No. 21 (1976), para. 34.

[366] *Gustafsson v. Sweden*, 25 Apr. 1996, R.J.D., 1996–II, No. 9.

[367] Para. 151.

[368] *Gustafsson v. Sweden*, 25 Apr. 1996, R.J.D., 1996–II, No. 9, para. 45.

[369] Para. 160.

any event the justified limitations on the alleged right to bargain collectively would arguably be identical to those on freedom of contract.[370]

He therefore said that while management and labour are in principle free to enter into such agreements as they see fit, they must, like any other economic actor, respect the limitations imposed by Community law, such as sex equality[371] and free movement of workers.[372] He continues that this could be seen as an application of the general rule that the exercise of a fundamental right may be restricted provided that the restriction in fact corresponds to objectives of general interest pursued by the Community and does not constitute in relation to the aim pursued a disproportionate and intolerable interference, impairing the very substance of the rights guaranteed.[373]

2.4 Collective Bargaining and Competition Law

The purpose of this discussion in *Albany* was to consider whether collective agreements on wages and conditions as well as those implementing Community directives could be shielded from Community competition law (Article 81(1) and (2) [ex Article 85(1) and (2)]). If collective bargaining had been a fundamental right then collective agreements might have been protected from Article 81,[374] although Advocate General Jacobs doubted even this.[375] However, since collective bargaining was not, according to Advocate General Jacobs, a fundamental right then in principle collective agreements risked being exposed to the full rigours of Article 81 [ex Article 85]: according to the Commission's submissions, collective agreements are, by their very nature, restrictive of competition since generally employees cannot offer to work for a wage below the agreed minimum, and they affect trade between Member States.[376] Such agreements would thus be prohibited and void unless

---

[370] Para. 161.

[371] See further Ch. 4.

[372] See further Ch. 3.

[373] Para. 162, citing Case C–44/94 *R v. MAFF, ex parte Fishermen's Organisation* [1995] ECR I–3115, para. 55.

[374] See the arguments of the Funds, the Dutch and French governments, and the Commission.

[375] Para. 163: 'The mere recognition of a fundamental right to bargain collectively would therefore not suffice to shelter collective bargaining from the applicability of the competition rules'.

[376] Para. 175. Advocate General Jacobs in *Albany* doubted this (para. 182). He said that collective agreements on wages, working time, or other working conditions, although they may restrict competition between employees, probably do not have an appreciable restrictive effect on competition between employers. As regards competition on the demand side of the labour market, normally each employer remains free to offer more advantageous conditions to his employees. As regards competition on the product or services markets on which the employers operate, first, agreements on wages or working conditions harmonize merely one of many production cost factors. Therefore only one aspect of competition is affected. Secondly, as follows from the practice of the Commission, proximity to the market of the factor in issue is an important criterion for assessing appreciability. In the case of collective agreements on wages and working conditions the final price of the products or services in question will be influenced by

exempted by the Commission under Article 81(3) [ex Article 85(3)]. The granting of such an exemption would be unlikely since that provision does not allow social objectives to be taken into account.[377] This result would occur despite the fact that 'there is international consensus on the legitimate and socially desirable character of collective bargaining'[378] since the main purpose of trade unions and of the collective bargaining process is to prevent employees from engaging in a 'race to the bottom' with regard to wages and working conditions.[379]

Collective agreements therefore present a conflict between the social rights of the Treaty and the competition provisions of the Treaty. As Advocate General Jacobs pointed out,[380] the authors of the Treaty either were not aware of the problem or could not agree on a solution.[381] The Treaty therefore does not give clear guidance on which policy should take priority. He said that since both sets of rules were Treaty provisions of the same rank, one set of rules should not take absolute precedence over the other and neither set of rules should be emptied of its entire content. He therefore suggested the following reconciliation: since the Treaty rules encouraging collective bargaining presuppose that collective agreements are in principle lawful, Article 85(1) [new Article 81(1)] could not have been intended to apply to collective agreements between management and labour on core subjects such as wages and other working conditions. Accordingly, collective agreements between management and labour on wages and working conditions should enjoy automatic immunity from antitrust scrutiny. He then proposed three conditions for *ipso facto* immunity:

First, as the Commission has pointed out, the agreement must be made within the formal framework of collective bargaining between both sides of industry. Unilateral coordination between employers unconnected with the collective bargaining process should not be automatically sheltered, whatever the subject of the coordination may be.[382]

Secondly, the agreement should be concluded in good faith. In that context account must be taken of agreements which apparently deal with core subjects of collective

---

many other factors before they reach the market. Thirdly, and perhaps most importantly, production factor costs are only apparently harmonized, because in economic terms labour, in contrast to raw materials, is not a homogeneous commodity. The fact that employees earn nominally the same wage does not mean that the real costs for their respective employers are identical. Real costs can be determined only when the employees' productivity is taken into account. Productivity is determined by many factors e.g. professional skills, motivation, technological environment, and work organization. All those factors can be and are influenced by employers. That is precisely the task of efficient management of human resources. Thus, competition on labour as a cost factor is in fact strong.

[377] Para. 175. Cf. para. 193, considered below, n. 384.
[378] Para. 164.
[379] Para. 178.
[380] Para. 179.
[381] Para. 179.
[382] Para. 191.

bargaining such as working time but which merely function as cover for a serious restriction of competition between employers on their product markets. In those exceptional cases, too, competition authorities should be able to examine the agreement in question.[383]

Thirdly, it is necessary to delimit the scope of the collective bargaining immunity, so that the immunity extends only to those agreements for which it is truly justified. . . . I would tentatively suggest as a possible criterion that the collective agreement must be one which deals with core subjects of collective bargaining such as wages and working conditions and which does not directly affect third parties or markets. The test should be whether the agreement merely modifies or establishes rights and obligations within the labour relationship between employers and employees or whether it goes beyond that and directly affects relations between employers and third parties, such as clients, suppliers, competing employers, or consumers. . . . Since those agreements have potentially harmful effects on the competitive process, they should be subject to antitrust scrutiny by the Commission or other competent authorities, which would examine whether there was in fact an appreciable restriction of competition. If so, the Commission should be able to balance the different interests involved and where appropriate grant an exemption according to Article 85(3) [new Article 81(3)] of the Treaty. Both the Court and the Commission have on occasions recognised the possibility of taking account of social grounds in that context, in particular by interpreting the conditions of Article 85(3) broadly so as to include concerns for employment.[384]

Thus, collective agreements between management and labour concluded in good faith on core subjects of collective bargaining such as wages and working conditions which do not directly affect third markets and third parties are not caught by Article 81(1) [ex Article 85(1)].[385] This is very much the perspective of a competition lawyer. Agreements which do not satisfy one of these conditions are caught by Article 81(1) [ex Article 85(1)] and will be subject to scrutiny by the Commission under Article 81(3) if notified.

The Court took a rather different, labour relations approach which respected far more the autonomy of the Social Partners. It did not follow the fundamental rights route but it did recognize the potential conflict between the social provisions of the Treaty and the Articles on competition. It began by observing that the Community's activities include not only 'a system ensuring that competition in the internal market is not distorted'[386] but also 'a policy in the social sphere',[387] and that one of the Community's tasks is to promote a 'harmonious and balanced development of economic activities' and a 'high level of employment and social protection'.[388] It then pointed to

---

[383] Para. 192.
[384] Citing Case 26/76 *Metro v. Commission* [1977] ECR 1875, para. 43; Case 42/84 *Remia v. Commission* [1985] ECR 2545, para. 42; *Synthetic Fibres* [1984] OJ L207/17, para. 37; and *Ford v. Volkswagen* [1993] OJ L20/14, para. 23.
[385] Para. 194.
[386] Art. 3(g).
[387] Art. 3(j) [ex Art. 3(i)].
[388] Para. 54.

the Commission's duties under Article 118 [new Article 140] and Article 118b [now amended Article 139] concerning collective bargaining and the role of the social dialogue under Article 1 SPA [now Article 136] and Article 4(1) and (2) SPA [now Article 139(1) and (2)].[389] It then said:

59. It is beyond question that certain restrictions of competition are inherent in collective agreements between organisations representing employers and workers. However, the social policy objectives pursued by such agreements would be seriously undermined if management and labour were subject to Article 85(1) [new Article 81(1)] of the Treaty when seeking jointly to adopt measures to improve conditions of work and employment.

60. It therefore follows from an interpretation of the provisions of the Treaty as a whole which is both effective and consistent that agreements concluded in the context of collective negotiations between management and labour in pursuit of such objectives must, by virtue of their nature and purpose, be regarded as falling outside the scope of Article 85(1) of the Treaty.

Thus, while the Advocate General thought that competition law applied to collective agreements but they were immune subject to three strict conditions being satisfied, the so-called 'rule of reason' approach,[390] the Court took the view that competition law did not apply at all (the *'per se'* legal approach) provided that the collective agreement aimed at improving working conditions.

The case itself concerned a collective agreement negotiated by representative organizations of employers and workers setting up a supplementary pension scheme, managed by a pension fund, to which affiliation was compulsory. The Dutch Minister of Employment had, on the request of the Social Partners, made affiliation to the scheme compulsory for all workers in the sector. The Court said this guaranteed a certain level of pension to all workers in the sector which contributed directly to the improvement of one of the conditions of employment, knowing their pay. Thus Article 85 did not apply.[391] As far as extending the collective agreement is concerned, as we have already seen, the possibility of giving *erga omnes* effect to a collective agreement exists in certain Member States[392] and in the Community itself (through a 'decision' of the Council of Ministers).[393] This was recognized by the Court in *Albany*.[394] The Court said that since the collective agreement itself was not caught by Article 85(1) [new Article 81(1)] the Member State was free to extend it to all workers in the sector.[395]

---

[389] Paras. 55–58. See above, nn. 322–325.

[390] See Vousden, 'Albany, Market Law and Social Exclusion' (2000) 29 *ILJ* 181; see also the note by Gyselen (2000) 37 *CMLRev* 425. On the rule of reason see Korah, *An Introductory Guide to EC Competition Law and Practice* (6th edn, Hart, Oxford, 1997).

[391] Paras. 63–64.

[392] See above, n. 325.

[393] See above, n. 325.

[394] Paras. 66 and 67.

[395] Although Art. 85 [new Art. 81] concerns only the behaviour of undertakings and not legislative or regulatory measures emanating from Member States, Member States are obliged

3. The Right to Resort to Collective Action

Collective action can take a variety of forms. While strikes are the most obvious expression of conflict, concerted action can take the form of overtime bans, go-slows, a work to rule, withdrawal of co-operation, sit-ins, and picketing. Workers may also refuse to handle products made by a firm in a dispute (blacking) to support workers of that firm. Collective action is not necessarily one-sided: management can lock workers out, the reverse of a strike, dismiss workers, or bring in others to do the strikers' jobs (blacklegging). These workers may be employed by a subsidiary located elsewhere in the Community and, exercising their right of free movement,[396] drafted in to assist the employer. More drastically, the employer may decide to close the plant and/or relocate the business.

3.1 The Right to Strike

Article 13 of the Community Social Charter 1989 recognizes the right to 'resort to *collective action* in the event of a conflict of interests' (emphasis added). This includes the '*right* to strike, subject to obligations arising under national regulations and collective agreements' (emphasis added). Consistent with the Romano-Germanic tradition, the Community recognizes the *right* to strike rather than the *freedom* to strike.[397] Freedom to strike means that the strike is legally permitted but no special privileges are granted: the strike is tolerated, but not privileged, and the legal limits of the strike are dictated by the general legal order. The right to strike, by contrast, means that the legal order of the State must take precautions to ensure the exercise of the right; consequently, the strike is privileged. This demonstrates that the legal order evaluates the pursuit of collective interests more highly than the individual obligations arising from the contract of employment. The importance of this right, and the recognition of the inequality of bargaining power between workers and employers, has meant that the right to strike is expressly recognized in the constitutions of many Member States. In Germany, by contrast, strikes and lock-outs are both respected as weapons of the same value in industrial conflict, leading to parity between trade unions and employers' associations. Such collective action is considered to be part of the broader framework of the collective autonomy to conclude agreements. A similar

under Art. 85 read in conjunction with Art. 5 [new Art. 10] not to take or maintain in force legislation capable of eliminating the useful effect of the competition rules which apply to undertakings. This is not the case here.

[396] Art. 39ff. [ex Art. 48ff.]: see Ch. 3.

[397] Birk, 'Industrial Conflict: The Law of Strikes and Lock-outs', in *Comparative Labour Law and Industrial Relations*, ed. Blanpain (3rd edn, Kluwer, Deventer, 1990), 406. The discussion that follows draws on this chapter. See also Wedderburn, 'The Right to Strike: Is There a European Standard?', in Wedderburn, above n. 260.

approach can be detected in the European Social Charter 1961, where the right to engage in collective action in cases of conflict of interest (Article 6(4)) falls under the general heading of the 'right to bargain collectively'.

In most countries the right to strike belongs to the employees who organize their interests collectively. Individual action is generally excluded. In Germany, Greece, and Portugal, the right to strike belongs to the trade unions. By contrast, in the UK the *right* to strike does not exist as such, but, subject to certain stringent conditions, trade unions are protected by immunities established by law when their members take certain forms of industrial action. These same immunities now do provide some protection for individual employees but they are likely to breach their individual employment contracts by taking any form of industrial action and can, in certain circumstances, be dismissed as a result. By contrast, in most Romano-Germanic countries, the contract of employment is merely suspended during the strike. As Table 8.1 demonstrates, in general lockouts do not enjoy the same protection as the right or freedom to strike. For example, in Portugal lockouts are prohibited by Article 60 of the Constitution. Strikes have a variety of objectives. They may relate to labour matters and are consequently directed at the employer (primary strikes), or they may be political, designed to express grievances about government policy. In most Member States political strikes are unlawful since they are not intended to achieve a collective agreement (Germany). Strikes in support of the primary strikes, described as sympathy or secondary strikes, are generally legal (except in the UK), at least if the interests of the sympathy strikers are linked to those of the primary strikers. The legality of the different types of strikes in the twelve Member States is considered in Table 8.1.

The Community Social Charter recognizes the right to strike 'subject to the obligations arising under national regulations and collective agreements'. The European Social Charter 1961 is expressed in similar terms.[398] These obligations relate to national rules concerning strike ballots (Germany, the UK), the need to announce a strike in advance (France in the case of public sector employees and the UK), the requirement that any action taken must be proportionate[399] (Denmark, Germany, and the Netherlands) and a last resort (Germany), and respect, where necessary, the peace obligation contained in the collective agreement (Germany and Denmark).

Article 137(6) [ex Article 2(6) SPA] expressly excludes Community competence (at least under Article 137) in respect of the right to strike or the right to impose lockouts. Thus, the Community will not be legislating on this legal

---

[398] Art. 6(4) recognizes 'the right of workers and employers to collective action in cases of conflicts of interest, including the right to strike, subject to obligations that may arise out of collective agreements previously entered into'.

[399] i.e. 'the use of the industrial action must be necessary, must be the suitable instrument to fulfil the intended purpose, and finally may not be an excessive instrument': Weiss, *Labour Law and Industrial Relations in the Federal Republic of Germany* (Kluwer, Deventer, 1989), 135.

basis. On the other hand, as we have seen,[400] Advocate General Jacobs suggested in his opinion in *Albany*[401] that the collective right to take action was a fundamental right.[402] Later he added, 'In my view, the right to take collective action in order to protect occupational interests in so far as it is indispensable for the enjoyment of freedom of association is also protected by Community law'.[403] In his view this is significant, for any impairment of the substance of the right, even in the public interest, might be unlawful.[404] This issue was acknowledged in Council Regulation No. 2679/98,[405] which set up an intervention mechanism to safeguard free trade in the single market and was adopted unanimously by the Member States following the Court's ruling in *Commission v. France*.[406] Article 2 provides:

This Regulation may not be interpreted as affecting in any way the exercise of fundamental rights, as recognised in Member States, including the right or freedom to strike.[407]

The scope of the collective action that can be taken is far from clear. The European Court of Human Rights relied on the phrase 'for the protection of his interests' in Article 11(1) of the European Convention on Human Rights in holding that freedom of association included the rights that were 'indispensable for the effective enjoyment' or 'necessarily inherent elements' of trade union freedom.[408] Article 11 therefore also 'safeguards the freedom to protect the occupational interests of trade union members by trade union action, the conduct and development of which the Contracting States must both permit and make possible'.[409] As Advocate General Jacobs pointed out, that apparently broad statement seems to cover only a core of specific activities. To date the only right expressly recognized by the Court of Human Rights has been to be 'heard' by the State.[410] On the other hand, a trade union has no right to be consulted by the State,[411] nor is the State obliged to conclude collective agreements,[412] nor does Article 11 necessarily imply a right to

---

[400] See above, n. 276.

[401] Case C–67/96, judgment of 21 Sept. 1999.

[402] Para. 139.

[403] Para. 159.

[404] Case C–280/93 *Germany v. Council* [1994] ECR I–4973, paras. 78 and 87; cf. paras. 162 and 163 in Case C–67/96 *Albany*, judgment of 21 Sept. 1999.

[405] [1998] OJ L337/8.

[406] Case C–265/95 *Commission v. France* [1997] ECR I–6959.

[407] Regulation 2679/98 was accompanied by a Resolution of the Council and representatives of the Member States of 7 Dec. 1998 on the free movement of goods [1998] OJ L337/10.

[408] *National Union of Belgian Police v. Belgium*, 27 Oct. 1975, Eur. Ct HR Rep., Series A, No. 19 (1975), para. 39.

[409] Ibid., para. 40.

[410] Ibid., para. 39; *Swedish Engine Drivers' Union v. Sweden*, 6 Feb. 1976, Eur. Ct HR Rep., Series A, No. 20 (1976), para. 40.

[411] *National Union of Belgian Police v. Belgium*, 27 Oct. 1975, Eur. Ct HR Rep., Series A, No. 19 (1975), para. 38.

[412] *Swedish Engine Drivers' Union v. Sweden*, 6 Feb. 1976, Eur. Ct HR Rep., Series A, No. 20 (1976), para. 39.

Table 8.1 Rules for Strikes and Lockouts in the Member States

	STRIKES						LOCKOUTS
Country	Political strike	Socio-political strike	Professional strike	Sympathy strike	Actions short of strike	Effects	
Belgium	legality		legal	legal	not legal	s.i.e.c.	permitted under restrictive conditions
Denmark	same rules as for professional strike		legal, if proportionate, only in case of conflict of interest	legal, if provided in C.A.	generally not legal	breach of employment contract	legal, breach of employment contract
France	not legal	allowed	legal	legal	not legal	s.i.e.c.	normally unlawful except in emergency cases defensive lockout may be justified
Germany	not legal		only legal subject to peace obligation and secret ballot	only exceptionally legal	not legal	s.i.e.c.	forbidden by law
Greece	not legal	allowed	legal	legal, if linked to the interests of professional strikers		s.i.e.c.	
Ireland			immunity depends on C.A.	probably lawful	not necessarily unlawful	unclear whether contract is breached or suspended	not of legal relevance, may mean breach or suspension of contract

Italy	legal under certain circumstances	allowed	legal	legal, if related to professional strikers	not legal	s.i.e.c.	retaliatory lockout may be lawful
Luxembourg	probably legal		legal, if preceded by conciliation	doubtful legality	doubtful legality	s.i.e.c.	recognized but legal status uncertain
Netherlands	not legal	allowed	legal, proportionality important	doubtful legality	doubtful legality	s.i.e.c.	not regulated, legal status uncertain
Portugal	not legal	allowed	legal provided certain conditions are fulfilled		doubtful legality	s.i.e.c.	forbidden in all forms
Spain	not legal	allowed	legal	legal, if linked to interests of professional strikers	not legal	s.i.e.c.	defensive lockout recognized under exceptional circumstances
United Kingdom			immunity system	no immunity		breach of employment contract	not of legal relevance, may be breach of employment contract

Source: Commission. Comparative Study on Rules Governing Working Condition in the Member States: A Synopsis SEC(89)1137, as amended.
Key: C.A. = collective agreement   s.i.e.c. = suspension of individual employment contract

strike, since the interests of the members can be furthered by other means.[413]

3.2 Prevention and Settlement of Disputes[414]

Most Member States, with the exception of the UK and Ireland, draw a distinction between disputes over conflicts of interests and disputes over conflicts of rights. While disputes over conflicts of rights concern the interpretation and application of existing contractual clauses, disputes over conflicts of interests relate to changes in the establishment of collective rules and require the conflicting economic interest to be reconciled with a view to reaching a solution on the basis of legal or collective procedures. In principle, strikes are permitted to resolve conflicts of interests between labour and management, but the courts, especially the labour courts, usually decide disputes concerning conflicts of rights. For example, in Germany the Labour Courts have sole competence for all disputes between parties to collective agreements concerning rights. Similarly, in Denmark a conflict of rights cannot be resolved by industrial action but has to be settled through a procedural system which is subdivided into two branches: industrial arbitration and the Labour Court. Broadly speaking, conflicts over the interpretation of collective agreements are settled by arbitration, whereas conflicts over an alleged breach of the collective agreement are dealt with by the Labour Court (or the arbitrator if the parties concerned agree).[415] However, in most Member States this distinction is less clear-cut and carries less practical weight.

The Community Social Charter 1989 encourages the use of alternative dispute resolution. Article 13(2) of the Community Social Charter 1989 recognizes that:

In order to facilitate the settlement of industrial disputes the establishment and utilisation at the appropriate levels of conciliation, mediation and arbitration procedures should be encouraged in accordance with national practice.

Member States recognize both judicial and non-judicial mechanisms for preventing and resolving collective disputes. Conciliation, mediation, and arbitration are the most common forms of non-judicial or third party intervention. These are distinct processes and may be distinguished as follows:

conciliation: a third party encouraging the parties to reach their own
agreement;

---

[413] *Schmidt and Dahlström* v. *Sweden*, 6 Feb. 1976, Eur. Ct HR Rep., Series A, No. 21 (1976), para. 36.

[414] See generally Blanpain, 'Prevention and Settlement of Collective Labour Disputes in the EEC Countries', Parts I and II (1972) 1 *ILJ* 74 and 143.

[415] See generally Commission, above, n. 295, SEC(89)1137.

mediation: a third party hearing the dispute and making formal but non-
  binding recommendations for resolving it;
arbitration: a third party hearing the dispute and making a binding decision.

Conciliation and mediation may arise from and have their legal base in the
obligatory part of the collective agreement. This suggests that the parties
themselves are primarily responsible for finding a solution to their conflicts.
This is closely related to the principles behind the peace obligation. Government mediation and conciliation services (or the Labour Court in Ireland) are
available in most Member States, but in most cases they perform a secondary
role.[416] Arbitration, by contrast, imposes a solution on the parties from outside and for this reason interferes with the autonomy of the Social Partners.
Consequently in Germany compulsory arbitration no longer exists,[417] since it
was considered incompatible with the constitutional guarantee of the freedom of association, and has been replaced by voluntary mediation. This
means that it is up to the parties to the collective agreement to decide whether
to establish a mediation procedure and, if so, the effects of such mediation.[418]

Similarly, in France some collective agreements provide for the procedures
and institutions of conciliation. French law also recognizes three voluntary
means of collective dispute-settlement: conciliation by the Conciliation Commission, arbitration, and the courts. In cases which go before the courts, the
judge may appoint a third party, whose role is closely akin to that of a medi-
ator,[419] to propose a compromise which the judges feel may lead to a settlement.[420] In practice conciliation, mediation, and arbitration are rare in
France but in Italy mediation by public authorities plays an important role.
However, political mediation conducted by the Ministry of Labour in cases of
national disputes has almost become a form of arbitration since the persuasive tactics adopted cannot in practice be refused by the Social Partners.[421]
In Denmark, by contrast, as an alternative to industrial action, conflicts over
the interpretation of collective agreements are settled by arbitration.[422] The
reference to national practice in Article 13(2) of the Community Social Charter indicates that dispute resolution, as with most matters affecting remedies,
is a domestic law issue, and at present the Community will not get involved.

---

[416] Ibid.
[417] However, since strikes and lock-outs are prohibited by law in the case of disputes between
works councils and employers, the matter can be referred to an arbitration committee. The
committee's decision is binding on the parties and has the status of a work agreement.
[418] Weiss, 'The Federal Republic of Germany', *Social Europe* 5/93, 59.
[419] Lyon-Caen, *France, European Industrial Relations Glossary* (Sweet and Maxwell, London,
1993), para. 500.
[420] Lyon-Caen, 'France', *Social Europe* 5/93, 112. See also Couturier, *Droit du Travail 2/Les
Relations Collectives de Travail* (Presses Universitaires de France, Paris, 1991), 420–34.
[421] Treu, 'Italy', *Social Europe* 5/93, 135–6.
[422] Nielsen, 'Denmark', *Social Europe* 5/93, 34.

C. CONCLUSIONS

The enormous difficulties faced by the EC in enacting measures relating to collective labour law bear testimony to Kahn-Freund's observation that 'individual labour law lends itself to transplantation very much more easily than ... collective labour law. Standards of protection and rules on substantive terms of employment can be imitated—rules on collective bargaining, on the closed shop, on trade unions, on strikes, cannot'.[423] The experience of the ILO and the European Social Charter is similar: according to Kahn-Freund, 'nothing could more clearly demonstrate the knowledge of the draftsman that collective bargaining institutions and rules are untransplantable'.[424] This he attributes to a different 'habitat of industrial relations' where the relations between management and labour are organized under the influence of strong political traditions, traditions connected with the role played by organizations on both sides as political pressure groups promoting legislation, and as rule-making agencies through the procedures of collective bargaining.[425] The EU is learning these lessons.

[423] 'Uses and Misuses of Comparative Law' (1974) 37 *MLR* 1, 21.
[424] Ibid., 22.
[425] Ibid., 20.

Index